Stayin' Alive

ALSO BY JEFFERSON COWIE

Capital Moves: RCA's Seventy-Year Quest for Cheap Labor
Beyond the Ruins: The Meanings of Deindustrialization
(edited with Joseph Heathcott)

Stayin' Alive

The 1970s and the Last Days of the Working Class

Jefferson Cowie

THE NEW PRESS

NEW YORK
LONDON

First published in the United States by The New Press, New York, 2010
This paperback edition published by The New Press, 2012
Distributed by Perseus Distribution

ISBN 978-1-59558-707-7 (pbk.)

The Library of Congress has cataloged the hardcover edition as follows:

Cowie, Jefferson R.
Stayin' alive : the 1970s and the last days of the working class / Jefferson Cowie.
p. cm.
Includes bibliographical references and index.
ISBN 978-1-56584-875-7 (hc.)
1. Working class—United States—History—20th century. 2. Working class—
United States—Social conditions—20th century. 3. United States—Economic
conditions—1971–1981. 4. United States—Social conditions—1960–1980.
I. Title.
HD8072.5.C69 2010
305.5'62097309047—dc22   2010010884

The New Press was established in 1990 as a not-for-profit alternative to the large,
commercial publishing houses currently dominating the book publishing industry.
The New Press operates in the public interest rather than for private gain,
and is committed to publishing, in innovative ways, works of educational,
cultural, and community value that are often deemed insufficiently profitable.
www.thenewpress.com

Composition by Westchester Book Group
This book was set in Adobe Caslon

Printed in the United States of America

2   4   6   8   10   9   7   5   3

for Aliya and Aidan
—living proof

Pike County, Kentucky, 1979

And fear the time when the strikes stop
　　　　while the great owners live—
for every little beaten strike is proof that the step is being taken.

—JOHN STEINBECK

Contents

Stayin' Alive

INTRODUCTION

Something's Happening to People Like Me

At only twenty-six years of age, sporting long sideburns, slicked back hair, and mod striped pants, autoworker Dewey Burton could barely contain his rage over the state of politics or his frustration with his job in the spring of 1972.

Dewey loved nothing more than customizing and racing automobiles, transforming old parts into dazzling metallic-flake creations, but he could barely tolerate his job at the Wixom Ford plant just outside of Detroit where he felt sentenced to a trivial role in assembling them. Satisfied with his pay, he was part of a widespread movement across the heartland fighting the mind-numbing tedium of industrial production. Reflecting the broad discontent on the floors of the nation's factories, some of which grew into open revolt, he remarked, "I hate my job, I hate the people I work for. . . . It's kind of stupid to work so hard and achieve so little."

Politically, Burton identified himself as a committed New Deal Democrat, but he was livid over plans to bus his son across Detroit in order to conform to the Supreme Court's idea of racial integration—policies driving his politics quickly to the right. Like the nation as a whole, Burton was simply being torn in too many directions at once. He was a figure in transition, the type of person journalist Pete Hamill had in mind when he wrote "The working-class white man is actually in revolt against taxes, joyless work, the double standards and short memories of professional politicians, hypocrisy and what he considers the debasement of the American dream."[1]

Dewey Burton may not have been the typical disgruntled worker of the 1970s, but the *New York Times* believed that he came pretty close. He proved to be an able ambassador to the newspaper's professional middle-class readership interested in the increasingly exotic state of disaffected blue-collar America. He first surfaced in a *New York Times* article on industrial discontent at the Wixom plant in 1972. Shortly thereafter, a reporter selected him to explain to an incredulous readership the reasons for northern workers' support for back-lash populist and presidential candidate Alabama governor George Wallace, to whom Burton had turned because of his opposition to busing. The *New York Times* returned to interview Dewey during the fall 1972 campaign, the 1974 midterm elections, and the presidential contests in 1976 and 1980. Smart and well spoken, Burton had a demeanor that merged proletarian and mod, greaser and beatnik into a synthesis of optimistic sixties unrest and claustrophobic seventies resignation that would be hard to sustain as the decade unfolded. As a result, Burton noted, "I received my fifteen minutes of fame four times."[2]

The media attention lavished on workers like Burton was part of a broad blue-collar revival in the 1970s, as working-class America returned to the national consciousness through strikes, popular culture, voting booths, and corporate strategy. Making sense of what *Newsweek* called the "far-ranging, fast spreading revolt of the little man against the Establishment" bordered on a national obsession. *Fortune*, along with countless other magazines and television news features, recognized the workers of the early seventies as "restless, changeable, mobile, demanding" and headed for "a time of epic battle between management and labor" given the "angry, aggressive and acquisitive" mood in the shops. As many big contracts expired, inflation ate up wage gains, and workers challenged the rules of postwar labor relations, the country witnessed the biggest wave of strike activity since 1946 (which was the biggest strike year in all of U.S. history). In 1970 alone there were over 2.4 million workers engaged in large-scale work stoppages, thirty-four massive stoppages of ten thousand workers or more, and a raft of wildcats, slowdowns, and aggressive stands in contract negotiations. Like so many other observers of the seventies labor scene, *Time* magazine connected the seventies' unrest to the battered ideals of the Depression decade. "Blue collar workers," the newsmagazine reported, "are gaining a renewed sense of identity, of collective power and class that used to be called solidarity."[3]

Despite the frequent analogies to Depression-era militancy that often cropped up in coverage of the nation's "blue collar blues," the workers bursting upon the national stage in the seventies were hardly the stock proletarian character of the 1930s popular imagination. They appeared less as social-realist heroes of the industrial age than in ways that were simultaneously profound and strange, militant and absurd, traditional and new, male and

female, insurgent and reactionary, as well as white, black, and brown. Whether
re-christened as the "hardhats," "the unmeltable ethnics," the "forgotten man,"
the "Silent Majority," the "working class majority," the "middle Americans"
or the "new militants" depended upon at whom the observer looked; whether
the Dewey Burtons of the world were in the midst of an industrial insurgency or political backlash depended upon where the observer stood. The
acid-dipped lyrics of urban jazz poet Gil Scott-Heron may have captured
the basic tension best: "America doesn't know whether it wants to be Matt
Dillon or Bob Dylan." Indeed, as the crosscurrents affecting Burton begin
to suggest, whether the country wanted to be led, tall in the saddle, to a restoration of the *ancien régime*, cowboy style, by Marshall Matt Dillon of the
television show *Gunsmoke*, or whether it wanted to meld the workerism of
Woody Guthrie with the New Politics of the sixties á la early Bob Dylan
remained one of the core dilemmas of the decade. "In the 1970s," labor leader
Gus Tyler declared, "fury comes easily to the white worker. He is ready for
battle. But he does not quite know against whom to declare war."[4]

I

Political forecasters in the seventies saw working people's hope layered with
anxiety and their traditions undermined by a confusing phalanx of new problems. The seventies had the potential, as two labor intellectuals put it, of
becoming "Labor's Decade—Maybe." Advancing the old class politics of the
thirties in concert with the new social movements of the sixties could make the
1970s "not the dawning of the Age of Aquarius," but "a new era for the workingman." Famed left wing intellectual Michael Harrington, trying to make
sense of the crosscurrents in blue-collar America, said that the nation was moving "vigorously left, right, and center at the same time."[5]

Burton found himself caught in the turbulence. After the tumultuous
1968 primary campaign and the disaster of the Chicago Democratic Convention, he readily toed the unions' line for their bread-and-butter man,
Hubert Humphrey. Regarding himself "as a union man coming from a long
line of F.D.R. Democrats," it seemed the only sensible position for a worker
to take. "People have been telling me since I was a child that when the
Democrats were in office, everybody was put to work," Dewey noted. That
1968 race, however, was the last time Burton would call himself an unwavering Democrat as busing all but shattered his faith in the mainstream of the

party. Extending the separate-is-not-equal logic of *Brown v. Board of Education* (1954), the Supreme Court decided in *Swann v. Charlotte-Mecklenburg Board of Education* (1971) that integrating school children through mandatory busing was an appropriate remedy for racial segregation in the public schools. And in Burton's Detroit, plans were to integrate not just the schools within the city, but the suburbs with the city. "What burns me to the bottom of my bones is that I paid an excessive amount of money so that my son could walk three blocks to school," he explained about his family's small bungalow on the edge of Detroit. The leafy affluence of the term "suburb," however, hardly matched the rows of plain-stoop homes of Dewey's Redford, a township hugging the border of Detroit where many streets, including the Burtons', still remained unpaved. "I'm not going to pay big high school taxes and pay more for a home so that somebody can ship my son 30 miles away to get an inferior education," he declared.[6]

Burton decided that the answer to the busing threat was to pull the lever for the pivotal political figure of the era, George Wallace, for the Democratic nomination for president in 1972. The governor of Alabama, who famously stood in the schoolhouse doorway to defend segregation and who swore never to be "out niggered" in politics, was busy rattling the stale presumptions of both major parties. As an independent candidate in 1968, Wallace drew together the segregationist South with anti-liberal northerners concerned about blacks moving into their neighborhoods, fearful of the riots, and feeling simply forgotten. His candidacy enabled the political transformation of a substantial slice of white working people to become dislodged from the Roosevelt coalition and move toward what Kevin Phillips famously called *The Emerging Republican Majority* (1969). By the time George Wallace returned as an insurgent candidate in the fragmented Democratic primaries in 1972, his performance was roughly equal to any major candidate. He earned Dewey Burton's vote en route to a victory in the Michigan primary on the day after he was crippled by the bullet of a would-be assassin in suburban Baltimore.[7]

Separating George Wallace's race baiting from his "stand up for the common man" theme is as difficult as untangling race from class in U.S. history, but his blue-collar rhetoric spoke to themes that no one else on the national stage addressed. Among northern wage earners like Burton, Wallace's populist anti-elitism, anti-crime, and anti-busing messages worked best, but his overt embrace of segregation, his snarling rhetoric, and petty resentments failed. In a typical stump speech, Wallace effectively stirred the pot of populist anti-elitism that had been simmering in American politics since Andrew Jackson:

> Now what are the real issues that exist today in these United States? It is the trend of pseudointellectual government where a select elite group have written guidelines in bureaus and court decisions, have spoken from some pulpits, some college campuses, some newspaper offices, looking down their noses at the average man on the street, the glass workers, the steel workers, the auto workers, and the textile workers, the farm workers, the policemen, the beautician, and the barber, and the little businessman, saying to him that you do not know how to get up in the morning or go to bed at night unless we write you a guideline.

At the heart of the Wallace phenomenon was ambiguity about his cause. As one trucker explained, "I'm for either him or the Communists, I don't care, just anybody who wouldn't be afraid of the big companies." While conservative strategists were originally skeptical of Wallace's "country and western Marxism," they quickly found it the key to their own populist appeal in the 1970s—a key that would eventually open the door to the white working class vote for Ronald Reagan.[8]

The DayGlo® "This Family WILL NOT Be Bused" sticker on the Burtons' screen door was a complicated thing. Many anxious old liberals and impatient New Leftists dismissed votes like Dewey's as clear racism, but his political choices cannot be dismissed so simply. Raised poor (the first indoor running water he had was when he moved from southern Illinois to Detroit as a teenager), Dewey nonetheless profited from generations of segregated housing patterns, silent white privilege, and occupational segregation. Still, he felt open to black people as both leaders and neighbors. He touted his black union local leader as "the best president we've ever had" and claimed that he would welcome anyone into his neighborhood. "If a black mom and daddy buy or rent a house here and send their kids to [my son] David's school and pay their taxes, that's fine. Busing black kids to white neighborhoods and white kids to black neighborhoods is never going to achieve integration. It's upsetting. It's baloney." Like Wallace, Burton also detested "welfare freeloaders," pointing to an unruly white family that lived down the block. His protest against liberalism had as much to do with control of his life, the fate of his family, and his modest and tenuous place on the social ladder as it did anything else.[9]

For working people, the social upheavals associated with the sixties actually took root in most communities in the seventies, which was not simply a different decade but a distinctly less generous economic climate. From a policy perspective, the Democratic Party faced a dilemma that it could not solve: finding ways to maintain support within the white blue-collar base that came of age during the New Deal and World War II era, while at the same time servicing the pressing demands for racial and gender equity arising from the sixties. Both had to be achieved in the midst of two massive oil shocks, record inflation and unemployment, and a business community retooling to assert greater control over the political process. Placing affirmative action onto a world of declining occupational opportunity risked a zero-sum game: a post-scarcity politics without post-scarcity conditions. Despite the many forms of solidarity evident in the discontent in the factories, mines, and mills, without a shared economic vision to hold things together, issues like busing forced black and white residents to square off in what columnist Jimmy Breslin called "a Battle Royal" between "two groups of people who are poor and doomed and who have been thrown in the ring with each other."[10]

The mercurial nature of the politics of '72 was such that when Wallace was eliminated from the race, Dewey voted for the most left-leaning candidate of any major party in the twentieth century, Democratic senator George McGovern. The choice did not come easily. The autoworker was genuinely stumped about whether incumbent Richard Nixon's Silent Majority or challenger George McGovern's soggy populism best represented his interests. It would be a betrayal of everything he stood for to vote for a Republican, he believed, but he had grave concerns about McGovern and his entourage of student radicals. He also sensed a "meanness" creeping into McGovern's campaign after he threw vice presidential nominee Tom Eagleton off the ticket due to his earlier problems with mental illness. Much of the labor movement, especially the hierarchy of the American Federation of Labor-Congress of Industrial Organizations (AFL-CIO), could not stomach McGovern's New Politics with its anti-war positions, youth movements, and commitment to open up the Democratic Party to wider spectrum of Americans. The labor federation, fearing for its traditional kingmaker role in the Democratic Party, fought the McGovern insurgency with every scrap of institutional power it could muster.[11]

Meantime, Richard Nixon, taking his cues from Wallace, was designing his own heretical strategy to woo white working-class voters away from the party of Roosevelt. His plans to build a post-New Deal coalition—the "New

Majority" he liked to call it—around the Republican Party in 1972 was based on making an explicit pitch for white, male, working-class votes by appealing to their cultural values over their material needs. His targets were men like Burton, who had first been dislodged from the Democratic mainstream by George Wallace. Despite Nixon's courtship of Dewey's vote, the autoworker remained suspicious of Nixon's loyalties. "Nixon hasn't proved anything to me when he raises the prices of new cars and freezes the wages of the people who build them," Burton explained about falling back on bread-and-butter Democratic politics with his vote for the left-leaning McGovern. "I really don't think McGovern will win," he finally concluded. "But maybe if we vote for him we can show Nixon what we want, what the working man wants." The majority of white working-class voters disagreed, selecting Nixon by wide margins over the most pro-labor candidate ever produced by the American two-party system.[12]

The early seventies' political confusion had its analogue in the discontent boiling up on the shop floors. Employees at the Wixom Ford plant where Burton worked were a minor part of a national epidemic of industrial unrest in the first half of the 1970s. They fought with supervisors on the line, clogged up the system with grievances, demanded changes in the quality of work life, walked out in wildcat strikes, and organized to overthrow stale bureaucratic union leadership. Yet it was a conflicted set of movements. As Dewey explained, workers were harnessed to union pay but longed to run free of the deadening nature of the work itself—and sometimes free of the union leaders who spoke on their behalf. "Once you're there, there's no other way to make as much money and get the benefits. Ford's our security blanket. I'm a scaredy-cat. If I leave, I lose eight years seniority," he lamented. Chained to his paycheck, he dreaded his future at the plant. "Each year I felt like I accomplished something. Suddenly I realized that I'm at a dead end and I'll probably be hacking on the line for 30 years." Burton's "mouthing off" at the plant had resulted in a string of disciplinary notices for relatively minor infractions, which blocked his hopes of improving his skills and position at Ford. Too "pushy" and outspoken, according to his foreman, Burton was trapped at the bottom of the industrial order. As one of his co-workers lamented, "There's only three ways out of here. You either conform and become deader each day, or you rebel, or you quit."[13]

Commentators often referred to the unruliness on the assembly lines as the "Lordstown syndrome," after the infamous three-week-long strike in 1972 by a group of young, hip, and inter-racial autoworkers at a General

Motors (GM) plant in Lordstown, Ohio, who battled the fastest—and most psychically deadening—assembly line in the world. "With all the shoulder-length hair, beards, Afros and mod clothing along the line," explained *Newsweek* of the notorious GM plant, "it looks for all the world like an industrial Woodstock"—suggesting the possibility of an upheaval in class relations for the seventies equal to those of race and culture of the 1960s. "At the heart of the new mood," declared the *New York Times*, "there is a challenge to management's authority to run its plants, an issue that has resulted in some of the hardest fought battles between industry and labor in the past." There were also new leaders to match the new temperament. Ed Sadlowski, for instance, a rank-and-file leader emerging from the ashen haze of South Chicago's steel works, preached what the *Village Voice* called "a populist message of class conflict and class consciousness that hasn't been heard in this country since the '30s." As he liked to put it, "There's a fire in the steelworkers' union, and I'm not gonna piss on it." When New York television talk show host David Susskind asked Dewey Burton and a panel of other discontented workers, "Who had the power to change the situation?"—management or the union—all four guests chimed in unison, "the rank and file."[14]

The old guard mostly found such militancy naïve, talk of the "rank and file" bordering on the mystic, and the challengers ungrateful for collective bargaining riches that the previous generation had already won for them. As the Steel Workers president I.W. Abel explained, "Young workers don't appreciate what the union has built. They didn't go through the rough times." Rejecting the continuous analogies between the seventies and the thirties, union leaders also feared the insurgents' alliances with "outsiders"—especially meddlesome liberals and young activists turning from the campuses of the sixties to the union halls of the seventies. Both the mainstream labor leadership and management seemed to understand—and endorse—historian David Brody's fundamental insight about postwar labor relations machinery, a system in which all issues were to be funneled strictly through statesman-like negotiations. "The contractual logic itself," Brody argued, "actually evolved into a pervasive method for containing shop-floor activism." That activism was exactly what insurgents hoped would make the seventies into a new era of working-class mobilization by bringing unions into the New Politics, delivering remedies to the new shop floor demands, and organizing more inclusive and dynamic unions. In contrast, the union bureaucracy saw the upheavals as threatening to its power and as crippling labor's ability to deliver the goods.

Yet the insurgencies of the early seventies, resisted so mightily by the union hierarchy, were the main source of whatever hope there may have been for updating the old order. The postwar collective bargaining machinery had delivered the goods, and nobody wanted to get rid of it. "People wanted to kick the machine. But they didn't want the machine to stop."[15]

Working class discontent was puzzling to a generation accustomed to assuming that "the labor question" had long been answered. The problems of workers and class may have once existed in the United States, went the dominant logic, but it was solved back in the thirties by union recognition and the enlightened New Deal state. The "liberal consensus," the reigning ideology of the postwar era produced by that bargain, was in fact premised on the assumption that the set of problems that haunted capitalism for one hundred years had been resolved in the technocratic settlement that recognized workers' representatives as junior partners in the success story. In a trenchant critique of the "ideology of the liberal consensus," however, Godfrey Hodgson exposed how class conflict may have been "contained" in postwar America, but "the abolition of the working class, in fact, was a myth." By the seventies, as workers grew restless with their containment, it became clear that the immense institutional achievements of the previous generation—from labor legislation to the building of big unions to the strength of the Democratic Party—were both sources of power as well as systems of constraint on the future fortunes of the American working class.[16]

The complexity of Dewey Burton's life cuts against the simplistic "hard hat" stereotype that dominated the decade and that was brought to life each week in the most popular sitcom of the decade, *All in the Family*. Dewey found little opportunity for leisure or entertainment, other than his passion for customizing cars, but, like the rest of the country, he never missed the break-through CBS show he and his wife, Ilona, affectionately referred to by the name of its iconic main character, "Archie." *All in the Family* served as a sort of national therapy session as the generations, the races, the genders, and the classes clashed over post-sixties values and politics in some of the finest, most controversial, and popular television ever created. His wife, Ilona, feared that the *New York Times* reporter saw her as too much of an "Edith"— inadequately liberated and at the mercy of the needs of her family even though she, too, clocked in for a full shift installing trim for GM. Despite Archie becoming the national symbol for the bigoted blue-collar worker, however, Dewey Burton saw nothing of himself in the main character. "He's a fool,"

Dewey reported about Archie. "He's taken hate and bigotry and turned them into the most funny things I know. It's like Mark Twain's satire—it's hilarious."[17]

All in the Family may have been the most important representation of white working-class men in popular culture during the early seventies, but it was hardly the only one. A multifaceted resurrection of blue-collar America appeared in commercial culture from Nashville to Hollywood, echoing the issues in the factories and the voting booths. In addition to America's weekly encounter with Archie, the top shows in the mid-1970s included *The Waltons* (return of the Great Depression); *Welcome Back Kotter, Good Times,* and *Sanford and Son* (life and poverty in the inner city); *The Jeffersons* (black upward mobility); *Laverne and Shirley* (working girls in the classless fifties), and *One Day at a Time* and *Alice* (working single mothers take on the world). The new shows' emphases on class-infused social problems were a far cry from their staid but popular predecessors like *Marcus Welby* and *Gunsmoke*.

Exaggerated pathologies of violent, angry white men received the bulk of the attention in popular culture during the first half of the decade, but the overall message was more akin to what The Temptations called the "Ball of Confusion" in the nation as a whole. The ideological breakdown was evident all around. Reporters descended on factories for special programs to explain the "blue collar blues," and filmmakers turned their lenses toward working-class themes across the spectrum—from Peter Boyle's portrayal of the neo-fascist *Joe* to Al Pacino's brilliant identity meltdown in *Dog Day Afternoon* to Jack Nicholson's use of the blue-collar world as a playground of authenticity in *Five Easy Pieces*. Similarly, the themes of country music, a genre that once expressed the simple longings of lost souls and broken hearts, became embattled terrain in the class wars of the 1970s. By mid decade, however, any faith in the future of the common man was becoming difficult to hold. Robert DeNiro's portrayal of the pathologically alienated Travis Bickle in *Taxi Driver*—based on the Warholian diary of the man who shot George Wallace solely for the fame it would deliver—provided the nation with a new and threatening vigilante anti-hero living outside the boundaries of civil society. Just as in the nation's politics and workplaces, there was a tug of war in popular culture over the meaning and political potential of the working class, a struggle not fully reconciled until the second half of the decade.

II

The hope and possibility marbled throughout the confusion of the early part of the decade began to fade into the despair of the new order emerging in the second half. "I wanted to be somebody," Dewey Burton declared in 1974. "It wasn't the money so much as that I just want to have some kind of recognition, you know, to be more tomorrow than I was yesterday, and that's what I was working for." In addition to plugging away down at the Ford plant, Burton had been trying to start his own custom auto painting business, chipping away slowly at a college degree, and even playing guitar. "He drove himself," Ilona explained. "He'd work all day and study all night and then take his books with him to work and read on his breaks." Looking a lot more "sixties" by the mid-1970s, with his long hair and black turtleneck, he decided to surrender his hopes for the future in order to "concentrate on today," as he put it. "It takes so much to just make it that there's no time for dreams and no energy for making them come true—and I'm not so sure anymore that it's ever going to get better," he explained with a poetic fatalism. His creeping despair resonated with what Peter Marin identified in *Harper's Magazine* in 1975 as a "new world view emerging among us," focusing on the self with "individual survival as its sole good." Burton framed the problem more succinctly. "I realized I was killing myself, and there wasn't going to be any reward for my suicide."[18]

When Dewey made those remarks in late 1974, he stood not simply at the middle of a decade but at a watershed between eras. The 1970s might appropriately be thought of as half post-1960s and half pre-1980s, but they were also more than that—they served as a bridge between epochs. A broad spectrum of observers, from conservative ("the decade that brought you modern life—for better or worse") to liberal ("the great shift in American culture, society, and politics") to postmodern ("the undecade that was perhaps the most important decade"), have formed a consensus that within the gloomy seventies we can find the roots of our own time. The period has been named "pivotal" not because of its monumental events, its great leaders, or its movements, but because society, from its economic foundations to its cultural manifestations, really did move in a new direction. It stands as a bookend to the New Deal era: that which was built in the thirties and forties—politically, economically, and culturally—was beginning to crumble barely two generations later. More than a time of mere fads for which it is mercilessly teased, it was a time of fundamental realignments.[19]

Part of Burton's "no time for dreams" sensibility was reconciling himself to his future on the line, but another part was more than personal—it was a national disposition. Historian Andreas Killen portrays 1973 as the year of the collective "nervous breakdown," a year full of dire news but also "alive with a sense of new possibilities and openings to the future, harbingers of an emerging new postmodern cultural configuration." It was "a deeply schizophrenic moment," he found, in which "reality itself seemed to be up for grabs." That year was the buildup to a troika of disasters that rattled the American psyche— the oil embargo that threatened the nation's supply of energy, the beginning of the stagflation that sapped the nation's economic strength, the president's 1974 resignation that drained its faith—and then the fall of Saigon in 1975 shattered the remains of national purpose. Writing in 1974, Michael Harrington noted "a collective sadness" that had descended upon the nation as if it were in mourning for a dying era—the promise of modernity itself slipping out of reach.[20]

Above all, the mid-1970s marked the end of the postwar boom. The years prior to the 1973–74 crisis had been the most economically egalitarian time in U.S. history, the point on the graph where the bounty was shared most equitably, and unemployment was at historic lows. The year 1972 was also the apex of earnings for male workers. Starting in the 1973–74 years, real earnings began to stagnate and then slide as workers began their slow and painful dismissal from their troubled partnership with postwar liberalism. By mid-decade the record-breaking strikes, rank-and-file movements, and vibrant organizing drives that had once promised a new day for workers were reduced to a trickle in the new economic climate. They were then replaced by layoffs, plant closures, and union decertification drives. White male workers' incomes had risen an astonishing 42 percent since 1960, but those incomes stagnated or fell for the next quarter century following the early seventies. Real earnings first stagnated and then were driven down by oil shocks and inflation; deindustrialization, plant closings, and anti-unionism; and a global restructuring of work itself that would continue over the ensuing decades. Most telling of the lost opportunities was that even the relative rise of women's wages since the 1970s was greatly attributable to the decline in male earnings.[21]

Burton too saw little hope or opportunity in the new emerging reality at mid-decade. Peering out from underneath what he called his "despondency," he framed the problem as effectively as any of the sociologists of the time. "Something's happening to people like me—working stiffs, as they say—and it isn't just that we have to pay more for this or that or that we're having to do without this or make do with a little less of that. It's deep, and hard to explain, but it's more like more and more of us are sort of leaving all our hopes outside in the rain and coming into the house and just locking the door—you know, just turning the key and 'click,' that's it for what we always thought we could be."[22]

Dewey Burton managed to make it to the polls for the 1974 midterm elections, but his heart was not in it. The nation delivered the famously liberal sweep to Congress in the wake of the Republican humiliation of Watergate, but the class of '74 consisted of a new breed of post-1960s, free-market, social liberals, who were skeptical of workers' needs and suspicious of their institutions. The new politicians, inspired to do something about urgent issues of race and gender inequality, also tended to be chary of structural solutions in an era of inflation. For Dewey, however, the problem centered less upon his political choices than the lack of meaning in the entire political process. His sentiments were echoed in sociologist Robert Nisbet's 1975 book *The Twilight of Authority*, which charted the decline of the political community in the deepest sense of the term. "All we see are enlarging aggregates of atom-like individuals whose disenchantment with politics and party has become translated into indifference, always a dangerous circumstance in a democracy," he argued in refrains of Tocqueville. Predicting a new militaristic Leviathan emerging from the toxic political seas, he lamented not the direction of the nation but the lack of one, not the politicization of culture but its vacuity. Dewey would have agreed. "You can't blame it all on the politicians," Burton argued in earthier terms. "But I wish just for once that one of them would say, 'now folks, I swear to God, if you'll elect me, I won't do a damn thing.' That's the fellow I'd vote for. Somebody who'd just let us alone."[23]

III

In 1976, Dewey Burton announced that he found someone whom he believed could deliver the nation out of its malaise: former actor, California governor, and long-shot presidential candidate Ronald Reagan. He explained that he was going to be a "primary jumper"—a Democrat voting in the Republican primary in order to support the California governor's bid to unseat President Gerald Ford from the right. In Reagan, Burton found the same freshness, independence, backbone, and scrappy spirit that Wallace had shown in 1972 but "without the shadow of racism behind him" that bothered Dewey about the Alabama governor. "Four years ago, it was all fire and brimstone—busing and the Vietnam War. And then it was Watergate," he recalled about the earlier contests. "Now there aren't any issues, except maybe the economy," he explained about both the rapid changes in the nation and the hollowing out of the political process by 1976.[24]

The workers down at the plant regarded Dewey as a "rebel" and a "radical" for backing what he saw as Reagan's boldness rather than staying within the Democratic Party. Dewey no longer had busing to worry about since the Supreme Court's decision in *Milliken v. Bradley* (1974) exempted the suburban districts outside of Detroit from any part in desegregating inner-city school systems, a decision that left a suffocating ring of white flight around impoverished major cities in America. Yet he continued to feel a powerful draw to the right. "Sure, I've got qualms deep down inside me about voting for a Republican," he explained. "But a man's got to grow up sometime," he remarked half-consciously brushing aside not just his own youth but the idealism of an earlier time. Reagan lost to incumbent Gerald Ford in the Republican primary that year, leaving Burton with what he found to be a rather unremarkable contest between Ford and Georgia governor Jimmy Carter. It had not been just any Republican that fired Dewey's imagination or drew his loyalty, as he showed almost no interest in Ford. The election was so dull to Burton that by 1980 he had forgotten for whom he voted back in the '76 national contest. "Silly, we voted for Ford," Ilona reminded him.[25]

The president of Burton's union, in contrast, held out grand—perhaps grandiose—hopes for Jimmy Carter, whom he believed to be a new hybrid liberal for a complicated political age. When the United Auto Workers (UAW) president endorsed Carter, he hoped he would be the guy who could tame the Wallace supporters, entice the black voters, and still offer up something for the industrial workers, all while using his Georgian charms to turn the South back around to the Democratic column. When Carter gained the executive branch after the Democrats had suffered a painful eight-year absence from power, many thought a resurrection in labor liberalism was in the making. Plans were hatched in the labor, civil rights, and liberal groups to revive the old New Deal formula through full employment legislation, labor law reform, national health insurance, and industrial policy. A new, shared economic foundation for politics, they hoped, might mitigate the divisiveness then tearing at the party. It was, however, a New Deal revival that never happened. Missing from the seventies' progressive agenda were policy innovations that could effectively draw together the economic politics of the thirties and the social politics of the sixties, mobilization strategies that might work with a post-Vietnam/post-Watergate electorate skeptical of the efficacy of the state, and policies that would not exacerbate the nation's main economic problem, stagflation. By late 1978, Carter had already lurched right in his efforts to beat back inflation and pinned the nation's problems not on material issues but on what he called a "crisis of the spirit."[26]

By the turning point election of 1980, Dewey Burton's earlier rebelliousness had melted into a defensive gratitude for the limited job security he possessed. Back in 1972, a unionized manufacturing job seemed like an existential dead end, but, in the twilight of the industrial golden age, that same job had become a rare and coveted source of security. The dwindling numbers of workers who had claim on those high-paying industrial jobs found themselves to be labor's new aristocracy—shrinking in numbers, paid beyond the imagination of the vast unorganized majority, and politically detached from those toiling in the swelling ranks of the non-unionized service sector. Dewey was certainly doing quite well. He had earned a slot painting parts and then, finally, a much-sought-after position in the skilled trades. His promotions, ironically, were partially management's reaction to his media fame. While he continued to pour his soul into building his T-bucket hot rods, Burton's advancements allowed him to move his family up and out toward the more comfortable suburbs further outside of Detroit. He had come to reflect AFL-CIO president George Meany's boast that modern union members have "a great deal more to lose" than in the past. With little concern for the unorganized or labor's dwindling power, Meany complacently explained, "The more of the world's goods a person has, the more conservative he becomes."[27]

Dewey Burton may have been a good deal more comfortable than he had ever been, but, as he might have told a complacent George Meany, he was also the last of a dying breed. "It's the first time in 16 years that I've ever been threatened with losing my job," he reported in 1980. Like much of the economy as a whole, the auto industry was in a tailspin as Chrysler turned to a federal bailout and Ford and GM slashed employment levels. "A lot of my friends lost their jobs. They won't never come back to the plant," he lamented about a layoff of 3,200 workers at the Wixom Ford plant—a pattern that rippled across the heartland. Organized labor lost not just the percentage of workers they represented in the economy, but, by the end of the decade, the problem had crossed into the loss of real numbers as well (and even then, dramatic growth in the public sector masked dramatic losses in the private sector). The complacency evident in labor's failure to organize new workers or to help create a more expansive working-class identity beyond the industrial core of the AFL-CIO became evident as organized labor's strength began to dissolve. Without a strong counter-presence in the growing and diverse service and clerical industries—as well as political reforms, new labor leadership, and new voices necessary to organize new sectors—the unions' ability to withstand the attacks from politicians and business leaders weakened along with their industrial base.

By 1980 Burton completed the most significant transformation in postwar political history: from New Deal faithful to icon of discontent to Reagan Democrat. In his mind, there was little choice for the 1980 general election. "Carter's had four years. He didn't stabilize the country. Don't give me no more promises. Let me try somebody else's promises for a change," he concluded in his last interview. "If Carter's so good for the working people, how come they're not working?" he demanded about the president's disastrously ineffective first and only term. Organized labor rallied to defeat Reagan, but Burton believed that the unions' political influence on him and the rest of the rank and file had greatly diminished over the course of the decade. He also knew that even the UAW's support for Carter was little more than "lukewarm"—if for no other reason than the union had supported Ted Kennedy's attempt to unseat Carter from the left in the 1980 primary. On the eve of the 1980 election, the *New York Times* concluded its decade-long look at one autoworker, noting, "Dewey Burton has become a happy man, and he will gladly vote for Ronald Reagan for president on November 4 . . . [even though] he is a strong union man, a Democrat by upbringing and conviction."[28]

Burton's choice for the presidency in 1980 helped usher in a new and complex era of working-class political history. The new, more populist right proved effective in offering cultural refuge for blue-collar whites, while also being the central protagonist in the new economic transformations devastating working-class communities across the heartland. At a time when the traditional working-class ally, the Democratic Party, offered precious little material comfort to working people, Ronald Reagan's New Right offered a restoration of the glory days by bolstering morale on the basis of patriotism, God, race, patriarchy, and nostalgia for community. The Reagan administration did squeeze inflation out of the economy but only by allowing historic levels of unemployment, industrial decline, and the decimation of the collective bargaining system—all of which combined to fight inflation by lowering wages and raising unemployment. After the president's attack on organized labor, most dramatically in the firing of over ten thousand striking members of the Professional Air Traffic Controllers Organization, and the restructuring of the tax schedule in favor of the wealthy, he looked a lot less like the working man's champion. In many parts of the industrial belt, the Depression-era analogy became true not in terms of working-class insurgencies as it had in the early seventies but, by the early eighties, in terms of material reality. As Dewey later confessed, "Reagan blindsided us."[29]

As in the political world, the range of working-class possibilities in popular culture was similarly diminished by the second half of the 1970s. Working-class story lines hardened into three options: escape one's class position; find ways to forget it; or, lacking any civic outlets, bury its pains deep inside. Tony Manero, the lead in the immensely popular and decade-defining film *Saturday Night Fever*, declared his loser buddies in Brooklyn to be all "assholes back there" before escaping to upwardly mobile Manhattan. His pals were left behind in a simmering racial and ethnic stew with neither a future nor any narrative sense of what might happen to them. The future belonged to the chosen ones who could get out. Not surprisingly, the urban professionals—the "yuppies"—would become for the eighties what workers had been for the media in the seventies. By 1980 the ruthless oil baron J.R. Ewing of the immensely popular television show *Dallas* eclipsed Dewey's beloved working-class Archie as the media's new totem for the new decade.

To absorb the narratives of popular culture of the late seventies was to relegate the working class to faraway times and places—including the most distant, the isolated hearts of working people themselves. The runaway popularity of Johnny Paycheck's country novelty song, "Take This Job and Shove It" captured the new powerlessness. The blue-collar anthem saturated the radio stations, workplaces, and bars of the nation during the second half of the decade. Despite the title, the song is less about open rebellion than it is about a "hidden transcript" of resistance that takes place internally, far from the outward contest of power relations that defined the first half of the seventies. The narrator is unable to act; his rebellion is only a fantasy: "I'd give the shirt right off of my back / If I had the nerve to say / Take this job and shove it!" The surface militancy of the song was actually more about what two sociologists dubbed the smoldering "inner class warfare" of the seventies, in which "struggle between men leads to struggle within each man." Bruce Springsteen followed up his Whitmanesque paeans of mid-decade escape with ballads of rustbelt workers who failed to make it out, left to struggle alone "in the darkness on the edge of town." Music, television, and film turned from the hopeful crosscurrents of the early years toward a rather unified message: save yourself or face irrelevance.[30]

IV

What many pegged as the promise of a working-class revival in the early 1970s turned out to be more of a swan song by decade's end. The fragmented nature of the labor protests—by organization, industry, race, geography, and gender—failed to coalesce into a lasting national presence. The mainstream labor movement failed in its major political initiatives. Market orthodoxy eclipsed all alternatives, and promising organizing drives ended in failure. Deindustrialization decimated the power of the old industrial heartland. The vague class alliances of the major parties began to lose their distinction. As hip-hop writer Nelson George put it, "The first story is full of optimism and exalted ideas about humanity's ability to change through political action and moral argument. The next story, the plot we're living right now, is defined by cynicism, sarcasm, and self-involvement raised to art. The turning point was the early seventies." By 1981, *Time* magazine predicted little more than "Gloom and Doom for Workers."[31]

The 1970s, mocked as an era of questionable fashion and bad politics, simultaneously appear both irrelevant and the foundation of our own time. Yet the history of class in America reveals the profundity in the nothingness of the decade, a wholesale transformation without a narrative. One of the great constructs of the modern age, the unified notion of a "working class," crumbled, and the new world order was built on the rubble. Issues from stagflation to racial backlash, Vietnam to deindustrialization, have been fingered as the culprit for the decline of the impulse that animated the chaotic great strikes of the Gilded Age, fueled the concerns of the middle-class reform impulse of the Progressive Era, finally built the New Deal, and then voted in the Great Society. Yet the seventies suggest the fragility at the heart of the self-definition of "the working class." It was a conceptual unity that could briefly but imperfectly be identifiable as a unionized voting block from the New Deal to the 1970s. It ultimately died of the many external assaults upon it, yes, but mostly of its own internal weaknesses.

As the decade drew to a close, people with literary flare and political drive were penning tracts such as French theorist Andre Gorz's *Farewell to the Working Class* and British historian Eric Hobsbawm's *The Forward March of Labor Halted?* An entire generation of postmodern thought blossomed on the gnarled vines of disappointment in the failures and rigidities of the post-1968 working class. But if there is hope to be found in the bleak history of the 1970s, it is in the idea that the very storm that left Dewey Burton's "hopes out in the rain" may have also cleared the air for the return of a broader, more vigorous and inclusive incarnation of the working-class ideal.[32]

Burton, as usual, had a simpler take. Speculating from his Florida home where he retired—getting out not long before the final closure of the Wixom plant—he explained, "As far as working people go, it's gone and it's not gonna happen again."[33]

BOOK ONE

Hope in the Confusion, 1968–1974

1

Old Fashioned Heroes
of the New Working Class

Clarksville, Pennsylvania. New Year's Eve, 1969

Early in the morning of the last day of the 1960s, three hired assassins slipped off their shoes and crept into the Yablonski home in southwestern Pennsylvania. One of the intruders pulled out a handgun and quickly shot the Yablonskis' twenty-five-year-old daughter Charlotte while she slept. The two others burst into the master bedroom and shot Margaret and then fired half a dozen bullets into their target, dissident mine workers' leader Jock Yablonski. In a moment when the assassins' carbine jammed, Jock may have scrambled for a shotgun loaned to him for his protection, but only a spilled box of shells remained of any chance he may have had to defend his family. As the sun rose on the new decade, the three blood-caked corpses remained untouched until several days later when the Yablonskis' son became worried about his family and drove up to the spacious fieldstone home to investigate.[1]

The grisly triple homicide quickly became the talk of the nation in the first weeks of 1970, and, as news spread through the coalfields, twenty thousand coal miners laid down their tools and walked off the job to protest the state of their union. Anyone keeping up with the news quickly connected the assassination to a campaign that had received widespread coverage across the country in 1969: Yablonski's unsuccessful bid to unseat the authoritarian president of the United Mine Workers of America (UMWA), Tony Boyle. Years later, it would be proved that Boyle arranged the Yablonski murders (by which time he would be trying to take his own life), but, well before any trials, observers concluded that the slayings were evidence of a once venerable union—the detonator of labor's explosive growth back in the 1930s—gone terribly wrong. As the *New York Times* later noted, Yablonski's martyrdom made him "not only a labor folk hero, but in death, the force for reform that he longed to be in the last years of his life" as he helped begin the greatest reform effort in U.S. labor history.[2]

The fifty-nine-year-old Yablonski had faced regular threats—and actual acts—of violence since he publicly charged Boyle with being "dictatorial" in his running of a "decaying" administration that was "riddled with fear," and displaying "shocking ineptitude and passivity" in his dealings with mine safety. "In recent years," he railed, "the present leadership has not responded to its men, has not fought for their health and safety, has not improved grievance procedures, has not rooted itself in the felt needs of its membership and has rejected democratic procedures, freedom to dissent and the right of rank and file participation in the small and large issues that affect the union." Worse, in an occupational culture in which there was a clearer division between us and them, between workers and bosses, than any other in the nation, Yablonski accused Boyle of an "abject, follow-the-leader posture toward the coal industry." The union leaders have "sat on their backsides so long," he concluded, that "they've let the fat come up between their ears and they don't know what the coal miner's problems are anymore."[3]

As Yablonski reeled off his indictment against his union, he captured the sentiments of a wave of rank-and-file rebellions moving through much of occupational life in the early seventies. The core issues in the mines, as across the nation, were less about pay than union democracy, quality of work life, health and safety, and fresh leadership. In other areas, it was about expanding into new sectors and organizing new workers—joining "Soul Power and Union Power" as the slogan for Hospital Workers in New York City put it. In contrast to the brutality in the UMWA, most of the labor leadership tended to be more sclerotic than violent, more bureaucratic than corrupt, and more complacent than cynical. Against the stasis, rank-and-file workers across organized labor were, as they used to say in the thirties, "on the march" in the 1970s. When the unrest peaked in 1974, before rapidly subsiding into history with little trace, the press had to find explanations for "the most massive epidemic of labor strikes since the years just after World War II."[4]

Unlike many other labor dissidents of the day, Jock Yablonski was not a rank-and-filer but a lieutenant turned revolutionary, a part of the machine turned reformer. He had been a member of the UMWA for almost four decades, having gone down into the pits at the age of fifteen and worked his way up to become president of his district and a member of the executive board of the UMWA. By the time of his death, he had not actively mined coal for a quarter of a century. When the press asked how Yablonski could have been complicit in Boyle's leadership for much of the decade only to suddenly don the mantle of an insurgent, Yablonski responded in words told to him by the legendary John L. Lewis. "When ye be an anvil, lay ye very still; but when ye be a hammer, strike with all thy will," Yablonski recalled his mentor's paraphrasing of the seventeenth-century poet George Herbert. "Today," he explained, "is the day I cease being an anvil." After risking his life's comforts and accomplishments to be on the ballot for union president in December 1969, he was defeated in a rigged election by almost a two-to-one margin. In defeat, however, the union monarchy believed that Yablonski still posed a threat as he began to organize the swelling discontent in the coalfields. So the orders came down from the inner-sanctum of the union to have him killed.[5]

Yablonski was also part of a wave of labor leadership that not only sought to reform the unions but was also sympathetic to much of the New Politics of the late 1960s. He served as a delegate to the 1968 Chicago Democratic Convention where he supported Senator Eugene McCarthy's peace plank in opposition to the party and union establishments—both of which were unmovable in their support for the Vietnam War and Lyndon Johnson's heir and labor's darling, Hubert H. Humphrey (who had embraced Boyle as "My friend, that great American" in his typically reflexive campaign rhetoric). In contrast to Jock's dovishness, the most prominent national labor leaders were militant hawks who attacked the "dirty" and "foul mouthed" protestors at the 1968 Chicago Democratic Convention. Yablonski, however, was so disturbed by the violence that Mayor Daley unleashed on the protestors that he went down to Grant Park to speak to the demonstrators. The following spring, at a rally at the University of Pittsburgh, he invited students to join not just in the working people's fight against wealth and privilege but also the struggle "to get the hell out of Vietnam!" at a moment when organized labor was one of the most aggressive defenders of U.S. foreign policy.[6]

In addition to riding the discontent boiling up from the mines and the Democratic Party, Yablonski also had support from high-profile allies rarely seen in mainstream labor circles in the postwar era. Two in particular, the consumer advocate Ralph Nader, connected to the wave of protest over black lung disease, and the combative liberal attorney Joe Rauh, suggested a vibrant new direction for labor in the 1970s. Nader had taken on the automobile industry in the middle of the sixties and proven the unsafe design of many American cars as well as survived GM's sustained efforts to destroy his reputation. Young people flocked to work with Nader in his Washington-based consumer safety advocacy group, which became known as "Nader's Raiders" for its efforts to root out corporate fraud and corruption. Rauh, the attorney for the UAW, was one of the most noted and scrappy lawyers in Washington. He constantly threw himself into the thick of key civil rights and labor insurgencies of the era, crafting the civil rights plank for the Democratic Party in 1948, serving as the attorney for the Mississippi Freedom Democratic Party's attempt to be seated in lieu of the segregationist regulars at the national Democratic Convention in 1964, and working to get a peace plank in the 1968 Democratic platform.[7]

Hundreds of miners gathered to lay the Yablonski family to rest in sub-zero temperatures in the pale, barren earth of western Pennsylvania. Present were only family members and rank-and-file miners—officials from the UMWA were told not to attend. No other labor organization bothered to send a representative. Father Owen Rice, Pittsburgh's "Labor Priest," remarked at the service, "All the horrors of the 1960s were brought home to us in this deed of infamy. . . . The killing of a controversial man echoes the assassinations of both Kennedys and Martin Luther King. Only this is worse because of cold-blooded premeditation." It was then and there that Yablonski's comrades, gathered in the Immaculate Church near where he was laid to rest, swore to end the "horrors of the sixties" by forming what would become known as Miners for Democracy (MFD) for the seventies.[8]

The spirit of the movement captured everything the unions needed to make the transformation from fading, brittle icons of the thirties to vibrant participants in the post-1960s world. They linked together concerns that resonated across basic industry: the "new" qualitative demands of health and safety, quality of work life, and union democracy. The causes were leavened with youthful energy, a sixties-style discontent, and an anti-authority mood created not by protesting the war but, more typically among the working class, from actually serving in it. In the case of MFD, the insurgents went on to defeat the UMWA's bureaucratic authoritarianism just two years later in a social movement that swept through Appalachia and straight into the union's headquarters. As labor lawyer Thomas Geoghegan explained it, MFD "was like nothing else in labor. It was Union Democracy, the New Politics, the whole Sixties Enlightenment. It was the whole sixties experience come at last to organized labor."[9]

Chelsea Hotel. Atlantic City, New Jersey, 1935

If workers' organizational power was going to be revived for the 1970s, it was fitting that it begin where it last began, with the coal miners. Back in the Great Depression, it had been another miners' leader, John L. Lewis, who placed himself at the center of the struggle for economic justice. As the *New York Times* noted in 1973, the UMWA, once the "battering ram" of the union movement, was poised "once again" to be at "the forefront of American labor." The famous 1935 meeting of the American Federation of Labor (AFL) in Atlantic City arrived at the culmination of two years of brewing "discord, dissension, division, and disunion" among the union leadership, in the words of historian Irving Bernstein, about the cause of industrial unionism. The tension was palpable at the Chelsea Hotel, where the forces demanding a massive push to organize basic industry—steel, auto, rubber, electrical— squared off with the lords of craft unionism who sought to defend craft skill, status, nativism, and skin privilege that had become the hallmarks of the AFL. While the dissident advocates of industrial unionism had the arc of justice on their side, the defenders of the status quo could point to the grave- yard of labor history, which was strewn with the dashed hopes of broad-based industrial unionism from the Knights of Labor through Eugene Debs' rail- way workers and onto the massive strike wave of 1919. In the dialectic of soli- darity and fragmentation in American labor history, fragmentation kept winning.[10]

The 1935 Atlantic City convention finally reached its dramatic peak when John L. Lewis, in an infamous, theatrical act of frustration, launched his famous right jab across the jaw of the defender of craft unionism, Big Bill Hutcheson, president of the carpenters' union. After Hutcheson crashed across a collapsing table, Lewis famously straightened his tie, lit a cigar, and went on to launch the Committee, later Congress, of Industrial Organiza- tions (CIO)—the acronym that would forever be connected to economic justice and the unprecedented growth of membership, power, and mission of organized labor. For a brief and exciting period, all of the issues that had divided workers—immigrant from native, skilled from unskilled, white from black, women from men, ethnic from "American," craft versus industrial forms of organization, and liberal from radical—were all mitigated, though far from eliminated. Workers flocked to the cause of industrial unionism, fight- ing off company goons, the National Guard, the courts, and the ideological, gender, and racial divisions within their own ranks.[11]

That said, as historian Nelson Lichtenstein has argued, "industrial unionism's moment of unrivaled triumph proved exceedingly brief." Only a matter of weeks after the CIO's famous victories at GM and U.S. Steel in 1937, the unions' radical challenge met some of the most deeply engrained aspects of American history—the organized strength of corporations, the problems of race, the disproportionate power of the Southern Democracy, and the political precariousness of liberalism itself. Even then, just when the project to organize mass industry began to falter in the recession and political attacks after 1937, the national mobilization for war alone saved the upsurge. By the end of World War II, the unions could count over one-third of all non-agricultural workers among their members, unparalleled political influence, a state tolerant of its activities, and a web of allies that added up to a remarkable position of power in the American establishment. For a historically unique moment in the long struggle of organized labor, the unions won—and won big.[12]

As steelworker's son Jack Metzgar recalled the semi-mythic impact of the mine workers on working-class communities across the industrial heartland, "Somehow, in one of the Steelworkers' fights, 'we' looked up and there were the miners, 'hundreds of them' marching arm-in-arm in support of the steelworkers—like the cavalry arriving. . . . The miners' union begat the Steelworkers union, and the Steelworkers' union begat all that was good in our lives." While many were critical of the compromises and constraints placed on unions after World War II, Metzgar could point to a complete transformation in his family's life—from their material well-being to his father's bearing toward supervisors on the shop floor. "If what we lived through in the 1950s was not liberation," he noted about the new opportunities the CIO delivered to places like Johnstown, Pennsylvania, "then liberation never happens in real human lives."[13]

Union-driven spending funneled money from the company to the family and to the community and, in the process, fostered a relatively affluent industrial working class, which often passed in American political discourse for the amorphous "middle class." The unions grew to be immense and effective bulwarks against the unlimited prerogatives of business, and, with the passing of each bargaining session and each strike, delivered unprecedented buying power to the nation's workers. The weekly earnings of non-supervisory workers increased 62 percent between 1947 and 1972 before stagnating indefinitely thereafter. The system provided constant improvement in the material well-being of unionized workers: inequality went down, wages went up, and the majority of working people who were not organized enjoyed a nice spillover effect. Working-class people had a collective voice and sharp enough elbows at the political table to demand a larger slice of the economic pie. Those wages spurred savings and consumption that, circulating in a pre-global context, helped create good-paying jobs for other working people.[14]

There were, however, costs associated with such success. One was rigidity, as unions staked their legacy not on racial justice, not on gender equity, not on quality of work life, not on union democracy, and not on expansion of the movement beyond the white, male, industrial sectors of the Midwest and Northeast—especially after the Cold War purge of the Left that had been the unions' conscience on issues of gender and race. The job of labor leaders was to support and grow, often quite vigorously, the promise of the existing Keynesian dream of full employment and broad-based consumption and, more often than not, fight off quite vigorously anyone or anything that challenged its basic structure—including at times the unions' own members.

The system provided a creeping liberation for workers that quickly tipped from social movement to technocracy. Labor in its mature phase was thought of as part of the new "industrial pluralism"—a recognized junior partner in the American enterprise. As the Communication Workers' Joseph Beirne put it, a union had become "a professional organization, expertly administered," and the labor leader "an executive, an administrator" surrounded with "economists, lawyers, public relations men, statisticians, accountants, social security and insurance specialist, teachers, recreation directors and geriatrists." That pluralism embraced a program of rational interests hashed out at the bargaining table, replacing social vision with a sundry of technical disputes. The organized, industrial, white, and male sectors enjoyed the benefits of a private welfare system, while the unorganized sectors—often women and people of color in service occupations—were left out of the club. The more the system worked for the organized, and the more the political advancement of working-class interests was blocked by Southern Democrats voting in unison with Northern Republicans, the more deeply unions focused on their contractual successes. The more the unions' "pork chop solidarity" worked, the more the leadership believed that their great breakthrough in the thirties and forties had turned the house of labor into a palace. And it had, but by the time the seventies came around, it became clear that the entrance was guarded and the foundation lay on shifting sands.[15]

As Jock Yablonski could readily attest, the hothouse of union leadership and democracy of the thirties had grown cold by the late sixties. The incumbent leadership, rather than rising to the challenge of incorporating the new so-cial demands of the sixties, feared a more capacious and aggressive vision for organized labor as little more than a threat to the success they already enjoyed. In dissent they often saw descent, and they acted accordingly. At the same time that unions delivered unprecedented affluence to the postwar working class, they bordered on what one critic called "a new feudal order in which loyalty was the highest and finest virtue, a hierarchy that fed off igno-rance and called it solidarity." In the case of the UMWA, John L. Lewis selected weak insiders to head the union rather than building toward a democratic union culture. "Great tyrants, jealous of their power," remarked one UMWA analyst about Lewis, "often surround themselves with men much less capable than themselves, men who do not pose a threat to their kingdom. The result is often disastrous." In the case of the miners, the disas-ter arrived in the form of the sinister figure of Tony Boyle who took over for Lewis in 1963.[16]

Consolidated Coal. Farmington, West Virginia, 1968

The fall of Tony Boyle began just five years after his anointment when a mine explosion in the autumn of 1968 entombed seventy-eight miners. The press descended upon the small village of Farmington, where a thin and gaunt Tony Boyle publicly revealed his indifference to the concerns of the rank and file. As one observer noted, "there were weeping wives and smudge-faced children aplenty to satisfy the nation's need for year-end sentiments . . . the miners saw themselves and their occupation assume new dimensions of importance in the nation's eyes." As brother miners lay buried and televi-sion cameras swarmed all over the small town, however, the UMWA presi-dent did the unthinkable—he let the coal operators off the hook. "As long as we mine coal, there is always this inherent danger," Boyle dismissed the affair to reporters. He then proceeded to proclaim Consolidated Coal to be "one of the best companies to work with as far as cooperation and safety are concerned." The workers and their families were astonished by his callous-ness. To anyone concerned about the fate of the miners, the quality of the company's safety record was not the issue—the dead miners were. In a single media appearance, Boyle revealed how out of touch the UMWA leadership was with the concerns of the rank and file and just how cozy the union had become with management.[17]

The events in Farmington contrasted markedly with the image of John L. Lewis in a similar explosion in 1951 at the Orient No. 2 mine in West Frankfort, Illinois. There, with 119 miners dead, Lewis donned a miner's helmet and went underground. He emerged with his cheeks blackened and the pain of the community's loss carved into his face. A photographer captured his grief in one of the most famous and compelling images of postwar labor leadership. "That picture just had to make coal miners feel so proud," Jock Yablonski told his son. "But that sonovabitch Boyle. With those people dead in the mine, how could that bastard stand up and praise the company's safety record the way he did?" In contrast to Lewis, Boyle appeared at the Farmington explosion perfectly dressed, with a rose in his lapel. He did not even want to speak with the victims' families.[18]

A less symbolic but more substantive catalyst driving the chemistry of rank-and-file anger was the UMWA's neglect of the centuries-old problem of black lung disease. The UMWA contract provided the usual pay increases that had become the hallmark of postwar collective bargaining, but it failed to deal with the concern that had become the center-point for many miners: pneumoconiosis. Breathing the fine black dust of the mines—a problem made worse by the introduction of new digging technology—slowly clogged the miners' lungs', halting ability to transfer air into the bloodstream. The disease left workers short of breath, spitting up a tar-colored fluid, and eventually, miserably incapacitated, then dead. As Ralph Nader put it, "The continuance of the black lung epidemic over the years without attention, prevention, or remedy parallels another disease—that afflicting the United Mine Workers of America leadership."[19]

The efforts of miners and widows to find remedies and compensation for the plague of the coal regions had been crippled by bad science, corrupt mine operators, complicit physicians, jaundiced insurance systems, and even worse politics. Old laws included such arcane requirements as proving the exact chemical composition and concentration of the dust inhaled decades earlier in order to prove that mining was the actual cause of the victim's ailments. Worst of all, it became clear the UMWA had been lackadaisical, some said cynical, in its approach to health and safety legislation. As one Harlan County miner explained, "You was taught, and I believed it, that coal dust was good for you. I'd actually feel proud when I could cough up a mouthful of that black stuff and spit it out." In the late 1960s, activist physicians, widows, victims of the disease, and young members of Volunteers in Service to America (VISTA) began to travel Appalachia organizing meetings in bleak high school gymnasiums and smoky union halls, where they showed slides of blackened and perforated lungs to throngs of horrified miners.[20]

As miners finally received the first careful and honest explanation regarding the nature of their disease, the misery of black lung transformed into a vibrant and effective social movement. By January 1969, the West Virginia Black Lung Association was formed. Members elected an African-American, Charles Brooks, as their president, a miner who had mortgaged his home to raise the money to begin lobbying efforts to win black lung compensation from the state government of West Virginia. The movement was not at all a charismatic organization but a nuts-and-bolts, grassroots operation of competent and hard working people. The technicalities of the disease, the ceaseless questions of causality, and the doctors' diagnostic tricks that had trapped victims in a never-ending cycle of deception were reworked into a sense of entitlement: if you worked the mines and had respiratory ailments then you were entitled to compensation. The black lung groups demanded a much more comprehensive set of measures and mechanisms than a union-supported bill. When the legislature refused to take more serious measures and the union backed the legislature's tepid bill, 95 percent of the miners in the state walked off the job in a wildcat action that lasted twenty-three days. By March 1969, forty thousand miners had stopped work—the largest strike for an occupational health issue in American history, which basically shut down all of commercial mining in West Virginia.[21]

The fight for black lung benefits rested on the power of the wildcat strike, which had all the power of a sacrament in the coal mines of Appalachia. As Robert Payne, a disabled black miner and evangelical preacher who was president of the Disabled Miners and Widows, explained, "The strike's the onliest weapon the rank and file has. . . . There wasn't no one person responsible for what happened in 1969. Everybody was responsible for it. It was all the miners and disabled miners striking to get this Black Lung law passed." West Virginia's Black Lung Strike forced the state's politicians to produce a better bill. The action proved the power of rank-and-file action, aided by a tightened labor market and key allies, against the combined forces of the companies, the state, and the hierarchy of the UMWA. The miners learned their lesson: they could act outside of the union bureaucracy and win. The shock waves from the workers' movements in West Virginia finally played a central role in moving federal legislation on black lung. The strike reverberated all the way to the White House, as President Nixon changed his position from a declaration that he would veto the Federal Coal Mine Health and Safety Act to a quiet and unceremonial signing of the bill into law on December 30, 1969. On the day that Nixon signed the bill, Tony Boyle's hired thugs plotted the murder of Jock Yablonski, who had been moved to action by the black lung activists.[22]

Another key factor in the success of the miners' reform movement—and all of the rank-and-file dissent—was the discontent of the young. By the late 1960s, fresh workers with new ideas poured into the pits as employment rates began to rise after slumping for much of the fifties and sixties. As one dissident miner explained, "Them's the ones that's in back of us, young miners." Echoed another, "The old blood's against us." As John Wampler, who worked the nightshift in Virginia's Dixiana mine, explained in terms that echoed throughout basic industry, "The young guy is looking for something more than his father got. You saw that most of the older men were for Boyle at Dixiana. Well, the younger guys don't want to talk against them but they're looking for a change." Miners for Democracy (MFD) proved very popular among the new miners, especially the returning Vietnam vets, who refused to obey arbitrary orders or take on unnecessarily dangerous tasks. They often wore an anti-corporate chip on their shoulder and made friends with the stream of hip and urbane VISTA volunteers arriving in Appalachia—much like white civil rights workers had in Mississippi a decade earlier. As MFD co-chair Harry Patrick put it,

> I think one of the highlights of our campaign was when you'd walk into a bath-house at new mines and you would see all these young kids with long hair and beards. And they were Vietnam veterans, practically to the man. . . . And they made no bones about where they stood. They would tell you right up "Damn right we need a change. Maybe you guys ain't the right guys, but dammit, let's change and we'll change you guys. You know, you guys don't do right, we'll change you come the next time around." And they were just a tremendous, tremendous asset to our campaign. . . . They'd talk to people. Most of them, their fathers was old coal miners. Maybe retired. They'd go up and say "Look, dad, you're crazy, hell, don't you know what they're doing up there?" It helped.[23]

The final, if elusive, variable in the eventual success of the miners' upsurge was the federal government. The hope for the insurgencies in coal and beyond rested, oddly enough, with a business-backed law, the 1959 Landrum-Griffin

Act (Labor-Management Reporting and Disclosure Act or LMRDA). The act provided for federal oversight of unions in order, claimed the law's advocates, to protect workers and industry from communism and corruption. It promised to shield union members from abuses with a "bill of rights" that guaranteed freedom of speech and periodic secret elections. Republicans backed the bill hoping that the more conservative rank and file would use the tools to oust their liberal leaders. Union dissidents, however, banked on the opposite: using the act as a valuable tool for getting federal oversight for free and fair elections, when, that is, they could get the government to budge on its promises at all.

Labor attorney Joe Rauh constantly badgered the Department of Labor to live up to the promise of the act and to intervene in the Yablonski-Boyle contest—but to no avail. "This, Mr. Secretary [of Labor George Shultz], is the sorry record of illegal conduct of the incumbent officer of the UMWA," Rauh explained in his last appeal to get federal oversight of the election in 1969. "That they intend to steal the election a week from tomorrow has been shown over and over again in these pages," he pleaded. "So, Mr. Secretary, these are your choices: You can allow the Boyle team to steal the election and start a long four-year process toward a new election with cold evidence which will cost the government millions of dollars and the union its democracy for another four years; or, Mr. Secretary, you can stand up, investigate, have an agent at every poll and make the LMRDA a reality." The refusal of the Department of Labor to intervene in the 1969 mine workers' election suggested that labor's original critique of the bill was right: that it was designed not to help unions but to further contain their power. Yablonski's sons would later point to the Secretary of Labor's "inexcusable inaction" as central to their father's death.[24]

After investigations began in the wake of the Yablonski murders, the Department of Labor finally demanded a new, free, and fair election slated to be held in 1972. To prepare, MFD, the organization born at Yablonski's funeral, had its organizing convention in Wheeling, West Virginia. There all the strands of discontent—including the Yablonski dissidents, the Black Lung Association, the Disabled Miners and Widows of Southern West Virginia, and the young—gathered in a genuine rank-and-file convention. The delegates traveled at their own expense and eventually selected a miner named Arnold Miller to pick up Yablonski's fallen torch for a federally mandated re-run of the stolen 1969 election, slated for 1972.

Arnold Miller was a lifelong member of the UMWA and president of his small local in Cabin Creek, West Virginia, before going on to serve as the president of the Black Lung Association. Although strikingly handsome, the scars of the twentieth century marked his body. He survived being shot during the landing at Normandy, only to be abandoned there by his commanding officers. A scar ran down half of his head and he had a deformed ear—despite twenty operations in Army hospitals. Then, by the end of the sixties, he too had become disabled by the coal dust clogging his lungs. He was also oddly shy, even taciturn, for one who was going to lead the most dramatic labor insurgency in U.S. history. "It's a man's life that shows what he is," explained a young shuttle car operator in Blacksville, West Virginia. "Miller don't have to say anything."[25]

Arnold Miller, along with Yablonski's old allies Mike Trbovich and Patrick Miller, who rounded out the MFD slate, traveled the coalfields and campaigned among miners scrubbing off the dust in the bathhouses, and visited an endless scattering of dingy, smoke-filled union halls tucked up in the maze of Appalachian hollows. Even after the news about Boyle and the indictments for corruption trickled out, the MFD candidates still had to fight off strong currents of complacency and blind loyalty to the old regime—a regime that had proved its ability to deliver the goods. For too long, the stubborn arrogance of a person like Boyle (or Lewis) and the collective discipline imposed by the union hierarchy had been regarded as the price for good contracts. "We knowed Tony done wrong," explained Leonard Sargent, a miner from Sophia, West Virginia. "Everyone knowed it. We figure that has to be changed. But I been in the mine for 38 years, since I was 17, and I think our best bet is to stick with Tony. This is a funny thing to say for a man who believes in democracy as much as I do, but we can't afford democracy in this union."[26]

Even more than the Yablonski campaign, MFD gathered a great deal of support from outside of the coalfields and the unions as intellectuals, students, and reformers of various stripes saw their hopes wrapped up in the MFD cause. The Boyle campaign against Miller continually pointed to one of the stock characters in the labor history melodrama—the "outside agitator." To many, especially the inner clique of the mine workers' union, the young MFD allies from the law schools, the student groups, and liberal organizations were little more than meddlesome hippies and communists. Indeed, the entire platform of the Boyle slate in 1972 was based on two ideas:

they could run the union better, and they would not let outsiders interfere with the union. The UMWA tried to whip up anti-MFD sentiments by attacking the radical students who had left the campuses in order to organize workers. Using defensive labels that would soon come to define much of white working-class politics, the union defamed "the malcontents, the rebels, and the sundry other freaky characters including hundreds of hippie-type OUTSIDERS and wealthy supporters of rich-man, tax-free foundations." Federal intervention triggered some of the deepest fears, which the pro-Boyle literature whipped up, as they described "the biggest and most dangerous outsider, one intent upon destroying this great Union"— the federal government—which "has its tentacles into every part of the UMWA."[27]

The federal government's monitoring of the balloting in December 1972 marked a new beginning. Union employees were forbidden to contribute union time or personal money to any candidate; the Department of Labor posted thirty agents at UMWA headquarters and thirty at district and sub-district offices; and young organizers and student radicals who were turning their hopes to the labor movement poured into Appalachia from all over the eastern seaboard to act as election monitors. MFD observers, according to attorney Clarice Feldman, scrutinized documents "with a vengeance right out of the Old Testament." Two weeks later, Miller was declared the victor. It was the first time in modern labor history that a union chose a national leader straight from the rank and file over an incumbent president.[28]

As a then left-leaning journalist named Brit Hume noted in *Ramparts*, "In retrospect, it might seem that their resounding victory was inevitable. But no one who stood on that frozen cemetery hilltop in the Pennsylvania coal fields three years ago and watched the coffins of Joseph, Margaret, and Charlotte Yablonski lowered into the ground could have believed that a rank-and-file triumph was inevitable by 1973." Indeed, it would not have happened without Yablonski's martyrdom. Had it not been for the high public drama of the murders, which triggered federal intervention, journalist John Herling lamented, "the anger and dismay of the coal miners, long used to frustration and accustomed to the misuse of the union's electoral process, would have only added to the slagheap of their hopelessness."[29]

With a rank-and-file leader now in charge of the UMWA, "a breeze of uncertainty," in journalist Nina Totenberg's terms, flowed through the hierarchy of the other unions. AFL-CIO president George Meany, who had once dismissed Yablonski as "just a kitchen boy who wants to get into the dining room," now faced dissidents in charge of one of the great historical unions in the movement (albeit one then outside the AFL-CIO). As Rauh noted with dismay, much of labor's officialdom had long been complicit in the UMWA's disregard for the insurgents and, implicitly, even the murder of their leader. "The trade union movement has watched this tragedy in silent acquiescence," he declared, "some leaders even with hostility to our cause." The pain of liberals like Rauh, who had staked their professional lives on the labor-liberal alliance embodied in groups like Americans for Democratic Action, was palpable. "In my opinion," he grieved, "the labor movement with which I have had such close and warm ties all my working life is cutting its own throat here."[30]

A year after Arnold Miller's electoral victory, the new UMWA president officiated over his first convention in December 1973. The event bubbled with democratic spirit and was full of the promise to be found in what one worker called the "tedious but glorious" experience of democracy. Three-fourths of the miners present were at their first convention, many of whom had been given a crash course in parliamentary procedure before arriving so they could be full participants in the proceedings (a radical departure from the ramrod parliamentary maneuvers and crushing of dissent at previous conventions). For the duration of the eleven-day long event, microphones were open to the floor, typically featuring long lines of miners patiently waiting their turn to speak, fumbling with notes they had written for themselves, and finally speaking to the brothers about matters ranging from rewriting the constitution to requesting subsidies for delegates who could not afford rooms or food during the convention. As Joe Rauh explained in his address to the convention, "your example has encouraged thousands of others inside and outside the labor movement to dream what they have been told were impossible dreams. It has shaken other union tyrannies. It has given hope to the unorganized who live in poverty and degradation. It has given strength to those who are battling on every front against injustice, greed, and special privilege. . . . Thousands are looking to you as a symbol of the instincts and worthiest visions of our nation." The union, it was often said from the floor, had been returned to its members.[31]

A participant-observer of the mine workers in the early seventies, labor attorney Thomas Geoghegan, noted that the MFD victory was one of the most important transformations—a "revolution" in his terms—in the lives of working people and that, strangely enough, it had emerged from people who were bedrock cultural conservatives. Suggesting something of the malleability of class identity, he noted, "A union of Baptists, church deacons, people in Appalachia, who had never heard a Bob Dylan song in their lives, the most tsarist, autocratic and backward union in America: *this* is where it started." The problem was how far could the spirit of reform and revitalization go? "The miners for Democracy are the first wave of the new labor insurgents to send shock waves of conscience rippling through the world of liberalism," explained union democracy advocate H.W. Benson. The question was, however, "Is it a passing flash or the first sign of changing times?"[32]

Steel Workers Local 65. South Chicago, 1973

To believe, as so many did, that the MFD struggle was more than a passing flash, one only had to look at the steel workers where an almost equally dramatic story was unfolding in the heart of basic steel. If ever there was a contest between the complacency of the golden age labor relations system and the insurgencies of the seventies, it emerged from the slate and fire skies over South Works Local 65.

Enter Eddie Sadlowski. Many believed that this young, third-generation steel worker from the dreary steel mill neighborhoods in South Chicago had the potential, as *Rolling Stone* proclaimed, to be "this country's next great labor leader." He was only twenty-five years old when he was elected president of South Works Local 65 and earned a great deal of rank-and-file support with a refreshing combination of youth, tough-talking populism, and street-wise class consciousness. He had organized and spoken out against the war at the national United Steel Workers (USW) Convention in 1968, declaring that "it is the sons of steelworkers that are dying in this meaningless war!" Then, in events that echoed the turbulence in the UMWA, Sadlowski launched a grassroots crusade for the directorship of District 31 in 1973, the largest district in the union, consisting of nearly three hundred locals scattered around the core of basic steel in Chicago and Gary, Indiana. His support rested on the Dewey Burtons of the steel mills. "What really irritates people is that we haven't kept up in terms of rights on the job, working conditions, and safety," reported one Sadlowski supporter. "It's what goes on during the eight hours you're in there. This is what constantly aggravates people."[33]

Labor history was alive in "Oilcan Eddie" Sadlowski. Joe Hill, Eugene Debs, Clarence Darrow, Mother Jones, John L. Lewis, and Paul Robeson were not dead historical figures but living American spirits to him. He would often invoke Steinbeck to explain the plight of the working class: "They can't beat us, Pa, 'cause we're the people." "That may sound corny to you," Sadlowski confessed to a reporter, "but I believe it." Burly, gregarious, and irrepressible, Sadlowski regarded himself loosely in the tradition of Progressive Era socialist Eugene Debs. His house was located about a mile from the Republic Steel works where the infamous Memorial Day massacre took place in 1937, and his basement was a veritable repository of labor history. He loved to share his memories of sitting around and listening to "bull sessions" of the older generation of workers during breaks. "We'd go into the shanties—you know the rest shacks—and we'd talk about anything . . . best damn conversations I ever had. Those guys had *minds*, you know? They had subtlety. Talk about anything . . . philosophy, politics. It was tough keeping up with them— you had to keep your mind honed, you had to be sharp to hang in with these guys. Some of the best public speakers I ever saw were in the mills." He detested the notion that the heart of organized labor was in contracts, pensions, and technocratic details. For him, it was in the movement, in the history, in the people, and in the shops. *Rolling Stone* called him an "old-fashioned hero of the new working class."[34]

In many ways, Sadlowski's campaign for district office paralleled that of MFD. In 1973, Joseph Germano's seat as head of the district was set to expire as a result of mandatory retirement. He had run the district for three decades as an "old style labor boss," consolidating his power over the district back in the days of the original rise of the USW. To succeed him, Germano picked assistant director Sam Evett, a second generation union bureaucrat who had never worked in the mills or even run for office. Evett had the support of USW president Abel, the outgoing Germano, Mayor Daley's political machine, and nearly the entire USW staff. Surmounting nearly impossible obstacles just to get on the ballot in the first place, Sadlowski's path to victory in District 31 unfolded like a chapter straight out of the MFD strategy manual.[35]

Sadlowski used the USW's Experimental Negotiating Agreement (ENA), which was often heralded as the future of modern collective bargaining, as the target of his criticism. The ENA required that the union would not strike basic steel when the contract expired but would instead submit to binding arbitration if an agreement had not been found by a specific date. In exchange, the workers received substantial wage increases. The agreement was designed to guarantee steady production levels that would not be hampered by strikes or by customers stockpiling steel during contract negotiations in anticipation of strikes. Stabilizing the system, USW president Abel believed, would also allow American steel to compete better with foreign steel, thus preserving American jobs by guarding against "import threats, stockpiling, plant shutdowns and prolonged layoffs." Forfeiting the right to strike, however, became one of the central bones of contention between the rank-and-file activists, who saw it as disarming the working class, and the union, which saw it as a reasonable bargain and a step forward in institutional strength by providing more security for steel labor.[36]

Sadlowski's slogan was "It's time to fight back." Under that banner, he drew together a wide array of disgruntled steelworkers—blacks, whites, Latinos, women, men—who were fed up with the Germano machinery and the lack of rank-and-file voice within the union. He hit the plant gates, amassed funds from small contributions, and railed against the union for being too cozy with management. He focused on the union's accommodation to speed ups, loss of jobs to automation, failure to appoint blacks to administrative positions (when they constituted one-third of the membership in the district), and against the conservative policies of AFL-CIO on the war.

The dissident steelworkers were particularly frustrated by the dead-end nature of industrial labor. "Guys who work in the mill, they'd give their right arm to get outta there. But they want something more than that paycheck," he noted about the limits of collective bargaining. "They got pride. They know this country can't do without their labor. Instead, these companies treat 'em like animals or throw 'em away when they're worn out or they find some machine to replace them. Everybody needs some cause to identify with. So you don't give up and let 'em run over you. The present labor leadership's failed in that." As throughout the early seventies, the thirties analogy resonated for Sadlowski. "The CIO—now that didn't stand for pensions and vacations—that stood for a vision of social justice and people's dignity," Sadlowski explained to an interviewer. Recognizing that Sadlowski was starry-eyed about the potential of workers in a technocratic age, the interviewer shot back, "You're a romantic." But Eddie knew where he stood. "Fuck you. It's romantics and fighters who change the world. Not all these take-it-easy types who sit on their dicks waitin' for it to fall into their laps."[37]

At the microphone Sadlowski tended to ramble and lacked the eloquent turns of phrase of his hero John L. Lewis. Yet he brought issues of race, the war, the environment, distribution of wealth and power, and quality of work life constantly to the forefront of his discussions. On issues of race, for instance, Sadlowski's leadership was particularly strong. Drawing a line between the union vision and the growing white backlash that competed for the white workers' allegiance, he exclaimed, "You can't be a union man and be a redneck. I just can't handle that kind of shit. A guy will come up to me and say nigger this and nigger that and I'll just unload on him—you don't know me, I can be a mean sonofabitch. There's no way you can be a union man and a racist." He saw the racial divide as management's tool. "The biggest thing management has had going over the years is this game of divide and conquer—especially between blacks and whites. Like my pa used to tell me about the sharecroppers down South. The black sharecropper would get a house that was just a little better than the white guy . . . but the white guy would get a dime more on a bale of cotton than the black. And so they'd always be jealous of each other about something and always fighting each other instead of the boss."[38]

Yet the highly masculine culture of even the most progressive leader like Sadlowski spoke to the depth of the problems of patriarchy in the labor movement and society at large. When journalist Judith Coburn interviewed him, she found the missing piece in his new working-class hero persona—a piece largely missing from the male-dominated insurgencies of the first half of the seventies in general: respect for the role of women. For all of his aggressive posturing on race, there was still a deep reservoir of sexism running through it all. As Coburn noted, "I'm reminded of the one thing that cramps my enthusiasm for Sadlowski. Although he makes obligatory statements when asked about women's rights, there are few women in his campaign organization. And at least until he gets used to having a woman reporter around, he's full of outrageous sexist tricks—blowing a kiss to end an interview, copping a squeeze here and there, making cracks about sharing motel rooms to save money. All 'in good fun,' and after a while he cans it, but, still."[39]

Just as the UMWA stole the election from Yablonski, however, so the USW stole the election from Sadlowski. "We were winning by maybe three, four thousand votes," noted Sadlowski supporter Clem Balanoff about election night in February 1973. "But then, about midnight, the results stopped coming in. . . . Now, in Chicago politics this can mean only one thing: It means they're stealing the election." And so they were. The day after the election, Sadlowski was still in the lead, but, when the results from a couple of key locals with shady pasts came in, the news arrived that Evett was the victor. Like the insurgent miners, Sadlowski turned to attorney Joe Rauh and the Landrum-Griffin Act to contest the elections. For eighteen months, the legal wrangling ensued, and the Labor Department finally confirmed what the Sadlowski supporters believed: there had been widespread fraud in the election. The District 31 contest was re-run in November 1974, with U.S. Department of Labor supervision, and this time Sadlowski won by nearly a two to one margin: 39,637 votes to 20,058. The *Washington Post* declared that "a new labor star has been born." People began to see the district election as a dress rehearsal for head of the entire USW organization, and Eddie Sadlowski as candidate for the 1977 race to be the next international president of the United Steel Workers of America.[40]

With their victory for the head of USW District 31, Sadlowski backers formed Steelworkers Fight Back in 1975 to win the presidency of the entire international union. "If Eddie wins," predicted oral historian and journalist Studs Terkel, "it will be the end of Meanyism and all that cold war crap in America." While the contest for the presidency of the USW was very real, by the latter half of the 1970s, as we shall see in Chapter 5, it was practically a different age for both the steelworkers and the miners.[41]

Chevy Vega Plant. Lordstown, Ohio, 1972

One of the most modern assembly lines in the world, stuck in the middle of a cornfield in northeastern Ohio, was named after a non-descript crossroads but became synonymous with a syndrome, a rebellion, and a crisis: Lordstown. The 1972 struggle over the pace of production among insurgent autoworkers at the Chevy Vega plant became the iconic conflict of seventies working-class history, bringing focus to simmering issues of alienation, industrial boredom, and the failure of postwar collective bargaining to take into account the quality of work life. It also brought to the national consciousness a new generation of workers created by labor's postwar success, those less concerned with increasing the size of their paychecks or negotiating better benefits than they were in achieving a more humane workplace. *Commonweal* called Lordstown "the most dramatic instance of worker resistance since the 1937 Flint sit-down." Ralph Nader proclaimed that Lordstown would do for workers "what the Berkeley situation of 1964 did for student awareness." The New Left believed it had found "a trial run of the class struggle of the '70s." Like the young miners attracted to MFD and the Sadlowski campaign, the autoworkers were informed by an anti-authoritarianism learned in Vietnam and outlooks less constrained by the racial attitudes that divided much of blue-collar America in the early seventies.[42]

Any understanding of Lordstown must begin with a union and an industry in transition. As if to mark the uneasy move to the new era, the famous president of the UAW, Walter Reuther, died in a plane crash in the spring of 1970. Reuther embodied both the hope and constraints of postwar labor liberalism—"the left wing of the possible" in postwar America. He could simultaneously loathe the constraints placed upon his political ambition by the cigar-chomping George Meany and the executive board of the AFL-CIO but also remain suspicious of the student movements who similarly bridled at the limits of liberalism. He could stand heroically at the March on Washington in 1963, advocate for the Memphis sanitation workers clutching their "I am a Man" signs in 1968, push for the "Model Cities" program in Washington, march with the farmworkers in California, and finance many aspects of the civil rights movement for much of the decade. But he failed to deal with racism in the auto plants, the whiteness of his own leadership, and the black militancy boiling up in Detroit. The story was similar in the realm of foreign policy. Reuther could personally be critical of the war in Vietnam but leery of allying with the anti-war cause animating the nation's youth (the organizing of whom he had originally helped to finance) for risk of breaking with Johnson and Humphrey, in whom he saw the promise of the next leap forward in domestic reform.[43]

Exasperated with the constraints, Reuther finally pulled the UAW out of the AFL-CIO in 1968, only sixteen years after he had been elected president of the CIO and thirteen years after playing a pivotal role in uniting the house of labor. Declaring the labor federation "historically obsolete," he promised a doubling of union membership in six years. "Why," asked Reuther of his colleagues, "should we, the largest union in the AFL-CIO, pay more than a million dollars a year in per capita [dues] for the privilege of being kicked in the ass by George Meany?" Sounding a lot like the miners' Jock Yablonski, Reuther attacked the AFL-CIO executive council's "complacency," "indifference," "lack of social vision" and the ways that labor leaders had become "increasingly the comfortable custodians of the status quo."[44]

While Reuther laid claim to the insurgent CIO legacy by pulling out of the AFL-CIO, his move led to a very strange and unpromising place: an alliance with the International Brotherhood of Teamsters. The result was a still-born creation of famously incompatible bedfellows: one the liberal darling, the other notoriously corrupt and muscle-bound; one having left the federation on principle and the other having been kicked out for racketeering in 1957; one was led by the most dynamic national labor leader of the postwar era, the other the hand-picked placeholder for Jimmy Hoffa as they dragged him off to jail. Together the two largest unions in America, both orphaned, formed an unholy, even farcical, new organization, the Alliance for Labor Action (ALA). The Faustian deal promised less of a new direction for American workers than it did a sense of desperate aimlessness on the part of the unions as they looked beyond the sixties. The alliance only lasted a few years before it collapsed under the weight of its own improbability. Yet the search for a new paradigm remained.[45]

Leonard Woodcock, who took over the presidency of the drifting UAW after Reuther died, inherited battle plans for a strike against the biggest corporation in the world, GM. It would grow into a titanic undertaking—the biggest auto strike since Reuther had taken on GM at the end of World War II. Some feared that with the discontent boiling up in the shops and Reuther gone, the stability of the system could be at stake. As Virgil Boyd, the vice chairman of Chrysler, explained, "It takes a strong man to keep the situation under control. I hope that whoever his successor is can exercise great internal discipline."[46]

There was little to worry about. The 1970 GM strike may have proved to be one of the costliest strikes in U.S. history, an immense affair—more than "just a strike . . . a crusade" explained journalist William Serrin—that lasted for two months. But it never exploded. The conflict took place largely within predictable boundaries of postwar collective bargaining. In Serrin's study of the GM strike, he somewhat mockingly portrayed it as a "civilized affair" that followed the rituals of postwar collective bargaining in which the two parties were "not enemies, nor, in a large sense adversaries" but shared a *"greater community of interest than of conflict."* In many aspects the 1970 strike lacked the proletarian drama that fired journalists' hearts. The only reason there were even pickets was to "maintain tradition" and public presence. Strikers had to attend required weekly classes in order, according to the leadership, "to rekindle some Depression-style enthusiasm in the younger workers."[47]

Judging by the results of the strike, however, the civilizing of labor relations was not such a bad thing. The workers won substantial gains in wages and benefits, pensions, the renewal of lost cost-of-living protections, and an idea that was immensely popular with the rank and file: "thirty and out"— giving employees the option of escaping the life-draining labor of the assembly work with a pension after thirty years on the job. In a classic exercise in golden-age collective bargaining, the strike delivered more money and less of one's life on the job, objectively good things for those on the line; but what remained unaccounted for was sizable: increased rank-and-file control over the plant, the union, and the industry.

The GM strike may have been the biggest conflict economically, with its loss of $1 billion in profits for the company and the near bankruptcy of the UAW, but the perfunctory performance of postwar collective bargaining rites hardly rattled the golden cage of postwar industrial relations. The real drama in the automotive industry centered on Lordstown when GM tried to figure out ways to compete with foreign carmakers. The postwar industrial boom was partially predicated on the United States' control over global production after the devastation of World War II. By the 1970s, that supremacy was being challenged, first in the most competitive sectors—garments, consumer electronics, and textiles—and then, finally, in the heart of American industry, the automobile. Small foreign cars gaining popularity in the United States contained only a "fraction" of the labor costs of American cars, GM argued, so the company's solution was to compete with innovative design and assembly strategies. The General Motors Assembly Division (referred to, appropriately workers thought, as GMAD) set up shop at Lordstown in 1971, in plants that had only been in operation since 1967. There they re-engineered the line to build a subcompact model, the Vega, to compete with small foreign cars. The wide array of new production technology promised the fastest assembly line in the world. The industrial engineers were replete with optimism about their accomplishment. GM officials claimed "The concept is based on making it easier for the guy on the line. We feel that by giving him less to do he will do it better." Morale around the new system was so high, the company believed, that managers professed they would be able to sell the first five thousand cars right at the end of the assembly line to the workers themselves.[48]

The chairman of the Lordstown bargaining committee could not have disagreed more, countering that the new system was "designed to break the back of the people." GMAD reduced the workforce, sped up the line, and introduced "get tough" disciplinary measures across the board. The speed of the line went from sixty cars per hour to make the old Impala to an unprecedented one hundred cars per hour for the Vega—one vehicle every thirty-six seconds. The workers balked at the speed and discipline by working strictly to rules, letting production slip by unfinished, pushing absenteeism and turnover to new highs, taking drugs and alcohol on the job, and engaging in a wide array of sabotage on the line. The workers reached the breaking point when management responded not with conciliation but with a zero-tolerance, get-tough policy with regard to any form of dissent against regulations or production requirements.

By January 1972, five thousand complaints choked the grievance system protesting the speed up of the line and the unjust treatment of workers. The workers demanded that GM rehire those laid off because of the re-engineering and "to be treated like American workers, human beings, not as pieces of profit-making machinery." When the local strike vote finally came in March 1972, it polled a rare 97 percent in favor of walking off the job, not for more money but for a more humane industrial relations system (rumored to be the largest pro-strike vote in the UAW's history). Ominously for management, much of the impetus and energy for the rise of the CIO in the thirties had not been drawn from wages or hours but, like Lordstown, the organization of the factory floor. "The underlying thrust" of the thirties unrest, explains Mike Davis, "was surprisingly non-economistic: in a majority of cases the fundamental grievance was the petty despotism of the workplace incarnated in the capricious power of the foremen and the inhuman pressures of mechanized production lines." Perhaps, many believed, the seventies would be the same.[49]

Like the other insurgencies, the Lordstown conflict was generational as the young, hip, and angry began to take over. The average age at the plant was only twenty-five years. As the treasurer of Local 1112, J.D. Smith, explained, "It's a different generation of workingmen. None of these guys came over from the old country poor and starving, grateful for any job they could get. None of them have been through a depression. They've been exposed—at least through television—to all the youth movements of the last ten years and they don't see the disgrace of being unemployed." Encapsulating a package of desires that simultaneously rested upon and challenged the accomplishments of the previous generation, Smith noted, "They're just not going to swallow the same kind of treatment their fathers did. They're not afraid of management. That's a lot of what the strike was about. They want more than just a job for 30 years."[50]

The strike only lasted three weeks in the spring of 1972, but the press had been following the buildup of discontent—or the "blue collar blues" as they constantly referred to it—for two years. The press—from *Harper's* to *Life* to *Time* to *Newsweek* to *Playboy* to *The Nation* to *Business Week*—angled for the meanings of the strike and the inner longings of the discontented and shaggy workers, while business leaders fretted about its implications. The *New York Times* labeled it the "Revolt of the Robots," the *Wall Street Journal* saw the "Utopian GM Plant" as "Paradise Lost." The Lordstown local president testified at the Democratic Party's platform committee, the Senate held hearings on "alienation," and the Nixon administration launched a national commission to study the problems it raised. The federal report, *Work in America*, confirmed that "many workers at all occupational levels feel locked in, their mobility blocked, the opportunity to grow lacking in their jobs, challenge missing from their tasks." The strike and the report initiated the "quality of work life" movement that sought to redesign work, introduce automation differently, and invest in "human relations" strategies, most of which continued to empower management, not workers—albeit with the appearance of a gentler hand.[51]

For commentators flocking to the auto plants, the assembly line no longer reflected, if it ever did, the social-realist armies of faceless workers—a homogenized force of machine tenders for a homogenized economy—but, rather, it suggested a search for individual expression within the machine. "The visual evidence of a new youthful individuality is abundant in the assembly plants," noted an observer for *Fortune* magazine. "Along the main production lines and in the subassembly areas there are beards, and shades, long hair here, a peace medallion there, occasionally some beads—above all, young faces, curious eyes." Those faces, explained the writer, were restless yet imbued with a lilting sense of both hope and entitlement. "Their eyes have watched carefully as dissent has spread in the nation. These men are well aware that bishops, soldiers, diplomats, even Cabinet officers, question orders these days and dispute commands. They have observed that demonstrations and dissent have usually been rewarded. They do not look afraid, and they don't look as if they would take much guff. They are creatures of their times." Dan Clark, an assembler at Lordstown, concurred. "They are too concerned with wages and petty things, where they are not concerned with man and the environment. They better start thinking of man's mind and his relaxation, because the life expectancy is going to be cut short if he has got to work in a plant like this now. You have got to have peace of mind." It was not just alienation from the assembly line but the way workers, influenced by the war, had become "disassociated with the whole establishment" as Local president Gary Bryner put it.[52]

The Lordstown workers became a collective national symbol for that new breed of worker and emblematic of a widespread sense of occupational alienation. People gravitated to the refreshing vision of youth, vitality, inter-racial solidarity, and enlightenment hidden from the public behind the likes of television's Archie Bunker, pro-war labor leadership, and the growing politics of the blue-collar backlash. Gary Bryner explained that the workers suffered from little of the racial resentment that had been the plague of working-class movements since their inception. "The young black and white workers dig each other. There's an understanding. The guy with the Afro, the guy with the beads, the guy with the goatee, he doesn't care if he's black, white, green or yellow." They smoked dope, socialized inter-racially, and dreamed of a world in which work had some meaning. Bryner himself ended his official phone calls from the union office with "Peace." The auto plants in Sweden, where workers got to do a variety of tasks and learn multiple skills, were regarded as some sort of distant industrial nirvana to the screw turners at Lordstown. "They just want to be treated with dignity," explained Bryner. "That's not asking a hell of a lot."[53]

In the end, it was not clear who actually won the Lordstown conflict. A relatively successful guerrilla insurgency shook the plant, but the UAW intervened with a much simpler and more modest goal than empowering workers and bringing democracy to the workplace: a return to the 1970 in-plant contract. In the settlement, almost all of the jobs that had been eliminated under GMAD were reinstated, and 1,400 disciplinary layoffs were dropped. The conclusion of the strike returned Lordstown to the pre-GMAD levels of production, basically fending off management's offensive but little else. "All we are asking for at Lordstown, Vega, and truck is what we already had," explained one worker. "Nothing more." And on those terms, the conflict ended in a complete victory for the workers.[54]

On the larger issues, however, it was at best a draw, if not a defeat. It did not do much about the issue that captured the nation's imagination— rethinking the world of work and power on the job. The potential of the mini-movement was gone. "The union and the company say everything's settled, but we had a strike," reasoned one Lordstown worker. "What did we achieve for it? We got the shaft in the last strike. We didn't know what we won and what we lost. When we asked the union we wouldn't get answers." The conclusion of Lordstown preserved the basics of the unwritten rule of postwar labor relations, and liberalism more generally, that higher compensation and thus consumption could be promoted but the organization of production was not to be touched—at least not until it was shaken to its core in the second half of the decade.[55]

Table Grape Industry. Delano, California, 1970

To believe that a new day was dawning for the American working class, one only had to witness events in the California grape fields in the summer of 1970. There, after five years of strikes, of national and international grape boycotts, of constant sacrifice on the part of farmworkers, of a dramatic *perigrinación* (pilgrimage) three hundred miles from Delano to Sacramento, and of Cesar Chavez' famous 1968 fast that brought the movement into focus, the union made the leap from having contracts with a handful of wineries to unionizing nearly the entire California table grape industry. The opening of the decade promised an advance in a sector, agriculture, among groups of people, Mexican and Filipinos, that expanded organized labor well beyond the industrial limits of the postwar paradigm. The labor settlement in Delano consolidated the farmworkers' control over the grape industry, but it was only the end of the beginning of their struggle to organize agricultural labor. The important work—expanding into other crops and learning how to function as a union rather than a social movement—remained for the new decade.

Trade unionists and students, liberals and radicals, consumers and politicians, all seemed to agree on *la causa* when they agreed on little else in the late sixties and early seventies. Yet the breadth of support rested on the fact that Cesar Chavez, leader of the farmworkers, labored within a broad set of unreconciled values: Gandhiesque leader of his people and president of his union, a hierarchical Catholic structure and a democratic ethos, a liberal charity and a grassroots social movement, an upper-West-Side-attraction and the gritty survival of *la huelga* (the strike). Throw into the equation the immense power of California agribusiness and the vicious attacks from the Teamsters who, as the UMWA's Arnold Miller explained, were going after the farmworkers' hard-won contracts "like wolves running after fresh meat," and we can begin to glimpse some of the problems that would bedevil one of the great seventies meldings of sixties-style civil rights movements and thirties-style class demands.[56]

Of all the tactics brought to bear upon the growers in the sixties, the most important was the United Farm Workers' (UFW's) ever-resourceful grape boycott. Here, ironically, the weakness of the 1935 National Labor Relations Act (NLRA), which had left agricultural workers out of its purview as a sop to southern political interests, proved beneficial. The Taft-Hartley amendments had eliminated the secondary boycott, which otherwise would have allowed unions to boycott firms who did business with an employer that was being struck—that is, boycott the secondary handler of a good. For the farmworkers, not being covered by the act meant that they could take their struggle from the fields to the secondary sight of the supermarkets that sold grapes. Working outside of the New Deal order, in essence, proved to be the workers' best hope and most successful strategy.

To get consumers to stop buying grapes, young farmworkers fanned out across the country with precious little knowledge of what they were doing or where they were going. They had even less money—often all they had was some buttons, bus fare, the names of a few friendly contacts, and a deep reservoir of soul. The long, drawn out boycotts they managed to run against the chain stores proved remarkably effective in bringing the grape industry to the bargaining table, and the sympathy they were able to elicit from supporters was astounding. "My strongest memory of going out on an information picket line in Toronto," explained a young Chicana named Jessica Govea who grew up picking crops in California's Central Valley, "was when I saw these two young white men walking toward me who reminded me of young white men in Bakersfield. I made myself strong and went up to them and said, 'Excuse me, could I ask you to help farm workers by not buying grapes?'" Her life in Bakersfield had trained her to fear Anglos, and she remained steeled for their response. "As if on cue," she continued, "they both turned around and showed me their jackets, which had giant United Auto Workers emblems on them. And they turned around and said, 'We're all for you. We're all for you.'" Govea's story is but one of a myriad of events that made the boycott successful in cities like New York, Chicago, Boston, Philadelphia, Detroit, Montreal, Toronto, and many other major urban markets, drying up the demand for the grapes and bringing the growers to the bargaining table in the watershed year of 1970.[57]

After the heroic phase of the sixties, farmworkers of the seventies had to perform the difficult feat faced by all social movements: finding stability and lasting institutional presence for the insurgent power of the social movement. During the five years of immense sacrifice of the sixties, almost all participants lost their homes and cars and anything else they owned, but, Chavez-the-spiritualist believed, they uncovered something greater. "I think that in losing those worldly possessions they found themselves, and they found that only through dedication, through serving mankind, and in this case, serving the poor and those who were struggling for justice, in that way they could they really find themselves," Chavez noted about their triumph. That level of sacrifice could not go on indefinitely. Trouble began to brew as the charismatic movement made an awkward peace with the more mundane world of contract negotiations, overseeing hiring halls, and dealing with jurisdictional disputes. The union hiring halls were chaotically run, and the growers, already angry over having lost control of their labor force, added inefficiency to their list of complaints. "Those were very awful days for everybody, I guess especially for me," remembered Richard Chavez about managing the new contracts. "We knew how to go out there and raise all kinds of hell and all that, but administration? We didn't have that kind of experience."[58]

As if to guarantee a rough transition to administrative life, another crisis immediately emerged for the UFW. At the very moment that they were still celebrating their grape contract signing in Delano in 1970, word came that vegetable growers had begun to sign secret sweetheart contacts with the Teamsters in order to avoid being organized by the UFW. Suddenly, what at first appeared to be a new day for farmworkers descended into the renewal of a horrible inter-union and inter-racial rivalry to control the row crops. By the time that the original 1970 grape contracts were up for renewal in 1973, the crisis had spread to a ground war to maintain control over the once-secure grape industry as well. The UFW, as journalist Jacques Levy put it, had become a "target for destruction." Out of the farmworkers' conflict with the Teamster-grower alliance in the summer of 1973 came some of the ugliest images in labor history: huge, white Teamsters and hired thugs, bellies hanging over their belts, allied with police in a bloody fight against Mexican, Filipino, and Arab farmworkers.[59]

By 1973, as the mine workers celebrated their victory, Sadlowski challenged the steel workers' official family, and the embers of Lordstown died out, the farmworkers were mired in a massive strike to try to retain the fields they thought they had secured in 1970. The battles with the Teamsters strained the workers' commitment to non-violence, and the UFW ended up losing contract after contract. By August, when the strike was called off, according to Marshall Ganz, "two strikers were murdered, while picketers endured 44 shootings, 400 beatings, and 3,000 arrests." The death of two strikers in the violence of that infamous summer of 1973 was too high a cost for Chavez, and the bitter struggles nearly destroyed the union. Racial antagonism between the Teamsters and the UFW replaced the inter-racial alliances that buoyed the UFW in the earlier years, and an inter-union rivalry now defined what was once widespread labor support for the farmworkers. Three years after what appeared to be the farmworkers' final triumph, the union's very survival was in question. By mid decade, the farmworkers' movement was fighting for its life, having lost 90 percent of its grape contracts—down to only 12 from 150.[60]

AFL-CIO president George Meany delivered a little of the old fighting spirit from above. In a rare display of anger not directed at the Left, he called the Teamsters campaign "the most vicious strikebreaking, union-busting effort I've seen in my lifetime. We're going to do anything that's necessary to keep that Union alive," which he did, providing a $1.6 million strike fund to help keep the UFW afloat.[61]

Yet the farmworkers' moment had turned. In the fall of 1974, the *New York Times* magazine ran a lengthy article asking, "Is Chavez Beaten?" The question was not rhetorical, as the *Times* answered affirmatively, providing further demoralization for the UFW. Others began to reason cynically that the size, power, and efficiency of the Teamsters might serve the farmworkers just as well as the UFW. Such compromises with authoritarianism ignored the central issue: that the Teamsters' contracts were routes for the growers to circumvent the UFW's hiring halls and regain control of the labor force. The idea that the Teamsters might best represent the farmworkers said something about the mid-decade shift in the nation's psyche, exposing, as Ronald B. Taylor pointed out at the time, "a disturbing national trend to accept the 'efficiency' of autocracy disguised as 'democracy.'" Yet the retreat was evidence of a deeper sense of surrender. As another commentator noted, the "charisma and the cause were wearing thin." "The public seems to have grown tired of causes," editorialized *Time* magazine. "Today, few housewives even know that Chavez has called for another boycott and still fewer observe it." In 1974, a Salinas Valley attorney recalled a colleague who worked passionately for the UFW for more than five years. In terms that foreshadowed the second half of the 1970s, he remarked, "He's in private practice now, doing well. I saw him recently. He doesn't give a damn now. He was most enthused when he talked about taking his wife and some friends to see *Behind the Green Door* and another porno film. It's the decadent seventies."[62]

Back in the 1930s, the key breakthrough that gave architecture to the labor unrest of the Great Depression was the 1935 Wagner Act, which helped workers achieve what they had not been able to do in the absence of federal protections. Without the state on the workers' side, however briefly, it is difficult to imagine the success of the CIO. The pattern appeared to be repeating itself four decades later in California, as reformist politics and labor upheavals in California once again flowed together in the creation of California's Agricultural Labor Relations Act (ALRA) in 1975. In that year, Governor Ronald Reagan, famous for self-consciously eating grapes while the cameras rolled, left the governor's mansion to make way for Jerry Brown, who had marched with Chavez and the farmworkers and whose campaign promises included legal protections for farmworkers. Given the immense power of California agricultural interests, any act was an extraordinary breakthrough— this one appearing to promise a new day to farm labor, enfranchising groups largely left out of the postwar system of labor relations: people of color, migratory workers, and agricultural workers.[63]

Unfortunately for the UFW, the breakthrough promise of legally protected free and fair elections quickly became an impasse. The new law cost the organization the boycott tactic and left it vulnerable to political appointees who would serve on the labor board. The dilemma of any union leader is to trade off rank-and-file mobilization versus state protection, and in the case of the UFW, the constant mobilizations had hit a wall of fatigue. Given the stranglehold that agribusiness had on California politics, it did not take long for the ALRA to reach levels of inefficiency and, later, control by agribusiness, that it had taken decades for the NLRA to reach. "Seventeen months after the farm-labor law went into effect," explained an exasperated Chavez, "most farmworkers have yet to realize the promise and protection of this good law. Instead, for most the law has been a cruel hoax." Although he often liked to fume at the failures of the act, it was one of the key tools they had left in the absence of the secondary boycott or the popular will to support one. While the numbers of farmworkers under contract did bounce back up with the ALRA, the farmworkers would never manage to regain the power and coverage they had in the early seventies. Rather than becoming an organizing tool, the act mostly solidified contracts that the farmworkers held. The union's membership and contracts increased somewhat while the act was managed by allies of the cause, but when those tables turned, the union lost much of its collective force and vision.[64]

The cause of unionization of the farmworkers—and related environmental concerns—did reemerge in the late seventies, but the union would never again reach the type of power in California agriculture that it briefly enjoyed in the early seventies. In the "twin souls" of Chavez's life—spiritual/civil rights leader and labor leader—the patron saint of *Chicanismo* continued to live on, bolstering the civil rights of Mexican-Americans akin to Martin Luther King's role among African-Americans, but the union cause died out. Like King's success in civil rights but failure to achieve economic rights in the late sixties, the rise and political might of the Mexican-American identity, as difficult an achievement as that was, fused more easily with American political traditions of individual civil rights than did the unionization of the farmworkers for collective economic rights and the material betterment of those who toiled in the fields. Emblematic of the broader problems of the second half of the 1970s, the fighting spirit of the union descended into the despair of authoritarianism and cultish tactics with no organizational or strategic vision.[65]

Farah Garment Factory. El Paso, Texas, 1972

"Not since the UAW took on Ford at River Rouge, not since John L. organized the coal fields of Pennsylvania, not since the truckers beat hell out of the Minneapolis 400," argued the *Texas Observer*, "has there been a strike like Farah." Although such rhetoric was typical of the labor history hyperbole of the early seventies, even the Amalgamated Clothing Workers (ACWA or Amalgamated) called the struggle to organize the mostly Latina garment workers in El Paso "the biggest strike and the biggest conflict and the biggest battle we have ever faced" since the first decade of the union's existence.[66]

Although the Farah strike was hardly the biggest labor dispute since the rise of the CIO, it was exactly what organized labor needed for the seventies: a drive to organize a group in desperate need of economic power (Mexican and Mexican-American women) which had been left out of the labor movement in a sector (garments) that had been migrating out of labor's industrial stronghold for the better part of a generation in a region (the Southwest) where organized labor had a very weak presence. The obstacles to unionization were immense, as Farah was located in one of the most difficult labor markets in the country, and run by one of the most virulently anti-union employers in the area. A victory in one of the biggest industries in the region would not just be both a geographic and demographic breakthrough for organized labor, but could also serve as a beachhead in a right-to-work state and in an area where the new "twin plants" or *maquiladoras* were being set up to take advantage of cheaper Mexican wages just on the other side of the border.[67]

With mixed successes, the Amalgamated had sporadically been sending organizers down to Willie Farah's immense garment factories since the late sixties. In May 1972, however, the workers took the matter into their own hands. Fed up with harassment, intimidation, and the firing of outspoken workers, the Farah employees spontaneously poured out of the San Antonio plant and then the larger El Paso operation. At first, the union felt the moment for a strike was premature and tried to get the garment workers back on the job. The workers would have none of it, and the union ultimately rallied to their side. By July 1972, the Amalgamated, self-consciously emulating the success of the UFW, declared a national boycott of Farah slacks that would end up continuing for another two years. As Margie Talavera explained, "for all the 3,000 of us that went out on strike, there were about two people waiting in line for the jobs. So you can imagine how hard it was to go out on strike, because there is always a replacement right away. People from across the border, people from everywhere, they are ready to scab on us right away."[68]

The strike and the boycott were immensely successful, as the public, in *Fortune* magazine's terms, came to see "the company's management as stubborn and reactionary, and Farah's workers as underpaid, exploited, and hungering for the benefits of unionism." Forty union representatives worked on the Farah slacks boycott in sixty different cities. The garment workers' story grafted readily onto the public's awareness of the farmworkers' fight, and the boycott had a sizable impact on the company's profits. A year after the first walkout, Farah's quarterly sales were reported down by $9.1 million from the previous year—aided by some bad business decisions and the fact that consumers could easily target Farah's products. The community proved very supportive to the Farah workers, most notably in the form of a courageous

Catholic priest, Father Jesse Munoz, who placed his church and moral authority on the side of the strikers.[69]

The local mobilization around Farah reached deep but took the better part of two years to win. With Our Lady of the Light church as strike headquarters, and the union organizing an immense national publicity campaign, the strike garnered a wide array of political allies—many of whom would have had little in common otherwise—including unlikely bedfellows such as Republican Nelson Rockefeller and Democrat John Lindsay, and AFL-CIO president George Meany and presidential candidate George McGovern. The famously autocratic and paternalist Willie Farah made matters worse for himself by relentlessly digging in his heels against the community organizing. In terms of publicity and positioning, it all worked in favor of the union. When a judge with the National Labor Relations Board (NLRB) issued a decision that accused Farah of "flouting the Act and trampling on the rights of its employees as if there were no Act, no Board and no Ten Commandments," Farah's fate was sealed.[70]

Yet the young Chicana workers could not escape the patriarchal residue of the labor movement. When the Amalgamated featured speeches by the Farah workers during the national boycott mobilization, they were typically flanked by the aging white, male union leadership. Despite the fact that the women on the line suffered the consequences of the two-year strike—as well as the stream of intimidation and harassment that went along with it—the public presentation of the Farah strikers was often "steeped in traditional union ideology," explained one study of the strike, that "glorified the male leadership of the ACWA." Ironically, even though the women strikers often served as supporting accessories to the male leadership in the pro-strike press put out by the Amalgamated, the women were often ambivalent about the union itself. The clothing workers' union nonetheless poured millions of dollars into the national campaign that finally brought Willie Farah to the bargaining table in 1974.[71]

When Willie Farah finally capitulated and the mayor of El Paso oversaw a card-check union certification process, the unions heralded the breakthrough as a "new chapter in American labor history." It was, of course, more complicated than that. The union had never managed to get a majority of strikers (due to the extreme level of intimidation at the plant, they argued). It was only when Farah agreed to bargain with the union in order to get the boycott called off (and the NLRB and El Paso civic groups off his back) that two-thirds of the workers joined the union. The costs were extraordinary—some say as much as $8 million in union funds to procure the victory over Farah. Many strikers felt the union signed too quickly with too soft of a contract given the levels of sacrifice they had made. The so-called happies, as the anti-union employees were known, also ended up having a strong voice in the bargaining, which further diluted the strikers' power. The ensuing three-year contract raised workers' pay, but it was somewhat offset by a 60 cents per hour hike in the national minimum wage. The Farah employees did get some increases in fringe benefits and a grievance committee, but the results, given two years of sacrifice, were a little thin. Many strikers felt that they were entitled to a much better contract and that the union had imposed this from above. "Eventually we found out that we didn't win," explained radical Farah activist Chuy Bustamante. "The union and the company won, we didn't win."[72]

Like so many labor activists in the early seventies, however, the Farah strikers believed that their efforts were the first round in much bigger things to come. Yet the promised beachhead for unions in the Southwest never got beyond the beach, and for reasons of poor management, fashion changes, and increased labor costs, the Farah plants began an infamous decline from industry powerhouse to the garment industry's sick man. The second round of contract negotiations in 1977 were plagued by layoffs, dwindling activism, divisions in the workforce, and bitterness that the Amalgamated was forcing the approval of weak contracts upon the rank and file. From the perspective of the Farah workers, explains Emily Honig, "one finds during the post-strike decades a record of job layoffs due to plant closures and relocation overseas, fragmentation of political networks, and near-dissolution of their union." It was a typical pattern across the nation. Even when everything went right for labor in the early 1970s, it still went wrong by mid decade.[73]

Gathering of Black Trade Unionists. Chicago, Illinois, 1972

One of the central problems for the labor movement was not simply how to incorporate women and minorities into unions, but how to make sense of class when race and gender are part of the totality. The plurality of answers to the synthesis—and the conflict and tactical differences among them—spoke of the obstacles to a more complex sense of post-sixties class identity.

In the fall of 1972, black trade unionists came together in Chicago for the largest gathering of African-American workers in history. Minority workers

had bridled under the AFL-CIO's leadership, and the federation's announcement that summer that the AFL-CIO would remain neutral in the
Nixon-McGovern race, which most took as an implicit endorsement of
Nixon, was the last straw. The result was the formation of the Coalition
of Black Trade Unionists (CBTU). William Lucy, international secretary-
treasurer of the American Federation of State, County and Municipal Employees (AFSCME) and the first president of CBTU, laid out the tricky
position of minority unionists before the 1,200 delegates at the founding
convention. "We don't want to be a thorn in anybody's side," he explained,
"but we don't want to be a pivot for anybody's heel." Another CBTU founder,
Cleveland Robinson, the Jamaican-born president of the small Distributive
Workers of America in New York City and an organizer of the March on
Washington, explained, "We understand that as working people, regardless of where we work, regardless of our stakes, we have a common destiny
together, and that binds us." Be that as it may, Robinson continued, "Too
much hypocrisy has existed for too long in too many places in our unions."[74]

Black workers and civil rights activists like Robinson and Lucy lived the
contradiction of the relationship between the potential of the union movement and its disappointing history on matters of racial justice. The CIO was
arguably responsible for the biggest material advance in African-American
lives in the twentieth century prior to the coming of the civil rights movement and often provided the legislative muscle for the breakthrough civil
rights legislation in Washington. The rest of the racial legacy, however, remained unconvincing. When workers of color turned to the streets in the
1960s, the unions remained far out of touch. When the March on Washington happened, the AFL-CIO was not there. When the farmworkers marched
from Delano, the federation did not support it. When the Memphis sanitation workers were on strike in 1968, melding civil rights and labor rights
into the perfect dialectical synthesis of the age, the AFL-CIO stepped only
cautiously toward the cause that cost Martin Luther King his life. When the
Poor People's Campaign encamped on Washington the following summer,
labor leaders still feared that large-scale mobilizations might upset the system and refused to support it. For black unionists, it was a deeply frustrating
legacy.[75]

Veteran labor/civil rights advocates like Lucy and Robinson envisioned a
future in which collective class identity could triumph over the divisions of
race, if only the unions could overcome their defensive whiteness. Somewhere between the power of organized labor and the vision of the civil rights

movement was the promise of a movement of movements. "Now the blacks and the Spanish-speaking people are asking for their day in the sun, but there is no massive effort to organize these workers," Robinson explained in his crisp Jamaican accent. That lack of faith was reciprocated, he believed, by minority workers' unwillingness to trust the unions. The biggest obstacle to organizing poor people of color, he believed, was "their lack of faith in established labor. They've heard promises and they've seen betrayals." Yet Robinson made it clear that the CBTU was not trying to go it alone. "We do not want anyone to feel that ours is a separate or a segregationist organization and that we are going our own way." Black workers were "part and parcel" of the labor movement, whose fate was intertwined with organized labor and their white brothers and sisters.[76]

CBTU's argument was with other veteran labor/civil rights leaders like the head of the AFL-CIO's A. Philip Randolph Institute, Bayard Rustin, who believed that black progress could be achieved solely *within* the house of labor—never as an outside critic. Rustin had been the primary architect of the 1963 March on Washington, building upon A.P. Randolph's original World War II era plan to bring the issues of discrimination and full employment to the nation's capital. Rustin believed that after the Civil Rights Act the movement had to shift, as he put it in a famous 1965 essay, "From Protest to Politics," that is, using coalitions to move from the streets to the corridors of political power. His belief was part of his life-long drift from socialist and pacifist circles in World War II to a rather brittle belief in the AFL-CIO's Cold War bureaucratic pragmatism. Those that criticized the racism of the unions or, worse, claimed the path to autonomous black revolution, he believed, unwittingly fed the rising power of the anti-union conservatives. Like Robinson and his fellow members of CBTU, Rustin believed that the black experience was part of a "broader class reality," but one that could only be addressed through a slow, grinding push through existing institutions in such a way as to not threaten the unions' hard-won stability. "The blacks have a choice," argued Rustin. "They can fight to strengthen the trade-union movement by wiping out the vestiges of segregation that remain in it, or they can knowingly or unknowingly offer themselves as pawns in the conservatives' games of bust-the-unions."[77]

Despite their differences, both the CBTU and the AFL-CIO's A. Philip Randolph Institute stood squarely against the fading power of black militants who advanced a Marxist-Leninist critique of mainstream unionism. The Revolutionary Union Movements (RUMs) in the auto sector, for instance, were not just aggressively critical of the automakers but of the UAW as well, which they saw as equally oppressive because of the union's complicity in the companies' speed-ups, unsafe working conditions, authoritarianism in the plants, and institutional racism. For black militants, it was a simple matter of connecting the dots from the local racism in the plants, to the UAW's bureaucratic complicity, to the failures of liberalism, onto the capitalist system, and ending with the imperialist war in Southeast Asia. It all folded into an irredeemable whole, a totality that held out the hope of uniting the colonized peoples—from Detroit to the third world—in shared struggle. Like so many other dissidents in the late sixties and early seventies, the touchstone of their analysis was the 1930s. As the preamble to the Jefferson Assembly Revolutionary Movement (JARUM) in Detroit read: "Just as in the 1930s when the rank and file joined in unity from the bottom up to form throughout the country the CIO, the time has come for the Rank and File once again to rid ourselves of the back-stabbing union leadership and their phony reforms. We demand that union democracy start from the bottom and go up."[78]

While the revolutionary rhetoric was hot and the posture of the separatists was militant, Robinson and Rustin were right that the long-term impact of the black radical movements was limited. Despite long being fetishized in the iconography of the Left, the RUMs found it impossible to win elections—even in locals with black majorities. Their uncompromising language attracted few followers. Indeed, their posture tended to inculcate more fear than solidarity. They alienated the older generation of black workers and were particularly contemptuous of all outside of their reach: liberals, reform-oriented black leaders, and, above all, backlash whites being drawn to George Wallace. By the dawn of the seventies, the allure of black power in the plants was rapidly fading. It briefly resurfaced in some of the wildcats in the auto plants in 1973 before disappearing altogether.[79]

The problem was similar when local black leaders took over the schools at Ocean Hill-Brownsville in 1968, under the name of community control, and kicked out white, often liberal, Jewish members of the American Federation of Teachers in the process. Rustin queried, "What will prevent white community groups in Queens from firing black teachers—or white teachers with liberal views? What will prevent local Birchites and Wallaceites from taking over *their* schools and using them for *their* purposes?" The key was finding a path beyond the zero-sum logic of racial separatism and getting working-class institutions to adapt to the new day. As will be explored in Chapter 6, both Robinson and Rustin would pour their hopes for that common ground into the late-seventies push for full employment legislation, which so many hoped would foment a revival of a broader and more inclusive New Deal-style politics.[80]

The shining star in the race-labor story, in fact the leading light of all seventies labor history, was in the public sector where many minority workers gained union representation. The representation of teachers, sanitation workers, office clerks, police, and firefighters rose dramatically in the sixties and seventies as the longed-for "movement of movements" really did emerge among government workers. As Joseph McCartin has deftly made the case, the history of public sector workers unravels our major assumptions about the "declension narrative" of union history, pointing to the fact that public sector success was the obverse of private sector failure: in lieu of decline there was growth, in place of isolation there was collaboration, rather than stale leadership there was dynamism. In contrast to the somnolence with which most unions greeted the sixties, AFSCME, reported *Fortune* magazine, "created an exuberant atmosphere in its Washington headquarters reminiscent of the CIO organizing drives of the Thirties. There is an élan to the organization, an air of bustle and excitement, a sense of great plans underfoot, and an evangelical zeal that one rarely encounters these days in the stately mansions of Big Labor."[81]

The thirties analogy was frequently invoked in the labor world of the late sixties and early seventies, but, in the case of government employees, the comparison held a little bit better. Buoyed by the fresh young leadership of Jerry Wurf, who took over AFSCME in 1964, the union enrolled women and minority workers interested in building material advances on the backs of the new social movements. Further enabled by President Kennedy's executive order allowing for federal workers to organize (and similar political achievements on the state level), the membership more than quadrupled between the mid-1960s and the early seventies. As Wurf explained, AFSCME's victory for the Memphis sanitation workers, which came at the cost of an immense social movement and the martyrdom of Martin Luther King Jr., was "our Homestead, our Hart, Schaffner & Marx, our Flint sit-downs." Yet the success among public workers, where snow-balling union density quickly reached beyond postwar highs in the private sector, was partially a product of an employer that was generally held to higher moral standards than those of the private sector.[82]

Yet it is exactly because public workers run so dramatically against the historical grain that their story is difficult to square with the rest of working-class history. Government employees, who might have been a model for the rest of the labor movement, typically failed to have the much-needed spillover effect on other workers or unions. AFSCME and Wurf tended to be regarded as barely tolerated mavericks and outsiders in mainstream labor circles—Wurf's biography is subtitled "labor's last angry man"—rather than the source of inspiration. In 1973, *Time* magazine reported that Wurf's admission to the AFL-CIO executive council in the autumn of 1969, meant "the vote usually ranges from 25 to 1 to 34 to 1, depending on how many other union chiefs are present to vote down Jerry Wurf." Also, from the perspective of their brothers and sisters in private jobs, public sector raises were costing them tax dollars—a problem that would become a crisis with the tax revolts at the end of the decade. The degree of separation of public and private sector tracks was clear by the end of the decade when one out of every eight strikes took place in the public sector.[83]

One of the fundamentals of the CIO analogy for public sector workers in the seventies was the push for a "Wagner Act for public employees." By 1975, however, the Supreme Court had dusted off the Tenth Amendment, renewing states' rights doctrine, in order not to extend the Fair Labor Standards Act to state employees, and thus digging the grave for any hope for a national public employee relations action. Just as the Supreme Court bent to the political winds in finding the Wagner Act constitutional in 1937, so the Court did the same in 1975—except with the opposite result. "The problem for labor," explains McCartin, "was that the political mood in 1976 did not favor extensions of new rights to workers, as it had in 1937." Although the public sector unions showed more life than most, their fortunes, too, faded in the second half of the decade.[84]

Public sector unions, especially AFSCME, are the exception that proves the rule of seventies history, profoundly suggestive of the path not taken for labor as a whole. As Jerry Wurf nailed labor's problem in 1974, "We can stand pat as a movement that represents a declining percentage of the workforce, and watch our influence over national direction slip away. Or we can make ourselves more relevant to the needs of workers in a postindustrial society, and become an even more substantial voice in the shaping of the future than in the past. If labor is weakened, society is more likely to close out the poor and the powerless whom labor seeks to represent." Yet even the public employee unions had largely reached as large a share of the workforce as they ever would by the first half of the decade when the double punch of the governments' fiscal crises of the late seventies and Reagan's attack on the Professional Air Traffic Controllers (PATCO) defined its apex.[85]

Office Buildings. Boston, Massachusetts, 1973

If the hopes of black workers were fragmented between allied but critical unionists like Robinson, defensive insiders like Rustin, and militants like the RUM groups, women faced similarly complex debates about the relationship among gender, class, and the union movement.

Karen Nussbaum, who eventually committed her life to organizing clerical workers in the seventies, began as a New Left anti-war activist who had taken work as a clerk and typist at Harvard in the early seventies. There she began to notice that the women's movement "was bubbling among working-class women" in the early seventies. This was not the professional middle-class feminism of the National Organization of Women, but a different breed of pink-collar, class-conscious feminism. Out of regular meetings and story sharing of the Boston area, clerical workers grew the organization 9to5, which, as Nussbaum described it, was to be "a women's rights organization on the job for women office workers."[86]

The organization began not as a union but as a simple citizens' advocacy group, which Nussbaum found to be too "ephemeral." As she explained, 9to5 would "organize groups to confront their bosses over maternity rights or discrimination and, inevitably, the boss would respond with, 'Well, that's very interesting. We'll get back to you.' And then they never got back to us. And that's when we began to understand. We said, 'We need something that forces them to get back to us. There should be a law about this.' And then, of course, we found out that there was a law. It's called the National Labor Relations Act, that if you organize a majority of people in the workplace, then the employer is obligated to bargain with you." When they approached a list of unions with their ideas of chartering their own local to organize women clerical workers, however, their ideas were met with indifference or hostility. "When we started," explained Nussbaum, "the union people scorned women. They didn't care to take the time with us women, who didn't know anything about unions."[87]

Nussbaum's original attitude toward unions tells much about the New Left's and the women's movement's hope for organized labor as the agent of historical transformation. "It never occurred to me that unions were a force for social change. . . . That was the milieu. That wasn't where the impetus for change was coming in society, and that's why it didn't occur to us that that's where it should be." Eventually, the advocacy group 9to5 became Local 925 of the Service Employees International Union (SEIU), a once sleepy union that would go on to become one of the few sources of growth and dynamism beyond the 1980s. The local, recalled Nussbaum, "had an organization that had the character and concerns of the working women's movement but the power of a trade union." The initial promise may have been great, but as Nussbaum lamented, "We never knew what hit us. We got smashed over and over. These businesses had not traditionally been unionized, and they were damned if they were going to be the first ones in the new wave."[88]

The challenge of women's rights also cut straight to the core of the old industrial unions. "The old time union slogan, 'Solidarity Forever,'" announced the *Detroit Free Press*, began "to quiver in the face of the Battle of the Sexes" when the mostly female staff of the United Auto Workers walked off their jobs—picketing one of the most progressive unions in the nation in March 1971. Balking at the paternalism and the wages offered up by the autoworkers, the clerical workers refused to be treated as "pea-brained women" and rejected the unwritten rule to "be good little girls and you'll get the goodies," as one striker put it.

After piloting the UAW through its enormous struggle against GM, the union executives did what they would never have dreamed of doing against fellow autoworkers: they crossed the picket line put up by their own clerical workers. At one point in the strike, Emil Mazey, secretary-treasurer of the UAW and one-time labor radical, flew into a rage, reminding the "little bitches" that "I organized this union before you were born," as he walked across their picket line dismissing the women strikers as "greedy and selfish"—exactly what critics said about the UAW. While clerical workers might have been the future of organized labor (and had been labeled as such by Reuther and many others), when the moment emerged, they seemed like little more than a nuisance, hindering the forward progress of the great (male) industrial working class. The indifference went all the way to the top. "Our general staff and I," explained President Leonard Woodcock in the usual justifications of the picket-line crosser, "we're not on strike and we'll go about doing our routine."[89]

Following the footsteps of the Coalition of Black Trade Unionists (CBTU), women formed the Coalition of Labor Union Women (CLUW) in 1974. Myra Wolfgang, who had been involved in the long history of labor feminism since she helped orchestrate a sit-down strike at a Detroit Woolworth's dime store in 1937, exclaimed from her position as chair of the first CLUW convention, "And you can call Mr. Meany and tell him there are three thousand women in Chicago, and they didn't come to swap recipes," which delivered the crowd to its feet with raucous applause. As the historian Dorothy Sue Cobble argues, the founding of CLUW has typically been framed as an expansion of second wave, 1970s feminism to the labor movement. However, seen from the longer arc of labor history, she explains, there was a tradition of labor-based feminism with deep roots in the twentieth century. "The advent of CLUW," argues Cobble, "does not represent the trickling down of feminist consciousness to working-class women. Rather, it was a realization of a long sought goal of labor feminists" who had deep roots in the history of the union movement."[90]

Just as the long-sought dream of an institutional home for labor feminism began to become a reality, however, tensions quickly emerged within the celebration of working-class sisterhood in Chicago. Divisions between professional middle-class feminists demanding equality and working-class feminists who advocated women's protective legislation in the workplace had barely healed from the debates around the Equal Rights Amendment (ERA) that passed Congress in 1972 (which the AFL-CIO tepidly endorsed a year later). Anne Draper, for instance, expressed her exasperation with the "hostility and condescension toward unions" expressed by "middle-class women's rights types." The non-labor feminists betrayed their class bias, she believed, seeing "unions, not as the struggling working-class combining on its own behalf against great odds" but "as a powerful, wealthy, entrenched institution of the status quo." Yet from the perspective of radical feminist, CLUW was dominated, like that of the labor movement more broadly, by the World War II generation. The young radicals preferred a more militant and "freewheeling" style of politics on the convention floor than the unions and simultaneously remained suspicious of both the ambitious professional middle-class feminists and the acceptance of the plodding course of bureaucracy and collective bargaining emphasized by the old labor feminists.[91]

Tactics for bringing gender into questions of class justice were as complex as those of bringing in race. Middle-class feminists, radical feminists of many stripes, and trade union women interested in maintaining a supportive role in the mainstream labor movement all jockeyed for position. As Susan Reverby, a member of the Boston CLUW chapter noted in *Radical America*, the problems within CLUW were a microcosm of the issues of labor politics broadly conceived in the early seventies: no shortage of ferment, but an absence of cohesion or direction. It was less of an insurgency than it was a maelstrom. "The 'left' is itself divided," noted Reverby,

> Many women in organized groups believe that the issues come down to a series of problems neatly subsumed under the "woman question." Other leftists accept the hierarchy within CLUW and follow almost any directive from the National because it is "the leadership." Still other women identify as socialist feminists but have by no means developed a complete analysis of what that means concretely for strategy and tactics in organizations like CLUW. This confusion on the left, combined with the obvious manipulations of the union bureaucrats, seems to have caused many progressive, but non-sectarian, rank-and-file women to abandon CLUW altogether.

As a result of the confusion, the fighting between the sectarian Left and the union-based leadership tended to drive away the rank and file. CLUW also restricted its membership to only those already under a union contract, thus cutting itself off from natural allies but also protecting itself from the turbulent pools of sectarian politics.

The problems were more salient at the 1975 Constitutional Convention where the atmosphere, like that of the nation more broadly, had changed greatly. Less than a third of the number of people who attended the first meeting made it to the 1975 convention in Detroit. With the memories of political in-fighting now coupled to a bitter recession, as one attendee put it, "One could sense an air of apprehension as 1,000 women unionists arrived in Detroit. . . . gloomy uncertainty contrasted with the air of anticipation, even exhilaration, that characterized CLUW's first founding convention almost two years ago."[92]

By the end of the decade, however, CLUW's numbers bounced back up. Even George Meany was ready to openly declare that he was a feminist. In 1980, Joyce Miller of the ACWA became president of CLUW and became the first woman to sit on the executive council of the AFL-CIO. The tragedy was, however, that women's long-overdue victories, and their rising presence in the unions in general, came just as labor began its period of precipitous decline. The limiting of CLUW's leadership to the old guard labor-feminist leadership may have spared the group's in-fighting, but it also meant, like many of the insurgencies of the era, the labor machinery from a by-gone era remained firmly in place.

The real problem was that the national narrative was shifting. Second-wave feminism had effectively framed gender as a central issue in civic life, but had difficulties sustaining a national dialogue on both gender and class and how one informed the other. Labor feminists were more of a curiosity or, more likely, just plain unionists. Karen Silkwood, for instance, was a young union activist who lost her life in the process of delivering secrets about health and safety violations at the Kerr-McGee plutonium plant in 1974 (and went on to be portrayed by Meryl Streep in the 1983 film *Silkwood*). As Tony Mazzochi, perhaps the most amazing union organizer of the post-sixties era, put it, there was little space for understanding Karen Silkwood as a worker and a unionist. "I have nothing against feminism," he said—and meant it,

> but Karen wasn't a feminist. She's been adopted by the feminist movement. . . . She has been portrayed as an anti-nuclear activist. She wasn't. She was involved in one simple activity; it was to save a local union at Kerr-McGee where the company was hell bent on destroying it. . . . Karen was solely a trade union martyr.[93]

Despite the troubled relationship between class and feminism, women were the real working-class heroes of civic and popular culture in the 1970s. Household workers, for instance, finally came under the Fair Labor Standards Act in 1974. Flight attendants rejected their role as highly sexualized "sky muffins" by organizing Stewardesses for Women's Rights. A string of remarkable women gained fame from their commitment to labor issues in the seventies. Like Karen Silkwood, Crystal Lee Sutton, who played a key role in the 1974 organizing of a J.P. Stevens textile plant in Roanoke Rapids, North Carolina, became a household personality. She was the focus of a *New York Times Magazine* piece and later an academy award–winning film featuring Sally Field as *Norma Rae*. Like *Silkwood*, the *Norma Rae* phenomena spoke more of women's individual emancipation than of collective labor rights (see Chapter 7).

The unions were hardly responsible for the long-standing gendered divisions in the labor market, but the lack of representation among women— and the occupations they tended to hold, often called the Pink Collar

Ghetto—was clearly evident in the weakness of women's earning power vis-à-vis men's. The ratio of women's earnings to men's had actually *fallen* since 1960—from 61 percent of men's earnings to 57 percent—as male breadwinners enjoyed the larger share of the pie afforded them by collective bargaining. In fact, women's relative earnings would not make gains until the eighties when men's income stagnated in the face of deindustrialization and deunionization.[94]

New Left Caucuses. Workplaces and Campuses, 1973

Self-identified "militants" from the anti-war, civil rights, and feminist movements began moving into the workplaces of America as a political act—"colonizing" or "industrializing" as they called it. These "proletarianized" New Left youth saw in the seventies revival of organized labor both a new route to political power denied them on the campuses as well as the hope of a democratic socialist future. The hope of many young radicals was that in the tea leaves of Lordstown and MFD, and the farmworkers and the Farah strikers could be read something greater than the simple job-conscious unionism that had been at the center of much of labor history—that the revolutionary transformation of society might be at hand.

As the activist Staughton Lynd explained in 1973, movement organizers, sensing the "critical weakness" in the efficacy of their campus politics to be their inability to make linkages with working people, "have recently begun trying to deal with working-class America. Collectives of former student radicals who have taken jobs in offices and factories are dotted across the nation. Others have sought to reach the same constituency from outside the workplace, organizing around issues like pollution and taxation." MFD and movements like that at Lordstown, Lynd explained, "symbolized the new restlessness. Unsure as yet about who the enemy is, or what the goal is, workers have begun to sense their power and make their feelings known." Young militants who entered the shops made ready allies with rank-and-file workers interested in transforming the union leadership, while creating both a source of constant annoyance to the institutional labor movement as well as a ready scapegoat for whatever lay beyond their control.[95]

The New Left activists may have moved beyond the campus in their echoes of the 1930s Popular Front of workers and radical intellectuals, but

they quickly ran up against the core dilemma of the American Left: no matter what one's hoped-for politics, radicalism often ends up being pragmatic
reformism. As one veteran colonizer, Steve Early, explained, "Most New
Leftists who entered the labor movement had hoped to win converts to socialism. But where radicals have been most successful in building a rank-and-
file base, it has often been through downplaying their politics and winning
acceptance on the basis of their performance as dedicated and effective trade
unionists." The bitter and constant enemy of the radicals was the real, but rather
abstract and monolithic, forces of "the labor bureaucracy," which to them was
the sole force holding back the dynamism of working-class revolution. As Jim
Green wrote of his time as part of the *Radical America* collective, their understanding of the bureaucracy "was not balanced with an explanation of why
union members often accepted business unionism or why they abandoned the
social unionism radical and progressive leaders advocated."[96]

The bureaucracy often did fail to respond to the rank and file, but to think
that the entire working class was on the brink of fundamental transformation with or without the much-maligned "union bureaucrats" was naïve. As
one student of the miners' insurgency put it, "From its inception, MFD was
reformist, not revolutionary. To criticize reformers for being reformist revealed more about the critic than the reformers. Doctrinaire radicals were
bound to be disappointed that they had not found a vanguard group of 'Mountain Marxists.'" The New Left generation that entered the labor movement
with high hopes often did good works—and made long and tedious marches
through the compromised terrain of labor's institutions throughout the decade. Like the Industrial Workers of the World before them who espoused
revolution but won tamer victories such as free speech rights or union recognition, or the Communists of the thirties who organized for revolution but
won the day for the CIO and the Democratic Party, the New Left's major
achievements were in the realm of outright reformism rather than radicalism. "To succeed on the shop-floor," recalled Early, "'colonizers' had to im-
merse themselves in what one longtime UAW dissident . . . calls 'the trade
union crap'—individual grievances, benefit questions, day-to-day workplace
problems and complaints."[97]

It became clear to the New Left by mid decade that the hodge-podge of
labor insurgencies, along with their much-vaunted potential for radical
transformation, were at an impasse. "We were actually aware by 1975 that
the rank-and-file rebellions of previous years were not going to coalesce into

a new kind of radical movement," Green explained, "and we knew that our emphasis on shop-floor spontaneity missed important political questions: questions about gender, culture, sexuality, and race relations."[98]

*   *   *

By 1974–1975, the various insurgencies, despite their energy and creativity, rarely found a place in the national discourse, achieved little lasting institutional presence in the labor movement, left almost no legacy in American politics, and, most significantly, failed to become an enduring part of the class awareness of the nation's workers. The ingredients for labor's renewal— new organizing, democratization movements, insurgencies among women and minorities, youth, and quality of work life issues—added up to less than the sum of their parts. When the hammer of the sixties struck the labor institutions of the thirties, the sparks flew in the 1970s but few caught fire.

"In contrast to Western Europe," Mike Davis argues, "where the insurgencies of 1968–1973 led to profound upheavals that set new agendas for the labor movement and recomposed its activist leadership, the American rank-and-file struggles did not succeed in re-orienting the unions towards 'qualitative' demands nor did they produce a distinct new layer of worker-militants." Rather, the thrust of the story was "the defeat of local insurgencies, or, conversely, their immediate cooption into the status quo," which "only left enduring legacies of frustration and demoralization." Organizations like the CBTU and CLUW continued on as the moral conscience of the official labor movement, and a smattering of determined New Leftists eventually made a long and compromised march to leadership positions of a movement that was long on the defense. Organized labor went on to become one of the most diverse institutions in American life, but, simultaneously, a greatly weakened one as it faced the onslaught of the second half of the decade. Most of the energy of the first half of the seventies simply dissipated into the harsh economic climate and airless cultural mood of the second half of the decade.[99]

The dramatically changed working-class world after 1974 will be explored in more detail in the second half of the book, but for now it is worth examining why the insurgencies failed to make a lasting imprint on American life. It was a far more complicated story than simply the melodramas of closing of factories and conservative political tactics. There are at least five pieces to that story, but all of them fit together into a single frame: the seventies were the ragged edge of the political shadow cast across the postwar land-scape by the crisis of the 1930s and 1940s. What appeared to be semi-permanent solutions during the promising years of the "liberal consensus" proved, by decade's end, to be brittle and unyielding, unable to adapt to new voices and issues. Few would have ventured to guess in the early seventies that labor's harmonic convergence back in the thirties and forties may well have been a singular set of events rather than part of an ongoing linear tri-umph of the liberal state. While labor and their liberal allies waited for their restoration, they were living through the end of an "interregnum between Gilded Ages." Indeed, many radical critics presumed labor-liberalism to be the enduring enemy against which they would have to fight. In retrospect, however, the New Deal's victory over past political and social traditions of working-class fragmentation proved a short-lived triumph over the jungle of the labor market. In the 1970s, despite the attempts to revitalize the para-digm, the culture, politics, and economy began to tilt back toward the pre-New Deal status quo of fragmentation, political division, and economic inequality from which the New Deal had originally emerged.[100]

More specifically, one of the key reasons for the failure of the uprisings and organizing of the early seventies in particular was that they were, symp-tomatic of the decade itself, too fragmented and dispersed to constitute anything close to a single or unified movement. Many forms of occupational discontent were scattered across the industrial landscape from Boston to Del-ano, but the movements lacked coordination, commonality, and cohesion. While many at the time liked to compare the unrest to the 1930s—often with more nostalgia than historical grounding—there was nothing remotely close to the degree of unrest or the level of national vision as during the for-mation of the CIO. What were easily seen as stirrings of renewal might better be understood as cracks emerging in the brittle edifice of the highly celebrated system of postwar industrial pluralism.

The social forces outside of the labor world also tended to be centrifugal rather than unifying. Again, the comparison with the thirties is apt. While class identity in the thirties competed with the darker populisms of Huey Long or Father Coughlin, the unique degree of cultural unity in the Great Depression far surpassed any similar moment in American history. Not only were the progressive labor forces in the seventies scattershot, but they had to compete with, and were readily overshadowed by, other issues on both the Right and the Left. Issues like the ERA, busing, abortion, and affirmative action, as well as the general trend of what would later be labeled

as "identity politics" or "rights consciousness," threw into question the limited definition of the "working class" that had originally empowered—but
fundamentally limited—the idea of class in postwar America. The reformed
and diversified versions of individualism in post-sixties America proved
more attractive than did the stumbling drive for collective economic rights.
With class identity growing feeble as the decade wore on, the more powerful
draw of individual rights against discrimination gained momentum. This
was particularly problematic, as we shall see, as the changes in politics continued to pry loose white male workers' economic identity and drive them
toward a more conservative cultural identity. Lost in the breech was the possibility of a vibrant, multi-cultural, and gender conscious conceptualization
of class.

In a militant defense of what already existed, labor leaders also did their
best to resist the pleas, attacks, democratization movements, and criticisms
coming from many corners. While the leadership's presumptions about race
and gender hierarchies hampered a more expansive vision, the problems
were even more troublesome as the existing power brokers believed they had
built a perfectible system and, accordingly, did most of what they could to
ensure the failure of those who challenged it. The murder of the Yablonski
family was merely the most heinous dimension of this. A range of issues
from African-American leaders claiming that "the AFL-CIO is not doing
its job for black workers," as CBTU's William Lucy put it, to Sadlowski
fighting for rank-and-file voice in the steel workers, to Lordstown workers
trying to push for a reconciling of issues outside of the paradigm of collective bargaining, posed a double struggle against both management and labor's "official family." Unlike any previous upheavals in American labor history,
during this one, the labor question already had its solution, and there was a
host of institutional interests invested in maintaining those solutions exactly
how they already existed.

Perhaps most importantly, the insurgencies of the first half of the 1970s
dissipated with remarkable speed with the mid-seventies recession. The unrest of the early decade was based on the most successful economy in American history—simply put, in terms of class power, most workers never had it
so good. Once the rug of economic success was pulled out from underneath
workers during the bitter recessions that began with the first oil shock in
1973, they lost their footing in their fights for solutions to their discontents.
Although the unions were able to outrun inflation with big settlements in

1974, raging inflation, rising unemployment, and a steadily declining economy allowed business to begin to get the upper hand. By the second oil shock in 1979, there was little fight left. The rebelliousness dried up not because the problems were suddenly resolved, but because the high expectations and stiff leverage offered by a tight labor market and a reasonably sound economy began to sag. Afterward, the economy drifted toward stagnation: industrial capacity plummeted, unemployment rose to its (then) postwar high, foreign competition eroded market position, rising interest rates prevented plant modernization, and holding down wages and benefits became the central goal of corporate strategies as inflation eclipsed unemployment as political enemy number one. While the New Left activists had railed against the way liberalism held back the rank and file from their militant destiny, it turned out that liberal economic success had been one of their key sources of power.[101]

Finally, the rapid shift away from labor activism was part of a larger cultural phenomenon, a change in the national mood, even a shift in eras. Joshua Freeman's description of New Yorkers who became "hard-hearted" in the "the harsh climate of prolonged recession and austerity politics" in the mid and late seventies holds true for much of the nation. The rapidity of the change in the nation's sense of destiny is one of the most profound yet unacknowledged transformations in American culture. The hope of renewing the postwar blue-collar dream meant breaking out of the structure that had simultaneously helped to create and limit it. That hope faded into the decade's widely recognized moods of malaise and self absorption, which were at the core of what Tom Wolfe called the "Me Decade."

All that was left, according to an anthropologist who studied the Lordstown workers, was a "mixture of rank and file discouragement and anger" that "vacillated between individual withdrawal and sporadic rebellion bubbling forth from the simmering pot of daily conflict." Workers, "sensing themselves to have less power and less hope of change" simply sunk into despair. A young Lordstown worker named Plato Babbas, who embodied much of the early hope for the new industrial working class, captured the mid-decade switch prevalent in so many sectors. As a young "freak" he allied with many radical causes, felt sympathetic to the women's and civil rights movements, and was part of the "dope-rock-long-hair scene" of the culturally "emancipated" working class. Babbas' thoughts after Lordstown foreshadowed the larger trends of the cultural exhaustion settling over the post-1973 world:

I think we're in an era where everybody is a kind of spectator. I don't know. Maybe that's just me. Boy I can't get it together to do anything. You watch the world around you. You watch the wars. You watch the corrupt politics. You watch the taxes. You're just so small. You can't change anything. I can't change anything out there [at the Lordstown plant]. How am I going to change the world?[102]

By mid decade, Dewey Burton would have understood.

2

What Kind of Delegation Is This?

Robert F. Kennedy, seated at the dinner table with a handful of journalists and photographers on the eve of the Indiana Democratic Primary, summarized the lessons he gleaned from his time among the voters in the tumultuous political spring of 1968. Peering from under his trademark forelock he declared, "It's class, not color. What everyone wants is a job and some hope."[1]

Many saw Kennedy as the only figure capable of serving as the common denominator for the increasingly complicated political equation of 1968. Lyndon Johnson, who had won in one of the biggest landslides in American political history four years earlier, had decided not to run for re-election. African-American voices were splitting between non-violent calls for integration and militant demands for black power, while major cities like Watts, Detroit, and Newark burned in the long hot summers of the decade. The war was going badly, and major campuses were engulfed in unrest. White working-class voters declared their sentiments in the 1966 midterms, which showed them moving quickly to the right. Segregationist Alabama governor George Wallace rode—and fomented—the backlash, winning over working-class whites from the mainstream of the Democratic Party.

"I think there has to be a new kind of coalition to keep the Democratic Party going, and to keep the country together," RFK told journalist David Frost. "We have to write off the unions and the South now. And to replace them with Negroes, blue-collar whites, and the kids. We have to convince the Negroes and the poor whites that they have common interests. If we can reconcile those hostile groups, and then add the kids, you can really turn this country around." Reporter Jack Newfield, a Kennedy believer, felt that

RFK's linking of law-and-order toughness and his charismatic populism was the only hope for progressive politics in 1968. Kennedy, he claimed, evinced the "same empathy for white workingmen and women that he felt for blacks, Latinos, and Native Americans. He thought of cops, waitresses, construction workers, and firefighters as his people. He respected their work ethic, and understood the limits placed on their fulfillment by the system." Unlike his opponent in the Democratic primary and fellow peace candidate Senator Eugene McCarthy, who made a more cerebral appeal to intellectuals and professionals, Kennedy made his pitch to the common folks. "And these working people trusted Kennedy," continued Newfield, "They identified with his patriotism, his toughness, his Catholicism, his sense of loss, his law-and-order background, his devotion to family."[2]

After Kennedy toured Spanish Harlem in 1968 with José Torres, the former world's light-heavyweight boxing champion, the pugilist pressed the senator on his motivations for seeking the presidency. "Why are you doing this? Why are you running?" queried Torres. "Because I found out something I never knew," Kennedy responded, "I found out that my world was not the real world." Indeed, Kennedy had famously been transformed from the family attack dog to social crusader in the years after 1963. His presidential campaign sought to channel that revelation and the new social movements, but do so in a way that would bolster rather than threaten the material and social standing of white workers, a group that felt itself threatened from every angle. Whether those threats were real did not matter—they were politically real, as George Wallace's third-party bid clearly showed—and they were central to any understanding of post-1968 American politics. For liberalism to survive, it needed to be saved from its radical critics, saved from its own disastrous war, saved from its anti-democratic tendencies, saved from racial polarization, and saved from its own self-referential world view, but, more importantly, it needed to preserve and strengthen the common denominators of economic justice that had originally given it life.[3]

The headlines in the late sixties focused on race—the long hot summers, the Kerner Commission, the Panthers—but Kennedy divined class as one of his central campaign principles directly from his experiences in the spring of 1968. Class had always been an elusive variable in American politics, but used loosely, undogmatically, and with just enough populism to deliver the message, there might be enough political gravity to draw together the competing forces of George Wallace, black power, Vietnam, student militants, and a national retreat from liberalism. His sense from places as diverse as the

New York ghettos of Bedford-Stuyvesant, the migrant labor camps in California, the factory towns in Indiana, and the rural poverty of Appalachia was that "a job and some hope" might do the trick.

Many believed RFK was "the last liberal politician who could communicate with white working class America," as Paul Cowan put it in the *Village Voice* or, as psychologist Robert Coles framed it, the final hope for the "miraculous: attract the support of frightened, impoverished, desperate blacks, and their angry insistent spokesmen, and, as well, working class white people." Many argued then and since, however, that Kennedy was chasing a chimera. There was no populist "black and blue-collar" coalition to be found or built in 1968; indeed, in many districts, such as those in the industrial northwest part of Indiana, RFK's political popularity was mortally weakened by his association with civil rights. As the distinction between "black" and "blue collar" unconsciously suggests, white men were "workers" in the popular political lexicon, and black people and women were others—nonworkers, welfare recipients, or worse. But *if* there was hope for blue-collar liberalism in 1968, it lay exactly with the type of coalition Kennedy believed himself to be building. He was trying, even if futilely and with minimum programmatic content, to bridge the divide that had defined much of the history of American politics.[4]

RFK's campaign to unite the forces boiling up from below emerged from an opening created at the top. Lyndon Johnson—who seemed to have proven the inviolate power of American liberalism in his landslide victory against Barry Goldwater in 1964—felt nothing short of besieged in the year of his presumed re-election. The Great Society president explained to historian Doris Kearns, in an appropriate cowboy metaphor, that he felt "chased on all sides by a giant stampede coming at me from all directions. On one side, the American people were stampeding me to do something about Vietnam. On another side, the inflationary economy was booming out of control. Up ahead were dozens of dangerous signs pointing to another summer of riots in the cities. I was being forced over the edge by rioting blacks, demonstrating students, marching welfare mothers, squawking professors, and hysterical reporters." Johnson, the consummate politician that he was, might have been able to handle all of that, but then, reported the president, "The thing I feared from the first day of my presidency was actually coming true. Robert Kennedy had openly announced his intention to reclaim the throne in the memory of his brother. And the American people, swayed by the magic of the name, were dancing in the streets. The whole situation was unbearable for me. After thirty-seven years in public service, I deserved something more than being left alone in the middle of the plain, chased by stampedes on every side."[5]

Unable to face the pounding hooves of revolt, Johnson refused to run in 1968. Once the chance to enter the primaries had safely passed, Vice President Hubert Humphrey finally entered the race, but he did so burdened with the same set of conflicts tearing at Cold War liberalism that forced Johnson to retreat. Humphrey's campaign slogan, "The Politics of Joy," was an awkward, even hollow, attempt to bridge the New Deal's "Happy Days Are Here Again" with the cultural liberation of the late sixties. The vice president was the embodiment of institutional liberalism, the darling of organized labor, the choice of the powerful, the deal makers' man, the recipient of the legacy of Vietnam at exactly the moment when the establishment was under siege.

For Kennedy the political opening at the top coincided with events on the ground to make the case for his gamble on the common denominators of class. The same spring RFK campaigned in Indiana, Martin Luther King Jr. had been in Memphis to support striking sanitation workers as a building block in his "Poor People's Campaign," a new march on Washington that would be "a Selma-like movement on economic issues." The march on Selma helped to push the Voting Rights Act into being, and King had hoped that the Poor People's Campaign could do the same for legislation aimed at economic justice. Although King and Kennedy were never close (indeed, King was harassed and spied on during John F. Kennedy's administration), Robert Kennedy admired King's commitment to unite poor whites and poor blacks into what the civil rights leader believed would be a "powerful new alliance" that transcended racial integration and placed social justice on an economic footing. As the historian William Chafe explains, King had come to a similar conclusion as Kennedy, that "class was as important to blacks as race." After King's assassination in Memphis, Kennedy delivered one of the greatest extemporaneous speeches of the era to a mostly black audience in Indianapolis, informing them for the first time of the murder of the civil rights leader. As the stunned crowd recovered from its horror, RFK famously pleaded, "Let us dedicate ourselves to what the Greeks wrote so many years ago, 'To tame the savageness of man and make gentle the life of this world.'"[6]

Concluding "it's class not color," Kennedy might also have been thinking about breaking bread with Cesar Chavez just two months earlier. In the town of Delano in California's Central Valley, RFK bore witness to the end of the labor leader's twenty-five day fast, which had brought focus to the farmworkers' struggle to build the same kind of movement capable of bridging economic and civil rights that King envisioned at the end of his life. Even opening the paper on that day before the Indiana primary, Kennedy would have read the news about "Bloody Sunday" the day before, as Parisian students took to the streets against Charles de Gaulle, soon joined in common cause by millions of workers who shut down the nation in solidarity with the students' demands. Race certainly mattered, the war mattered, the demands of youth mattered, but without finding common denominators, the many causes of the 1960s would have a hard time making the leap to lasting political form.[7]

While Kennedy believed that an appeal to class could pull together blue-collar whites, blacks, and Latinos, he had very little faith in the primary vehicle for class interests, the mainstream labor movement. Unlike many older Democratic Party leaders, he had none of the knee-jerk commitments to organized labor that figures like his unofficial opponent, Vice President Hubert Humphrey, regularly displayed. The AFL-CIO had given Kennedy its highest rating based on his voting record, but the federation proved very hostile to his candidacy and, unlike the radical French unions, despised the student movement that Kennedy was turning to for part of his base. RFK was keenly aware that some unions, like the more progressive UAW, would be key elements in the success of the Indiana primary campaign. As Newfield explained, however, "To Kennedy's eyes, the AFL-CIO leadership was committed politically to Lyndon Johnson, committed emotionally to the Vietnam War, and not committed at all to organizing the new, invisible poor."[8]

Without a shared economic vision, white working-class interests easily became racial resentments. Journalist Pete Hamill described the darkness stirring in the soul of the white working class in 1968: the "cab-drivers, beauticians, steelworkers, ironworkers, and construction-men so beautifully romanticized by generations of dreamy socialists," he explained, could be an "ugly bunch of people." The specter that roused such fears in 1968—and in 1972 as well—was the candidacy of Alabama governor George Wallace. The man who famously stood in the schoolhouse doorway to defend segregation was busy rattling the stale presumptions of both major parties. As an independent candidate in 1968, and again as Democratic primary challenger in 1972, Wallace drew together the segregationist South with anti-liberal northerners fearful of blacks moving into their neighborhoods, questioning the protests and the urban riots, and feeling, above all, simply forgotten. Wallace would ride those sentiments to a 21 percent share in a national poll in 1968, only seven points behind Democratic candidate Hubert Humphrey, just a month before the main election. "The support he was drawing in 1968," suggests historian Michael Kazin, "looked to many liberals like a fascist movement on the rise." In the end, Wallace won 13.6 percent of the vote, and his segregationist message helped him carry five southern states (four of which Barry Goldwater had carried four years earlier). His earlier inroads into the white ethnics in the urban north had been foiled—primarily by labor's informational campaign against him—by Election Day.[9]

Some of the reasons for the erosion of Wallace's support are suggestive of some of the characteristics of the blue-collar backlash. Among northern wage earners, his populist anti-elitism—"stand up for the common man" was his slogan—spoke to the powerful undercurrent of resentment. His racially coded language also served him well. But his embrace of segregation, his terrible record on labor rights and his selection of a vice presidential candidate who appeared ready to push the button, failed him. When the UAW launched a campaign against him—exposing the dismal level of workers' rights and compensation in Wallace's Alabama—it helped to turn the tide in the industrial north. Undoubtedly, his common man rhetoric spoke to themes that no one else on the national stage addressed—especially after Robert Kennedy was killed. As one welder noted in 1970, "Now people say we're only out for ourselves and we're against the Negroes and all that. Well, I don't know. I've never been asked. If they did come around and talk with us at work and ask us their question, I'll bet we'd confuse them. One minute we'd sound like George Wallace, and the next we'd probably be called radicals or something." There seemed to be a promising potential political space between the race and class dimensions of the labor question in the late sixties and seventies. As Oklahoma populist Fred Harris speculated later in the seventies, it was dangerous to leave the white working-class off the political table while solely emphasizing the needs of minorities—however real those needs were. The "blue collar worker," explained Harris, "will be progressive as long as it is not progress for everyone but himself."[10]

The old men of organized labor, however, found Kennedy's campaign just as dangerous and unpredictable as Wallace's politics of race and rage. They kept close tabs on him, his strategy, and his prospects, following developments with a combination of fear and disdain. Political strategists sent to Indiana to tail the Kennedy campaign ruefully reported to AFL-CIO president George Meany that, given the political lay of the land in 1968, Bobby "*can* make it *if* everything falls his way." They found troubling his "highly emotional style," which was "not at all cool like JFK. He excites instant hysteria." They felt more comfortable with the way his older brother "relied heavily on the individual collection of party leaders" rather than Bobby's attempt to move the party elite through that most dangerous of forces, "mass popular appeal." A Committee on Political Education (COPE) memo dripped with contempt for the populism Kennedy unleashed in Indiana. "Will the morons who throng about Kennedy seeking to touch the hem of his garments outvote the provincial morons who can't vote for an 'Easterner'?" the strategists asked rhetorically. RFK's direct appeal to the electorate may have grated on the AFL-CIO bureaucracy, but labor's attempt to rally the regulars behind Indiana governor Roger Branigan as a stand-in for Vice President Humphrey proved a tepid and ineffectual alternative.[11]

The night following his "class not color" remark, Kennedy, boosted by family money and dragged down by hostile local press, found out that he won the Indiana primary. His defeat of Eugene McCarthy as well as favorite son Branigan suggested that a class-based coalition could be stitched together even in a conservative state like Indiana and even in a stormy election year like 1968. Jubilant over his victory, Kennedy thought about the working people he encountered on his exhaustive tour of the state. "I loved the faces here in Indiana, on the farmers, on the steelworkers, on the black kids," he remarked. Asked by reporters to describe the meaning of his victory, he proclaimed, "That I really have a chance now, just a chance, to organize a new coalition of Negroes, and working-class white people, against the union and party establishments."[12]

RFK's internal polling in Indiana showed that, indeed, income was the "most important factor in the Kennedy vote." He did very well among lower-income groups, blacks, protestant blue-collar whites, and even German and Italian Catholic voters. When it came to the "ethnics" of Eastern European descent, he showed considerable weakness. These were white working-class voters that actually lived in and around African-American workers in the steel mills in northeast Indiana and who appeared to reject him because they associated him too strongly with the advancement of blacks and the destabilization of the Democratic Party. A sober review of the polling suggests that perhaps the RFK coalition could be built, but it did not yet really exist. The ethnic industrial working class remained politically volatile, but conscious strategy could close some of the race-class divide in Democratic politics.[13]

Robert Kennedy did go on to win all of the succeeding primaries, with his single setback in Oregon, finally storming California to the sounds of Mexican-Americans chanting "Viva Kennedy!" and throngs of African-Americans reaching to touch him as his motorcade drove through Watts. At his victory gathering at the Ambassador Hotel in Los Angeles, he flashed a peace sign and said, "Now, on to Chicago and let's win there." Hanging on Kennedy's last public utterances was the hope of a different kind of convention than the violence and chaos that marked Chicago '68, where the regulars locked out the voices of dissent and the New Left came to believe that there was little in the party worth salvaging.

As Kennedy proceeded to the hotel pantry, a young busboy named Juan Romero, anxious to greet the senator, extended his hand to his hero. Suddenly, shots rang out and Kennedy collapsed with three bullets in his body. Paul Schrade, an outspoken young UAW strategist working on the Kennedy campaign, also took a bullet to his skull. As Kennedy crumpled to the floor, Romero held his head and tried to comfort him. The hotel worker pulled a rosary out of his pocket and pressed it into the senator's hand. Kennedy was unable to hold it, so Romero wrapped the rosary around Kennedy's thumb. As they carried Robert Kennedy away in the stretcher for the final hours of his life, the immigrant busboy's rosary remained dangling from Kennedy's hand.[14]

I

Although Kennedy won almost all of the 1968 primaries, the nomination quickly reverted to labor's man, Hubert Humphrey. The vice president had, all along, controlled more delegates in the old insider system of the pre-reform era. The Kennedy campaign's hope had been that those delegates would change their mind in Chicago when they saw the strength of the Kennedy campaign. As the nomination process moved out of the streets and back to the smoke-filled rooms in Chicago, however, Humphrey and labor managed to wrangle two-thirds of the delegates with a mere 2 percent of the primary vote while Mayor Daley's police mercilessly and violently crushed the protestors outside of the convention.

With the Kennedy insurgency no longer a concern, there was yet another threat on the political horizon—this one from George Wallace, who threatened to siphon off Humphrey's blue-collar vote. George Meany's lieutenant

Al Barkan was in a panic over Wallace's "alarming inroads among union membership, deeper even than that among the public at-large" as he noted in a confidential memo to his boss. "Never before has the trade union movement developed so much political muscle and organizational sophistication," explained veteran labor journalist John Herling. "Yet never before has organized labor seemed so ineffectual in combating an appeal to fear and prejudice as personified, for many, in George Wallace."[15]

Because of the divisions, disarray, and disaffections within the Democratic Party in 1968, labor took over the party—almost completely. It was only the AFL-CIO's massive investment in Humphrey—and against Wallace—that brought the vice president close to beating Richard Nixon in a pale and anticlimactic general election that failed to reflect the nation's many concerns surfacing just months earlier. The Democratic Party in the 1968 general election was, practically speaking, a labor party, supported almost solely by the institutional power and financial resources of the AFL-CIO. As George Meany accurately noted, "Now after the convention in 1968 the Democratic Party was in a shambles. All Humphrey had was us. I mean the only thing he had, really, in the way of machinery to get people to the polls and try to get them to vote for him was the trade union movement." There was no money, little party discipline, continued disagreement on Vietnam, and local party leaders alienated from the national ticket. As one veteran in the Humphrey camp said, "Labor, and only labor, came damn near doing it for Hubert. The Democratic Party is a labor party" (albeit one that was having trouble reaching its members). Meantime, Nixon ran a bland and featureless campaign, trumpeting little more than the "law and order" issue, and successfully banking on his opposition's complete disarray. The national contest may have been a narrow loss for the Democrats, but for labor it proved that union muscle alone could move the politics of the nation. It may have been a tough time for the national ticket, but it proved labor was now the uncontested big boss in the Democratic Party.[16]

Both the promise and failure of organized labor as a political institution were evident in the 1968 election. On the one hand, the unions proved the power of their vast network of political machinery. On the other, their uncompromising support of the war in Vietnam, their hesitance to enlist the new social movements of the sixties, and their deep skepticism of anyone, such as Robert Kennedy or Eugene McCarthy, who might upset the delicate balance of *their* specific and narrow version of liberalism, demonstrated a debilitating set of weaknesses. Just when the unions got their hands firmly on the levers of the Democratic machinery, they slipped from their grasp. By 1972, organized labor was frantically trying to regain control, only to expose their provincialism in the process when they sought to subvert the nomination of Senator George McGovern for head of the Democratic ticket.[17]

II

When Allard Lowenstein—the young, driven, left-liberal gadfly—approached Kennedy about running in 1968 in a "Dump Johnson" movement, Bobby recommended that he pursue instead a quiet, plain-spoken senator from South Dakota named George McGovern. "George is the most decent man in the Senate. As a matter of fact," Kennedy added, "he's the only one." When Lowenstein pointed his seductive powers toward McGovern, the senator had already calculated that he could not address national issues and constituencies—the cities, the war, the students, the urban workers—without sounding like "a madman or a socialist" to his rural constituents back home. This was doubly true since it was clear that he would be running largely as a sacrificial candidate to the anti-war cause. "I saw the decision to run for the presidency as synonymous with resigning from the Senate," he later explained. The anti-Johnson forces eventually found their man in Eugene McCarthy and, after the New Hampshire primary, Kennedy as well.[18]

After Robert Kennedy's assassination and the disastrously bloody convention in Chicago, McGovern was haunted by his decision not to heed Lowenstein's original suggestion to run. As it was, he did end up running, but only a small, eighteen-day campaign as RFK's proxy in the weeks just prior to the convention. He received a mere 146½ votes in his "adventure," as campaign chronicler Theodore White put it, "to keep aglow the flare of conscience Robert Kennedy had lit in the spring of that year." As the conventioneers deserted Chicago and headed back to their homes, White appeared at the senator's hotel door. "How does it feel to be the guy that booted away the presidency of the United States?" he queried McGovern. "If you had run, Bobby would never have gotten into it. Johnson would still have withdrawn. Humphrey would have been no more electable than he is today. And so the convention would have turned to you, because, unlike McCarthy, you were respectable to the regulars. And if you rather than Humphrey were the nominee, with Bob Kennedy alive and campaigning for you, then." White's narrative was too tight, there was not enough contingency, and it grossly overstated McGovern's power and appeal in 1968—even though Kennedy himself had said he would not have entered the race had McGovern been in it. In the back of McGovern's mind rolled the sense that he had betrayed his instincts and passed up his destiny. In Chicago, George McGovern committed himself to making the effort real in 1972, convinced that he could defeat the opposition within his party, and do so in the populist mold of Robert F. Kennedy.[19]

George Stanley McGovern was born in the tiny village of Avon, South Dakota, in the summer of 1922. There his father served as the minister in one of many churches across the plains of South Dakota that he built with his own hands. Six years later, the family moved to Mitchell, where Reverend Joseph McGovern built his last church and the future senator spent the remainder of his upbringing. George's father preached as a Wesleyan Methodist; his fundamentalism looked more toward faith than damnation, and his sermons—as well as his parenting—emphasized the type of discipline that built both lives and communities. He organized his congregations the way his son would later build the state's Democratic Party—through hard work, sacrifice, fine oratory, and a great deal of neighborly travel. The family often lived on the edge of poverty during the Great Depression, and George inherited nothing besides his family's sense of hard work, Christian charity, and ability to speak to the people. He graduated from Dakota Wesleyan University—a school right in Mitchell with an enrollment of only five hundred students. The small town bubble burst when he departed for training to become a bomber pilot in World War II, from which he returned a hero, having won the Distinguished Flying Cross and other honors during perilous raids over Germany and Eastern Europe.[20]

The young war hero returned home and did the expected: he enrolled in seminary to follow in his father's footsteps. He soon grew dissatisfied with the limits of the clerical world, however, and turned to graduate study in history at Northwestern for more secular answers to the nation's problems. There he got involved in Henry Wallace's third-party campaign, including attending the Progressive Party Convention in Philadelphia, only to become disappointed that accusations of Communist infiltration were too true. With the labor question still pressing the nation, and the rise of industrial unionism still fresh as one of the most central developments in twentieth-century history, it is not surprising that McGovern wrote his doctoral dissertation on the topic of labor. Under the direction of Arthur Link, the devoted Woodrow Wilson scholar, he selected as his subject one of the most notorious clashes in labor history: the Colorado coal strike of 1913–1914, a conflict that included the notorious Ludlow Massacre.

Some of McGovern's relations with labor, even aspects of his political personality, are foreshadowed in his PhD dissertation, which long remained one of the best examinations of events at Ludlow. The Colorado miners were, indeed, as McGovern wrote, "virtual industrial serfs" employed by "mining barons whose law of life was an unchecked, competitive capitalism." The marriage of mining and politics in Colorado did, as young McGovern argued, create a sort of industrial "despotism" of the mining districts. Rarely in American life had class conflict played itself out as clearly—and violently— as in the western mines. It was in Ludlow that an amalgam of Colorado militia men, hired detectives, and coal company guards, all doing Rockefeller's bidding, shot and burned to death twenty people, including a dozen women and children. The starkness of the tale served McGovern's personality. "It is one of McGovern's greatest strengths—and some would say, among his most glaring weaknesses—that on certain issues he does see politics in moral, almost apocalyptic terms. Later Vietnam would be that way for him. It would summon up a sort of ministerial outrage, which in turn would produce denunciations of a fervor and intensity worthy of his father's pulpit." Not surprisingly, by the time he was on the national ticket, the labor issue he liked to emphasize was Lordstown.[21]

Following the completion of his dissertation, McGovern returned to teach at Dakota Wesleyan before he answered the call to rebuild the moribund South Dakota state Democratic Party. It was a daunting task—there were only 2 Democrats in the 110-person state legislature. Just as his father built a series of churches across the plains, George McGovern slowly created a party out of mountains of index cards and countless personal calls where previously there had been close to none. By building web-like connections to the people of his district, he went on to win a seat to the House of Representatives but then lost a Senate bid in 1960. In honor of McGovern's sacrifices for Kennedy's presidential campaign that year, which helped him to lose his own senatorial bid, John F. Kennedy—largely at Bobby's insistence— appointed McGovern head of the Food for Peace program. By sending U.S. agricultural surpluses to developing countries, Kennedy hoped to both drain off excess production and sweeten the deal for developing nations leaning toward the United States in the Cold War. It also introduced McGovern to some of the real reasons for the instability of the third world, where he saw first hand the impact of economic underdevelopment and hunger that plagued those regions—lessons readily applicable to Vietnam. He finally won his Senate seat in 1962, and became the first senator to criticize involvement in Vietnam in September 1963. Although he voted for the 1964 Gulf of Tonkin Resolution in order to unify support for Johnson and stave off Goldwater, it was a vote he regretted.[22]

Despite a remarkable pro-labor voting record that placed him among labor's most reliable allies in the Senate (especially considering he was from a rural state), McGovern had a conflicted relationship with organized labor even before his 1972 presidential bid. Most notably, of course, was his opposition to the war and growing alliance with the peace movement, both of which were intolerable to the gray cold warriors of the AFL-CIO. He had also taken Bobby Kennedy's place against labor's beloved Humphrey in Chicago, attempting to serve as a spoiler for a man who had once served as his political mentor in his early days in Washington. In 1970, on the day before the Cambodian invasion, he introduced the McGovern-Hatfield Amendment to a military procurement bill, which served as the political focus for the peace wing of the party by requiring a timetable for an end to the war. On the day of the vote, he spoke before a packed and hushed Senate, declaring "Every Senator in this Chamber is partly responsible for sending 50,000 young Americans to an early grave. This Chamber reeks of blood." The vote went down to defeat by a vote of thirty-nine to fifty-five.[23]

If opposition to the war was not bad enough in the jaundiced eyes of the AFL-CIO leadership, the critical blow to the McGovern-labor relationship came when the senator chaired the committee charged with reforming the delegate selection process after the disastrous 1968 Democratic Convention. Almost everyone figured that chairing the reform commission was a thankless job that could only alienate party regulars and, most likely, destroy presidential aspirations. McGovern, however, believed he could heal the rift between the Humphrey regulars and the Kennedy-McCarthy wing of the party and do so by genuinely reforming the party rather than putting on the political show everyone expected. "In the past, when political parties have had a choice between reform and a quiet death, they have almost invariably chosen death," declared McGovern. He struggled against the view that the reform commission merely housed the orphans and mavericks of 1968 by being as inclusive to the traditional concerns as he could. To the Democratic power brokers, however, the reform committee appeared to be little more than a plot to allow the barbarians of the sixties through the gates.[24]

Labor and many of the party regulars, to their detriment, did not respond kindly to the reform commission. The leaders of the AFL-CIO, who would later be the most savage critics of the outcome of the reform process, simply boycotted the proceedings. Many regulars ignored the hearings and deliberations on the not-so-far-fetched assumption that the entire project would be for naught. The Steel Workers' I.W. Abel, labor's official appointee to the commission, did not even bother to show up for a single meeting, and other labor leaders refused to participate in hearings. "By remaining aloof from the reform effort," recalled McGovern, "labor not only forfeited its considerable influence but also helped maintain the divisions within the party that had opened in 1968. Labor kept itself isolated from what had become the dynamic mainstream of the party and encouraged others to ignore or oppose reform." A generation of neo-conservatives would blame the reforms for alienating the center of the party, but few took into account the need for new voices in the party or the regulars' unwillingness to engage the process and mold it toward more palatable ends. AFSCME president Jerry Wurf, one of the few members of the AFL-CIO executive board in favor of the reforms, saw the commission as a tremendous opportunity for the unions, the party, and the new social movements to advance together. Rather than participating, Wurf explained, "labor sulked, and that is tragic and rather pitiful." He continued, "We had a golden opportunity to bring working families access to power through the Democratic Party—and we blew it."[25]

The reform hearings, according to one student of the process, revealed a terrifying picture of the Democratic Party with "tales of greed, abuse of party office, meaningless elections, closed party forums, and servile decision-makers." The lifeblood of the system was patronage, the ends were spoils, and the system worked like well-oiled machinery. To combat this, the commission settled on two major changes that brought the process out of the smoke-filled rooms. First, the party would require affirmative action in the delegate selection process so that women, minorities, and youth could break into the system. Although they attempted to avoid formal quotas to achieve their goals, they largely failed and ended up with a de facto quota system. The second aspect was the direct election of delegates through either primaries or caucuses. Delegates would therefore be much more diverse, much less connected to traditional power structures (whether unions or urban machines), specifically pledged to candidates, and selected by much larger numbers of voters than in the old process ruled by insiders. Many argued that the open party would be much more white-collar—more "new class"—than working-class since blue-collar institutions like labor and the urban machines would not be represented in their previously uncontested ways. No one knew exactly what the reform process would mean in the long term, but it certainly appeared to be the dethroning of the old guard that had left itself so vulnerable to the debacle in Mayor Daley's Chicago in 1968.[26]

For labor, the biggest impact of the reform commission was its undoing of the central power-broker role that unions had enjoyed in the Democratic Party, which they had nearly perfected in 1968. Labor strategists saw their job as fending off the influence of the "kids, kooks, Communists and other far-out 'kinky' left liberals," in the words of COPE director Al Barkan, who were infiltrating the party. As one AFL-CIO political operative put it smugly, "We are the kingpin of any possible presidential election for a Democrat, and very likely the only cohesive force that can assure relatively progressive majorities in the House and Senate." After 1972 no labor leader would ever again be able to say that about presidential politics. The '72 election year marked a key point not in the simple conservative turn of labor's politics, but rather in the fragmentation of labor's political voice.[27]

Although McGovern modeled his insurgency on Kennedy's, he was missing key elements of '68. RFK might have been able to win the nomination without organized labor, but McGovern could not. He could hire Kennedy's advisors and strategists and tap into his political infrastructure, but he could not manage to lead them. Where Kennedy sought to channel the power of the social movements, McGovern seemed controlled by them. In lieu of Kennedy's charisma, McGovern was saddled with plainness. The senator from South Dakota was, furthermore, often regarded as a one-issue candidate at a time when Richard Nixon seemed in control of that issue, the war in Vietnam. It was also four years later, and the public was that much more tired of social upheavals, the movements were that much more ready to take over mainstream political institutions, and busing had become a millstone for the Democratic Party. Moreover, McGovern was stuck with all of these problems and, just like Bobby, could not win the group that had nearly done the job for Humphrey four years earlier: organized labor.[28]

McGovern's largest failure as a national politician was the obverse of where Kennedy and Wallace both understood their strengths to be: his appeal to working people. Where RFK could build some shaky bridges between the New Politics and the Wallace supporters and between the white working class and workers of color, McGovern later confessed that he could never gain more than "erratic" support among factory workers. "You just didn't know what would reach them," he emphasized. Despite the exasperation, campaign manager Gary Hart knew that it was the white working-class that held the balance of power in the election. "Somehow he had to get to 'the people,' the workers, the blue-collars," he mused about McGovern. "Muskie would get the regular Democrats, McGovern would get the liberals and the 'peace people'; in between was this vast multitude, this turned-off majority, over-taxed, distrustful of politics and politicians, worried constantly about layoffs, knowing that bankruptcy was one operation, one hospital-visit away. They would nominate a Democrat; they would elect a president."[29]

A strategy memo from documentary filmmaker and Kennedy insider Charles Guggenheim captured the essence of McGovern's challenge. He had to get beyond the movement people, Guggenheim argued, and reach outside of the New Politics and the anti-war forces:

> The necessity to turn your concerns to the "forgotten man" in America cannot be overemphasized. You have certainly earned and have the respect of the young and thinking liberal. You may have the farm vote . . . but the vast throng of hard-working urbanites, the fellow who pays most of the taxes, reads the Reader's Digest, and is on the cutting edge of most of today's social reforms, really doesn't know what to make of George McGovern of South Dakota. You enter national politics with your own coalition, but it does not include the people who won for Bobby in Indiana, Nebraska, and South Dakota and defeated him in Oregon. It does not include the people that Norman Rockwell painted.[30]

III

Professional political commentators and intellectuals, generally agreeing that 1972 was going to be a watershed year, divided into roughly three strategic/philosophical positions that sought to capture the people Guggenheim had sketched out. Each had a different take on the nature of the politics of class in the 1970s, and most contained more than a little bit of political fantasy.

A survey of the range of strategies for capturing working-class votes illustrates the complexity and contradictions of blue-collar vote harvesting in 1972.

Fred Dutton, a man of considerable gravitas, having worked for JFK, California governor Pat Brown, and Bobby Kennedy before joining the McGovern campaign in 1972, staked one important position: the New Politics. He envisioned a voter insurgency in 1972 pulsing through the entirety of society, destabilizing old hierarchies, and pushing toward a youthful, individualistic emancipation from staid cultural norms. The new historical epoch, he calculated, was in search of a Rooseveltian figure that could give voice to the unprecedented upsurge of youth culture in a way that Franklin Delano Roosevelt institutionalized the economic demands of the working-class in the thirties. This was partially the great hope of the Twenty-Sixth Amendment, which had lowered the voting age to eighteen in 1970. "If the older America has more votes, money, experience, and guns at present," he argued, "the new elements have still-unfathomable energy, growth, imagination, and time on their side." Rather than the politics of material security, Dutton advocated the politics of fulfillment. In lieu of the old shibboleths of peace and prosperity, the slogans of the New Politics would be "*Live!*— perhaps even *Love!*" Like so many who emphasized youth in the sixties, Dutton tended to view young people as part of a single (affluent) class.[31]

Dutton's political shortcomings were most evident in his treatment of the Wallace phenomenon, which almost all other political strategists of the period regarded as the key to the future in one way or another. He failed to see the core of Kennedy's appeal in the blue-collar vote—preferring to emphasize the youth; rather than tapping into the Wallacites' anger, Dutton chose the most dangerous path of dismissing it. "Wallace is important as a symbol of the elemental—and malevolent—forces infecting the body politic," Dutton explained. That, it turned out, was enough to dismiss the governor along with the entire, slightly sinister and unreliable, white working class. Besides, he argued, working people had entered a post-material phase just like the rest of the nation. "A 'union man' not long ago connoted a craftsman or factory worker who lived in a crowded section of an industrial town, worked long hours, had little free time, and could generally claim only elementary school training," Dutton claimed. "The union member of the 1970s must far more often be thought of as a leisure-seeking suburbanite with a high school education and a strong concern about his own identity and status." Workers and union members, just like the rest of the nation, would be drawn to the polls

on the grounds of social style, attitudes, and the promise of personal liberation.[32]

Dutton's tossing of the white working-class anger into the dustbin of history was a more sophisticated version of Charles Reich's *The Greening of
America*, which promised a "revolution by consciousness" that would produce
a "'new head'—a new way of living—a new man." The messy world of coalitions, elections, organizing, wealth, power, and conflict was to melt away as
a painless—if preposterous—do-nothing revolution took hold of the American soul. "There is nothing on the other side," explained Reich; "there are no
enemies" as all members of society will want the psychic bounty available in
what he called the higher state of "Consciousness III." Square America will
fall because "there is no class struggle; today there is only one class. . . . We
are all the proletariat, and there is no longer any ruling class except the machine itself." He continues, "the fact that the exploited blue-collar worker is
a chief opponent of change is in a sense an optimistic sign, for his consciousness clearly does not rest on economic interest, and is therefore just as clearly
subject to change." Who could oppose the rosy allure of the coming cultural
revolution? "Even businessmen, once liberated, would like to roll in the grass
and lie in the sun. There is no need to fight against any group of people in
America."[33]

A dramatically different strategic position on the working class, one that
regarded the Dutton/Reich position as madness, argued the opposite: that the
harder a candidate ran *against* the new cultural trends, the better the chances
of success with white working-class voters would be. This was laid out most
forcefully in Richard Scammon and Ben Wattenberg's *The Real Majority*
(1970), which argued that Democrats needed to pander not to the new social
movements but to the nation's deep social conservatism in 1972—and to do
so quickly and aggressively. "The great majority of the voters in America are
unyoung, unpoor, and unblack," the authors famously proclaimed; "they are
middle-aged, middle-class, middle-minded." Blue-collar voters had no interests in the type of cultural liberation offered by Dutton or Reich. In contrast, they believed, working-class voters were motivated by fear of those
same issues, which they lumped into a single rubric: the social issue. It included ills such as crime, race, youth culture, pornography, sexual liberation,
and, perhaps above all, the racialized hot-buttons of protests and riots. The
rising social issue, they believed, was not yet liberal or conservative, Right or
Left, but a "new factor in the political equation." The "paradox of attitude in

the seventies" was that while the electorate was conservative on the social issue, it tended to remain solidly liberal on bread-and-butter issues. They calculated that anyone associated with the New Politics was in danger. Any candidate attempting to form a new-left coalition of young, black, poor, and intellectual, Scammon and Wattenberg believed, while "relegating Middle Americans and especially white union labor to the ranks of 'racists,'" was doomed to failure.[34]

Although there were clear political truths that ran through Scammon and Wattenberg's logic, the problem with their analysis was two-fold. First, their study was not about leadership but about strategy. Nowhere did the study discuss the ideals of policy, governing, or leadership—only how to win by running a negative campaign against the major social changes of the day. At best, their tactics could simply offer a social restoration with no clear vision of how it bettered society; they could win votes but not search out solutions; they could pander to fears but could not find a way to incorporate the solutions to the problems of the seventies into a meaningful Democratic agenda. Second, as shown in the next chapter, the social issue agenda actually helped pave the way for a New Right to push through relatively unpopular economic policies under the cover of traditional cultural values. In sum, although Scammon and Wattenberg aimed the *The Real Majority* at preserving Democratic power, it worked for Nixon and Reagan, figures who could run more effectively against the new social movements with, in contrast to the Democrats, no political cost.

A third and final position available to McGovern looked to a revival of economic populism. Jack Newfield and Jeff Greenfield, in their study *A Populist Manifesto: The Making of a New Majority*, rejected embracing the "fairy tale" of cultural liberation as proffered by Dutton and Reich but also attacked the jaundiced strategies purported by Scammon and Wattenberg. In contrast, Newfield and Greenfield looked to the new coalition that Robert Kennedy had attempted in 1968 as the template for the seventies. The book was even dedicated to the late senator, and it was his spirit they attempted to channel. Populism is arguably the deepest and most passionate vein in American politics, one that pits the people against the interests in "a language whose speakers conceive of ordinary people as a noble assemblage not bounded narrowly by class," according to its most astute scholar Michael Kazin, and who "view their elite opponents as self-serving and undemocratic, and seek to mobilize the former against the latter." The plan was to unite the intellectuals and the minorities, along with the newly en-franchised youth, with the older concerns of the white ethnics and the labor unions.[35]

Like Scammon and Wattenberg, Newfield and Greenfield put the white working class squarely at the center of their analysis but did so on a material rather than cultural basis. "Despite all the ethnic and racial divisions, blue-collar workers were progressive during the 1930s and 1940s," they argued. "There is no reason why they can't be again." The authors admitted, however, that the revival of economic populism was far from certain. "Working-class whites and blacks are separate armed camps in Cicero, Illinois; school buses are bombed in Pontiac, Michigan, in an effort to halt racial busing. In 1968, New York watched as teachers—mostly Jewish—battled parents' groups—mostly black and Puerto Rican—for control of the city's schools." But, they calculated, more than racial animosity was at play. "Certainly the jobless youth in Watts and the steelworker laid off his job in Gary have more in common than antilabor millionaires like Senators James Buckley and William Brock III have in common with those blue-collar workers who voted for them." They advocated a populist and loosely based class appeal, but the problem was that populism depended upon broad-based and widespread community movements as well as a charismatic figure to unite the people's passions. Without the person and the movements, populism tended to be a rather diffuse sentiment. And, as it was, the American populist in 1972 was George Wallace.[36]

Oklahoma populist and former Democratic National Committee national chair senator Fred Harris also believed the populist angle would be the best hope for 1972. Buoyed by the optimism of the 1970 midterm elections, which offered little boost to Nixon, he extrapolated forth a new populism boiling up in America, a discontent that could be channeled into rebuilding the Democratic Party. "The 1970s can truly be the Decade of the People if we will move vigorously to do two things: return power to the people—open up our political parties, decentralize authority, broaden popular participation in political and other processes, and expand the people's control over government and other decisions; and if we will remember that there are no purely political choices, only moral ones."[37]

Although McGovern was often branded a populist, in balancing these perspectives, he ended up on the weak side of all three positions. He naively believed himself to be working in the populist tradition advocated by New-field and Greenfield, while simultaneously appearing to be captured by the youth-and-movement ideas of Dutton and Reich, and allowing those inside and outside of the party to attack him with the ideas in Scammon and Wattenberg's *The Real Majority*. As one staffer remarked, "McGovern's preoccupation with the youth cult led him to accept unquestioningly Fred Dutton's opinion that the new 18-year-old vote would control this election and that we would win simply by registering millions of new voters. . . . He so jealously guarded his position on the left that he never noticed no one else was there—except his staff." Campaign strategist Frank Mankiewicz later admitted that the basic mistake of the campaign was that "We were always subject to this pressure from the cause people. We reacted to every threat from women, or militants, or college groups. If I had to do it all over again, I'd learn when to tell them to go to hell." The activists also hamstrung McGovern's ability to make a pitch to the party regulars with whom he had shown considerable ability to work during the sixties. Moreover, by working toward the cultural Left, McGovern also allowed Richard Nixon to claim the conservative social-issue ground that Scammon and Wattenberg had originally tried to preserve for the Democrats.[38]

IV

McGovern, keenly aware that he did not have the political appeal to sweep into the primaries at the last minute like Robert Kennedy, declared his bid for the nomination in January 1971—earlier in the process than any candidate since Andrew Jackson. People who described the campaign often resorted to terms of guerrilla warfare—a long-term series of tactical hit-and-run battles waged by a small rag-tag people's army against the well-trained and well-financed troops of the Democratic regulars. Gary Hart, a Colorado attorney who had worked for Kennedy in 1968, became McGovern's campaign manager. Although he looked more like a hip, young, and handsome Colorado ski bum, he preferred to imagine himself as Kutuzov of *War and Peace*, who had to attack and win anywhere and everywhere. Hart laid his cards on the table about the popular perception of McGovern's chances this way: "He is a nice man, decent, honest, perhaps even courageous; he says what he thinks and is right on the issues before any of the others. *But* he can't win. He is from a small midwestern state; he has no money; he has no standing in the polls; he doesn't have the backing of organized labor or any substantial element of the Democratic Party or any of the constituent elements of the traditional Democratic coalition. Worse still, he is a 'one-issue candidate'—the war—and that issue will be gone by 1972. But above all, *he does not have charisma*." To win, remarked gonzo journalist Hunter S. Thompson, McGovern would need "at least one dark kinky streak of Mick Jagger in his soul." Jimmy the Greek, the Las Vegas odds maker, gave the senator 200 to 1 odds of winning the 1972 Democratic nomination.[39]

If George McGovern was known nationally in 1971 and early 1972, it was as a spokesman for the anti-war movement and his attacks on the bloated defense budget, which he advocated cutting by 40 percent. It was solely his passionate stand against the war, including amnesty for evasion of the draft, that could elevate his oratory above his otherwise flat, often nasally, twang and toward tones of righteousness. The peace dividend, he argued, plus closing tax loopholes and taxing inherited wealth, could be used to build federal full employment policies and provide for national health care. He was strong on agricultural subsidies and advocated massive investment in urban public transportation. In essence, George McGovern ran not only as a peace candidate but as a European-style social democrat.

McGovern's signature economic policy, however, was one long, blundering disaster called the Demogrant. In an echo of Nixon's Family Assistance Plan, this promised $1,000 to every single person in the United States—men, women, and children from the filthy rich to the destitute poor. A family of four, for instance, would receive $4,000 (over $20,000 in 2009 dollars), and there would be no welfare; their tax obligation would begin at any dollar earned beyond $4,000. Plans to redistribute money to the poor through various "negative tax" schemes were everywhere on the political landscape of the early seventies—from Nixon's Family Assistance Plan, to congressional Democrats who had been advocating $3,000 to $4,000 grants to the poor, to more radical redistributive plans of the National Welfare Rights Organization (which wanted to guarantee every family $6,500 per year). McGovern's "giveaway" was going to be available to all citizens (quietly recouped from the stable and affluent through taxation) and was, in reality, little different than Milton Friedman's negative income tax that had been a pet project of the conservative movement. In McGovern's hands, however, the same idea advocated by a conservative economist like Friedman appeared to be a massive giveaway, especially when the campaign remained mired in confusion as to who would gain and who would lose under the plan. Already "soft" on foreign policy, the muddled presentation of the Demogrant left the candidate vulnerable to the charge that he was weak on economic policy as well. His attempt at economic populism went down as another confusing Washington scheme rather than anti-elitist leveling.[40]

The senator's attack on economic privilege tended to be eclipsed by his association with a different kind of elitism—that of the new cultural values. Here he fought against a set of political phantoms that became known simply as the "McGovern trilogy:" the three "A's" of "Amnesty, Acid, and Abortion." Senate Minority Leader Hugh Scott first hurled the three A's at McGovern and they stuck like a grand jury indictment. Their political brilliance was in their abstractness—the three A's captured fears and resentments without ever touching specifics—and they became central to the idea of McGovern's permissiveness. Most of the accusations implied in the three A's were either not true or not central aspects of McGovern's platform, but they grafted readily to the McGovern narrative. He was intentionally vague on abortion (though privately in favor of choice). He never advocated the legalization of marijuana (the misguided "acid" reference), but his daughter was arrested on possession charges. McGovern did remain publicly committed to amnesty for draft resisters (consistently his biggest applause line on the campus circuit), an issue that consistently overshadowed his own record of war heroism, which he did not feel comfortable running on. Despite the reality, the candidate's association with youth and the college crowd seemed to make the McGovern trilogy axiomatic to the company he kept.[41]

Senator McGovern may have been hampered by the social issue and occasionally bungled presentations of himself and his ideas, but his path to the nomination was strategically sharp, grassroots based, and hard won against great odds. There were more than simple glimmers in 1971 and 1972 of McGovern the new hope, the "thinking man's Wallace," the type of person that Newfield and Greenfield hoped would rise to the challenge of renewing a populist coalition for the seventies. But he faced a tough field of Democratic heavies. Edmund Muskie, who had out-polled Nixon as early as 1970, was the clear frontrunner for the Democratic nomination and was committed to run in all states. Muskie was the man to beat, but he ran as a centrist in a year when the center had largely fallen out of the party. Humphrey appeared to be simply old—not in a chronological sense, but as part of a by-gone era. That left George Wallace, running as a Democrat in '72 rather than as an independent as he did in '68, and a large group of also-rans, including Mayor John Lindsay of New York, Senator Henry "Scoop" Jackson of Washington, Congresswoman Shirley Chisholm, and Eugene McCarthy among a host of others.

The strategy to beat these opponents, dreamt up largely by Gary Hart, played out brilliantly at a time when real primary strategies under the reform system were untested. He would pour all of his efforts into the New Hampshire primary, hoping for a good showing, then largely skip the Florida contest where Wallace would clearly be strong. He would then rely upon a massive and long-standing organizing campaign in Wisconsin where he planned to win as a "set-piece breakthrough" based on momentum from a strong showing in New Hampshire. After that, the strategy went, he would sweep Massachusetts, Nebraska, and Oregon. His big prizes would then come in California and New York, maybe picking up Ohio along the way. Given that all the other candidates had their plans too, it worked with remarkable precision. The reason may have had less to do with the strategic brilliance of the campaign, than with McGovernites' ability to exploit a party that had lost its core. By the spring of '72, it was clear that McGovern had not so much galvanized the party as managed to squeak ahead in a party divided into equal thirds—McGovern on the left, Muskie then Humphrey in the center, and Wallace on the right.[42]

The McGovern team opened with an electric campaign in New Hampshire. Although attacked for making ghostly radio ads out of a 1968 recording of RFK's endorsement of McGovern, the spirit of Kennedy and McCarthy's insurgent campaigns were present in more positive ways. As the *New York Times* headline summarized it, "For Muskie, Mild Support; For McGovern, Intensity." The moment when things came together for the candidate was his tour of the four-story J.F. McElwain shoe factory in Manchester. There he broke out of his pattern of rural, suburban, and college town support and into the core of Muskie's urban working-class constituents. The shoe workers were intrigued by McGovern's interest in ending the war, talk of wanting better pay and retirement benefits, and demands for some sort of solution to foreign imports of textiles and shoes that threatened the core of New Hampshire's industrial economy. As Gary Hart rosily remembered, "He was beginning to capture the imagination of the workingman." Early on in the campaign the McGovern forces had claimed that 10 percent of the vote share in New Hampshire would be a victory, but they grew to within 5 to 6 points of Muskie in areas of his strength. McGovern won 37 percent to Muskie's 46 percent, making it one of those primary losses that was actually a "win" for the insurgent.[43]

Race proved to be a dangerous trap for McGovern, and the bait was busing. He enjoyed moderate success with African-American voters but paid a high price among white voters for his commitments to racial equality. Most Democratic candidates vaguely followed suit or tried to dodge the issue, but it placed them in very awkward situations—busing appealed to most blacks (although many argued instead for increase in funding to black schools) and warmed the hearts of professional middle-class liberals but was met with anger by white working-class voters whose children would be bused. When the issue got hot, McGovern tried to dismiss it as either a red herring or a "minor flap" or a case of simply having to abide by the courts' decisions. McGovern never understood the depth of white working-class fear—the type that would explode in Boston just a couple of years later. As he told an angry working-class voter in Boston who pestered him on busing, "You may discover what President Nixon and George Wallace have done is take this issue and blow it up all out of proportion. I think they want us to forget about unemployment and inflation and crime and make us think that Public Enemy Number One is the old yellow school bus. Beware of any issue on which George Wallace and Richard Nixon agree." He never grasped the fear the issue instilled in white, blue-collar property owners (even though actual busing efforts were few and small at the time). As conservative columnists Roland Evans and Robert Novak put it, "At issue here is a gap between what really bothers the white working man and what the McGovern liberals think bothers him." Here McGovern the anti-war crusader found himself lost in the quagmire of America's domestic "Vietnam of the seventies."[44]

McGovern certainly overplayed his hand when he declared that "busing is not even a real issue," but his attempt to defuse the explosive issues of integration by refocusing on the shared political terrain of material interests was not only the high moral ground—it was his only option. "Here is where I think people have to stop and think," he explained, "whether voting for George Wallace and stopping the buses is really going to give them all the other things they want: jobs, homes, healthy families, better schools, safe communities—futures they look forward to with pride." No matter how well-intentioned, however, busing was an absolute political disaster. Busing, according to Thomas and Mary Edsall, "fell like an axe through the Democratic party, severing long-standing connections and creating a new set of troubled alliances: white, blue-collar northerners with southerners against blacks and upper-middle-class liberals." Support for it was a difficult case to make to white working people who felt that integration was taking place on their backs. Immediate defense of white identity, home, and school readily trumped the abstract hope of a better world someday.[45]

McGovern also found himself completely surrendering the southern states to the opposition. Between Wallace running as a Democrat and the realignment of the once solidly Democratic South toward the Republican Party after the Civil Rights and Voting Rights Acts, there were few McGovern votes to be found. The left-liberal hope had long been to reshuffle the party structure in America by pushing out southern white conservatives and enfranchising blacks in order to make the Democratic Party a truly progressive—class-based—force. When the Voting Rights Act passed in 1965, Walter Reuther explained that "the achievement of democratic franchise and full citizenship rights by millions of southern Negroes will drastically shift the balance of political power in the thirteen southern states. . . . This will accelerate the historic process of bringing about a fundamental political realignment of forces in the United States." Unfortunately for Reuther's hopes, a realignment was in the works, but it was a white southern exodus toward Wallace and then out of the Democratic Party—for which the enfranchisement of African Americas could not compensate—and the creation of a new Republican, and still very anti-union, South. In the North, the process was much the same, in less dramatic terms, as affirmative action, union integration, busing, suburban-urban segregation, and other state efforts to integrate blue-collar life alienated much of the white working class.[46]

The crowded Florida primary was indicative of the change. It predictably went in a lopsided victory for George Wallace, who spent most of the campaign successfully railing against court-ordered busing. The Wallace victory was decisive, earning him 42 percent of the vote and a victory in every county against a large gaggle of party regulars and challengers. Most of the candidates bitterly attacked Wallace's bigotry, but McGovern smartly interpreted the governor's victory as a broader symptom of alienation. "I believe the Governor is an extremist," he declared. "But I believe many of the people who supported the governor did so because they are deeply frustrated and disgusted with the way their government is ignoring their concerns and interests." The vote for Wallace was "an angry cry from the guts of ordinary Americans against a system which doesn't seem to give a damn about what is really bothering people in this country today." The Wallace vote was not just about busing, he argued, "It was a vote to stop the whole damn Democratic Party and make it listen to the people for a change—instead of just to political strategists." He then made what FDR called "the forgotten man" the center of his campaign. To the working people of Wisconsin, he proclaimed,

> I have walked through the stench of the paper factories and the steady noise of the shoe factories of New Hampshire—not just smiling and handing out buttons, but stopping to listen.
>
> I have gone down into the coal mines of West Virginia, felt the cold winter air blowing through the shaft, and smelled the coal dust that can explode on a moment's notice if safe working conditions are not properly maintained.
>
> I have been in a thousand crowded big-city neighborhoods, fast-changing suburbs, farms, towns, and homes. I have come to a new appreciation of the pressures, the concerns, and the hopes of ordinary American workers.
>
> I know that this country is kept going day in and day out by hard-working men and women, not all of whom love their jobs by a long shot but who do them because doing a job well is something to take pride in—in and of itself.
>
> I know that the working people of this country are being asked to give everything for their country—including their sons' lives in a confusing war that no one wants—and feel their government is not giving them much in return.[47]

When the campaign finally landed in Wisconsin, it rested on a year-long project of on-the-ground organizing. Skipping Florida allowed the campaign to spend "incalculable" time and money in Wisconsin where the campaign hoped to catapult McGovern into frontrunner status. The candidate traveled tirelessly there and was buoyed by a tremendous citizens' campaign—allegedly comprised of a statewide army of ten thousand volunteers assembled by the young and nerdy political organizing genius, Gene Pokorny. When the returns poured in, there was dancing in McGovern's Wisconsin campaign headquarters as the senator won 30 percent, Wallace 22 percent, Humphrey 21 percent, and Muskie only 10 percent. Hart noted after the Wisconsin victory that "it was a whole new ball game."[48]

Despite the success, the campaign could neither escape nor control the loose cannons of 1968 and 1972—the white blue-collar voters on whom national success depended. As McGovern explained *publicly* during the Wisconsin campaign to skeptical interviewers on CBS's *Face the Nation*, "I have strong support among the autoworkers, among the construction workers, among working people of all kinds, and I predict that when the votes come in Wisconsin on Tuesday that you're going to see that the—McGovern's base of support is very wide, and that it embraces all segments of the population." The campaign did win broadly, even in what Gary Hart called the "Archie Bunker" areas in south Milwaukee's blue-collar Fourth District. While it looked good on the surface, however, McGovern later revealed that he was absolutely staggered by his battle with the Wallace forces in the Midwest:

> The first warnings of a possible Nixon landslide in 1972 were sounded in the series of surprising victories by Governor Wallace in the Democratic primary elections early in the year. . . . In every state where Wallace made a serious bid, I was startled by the strength of his appeal. In factory after factory, I found Democrats giving open commitments to Wallace. Indeed, even in a progressive State like Wisconsin where I had a superb grassroots organization, it was Wallace who gave the toughest competition. . . . In traditionally Democratic power bases such as Michigan, Wallace walked off with first place. If he had campaigned hard in Pennsylvania and Ohio, he would have rolled up impressive percentages. . . . These early signals should have been clear warning to the Democratic nominee, no matter who he was, that without the support of Wallace's followers, there was little chance for victory in November. The only other formula for a possible Democratic victory was for Wallace to run as an Independent as he had in 1968, thus siphoning off the right-wing Democratic vote which otherwise would go to Nixon.

Surprisingly, given the depths of Wallace's support in Wisconsin, the Alabama governor had barely campaigned in the state. He arrived late, campaigned for one paltry week, and disappeared with a sizable plurality of the vote. McGovern won Massachusetts shortly after Wisconsin, which made him the national leader. In reality, however, as the primary process rolled across the nation, the deeper indicators suggest that it was more of a three-way tie among Humphrey, the rising centrist taking Muskie's place, George Wallace, and McGovern.[49]

On May 15, 1972, Wallace was shoring up his position as the front-runner in Michigan and Maryland, campaigning in suburban Maryland against the "social schemers" and "ultra-false liberals," inveighing his constituents "to shake the eyeteeth of the Democratic Party. Let's give 'em the St. Vitus dance. And tell 'em a vote for George Wallace is a vote for the average citizen." He stepped down from the podium and moved into the crowd of supporters. There, a young man named Arthur Bremer, motivated by little more than fame and notoriety, shot him at point-blank range. The next day, voters, including Dewey Burton, gave both states to the governor. For those concerned about the politics of working people, Wallace's victory in Michigan, the core of the industrial Midwest and UAW stronghold, was particularly disconcerting. Bremer's bullet, however, not only forced Wallace out of the race but left him paralyzed and wheel-chair bound for the rest of his life.[50]

To freeze events at the attempt on Wallace's life is to see a party that had more or less been torn into equal thirds. McGovern led the delegate count, but if one were to bulk the state primary votes into a national popular vote at the time of the shooting, Wallace would have been the leader. As of May 16, 1972, Wallace had 3,354,360 votes, Humphrey 2,647,676, and McGovern only 2,202,840. McGovern was building his bank of strategic delegate votes through his grassroots campaign, while Humphrey battled to keep the regulars at his side, and the ragtag Wallace campaign continued to stymie both. This was clearly not the moment of triumph for a new Democratic majority, but rather symptomatic of a party that could not find a unified voice to speak to the issues of the majority of working people. McGovern did not manage to move ahead of Wallace in the popular vote until June, when, with the Alabama governor paralyzed, he won New Jersey, New Mexico, South Dakota, and barely squeaked past Humphrey in California. In short, McGovern's strength appears to have been more of a byproduct of the Democratic Party's weakness.[51]

The McGovern insurgency was stuck. It neither had a strong enough "new" coalition to make it without the party regulars or the leverage to demand that the regulars' survival depended upon them moving toward him. So, as the senator began to chalk up his many primary victories, he had to confront the problem of any insurgent candidate: whether and how to make peace with the party establishment. If he did not, he had to balance his New Politics with the Wallace voters, to become the honest insurgent, the fresh but viable underdog who could make the rest of the voters come to him. He would, in short, have to solidify a coalition based on the New Politics. This risked standing on absolute principle and, most likely, making the election a crusade over a fatal ideological purity—what the regulars liked to call the "Goldwater of the left" problem. Alternatively, he could attempt to make peace with the Democratic machinery but then risked alienating his most dedicated activists. Most insiders agreed with strategist Gordon Weil who predicted "reconciliation with the Regulars was doomed to failure."[52]

Shunning the advice of "the more rigid purists in my camp" McGovern decided to make a play for the party regulars in the spring of 1972—and the regulars meant organized labor. "I think I've got the skill and the common sense to quiet the fears of those people and bring them on board at some point," he told the *Washington Post*'s David Broder. Yet he carefully reassured his supporters that this was not a sellout. "No labor leader, no party leader is going to get me to change my position on the war, or the need for tax reform, or the need for a major reallocation of resources from the military to civilian purposes to achieve full employment. Those are three things I would not compromise on." Try as he might, however, labor was not going to budge. "Labor is often credited with veto power over the choice at the Democratic convention," Broder noted, and by July 1972, the person the AFL-CIO leadership seemed to hate the most in the free world was Senator George McGovern. The *New York Times* put it more problematically, "Selling this [McGovern package] to George Meany and the labor organization, which is about the only effective political organization the Democrats have, will not be easy, and it will not be very popular either with Meany or other Democratic candidates who think pot, abortion and amnesty are explosively dangerous issues."[53]

There were, however, cracks beginning to show in labor's unanimity against McGovern. In the pivotal California primary, the site of RFK's victory four years earlier, the race came down to Humphrey and McGovern. Robert J. Keefe, the AFL-CIO's operative in California, admitted that California's labor leaders were a bit exasperated with their old friend Hubert Humphrey. "We're doing all we can. But they're tired of Humphrey, he's been around too long. They say, 'Oh, Goddamnit, here he is broke again, we've been pulling his chestnuts out of the fire for years.' All he's got going for him here is what we're putting out for him—our mailings, our membership lists." Although the unions worked hard for Humphrey, he came in a tight second to McGovern. Then the left-leaning Oil, Chemical and Atomic Workers endorsed McGovern in May, the first union to do so. By June, the union doves formed Labor for Peace in St. Louis, demanding immediate withdrawal from Vietnam. There, over one thousand delegates tried to weave a path between the growing radicalism of the peace movement and the intransigence of the mainstream labor movement. "In common with the overwhelming majority of Americans," the call from Labor for Peace declared, "the working people of our country are plain sick and tired of the cruel and senseless war in Viet Nam." The organization would serve as a foundation for the later creation of the National Labor Committee for McGovern-Shriver.[54]

The AFL-CIO entered the Democratic Convention in Miami Beach geared to defeat the McGovern forces. Although, by all rights, McGovern had the nomination locked up, the federation militantly pursued its own "sectarian view" by attempting to silence the new voices and destroy McGovern's chances of gaining the nomination and, later, the presidency. In the process, the federation damaged itself beyond repair. After 1972, the unions would be unable to reproduce what the United Steel Workers' president, David McDonald, proudly described as his role in the 1960 Democratic Convention, where he "chivvied and bullied and pleaded and traded and threatened and maneuvered on the convention floor" to get the votes for the candidates of his choice. In their 1972 overreach, the labor chiefs watched the power they had solidified in '68 slip away.[55]

V

"What kind of delegation is this?" sneered George Meany upon seeing the New York delegation at the first Democratic Convention since the reform commission. "They've got six open fags and only three AFL-CIO people on that delegation! Representative?" As another labor leader put it at Miami, "There is too much hair and not enough cigars at this convention."[56]

Indeed, the complexion of Democratic politics had changed. The results of the reform commission meant that women had moved from 14 percent of the delegates in 1968 to 36 percent in 1972, people under thirty went from 2 to 23 percent, and blacks increased from just over 5 percent at the Chicago convention to 14 percent in Miami. Ironically, there were more labor leaders and more delegates carrying union cards on the floor in Miami than there had been four years earlier in Chicago, but those labor delegates were not AFL-CIO lieutenants but acting independent of labor's command and control. Moreover, the political action moved toward the endless stream of caucuses that labor did not influence: the Black Caucus, the Women's Caucus, and the Latin, Youth, Senior Citizen, and Jewish caucuses. The party nonetheless rolled out the red carpet for labor, with more box seats, telephones, a special trailer behind the podium, floor passes, etc., than any other group. As AFL-CIO political consultant Bob Keefe lamented, "Labor had more delegates and less influence than ever before."[57]

While offering constant sneers about McGovern's cultural politics, the unions risked appearing completely disingenuous unless they could mount a specific and aggressive attack on Senator McGovern's record on real labor issues. It was next to impossible, however, because he had one of the best pro-labor voting records in the Senate. COPE, the political arm of the AFL-CIO, had determined that McGovern had voted "right" with labor's interests 93.5 percent of the time, just over a point less than Muskie, three points less than Ted Kennedy, but admittedly not in the range of the genuflecting Hubert Humphrey who could boast a 98.6 percent pro-labor record. McGovern not only had a golden voting record, he was also the first presidential candidate to support collective bargaining for public sector workers and the first to criticize Nixon's wage and price controls as placing an unfair burden on workers. Anyone familiar with his dissertation, at that point just published as a book, also knew that his heart was on the side of the working class. Furthermore, McGovern aside, the 1972 Democratic platform reflected rather perfectly the AFL-CIO's requests on bread-and-butter issues, though not, of course, on Vietnam.[58]

So, the AFL-CIO set about transforming one of the most pro-labor Democratic presidential nominees in U.S. history into an anti-labor hack. In Miami, the unions circulated a venomous but "anonymous" fifty-page white paper entitled "The McGovern Record: A Critical Appraisal" that assailed him as an enemy of unions and the working man. The document, evidence from which made it in all the major newspapers, claimed that McGovern had "repeatedly voted wrong on legislation affecting working people in the trade union movement." The core of the criticism was McGovern's 1965 vote against a cloture motion that would have permitted a vote on the repeal of section 14(b)—the infamous right-to-work clause—of the Taft-Hartley Act. Liberals had assembled a majority in favor of repealing the notorious provision that had helped the South remain non-union, but it was clear at the time that they did not have enough votes against a certain filibuster. Any vote in favor of repealing 14(b) could have been very detrimental to McGovern in South Dakota (a farm state where 14(b) was part of the state constitution), and there was clearly no reason to do it if there were not enough votes to push the bill over a filibuster. It was a reasonable position not to waste a tremendous amount of political capital for what was certain to be no legislative gain. Meany had even absolved him of the vote at the time. In 1971, on the *David Frost Show*, McGovern had nonetheless declared the vote to be a product of "the worst advice I ever got," in which he had betrayed "my own convictions, my own instincts." Moreover, since declaring his candidacy for the nomination, he had vociferously declared his desire to repeal 14(b) once in office. While the depth of his regret over his 14(b) vote smacked of election year pandering, his desire to have 14(b) repealed was not a conversion of political necessity but a position consistent with his entire political career.[59]

In addition to the 14(b) vote, the AFL-CIO's white paper resorted to distortions of his record on Landrum-Griffin (1959) and minimum wage, and then proceeded to drag out several other votes that were so insignificant that COPE did not even count them in its regular tallies. The fifty-page denunciation got closer to the rub when it attacked his position on Vietnam and grain shipments to the Soviet Union, but the thrust of the document was gross inflations of the tiny failings of his labor record. The contrast with other politicians was astonishing. LBJ, whom labor loved, had actually voted for the unions' most hated law, Taft-Hartley, and as a senator, his COPE rating had only been in the low sixties. Richard Nixon, with whom the AFL-CIO leadership was rapidly growing very cozy, had a COPE rating in the twenties. Despite the incivility, McGovern's labor attaché urged patience and hope in Miami. "Meany and Al Barkan are going through a menopause—but probably will recover when they leave this atmosphere. So please—no anti-Meany statements, no labor 'bosses' etc. . . . It's hard to bear their dirty tactics—but let's hold for a while longer." Such optimism may have been the only option, but it went unrewarded as labor's bitterness only escalated.[60]

It was all a charade. At stake was not hair or cigars or sexuality or 14(b) or any other issue, but power. Examining the events unfolding in Miami, labor journalist John Herling argued, "there was no way" for the AFL-CIO "to retrieve a position of influence in the decision-making process at the convention." The labor leadership could have "made an adjustment to political reality" and attempted to ride the new wave to new forms of coalitional power, but instead, explained Herling, "George Meany and others became fixed in their determination *not* to be flexible." They dug in, clinging to principles that were as old and unwavering as the labor leadership itself, continuing to argue that McGovern was anti-labor despite the obvious record. The truth was that they knew McGovern owed them nothing and that the party was now "open," as everyone called it that year. They saw him as the man who had steered the way to labor's diminished power, even though he had invited them along for the ride. McGovern had not only defied the rules that had kept them in power, but he had literally rewritten them.[61]

The particularly disingenuous idea developed at the Miami convention that perhaps McGovern could be stopped by splitting the California delegation. So, labor spearheaded the Anybody But McGovern forces by turning to the one channel they thought they might still be able to control: the Credentials Committee (the same committee that had refused to seat the black Mississippi Freedom Democratic Party in 1964). McGovern had barely beaten Humphrey in California—a state-mandated winner-take-all primary— which put McGovern over the top for the national nomination. California's winner-take-all rules were technically in violation of the reform requirements, but everyone recognized this and ran there knowing that the victor would take all of the state's delegates. Since McGovern won California with only 44 percent of the primary vote, however, the regulars hoped that by controlling the Credentials Committee, they could prevent McGovern from getting all of the delegates and scuttle his nomination. It was a vicious parliamentary attempt to change the rules after the game was over. The result was extremely complicated parliamentary maneuvering, in which, ironically, the reform rules were used by labor against McGovern, then by McGovern against the regulars. The events in Miami were the stuff of party whips, floor fights, and committee wrangling to the point of exhaustion of all concerned.

When the regulars sought to split California, the reformers then turned on the Illinois delegation. The Cook County delegates were some of the last representatives of old-school politics, hand picked by the Daley machine, and technically also unqualified under the new rules. Attempting to counter the move on California, the McGovern forces managed to have their handpicked alternative delegation replace them even though the original group had at least been voted in by the people of Cook County. To the public, this looked like the worst sort of social engineering that the New Politics had to offer. As the Chicago delegation was taken over by women, youth, and minorities (and, most notably, Jesse Jackson), *Chicago Sun-Times* columnist Mike Royko landed some of the best rhetorical barbs of the decade. "I just don't know where your delegation is representative of Chicago's Democrats," he puzzled. "Anybody who would reform Chicago's Democratic Party by dropping the white ethnic would probably begin a diet by shooting himself in the stomach." This quote reverberated for decades as representative of the Democrats' eviction of the white working class from its core constituencies, but it is rarely explained that the movement was a product of both the failure of the Daley delegation to follow the new rules and, more importantly, only a last-minute defensive parliamentarian maneuver against the regulars' attempt to steal the California delegates.[62]

Hunter S. Thompson, in his indomitable, hyperbolic style, described the scrambling to defeat McGovern in Miami "like a scene from the final hours of the Roman Empire: Everywhere you looked some prominent politician was degrading himself in public" in frenzied but futile attempts to maintain the old order. The regulars scurried around attempting to cut any deal on any terms to try to deny Senator McGovern the nomination on the first ballot. The "Meany/Daley crowd" did not care who they ended up with or whether their alternative stood a chance of winning. All that mattered, according to Thompson, "was *keeping control of The Party*; and this meant the nominee would have to be some loyal whore with more debts to Big labor than he could ever hope to pay." By the time that McGovern finally survived the regulars' attempts to deny him the California delegates, Thompson fantasized the reaction of an apoplectic George Meany. The labor autocrat, he mused, must have "raged incoherently at the Tube for eight minutes without drawing a breath, then suddenly his face turned beet red and his head swelled up to twice its normal size. Seconds later—while his henchmen looked on in mute horror—Meany swallowed his tongue, rolled out of chair like a log, and crawled through a plate glass window."[63]

McGovern survived the procedural challenges to his nomination, but the convention continued to fume, boil, and occasionally explode. There were the ceaseless protests by every fringe group and coalition who now made McGovern their new focus of discontent, revealing the already hardening orthodoxy of much of the New Politics. "Scarcely one of them had spent one minute helping McGovern in his uphill struggle," Hart recalled about the many protest movements at the convention. "Chanting, pleased to have a focus for their wrath, roused occasionally by flamboyant, irrelevant rhetoric, they called for the candidate's appearance, or his head." Georgia governor Jimmy Carter was out organizing the governors to resist McGovern's nomination, while the black leadership, the women's leadership, the Chicano leadership all made incalculable demands, followed by endless strategy sessions and caucuses, petty feuds, and accusations and counter-accusations about who was destroying the party. All the while, lamented McGovern, middle America was watching on television where they "saw a lot of aggressive women, they saw a lot of militant blacks, they saw long-haired kids, and I think the combination, which helped win the nomination for me, I think it offended a lot of them."[64]

Following tradition, the issue of a running mate, a figure that might still help to bridge McGovern and the party regulars, was still not resolved until the day McGovern was scheduled to receive the nomination. Ted Kennedy was the silver bullet vice presidential candidate, but after teasing the campaign with the possibility, he finally refused. Next on McGovern's list was the unprecedented—a union leader—president of the UAW, Leonard Woodcock. Originally a Muskie backer, Woodcock was supportive of McGovern and head of an enormous and progressive union. McGovern had invited Woodcock to his home earlier to discuss the possibility, and the labor leader was clearly intrigued. On the surface, this appeared to be a way to shore up rank-and-file blue-collar support, even if it did not necessarily warm McGovern to the rest of the AFL-CIO leadership since the UAW had pulled out of the federation because of its knee-jerk anti-communism. However, Woodcock's nomination ran into criticism from within the UAW, and it clearly would check any possibility of a still-hoped-for rapprochement with the federation. The idea that a Woodcock nomination could heal the divisions, reported the *New York Times*, was "scoffed" at by leading AFL-CIO officials.[65]

The final selection would be recorded as one of the most famous bungles in postwar American political history. The penultimate choice for the vice presidential slot—not arrived upon until almost 4:00 PM on the day of McGovern's acceptance speech—was Senator Tom Eagleton of Missouri. The last-minute selection, made in the aftermath of the all-consuming floor fight over the California delegation, was believed to be the perfect option at the time: he was a Catholic, from a border state, had connections to labor, was a vigorous campaigner, and had the support of a wide array of Democrats. Unlike many others—including first choice Ted Kennedy—he also wanted the job very badly. To the insurgents, the Eagleton selection smelled like the beginning of McGovern's sellout to the party establishment, but to most analysts the choice appeared to be a realistic tactic to help position McGovern in the national race. His vice presidential choice settled, McGovern looked forward to his acceptance speech to heal the many rifts in the party.

The night of McGovern's acceptance speech encapsulated all that was good and great about his campaign as well as much that was silly and flawed. Rather than moving swiftly to the main event, the night of the nominee's acceptance speech opened up the opportunity for symbolic power plays, posturing, and convention-floor theater that trumped the much-needed party unity for McGovern. Unprepared television viewers tuned in at prime time and saw the new chaotic diversity of the convention: the long hair, the dashikis, the overempowered youth, and the afros—all interspersed with the straight suits and the dour faces of the suited party regulars and the disappointed Wallace supporters. The New York delegation demanded debate over further reforms, and the open rules required debate over the vice presidential slot. Against Eagleton, delegates put forth a wild assortment of icons, jokes, and dreams: Ralph Nader, Benjamin Spock, the Berrigan brothers, Cesar Chavez, Jerry Rubin—even Chairman Mao, Margaret Mitchell, and Archie Bunker. By the time Eagleton was finally nominated and the dignitaries and conceding candidates had spoken, most of the nation was fast asleep. When an exhausted but triumphant McGovern finally took to the platform in Miami, it was nearly 3:00 AM. It may have been the most open convention in American history, but the nominee had already lost his best chance to reach a national prime-time audience.

The convention hall madness subsided as McGovern dug deep and managed to galvanize the convention with a stunning speech centered on his campaign theme, "Come Home America." "My nomination is all the more precious in that it is the gift of the most open political process in our national history," he rightly declared; "This is the nomination of the people." He melded the cultural rebellion of the sixties to the traditionalism of the scriptures, the youth that supported his campaign to his own Methodism: "In Scripture and in the music of our children we are told: 'To everything there is a season, and a time to every purpose under heaven.' . . . And for America, the time has come at last." As he turned to close his speech, his flat Midwestern tones came to life: "Come home to the belief that we can seek a newer world. And let us be joyful in the homecoming." He closed with a reference that arced from the New Deal to the 1960s by quoting Woody Guthrie's "This Land is Your Land"—which, not incidentally, had also been Robert F. Kennedy's campaign theme. As the journalist Theodore White recalled, "It seemed barely possible, just faintly possible, in the exhaustion, the giddiness, the evangelical moment, that this George McGovern, the prophet, was indeed a serious candidate for the Presidency."[66]

Richard Nixon watched the proceedings from Washington, jubilant over the pandemonium and disarray of his opposition in Miami. He noted in his diary that he now had a "chance not just to win the election, but to create the New Majority we had only dreamed of in 1970. Only organized labor and George Wallace remained in doubt." He had little to worry about. Wallace was unable to run as an independent, which would have sliced into Nixon's votes, and the AFL-CIO got straight to work distancing itself from the Democratic nominee while growing ever cozier with the president.[67]

After the convention, the *New York Times* continued to regard labor as the "immovable boulder in Mr. McGovern's path toward the presidency." Meany quickly assembled his executive council—consisting of the presidents of the major unions. There he orchestrated an unprecedented vote in favor of remaining neutral in the national presidential race. The vote was twenty-seven to three (the dissidents were Jerry Wurf of AFSCME, Al Grosspiron of the Oil, Chemical and Atomic Workers, and Paul Jennings of the Electrical Workers). At a press conference two days later, Meany declared, "I will not endorse, I will not support and I will not vote for Richard Nixon for President of the United States. I will not endorse, I will not support and I will not vote for George McGovern for President of the United States." Then in jest, he suggested, "If old Norman Thomas was only alive." When pressed, he admitted that he had never voted for Socialist Party candidate Norman Thomas when he had the chance, arguing that "there was a fellow named Roosevelt around in those days." Evidence is, however, Meany voted for Governor Dewey in 1944, against both FDR and Thomas. Labor's new-found sympathy for Richard Nixon was a long way from what Barkan had derided back in 1968 as "the same old double-plated, triple-coated, four-faced and five-ply phony faker [Nixon] has always been."[68]

The unions were blindsided by the success of the youthful, multi-cultural energy of the New Politics and unable to reclaim their 1968 power broker role. "The real concern," Jerry Wurf concluded, "was participation and access, the AFL-CIO's vested interest which ignored the rich opportunities for workers and their unions in the more open, 'new' party." Joseph Beirne, president of the Communication Workers of America (CWA), a former hawk and Meany supporter, concurred. "For whatever reason, organized labor has lost its position as 'honest broker' in the Democratic Party," he reflected about the convention. "The COPE leaders live in the dreams of the past where they wheeled and dealed in politics." Indeed, an internal AFL-CIO memo explained that the main priority after the nomination was "to regain control of the machinery after the election," which first required defeating George McGovern in the national race.[69]

As if McGovern's labor debacles were not enough, it came out not long after the convention that his vice presidential selection, Tom Eagleton, had a history of mental illness that had led to electro-shock therapy. Suddenly the costs of the California delegate fight, which forced a haphazard vice presidential selection process, became crystal clear. McGovern quickly announced that he was "1,000 percent for Tom Eagleton" and had "no intention of dropping him from the ticket," phrases he would soon regret. When Eagleton refused to do the right thing and step down on his own, McGovern eventually had to kick him off the ticket. McGovern's handling of the Eagleton affair made him look not simply radical as many accused, but radically incompetent, even cynical. His strongest asset—the generally held belief that he was genuinely an honest and fair person who was different from other politicians—was lost. It planted the idea that McGovern might just be another politician who would do anything to get elected.[70]

The blow from the Eagleton affair seemed to seal McGovern's fate as the news rippled across the political world. As the Democratic Party burned, Nixon's Bob Haldeman quietly noted in his diary, "The P[resident] played golf this afternoon with George Meany" where the AFL-CIO president expressed his "'real hatred' for McGovern." Texan John Connally, who headed up the defecting "Democrats for Nixon" group, decided, "We might well say that this was the day the election was won." It was the final piece in what Dan Carter called Nixon's "hat trick:" neutralizing Wallace, who now appeared certain not to run as an independent; preventing McGovern from getting labor's support; and, finally, profiting from a gaff big enough to undo the one thing the senator had going for him—integrity. McGovern received no political bounce from the convention. It was only late July, and already commentators thought they could hear the death rattle of the McGovern insurgency. He turned in desperation to Kennedy hand Sargent Shriver to fill the vice presidential slot.[71]

VI

As much as the primary process showed a divided Democratic Party without a unifying message for working people, the ensuing national campaign showed that the AFL-CIO faced a similar dilemma. In August, the National

Labor Committee for the Election of McGovern-Shriver officially broke away from the AFL-CIO neutrality decision. It included unions of many stripes: those that had been critical of the federation's stance, unions that had voted along with the neutrality position, and those outside the federation such as the UAW and the National Education Association. The feud between the McGovern coalition and the AFL-CIO basically ripped organized labor's political voice right down the middle, as unions that added up to half the AFL-CIO's membership (and half the executive council) ended up endorsing Senator McGovern. Meany faced further revolts from the labor councils and state federations across the country.[72]

Ironically, George Meany had risen to national prominence in 1955 when he and Walter Reuther healed the rift in the historically divided house of labor by bringing the AFL and the CIO together into one federation. While threats of splits and moves to bolt were constants in the palace intrigue of postwar labor history, only a generation after reunification organized labor was again seriously divided. The *New York Times* labor beat reporter A.H. Raskin noted with prescience in the fall of 1972, "For the first time since Meany scored a monumental personal triumph in 1955 by ending two decades of warfare between the AFL and CIO, unions are running their own political action drives, free from the Meany yoke. That heady experience almost surely will wind up in a resolve to go it alone in future campaigns and thus deprive the parent federation of its main reason for being. The great unifier may wind up in labor history as the great disintegrator." Victor Gotbaum, leader of the powerful New York City AFSCME local, put it best: "Meany today is a lion who is roaring but nobody is listening. . . . He promotes a myth of labor solidarity. But today we are a movement of movements." What appeared to be a permanent realignment in the politics of class power stemming from the upheavals of the thirties and forties was, by 1972, proving to be a relatively brief and exceptional period born of one-time success.[73]

To many, organized labor's militant intransigence around the New Politics was both ironic and tragic. By the 1970s, the new activists of the sixties were largely doing what they had been told to do by their elders: moving out of the streets and pressing their demands within the mainstream political process. As Eugene Glover, the secretary-treasurer of the Machinists Union lamented, "Hell, we used to complain that the young people were running around the streets, demonstrating to no effect, and rejecting the 'system,' whatever the hell that is. But now they have come into the political system. We got mad because they have outsmarted us. They did a whale of a job in organizing and throwing us a thing or two. They beat us at our own game. What are we afraid of? They are our sons and daughters."[74]

By August 1972, the campaign's larger institutional problems had been fixed, but the crisis of the campaign's larger blue-collar appeal still loomed. The AFL-CIO neutrality problem was behind them, the vice presidential selection crisis was over, and they were enjoying the support of the organization of Labor for McGovern-Shriver. At that point, however, the campaign staff turned to outright panic over the issue that had haunted the McGovern movement from the very beginning: the campaign's inability to reach white working-class voters. McGovern hammered away at the disparities in the labor records between Nixon and himself, but it never seemed to make a dent. The political narrative had already been cast. A shocking August poll showed that 61 percent of respondents "expressed considerable confidence" in Nixon on the issue of "making the government pay more attention to the problems of the working man and his family." Internal Democratic polls indicated that the Catholic vote was trending as low as 23 percent for McGovern, and the manual labor vote dipping as low as 35 percent.[75]

As one frustrated confidential memo noted to the senator, "by this time, you've been told 'ad nauseam' how much trouble you are in with the conservative, ethnic, vote in the big states because of your outspoken positions on the war (including the amnesty question) and your 'softness' on the social issues (crime, welfare, abortion, etc.)." Even though such working-class voters believe that they had been sold a bill of goods on the war, the memo explained, "such straight-out moral condemnation still runs right against the grain of their strong sense of patriotism and respect for flag and country." The issue Wallace tapped into was the one they could not escape: "Resentment against outside bureaucrats, experts, planners and liberal politicians is constantly on the increase because their proposals usually end up costing ethnic groups more than they cost anyone else. . . . It would be difficult to exaggerate how painful it is for such whites to hear the accusations that they are racist or reactionary." The answer to the crisis was to work harder and listen more earnestly: "you must go into their neighborhoods, listen to the fears of crime and drugs, their frustrations with jobs and housing, their anger at unresponsive and distant government, and speak back to them in their own language with *emotion*."[76]

Others, such as Jean Westwood, chair of the Democratic National Committee, concurred. Noting that the Democratic voters were moving rapidly toward Nixon—"Resistance to the ticket is *not* based on our being *radical*, but on our identification with *'them'*—with the educated liberals," explained Westwood in continuing echoes of the Wallace problem. While the campaign believed there was general support for tax reform and cutting defense among workers, the problem was vision: "It is a matter of morale, pride in the direction of the country, a feeling of workingman's solidarity with leaders. It's this last that we must rekindle." Pinpointing some of the elements in the working-class upsurge of the time, "In the 1970s these white working people are asking and need the attention Blacks and Chicanos got in the 1960s. If they get it from Democrats, all sectors of population will advance. If not, the G.O.P. will win and no one will advance. In short, we face the most serious challenge to progress since 1932." Yet hope remained for a Truman-like surge. The answer Westwood proposed was the Bobby formula: "*Make yourself the candidate of working people with particular stress on Jews and Catholics—in coalition with Blacks, Chicanos, young people, and liberal suburbanites.*" Get out in the streets and talk to the "beauticians . . . firemen, policemen, truckdrivers, worker's suburbs, bowling alleys, church basements, working class picnic and amusement areas, factories, talks with working wives, emphasis on men who hold *two* jobs." As another advisor admonished, McGovern needed to get to the "average working citizen," get tough like Bobby Kennedy or Harry Truman, and "ditch the movie stars, celebrities, moneyed crowd, etc."[77]

McGovern aides Kenneth Schlossberg and Gerald Cassidy were exhausted, bitter, and "indignant" about the worker issue. The failure to reach blue-collar voters was the foundation of their indictment of the campaign. "They never tried to understand the Wallace vote," said Schlossberg. "Our people deluded themselves. They were angry when we pointed out that the workingman resented us." They asked for a quarter of a million dollars to reach the blue-collar vote, and they ended up with only $12,000. The Nixon figure for the same constituency was closer to $2 million. "McGovern," said Schlossberg, "doesn't understand the East. He finally got to be able to deal with blacks in a meaningful way, though he never turned them on. He didn't resent them the way he came to resent the ethnics. The ethnics were the opposition, and his people shared his resentment—it became a campaign which couldn't understand its own vote."[78]

If only the working-class voters were like those McGovern encountered at Lordstown, site of the famous rank-and-file rebellion against automation, then McGovern might have had a much better time among the blue-collar voters. He had been at Lordstown on multiple occasions, where he was greeted with "clenched fist" salutes and choruses of "right on"—especially when he declared that "we don't want workers to be treated like robots or machines." His appearances were extraordinarily well-received at the "boisterous union hall, dominated by young and long-haired workers." As a UAW leader from Cleveland remarked at an appearance in August, "Your voting record on measures that the UAW believes in stands at 95 percent and Nixon's stands at 13 percent. It's awfully easy for even a plumber to understand those figures," he exclaimed, taking a jab at one-time Bronx plumber George Meany. At a place like Lordstown, McGovern found the young, lively, anti-war workers to be the working-class that he wanted. McGovern pointed to a button he saw in the office of Gary Bryner, the local union president—"Freeze War Not Wages" it said—referring to Nixon's attempt to freeze wages in order to curb inflation. "If you stop to think about it," reflected the senator, "that embraces two of the most important issues that we are going to be addressing in 1972."[79]

McGovern blasted away at Nixon's record on labor and employment issues but to no avail. The final battle for the hearts and minds of the blue-collar voters took one of its most potent forms in national television ads. George McGovern's advertisements were made by filmmaker Charles Guggenheim, who had made films for the Kennedy candidates as well as McGovern's senatorial bid. They were rich, generally well-crafted *cinéma verité* pieces, displaying McGovern among the people in factories, neighborhoods, and schools. Each showed McGovern rubbing shoulders among small crowds of workers and common folks, answering their questions directly and honestly, exactly as his campaign workers requested. Each ended with a deep voice over: "McGovern. Democrat. For the People." Several of the most popular of them were filmed at the Lordstown auto plant, reflecting the resonance between the insurgent senator and the disgruntled autoworkers. "We're getting laughed at for workin'," exclaims one autoworker to the candidate; those collecting welfare are "laughing at our society." Borrowing the Kennedy combination of opportunity and toughness, McGovern parries the Wallaceite thrust, arguing that those who "don't want to work" should get "no public support" because he is going to make jobs available to everyone. A satisfied smile then quickly creeps across the face of the autoworker. Unfortunately, the *cinéma verité* material continued the feel of the populist primary and failed to project McGovern in a presidential light. Social realism was not what working-class voters seemed to want. As Guggenheim later had to admit, "Someone who is down with the people and more informal, rubbing shoulders with everyone, is less attractive as a presidential candidate in the general election than he would be in the primaries. . . . In hindsight, I don't think [continuing the style in the general election] was the right thing do."[80]

For Nixon, media testing had shown that advertisements coming from a group called "Democrats for Nixon" were more powerful than from the Committee to Re-elect the President (which gained the notorious acronym CREEP). Nixon regarded the set of ads made under that banner as the best political commercials he had ever seen. The most popular of them featured a construction worker—complete with hard hat—looking down from scaffolding high above the city. He is the New Deal's working-class hero, sitting down to survey the city with his brown-bag lunch. The voiceover then explains to him that George McGovern had recently submitted a welfare bill to Congress that "would make 47% of the people in the United States eligible for welfare. Forty-seven percent. Almost every other person in the country would be on welfare." The worker, sandwich in mouth, is quietly flabbergasted. The voiceover continues, "And who's going to pay for this? Well, if you're not the one out of two people on welfare, you do."[81]

In contrast to McGovern's man of the people, Nixon's campaign was a highly orchestrated series of appearances of "the President." One of his surreal ads began with pictures of butterflies and featured young people frolicking on the beach to the tune of "Nixon Now." Journalist David Broder called Nixon a "touring emperor" rather than someone engaged in a contest of ideas about the future of the nation. With Nixon saying almost nothing, it meant the press had extra time to criticize McGovern, whose openness left him vulnerable to anyone wishing to have a swing at him. "In the end," explained journalist Timothy Crouse from the view of the Nixon press corps, "Nixon's 1972 non-campaign was a triumph of pubic relations. Agnew was calm and conciliatory. The President was Presidential. Peace was at hand. The press had become too weak, frightened, and demoralized to try to dent the Administration's handsome veneer."[82]

VII

On Labor Day, the traditional kickoff of the Democratic Party's campaign season, McGovern connected his campaign theme—"Come Home America"—to one of his many hair-raising missions as a bomber pilot in World War II (an experience that, oddly enough given the defining aspect of the Vietnam War, he had not yet exploited). McGovern's plane, the *Dakota Queen*, had been badly hit in a bombing run to Czechoslovakia. With an engine in flames, the dead propeller cartwheeling around uncontrollably, and the plane vibrating madly, McGovern told his crew, "Prepare to bail out." He managed to get control of the plane, and declared, "Resume your stations. We're going to try to bring her home." Acknowledging that his campaign was also severely weakened by enemy fire, he declared, "Democrats who are fainthearted and to those who are anxious to fight on, and to people everywhere who share our cause: 'Resume your stations, we're going to bring America home.'" While he was able to bring the crippled *Dakota Queen* to a miraculous emergency landing on the island of Vis in the Adriatic, he had less success landing his campaign back in the United States. The "Come Home America" slogan attempted to connect to the vague but widespread feeling that the nation was off course, but it fell flat in the sense that the home McGovern had in mind—a land of peace, a politics of class, a culture of tolerance, and a campaign of meaning—had been, at best, elusive dimensions of American politics.[83]

Many McGovern staffers were failing to remain at their battle stations. The once unstoppable McGovern machine had dissolved into an undisciplined group full of in-fighting, saddled with petty, jealous, and indecisive leadership. Many of the regulars—Hubert Humphrey, Ted Kennedy, and Richard Daley—had finally come on board, but it merely added up to what Hunter S. Thompson called the campaign's "false dawn." All the formulas that worked to capture the nomination seemed to backfire on the national level. The press story, according to one insider, was "no longer McGovern, presidential nominee" but "McGovern-in-trouble."[84]

As the campaign sunk into a culture of defeat during the autumn of 1972, the policy positions of the politician began to be replaced by the jeremiads of the prophet. The less McGovern's economic programs and his profound desire to end the war appeared to be moving the country, the more the senator returned to his roots as a minister—in its updated form as political martyr—calling a nation home to first principles. McGovern seemed mystified by voters, including a large swath of the Democratic Party, who seemed to prefer a president of war, corruption, and aloofness rather than the moral vision of a man of the people. His speeches had always been peppered with biblical phrasing, but now, with defeat likely, an Old Testament McGovern demanded that the people rise to follow him out of the political wilderness. His congregation may have become the nation, and his sermons may have gained a Catholic edge, but George McGovern seemed to be fading back into the mission and rhetoric of the small churches his father had built on the prairies of South Dakota. *Newsweek* called it "McGovern's Politics of Righteousness," noting that the senator "has turned more furiously evangelical than any major party candidate since William Jennings Bryan."[85]

Richard Nixon, he implied, was an agent of not just *political* death and darkness, but *spiritual* death as well, who had led the people away from the promise of America. On the war, he railed against four more years of "barbarism," reminding Americans of the "thousands of Asians" who were "burning, bleeding, and dying under the bombs that fall from American planes." "What is it," he queried the nation, "that keeps a great and decent country like the United States involved in this cruel killing and destruction? Why is it that we cannot find the wit and the will to escape from this dreadful conflict that has tied us down for so long?" he asked. McGovern found Nixon's formula of sparing American casualties by engaging in the massive carpet-bombing campaigns morally reprehensible. In an address titled "They, Too, Are Created in the Image of God," McGovern subverted the logic of nearly two hundred years of imperial conquest by boldly equating the value of an Asian life to an American life. "Come with me," he declared, "and we will bring America home to the great and good and decent land our people want it to be." In a nationally televised address on the economy, he was explicit: "I want to claim the promise of Isaiah: 'The people shall be righteous and they shall inherit the land.'"[86]

At Wheaton College, he attempted to promote the social dimension of the evangelical tradition. He looked not to the unions as agents of social change but, in an unconscious link to the pre–New Deal years, to the social gospel. "The most notable advances of the eighteenth and nineteenth centuries—the fight for decent labor conditions and against slavery, and the efforts for prison reform—seemed to flow from the evangelical tides in society which preceded and accompanied them. . . . Today the conscience of our nation must be touched anew." The nation itself was a voyage—one tempo-

rarily adrift. "America was founded as part of a spiritual pilgrimage," Mc-
Govern declared, "Our forebears stood against the eternal night and affirmed
that there is a purpose to life—that people can find fulfillment and glory in
their dreams. And the wish of our forebears was to see the way of God prevail.
We have strayed from their pilgrimage, like lost sheep. But I believe we
can begin this ancient journey anew." McGovern then invoked John Winthrop's stirring sermon to the Puritans on the deck of the *Arabella*: "We
shall be a city upon a hill, the eyes of all people upon us; so that if we shall
deal falsely with our God in this work we have undertaken and so cause
him to withdraw His present help from us." For McGovern the invocation
of a city on a hill came with an absolute conviction that America had
veered from the path of spiritual righteousness. The vote on Tuesday, he
claimed on the eve of the election, will be "a day of reckoning and judg-
ment." Eight years later, Reagan would later invoke the same sermon as an
affirmation of national greatness.[87]

Despite his millennial exhortations, the polls did not budge. The one hope
had been that he might be able to tap into the disgruntled populism of the
Wallace votes akin to his brilliant victory in the Wisconsin primary, but
those votes clearly went to Nixon. As one South Carolina Democrat put the
calculus, it was a turn away from the sixties. "McGovern smacks of yesterday—
the Kennedys and integration and Martin Luther King and all of that—and
Nixon is a man that Wallace people conceived of as at least a little closer to
their man." The strains of honest prairie populism were lost under the debacles at the Democratic Convention, the Eagleton affair, Nixon's announcement that "peace was at hand" and, above all, an unwillingness of blue-collar
America to throw its lot in with "the sixties." "So Senator McGovern," concluded the *New York Times*, "was left with his pleas for decency and defense
cuts and tax reform and a new social agenda of governmental exertion. But
among many traditional Democrats and the bulk of the Wallace constituency, these positions faded into the impression that he was a $1,000-give-away
do-gooder, a friend of rebels and malcontents or just plain blacks, an opponent of the traditional virtues and of some less than virtuous but hallowed
ways of doing business."[88]

On November 7, 1972, Senator George McGovern lost every state save
Massachusetts and the District of Columbia in one of the biggest landslides
in American political history. Nixon won with 62 percent of the popular
vote, forty-nine states in the Electoral College, 57 percent of the manual

worker vote (a twenty-two point increase for Nixon since 1968), and 54 percent of the union vote (a twenty-five point gain since 1968). He was even the first Republican to receive a majority of Catholic votes. Later election analysis suggested that eight out of ten individuals who voted for Wallace in 1968 chose to cast their ballots for Nixon in 1972. Clearly, try as he might, McGovern was not able to win over the volatile white, blue-collar worker. Labor, too, was in disarray. Floyd "Red" Smith, president of the Machinists and a leader of the Labor for McGovern forces, put it this way: "If the newsmen are right, about half the wage earners in the United States voted for Richard Nixon last week; the other half voted for George McGovern. In my lifetime, the trade union movement has never been so divided in a national election."[89]

Clearly, a majority of workers voted for Richard Nixon, but often overlooked in the 1972 election analyses (and into the elections of the eighties as well) was that professional middle-class and white-collar voters went for Nixon at significantly larger percentages than did the union or the manual worker categories. Compared with the voters of the professional middle class, there actually were a relatively large number of working-class voters supporting McGovern. The 1972 election was certainly a national repudiation of McGovern, but while 46 percent of manual workers voted for McGovern, only 31 percent of professional and business people did, and 36 percent of white-collar voters did. Forty-nine percent of those at the bottom of the educational rungs went for McGovern, while only 37 percent of the much-discussed college-educated vote pulled for the senator. The candidate's inability to reach a majority of the exact constituency on whose behalf he had spoken, to whom he had devoted his dissertation, on whom everyone knew the election hinged, however, made the campaign for the working-class vote a failure.[90]

Although McGovern initially appeared as a likely candidate to pull off RFK's political balancing act, the legacy of his campaign grew to become a damning metaphor for any form of Democratic boldness. Despite his commitment to real material concerns of working people, a long-standing intellectual interest in labor issues, and an exceptional pro-labor voting record, McGovern's candidacy created an enduring, if distorted, political template for what the white, male American working class was not: radical, effete, movement-based, anti-war, and, perhaps most profoundly, Democratic.

After the election, everyone held a grudge. Asked in November what he would do for the future of the party, McGovern lashed out uncharacteristically, "I would do whatever I could to make sure that the wreckers, like [COPE Director Al] Barkan and Meany, don't come back into a dominant role in the Democratic party." Barkan responded in kind by trying to purge all the "crazies" of the New Politics from the labor leadership, as one observer explained it, "with the same zeal the old unionists had used to purge communists from their ranks in the thirties and forties." McGovern's campaign manager, Gary Hart, went on to run successfully for the Senate in 1974 and then unsuccessfully for the presidency as a "New Democrat." Certainly one of the defining features of Hart and the new breed, was, at best, an ambivalent relationship to organized labor and, at worst, open hostility toward the natural people who he believed ought to have been firmly behind the McGovern campaign. As Hart explained the new mood for the congressional class of 1974, "we're not just a bunch of little Humphreys."[91]

Reflecting on the results a month after the national election, McGovern recalled a "young black man who told me late one night in New York: 'This election is going to break your heart. People aren't as decent as you think they are. They don't like black people; they're resentful of the kids, and they want to forget about the poor. They don't care about peace and human rights and the Constitution. Every guy is just trying to make it for himself.'" McGovern had to agree. "I can only say that I found these attitudes all too often. I found too much apathy and cynicism and not enough concern and guts even among many young people—too pampered, or too prematurely weary to care." Polls confirmed the disinterest. Astonishingly, an October 1972 poll showed that 55 percent of the public saw Nixon as the "peace candidate," and only 30 percent gave McGovern the same title. Even after the Watergate break-in, more voters even identified Nixon as more likely to have an "open and trustworthy" administration, to be a "logical and clear thinker," and to be the one who "listens to what other people say." Campaign staffer Richard Dougherty acidly noted that "Nixon offered no improvement in the life of the people but only empty and ersatz satisfactions to their angers and bewilderments." The Nixon campaign's successful gimmick, he concluded, was "Let 'em eat revenge."[92]

The political events of 1972 both loosened the political bonds of working-class voters to the Democratic Party and fractured labor's ability to make a unified political stand—let alone rule the party. McGovern also understood that the Nixon administration had been orchestrating a very focused attempt to romance the New Right worker. As the next chapter will show, the president had done all he could to insure that the working-class vote would be removed from material concerns and placed on cultural terrain as key steps toward building the president's beloved "New Majority." As things continued to fall apart for the New Deal coalition just thirty-six years after its birth—barely two generations—Richard Nixon lectured his advisors about the new world of the 1970s. "The real issues of the election are the ones like patriotism, morality, religion—not the material issues," the president explained. "If the issues were prices and taxes, they'd vote for McGovern. We've done things labor doesn't like. We've held wages down. But they'll support us for these other reasons."[93]

3

Nixon's Class Struggle

H.R. Haldeman, Richard Nixon's chief of staff, called it the president's "long philosophical thing." As Washington sweltered in the hot July of 1971, a year before George McGovern would receive the Democratic nomination, Richard Nixon gathered his advisors together to explain the core premise of his domestic political strategy: winning working men to what he liked to call the "New Majority." Few issues in domestic politics stirred his passions more deeply. Although his team would go down in history most famously for the crimes of Watergate (which barely emerged in the 1972 campaign season), in the summer of 1971 they believed they were brewing a permanent realignment in the political cauldrons of the White House—one that would finally bring an end to the Roosevelt coalition.

"When you have to call on the nation to be strong—on such things as drugs, crime, defense, our basic national position," Nixon declared to the assembled political wizards gathered about him, H.R. Haldeman, John Ehrlichman, George Shultz, John Connally, and Charles Colson, "the educated people and the leader class no longer have any character, and you can't count on them." Nixon always detested the eastern elite, whom he saw as impotent and effete, and envisioned the working class as the only constituency with the "character and guts" to meet the many crises of the day. "When we need support on tough problems," he declared, "the uneducated are the ones that are with us." Because the president felt that the deepest reservoir of character in the nation consisted of those who "offer their back and their brawn," he rejected the proposals from many of his advisors to do what Republicans were supposed to do: attack organized labor. He explained that it was "vital that we continue to recognize and work with [workers] and that we not attack unions which represent the organized structure of the working man."[1]

In Nixon's class analysis, workers were the counterpoise to the eastern establishment for which he had nothing but bitter contempt. When the crises hit, Nixon concluded, the business and academic leaders simply "painted their asses white and ran like antelopes." The so-called managers were not what the country needed—the historical moment beckoned for what he called the "two-fisted" types. It was in workers and the labor leadership—the traditional backbone of New Deal politics—that new faith and renewal could be found for the Republican Party. They may be "shortsighted, partisan, [and] hate Nixon politically" but in the end, the president concluded, "they are men, not softies." As Nixon theorized his plans for the future, he declared, we "need to build our own new coalition based on Silent Majority, blue-collar Catholics, Poles, Italians, Irish. No promise with Jews and Negroes. Appeal not hard right-wing, Bircher, or anti-Communist." He sensed the moment and devoted his presidency to making the New Majority out of such sentiments. His sole domestic political goal was to disassemble the Roosevelt coalition and to rebuild the pieces into his own modern coalition. All else—the Watergate break-in, the liberal domestic policy initiatives, much of his entire domestic presidency—derived from that central principle.[2]

By the fall of 1972, Nixon would prove very successful in shifting what FDR called the "forgotten man" away from his bread-and-butter material concerns to the shared terrain of culture, social issues, and patriotism. This was not simply just cynical political manipulation—although there was plenty of that. Rather, it was something he really believed in: that the people's natural political alliances stemmed from their values (and that they were highly exploitable politically). "The Roosevelt coalition was just that—a coalition," he intoned to his advisors. FDR "played one against another—big city bosses, intellectuals, South, North. By contrast, our New American Majority appeals across the board—to Italians, Poles, Southerners, to the Midwest and New York—for the *same reasons*, and because of the same basic values. These are people who care about a strong United States, about patriotism, about moral and spiritual values." There may not even be consensus on what "those moral and spiritual values ought to be," Nixon confessed, "but they agree that you ought to have some." They were ironic words for a president who would have to resign in disgrace two years after the election, but

they were terms he believed to be bedrock political truth. While FDR intoned against elites as the "economic royalists" who wanted to form an "industrial dictatorship," Nixon knew in his very soul that working people
would rally against a new kind of elite—a liberal cultural elite "who want to
take their money, and give it to people who don't work." As he concluded,
"These are not just southern or ethnic notions—they're American to the
core."[3]

Nixon's thinking about workers inverted that of Woodrow Wilson, his
presidential hero and model. Wilson had sought routes for workers to establish "progressive improvement in the conditions of their labor," ways they
could "be made happier" or "served better by the communities and the industries which their labor sustains and advances." Nixon, in contrast, stood
the problem on its head—ideal rather than material—by making workers'
economic interests secondary to an appeal to their moral backbone, patriotic
rectitude, whiteness, and machismo in the face of the inter-related threats of
social decay, racial unrest, and faltering national purpose. His cultural formulation of workers' interests meant he was not going to break much new
legislative ground in the name of the working class, but as it became clear,
he was also not going to launch an open offensive against organized labor or
the key institutions of collective bargaining in the United States. Indeed, it
was not long after his musings that he declared that there would be "no more
rhetoric from the Administration [that] contained any kind of anti-union
implications." In formulating such an appeal, Richard Nixon may have been
one of the most class aware presidents of the postwar era, even if that awareness never sought to improve conditions for the American working class or
the fortunes of organized labor. He would make the Republican Party a bit
less receptive to the needs of Wall Street and, at least rhetorically, much
more open to the men of the assembly lines.[4]

Richard Nixon's attempt at working-class populism may have been the
loneliest in American history. A politician who ironically had a class background closer to his hoped-for constituency than the more popular figures of
John F. Kennedy or Franklin D. Roosevelt, he was, in speechwriter William
Safire's estimation, a "man born with a potmetal spoon in his mouth fighting a Rockefeller for the nomination and a Kennedy for the Presidency."
Humble origin, however, does not a populist make. As biographer Richard
Reeves explains, Nixon was "a strange man of uncomfortable shyness, who
functioned best alone with his thoughts and the yellow legal pads he fa-
vored, or in set pieces where he literally memorized every word he had to

say"—hardly the characteristics of a man of the people. His was a "cramped version of populism," based on who he was aligned against not what he was for, and it tapped into his own grinding anxiety rather than his faith in the working class. Lonely, isolated, and smart, the brooding workhorse of post-war America came to believe that groups and interests could be politically manipulated from the inner-sanctum of the White House. As Reeves argues, "he gloried in cultural warfare, dividing the nation geographically, generationally, racially, religiously," often believing that the genetic code caused voters to act in pre-determined ways.[5]

By the 1972 campaign, he would have strategic appeals laid out to thirty-three separate ethnic voter groups ranging from the Armenians and Bulgarians to the Syrians and the Ukrainians—all united around the need for some vague sense of values. Nixon believed that he could bring those ethnicities together; surmount economic disagreements with organized labor; and, by presenting his cultural vision at his particular historical moment, become the workingman's president. And he was, to a large extent, correct.[6]

I

The origins of what Nixon's men called the "blue-collar strategy" were rooted in a more vague but famous appeal to the "Silent Majority." Barely squeaking past Hubert Humphrey and a Democratic Party in complete disarray after the 1968 Chicago convention, he turned toward sharpening his appeal to what he first called the "Silent Americans." He launched a secret group called the "Middle America Committee" in the fall of 1969 to help the Republican Party reach the "the large and politically powerful white middle class." That constituency, they reasoned, was "deeply troubled, primarily over the erosion of what they consider to be their values."[7]

The National Moratorium to End the War on October 15, 1969, provided a chance for Nixon to take his strategy to the next level. The flavor and hue of protest suggested that criticism of the war was going mainstream. The massive mobilization against the war received favorable press coverage and appeared to be a public relations disaster for the pro-war administration. "Enough educated and affluent Americans turned against [Nixon]," former *New York Times* reporter Max Frankle argues, that "criticism ceased to be 'radical' and the president had to vie with critics for attention on the news." With the anti-war cause clearly no longer a fringe cause, he had to win back the hearts and minds of the people. So, in the early hours of the morning about two weeks after the moratorium, Nixon toiled to find the right words for his national television address to defend his policies in Vietnam. It was then that he struck upon his famous appeal to "the great silent majority of my fellow Americans." While it began as a counter-attack on the anti-war movement, it crystallized as a key domestic theme that would run through his presidency all the way through the 1972 campaign.[8]

The Silent Majority rhetoric also meshed neatly with the more venomous posturing of Vice President Spiro Agnew, who had a field day attacking the "small and unelected elite" of the press and the "effete corps of impudent snobs who characterize themselves as intellectuals." The nation's newspapers and television stations, argued Agnew, had played up the scourge of dissent in the nation while ignoring the hardworking Americans who did their jobs and paid their taxes. He tarred the media elite, with his trademark alliteration, as the "nattering nabobs of negativism" who had formed "their own Four H club—the hopeless, hysterical, hypochondriacs of history." Pat Buchanan, a young reporter who had become a sort of political valet to the president, reveled in Agnew's success. The vice president, he wrote to Nixon, "has become the acknowledged spokesman of the Middle American, the Robespierre of the Great Silent Majority." The press sheepishly covered Agnew's rhetorical offensive. The cover of *Time* magazine that November even showed thousands of clean-cut white people at the Washington Monument celebrating Veterans Day with the headline "Counterattack on Dissent." An influential young billionaire name H. Ross Perot then dumped half a million dollars into an advertising campaign to send letters of support to the White House.[9]

As it was for Robert Kennedy and then George McGovern, the key to Nixon's political universe between 1968 and 1972 was the Wallace voter. Wallace's oratory during his 1968 campaign, running under the banner of the American Independent Party, earned him the moniker of "Cicero of the cab driver" from one journalist because of his ability to tap into the anger, disenchantment, and racial resentments of white blue-collar America. As the governor's biographer argues, Wallace was able to draw together the social and racial problems of the late sixties and early seventies in inextricable ways. "Fears of blackness and fears of disorder—interwoven by the subconscious connection many white Americans made between blackness and criminality, blackness and poverty, blackness and cultural degradation— were the warp and woof of the new social agenda." Working-class liberals still constituted a strong bloc, but they were growing suspicious of changes afoot and feeling forgotten in the mix. Better than many Democrats, Nixon, like Wallace, figured out that much of the backlash was a simple search for secure ground in the cultural storms.[10]

The Wallace voter offered the key to more specific plans for romancing the working class beyond the Silent Majority. Kevin Phillips, the precocious young Nixon advisor who read his computer printouts with the intensity of a biblical scholar, believed that the secret to American politics was "who hated who." The Bronx-Irish strategist understood the essential cultural conservatism of the white ethnics and boldly posited that the manipulation of race and culture would provide for what he called the *The Emerging Republican Majority* (1969). In that famous manifesto, Phillips argued that Nixon's narrow victory over Hubert Humphrey in 1968 was not the political fluke that it appeared to be; rather, it represented the beginning of a major ethnic and regional political realignment. The Wallace voters were not a one-time move away from the Democrats but part of a permanent realignment toward the Republicans. To look at simple election returns of the two major parties was to miss the point. The solid Democratic South was crumbling under the Democrats' commitment to racial equality and cultural values, he believed, and, by adding the Nixon votes to those cast for George Wallace, one could see a nation "in motion between a Democratic past and Republican future." A less prominent argument in Phillips' famous book looked beyond the Southern Strategy and considered the possibility of mobilizing the votes of northern industrial workers. "Successful moderate conservatism is also likely to attract to the Republican side some of the northern blue-collar workers who flirted with George Wallace but ultimately backed Hubert Humphrey," Phillips calculated.[11]

The problem was that working-class voters feared that a Republican administration would do away with popular New Deal programs—from social security to collective bargaining. Phillips' version of conservatism was nothing like what it would soon become; he advocated, for instance, programs ranging from national health insurance to aid for declining industrial regions. If Nixon could dispel the notion that his party and his presidency were anti-worker, cleverly manipulate the race issue, and peg the label of "elitism" on the liberals, it followed, he could build a post-New Deal coalition that transcended the Southern Strategy. As Nixon appeared soft on labor, liberals lost their bearings with (another) new Nixon. As labor insider John Herling reported in the spring of 1969, the new president "certainly is not behaving according to the pattern both friend and foe set out for him as he advanced to the White House. In the area of labor-management relations, there has been no sizzle and crackle and lopping off of heads, no snarling that 'We've got you now, bub.'" The roots of a New Right lay, Phillips contended, in the hope of "a new coalition reaching across to what elite conservatives still consider 'the wrong side of the tracks.'" The Wallace vote of 1968 was merely a "way station" for blue-collar Democrats drifting into the Republican Party—and the future of republicanism rested upon the "the great, ordinary, Lawrence Welkish mass of Americans from Maine to Hawaii."[12]

The Wallace voter was a dangerous and confusing character for any candidate. On the issues of class and economics, the Wallace voter tended to see the Democrats as the party of the center—accepting and depending upon much of the economic gains of the New Deal programs; but on race and law-and-order, that same voter would need the most conservative elements of the Republicans. The question was which element was stronger—culture or economics? As Scammon and Wattenberg explained in *The Real Majority* (1970), from the hypothetical position of the ten million people who voted for Wallace in 1968, "'Law and order' beats 'bread and butter'; social beats economic. Keep your tainted federal dollars if it means putting my kid in school with the colored." For the millions of voters who originally leaned toward Wallace but voted for one of the two-party candidates in 1968, however, in the end the calculus went in the other direction—the politics of economic interest generally trumped the social issue. But, as the pugnacious liberal journalist Pete Hamill described Wallace supporters in 1968, it may have been more basic than the false binary of economics versus culture. As so often in populist movements, the Wallace movement had more than a hint of the promise of a restoration of a lost golden age. As Hamill argued,

> There was little mystery to them. They were my own people, lower middle-class people who worked with their backs and their hands, who paid dues to a union that was remote to them, people who drove a cab or tended bar one night a week to make ends meet, people who went hunting with the boys on vacations, people who handed their infant children to their wives while they applauded the candidate. Most of them seemed to make about $125 a week and were struggling to pay off GI loans on their homes. . . . They want change; the America they thought was theirs has become something else in their own lifetimes, they want to go back. A lot of the people attracted to George Wallace are just

people who think America has passed them by, leaving them confused and screwed-up and unhappy.

The vague populism of the Silent Majority, the sentiments of the Wallace followers, and the outlook of the voters Phillips scrutinized all lacked the class edge that Nixon would soon develop to his political calculations.[13]

The document that moved Nixon's thinking from these broader appeals to a more specific blue-collar strategy was another provocative essay by the liberal journalist Pete Hamill titled "The Revolt of the White Lower Middle Class." Nixon read the 1969 piece in *New York* magazine only a few months after taking office, and by all accounts he was deeply moved by its street-wise view of the issues. The article exposed the unrecognized rage coursing through the New Deal bulwark. It allowed the president to move Phillips' thinking, and the president's own impulses, from an abstract possibility to a concrete strategy by clearly identifying a set of political resentments in the urban north ready for plucking. While Hamill did not mince words about the racist expressions of white working-class anger in 1969, like Nixon, he concluded that it was less race, per se, which drove phenomena like northern blue-collar support for George Wallace, than it was workers' belief that they were not respected and that society had focused its attention and resources on other, noisier, groups. The urgency of the war, civil rights, and the rising women's movement were threatening the privileged centrality of the old New Deal base—the white ethnic working class. "It is imperative for New York politicians to begin to deal with the growing alienation and paranoia of the working-class white man," Hamill explained in this strategic Rosetta Stone; he "feels trapped and, even worse, in a society that purports to be democratic, ignored." In concluding words that must have leapt from the page into Richard Nixon's mind, the author wrote, "Any politician who leaves that white man out of the political equation, does so at very large risk."[14]

Hamill's work was complemented by an intellectual resurgence that made the promise and pathologies of white, blue-collar men a veritable genre in the early seventies. Works such as Peter Schrag, "The Forgotten American" in *Harper's Magazine* (1969), Patricia Cayo Sexton and Brendan Sexton, *Blue Collars and Hard-Hats* (1971), Richard Sennett and Jonathan Cobb, *The Hidden Injuries of Class* (1972), Andrew Levison, *The Working Class Majority* (1974), Studs Terkel, *Working* (1974), Lloyd Zimpel, *Man Against Work* (1974), E.E. LeMasters, *Blue-Collar Aristocrats* (1975), and all too rare entries on women like Louise Kapp Howe, *Pink Collar Workers* (1977) suggest a small chunk of the blue-collar revival among intellectuals. Yet it is likely that Richard Nixon learned his lessons less from Hamill and the others than he had his preternatural political instincts confirmed by the intellectuals—the exact type of affirmation he relished.

Nixon circulated the Hamill article widely among his strategists. George Shultz's Department of Labor studied the issues in greater empirical detail, and delivered *the* document of reference in the administration's debates over the labor question, a paper titled "The Problem of the Blue-Collar Worker." More commonly known as the "Rosow Report" after its author, Assistant Secretary of Labor Jerome M. Rosow, it was delivered to the president in April 1970. The brief clearly made the case for material concerns, arguing that white lower-class workers were "on a treadmill, chasing the illusion of higher living standards." A worker's "only hope seems to be continued pressure for higher wages," admitted Rosow, and "their only spokesmen seem to be union leaders spearheading the demand for more money wages." The author concluded that these workers "are overripe for a political response to the pressing needs they feel so keenly." The report admitted, "People in the blue-collar class are less mobile, less organized, and less capable of using legitimate means to either protect the status quo or secure changes in their favor. To a considerable extent, they feel like 'forgotten people'—those for whom the government and the society have limited, if any, direct concern and little visible action." Rosow's solutions to the problems he outlined made up an unimaginative stew of policy ideas to better workers' lives materially: education, childcare, tax policy, and workplace regulations. "Our system of values signal that something is very wrong when conscientious, able, and hard-working people cannot make it." The more conservative members of Nixon's staff were horrified by the whole idea of the report—it was much too redolent of the old New Deal. "The Rosow Report is a blue-print for an expanded welfare state," complained aide Tom Huston; "It envisions a program which we cannot afford politically or budgetarily." The key, he argued, would be to "develop a rhetoric which communicates concern for the legitimate claims of this class, yet avoids any incitement to the baser instincts of man afraid."[15]

Nothing remains a secret in Washington for long, and one of the twenty-five copies in circulation made it into the hands of the *Wall Street Journal*. "Secret Report Tells Nixon How to Help White Workingmen and Win Their Votes," proclaimed the title of the exposé. "President Nixon has before him a confidential blueprint designed to help him capture the hearts and votes of the nation's white working men—the traditionally Democratic 'forgotten Americans' that the Administration believes are ripe for political plucking." While the article covering the strategy was forthright, the paper's editorial on the subject dripped with contempt. Calling the news of the strategy "depressing" and the plan as having "a sense of absurdity," the newspaper condemned the new direction for the Republicans by suggesting that alienation was too complex an emotion for presidential politics. Workers were simply the next group to claim the fashionable badge of alienation, the *Journal* claimed, and even if it was a real emotion, the newspaper questioned whether it was at all curable. It preferred to place a chunk of the blame on "the big labor unions," which were once a "fountain of so much security" and now "may also contribute to their alienation."[16]

The question was, despite the obvious need for material betterment contained in the Rosow Report and despite the remarkably objective multiracial definition of the blue-collar vote it contained, could the administration chuck the material issues it raised and succeed in winning white working-class votes solely through cultural and social appeals? Putting the pieces together, the president and his staff agreed that the political moment supported three basic, interlocking propositions. First, the white working-class vote was politically up for grabs, and Nixon could be the leader to knit them into a new political coalition—essentially giving mainstream legitimacy to Wallaceite sentiments. Second, while Rosow's report brought up significant bread-and-butter issues and argued that any concern for workers had to include two million blacks "who share many of the same problems as whites in their income class," it was neither the entire working class nor its material grievances on which the administration would focus. Rather, it was the "feeling of being forgotten" among white, male workers that the administration would seek to tap. Finally, policy and rhetoric would be formulated that did not require federal expenditures or even wage increases—the politics of recognition and status would be enough. The struggle for the Nixon administration would be to ferret out non-material political responses to the "pressing needs" they knew workers experienced and, as inflation became a priority, in fact placing restraints on workers' wage demands. The key question remained for the administration: was this to be a strategy to draw out workers only or might even the unions—whose entire identity was largely wrapped up in delivering the material goods to the rank and file—also be brought on board?[17]

II

Then came the proof. Just weeks after the internal release of the Rosow Report, Richard Nixon's wildest dreams for the blue-collar strategy found their popular manifestation. Beginning in early May 1970 and lasting much of the month, New York City construction workers turned out in the streets in a frenzy of "jingoistic joy" aimed against the war protestors and "red" Mayor Lindsay, and in support of Nixon's policies in Southeast Asia. The protests began when brightly helmeted construction workers, many wielding their heavy tools, pushed through a weak line of police and violently descended on an anti-war demonstration called after the killings at Kent State. The workers' goal, besides venting their rage, was to raise a flag lowered to half mast to honor the four slain students in Ohio. They then proceeded to storm the steps of City Hall, chasing student protestors through the streets of the financial district, and bloodying around seventy people in the process. While demonstrations continued on lunch hours throughout the month, the culmination of the conflicts came on May 20 when the Building and Construction Trades Council of Greater New York sponsored a rally—the previous actions had no open sponsorship—and delivered around one hundred thousand supporters in a sea of American flags, declaring their support for the war effort. Complete with a concrete mixer draped with the slogan "Lindsay for Mayor of Hanoi," and signs declaring GOD BLESS THE ESTABLISHMENT and WE SUPPORT NIXON AND AGNEW, the protests delivered to the national spotlight both the hard-hat image and the resentment Hamill pinpointed the previous year. *Business Week* called the original hard-hat revolts the "three days that shook the establishment," but it was more like three days that affirmed it.[18]

The pro-war worker was an unfair stereotype, which, upon close examination, suggests something of the class divides of the anti-war movement. Certainly there were plenty of blue-collar Americans who agreed with John Nash, a Newark printer interviewed during the protests, who chalked up support for the war as simple duty to country. "I'm backing the President all the way. My boy goes into service Dec. 7. . . . I'm proud of him. It's a chance we all had to take. It's his turn." But polling data belies the myth of a uniquely pro-war working class and consistently shows, in fact, that manual workers were more opposed to the war and more in favor of withdrawal than were the college educated. An amalgam of polls, interviews, and reports suggests that it was less support for the war among pro-Nixon workers than it was class resentments aimed at the approach, privilege, and lack of duty among the protesters. With college a reasonable class signifier in the sixties, the college draft deferment tore a fairly clear class divide between those who were forced to serve and those who were not—in an era in which many families were barely more than a generation out of poverty. Thus much of the psychology of the backlash trended more toward that of class antagonisms, guilt, and victimization than an actual stand on foreign policy. As historian Christian Appy, reports, "To many veterans, the protest of college students felt like moral and social putdowns, expressions not of principle and commitment but simply of class privilege and arrogance." As one tradesman confirmed, "Here were these kids, rich kids, who could go to college, who didn't have to fight, they are telling you your son died in vain. It makes you feel your whole life is shit, just nothing."[19]

What mattered most to the Nixon administration was that the protests suddenly gave their ideas about the working class palpable imagery and potent political symbolism. "This display of emotional activity from the 'hard hats,'" argued Nixon's aide Steve Bull, provided an opportunity "to forge a new alliance and perhaps result in the emergence of a 'new right.'" Strategically, the idea was to avoid the treacherous waters of workers' inflationary wage interests by addressing a powerful and rising tide of cultural conservatism. "The emphasis," continued Bull, "would be upon some of these supposedly trite mid-America values that the liberal press likes to snicker about: love of country, respect for people as individuals, the Golden Rule, etc."[20]

The hard-hat protests and the stereotype of the hawkish working class was yet another twist in a long line of manipulations of the working-class image—whether it was the Left's revolutionary agent or the Right's neo-brown shirts. As two sociologists explained at the time, "the whole idea of the 'hard hat'—the superpatriot, the racist workingman" served to hollow out the humanity of the wearer and replace the person with a political symbol: "a thing, with an empty head hidden beneath, a part of a mass over which the 'educated' or 'enlightened' person towers." The right wing's new essentialization was as reductionist as the Old Left's equally simplistic "proletariat"—both mere instruments for others to wield for their own political purposes.[21]

The timing of the protests could not have been more fortuitous. The White House was literally and figuratively under siege in the wake of the bombing of Cambodia. Chuck Colson called the White House a "bunker" as tear gas drifted in from the streets, and the secret service resorted to ringing the grounds with buses in order to protect the president. With protestors and the press attacking the White House, the hard hats came to Nixon's aid, bolstering the sagging *esprit de corps* of the administration. The workers, Nixon exclaimed, "were with us when some of the elitist crowd were running away from us. Thank God for the hard hats!" As Haldeman noted, Nixon "thinks now the college demonstrators have overplayed their hands, evidence is the blue collar group rising up against them, and P can mobilize them," he explained optimistically as Washington lay in a fog of tear gas.[22]

Nixon seized upon the moment to uphold traditional values in the face of cultural upheaval: a discussion about manly citizens who work and support their country in opposition to the effete non-citizens who loaf, protest, and undermine the national purpose. As Peter Brennan, head of the New York building trades who helped orchestrate the hard-hat protests, explained to Colson (and Colson to the president), the "hard hats" cheering for the president did not correlate directly to votes. They did not like Nixon's economic policies and feared his push on civil rights. "What is winning their political loyalty," Brennan explained,

> is their admiration for your masculinity. The "hard hats," who are a tough breed, have come to respect you as a tough, courageous man's man. Brennan's thesis is that this image of you will win their votes more than the patriotism theme. The image of being strong, forceful and decisive will have a powerful personal appeal with the alienated voter.[23]

Many have suggested that the rampaging protests of the tool wielding tradesmen emerged from Nixon's kit of dirty tricks. Although this appears not to have directly been the case, the administration was certainly ready and willing to exploit the uprisings and, when necessary, foment more. Haldeman, aggravated by the continued presence of Viet Cong flags at the president's appearances, arranged for the illusion of spontaneous blue-collar types to descend upon flag-waving protestors so that they could be quickly removed. "The best way to do this is probably to work out an arrangement with the Teamsters Union so that they will have a crew on hand at all Presidential appearances, ready, willing, and able to remove Viet Cong flags, physically." At other times Nixon approved of having Teamsters "go in and knock [protestors'] heads off." Haldeman suggested hiring "Murderers. Guys that really, you know . . . the regular strikebusters-types . . . and then they're gonna beat the [obscenity] out of some of these people." Haldeman's "to do" list in his copious yellow note pads even included "Get a goon squad to start roughing up demos" as part of the appearance of a broader revolt of the Silent Majority against the vocal minority. (There are several references to "those eight thugs" in the documents, suggesting some familiarity and use of them, and curiously Abbie Hoffman [the butt of many anti-Semitic remarks from Nixon and his advisors] did get a broken nose from unknown assailants two days before the "thugs discussion.")[24]

Whatever covert tricks the administration may have engaged in, the Nixon staff certainly made the most of *overt* operations. No sooner had the protests come to their conclusion than Nixon had invited twenty-two New York union officials, led by New York Trades Council president Peter Brennan, to the White House for a chat. The union leaders presented the president with a small metal flag for his lapel and a hard hat labeled "Commander in Chief" as well as a similar helmet for the commander in Vietnam, General Creighton W. Abrams. "The hard hat," they explained, "will stand as a symbol, along with our great flag, for freedom and patriotism to our beloved country." Nixon briefed the group on the progress of the war and "was visibly moved" when one member of the delegation, whose son had been killed in Vietnam, said "if someone would have had the courage to go into Cambodia sooner, they might have captured the bullet that took my son's life."[25]

III

Richard Nixon is often described as the "last liberal," but he, and anyone else at the time, would have chafed—if not been revolted—by the idea. "His heart was on the right," explained William Safire, "and his head was, with FDR, 'slightly left of center.'" It is only in historical perspective of the post-Reagan era that he can be seen as liberal. He was certainly the last president to function within the liberal paradigm, but it was a paradigm he sought to undo, not to promote. He was, however, not a political ideologue but a strategic opportunist, a tactical pragmatist, who made peace where he needed in order to exploit the political space between the congressional liberals and the hostility of more conservative Republicans. His domestic policy vision was mostly one of disinterest, except where it overlapped with his plans for the New Majority. On issues such as busing, his opposition allowed him to score easy points against liberals. In other areas, however, he seemed at the forefront of expanding the Great Society. He liked to compare himself to the British prime minister Benjamin Disraeli, the nineteenth-century Conservative, known for launching liberal initiatives as a way of controlling the reform process. His "liberalism" involved pre-empting liberal legislation with his own policies, while simultaneously using those more tepid liberal initiatives to draw voters to his new coalition. The president's "baffling blend of Republicanism and radicalism," in the terms of the *New York Times*, was the result: a conservative opportunist governing in a liberal paradigm with the goal of building the New Majority.[26]

The signing of the Occupational Safety and Health Act (OSHA) in December 1970 was a case in point. The new administrative office set up mechanisms for enforcement of safety and health on the job—a response to the roiling concerns about non-wage aspects of the employment relationship. President Johnson had proposed a workplace safety bill that never passed, but as the environmental and consumer safety movements took hold (the Environmental Protection Agency [EPA] was created in the same year), the momentum for OSHA grew. It was an unwelcome and intrusive intervention in the workplace for most employers and Republicans. Nixon, however, declared that it was "probably one of the most important pieces of legislation, from the standpoint of the 55 million people who will be covered by it, ever passed by the Congress of the United States." Needless to say, it dovetailed flawlessly with his desire to woo his new constituency.[27]

Perhaps the most intriguing piece of the Nixon domestic program, one that never made it to political daylight, was his welfare reform initiative known as the Family Assistance Program (FAP). Most of Nixon's domestic policy was based on his "New Federalism," which sought to increase funding but to do so by distributing power away from the federal bureaucracy and toward state and local governments. FAP, however, was slightly different. The program was based on a guaranteed annual income (of $1,600 for a family of four) that cut at the heart of the flaws in the Aid to Families with Dependent Children (AFDC) program, which was believed to penalize work and create a large bureaucracy. It had been a long-standing dream of free-market conservatives, like Milton Friedman, who called it a "Negative Income Tax." With a national guaranteed income, people could still work, and be encouraged or even required to do so, but nobody would fall below the national standard. The fundamental idea was simple, but the details were mind-bogglingly complicated and political—work requirements, break-even points, taxation rates, actual costs, the amount of assistance—all of which seemed only of interest to Democrat Daniel Patrick Moynihan, who joined the administration to try to deal with the welfare mess. Here, Nixon failed as the American Disraeli, as the bill was too much for conservatives and not enough for liberals, especially those influenced by the National Welfare Rights Organization, which demanded the most generous bill it could get. Or, perhaps, he was as shrewd as ever. As the bill stalled in Congress, Haldeman noted in his diary: "About Family Assistance Plan, [President] wants to be sure it's killed by Democrats and that we make a big play for it, but don't let it pass, can't afford it." Nixon gets the credit for the idea; Democrats get the blame for its failure.[28]

Another measure of Nixon's moderation on domestic policies was his response to the labor upheavals that marked the seventies. If he were interested in a showdown with the unions, there was no better opportunity than when the postal workers launched the first substantial strike against the federal government in U.S. history during the spring of 1970. *Time* magazine called it "The Strike that Stunned the Country"; the papers called it "postal anarchy." A New York City postal worker with twenty-three years on the job still made 25 percent less than the income level necessary for a moderate standard of living as defined by the federal government. Long-standing complaints about poor wages remained unmet, and many feared that Nixon's plan to turn the U.S. Postal Service into an independent government corporation held out little promise to change the situation. Postal workers were typically regarded as good and loyal civil servants, and their union, like those of other federal employees, was little more than a toothless lobbying organization that could neither bargain nor legally strike—only, as the workers called it, partake in "collective begging." Joining an illegal strike against the federal government was not without substantial risk: postal workers risked fines of up to $1,000, jail time of up to a year, and automatic dismissal.[29]

In March, however, postal workers shocked the nation as they walked off the job in New York, New Jersey, and Connecticut, followed by stoppages in major cities across the country in demand of wage increases and collective bargaining procedures. The Nixon administration declared, "What is at issue then is the survival of a government based upon law." Yet the administration carefully called it a "work stoppage" rather than a strike so as not to antagonize the situation, since a strike by federal employees would be illegal. Nixon did send in 25,000 unarmed members of the National Guard to move the mail (though without much success). The federal government's intervention sparked a back to work movement in most sites except for New York City, which remained out in defiance of the federal government. George

Shultz, Nixon's secretary of labor, captured fears of rank and file power in the early seventies in his opening salvo in the conflict. "There's only one thing worse than a wildcat strike," he declared, "a wildcat strike that succeeds." And this *was* a wildcat that largely succeeded, potentially tipping the balance toward a runaway rank and file rather than the sober and statesman-like union leadership on which the post-war paradigm of labor relations depended. Nixon's conciliatory caution with regard to the postal strike would stand in dramatic contrast to another public workers' dispute ten years later, that of the Professional Air Traffic Controllers Organization (PATCO), when Ronald Reagan summarily fired thousands of striking employees. The comparison suggests much about the transformation—and disempowerment of workers—wrought by the 1970s.[30]

IV

In an unprecedented and risky gesture at the end of the summer of 1970, Nixon tried to move beyond the rank and file by reaching out to court the AFL-CIO leadership. In a large public gesture, he invited George Meany and sixty other labor leaders to the White House for dinner on Labor Day. It was an extraordinary and curious event: a Republican president not just flirting with the common man, but now romancing the highest ranks of organized labor's leadership. William Safire once described Nixon and Meany as "diametrically allied"—a fundamental mutual admiration, agreement on cultural authority, and a deeply shared Cold War mentality, all of which was undermined by a constant distrust and disagreement on domestic economic policy. Prior to the dinner, Meany helped to lay an amicable groundwork in a pre–Labor Day interview. Admitting that the administration was making "a very definite pitch" to win over workers, he helped push the effort forth by declaring that "the Democratic Party has disintegrated" and what remained was being taken over by "extremists"—long before George McGovern even had the standing of a dark horse. The president did not make any bold initiatives at the gathering—inviting Meany into the White House was certainly risky enough—but instead focused on the fundamental point of agreement between the administration and the AFL-CIO: the Vietnam war.[31]

Following a round of golf between Meany and the president, Nixon had his chance to preach to labor's Cold War choir during dinner. "The message of our time is that a strong, free, independent labor movement is essential to the preservation and the growth of freedom in any country in the world," lectured the president. Turning his attention to the AFL-CIO president, Nixon raised his glass to George Meany and proffered a parallel between the recently deceased Vince Lombardi, whose funeral Nixon just attended, and the aging labor leader. Meany, he explained "has stood like a pillar in the storm—strong, full of character, devoted to his church, devoted to his family, devoted to his country, whether the president is a Republican or a Democrat, standing with that President and his country when he felt that that served the interest of freedom, that kind of freedom which is so essential if a strong, free labor movement is to survive." Nixon and his guests then retired to the South Lawn where they joined six thousand union families for a performance of the *1812 Overture*.[32]

If only Nixon could go to China, perhaps only Nixon could have brought labor into the Republican White House on Labor Day as well. Haldeman privately noted that the dinner was a "real coup," and no sooner had the posturing ended and the East Room been cleared of the dirty dishes than the memos began to flow through the White House about hopes and strategies to capitalize on the new labor-Republican linkage. Haldeman dashed off a memo regarding the new "resource to be cultivated" and argued that, given the success of the evening, he and the president felt that the most efficient route to the blue-collar vote would now be through sympathetic labor leaders. The administration's plan was to proceed by sifting through the labor leadership to figure out which "are worth cultivating" and "picking them off one by one." As Haldeman summarized, "there is a great deal of gold to be mined." He passed responsibility for the initiative onto Charles Colson, and he noted, "As you can see from all of the above, [the President] is most anxious to move hard, fast and extensively in this whole area, and he is counting on you to see that this is done."[33]

"I will take this one on with real delight," Colson responded to the challenge of wooing labor to Nixon's side after the Labor Day dinner. Chuck Colson, who looked like a cherubic and mild-mannered accountant, was, in his own description, the "toughest of the Nixon tough guys." Labeled the administration's "hatchet man" by the *Wall Street Journal* years before Watergate, Colson went down in history (and to prison) as one of the masterminds of Nixon's dirty tricks. Behind his thick, black glasses was a calculating political mind that never deviated from its goal. With the same faith and conviction he would later declare for the Lord during his post-Watergate incarceration, Colson's effectiveness led Nixon to make him his "political point-man" in 1970. He chose Colson, explained the president, because he was "positive, persuasive, smart, and aggressively partisan" with an "instinct for the jugular." When Nixon complained to Colson, he "felt confident that something would be done"—a fact that suggests something of the central importance of the blue-collar project to the president. The two men also shared a similar class background and a history of aggressive upward mobility. "Nixon and I understood one another," explained Colson, "We were both men of the same lower middle-class origins, men who'd known hard work all our lives, prideful men seeking that most elusive goal of all—acceptance and the respect of those who had spurned us in earlier years." In turning his considerable energies toward the president's request, however, Colson may have underestimated the task before him. "We have succeeded in splitting large parts of the labor movement away from the Democratic Party," Colson wrote. "We have not won them over to the Republican Party; but the reservoir of goodwill and support for the President, both as an individual and as a President, is the basis for a permanent alliance." Conceding that getting labor to advocate for the president in the near future would be difficult, the strategist concluded that, "Our immediate objective is to keep Labor split away from the Democrats. Our long range target is to make them part of our 'New Majority.'"[34]

Despite the success of the Labor Day dinner, Colson knew that the leadership was not enough—that the rank and file were the real voters. "As a general policy we must always keep in mind that romancing the union leadership is only one part of the task. . . . We need to cultivate the leadership by our individual activities and the rank and file by both our policies and our reaching out to the state and local apparatus." He concluded the plan of action should be to continue courting sympathetic union leaders—including maritime unions, Longshoreman, Seafarers, the building trades, federal employees, Teamsters, fire and police, the Retail Clerks, and even the staunchly liberal UAW. In the UAW case, he tacked differently. Given that the "socialist" leadership would never be won to the Republican side, he would turn to the rank-and-file autoworkers who were "among the most conservative in the union movement." Combining the major intellectual themes of the administration's strategy, he explained, "our task, therefore, is to cultivate local leaders, who are strongly patriotic, anti-student and keenly aware of the race question."[35]

Nixon scrawled "good," "yes," and "do it," to most of Colson's suggestions, and his memo essentially stands as a blue-print for the administration's actions to implement the Rosow Report from the 1970 midterm elections through the 1972 national campaign. The easy stuff was simple Rockefeller-like invitation and flattery that would hopefully make its way back to the rank and file. Colson suggested appointing representatives of organized labor to "every commission we announce," having an administration official at every labor convention, considering the appointment of a trade unionist to a top post in the administration, having regular meetings with top union economists, and fixing prospective indictments of friendly labor leaders. In sum, explained Colson, "If we bring them into the advisory process in this way we then make them a part of our policy formulation rather than natural adversaries." He went so far as to suggest that in order to find some common ground beyond Vietnam and the Cold War, the administration should consider backing a "pro-labor" bill to prove its mettle.[36]

The most cost-free angle, however, was going to be the most effective: not being silent on the Silent Majority. One of Nixon's fundamental beliefs had always been that the appearance of action—the manipulation of the image—was at least as important, if not more so, than the reality of it. An exasperated Nixon once remarked to his staff that he wanted "everybody here now to start thinking politically, instead of worrying about running things well." He had always been uninterested in the intricacies of domestic policy but absolutely driven by his desire to build his New Majority. That balance, John Ehrlichman estimated, meant that Nixon spent "half his working time on the nonsubstantive aspects of the Presidency." The administration therefore sought to control the discourse on the labor issue. "Of crucial importance is getting out the right line to the press," Colson continued, advising that administration publicist Herb Klein "should have a regular media briefing for the labor press particularly on key economic issues." The real key would be to build a sense of working-class movement on behalf of the president. "Friendly columnists should keep talking about how Nixon is winning the workingman's vote and how this Administration is pro-workingman, not anti-labor as other Republican administrations have appeared to be," Colson noted. "The more that the rank and file read that we are winning the labor vote, the more they are psychologically adjusted to getting on the band wagon." They went out of their way to make sure the bandwagon was big by ensuring that the "working man" and "building America" themes regularly appeared in the speeches of all administration representatives and mailing the Rosow Report to Republican candidates throughout the country to include them in the new strategic vision.[37]

Nixon was well aware of the right-left tensions within the trade union movement dating from his time in the Eisenhower administration and sought to exacerbate that split by simultaneously courting the right-wing unions and attacking the Left within the labor movement. Calling the UAW and the International Ladies' Garment Workers' Union (ILGWU) leadership "not only hopeless Democrats, but also hopeless pacifists," he countered Colson's more blanket approach, suggesting that "we simply are not going to make any points by trying to get along with the congenital left-wingers of the labor movement." The administration did try, however quixotically, to return to old McCarthyite tactics by asking the Department of Justice to "initiate and sustain a major attack on left wing/Communist infiltration of the labor movement." Nixon's people never made headway on this angle for one simple reason: they could not find very many Communists. They did have more reality-based concerns about New Left activists and splinter group militants moving into the unions, but this hardly constituted the heady issue they needed in order make a meaningful public show. As an intelligence memo to John Dean explained, "CP infiltration of, and influence in, the labor movement is minimal. . . . I do not believe it would be appropriate to launch any 'major attack' upon CP influence in the labor movement." Even J. Edgar Hoover, capable of finding subversive threats where they did not exist, had to admit, "CP influence can't be gauged." The administration still maintained its vigilance against radical influences and appeared to work in concert with the AFL-CIO hierarchy whenever it could. Lacking Communists, the administration still kept progressive unionists on its infamous "enemies list" and vented its anger and conspiratorial venom at the dismal employment reports by purging the Jews and the Democrats from the Bureau of Labor Statistics.[38]

V

Nixon campaigned hard for Republican candidates in the 1970 midterm elections, but the results were disappointing. The Republicans did pick up two of the seven Senate seats that would have been necessary for a majority. That was reasonably successful given that sitting presidents tended to lose seats in the midterms. The rest of the story was bleak, however, as they lost a net of nine seats in the House and eleven governorships. Tilting against "permissiveness" and following Phillips' advice of using "patriotic themes to counter economic depression" in order to get a response from the unemployed had not done the trick. As unemployment tipped toward 6 percent and the GM strike paralyzed the auto industry, furthermore, labor did its traditional job of beating up on Republicans. As a result, not everyone was as excited about the blue-collar strategy as the key players in the strategy like Charles Colson or Pat Buchanan.[39]

Indeed, the administration was marbled with old-school Republicans itching to discipline labor economically and politically with a good old-fashioned showdown. The failures of the 1970s elections sparked a battle of the memos that attempted to come to terms with the bedrock issues a New Right faced with regard to labor issues: Was the effort to co-opt labor futile, given the unions' traditional interests, or was there a real opportunity to re-mold American politics? Analysts and advisors spread out in a spectrum of opinion from Colson who fought militantly to continue efforts to woo labor to Acting Treasury Secretary Charls Walker who saw the effort as foolish.

Walker crafted an influential memo to Nixon in November recommending "for economic and political reasons, the Administration [ought] to take a more antagonistic stance towards organized labor." Walker's logic was fairly tight from a traditional Republican point of view. Economically, wage settlements were outpacing productivity gains in core industries, and thus the sought-after combination of price stability and full employment could not be achieved without "reducing the power of some major unions." This meant that it was time to "take off the gloves" and "enter into open battle." This view, continued Walker, is "very widely held by our traditional constituency" and the prudent thing to do on economic grounds. Fundamental conflicts over inflationary wage pressures, a problem Federal Reserve Chairman Arthur Burns had been trying to push to the top of the agenda for months, meant that organized labor was never really going to be part of the New Majority. "There is little to lose—and perhaps much to gain," Walker argued, "by getting 'tougher.'" Even Walker wanted to ensure the continuation of the "common man" theme, however, concerned that the new attack strategy "not be aimed at the 'working man'" but at those institutions and leaders damaging to the stability of the economy and that cut across workers' own long-term interests.[40]

Nixon noted "Excellent Analysis" on several points of Walker's memo, and it prompted him to launch a reconsideration of the romancing the New Right worker concept among his chief advisors. His memo hit the nub of the issue when he postulated that the whole concept that "labor would leave the Democrats and join us" was simply "wrong." The unions' goal would not be to support Nixon in 1972 as Colson and others hoped, but rather "to move the Democratic Party in its direction, supporting a centrist candidate such as Muskie." Here Nixon noted "Probably true." There was only one problem with Walker's analysis, noted Nixon in the margins: "But [they are] with us on national Defense." Without Vietnam, the "common man" strategy might not have survived the trial stage.[41]

Elder White House intellectual, speech writer, and former *Time* editor James Keogh took a slightly different tack: the effort to woo the leadership was futile, but there might be more support to be mined by differentiating the rank and file from the leadership. "We had a big Labor Day dinner for [the AFL-CIO leadership] and in other ways sought their favor. In return, they went out and bludgeoned us with rhetoric and money spent for the opposition. I have no doubt that they will continue to oppose the President politically right up to and including 1972." Keogh certainly expected quick results given the short time between Labor Day and the midterm elections, but his basic point had merit: it was a no-win situation given that other, more natural Republican allies would be alienated by Nixon's courting of labor. There was hope, however, in exploiting the anti-establishment mood by taking advantage of tensions between the rank and file and the labor leaders. That, Keogh argued, is where the administration should place its emphasis. "I hold the belief that even the rank and file labor union member tends to look with suspicion on the big labor leaders, having transferred to them a considerable portion of the dislike that goes towards the bosses." Rather than scrapping the whole blue-collar concept, "I wind up concluding that it is politically wise for us to seek the support of the rank and file of organized labor but that it is a risky affair for us to hold hands with the big labor leaders."[42]

Chuck Colson countered all opposition in a passionate defense of the rise of the workingman's right, siding forcefully with other blue-collar militants who wanted to continue to push fully toward bringing labor on board. "There is no profit in being antagonistic simply for the sake of being antagonistic," he argued, "nor to please those Republican businessmen and bankers who still believe that being anti-labor is part and parcel of Republican orthodoxy." Playing to the president's sympathies on foreign policy, Colson stressed, "labor has been our strongest ally on the most vital issues which confront this Administration—the fight against neo-isolationism—the ABM, SST, Cambodia, Hatfield-McGovern, and the Defense Budget." Even on fighting inflation, Colson argued for an even-handed approach requiring getting tough on business and government too. Most importantly, when it came to the tension between labor moving the Democrats to the center or joining the Republicans, there was no reason not to think the administration could not still win the tug of war: it was, he argued hopefully, "unwise to prejudge this one."[43]

Given the public fight labor gave Nixon in the 1970 elections, Colson confessed that "some will also say that I have lost my mind," but the evidence was still strong. Analysis of the 1970 midterm elections demonstrated the importance of the blue-collar vote but also its volatility. The administration's state-by-state breakdown showed that the blue-collar and middle-income votes varied dramatically depending upon the race, while most of the other categories remained relatively constant. In the races won by Republicans, the blue-collar vote was often responsible. The opposite was also true: in the races they lost, the party did poorly with the working-class vote. As Colson concluded to Haldeman, "The blue collar, middle income vote is volatile, and will swing to us if we play the issues correctly. . . . There is an emerging conservative, middle class/labor vote." Appealing to the president's ambitions, Colson extrapolated some wishful thinking from the data. "You have made an historic breakthrough in the old Roosevelt coalition of the 'have nots,' labor, the poor, the minorities. . . . you are winning the respect—and I believe the votes—of working men."[44]

It was not until the following summer, 1971, however, that the president finally put the matter to rest by siding decisively in favor of the hard-hat strategy. And decisive it was. Incredibly, even when polling data showed that the moment was ripe to attack labor, the administration bit its tongue. "The public in general and union families in particular are now ripe for a major uprising against the leadership of organized labor," claimed pollsters commissioned by the administration. All of the issues and sentiments were in place for a large-scale public revolt against crippling strikes, inflationary wage demands, and the undemocratic structure of some key unions. All measures demonstrated significant anti-labor gains since the 1969 poll, even, and most dramatically, in union families. "Surprisingly enough," concluded the poll results, "those closest to unions appear to share, often to an even greater degree, the feelings of the general population." But the pro-labor strategy was set—there would be no attack. As Colson concluded in a private memo after Nixon's decision, "This President, regardless of what the business community urges, what the polls show, or what Republican orthodoxy would dictate, is not going to do anything that undermines the working man's economic status."[45]

VI

Despite the flow of optimistic rhetoric and symbolic concessions, real-life labor issues plagued the administration, often putting the president in the odd position of being economically at odds with the interests of the labor movement while still allied with the AFL-CIO leadership on social issues and foreign policy. Contrary to both evidence and traditional Republican policy, Nixon's advisors pursued the blue-collar strategy even when it appeared to be failing before their eyes. The biggest problem was finding ways to continue the hard-hat angle while figuring out ways to discipline what was just beginning to compete with the administration's concerns about unemployment: inflation. And the president's staff had already decided what caused inflation—the economic demands of its hoped-for new ally, organized labor.

The building trades may have been the source of hard-hat national pride, but they were also one of the prime sources of pre–OPEC (Organization of Petroleum Exporting Countries) inflation. Wage increases in the industry were far outpacing those in manufacturing, and the powerful but fragmented craft unions prevented any easy top-down response to what was beginning to be an inflationary crisis in the industry. Nothing was more inflationary to construction users than the hated Davis-Bacon Act. The act, which requires contractors working on federal construction projects to pay the highest prevailing (thus union) wages to its workers, had been regarded as an inflationary pressure in the construction industry for many years. In February 1971, Nixon suspended the act after failing to get the unions to agree to a voluntary solution to rising labor costs. Even though the *Wall Street Journal* reported that the suspension "seemed to have undone all the administration's careful cultivation of the blue collar vote," the president was not plunging into the political darkness. The suspension had been secretly vetted ahead of time with all of the major building-trades leaders as well as George Meany, Lane Kirkland, and Teamster president Frank Fitzsimmons, among over a dozen others. Although New York City building trades leader Peter Brennan felt that there were other options that could have been pursued, he was kept tightly in the loop of the administration's decisions and still promised to "deliver 90% to our side in 1972." In ending the wage guarantee in the industry, the president had the agreement that leadership would grouse but not fight, and so his crafting of his official statement on the suspension in pro-worker terms would not seem completely absurd. "While some might wish to blame management or labor unions for this inflationary syndrome, we must recognize that, in fact, they are its victims," argued the President in his official statement. "The person who is hurt most by this pattern of inflation," he explained, "is the construction worker himself. For as the cost of building increases, the rate of building is slowed—and the result is fewer jobs for the workingman."[46]

Many saw Nixon's suspension of Davis-Bacon, oddly enough, as a victory for labor. The *New York Times* editorialized that the suspension meant that "The Construction Unions Win" because the administration's solution was really a tepid response to a situation that demanded more draconian moves. True, Nixon may have pulled his punches somewhat in order to avoid alienating his new allies. The administration put the act back in place barely over a month after rescinding it, obtaining the voluntary controls it had originally hoped for as the suspension got the attention of the unions "the way a two-by-four gets the attention of a mule" explained Labor Secretary Hodgson. The new "voluntary" controls by labor-management boards included heavy governmental pressure to control wages but gave the administration room to wiggle in order to placate friends in need. It did work, modestly, as first-year contract negotiation wage and benefits increases fell from 19 percent to 11 percent.[47]

Typically, if Nixon is remembered for his relationship with the building trades, it is usually for his Machiavellian support for the Philadelphia Plan. That emphasis is somewhat misplaced. Secretary of Labor George Shultz did explain to Nixon that the federal plan to integrate the building trades would help foment conflict between two core constituents of the New Deal coalition—labor and blacks. The idea of the program had lingered since the Kennedy administration as a reaction to grassroots organizing for integration of the trades in Philadelphia, and the president was always "tenuous" on the plan. His endorsement of it probably had more to do with outflanking the liberals and trying to flood the inflation-minded labor market—the same problem he struggled with in suspending Davis-Bacon—than anything else. His advisors explain that Nixon's commitment to the plan was always very limited, and most importantly, it was "short lived." As William Safire explained, the Philadelphia-type plans "lasted for a couple of years, until Charles

Colson's appeal to labor as a bloc in the 'new majority' took these matters out of [Attorney General] Mitchell's hands." Colson's blue-collar strategy won out, resulting in Arthur Fletcher, the plan's biggest advocate, being moved from the Labor Department to the United Nations.[48]

The biggest point of conflict was controlling wages in order to keep down inflation, which came to a head with the administration's New Economic Policy (ironically, the same name as Lenin's policies for the Soviet Union in the 1920s). Controlling wages and prices were of national concern, and one of the most popular ideas was to put federal controls on both. Nixon officially opposed such drastic measures, which smacked too much of World War II era government intervention. Labor traditionally opposed freezes largely because it was much easier to control wages than prices, and, of course, it violated one of the basic functions of unions, the freedom to negotiate contracts. Controls were an immensely popular idea among voters, however, and the AFL-CIO president publicly, if tepidly, endorsed controls on the presumption that Nixon would never actually implement them. If Meany had to have controls, the type he preferred were akin to the aggressive form used during World War II in order to ensure that prices as well as wages were kept down. When the president did what the polls had been telling him was popular, and what appeared to assist his re-election hopes— declare a ninety-day wage-price freeze in August 1971 (when he also most famously took the dollar off the gold standard)—what little shared common ground there had been quickly evaporated. The unions felt that corporations would easily raise prices well beyond the level that wages were pushing them up anyway, so it was easy to assume that wage-price controls were a way of disciplining wages. When the administration ruled that 1.3 million workers scheduled to receive wage increases negotiated before the freeze would not get their pay, labor's position hardened. Leonard Woodcock, president of the UAW, declared, if the administration "wants war, it can have war."[49]

The rupture between the AFL-CIO and the administration on the wage-price freeze forced the administration to tack away from the leadership strategy and back to the rank-and-file approach. Meany's open hostility to the freeze as a rich-man's plan showed his overreach, Nixon believed, and the rank and file—and certainly the public at large—was with the president on the freeze. As the *Washington Post* reported, Meany's battle with the president was a "gamble . . . by no means fully shared by American wage earners." The labor leadership's anger, however, was deep. When Shultz and Hodgson went to the AFL-CIO headquarters to explain the program, one labor official told Shultz, "When you take your ass out of here, get measured for a pair of tin pants because you are going to need them" implying that they would need extra protection where the unions were going to kick them. But labor had clearly fumbled the popularity of the freeze. As Herbert Stein recalled, the ninety-day freeze, which even Nixon was ambivalent about, "had instantly become the most popular economic action of government that anyone could remember."[50]

Given the popularity of the freeze, the AFL-CIO had to concede this round of political chess. Nixon knew that "Meany's overplayed his hand, and that's why he came back." Still, he admitted, "no program can work without labor cooperation" and the president welcomed union leaders in to shape Phase II of the controls to go into effect in November 1971. With Meany's reluctant buy-in on Phase II, Nixon launched a Price Commission and a Pay Board, with five members each from labor, business, and the public on the Pay Board. Meany was able to shape the board to his plans, including autonomy from the federal government, simply by threatening to walk out, after which the Nixon people had to appease the feisty plumber's demands. In fact, at the first meeting, Meany kept his overcoat on, claiming that it was chilly in the room but giving the appearance he was ready to walk out at any moment. The Pay Board remained deeply divided, and when the majority voted to deny retroactive payment of a wage increase negotiated to take place during the freeze, Meany stopped in his tracks. The sanctity of the collective bargaining contract had been violated. Nixon refused to meet with Meany on the issue to cut a deal. Nixon's advisors had already concluded that Meany will "spring lots of his opposition when he thinks it will do the most damage." Meany and the other labor leaders walked off the pay board in protest. Nixon, never one to take the high road, found himself resentful about "all those free breakfasts I gave that son of a bitch" during his attempts to win his support.[51]

VII

The real issues at stake devolved into a nasty symbolic showdown at the AFL-CIO convention in Florida. Toasts to the labor-Nixon relationship of the year before were soon overshadowed by a public relations double-cross in Miami. At the very last minute, Nixon decided to accept a *pro forma* invitation to address the labor convention, creating the forum for an ugly clash between two monumental egos and viscerally political animals around one issue: who was the voice of the American worker, Nixon or Meany? The administration decided the day before the convention to make a macho public relations play on what they called the "'Daniel into the Lions' Den' thesis"—a gutsy president strutting into the fortress of his enemies to boldly set the opposition straight. He planned on having a boilerplate speech to release—covering all the "dull routine standard stuff" that the administration had done for labor. The plan was for Nixon to get up to the podium, claim he stood behind everything in the official speech, then toss it aside and speak to the workers from his heart. In reserve, he had all of the "good stuff" about the dignity of the working class that had been building up in the blue-collar strategy that would be unleashed in a staged and memorized but "spontaneous" outreach to the common man—"straight from the shoulder, the way they like to hear it."[52]

Meany, in an era in which the machinations of organized labor were always big news, had other plans for the president—the lion's den was actually a trap. The day before Nixon's arrival, Meany slammed the entire administration in his keynote address, going so far as to claim that "we have no faith in President Nixon's ability to manage the economy of the nation." The next day, even though George Shultz had been assured that Nixon would be extended all of the "courtesies," Meany was ready to humiliate the president on labor's turf. Nixon walked into the convention with only a terse, one-sentence announcement, the band had been removed so they could not play "Hail to the Chief," the television cameras had been banned, and the president of the United States was seated in the second row on the platform behind Meany. He looked exhausted, having stayed up much of the night memorizing his allegedly extemporaneous speech. Meany had instructed the crowd not to respond to what Nixon said and even tried to get the executive council not to sit on stage with him, which the members rejected. Otherwise, it was the master snub. The audience occasionally applauded, but also snickered and groaned at the idea that the wage-price freeze was a success. When the pseudo-words-from-the-heart were over (which Meany recognized as a "corny act" that was "as old as the Republic"), the president moved to begin shaking hands with the conventioneers when Meany gaveled the convention to order and all but pushed Nixon out. Meany's ability to play both ends off the middle surfaced a couple of hours later when George McGovern took the stage and attacked Nixon's economic policies. Although Meany hated the senator's dovish foreign policy and would soon try to destroy his candidacy, he proclaimed to the convention, "Now we've heard the real gut issue."[53]

After events in Florida, Nixon's advisors became obsessed with the public spin on the humiliating appearance. The *New York Times* reported that the audience "reacted with polite hostility, punctuated occasionally by derisive laughter." Haldeman noted that there was "more emphasis on the rebuff by the labor people than on the P's courage," so the strategy became to change the news story to a "labor is rude to a courageous President." Nixon's immediate reaction was that "we can't make peace with the labor unions," but the president and his advisors agreed "not to martyr Meany or drive the union members to support him." They would continue the effort to woo the rank and file and hopefully let Meany hang himself. Editorial opinion, telegrams, and the polls after the convention showed little improvement for the president's actual ratings but clearly showed that the public had strong support for Nixon over Meany in the affair. In the aftermath, George Shultz, arguing against launching vengeful anti-labor legislation, explained, "we may be on the verge of a spectacular breakthrough, because our strategy, which was to neutralize the headquarters and to woo the locals, is working and now . . . the headquarters are falling apart at the seams and Meany's power is waning." They had to be very careful, Shultz was convinced, "not to send anti-labor signals from the White House and give Meany the leverage to get back on top." The *Los Angeles Times* summed it up best with a cartoon of Nixon and Meany arm wrestling—with Nixon winning.[54]

After Nixon's Florida speech, the president noted to Haldeman that "it'll be hard to make the Hoffa move right now," but move he did. Barely a month after the debacle in Florida, he cemented his relationship with the most trusted of his blue-collar backlash supporters, Frank Fitzsimmons of the Teamsters, when the president released Jimmy Hoffa from prison just before Christmas 1971. The president's commutation of his sentence included a proviso that Hoffa could not return to his lifeblood, union business, until 1980—the end of his original sentence. Hoffa claimed not to know about this stipulation in the terms of his release, learning about it only when reporters peppered him with questions once he was outside the penitentiary gates. He quickly concluded what many of his biographers believe, that a deal had been struck between Teamster president Frank Fitzsimmons and the Nixon administration (probably engineered by John Dean and the indomitable Charles Colson) to prevent Hoffa from returning to office. Hoffa showed no resentment toward Nixon but did vent considerable anger at Fitzsimmons, the person who was supposed to sit passively in Hoffa's place while he was in jail. In essence, "Fitz," as he was known, had gone from Hoffa's hand-selected puppet and place-keeper to, in Hoffa's words, a "liar" and a "double-crosser." But the Nixon administration loved Fitzsimmons: he was more New Majority than Meany, less volatile and skittish than other labor leaders with the exception of Brennan, far less independent than Hoffa, and believed to be capable of delivering an enormous bloc of votes to Nixon. He was simultaneously powerful, but sycophantic and highly seducible—the perfect and certainly the favorite lieutenant in Nixon's battle plans for the New Majority.[55]

The alliance with the Teamsters helped the administration defeat the farmworkers in California, a union that had been "targeted for destruction" by the Nixon White House. When the administration realized the consumer boycott gave the farmworkers leverage outside of the confines of the NLRA, they tried, unsuccessfully, to bring agricultural workers under the act's purview. Chuck Colson then helped orchestrate the Teamster war against the UFW. As Cesar Chavez tried to make public at the time, memos had already leaked showing that Colson had ordered the Justice Department, the Labor Department, and NLRB to stay out of the Teamster-farmworker disputes unless "you can find some way to work against the Chavez union." Another Colson memo explained, "The Teamsters Union is now organizing the area and will probably sign up most of the grape growers this coming spring and they will need our support against the UFW." The Teamsters supported Nixon, and Nixon supported the Teamsters in a joint effort to foster a working-class Right and defeat the Left.[56]

Despite Nixon's Machiavellian success with the Teamsters, labor leaders seemed to be snubbing the president's overtures by early 1972—especially when an exasperated Meany finally walked off the Pay Board in March (for which Nixon privately promised him a "kick in the ass"). As Colson aide George Bell saw it, "As I analyze our campaign in terms of support for the President from organized labor, it seems to me that on a national basis, we are in rather poor shape." The national leadership situation seemed in disarray, and the best hope was for a few endorsements from small independents and maybe some neutrality from a couple of large unions. The blue-collar strategy limped along into the 1972 election, vacillating between wooing the leadership or drumming up the rank and file. By the summer campaign season, the administration's strategic plans to win the hard hats looked good only compared to the disarray of the Democratic Party's relationship to its blue-collar base.[57]

VIII

Although George McGovern was en route to a highly contested Democratic primary victory, the man that the AFL-CIO hierarchy loved for the Democratic nomination was Henry "Scoop" Jackson—cold warrior extraordinaire, the "Senator from Boeing" as he was often called. In a speech in New York City (written in part by Ben Wattenberg, co-author of *The Real Majority*), Jackson laid out the problem in a distinctly Nixonian way. "The working people are also under attack from the left fringes, by people who would like to take over the Democratic Party. If this takeover were to succeed, the Democratic Party will lose in 1972 and be in deep trouble for years thereafter." Without directly naming George McGovern, he went on, "There are some people in the Democratic Party, who, intentionally or not, have turned their backs on the working man. They are either indifferent to him or downright hostile. Their cocktail parties abound with snide jokes about 'hardhats' and 'ethnics.' They mouth fashionable clichés about how workers have grown fat and conservative with affluence, and how their unions are reactionary or racist."[58]

Nixon did his best to ensure that a cultural conservative/hawk like Jackson or a moderate like the presumed front-runner Muskie would *not* get the nomination. Nixon wanted to run against an "extremist" like McGovern, so the Committee to Re-elect the President subsidized McGovern's campaign with a few surprises from the administration's bag of dirty tricks. Nixon operatives had planted the notorious "Canuck" letter that helped undermine centrist Muskie in New Hampshire by claiming he had used derogatory remarks against French-Canadians. When he went on the counter-attack, his emotions heightened while defending his wife against mean-spirited editorials. Then he appeared to weep as the New Hampshire snow fell on his cheeks. At the time, it was portrayed as a "breakdown" that made him appear fragile under stress. Also during the New Hampshire primary, the Nixon people made late night and early morning phone calls soliciting support for Muskie from people claiming to have just arrived from Harlem to help with the campaign. In Florida, Republican operatives put up posters saying "Help

Muskie in Busing More Children Now" by a fictitious group called the Mothers Backing Muskie Committee. The tricks went on through the primaries and, of course, culminated in the break-in at the Watergate hotel to bug Democratic Headquarters in June 1972.[59]

The most important thing that Nixon *may* have done in the realm of dirty tricks was to make sure that George Wallace ran as a Democrat rather than an independent. The Alabama governor ran as an independent in 1968, and the race between Nixon and Humphrey was deemed too close. If Nixon could ensure that Wallace would carve votes out of the Democratic Party, and let his populism give the party fits throughout the primary process, then 1972 would be in the bag. Nixon may have made material and political contributions toward that end. A large-scale federal investigation had been launched into Wallace's taxes. It looked like indictments would be forthcoming for his campaign supporters and his brother Gerald. Then on April 30, 1971, with no explanation, federal prosecutors announced a recession in the presentation of witnesses to the grand jury. Two weeks later, Nixon and Wallace met on the presidential helicopter. Then, according to columnist Rowland Evans, Postmaster General Blount was in Alabama for discussions— allegedly over shared interests in keeping a liberal Democrat out of the White House. The Grand Jury reconvened four months later, but by then only a handful of Wallace associates were indicted—all but one of whom had already broken with Wallace. In January 1972, the Justice Department declared it was dropping its investigation of Gerald Wallace. The next day, George Wallace announced he would be running as a Democrat. Although it may never be clear exactly what happened, events made it so that the Wallace candidacy was an asset for Richard Nixon. After the attempt on Wallace's life, Nixon sent John Connally to find out if he would run then as an independent. Wallace was in no shape to do so. Connally noted, "We might well say that this was the day the election was won." Nixon agreed to pay Wallace's staff for the remainder of the year.[60]

White House operatives viewed the messiness of the 1972 Democratic Convention as the final piece in their plans to build the New Majority. "McGovern's victory is not a popular victory; it is more a coup d'etat of the Democratic Party, where a youthful leftist and suburban leftist elite has deposed and ousted the traditional Catholic and Jewish leadership of the Democratic Party," explained Pat Buchanan. Speechwriter William Safire saw it as the obverse of 1964: "As Barry Goldwater was Lyndon Johnson's gift from the Gods, George McGovern was Richard Nixon's." By the summer of 1972, Richard Nixon, the man George Meany had called a "union hater" who would "make Taft-Hartley and Landrum-Griffin (labor laws) look pro-labor" back in 1968 appeared to be organized labor's new best friend.[61]

Labor leaders frequently spoke of the "kooks" and "fairies" attending the convention, but one of the more infamous of his nasty rhetorical moments came when a crusty, bitter, and immobilized George Meany described the debacle of the Democratic Convention in Miami to the national convention of the USW. Here Meany succumbed to the same cultural low-balling as Nixon, perhaps ironically contributing, in a small way, to the long-term decline of the economic dimensions of working-class identity. "We listened to the gay lib people—you know the people who want to legalize marriage between boys and boys and girls and girls," he declared in an attempt to gain support for his neutrality strategy. "We heard from the abortionists, and we heard from the people who look like Jacks, acted like Jills and had the odors of Johns about them." His snide rhetoric seems to be evidence for the idea that the New Politics-labor split was, in essence, about cultural values. It was, however, a play straight out of Nixon's book: rev up the troops for cultural battle even if the war was about political power rather than relevant issues. It did the trick. The conventioneers passed the non-endorsement resolution by voice vote, "with a considerable volume of disagreement from McGovern supporters."[62]

George Shultz, by then secretary of the treasury, increased his regular contacts and golf games with Meany in the summer of 1972 as the national campaign season approached. The conversations remained undocumented, but suggestions from the AFL-CIO hierarchy about how to campaign made it to the president through such back channels:

> The unions share Nixon's position on busing. Don't talk about defense in terms of jobs, talk about national security. Continue to fight the idea of amnesty. Don't worry about vetoing things like the clean water bill—'they don't want to be put out of jobs by environmental kooks anyway.' Run against inflation—not on the grounds that it's been solved. Most of all, they said, 'Stop pitching directly for the support of Democrats. It makes it seem like you're trying to break up the Democratic Party. You'll get more Democrats to vote for you if you don't remind them about being Democrats, or suggesting that you are a threat to the long-term continuance of the Democratic Party.'[63]

IX

Once George McGovern's nomination was secure, his candidacy gave the president the latitude necessary to portray himself as the candidate of the workingman and the Democrats as captured by the most effete and decadent elements of the permissive new liberalism. As the administration's "Assault Book" for the fall presidential contest argued,

> As the campaign progresses, we should increasingly portray McGovern as the pet radical of Eastern Liberalism, the darling of the New York Times, the hero of the Berkeley Hill Jet Set; Mr. Radical Chic. The liberal elitists are his—we have to get back the working people; and the better we portray McGovern as an elitist radical, the smaller his political base. By November, he should be postured as the Establishment's fair-haired boy, and RN postured as the Candidate of the Common Man, the working man.

Half jokingly, Buchanan and the other strategists suggested pushing even further into the lion's den, by suggesting that the Republicans take over the traditional place where Democrats launched their fall campaign: "How about RN going to Cadillac Square on Labor Day this year!!" McGovern helped by being unwise enough to tease that he would renounce his 1965 vote against the repeal of 14(b) of Taft-Hartley (the "Right-to-Work" provision), a relatively minor flaw in a pro-labor voting record that the AFL-CIO had bludgeoned him with, if Meany would proclaim that he was incorrect about Vietnam and the Cold War. This, of course, was a gold mine for the Nixon administration as all the staff had to do was wait for reporters to ask whether Meany, probably the second most prominent cold warrior in the country after Nixon, would renounce a lifetime of militant anti-communism.[64]

The proof of Nixon's newly found mettle on the labor issue came during the Republican platform fight. Ever since the New Deal, it had been Republican orthodoxy to claim to defend the nation and free enterprise against the corrupting forces of the labor bosses. They extolled the virtues of the core anti-labor laws, Taft-Hartley and Landrum-Griffin, "as if they had been written into the Constitution," explained Theodore White. When the Republican delegates on the Platform Committee gathered together to polish up the old anti-union shibboleths in 1972, however, they were stopped in their tracks by Richard Nixon. In his passionate desire to seduce the blue-collar vote away from the Democrats, he sent John Ehrlichman to oversee the crafting of the platform to ensure that the party would unilaterally end its official war with labor. As a result, the platform praised "the nation's labor unions for advancing the well-being not only of their members but also of our entire free-enterprise system." It was Nixon's less famous détente. "We salute," declared the Republican platform, "the statesmanship of the labor union movement." The man who declared he came to Congress "to smash the labor bosses" in 1947 was now declaring "There will be no anti-labor plank in this platform."[65]

However symbolic, the changes in the Republican platform were as concrete a gesture as Nixon made to his new constituency. The working-class appeal worked much like the campaign as a whole: a series of behind-the-scenes maneuvers tied together by imperial pronouncements. His nomination was more of a minute-by-minute planned coronation—complete with planned spontaneous demonstrations—and his campaign went down in history as the non-campaign, one that looked much more like a made-for-television tour. As the journalist David Broder accused, "The editors of the country and the television news chiefs ought to tell Mr. Nixon in plain terms, that before they spend another nickel to send their reporters and camera crews around the country with him, they want a system set up in which journalists can be journalists again, and a President campaigns as a candidate, not a touring emperor."[66]

As the election approached, Secretary of Labor James Hodgson tried to summarize Nixon's working-class appeal in an appearance at New York's Dutch Treat Club by arguing that "the worker's liberalism had been tied to bread-and-butter economic issues [and] when those issues were crowded from the center stage by more extraneous sociological concepts, the workers began to question sharply just where his self-interest lay." But even for white male workers, the Republican Party offered little of "bread-and-butter" value—comfort and solace but precious little bread. In many ways, the blue-collar strategy offered the worst type of identity politics—place of pride but place without economic substance.[67]

In the final push to get out the blue-collar vote for Nixon, the administration had one hundred thousand little stickers delivered to New York City that declared simply, "NIXON" above a hard hat emblazoned with an American flag. The campaign decals were designed to be just the right size to be placed on a workers' hard hat. There was, however, a problem: "*NO UNION BUG*" (the symbol that shows they were printed by a union firm) proclaimed a memo on one of the stickers, "*They're useless.*" The stickers never saw the light of day. While the Nixon people were able to marshal all of the symbols and pageantry of the blue-collar strategy, the underlying bedrock principle of unionism—protection of jobs and wages through solidarity—still remained an alien concept.[68]

When Richard Nixon won the largest electoral victory in American political history in 1972, he sat hidden away in his favorite office in the Executive Office Building alone with his devoted advisors, Bob Haldeman and Chuck Colson. Bob Haldeman dutifully thumbed through reams of election returns to tally the exact size of the president's landslide, calculations that would eventually lead to 62 percent of the popular vote, forty-nine states in the Electoral College, 57 percent of the manual worker vote, and 54 percent of the union vote. The increases in union and manual votes were some of the largest jumps in any category in that four-year interval, suggesting something particularly remarkable about the voting behavior of workers that year—whether due to the success of Nixon's strategy, the announcement that "Peace was at hand," the many failings of McGovern's campaign, or all three. The president himself certainly believed it was a strategic breakthrough. Basking in the private moment of a public victory, Nixon raised his scotch and soda to Charles Colson. "Here's to you Chuck," exclaimed the victorious president, "Those are your votes that are pouring in, the Catholics, the union members, the blue-collars, your votes, boy. It was your strategy and it's a landslide!"[69]

Writing in the halcyon days between Nixon's victory and the public imbroglio of Watergate, pamphleteer Patrick Buchanan claimed in a book titled *The New Majority*, that "the ideological fault that runs beneath the surface and down the center of the Democratic Party is as deep as any political division in America." The blue-collar, lower-middle-class ethnics and white Southerners "who gave FDR those great landslides" are now in rebellion against the "intellectual aristocracy and liberal elite who now set the course of their party." The 1972 election was for Nixon and the Republicans much like the 1936 election was for Roosevelt and the Democrats: the delivery of the common man to the party of Nixon. The election was, Buchanan claimed, a fundamental, semi-permanent realignment: "a victory of 'the New American Majority' over the 'New Politics,' a victory of traditional American values and beliefs over the claims of the 'counter-culture,' a victory of the 'Middle America' over the celebrants of Woodstock Nation."

Although his triumphant rhetoric came as the administration was about to crumble under the Watergate scandal, Buchanan claimed that 1972 "makes the long-predicted 'realignment of parties' a possibility, and could make Mr. Nixon the Republican FDR" and the New Right "the successor to the Roosevelt coalition."[70]

Charles Colson compared the victory celebrations to those of Andrew Jackson, when the doors of the White House were thrown open to the popular classes, but this time the elites were not the capitalists but the cultural elite:

> Christmas time at the White House, 1972, signified the changing of power from the citadels of the Ivy League, the Wall Street law firms and the mass media complex, to Main Street USA. The ordinary folks from the heartland— the shop steward, the electrician, the farmer—were the honored guests of an American President for the first time in generations. . . .
>
> The People filing through the White House the week before Christmas included the head of the Pittsburgh Boilermakers local, officers of the Polish American congress, an Italian-American priest, Teamsters officials, the head of the Policemen's Benevolent Association—the people who really form the heart of the New American Majority.

It seemed the counter-revolutionary moment might be at hand—"To the Nashville Station," chided the *National Review* in a country-and-western reordering of Edmund Wilson's *To the Finland Station*, an account of left-wing revolutionary emancipation. As the forward march of progressive politics seemed to be taking on a distinctly middle-class hue, and workers mobilized in a reactionary front, columnist Mike Royko declared that it appeared like Marxism "turned upside down." William F. Buckley's *National Review*, which was ambivalent about aligning its high-brow brand of conservatism with the new populist conservatism, envisioned Nixon's coalition as "the direct political descendents of Sockless Jerry Simpson, Mary Yellin' Lease, and General James B. Weaver," the populists of the 1890s, who were "bubbling with socio-cultural grievances" against the monopolies and trusts, but also the establishment and the modern world order as well. That very same energy, poured into defeating evolution in Dayton, Tennessee, in the Scopes trial, went underground in the era of the New Deal only to return under Nixon. "Plainly," continued the *National Review*, "the New Majoritarians are themselves descendants of the anti-modernists and anti-cosmopolitans" whom Williams Jennings Bryan defended against science and the modern world.[71]

X

Nixon entered his second term convinced that he could rely on the working-men's votes. He followed Eisenhower's move to bring a building tradesman into the cabinet by quickly tapping Peter Brennan, promoter of the hard-hat protests, to be his new—and rather incompetent—secretary of labor. The appointment of "Mr. Hardhat" not only fulfilled the long-standing idea of placing a labor leader in the administration, but also Brennan, the loud, tough-talking Bronx Democrat, in many ways symbolized the movement of a key constituent from the party of Roosevelt to an awkward position in the New Right. As a high-ranking building trades official and Democrat remarked, "It is a very clever move. It shows Nixon's hell-bent on reorganizing the Republican Party to include trade union elements. He's intent on breaking up the monolith of labor support for the Democrats." Colson reported that Brennan's goal in taking over the position would be to help the Republicans gain labor's "permanent allegiance," though Brennan later ended up feeling "very frustrated, like a caged lion."[72]

The Nixon administration had not counted on the weight of economic reality dragging down their lofty rhetorical appeals in the second term. The wage and price controls largely failed to provide a long-term tool for stabilizing the economy. The expansive economic policies also helped fuel inflation in the economy, which tipped to 8 percent in 1973. The real tragedy for the economic hopes of the administration, however, came from abroad. The developing world bit back in the 1970s from Saigon to Tehran, but no bite was as crippling as the OPEC decision to raise the price of oil.

The economic shocks of 1973 rattled the hopes of the blue-collar strategy, but Watergate destroyed them. The administration quickly became obsessed with covering up what John Dean reported to Nixon in March 1973 as the "geometrically" compounding "cancer" on the presidency. The AFL-CIO grew increasingly critical of the president with each new revelation about its abuse of power surrounding the Watergate scandal. Then, in an odd coincidence, the federation's convention took place on the same weekend as Nixon's "Saturday Night Massacre" in October 1973. George Meany reported that "This Administration has cast a dark shadow of shame over the spirit of

America. After five years of Richard Nixon, this great and once-proud nation stands before the world with its head bowed—disgraced, not only by its enemies abroad, but by its leaders at home." Already assembled in Florida, the executive council quickly gathered to ask for Nixon's resignation.[73]

The conservative *National Review* could barely hold back its venom at Nixon's squandering of the New Majority and the conservatives' political fortunes. In 1972, the journal was suspicious that the Republican Party could become the vehicle of a new governing coalition, but a year later, "Richard Nixon and the circle of political geniuses with whom he has surrounded himself have managed to devastate that possibility." With polling reaching all-time lows for Republicans in 1974, organized labor back in the Democratic column, and the blue-collar ethnics returning to their traditional party, it appeared that the administration had trashed the natural course of history. With Watergate, "what Nixon and his people have accomplished is to stand athwart history and sidetrack the formation of a new, dynamic non-liberal majority. It has been an astonishing accomplishment, achieved against all odds." Yet the *National Review* had changed its tune from snubbing the idea of blue-collar conservatism to naturalizing it. The magazine actually failed to give the president enough credit for sensing the prevailing political winds in the first place. As Nixon's speechwriter, William Safire, recalled, "With brilliance, panache, subtle understanding, and nefarious connivance, the new majority had been fused together, destined to hold sway for one election year; then, after Watergate, Meany would decide he had a good villain in Nixon, and the carefully built coalition would be smashed to smithereens"—yet only, one might add, for the duration of a couple of election cycles.[74]

XI

Richard Nixon was simultaneously the last president to work within the logic of the New Deal political framework of material politics, the first postwar president to try to recast the ways in which workers appeared in American presidential strategy, and the last to court labor seriously. While "struggling to change the political fortunes of the presidential Republican party by dressing it up as the congeries of the silent rather than the rich or propertied," in David Farber's formulation, Nixon helped to push the concept of "worker" out of the realm of production and helped drive a long process of deconstructing the postwar worker as a liberal, materially based concept. Knowing as he did that there was not a single working-class identity or a pure working-class consciousness, he sought to build political power out of new forms of discontent. As sociologist David Halle and others have argued, class consciousness, nationalism, and populism all have very blurry and overlapping edges; they bleed into one another and shape the presentation and representation of different sources of social identity. At any of the sources of workers' thinking about themselves, explains Halle, "there is an identity that contains the seeds of both a progressive and a reactionary response, and which one is dominant will depend on the possibilities people are presented with." Nixon grasped this basic sociology and sought to recast the definition of "working class" from economics to culture, from workplace and community to national pride. En route to his hoped-for New Majority, he paved the way for a reconsideration of labor that, in its long-term effects, helped to erode the political force, meaning, and certainly economic identity, of "workers" in American political discourse.[75]

As graceless as Nixon's ideas and plans might have been, he did attempt to fill a void in the nation's discussion of working people by drafting a powerful emotional pageantry around blue-collar resentments. In contrast, as the Democratic Party chased after affluent suburban voters and social liberals, historian Judith Stein argues, its leaders failed to "devise a modernization project compatible with the interests of their working-class base." Indeed Nixon may have been the last president to take working-class interests seriously, but his was less a "modernizing project" than a postmodernizing one. Lacking both resources and inclination to offer material betterment to the whole of the American labor force, Nixon instead tried to offer ideological shelter to those white male workers and union members who felt themselves slipping through the widening cracks of the New Deal coalition. In the end, Nixon's efforts were based too much on undercutting the opposition than building his own vision, and they were too subterranean for a time that cried out for explicit leadership. He sniffed out the anger and resentment of a constituency in drift only to try to win them with his own definitions of their problems.[76]

Nixon also based his strategic reasoning on political blocs that conflated workers with unions—a hypothetical unity that Ronald Reagan would successfully bifurcate a decade later. Nixon seemed to feel that all he had to do was command his aides to do the right things, get his representatives to say what people wanted to hear, woo the right leader, and pull the right political levers to draw the right blocs into his realignment. If the project to build the New Right worker was incomplete, as Jonathan Rieder suggests, "the crafting of a new culture of the Right, one more self-consciously grounded in appeals to the working and lower-middle classes, did not occur full-blown overnight." As one Democratic strategist explained at the time, "Nixon gnaws around the edges of a worker's life. He hasn't touched the central trade union part. But he gnaws a little at the Catholic part, a little at the Polish part, a little at the patriotic part and a little at the anti-hippie part. After a while, he has an awful lot of that worker."[77]

In December 1972, still basking in the afterglow of the election, Chuck Colson telephoned the president to report that they were receiving the "damnedest fan mail" about the appointment of Peter Brennan as secretary of labor. "You mean," said Nixon, "they finally think the appointment of a working man makes them think that we're for the working man? They talk about all the tokenism—we appoint blacks and that but they don't think you're for blacks. Mexicans, they don't think you're for Mexicans. But a working man, by golly, that's really something." Yes, explained Colson, "This kind of locked it up." As Colson continued, "The fundamental dichotomy here, the fundamental cleavage within the Democratic Party is such that with what you're doing to build the New Majority, and what I hope to help you do, I think we're going to keep them split, and I'm awful bullish about what we can do in this country."

"They may not ever become Republicans," Colson summarized; "but they're Nixon."[78]

4

I'm Dying Here

Merle Haggard and his band, the Strangers, stumbled toward the stage in matching powder-blue polyester suits. Readying for the gig, Hag pulled his mud-stained Stetson over his bleary eyes, obscuring both his smooth-faced good looks and a fifties-style pompadour grown loose and shaggy with the 1970s. When they arrived at the Nixon White House for the show, the band was on its third day of playing and partying during one of the "wildest tours" of the troubadour's career. As Haggard recalled, he and the boys showed up at Pat Nixon's 1973 birthday celebration "hung over, dead on our feet, and walking around in a daze"—hardly the picture of small-town morality that the president hoped to promote by inviting the country singer to perform.

Once on stage, Hag immediately sensed that he was in for a cool reception and silently wished he was anywhere other than in the presence of the president and his entourage. "I felt like I was coming out for hand-to-hand combat with the enemy," he recalled about the White House audience. As the band banged their way through the first two numbers, Haggard scanned the stiff, black-tie crowd for any signs of awareness of what he and the band were up to, but the audience simply sat there like "a bunch of department store mannequins." Digging deep into his bag of tricks, he turned to the Jimmy Rodgers classic "California Blues" in hopes that a song about the home state he shared with Nixon might do the trick. No luck there. Clearly the president, he concluded, "hadn't hung out at the same places I did." As Hag summed up the appearance, "I didn't expect the crowd to be as receptive as a Texas honky-tonk's, but I didn't expect them to be embalmed either."[1]

Merle Haggard's invitation to the White House was not because Richard Nixon was any kind of fan of country music—quite the opposite—but because it was part of the administration's continuing schemes to bolster the president's blue-collar appeal. Steel guitars may not have made Nixon's heart soar, but building political majorities did. Nixon's lieutenant Bob Haldeman, however, had to confess defeat to his diary that night. "The 'Evening' was pretty much a flop because the audience had no appreciation for country/western music and there wasn't much rapport," he wrote, "except when Haggard did his 'Okie from Muskogee' and 'Fighting Side of Me' numbers, which everybody responded to very favorably, of course." Indeed, Nixon's tin ear on the distinctions between country musicians surfaced when Johnny Cash was invited to play the White House earlier in the administration. The president's handlers requested that Cash play the backlash classics (written and performed by others) "Okie" and "Welfare Cadillac," both of which he refused to do, resulting in a minor tempest in the press. As Nixon confessed during Cash's appearance, "I'm no expert on music. I found that out when I told him to sing 'Welfare Cadillac,'" which, Cash's biographer explains, Johnny refused because he did not write it and "the song appeared to mock the poor."[2]

The path toward linking the Republican elites and the music of the common man might have been a rough one, but unlike many liberals who dismissed the twang, sentimentality, grit, and reactionary tendencies of country music in the early seventies, the White House overlooked its own musical tastes, convinced that country music could be marshaled in the fight for its New Majority. Country music, traditionally a southern working-class chronicle of lost souls and cheatin' hearts, had become valuable cultural territory in the decade's national political wars.

Nixon's attempt to build a cross-class cultural alliance was a paler shade of its opposite, a fun house mirror incarnation, of the 1930s Popular Front. During the Great Depression, artists, writers, performers, and intellectuals joined together in what Michael Denning called, in somewhat exaggerated terms, the "laboring of American culture." The worker and the CIO were the cause, and burying the sectarian hatchets of the Left in favor of the New Deal was the mood. By the early seventies, however, there was less a popular front than a cultural war as to what the "the worker" might be, as artists did battle over his (mostly, *his*) allegiance and representation. Nixon's tapping into performers like Haggard suggested the inverse of the Popular Front—

the emergence of a top-down cultural front for the Right. On the Left, in contrast, overtures from the counterculture to the working class were weaker—and sometimes hostile. Occasionally New Left filmmakers or countercultural performers offered the possibility of a cross-class alliance akin to the college students who entered the labor movement during the insurgencies of the early seventies. The country-rock movement or films like *Five Easy Pieces*, for instance, looked to blue-collar culture as a source of authenticity for a movement lacking roots and grounding. Others, who chose art over partisanship, like Sidney Lumet in his film *Dog Day Afternoon*, suggested that the problem may have been beyond politics—that, truth be told, there was a wholesale meltdown in working-class identity. Parts of the working class did go Right, parts did go Left, but mostly the "working class" in early seventies popular culture failed to congeal in a visible public form.

In the thirties, the Left had Okie troubadour Woody Guthrie; in the seventies, the Right had Merle Haggard and the number one hit on the backlash billboard, "Okie from Muskogee." "We don't smoke marijuana in Muskogee / We don't burn our draft cards down on Main Street," Haggard sang, "Cuz we like livin' right and being free." The same year that the Woodstock Nation basked in love, pot, and mud, at nearly the same historical moment that the lurking violence of the counterculture revealed itself at the bad trip at Altamont Speedway, and in the year that Black Panther Fred Hampton was gunned down in his bed by the Chicago police, the number one hit on the country charts celebrated a place where "We don't make a party out of lovin'" and "football's still the roughest thing on campus." It not only made Haggard into a hot commodity among Republican strategists for celebrating "a place where even squares can have a ball," but propelled him into stardom. His booking fees went through the roof, and the tune opened the floodgates to a wave of songs celebrating a defensive, chip-on-the-shoulder belligerency from other artists. It also created a stereotype of what Merle Haggard's music was about, which he struggled against for the rest of his career. As the *New Yorker* explained, "It is an unfortunate irony that Merle Haggard, probably the most musically diverse singer in country music, should be inextricably linked with a casual ditty—a passably catchy tune—that shifted attention from his musicianship, which is highly articulate, to his politics, which are not."[3]

Class consciousness had always been weak in country music, but its new populism meant that the genre in the seventies was typically contemptuous of those who did not work (on either end of the economic spectrum), suspicious of outsiders and strangers (whether by geography, race, or conviction), and antipathetic toward the uprooting of tradition (which tended to get pinned more on the state than the market). The new country attitude, the "redneck rebellion," was recasting American political iconography in the early seventies. The tensions between, on the one hand, a longing for roots and tradition, and, on the other, the maelstrom of modernity, gave country music "an appealingly rebellious yet conservative political identity for America's modern white working class." This happened at just the moment when key aspects of southern culture were becoming national culture. The easy battles of the early seventies were cultural more than economic, so that rebellious Americanism tended to be aimed at the permissive liberal/radical elite who served all too easily as the enemy of tradition. By emphasizing the cultural dimensions of working-class life over its material base in the early seventies, country offered a lot of rebellious attitude but certainly not much threat to capitalism.[4]

Not long before, country music had mostly been apolitical. Here again Nixon took his populist cues from George Wallace, who reportedly had a country act in every political rally since 1958. Wallace had even invited Hag to join his presidential campaign. Many country music fans were certainly drawn to Wallace's message, but it was not because the genre was innately reactionary prior to the seventies. The Alabama politician had simply sought out Nashville's support as no previous candidate had ever done. His rallies bordered on stage revues, with country performers, the bouffant-haired "Wallace girls," and the knee-slapping lines of the man himself. As Bill C. Malone argues, "Wallace and the country musicians shared a common ground, apart from ideology, in their origins in the southern working class with their common accents, religion, food tastes, and social memories." The candidate, he notes, "played the role to the hilt." Subsequently, any major country act that endorsed a candidate came out for either George Wallace or Richard Nixon in 1968 and, by 1972, the entire country music establishment became associated with the semi-mythic "Silent Majority." By the dawn of the seventies, as Malone argues, "for the first time in its history, country music began to be identified with a specific political position, gaining a reputation for being jingoistic and nativistic music."[5]

Rednecks and good ol' boys were suddenly everywhere—not just in country music but in movies like *Smokey and the Bandit* (1977), television shows like *The Dukes of Hazzard* (1979), and even political iconography in the form of Jimmy Carter's alter ego, brother Billy Carter. The term had moved successfully from pejorative to point of pride, with some exceptions such as the horrors of *Deliverance* (1972), in which the rural poor remained a frightening "other" to four adventurous Atlanta businessmen—not yet their cultural allies in a fight against the hippies as they would be in most seventies productions. The South was no longer a place inhabited by innocents as in the sixties with *The Andy Griffith Show*, *The Beverly Hillbillies*, or *Petticoat Junction*; by the seventies the southern white worker had become variously a defensive militant, a rebellious outlaw, or, most often, the most distinctly American of all groups. The redneck maintains a paradoxical combination of rebellion and patriotic nationalism—the state is his enemy, the nation his mystical identity—forged in honest if "alienated, body-wrecking, and mind-numbing" manual labor.[6]

So it is easy to understand that Nixon's entourage might not have grasped much of the material reality of Haggard's music, but they felt fine trying to tap into its populist resentments. They heard the anti-counterculture traditionalism, but they failed to see how Hag's fingernails still curled and bent because of prolonged exposure to the chemicals he used during his labors in the San Quentin laundry. They smelled political opportunity, but they did not recognize a character who really did seem like part of a Steinbeck novel. They sensed the potential for mobilizing Okies in support of the war and against the protestors, but they probably never noticed the initials PBS tattooed on his wrist, for Preston Boy's School, the juvenile home where he was imprisoned at the age of sixteen. And, while Nixon's men were more than a little familiar with political crimes, they knew little of the world in which stealing cars, breaking and entering, or doing hard time for material reasons were not uncommon. What Nixon's people saw in Hag's song was one thing: a rising star of a new anti-elitism, one pointed at cultural values and away from those responsible for economic conditions.[7]

Nixon was not alone in his calculations. It had only been a year before the White House gig that California's governor Ronald Reagan had granted Haggard a full and unconditional pardon for his long and sordid list of felonies and misdemeanors, which had led to the artist's incarceration in San Quentin. Haggard really had "turned twenty-one in prison" (in solitary confinement next to the condemned Caryl Chessman, in fact) just as he sang in his hit "Momma Tried." Back when many country singers really were outlaws, not just packaged as such, Haggard longed to escape the chains of his nefarious past rather than wear them as false badges of honor. Returning from prison to his beloved Central Valley, he helped build on Buck Owens'

"Bakersfield Sound" in the 1960s as a roots-based alternative to the slick, corporate-country music of Nashville. Despite his string of country music successes, he did not feel complete until the day that Reagan forgave his crimes. "I was no longer ex-convict Merle Haggard," the singer declared proudly about Reagan's pardon. "I was Citizen Haggard. I had outlived my past." Repaying the favor, Haggard appeared on a televised Republican fund-raiser with Reagan. His appearance on behalf of Reagan was an act of loyalty to those who stood in his corner—one of the more prized characteristics of working-class culture. "A lot of Democrats didn't think that someone who sang for a workingman's rights, as I had, should try to help a Republican win office. I don't judge a man by his politics, any more than I judge him by his color," Haggard recalled. "Reagan helped me in a way no one else had and no one else could. So when he called on me, his friend, for a favor, I was there—will be again should he need me."[8]

Ironically, the origins of the song that propelled Haggard and working-class identity itself to right-wing political fame were more circumstantial than consciously partisan. On tour, Haggard and his band motored past the exit sign to Muskogee, Oklahoma—presumably in a cloud of their own smoke—when one of the band members facetiously called out, "I bet they don't smoke no marijuana in Muskogee!" This quip led to a series of satirical riffs on what else they did not do in small town America besides dope: protest, burn draft cards, tolerate men with long hair and sandals, or riot on campus. But they did, the song finally declared, "fly old glory down at the court house" because they "like livin' right and being free." What started out as a joke among the punchy and road-weary musicians quickly evolved into a novelty song and then, rather unexpectedly, into a political anthem that helped to define the politics of a white, male working class drifting away from the politics of economic empowerment toward those of cultural pride and social resentment. The runaway success of the tune was a little unexpected. The first time Hag performed the number publicly, he had to play it three times in a row to a demanding crowd. Clearly, he had hit a populist nerve as his song shot to the number one position on the country charts. Newly elected president Nixon sent Haggard a note of congratulations, and Reuters proclaimed that "Haggard has tapped, perhaps for the first time in popular music, a vast reservoir of resentment among Americans against the long-haired young and their underground society. Those who condemn the hippies' refusal to work, their drugs, pacifism and eccentric costume, have taken the song as an anthem of their unvoiced approval for the traditional values of small-town America."[9]

As for so much of the seventies working-class revival, hovering in the background of Hag's thinking was the Great Depression. In the thirties, the issues somehow seemed clearer, the struggle more concrete than the diffuse and complicated issues of the seventies. "There were so many things I loved about the thirties," Haggard explained, "I could find many reasons for wanting to live back there. . . . America was at the dawn of an industrial age, coming out of a depression into war. . . . Then again, the music was young. So many things were being done in music; it was wide open back then, electronics had not yet been involved, and basically it was *real*." Haggard was often praised for his Guthriesque odes to the era, such as "Mama's Hungry Eyes" and "They're Tearing the Labor Camps Down." His fascination with trains, his association with the Okie experience, his desire for a simpler time, are all suggestive of the nostalgia for lost tradition that permeates country music. It also hints at the shadow that the Great Depression cast over the present—it was both celebrated as a time of struggle but feared as something that could return. James Talley put that fear at the center of his song, "Are they Gonna Make Us Outlaws Again?" Dolly Parton framed the ambivalence of nostalgia for the Depression best in the title to her oft-covered song, "In the Good Old Days, When Times Were Bad."[10]

I

By the 1970s, "Okie," like the term "redneck," had become nationalized. Once it referred specifically to the uprooted peoples of the Southwest who headed to California during the Great Depression—most famously illustrated in Steinbeck's *The Grapes of Wrath*—but the ideal had grown from a specific group of down-trodden migrants to a conglomerate of American identity. The Okies were less a piece of American history bound in time and place than they were a collage built from fragments of collective memory, history, and current events: the Depression, Dorothea Lange's photographs, John Steinbeck's fiction, Woody Guthrie's music, John Ford's film, and Merle Haggard himself. By the 1970s, Okies had grown from marginalized and impoverished southwestern migrants to a broader idea, as James Gregory put it, of a "people who have known suffering, who are tough enough to rise above it, who can be guilty of redneck intolerance, even as they never forget the 'essentials,' namely, that ordinary folk are the guts and sinew of American society." The identity was no longer tied to region or time, but had become the title of an American working-class pastiche, "constructed out of symbols appropriated from the heritage of an entire nation."[11]

Like the Nixon-McGovern campaign itself, the canonization of Okies and rednecks in the seventies marked the triumph of the "reddening of America" over the counterculture's "greening of America." The old defiant regionalism became a murkier but appealingly defiant nationalism, a populist conservatism that held federal programs, urban life, women's rights, and "special privileges" for blacks in bitter contempt. Not surprisingly, however, the growth of country-based nostalgia served to cover the tracks of more profound issues that were recasting southern distinctiveness into American homogeneity: urbanization, suburbanization, Republicanization, and the growing dependence on federal dollars of the Sunbelt economy. In the 1974 book *The Americanization of Dixie*, John Egerton writes, "The South and the nation are not exchanging strength as much as they are exchanging sins; more often than not, they are sharing and spreading the worst in each other, while the best languishes and withers." That was certainly the case in the national discourse over working-class identity. What writer Kirkpatrick Sale called *The Power Shift* from the Northeast to the South rested *not* on a national commitment to the small-town Muskogee ideal, but on the realities of investment in the Sunbelt: corporate agribusiness, federal defense dollars, aerospace, oil, and tourism.[12]

In celebrating the trials and tribulations of the hard life, "redneck chic" functioned as a cultural antidote to the economic and demographic changes of the seventies. The country and western records—and the cowboy boots, Confederate flags, tickets to stock car races, and chances to ride mechanical bulls—sold in much greater numbers than could be sustained by the genuine article. It was really the spread of the "demi-rednecks," as Bruce Schulman calls them, who adopted the posture of Nixon's conservative working-class populism as a tamed and sanitized form of rebellion against an increasingly homogenous and effete national world of suburbs, service work, and corporate consolidation.[13]

"The Second War Between the States" for investment, as a *Business Week* headline dubbed it, had its own pop culture variation: a regional battle of the bands. "Southern man, better keep your head," sang Neil Young in his indictment of Dixie, "Southern Man" (1970); "Southern change gonna come at last." His references to the "bull whips crackin'" were a decade late (and implied the South alone had the corner on American racism), and, to white southern ears, certainly sounded pious and contemptuous—a ready formula for raising the hackles of regional defensiveness. The members of Lynyrd Skynyrd responded in kind to "Southern Man" as well as Young's follow up "Alabama" (1972), telling audiences to "turn it up" as they launched into a defense of the homeland, "Sweet Home Alabama" (1974). Skynyrd, a Florida group playfully named after the lowest form of authority, the band mates' high school gym teacher, had captured the new southern rock sound better than any other. They fired back,

Well I heard Mister Young sing about her
Well, I heard ole Neil put her down
Well, I hope Neil Young will remember
A Southern man don't need him around anyhow

While Skynyrd told Neil to mind his own business, they also admitted there were problems. "In Birmingham they love the governor / Now we all did what we could do," they sang about George Wallace followed by an ambiguous "boo, boo, boo." Symbolic of something larger about the early seventies, Young, and almost everyone else, had to admit that Skynyrd had the better song even if the politics were less uplifting. Like the revival of ethnic identities—Kiss Me, I'm Italian or Irish or Greek the t-shirts used to say—the sentiments at the foundation of "Sweet Home" and the Confederate flag hanging behind the band crossed the line between an affirmation of whiteness and a subjugation of blackness. In 1975, the members of Skynyrd stood on stage before thousands of fans in Tuscaloosa and accepted honorary positions as lieutenant colonels in the Alabama state militia. The governor presenting was George Wallace.[14]

For all of the backlash impulses in "Sweet Home Alabama" it was, like Haggard's "Okie," an outlet for pride more than anything else. "My father came from the [Muskogee] area," Haggard explained, "worked hard on his farm, was proud of it and got called white trash once he took to the road as an Okie." Born in a boxcar to migrant parents in Oildale, California, Haggard staked his identity and the meaning of the song most directly to the chorus. "Listen to that line," Hag explained, "'I'm *proud* to be an Okie from Muskogee.' Nobody had ever said that before in a song."[15]

Richard Nixon understood. He sent speechwriter William Safire into the occupational wilderness to speak to some real workers and return with material on the importance of working class pride. "What's happening to the willingness for self-sacrifice that enabled us to build a great nation, to a moral code that made self-reliance part of the American character?" Nixon asked in his Labor Day radio address. "We must give more respect to the proud men and women who do work that is all too often considered 'menial.'" Indeed, at its heart, Haggard's immensely popular song was in the same "forgotten man" category as Pete Hamill's expose, Chuck Colson's strategies, Scammon and Wattenberg's political analysis, and George Wallace's campaign. Pride in work often remained directly or indirectly a main theme in all categories. "The lyrical insistence on the heroic qualities of blue-collar jobs," wrote two critics of the decade, "may be an ideological assertion of working-class worth in the face of urban white-collar ways." The inability of McGovern, the Left, or the liberals to make more than minor headway with this tension—while the Right basically cleaned up—is the essence of working-class political and cultural history of the seventies.[16]

Robert Altman's 1975 film *Nashville* attacked the faux folksiness and artificial grit of the seventies Southern cult and revealed the Nixonesque manufacturing, commodification, and broadcasting of a Warholian festival of the people. The movie may have been set in Nashville, with rootless characters descending upon the city like moths to a vague light of fame and power, but, like the new country attitude itself, the city only serves as a cultural hub for its real subject, America. *Nashville* moves, agonizingly, toward a vivisection of politics, country music, and the dissolution of the national narrative in what one critic called "an X-ray of the era's uneasy political soul." For the viewer, Altman creates a craving for authenticity that is never satiated with anything more than empty cultural calories and political junk food. Social critic Christopher Lasch might well have been watching *Nashville* when he noted in the seventies, "Today Americans are overcome not by the sense of endless possibility but by the banality of the social order they have erected against it."[17]

Throughout the movie, a truck fitted with a loudspeaker makes announcements about the coming of the "Replacement Party," although, appropriately enough, nobody seems to listen to the obnoxious political drumbeat. While the political campaign might resonate with the candidacy of a George Wallace, there is really no sense of what the candidate of such a party might stand for; yet everyone is expecting some sense of deliverance. Conflict

between generations, the emptiness of death, the vacuity of politics, and the
pre-fabrication of social life are all captured in the film's chaotic *cinéma
verité* style, oddly enough, in a society without much *verité* to offer. In one of
the great platitudes of a movie awash in discomforting platitudes, one character sings over all sorts of strife in the studio, "We must be doing somethin'
right to last 200 years"—the best that can be mustered on the eve of the nation's bicentennial. In the end, the loose strands of the film come together in
a festival of politics that ends with the film's single moment of awful authenticity when an assassination rips through the rally. The tone of the film
abruptly changes with this echo of the sixties, as devastation, blank looks,
and a song actually sung from the heart overtakes the vacuous culture that
had dominated the film. Given the terror of reality, it is no wonder that the
characters of *Nashville* choose to live the cultural lie. "You may say that I
ain't free," triumphantly twangs the unifying aural backdrop to the film,
"but it don't worry me."

Yet the weightlessness of *Nashville* may not have been so surreal, as it only
matched Richard Nixon's performances of reality. In the spring of 1974,
when Nixon's presidency was in the throes of the Watergate crisis, he went
on the road to save his faltering reputation by turning to the real city of
Nashville to shore up his support with the common horde. With the House
Judiciary Committee about to launch its impeachment inquiry, Nixon attempted to soften up his congressional critics by appealing directly to the
people. Part of his strategy consisted of appearing on the stage of the Grand
Ole Opry and performing yo-yo tricks with country legend Roy Acuff. (As
one critique quipped, the silliest image of a president, that of Calvin Coolidge in a war bonnet, could now be laid to rest with the new image of
the leader of the free world twirling a yo-yo.) With George Wallace seated
prominently in the front row, Nixon told the audience, "Country music radi-
ates a love of this nation—patriotism." "The Peace of the world for generations," he continued, "maybe centuries, may depend not just on our military
might or wealth but on our character, our love of country, our willingness to
stand up for the flag, and country music does just that." Although not enough
to save his presidency, for reasons stretching deep into the American psyche,
such paeans to the *herrenvolk* republic resonated more effectively than George
McGovern's quoting of Woody Guthrie's "This Land is Your Land" at the
Democratic Convention.[18]

The ever-shrewd Nixon intuitively grasped the nationalization of the
southern working-class identity, as his infamous "Southern Strategy" to

complete the conversion of the region from Democratic to Republican showed. "The South," he argued in a private session with advisors, "is finally teaching the Democrats a lesson—not because they think I'm a racist, they know I'm not, but because they're proud, because they care about a strong national defense, about patriotism, about life-styles, about morality. I don't satisfy 'em on race. But southerners have basically the same sort of characteristics as a lot of union leaders—a belief in abiding by the law, and respect for the presidency."[19]

II

In the public imagination, semi-mythical places of country attitude like Muskogee, Oklahoma, evolved into a political and geographic counterpoint to Woodstock, New York, site of the famous 1969 music festival. One was southern, western, gritty, masculine, working class, white, and soaked in the reality of putting food on the table; the other was northern, eastern, radical, effete, leisurely, affluent, multi-cultural, and full of pipe dreams. One was real, the other surreal; one worked, the other played; one did the labor, the other did the criticism; one drank whisky, the other smoked dope; one built, the other destroyed; one was for survival, the other was for the revolution; one died in wars, the other protested wars; and one was for Richard Nixon, the other was for George McGovern. It was that sense of reality, a grounding in life's lived circumstances, that gave the productions of the cultural Right their authority—even when they were being manipulated, and drained of content, from the top.

The press referred to two separate events in the early seventies, with dramatically different contents, as the "Workers' Woodstock." One was Lordstown, where auto workers attempted to recast the meaning of work and their relationship to the assembly line in a youthful and inter-racial rebellion against GM. The other was the construction workers' counter-demonstration in New York against the anti-war protesters after Kent State. That both of these incidents, with nearly diametrically opposed political implications, were labeled as the "Workers' Woodstock" by different commentators is suggestive of the complex tensions running through northern, industrial working-class identity. While the reactionary "Woodstock" of the hard hats received more media play than did the Lordstown-type insurgencies, there were some promising spaces of compromise and reconciliation in the cultural fragmentation. If the hard hats were on the right and Lordstown workers on the left, if Muskogee was country and Woodstock was rock 'n' roll, then the new thing called "country rock" might have been the dialectical synthesis of the age for the labor Left. It was, perhaps, the musical equivalent of the New Left colonizers who went to the plant gates to organize workers or akin to rank and filers like Eddie Sadlowski or Arnold Miller who united the thirties and the sixties in their insurgencies against the official families of the establishments.

When facing cultural exhaustion, rock innovators typically refresh the genre by dipping into either of its two main tributary streams: African-American blues or white country ballads. In the early seventies, it was country music's turn. Rock 'n' roll had lost much of what had given it authenticity by the early seventies, having largely drained the current of black blues reinvented and redelivered to American shores by the British invasion. As an antidote to the narcissistic culture of bloated guitar solos, stadium audiences, hard drugs, and private tour jets that would go on to dominate corporate rock of the decade, the innovators of the era turned to white country music for inspiration and to rekindle the lost sense of authenticity.

The creation of country rock that dominated the early seventies was, symbolically and culturally, the type of cross-class alliance on which working-class success had always depended. According to *Rolling Stone* editor Jann Wenner, it was "the music of reconciliation," an attempt to fill the gap between the rock 'n' roll Left and the country Right, between the grand designs of the youth movement and the grit of people who worked for a living. At worst, explains Peter Doggett, rock's tendency to incorporate "a banjo or a blare of bluegrass harmonies became a self-conscious totem of American identity, a statement that the artist was speaking for a nation, not a youth movement or cultural elite." The synthesis of country, rock, and pop was at least as old as Hank Williams, however, and the genealogical thread ran through Sun Records to Dylan's *Nashville Skyline*, and it stumbled toward maturity when Bob Dylan appeared on stage at the Grand Ole Opry with Johnny Cash in 1969. It arguably peaked with Gram Parsons' solo albums of the early seventies and the growth of "Redneck Rock" in Austin, Texas, before quickly fading into the "peaceful easy feeling," the campfire mellowness, the enlightened apathy, of bands like The Eagles. For all of the liberal criticism of redneck culture for the debasing of the urbanity of American civilization—what one writer called the takeover of "Red Necks, White

Socks, and Blue Ribbon Fear"—few have adequately explored the failure of the Left to create an alternative cultural synthesis that could appeal to the white working class.[20]

Arguably, there may have been more space for a cross-class cultural alignment than a quick survey of the era might at first suggest. Haggard, like much of the backlash, was more complex and ambivalent than the belligerence and resentment suggested in the lyrics of "Okie." As Haggard later explained, the song made "me appear to be a person who was a lot more narrow-minded, possibly, than I really am." Even the Grateful Dead loved his stuff and had once embraced him as the new Woody Guthrie. As Jerry Garcia explained, "We're kind of on the far fringe of it, but we're part of that California Bakersfield school of country-and-western rock 'n' roll—Buck Owens, Merle Haggard. We used to see those bands and think, 'Gee, those guys are great.'" Haggard even expressed some sympathy for the counterculture and, like many working-class Americans, uncertainty on the war, while never wavering in his belief that the protestors' methods were wrong. "I don't mean if they could have changed the whole world situation that it might not have been better," Haggard explained, "[but] it irritated me a little bit to see 'em roaming the streets and bitching and burning and not really coming up with any answers to anything. So some of the frustrations came out in different songs." He even attempted to temper the message of "Okie" in his follow-up recording, "Irma Jackson," a tale of inter-racial love— "there's no way the world will understand love is color-blind," he sang—but the record machinery refused and demanded more redneck anthems. They got them in the militant singles "The Fightin' Side of Me" and "Workin' Man Blues."[21]

Meanwhile, the search for a politics of authenticity that informed, and ultimately failed, the Port Huron generation had collapsed in the face of formal politics by the 1970s. Out of that rubble emerged a more achievable but limited individual, cultural liberation. The turn in rock 'n' roll toward what Mark Marqusee calls "the release of inhibitions, in self-expression and communal joy" in the late sixties also meant a turn away from art grounded in tradition, in community, and hard work celebrated by artists like Cash and Haggard. Working people largely believed that a good time could certainly be had, but communal joy—and certainly the release of inhibitions—were misguided goals. Bob Dylan's 1967 experiments that became known as the "Basement Tapes" reflected the advance party of a generation's voyage that had given up on people's politics. The artist who began in the guise of working-class hero Woody Guthrie and who debuted for many at the March on Washington ended in the individual cultural release but with "no popular-front optimism" and "no faith in progress, democracy or the people." Dylan's path in the sixties was largely a retreat from what he saw as stale and deadening political realities, and toward the pursuit of the "politics" of innocence, spontaneity, and personal authenticity. As Marqusee boldly argues, such a "retreat may be a palliative, but it is not a cure."[22]

Gram Parsons, one of the creative forces behind country-rock, consciously avoided protest songs in favor of what he liked to think of as "Cosmic American music." Parsons was a Southerner from old money who could readily afford to drop out of Harvard to explore drugs and rock 'n' roll. Willie Nelson described him as the "real link between country, rock 'n' roll, blues, that whole thing." Having lived in the eye of the psychedelic storm of California rock in the sixties, Parsons searched for a rock 'n' roll identity that could fuse the history of music from Elvis to Merle. With his own mournful rural themes, steel guitars, and wistful lyrics, as his biographer explains, Parsons "tried building bridges, by way of music, between rock and traditional country—two worlds separated by age, politics, life-style, and musical tastes." Troubled by the rootlessness of his generation, Parsons attempted to reconstitute the dissolving sense of self he witnessed around him by infusing his music with the richness of traditional country forms. In his 1973 "A Song for You," he envisions saving his aimless generation by seeking refuge among the rural people. He asks for guidance to the dance floor—even if people will not tolerate his looks or his habits:

> Some of my friends don't know who they belong to
> Some can't get a single thing to work inside
> So take me down to your dance floor
> And I won't mind the people when they stare
> Paint a different color on your front door
> And tomorrow we will still be there[23]

The Confederate flag hanging behind the band during his performances was a reminder of his geographic background, but his life's material circumstances were the opposite of those that informed Haggard's sensibilities.

But Parsons loved Hag. "Merle Haggard is a great artist and a great person, a great human being. Great everything," proclaimed Gram Parsons about his hero. Having survived the kind of life that Johnny Cash only wrote about, Haggard was the real deal for Parsons. Gram Parsons blew his chance, however, like he blew his life. When Parsons showed up at Hag's place in Bakersfield hoping to convince him to produce his next album, the Bakersfield legend would not have anything to do with him. Although the details of the story are highly contested, journeyman player Chris Hillman put it this way: "Gram was drunk. So Merle quit." It's not like Hag knew his alcohol—"Tonight the Bottle Let Me Down" rings personal—but what remained of craft pride among country music meant being able to crank out saleable music in a reasonable time—not by showing up in the studio either drunk or on smack, and Parsons liked to do both. As Richard Doggett asked rhetorically, "Why should the poet of the American working man waste time on a hippie who wanted to be a country star?" The working class was not the cultural Left's playground. Parsons died of an overdose not too long afterward, with alcohol and chemicals numbing him to death in a cement motel room in Joshua Tree, California, when he was twenty-six years old.[24]

As the quick answers to the questions of the sixties never came, the political Left looked to organize workers during the insurgencies of the early seventies, but much of the counterculture began to make plans for an exodus—be it to colonize farms in Vermont, build utopias in Mendocino County, or make a more metaphorical retreat into their own communal consciousness. The national consciousness proved less responsive to the baby boomers' demands than they had been raised to believe, which resulted in fantasies of leaving and starting anew. This was fueled by the impending sense of a possible nuclear—and certainly social—apocalypse that haunted the Cold War political imagination.

David Crosby's "Wooden Ships," written along with an ensemble of sixties rockers on his boat off the coast of Florida, best captures the sentiments of searching out a higher plain on which to rebuild civilization afresh—far from the common man who drags him down. The song begins with the muffled dialogue of two post-apocalypse survivors meeting and then moves quickly, and brightly, to the narrators' collective and harmonious search for a land on which to launch a new society far from the wreckage and the madness of that which they must leave behind. There are "Wooden ships on the water, very free, and easy / Easy, you know the way it's supposed to be." To find that paradise, however, the old corrupt world that refuses to follow the enlightened path must be abandoned:

> *Go take a sister, then, by the hand*
> *Lead her away from this foreign land*
> *Far away, where we might laugh again*
> *We are leaving, you don't need us*

Yet not everyone with similar sentiments agreed. Like a Bobby Kennedy delegate who did not know the campaign was over, Jackson Browne penned his brilliant 1973 song of vigil "For Everyman" as the seventies' direct response to the exodus of "Wooden Ships." Browne, keenly aware that the many ways in which the idealism of the sixties was hardening into the cynicism of the seventies merely increased the impulse to flee, took an anti-sixties position: he would remain to play out political fate with those whom FDR called "the forgotten man." Browne knew both the emptiness of retreat as well as the improbability of success without building some sort of democratic majority—despite the cultural differences.[25] He was so convinced that his song was the statement of the decade, in fact, that the typically cautious Browne blurted out to an interviewer that he was working on the "motherfuckin' hit of the seventies."

Perhaps Browne was not completely convinced of his own stated convictions, but he knew that he had chosen the only viable option: a lifelong alliance with people he neither understood nor with whom he could always agree. His voice has a reedy equivocation to it and the lyrics honor the desire to run, both of which add ambivalent dimensions to his determination to work it out with the Silent Majority:

> *Everybody I talk to is ready to leave*
> *With the light of the morning*
> *They've seen the end coming down long enough to believe*
> *That they've heard their last warning*
> *Standing alone*
> *Each has his own ticket in his hand*
> *And as the evening descends*
> *I sit thinking 'bout Everyman*

Anyone who thinks they can make it without those whom the Old Left liked to call "The Masses" are free to make a go of it, but, reminds Browne,

Somewhere later on you'll have to take a stand
Then you're going to need a hand

We rise and fall together, he notes, as he reminds his listeners of the futility of a holier-than-thou politics of marginal groups. As one critic put it, Browne "internalized the remains" of Bob Dylan's search for answers "and still dares to hope for solution" in the lingering twilight of post-sixties hope. He notes that his commitment to the people is antiquated—it was "Long ago," he admits, that "I heard someone say something 'bout Everyman."[26]

The album by the same name, *For Everyman*, is thematically wound around the problem of confronting what to do about the counterculture's inability to bend the regular folks to their will. He has the problem right, but the futile ache in much of the album reveals his despair about linking common man and counterculture. In a track that comes earlier in the album, "Our Lady of the Well," he actually does leave and has fled to some form of indigenous community or commune (referred to simply as "people in the sun"). He admires the way they live there and craves it for himself, lamenting, America is in the shadow of "a cruel and senseless hand," but he takes faith that there are "some hearts" in which "love and truth remain." His exile cannot last since he remains wedded to the people of his country to whom he must return. Jackson Browne's courage to remain with "everyman," even though he is neither comfortable nor even convinced it will lead to a brighter day, is unique in seventies popular culture. It might be an old-fashioned concept to build some semblance of solidarity with the common horde, but he has no other option if he is to live a socially and politically fulfilling life other than to stand together with the Wallaceites, the hard hats, and the people who returned Nixon to a landslide second term.[27]

As rock 'n' roll emerged from the fads of the psychedelic scene in the late 1960s, Robbie Robertson, the great guitar virtuoso for The Band, was another of the era's leaders in both the white roots revival and a more progressive cross-class alliance. Critic Greil Marcus effectively describes The Band's momentum: "against a cult of youth they felt for a continuity of generations; against the instant America of the sixties they looked for the traditions that made new things not only possible, but valuable; against a flight from roots they set a sense of place." While vocal young Americans spent the decade displaying badges of alienation, decrying Amerika, and worshiping in the cult of cultural innovation, as Canadians The Band could embrace the "land that had kicked up the blues, jazz, church music, country and western, and a score of authentic rock 'n' roll heroes." Displaying an almost mystical connection to the rich Gothic complexities and midnight energy of all things American, Robertson wrote "King Harvest (Has Surely Come)" from a hideaway in Woodstock, New York—at about the same time Hag wrote "Okie" and after Robertson had finished reading the Okie epic, *Grapes of Wrath*.[28]

Robertson, whose credentials might suggest another, more contemptuous, path, holds out for a very different concept of the working-class community than others of his generation. In "King Harvest," the indignities of working-class life are overcome not in Haggardesque cultural pride, but in affirmation of the land and the power of the labor union. The song, optimistic, full of desire, and grounded in its setting, declares its labor commitment through an idealized historical community with the shared understandings necessary for social life. Here, the culture that country music celebrated requires economic defense:

> *I work for the union 'cause she's so good to me;*
> *And I'm bound to come out on top, that's where I should be.*
> *I will hear ev'ry word the boss may say,*
> *For he's the one who hands me down my pay.*
> *Looks like this time I'm gonna get to stay,*
> *I'm a union man, now, all the way.*

The setting is the rich time of harvest, the real time of life's fulfillment, in which it is the land itself that offers the worker a future, if only the boss can be controlled: "And then, if they don't give us what we like / He said, 'Men, that's when you gotta go on strike.'"

The longing at the center of the self-titled album, *The Band*, is a product of its unresolved tension between the experiences of different eras—the confusion of the present and the search for roots in the mystics of working-class history. The album was "made to bring to life the fragments of experience, legend, and artifact that every American has inherited as the legacy of a mythical past," writes Greil Marcus. "The songs have little to do with chronology; most describe events that could be taking place right now, but most of those events had taken on their color before any of us was born." The mood and the feel of the song make the same bridge between the thirties and the dawn of the seventies as did Merle's "Okie." As Robertson explained in less abstract terms, the song attempts to recapture the original vision of what organized labor was supposed to be about—before Tony Boyle's thugs made the cover of the papers for murdering dissident mine workers' leader Jock Yablonski and family and before the stale bureaucratic unionism of George Meany. "It's just a kind of character study in a time period," explained Robertson. "At the beginning, when the unions came in, they were a saving grace, a way of fighting the big money people, and they affected everybody from the people that worked in the big cities all the way around to the farm people," he continued. "It's ironic now, because now so much of it is like gangsters, assassinations, power, greed, insanity. I just thought it was incredible how it started and how it ended up."[29]

The Band's uncanny ability to tap into American culture—and to play with the past in such a way as to make it feel like the present, that is, to blur the Depression and the early seventies—is based, as John Street argues, on a paradox. The Band and other more class conscious artists' "success in creating a sense of community and in evoking past images to forge contemporary links also led to their failure in the mass market." Robertson's working class is captured through the same hazy lens as George McGovern's. Labor is fine when it is idealized, when it is pure in the struggle, but much less attractive in compromise, relative affluence, and in its institutionalized form. It was the problem of the New Left encapsulated; the same issue that concerned Jackson Browne. "The community they helped to forge identified itself *against* the rest of the people," continues Street, "not as part of them." Robbie Robertson attempted to recapture the power of workers' collective action for the seventies but did so for a rather limited and elite audience. Haggard, in contrast, played to a mass audience mobilized by images of cultural pride and individualism. White working-class America wanted more Muskogee and less Woodstock—even when Woodstock attempted to speak in their terms.[30]

While some popular music sketched out the possibility of a greater connection between Muskogee and Woodstock, the country-rock reality fell to less compelling or interesting products. The music's final commercial form, as the wonderfully acerbic critic Robert Christgau argues, is based largely on a "reactionary individualism" that followed on the heels of the failed collectivism of the sixties. That collectivism, we might add, purported to thrive without the white working class in the first place. The commercial apex of seventies country rock, the music of The Eagles, explains Christgau, "bespeaks not roots but a lack of them, so that in the end the product is suave and synthetic—brilliant, but false."[31]

Rather than bridging the cultural and racial upheavals of the sixties and the economic dilemmas of the seventies, the bulk of the country-rock synthesis of the seventies "excises precisely what is deepest and most gripping about country music—its adult working-class pain, its paradoxically rigid ethics—and leaves bluegrass-sounding good feelin'." John Fogerty of Credence Clearwater Revival—a Californian who adopted his own very effective southern voice—understood the bad faith that underlay much of rock's colonization expeditions into roots music. Unlike the "love and theft" that went into white appropriation of the blues, much of the country influence came from love, theft, and a certain contempt. "We're all so ethnic now, with our long hair and shit," declared Fogerty with a refreshing dose of reality; "But when it comes to doing the real crap that civilization needs to keep going, who's going to be the garbage collector? None of *us* will."[32]

The condescension of the seventies bourgeois dream of escaping the grit of daily life was best expressed in Richard Bach's *Jonathan Livingston Seagull*. The pop-schlock classic of the new individualism of the seventies—number one on the bestseller list for 1972 *and* 1973—examines the spiritual awakening of a seagull, who must become an outcast in society in order to learn to fly and soar in absolute freedom. Like the generation that made the book popular, Jonathan cannot understand the grinding struggle for subsistence and longs for something more. "We can lift ourselves out of ignorance, we can find ourselves as creatures of excellence and intelligence and skill. We can be free! *We can learn to fly!*" he exclaims. To do so, he must abandon his fellow gulls sentenced to "screeching and fighting with the flock around the piers and fighting boats, diving on scraps of fish and bread." He chooses to reject the ceaseless material struggle within the community as well as the idea, as his father tells him, that "we are put into this world to eat, to stay alive as long as we possibly can." By abandoning the life of work in favor of his own spiritual emancipation, he echoes Reich's *Greening of America*: "I am a perfect, unlimited gull!" Jonathan obtained his freedom from the daily scrabble for fish just as almost every indicator of the nation's material well-being— wages, prices, unemployment—was getting worse. His individual freedom is not far from that of The Eagles. As they sing on "Earlybird," "high up on his own, the eagle flies alone / and he is free." "But," as Peter Doggett quips, "as Merle Haggard could have told them the working man still had rent to pay."[33]

The search for a connection between working-class reality and sixties dis-sent, between the weight of blue-collar authenticity and the impatient dissent of the New Left, between a new Popular Front and the New Majority, is more fully explored in its cinematic form by Jack Nicholson's character Bobby Dupea, the rootless hero of the classic film *Five Easy Pieces*. Like Gram Parsons, Dupea is from wealth but looks for authenticity in the blue-collar experience. Bobby is a concert pianist and the wayward son of afflu-ence who escapes the coldness of his family of classical musicians by working as a rigger in the California oilfields. Like Gram Parsons, he wants to be taken down to the blue-collar dance floor. He lives with a waitress whose musical tastes tend toward Tammy Wynette, bowls with his buddies, drinks, plays cards, and indulges the full range of working-class pursuits. He is in-capable of fully entering working-class culture, however; like Victorian Londoners exploring the East End, the thrill of discovering the other was often tempered with disgust. When Bobby gets into a fight with his closest friend, he lets all of his class condescension foam out. "I'm sitting here lis-tening to some cracker asshole, lives in a trailer park, compare his life to mine!" There is simply not enough identity there to solve the urgency of the post-sixties identity crisis; like Parsons, Dupea is a tourist, not a student of working-class culture.

Five Easy Pieces is full of an odd cast of characters, each handicapped in some capacity, each in search of identity and place, but most of whom have little capacity to love and are incapable of asking for it. Bobby detests bour-geois culture but finds working-class culture something he merely dips into when necessary, something inadequate to his needs beyond serving as a mere playground. Bobby's upper-crust father is both crippled and mute—the symbolism here not so abstract—and the only psychic salve Bobby can find for his familial alienation is in the limited authenticity he finds in slumming. When Bobby's ditzy but genuine waitress girlfriend is criticized by his brother's friend, he lets loose with a full defense of her. She is, after all, the only character in the film capable of love. "Don't sit there pointing at her. I said don't point at her, you creep! Where the hell do you get the ass to tell anybody who the hell's got it or has class or who or what she typifies. You shouldn't even be in the same room with her, you pompous celibate. You're totally full of shit. You're all full of shit."

Bobby, unable to sustain his vigil with every man and woman, chooses, like David Crosby, to head off on his own. Abandoning the only source of authen-ticity in the movie—his clingy, loving, country-music singing girlfriend—at a gas station in the Northwest along with his wallet, his coat, and his car, he hitches a ride with a trucker headed north. Unable to bridge the cultural space between his working-class lifestyle and his affluent past or to open himself up to love of anyone, he chooses a cold and isolated individualism. As the truck pulls out, the driver tells him, that it is going to be "cold as hell" where they are headed. There is no cross-class, cross-cultural alliance to be had. As the film ends, Bobby's chilly isolation will only become all the colder and lonelier, his dissent and anger more rootless than when he began.

III

The attempts of artists like Parsons, Dylan, and Robertson, and characters like Bobby Dupea to ground themselves in working-class traditions—however awkward—were rare. Most movies, songs, and television productions tended to evince a bitter contempt, a deep-seated psychological anger, toward white, male blue-collar America. They chose to create caricatures of the Wallace voters, the anti-busing protestors, and the hard-hat demonstrators rather than explore the equally prevalent workers who rocked the nation in the biggest strike wave in postwar history. Many in film and television seemed ready to punish and humiliate the white working class for their political failures—as well as making them a repository for their own rightward drifting tendencies. In essence, workers' reticence to mobilize against the war and their mixed—at best—record on civil rights and black power movements made them the enemy to many professional middle-class makers of popular culture.

At times, the level of condescension was astonishing. In one of the most innovative films of the era, *Easy Rider*, two chopper-driving hippies (Peter Fonda and Dennis Hopper) score cash in a drug deal and then embark on a discovery ride across America. Motoring into the past (they drive east not west), the heroes have already admitted that somewhere along the way, "we blew it." But the search continues. As the promotional materials for the film proclaim, "A man went looking for America and couldn't find it anywhere."

The heroes did find what they believed to be the fate of America in the wrathful hands of the southern working class. As the heroes steer their choppers on the highway, along comes a pickup truck with two surly looking rednecks in it. It is almost impossible to not see these characters as a quote from *The Grapes of Wrath*—they have the same body types, looks, and, though updated, mode of transportation. When one of them pulls a shotgun off the rack and blasts the hippie heroes off their motorcycles, it was explicitly designed to incriminate reactionary working-class politics. The film ends with the camera panning from the air, looking down on Wyatt's (Peter Fonda's) motorbike in flames and the sixties dream road trip coming to an end— killed by the anger of the working class. As Terry Southern, an author of *Easy Rider*, explained in incredibly tortured logic, "In my mind, the ending was to be an indictment of blue-collar America, the people I thought were responsible for the Vietnam War."[34]

To believe that the stage was being set not just for populist conservatism but even for fascism, one only had to believe any of a number of films that caricaturized white guys in the first half of the decade. These movies lend credence to Barbara Ehrenreich's conviction that professional middle-class creators of popular culture in the decade were using working-class subjects as a vehicle for their own macho anti-liberal impulses. Much of the working-class cinema of the seventies, she argues, was a simple projection of "middle-class anxiety and prejudice" that was largely hostile to its subject. Portrayals of blue-collar characters helped to legitimize the middle-class's own rising conservatism by creating "a working class more suited to their mood: dumb, reactionary, and bigoted." While very compelling and often right, Ehrenreich overbuilds her argument. In her zeal to protect workers, she overlooks the genuine sources of some of the caricature of blue-collar behavior and fails to see that much of the most mean spirited of the genre that she wants to pin solely on middle-class values was simultaneously a byproduct of the failures of the New Left and the real limits of working-class identity.[35]

The notorious title character in the 1970 film *Joe*, a machinist played by Peter Boyle, is the nastiest example of the anti-worker genre. It is not hard to see cultural producers (in this case, writer Norman Wexler, a former advertising agent who would go on to write *Saturday Night Fever*) projecting all of their venom about the ills of society onto the white working class locked in a Wallaceite rage. *Joe* was re-titled and reformulated to emphasize backlash themes after the hard-hat revolts in Manhattan and then rushed to release two months after the protests. The red, white, and blue credits open with a country song playing, "Hey Joe, don't it make you want to go to war . . . once more?"

When we first meet the title character, he is perched on his barstool in the middle of a drunken tirade at the American Bar and Grill. "I sweat my balls off forty-hours a week in front of a fuckin' furnace and they get as much money as I do—fer nuthin'," Joe declares. "All you gotta do is act black and the money rolls in. Set fire to the cities, burn a few buildings, throw a few bombs and you get money and jobs. . . . And the kids, the white kids, they're worse than the niggers. Money don't mean nothing to them." With a picture of the American flag being raised at Iwo Jima in the background, he declares, "Forty-two percent of all liberals are queer—that's a fact—the Wallace people took a poll."

When Joe repeatedly rants that he would like to kill a hippie, a new patron at the bar explains quietly and almost unconsciously, "I just did." Joe thinks he is kidding, but we have just seen the WASPy, Cadillac-driving advertising executive Phil Compton murder his daughter's despicable junkie-hippie boyfriend, which Joe will later declare to be a "humanitarian act." Joe eventually teams up with his new and affluent buddy in a tour of the hippie underworld in search of Compton's runaway daughter (Susan Sarandon's debut role). The film quickly becomes a white working-class exploitation film, but one that makes the class discrepancies between the two anti-heroes perfectly clear. Joe makes $160 per week, while the advertising executive Compton pulls in $60,000 per year ("The fuckin' president of my union pays himself that amount of money!" Joe declares incredulously.) The two men are different in virtually every single aspect of their lives, except for their shared hatred for the counterculture. The masculinity of both men is threatened by the entire package of the sixties—though for different reasons—and makes for a common alliance for the purpose of eradicating the menace. Joe admires Compton's "balls" for actually acting on his murderous impulses, and Compton—like Bobby in *Five Easy Pieces*—finds a refreshing well of reality in his dalliance with the working class. The odd alliance is not unlike that of Merle Haggard and Nixon/Reagan, as working-class Queens and the Upper East Side are allied against a ridiculous caricature of the squalid, filthy, drug-infested bohemia of the East Village.

Like the narrator of "Okie from Muskogee," Joe feels that he must defend himself or see all of his hard work gain him little more than a new place at the bottom of the cultural pecking order. "These kids shit on you," he declares. "They shit on everything you believe in." The story ends—after the two get stoned and indulge in a highly improbable orgy with some hippie chicks who rip them off—at a farmhouse. Compton and Joe are armed with Joe's precious gun collection, and the commune dwellers beg for their lives fleeing into the snow. For a brief moment, however, it appears that Compton might shoot Joe, that the class animosity between worker and elite might trump their cross-class bonding over the cultural crisis. "What are you going to do, you wanna shoot me? Well where's that going to get you? If you wanna shoot somebody, shoot them!" Joe exclaims. "Look Compton, there's only one way out now—clean—that means everybody. At this point it can get to be fun," Joe sneers as he unloads his rifle into the cowering and defenseless hippies. "It's your ass now, Compton!" he repeats over and over as he blasts away at kids all over the place. In the final scene, with Joe's words echoing in the executive's head, Compton shoots his own daughter in the back as she tries to flee the mayhem.

The film certainly hits the mark for the culture industry as a whole. As *Variety* argued, "Commercial prospects seem bright indeed" for working-class exploitation films such as *Joe.* The appeal of the film should "stretch across the board, from the mass of blue-collar workers whose feelings are here given full expression . . . to knee-jerk liberals who can be patronizing and shocked at the same time, to the truly concerned who may wonder at the current divided climate in which a film like this is classed as entertainment." *Time* gushed that it was "a film of Freudian anguish, biblical savagery and immense social and cinematic importance," while the Academy of Motion Picture Arts and Sciences gave it a nomination for best screenplay. As *Village Voice* film critic J. Hoberman summed up the film, it was more than Ehrenreich's idea of middle-class projections, but a combination of fantasy and history—a domestic My Lai massacre. "In giving on-screen presence to those blue-collar workers whose income was eaten away by wartime inflation even as the counterculture eroded their moral code, 'Joe' developed in tandem with the social spectacle." It was also semi-prophetic in the unlikely alliances it portrayed. By the end of the decade, a Reaganesque cross-class alliance would be built—white worker and rich man in common cause—to repeal the 1960s.[36]

One of Joe's more endearing neighbors in Queens—in geography as well as ideology—was television's iconic working-class anti-hero, Archie Bunker. More than another product to roll off the white backlash assembly line, *All in the Family* was a brilliant departure that transformed the sitcom genre. In one of the most daring moves in postwar television, CBS introduced the nation to *All in the Family* in 1971 with a special announcement about the potentially shocking content of the show—"a humorous spotlight on our frailties, prejudices, and concerns"—while a battery of temporary telephone operators were in place to field complaints from the public about the controversial show they were about to see.

When not lost in a tangle of malapropisms, Archie could be found railing against what he called spics, spades, hippies, hebes, pinkos, chinks, polacks, meatheads, and fags, while trying to maintain his sanity living with his useless "bleedin' heart" son-in-law, his "weepin' Nellie" daughter, and his "dingbat" wife. Archie is constantly under assault living with the vaguely New Left Mike and Gloria as well as his morally sincere wife Edith, struggling to remain king of his tawdry row house. We know little of what Archie does everyday in the world, except that he works on a loading dock, where he has achieved some status as a minor foreman but must moonlight as a cabbie to make ends meet. Although many viewers expressed sympathy for the reactionary rants of Archie Bunker, even going so far as to slap "Archie for President" bumper stickers on their cars (he even received votes at the 1972 Democratic Convention in Miami), he was clearly created and widely interpreted to be the historical relic, the pop icon of the "authoritarian working-class," who fought and railed against the New Politics of the 1960s.

The very first episode, "Meet the Bunkers," revealed the core tensions that would be played out in the coming years. The cigar-chomping Archie returns home, railing against the "bleeding heart" sermon they had to sit through at church. It does not take long before Mike ("Meathead") and Archie begin to mix it up. Mike tries to defend his study of sociology at college, explaining to Archie, "I just want to learn how to help people." Archie retorts, "Your mother-in-law and me is people. Help us and go to work!" Mike attacks Archie on the old "law and order" issue, arguing, "You know why we have a breakdown of law and order in this country, Archie? Because we got poverty, real poverty. And you know why we got that? Because guys like you are unwilling to give the black man, the Mexican American, and all the other minorities their just and rightful hard-earned share of the American dream." His stiff speech came straight from the campus soapbox. Archie does not relent. "Now let me tell you something. If your spics and your spades want their share of the American dream, let them go out and hustle for it just like I done. . . . I didn't have no million people out there marching and protesting to get me my job!" As usual, Edith gets the last word in, innocently unraveling Archie's bigotries and exposing his racial privileges. "No," she says, "his uncle got it for him."[37]

Archie is an inversion of the noble and suffering proletariat; he has only scant economic identity but an enormous racial one. Creator Norman Lear certainly saw the show as an exorcism of his own father's parochial world view in order to free up the power of the new social movements. Some worried that Archie's endearing, almost accidental, charm made his racism tolerable. As son-in-law Mike explained to Sammy Davis Jr. when he guest-starred on the show, Archie's "not so bad. He wouldn't burn a cross on your lawn." "No," replies Davis, "but he might stop to toast a marshmallow." When the bowling team that Archie desperately wants to join chooses a black guy instead of Archie, his buddy explains, "The world is changing." Archie stares at him in his hapless way, and says, "And every time it changes it gives me another kick in the butt."

Others argued that rather than the audience recognizing the satire, they saw Archie as a lovable victim of the forces he fights against. By asking the audience to side with him, many claimed, *All in the Family* drained the urgency of the social issues of the day. Nobody really knew whether people tuned in to laugh with or at Archie, but limited evidence suggests that *All in the Family* was a bit of a political Rorschach test—viewers sided with whomever they already believed in (and, in reality, Edith really scored most of the points).[38]

In *All in the Family*, the idea of the white working-class male was lumped with all that was retrograde in post-sixties American life. But Archie's backlash politics and murky nostalgic logic—"guys like us we had it made, those were the days," he sings, oddly longing for the pre–New Deal days of Herbert Hoover—are symptoms of something more profound than the simple racism of his "spics and spades" rhetoric (had Norman Lear got it right, the song would have looked back to the pre–Great Society days not pre–New Deal, to Eisenhower not Hoover). As Carroll O'Connor explained to *Ebony* magazine, Archie's bigotry is the product of a character whose

> world seems to be closing in on him. And you laugh as you watch him, but that man is in pain. You're laughing at a man in pain. *You're laughing at a loser*; a loser because of his misconceptions. He conceives that all these things are a threat to his life. And all these things are beating down on him. That life in the United States is no longer livable for him, for Archie Bunker.

Archie, on the losing end of history, was one of the most prominent fictional figures in the postwar drift of the idea of "worker" from a materially based to a culturally based concept, from the vanguard to the rearguard of history. Although doubt and fear may undergird Archie's rigidity and pride, we as audience members know that Archie, and all of his actions and attitudes, are headed for the dustbin of history. Whether one wanted to rail against that doom or celebrate it, whether one thought Meathead was on track or a deluded do-gooder, Archie's future seemed certain to all.[39]

When E.E. LeMasters did his participant observation at a working-class tavern for the writing of his book, *Blue Collar Aristocrats* (1976), his conclusions might as well have been about Archie:

> One has the feeling that eventually these men are going to lose their fight against social change (out of deference to them *we* will not call it progress). They are opposed to sexual equality, racial equality, mass production of houses, and many other features of modern society. In a very real (or literal) sense, these men are reactionary—that is, they yearn for the America that began to disappear yesterday or the day before. One can see this in their attitude towards women, in their gloomy view of the welfare state, and in their hostility toward blacks demanding equality.

Yet, in a 1976 episode, Archie, brooding over the Democrat Jimmy Carter's White House victory, may have had the last laugh when he warned that liberals would not be so happy when Ronald Reagan won in 1980. The prophecy was supposed to be an attempt at absurdly dark humor.[40]

For *All in the Family* and the many shows it spawned, the generation gap merged with class distinctions as the new generation seemed less held back by class than by culture. Mature white working-class men in popular culture, therefore, would be hard-pressed to have values in any enviable sense. This came to the fore in August 1974, when actor Carroll O'Connor refused to show up on the set while replacement workers did the jobs of striking electrical equipment operators at CBS. His nearly month-long show of solidarity single-handedly halted production of *All in the Family*, earning him the wrath of the producers, television critics, and fans alike. Meantime, his otherwise politically progressive co-stars saw little wrong with going to work in the midst of a strike and treated O'Connor as a bit of an oddity. "I don't think he has any support anywhere," remarked Jean Stapleton who played Edith; "It was very noble-sounding, but not, uh, wise." O'Connor, on the other hand, portrayed himself as constitutionally incapable of crossing a picket line. "I will not work with strike-breakers," he declared, "It's a matter of principle for me. I simply refuse to work with any-body who takes money to do a union man's job while that man is on strike. I call them scabs and I'm surprised that these management people [brought in to do the electrical workers' jobs] allow themselves to be used that way." He concluded, "I could no more go into a building and work with scabs than I could play handball in church."[41]

Despite the profound differences on post-sixties politics, both O'Connor and his character Archie Bunker shared a certain painful and growing irrelevance. When it came to this real-life work stoppage, O'Connor was conscious of heading for the same relic status as Archie—not because of his bigotry, but because he believed in unions. O'Connor had, at one time or another, been a member of seven different unions, including the Newspaper Guild, the National Maritime Union, and, of course, the Screen Actors Guild and the American Federation of Television and Radio Artists. "My whole life ever since I was seventeen, eighteen," he explained, "I thought of myself as part of a labor movement. I've been very labor and union-oriented since the time I was a kid. I can remember being told by Mike Quill, Joe Curran, and Sydney Hillman, 'don't cross a picket line' and they didn't tell me personally but they told the whole labor movement, and that was part of my history. I can't expect young kids in my show who grew up in the 50s and 60s to know anything about that and to have any sympathy for it."[42]

As many commented at the time, it seemed out of character for Archie to go on strike in the show or for O'Connor to support a real strike. For those acts to make sense in the narrative of post-sixties America, their actions would have to be placed in a framework in which they were either victims of injustice or possessors of nobility. But Archie was the wrong type of victim and O'Connor had the wrong kind of nobility for the seventies. As the brilliant creator and producer of the show, Norman Lear, explained about Carroll O'Connor's quixotic honoring of the picket line, "Carroll is convinced the world is marching in one step—against him." And it was.[43]

Ironically, the real-life labor dispute at CBS prevented O'Connor from taping a four-part set of shows centered on another strike—this one down at Archie's plant. Entertainment mixed with social issues in the 1970s as much as—or more than—any other time in the twentieth century, but here was a remarkably tight and complex intermingling of pop and real life. "Don't be telling me what to do, I'm an old trade union man, have been since before you were born," Archie explains to Gloria in the same language O'Connor spoke of the real strike. The irony of working on a show troubled by the same issues as those being played out on the screen was not lost on O'Connor. "To be looking at strikebreakers behind cameras, and to be asked to be funny, particularly in a show in which the same conditions being portrayed are those *lived* outside the studio . . . I can't act in that situation," lectured the actor.[44]

The four installments of *All in the Family*, finally made once the strike was settled, centered on Archie's union going on strike over wages and cost-of-living adjustments—exactly the reasons that the International Brotherhood of Electrical Workers (IBEW) was striking CBS. At the end of the made-for-TV dispute—during the entirety of which Archie could not grasp the difference between a flat raise and a cost-of-living adjustment—Archie boasts of winning a 15 percent raise. "Let's have a toast to the good old US of A, where everybody gets his slice of the pie. All you gotta do is do your work, and in the end ya get it," he declares as the laugh track humiliates him. The truth was that once the new settlement was adjusted for inflation, Archie and his crew were still behind in real terms. "Archie thinks he's 15% ahead," son-in-law Mike points out quietly to Gloria, "but he's already 5% behind." Archie, and his union (seemingly incapable of bargaining for real wage gains), are the fools as the show ends with everyone knowing that Archie really lost the strike—everyone, that is, except Archie.[45]

President Richard Nixon hated the idea that people were laughing at Archie Bunker. In a meeting with John Ehrlichman and Bob Haldeman, he described an episode in a private (but of course taped) conversation in which he saw homosexuality everywhere. Mike, the son-in-law, the president explained with no evidence, "apparently goes both ways." In the episode that got Nixon's attention, an old buddy of Archie's, a former football player, turns out to be a "fairy," Nixon explains. The laughs, however, are on Archie for his own fear of what his buddy had become. Nixon and his men cannot believe this should be happening to a "hard hat." Then, as the three statesmen sat on the edge of their own crumbling *Pax Americana*, Nixon's analysis of popular culture slipped into an interpretation of history that managed to meld the rise of homosexuality with the fall of empire. "You know what happened to the Greeks! Homosexuality destroyed them. Sure, Aristotle was a homo. We all know that. So was Socrates." In contrast, the "strong societies," like Russia, "Goddamn, they root 'em out. . . . Homosexuality, dope, immorality, are the enemies of strong societies. . . . We have to stand up to this," Nixon declared.[46]

Lonely, angry, anti-liberal men like Joe and Archie haunted the screen in the seventies but rarely so blatantly than in the many vigilante films of the decade, such as the infamous *Dirty Harry* (1972). Harry Callahan is a tough, fanatical, even sadistic, cop, chasing after a long-haired pathological criminal named Scorpio who sports a peace belt buckle. He stalks less the mean streets of San Francisco than he does the permissive ones—the city known for its tolerance of dope, hippies, homosexuals, and black radicals. Harry is as exciting as he is frightening, part supercop and part misanthropic maniac with a .44 Magnum, who has to fight both bad guys and the limits of the Warren Court. Most critics dismissed the "fascist medievalism" of *Dirty Harry* that made Clint Eastwood the number one draw at the box office in 1972. Critic J. Hoberman, however, sees it as a sort of class-based Vietnam allegory. "Grunts sent in-country to search-and-destroy slogged, sometimes for weeks, through rain forest and rice paddy to endure the cannon-fodder terror of serving as live bait—drawing VC fire so that American air power could target the enemy." Urban crime—even occupational life itself—was similar, where the system allegedly created an unwinnable scenario because of victims' rights and clay-footed liberals afraid of doing the wrong thing. "The complications of urban life were solvable by direct action," explains Hoberman of the film, "if only the radical chic fools who run the show would stand aside."[47]

If Dirty Harry is the "Last Cowboy" who emerges from "the Great Society's rumble at the twilight of liberalism," it is no surprise that the following year Eastwood directed himself in a Western with a similar message: *High Plains Drifter* (1973). If ever there was an anti-bourgeois film of the era, this was it. Citizens of the tiny western mining town of Lago are cowering and spineless, lost in corruption and collusion with power, and afraid to fight against the gangsters that terrorize it. The mine owns everything, the preacher is corrupt, the law establishment is useless, and the town is haunted by the memory of its own passivity when the bad guys whipped to death the old sheriff. To protect itself, the town must hire killers. In the opening scene, as The Stranger (Eastwood) rides into town, a hooker is rude to him, so he rapes her. Needless to say, an encounter with a real man leaves her breathless and with bosom heaving. Clint, having already straightened patriarchy out by putting mouthy women in their place, is clearly qualified to lead the weak-kneed citizens against their own fears. Judith Crist rightly understands *Drifter* to be "the Middle America R-rated substitute for *Deep Throat*, it's male sexual fantasy restricted, in our grand Puritan tradition, to the rape of a whore and the instant seduction of a 'good' woman and then sublimated in all sorts of virility rites from straight shooting to torture to fire, with an orgy of violence and bloodletting for climax." Yet, he is also the protector of the underdogs—the Indians, the midget, and even the Mexicans. As in a related Eastwood film a year prior, *Joe Kidd*, "Eastwood cast himself as a fantasy RFK, a tribune for Chicanos as well as hard-hats," whose law-and-order toughness can unite people and destroy enemies.[48]

There was no greater indictment of working-class patriarchy and violence than Martin Scorcese's feminist outing, *Alice Doesn't Live Here Anymore* (1974). Alice's husband is little more than another mean-spirited, violent, seventies redneck son of a bitch who cannot be pleased. Their bed is cold, and even when he comforts her from the pain she feels, he merely grabs her breast. Alice discusses with her friend whether she could live without a man—establishing the theme of the film—just before she learns that he has had an accident in his delivery truck and died. With Alice suddenly liberated from the terror of her life, viewers get to see not just Alice but other working-class women she meets struggle to get out from under blue-collar patriarchy. But every male relationship she stumbles across is tainted with violence. "Don't ever tell me what to do—I'll bust your jaw!" one potential (adulterous) mate tells her when she tries to escape him. When she finally finds a job at Mel's café after striking out on the road to start a singing career, she finds working-class pain everywhere. Yet Alice finds her path out in the classic Hollywood theme of class mobility. Her savior, Kris Kristoferson, is not perfect and, as a ranch owner, not exactly wealthy. But he has the means and the cultural resources to support her path of discovery (a tacky red, white, and blue tapestry of both Kennedy brothers hangs in his house to remind us of his liberalism). Only by leaving the white male working class behind, this film argues, can blue-collar women—and society as a whole—find release.

IV

In the end, the major storyline of the seventies white, male working-class identity was about failed linkages with youth movements, about racial and cultural backlash, about vigilantism, and about insurgency. Mostly, it was about how these centrifugal forces led *not* to an image but a breakdown, not a unity but a social deconstruction, not an idea but a reaction. The remains of the working-class hero of the 1930s were pulled apart into its fragments in the early 1970s, and, rather than leaving a single figure, it left disarray. In no piece of popular culture was the psychic meltdown of blue-collar identity more evident than in the film, and the reality that made it, of *Dog Day Afternoon*. The lead character, a blue-collar bank robber played by Al Pacino, is sexually confused and economically vulnerable, incompetent, alone, and, above all, doomed. When his mess of a life becomes a spectacle, he just keeps repeating, "I'm dying here."

The film was based, in extraordinarily minute detail, on exactly the type of breakdown in both masculinity and law and order that made Nixon's blood boil. On August 22, 1972, two armed men, the leader a Vietnam vet with a world of trouble and not enough money, entered a branch of the Chase Manhattan Bank in Brooklyn, New York, with the intent to rob it. After that, everything went wrong. When the robbery went awry, the men, John Wojtowicz and Salvatore Naturile, turned to taking the bank employees hostage. The ensuing spectacle was one of the most bizarre events in a decade marked by bizarre events. The negotiations over the hostages became carnivalesque as helicopters buzzed the air, hundreds of policemen formed barricades around the bank, and over three thousand spectators assembled in an all-night vigil to watch and cheer and boo for Wojtowicz.

Once the hostages had been taken, the handsome Wojtowicz boldly walked out into the street to jeer and taunt the police and the FBI, order pizza, throw money to the crowd, ham it up for the television cameras gathered, and receive the adulation of the throngs assembled to watch—and mostly support—the robbers. One of the demands that Wojtowicz made was that his (male) wife, Ernest Aron, be brought to him from the psychiatric ward of a Brooklyn hospital so that Wojtowicz could take him on their escape to a foreign country. Once safely out of the country with the loot, Wojtowicz could afford to pay for Aron's sex change operation. Meanwhile, his other (female) wife watched the whole affair on television from their cramped apartment in utter disbelief. Although Wojtowicz constantly threatened to send dead bodies out if the authorities did not meet his demands, the robber treated the bank tellers with respect—presumably because he had been a bank teller himself. The affair ended in the dawn hours at JFK Airport. Hoping to board the plane they had demanded to whisk them away from their botched robbery, Naturile was killed by the FBI and Wojtowicz surrendered.[49]

The 1972 Brooklyn spectacle required little embellishment to become the brilliant Sydney Lumet film *Dog Day Afternoon* (1975)—which, along with *Nashville*, was one of the best explorations of the explosion of social identity of the decade. Long before anyone was talking about making a movie about the affair, *Life* magazine had already noted that John Wojtowicz had the "broken-faced good looks of an Al Pacino or a Dustin Hoffman," and it was Pacino who played Sonny in the finest performance of his career. What makes *Dog Day Afternoon* a particularly good film, however, is that, unlike almost all of the proletarian dramas of the seventies, this one is less projection and more exploration. The film was part of director Sydney Lumet's ongoing project to explore characters struggling for "self-definition and self-understanding" rather than an empty vessel into which ideology could be poured. *Dog Day* manages to combine the existential crisis of film noir, the documentary tradition of the Great Depression, and the populist gangster motifs of the thirties into one of the finest prole films of the decade.[50]

Lumet artfully sets the stage with lingering opening sequences that capture the class distinctions of urban life. Before we are introduced to any characters, the camera walks the viewer through the contrasts, as one critic put it, "between those who have the time and money to play in the heat and those who are left to swelter in it. If one man suns himself on the beach, another lies prostrate on the sidewalk in the sun; if one man waters his lawn, another uses a hose to keep the garbage on the street away from his door." The dogs rummaging through rubbish, the construction workers, and the old guys arguing in lawn chairs captures the diversity of Brooklyn working-class life without being heavy handed or didactic. Jet planes whisk the affluent across the sky, but, as we find out, they will never get to be used by Sonny and Sal ("they're always screamin' overhead but never for you," Sonny later declares). Sitting at just another point in this geography of class distinctions and contradictions are the protagonists of the film, particularly Sonny, the working-class everyman, who is scrambling to find a way out of the dire straits in which he trapped. The robbery, which he planned in order to rescue himself and those he loved, will end up as one more out-of-control event in an already out-of-control life.[51]

Sonny is clearly a working stiff who cannot make it: he is a classic ethnic, Catholic, urban dweller, a Vietnam vet, a toiler in the service sector, a member of the working poor with a wife and kids on welfare. He is trapped in an impossible web of relationships from which he cannot escape, powerless to change his fate. Sonny is smart, even lovable, but he is entering the equivalent of social quicksand—the more he moves and the more he resists, the deeper he sinks. The bank clerks occupy the same place as Sonny; they are totally subject to rule from above and obviously indulge in a vicarious glow at Sonny's bold exploits. But his identity is clearly in a vortex of confusion: he has two wives, one male and one female; he loves a man but wants him to be a woman; he fails as a thief but succeeds as a spectacle; and he clearly respects his fellow workers but threatens to kill them. Lumet has the guts to reject the fantasy and show the futility of the two major themes of the era: escape and vengeance. As Sonny repeats throughout the movie, he cannot stand "the pressure." "I am dying in here," and "we're dying in here" are the constant refrains. If *Nashville* suggested that country music created artificial tradition to cover the absence of it, *Dog Day* admits that tradition itself is gone.[52]

The film hinges on a contrast between the warmth of local human relationships and the coldness of the world beyond the space that Sonny controls. There is a strong bond of mutual trust between Sonny and the local cop Moretti (Charles Durning), who scream at each other like family members, lose the assumed posture of control both are struggling to keep up, and treat each other as human adversaries. As the real bank manager said to Wojtowicz and Naturile, "I'm supposed to hate you guys, but I've had more laughs tonight than I've had in weeks."[53]

In the course of a single cinematic moment, three occurrences take place: the lights in the bank go out; darkness falls outside the bank; and out of that inside-outside darkness, a new voice speaks to Sonny through the bullhorn. It is the stone cold FBI agent who has taken over for the neighborhood cop, a cool figure who now seems significantly more ominous and threatening than Sonny the criminal. The only illumination left is the FBI's floodlights—and their function is not to clarify but to confuse and disorient Sonny, who has managed to rule the afternoon stage with his charismatic theatrics. The true power structure has arrived and taken the situation away from the locals. The shot from a helicopter reveals that Sonny only holds a few yards of turf, maintained by a precarious social and psychological performance, and dwarfed by the economic and political world in which it is enmeshed.

When a television reporter interviews Sonny, he is at first very excited to see himself on TV, but then he becomes angry at the lack of point to it all.

Just when the plot begins to turn explicitly on the issue of economic inequality, it drops the subject:

Reporter: "Why do you feel you have to steal for money? Couldn't you get a job?

Sonny: "Uh, no, doing what? Ya know, ya know, if you want a job you gotta be a member of a union, see if you got no union card, uh, you don't get a job."

Reporter: "What about nonunion occupations?"

Sonny: "What's wrong with this guy?" Sonny turns to the bank tellers, who laugh and scoff at the reporter's ignorance. "Whaddya mean non-union, like, like what? Like a bank teller? You know how much a bank teller makes a week?" (The women laugh, mouth off, hands on hips, say "not much.") "Not much. A hundred and fifteen to start. You gonna live on that? I got a wife and a couple of kids to take care of, how'm I gonna live on that?

Whaddyou make a week?"

Reporter: "Well, I'm here to talk to *you*, Sonny. . . . You could give up."

Sonny: "You ever been in prison?"

Reporter: "No."

Sonny: "No? No? No, well let's talk about something you fucking know about—how much you make a week? That's what I want to hear!"

Suddenly, as the confrontation becomes concretely about the class difference between Sonny and the television reporter rather than the sexually charged street spectacle, the television station shuts off the broadcast. The material reality of Sonny's world is silenced, and cartoons take their place on the screen.

Outside, the carnival carries on as Sonny revels in a type of outlaw status that is a revised and desperate version of the mainstay of early Depression film and song. In the gangster cycle of movies of the early thirties, the criminal typically hungers for personal success, but he can no longer fulfill his goals within the bounds of a corrupt society and must pursue them through crime. "The traditional good guy whose success affirms society," argue Roffman and Purdy in *The Hollywood Social Problem Film*, "had been transformed into the good bad guy whose success questions society." In truly populist terms, all means to success are unlawful, as in Woody Guthrie's classic folk song, "Pretty Boy Floyd." Guthrie paints Floyd as a Robin Hood figure who left $1,000 tips, paid the mortgages on failing farms, and bought Christmas dinners for the families on relief. Following the pattern, Sonny showers the crowd with cash and whips their anti-authority impulses into a frenzy. Sonny chants, "Remember Attica! Attica! Attica!" referring to the 1971 upstate New York prison rebellion that ended in the state's massive use of deadly force against the prisoners. In their response, he feels the mercurial power of the crowd as he reminds them of the viciousness of state authority in the 1970s.[54]

Ironically, Sonny gets caught and Sal killed because of their moments of trust in the system—they forget Attica. Sonny makes the wrong move by trusting the FBI over the more humane local authorities. As the car carrying the robbers and their hostages moves away from the bank, Lumet explains, we are left with a "crazy collage of contradictory elements that increasingly make up our public reality." At the airport, Sal, in a moment of blind trust, lowers his gun at the FBI agent's request ("so that we don't have any accidents"). The agent then reaches for a hidden gun and kills him. He has left the womb of the neighborhood, and faith in the alien power structure, however momentary, brings them down.

The noted literary critic Fredric Jameson, in a famous essay on *Dog Day Afternoon*, argues that the film works as an allegory of class. Jameson clearly divides the film into two completely separate narrative tracks. The first is Sonny's crisis around his alienation, frustration, and inability to communicate; and the second is one of the class structure based largely on what happens in the setting *around* Sonny. The main character's role, Jameson argues, "is that of a mere pretext for the colonized space that is the branch bank, with its peripheralized and marginalized work force." What then moves "to occupy the film's center of gravity is the action outside of the bank itself, and in particular the struggle for precedence between the local police and the FBI officials." Here Jameson sees the cold and bloodless FBI agent and the branch bank itself as representatives of a multinational power structure that is colonizing the local community in Brooklyn. Local forms of authority and power are impotent in the face of the emotionless control of the multinational corporation and its henchmen.[55]

Jameson is right that *Dog Day* has a lot to teach about class in the seventies, but he is looking too hard for his allegory, and, in so doing, ends up imposing class where there is some and ignoring it where there is much. The wonderful opening scenes of urban squalor, in classic social-realist terms, explain that what we are about to witness is part of that setting. The "existential" crisis cannot be separated from the larger crisis of class in the 1970s. Rather than a two-track narrative, Sonny's existential spectacle is the identity crisis of the working class itself—an identity in a public tailspin. Sonny robs the bank because, as he repeats tirelessly in the film, he is "dying" because "everyone needs money" from him, because the "pressure" is unbearable. He cannot escape the paralyzing set of relations that he is in, but he also cannot find love in them either.

Sidney Lumet would again explore the anger in the chaos two years later with his classic *Network* (1976), delivering to the nation the rebellious but futile yell, "I'm mad as hell, and I'm not going to take it anymore!" The anger of the character Howard Beale, who is about to be fired from his job for bad ratings, turns to plans to kill himself on the air. Although this taps into a sort of free-floating anger, there is no real agency; all that is left is the reality of the corporation, accountable to no one, and uncontestable except through the media outlets it owns and controls. Beale's popularity and job security go back up when he threatens to commit suicide on the air, but eventually the audience grows bored with the harangues of the "Mad Prophet of the Airwaves." In the end, he is gunned down on the air by Maoist terrorists sponsored by the network itself. Even revolutionary resistance is readily contained within the hermetic media world of the 1970s, foreshadowing the conservative media populism that would begin to emerge in the 1980s.

V

Even in the new seventies creation, the "blockbuster," one could view the demise of the working-class subject. Critics agree that Spielberg's 1975 film *Jaws*, which terrified moviegoers across the nation with images of a great white shark stalking the waters outside the peaceful resort community of Amity Island, reflects the mysterious fears haunting post-Watergate, post-Vietnam, post-civil rights America. In *Jaws*, it is clear that something has gone terribly wrong in America—something out there, threatening, upsetting, terrifying to a set-piece of small town life. The city leaders, most prominently the small-town mayor, even engage in their own little Watergate-type cover-up of the shark attacks in order to insure that the tourist trade continues unabated during the most profitable part of the season. Whether the hidden problem was inflation, urban decay, racial unrest, or unemployment really did not matter. As film analyst Peter Lev argues, disaster films like *Jaws* are "a conservative response which 'solves' the 1970s malaise by drastically simplifying and reframing it" into a concrete natural threat that can be defeated. It is also a suggestion of how deep and wide the "last days" problem was for workers in 1970s popular culture.[56]

Jaws turns on two key questions: who will kill the economic and political nightmare haunting the island and who will be killed by it? When a $10,000 reward is offered for the killing of the shark, every idiot with a gun and a boat heads out into the waters to hunt the beast. As a group, however, they are little more than an incompetent flotilla of Archie Bunkers—stupid, disorganized, and directionless stereotypes of mob behavior—pitted in an ugly one-against-all contest that results in their over-stuffed little boats ramming into one another, each hunter seemingly as intent on killing each other as much as they are focused on their prey. The collective failure of the greedy and disorganized common man leaves the project of saving the community up to greater men. Enter Quint (Robert Shaw) a crusty old sailor and World War II vet who halts a chaotic town meeting by slowly screeching his fingernails down a chalkboard. The scruffy working-class hero has returned from exile to save the town.

As the plot develops, two other characters will join Quint on his boat: the police chief (Roy Scheider), a water-fearing father figure who has left seedy New York City to raise his family in tranquil Amity, and Hooper (Richard Dreyfuss), the young and affluent scientist brought in from outside. A competition emerges to see which brand of patriarch will rid Amity of the shark: rational father figure escaping urban rot; old working-class hero with his grizzly voice and a penchant for singing foreboding sea chanteys; or young possessor of technical knowledge, gadgetry, and capital. At first when young scientist Hooper tries to convince Quint to include him in the great hunt, Quint tries to scare him off with boastful tales of the hardship and terror that they will face at sea. Hooper's sissy boy ways, Quint growls, will not be up to the task of shark killing. To this Hooper exclaims, "Don't give me that working-class hero crap!" and is eventually allowed to join the expedition armed with piles of the latest wizardry designed for shark catching—an obvious affront to Quint's reliance on skill, tradition, and intuition.

Accompanied by the nervous but brave Chief Brody, the three set out for the deep to slay that which haunts both the commerce and peace of Amity. By the time the man-versus-nature scenes of the film are over, Quint, the working-class hero, is dead. Hooper survives, but it is Brody who rises to the occasion to kill the shark. The early collective blue-collar effort to kill the shark has failed; the eccentric but masterful working-class hero of a previous generation is dead; and only two figures remain. The rational family man, Chief Brody, is the hero, due largely to his sense of duty and his ability to remain aloof from the politics and civil society of the island—a patriarchal strong man who has finally risen to the occasion. His success is supported by the twin pillars of Hooper's character: affluence and technology. The subtheme of class in the 1970s is complete in a savagely apolitical way. It is classic suburban Spielberg—a world in which labor is accomplished someplace else. While other filmmakers would have his characters in a bloody brawl over the working-class identity, Spielberg simply has the working class surgically removed from his lens. Although he would later revive the "greatest generation" as soldiers, he first had to kill it as workers. The end of *Jaws* is, indeed, "pulp story hokum" in the works of one critic, but Hollywood seemed on a mission to destroy the working class in the 1970s in a host of similar efforts.[57]

VI

The nation found its transitional working-class hero, perhaps the unrestrained id of its seventies working-class consciousness, when an obscure young greaser-poet named Bruce Springsteen rose from the grimy club scene along the declining Jersey shore to appear on the cover of *Time* and *Newsweek* simultaneously in 1975. Springsteen captured the power and glory of rock 'n' roll to deliver the faithful from all that held them back—his music, as *Time* put it, "primal, directly in touch with all the impulses of wild humor and glancing melancholy, street tragedy and punk anarchy."[58]

After two jazzy, lyrically packed albums, *Born to Run* (1975) was the artist's first fully realized and explicitly blue-collar statement, sounding, as one critic put it, "like a '57 Chevy running on melted-down Crystals records [that] shuts down every claim that has been made for him." The record was, indeed, a pile of one-hit wonders distilled into their rock 'n' roll essence. Springsteen remolded them into something grander than the original ingredients, creating both an elegy to the hurt of the seventies and an anthemic paean to the emancipatory impulse. The biggest virtue of Springsteen's music, other than marathon live performances that came off like a crazy soul-punk review, was showing signs of life in a life-less moment. He seemed to emerge from the ashes of the burned-over decade, as a romantic in an age that had lost its ability to love. Springsteen was a skeptical believer in the American project crawling out from the crumbling infrastructure of postwar hope, "Trying in vain to breathe the fire we was born in."[59]

While most interpretations of working-class life in popular culture were crafted from a middle-class perspective about what to do with the working class, how to deal with it, or define it, Springsteen's *Born to Run* was different. This was a voice that emerged *from* it. His father, never quite able to break into the stability of that CIO-based blue-collar golden age, was left to drift from job to job in the postwar era, driving a bus, working in a rug mill, being a prison guard. Springsteen's was not an intellectual family—his source material was the grit of life, and, equally important, all of popular culture from AM radio to B movies. While his intellectual material came from small town, blue-collar America, his emotional energy came from inter-generational anger and fear of unfulfilled dreams—nothing resembling politics. Springsteen's message was simple: get out. Find the psychic wherewithal to leave it all behind. "The door's open," he taunts his girlfriend in the opening track, "Thunder Road," "but the ride it ain't free."

Born to Run is therefore not about work or community but about escape from both. You may "get to work late and the boss man's givin' you hell," but "somehow you survive 'til the night" where liberation is found in the streets. Emancipation from the "death trap" and the "suicide rap" is outside of the deadening confines of the community, outside of the life-draining world of work, and somewhere on the road: "Hell all day they're busting you up on the outside" he concludes in the song "Night," but the answer is to "run sad and free / Until all you can see is the night." He lays down the gauntlet for those lost working-class kids too late for both postwar prosperity and the fantasy life of the sixties: save your own soul. There are no promises. His car impatiently rumbling and his hope somewhere else, he pleads with his girl to join him. "The only redemption I can offer, girl, is beneath this dirty hood." The opening cut hits its crescendo with a problem that would haunt popular culture for the second half of the decade: "It's a town full of losers / And I'm pulling out of here to win." Springsteen offers a romantic restoration of the Whitmanesque ideal but only for those who are strong enough to join the "last chance power drive."

Born to Run emerged at a very specific juncture when the nation's soul had bottomed out. "I was writing in a particular moment when people had sort of their legs cut out from underneath them," Springsteen explained about that pivotal 1974–75 turning point.

> People weren't sure where to stand or where the country was going or what we were about, and a lot of that searching for home and searching for place— that's what all the characters are doing. They're leaving something—they're leaving something and they're going somewhere they don't know where they're going. . . . They're in the middle, they're in the no-man's-land between here and there. . . . [*Born to Run*] managed to combine a certain youthful optimism with a certain mount of weariness and a spiritual searching, people moving through a pretty dark world.

But what, it might be asked, of those who are left behind? What about those who were not "the chosen ones"?[60]

Later, Springsteen would try to make sense of life for the vast majority of those working people who stayed behind, lost "in the darkness on the edge of town." At the decade's pivotal midpoint, however, individual emancipation moved to center stage in popular culture. *Born to Run* helped set the tone for the second half of the decade, which celebrated those upwardly mobile working-class heroes who got out. Those that were left behind, however, remained in their class position, often slipping down the economic ladder. While Nixon, McGovern, and Wallace at least fought for the hearts and minds of working people, by the second half of the decade, working people would slip out of the political equation—except as a force that required economic discipline. By the end of the decade working people would possess less place and meaningful identity within civic life than any time since the industrial revolution.

The hard hat becomes a coveted political symbol. Hubert Humphrey, labor's favorite, receives roses and a monogrammed helmet from Pennsylvania steelworkers. Richard Nixon waves his famous double V for victory at construction workers, key elements of his "New Majority." George McGovern, searching for working-class votes, autographs another worker's hard hat.

SOUTHEAST CHICAGO HISTORICAL SOCIETY

GREY VILLET / GETTY IMAGES

The faces of insurgency. Ed Sadlowski, rebellious steel workers' leader, poses with South Chicago's Wisconsin Steel in the distance. The mill would be shut down by decade's end. Arnold Miller, standard-bearer in the Miners for Democracy's closely watched campaign, seeks out votes among the rank and file. Posters support a national boycott and local strike at El Paso's Farah garment factory. This action and its vivid iconography melded labor and feminism in ways that proved difficult to sustain as the decade wore on. Finally, in the summer of 1973, violence and repression halted the United Farm Workers' progress. Two workers, Juan De La Cruz and Nagi Daifallah, were killed. Daifallah's casket is accompanied here by his Yemenese compatriots.

Democrats struggle to unite at the 1972 convention. Senator George McGovern, dwarfed by images of RFK, JFK, and Truman, accepts the nomination of a party in disarray. A George Wallace supporter carries his support into the convention, even though the Alabama governor had been crippled by an assassin's bullet that spring.

The question that vexed the McGovern campaign. (Opposite) Shunned by the AFL-CIO, McGovern still managed to rally half the unions to his side. The handwriting at the top of this flyer notes that 10,000 copies were made to bring the battle to the heart of Wallace country, Hialeah, Florida. In the end McGovern, one of the most pro-labor candidates ever nominated through the two-party system, failed to win a majority of workers' votes.

THIS REPRINT FROM "THE MACHINIST" DONATED TO THE McGOVERN COMMITTEE BY FRED SWICK

The Labor Committee for the Election of McGovern-Shriver plans to publish this as a paid advertisement in several newspapers across the country.

If you work for a living...

HOW IN HELL CAN YOU VOTE FOR NIXON?

Unfair Taxes Under Nixon

The Nixon Administration has pushed through corporate tax cuts worth $80 billion to the corporations over 10 years. Now individuals pay 77 percent of all federal income taxes—7 percent *more* than they paid when Nixon took office. But corporations pay only 23 percent of all federal income taxes—7 percent *less* than they did in 1969.

Soaring Prices Under Nixon

During the first three and a half years of the Nixon Administration, the cost of living has soared 17.5 percent, by official government figures. Food continues to cost more and more. Nixon's Secretary of Agriculture says that's good because the rich can buy more steaks. The U.S. sells so much wheat to Russia the baking corporations want to charge more for bread. American workers can't afford Richard Nixon.

More Unemployment Under Nixon

When Richard Nixon was elected President, there were about three million unemployed. Now there are more than five million. *Millions* more are forced to work part-time. In some areas of the country, the unemployment rate is over 10 percent. But Richard Nixon still opposes government programs for jobs for people who need them.

Wages Frozen Under Nixon

After announcing he would not impose wage and price controls, Richard Nixon did a turnabout. He slapped on wage controls that tore up fairly negotiated contracts and put a 5% ceiling on wage increases. Meanwhile, corporate profits have surged to an all-time record high.

How McGOVERN Will Help The Worker

• George McGovern has one of the best pro-labor voting records of any member of Congress—94.1% right.

• George McGovern is a leader in the fight for tax reform and for closing tax loopholes. He believes a bologna sandwich should be just as tax deductible as a martini.

• George McGovern has a positive economic policy of full employment to provide meaningful and useful jobs for every person who needs to work.

• George McGovern will work to stop runaway food prices by putting a lid on exorbitant profits and by breaking up the big monopolies that put the squeeze on the consumer.

• George McGovern has long recognized the need for protecting the health and safety of American workers. He would enforce tough safety standards to carry out the intent to the Occupational Safety and Health Act.

• George McGovern is a leading advocate of improved health care for all Americans. He is a co-sponsor of the National Health Insurance Act and has worked to hold down the cost of medicine.

LABOR COMMITTEE FOR THE ELECTION OF McGOVERN-SHRIVER

1925 K Street, N. W., Washington, D. C.

Joseph D. Keenan	Joseph A. Beirne	Howard D. Samuel
Chairman	*Secretary-Treasurer*	*Executive Director*

International Union of United Automobile, Aerospace and Agricultural Implement Workers of America (UAW)

Bakery and Confectionery Workers International Union

International Union of United Brewery Workers

International Chemical Workers Union

Cigarmakers' International

Amalgamated Clothing Workers of America

Communications Workers of America

Coopers International Union of North America

Graphic Arts International Union

International Union of Electrical, Radio and Machine Workers

United Furniture Workers

United Glass and Ceramic Workers

United Hatters, Cap and Millinery Workers International Union

Allied Industrial Workers

International Jewelry Workers

International Association of Machinists and Aerospace Workers

Amalgamated Meat Cutters and Butcher Workmen of North America

International Molders and Allied Workers Union

The Newspaper Guild

Oil, Chemical and Atomic Workers International Union

International Brotherhood of Pottery and Allied Workers

International Printing Pressmen's and Assistants' Union of North America

Retail Clerks International Association

Retail, Wholesale and Department Store Union

United Rubber, Cork, Linoleum and Plastic Workers of America

Service Employees International Union

United Shoe Workers of America

American Federation of State, County and Municipal Employees

American Federation of Teachers

Teamsters Local 688

American Federation of Technical Engineers

Textile Workers Union of America

Transport Workers Union of America

Upholsterers' International Union of North America

International Woodworkers of America

Competing sources of power. A 1975 rally packs RFK Stadium in Washington, D.C., to demand full employment legislation. The protestors shouted down stalwart liberal speakers like Hubert Humphrey, preferring to take matters into their own hands. A laughing George Meany, flanked by the aging AFL-CIO leadership, struggled to keep social change contained in the weakening systems of power the union leadership controlled.

Cultural politics. In the throes of the Watergate scandal, Richard Nixon turns to the people by playing at the Grand Ole Opry in 1974. Merle Haggard's song "Okie from Muskogee" defined the backlash genre and helped refocus working-class identity from material to cultural concerns. As governor, Ronald Reagan pardoned Haggard for his crimes. In 1976, Reagan demonstrates his patriotic faith and indomitable acting ability, en route to making the Republican Party open to "the man and the woman in the factories."

Splinters of pop working-class identity. Devo, named after the backsliding process the group called "de-evolution," emerged from what had once been one of the biggest union towns in the nation. Sally Field becomes a symbol of individual feminist liberation rather than working-class heroics. Here her image is used to advertise a new brand of non-union jeans. Bruce Springsteen, the working-class icon of the 1980s, drowns the pain of blue-collar communities under siege with chants of white patriotic masculinity—"Born in the U.S.A."

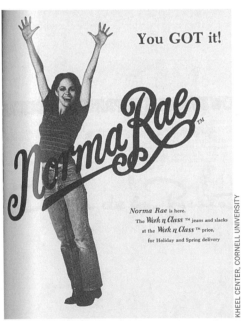

You GOT it!

Norma Rae™

Norma Rae is here.
The *Work n Class* ™ jeans and slacks
at the *Work n Class* ™ price,
for Holiday and Spring delivery

BOOK TWO

Despair in the Order,
1974–1982

5

A Collective Sadness

In the early hours of a dreary February evening in 1977, Michael Harrington turned up his collar and trudged across his beloved Greenwich Village. As he wandered through the drizzling rain, the aging radical found himself recoiling viscerally at the scenes of decadence and demoralization before him. "Panhandlers accosted me; junkies huddled in doorways near their haunt on Sixth Avenue and Eighth Street; a graying burly black man stood with a liquor bottle in his hand mumbling incoherently, oblivious to the rain." His mental snapshots of poverty in 1977 contrasted vividly with those of his most famous work, *The Other America* (1962), a study that exposed how the poor were rendered invisible by the glow of postwar splendor. His earlier work proved a spur toward the War on Poverty, but his reflections on that grey winter evening fifteen years later focused less on the callousness of the affluent society or the inequities of capitalism itself than on the failure of his generation of leftists to answer so many of the questions they had originally posed about American society. *The Other America* was a call to arms; Harrington's hand-wringing in 1977 was a reckoning with the failures of the battles. "Are my friends and I," he queried rhetorically, "the radical critics of this system, partly responsible for these shattered people?"[1]

Harrington, a figure awkwardly bridging Old and New Left traditions, now the left-wing elder groping for answers in the seventies, was haunted by an eerie sense of responsibility for the decrepit state of civil society, not just in the crumbling streets of New York but in the nation as a whole. The radicalism of the sixties had collapsed with only a partial victory, he feared, leaving a value-less freedom standing amidst the political rubble. "We radicals had mocked the old verities and preached a new freedom, only our negatives were more powerful than our creativity," he confessed. "We proposed that men and women find their purpose within themselves, that they disdain all traditional crutches, like God and flag. But were we then to blame because many seemed to have heard only that the old constraints had been abolished and ignored the call to find new obligations on their own?" The oversupply of big questions, the paucity of even small answers, and liberals' inability to cope with the economics of the seventies, Harrington sensed, were creating new opportunities not for his beloved Left but for a resurgent Right. Conservatives, he feared, were setting to work rejuvenating the political potency of those old standbys of God and flag, while liberals and the Left were building a complex and towering social agenda on a collective economic vision that was on the verge of collapse.[2]

Continuing across lower Manhattan, he reflected on how the scenes unfolding before him contrasted markedly with the vibrant Village culture of dissent of his youth during the forties. "The drinking, the flouting of established sexual mores and the breaking of literary and artistic rules were all part of a serious, often joyous, commitment to antivalues," he recalled. "The disorder I encountered in Greenwich Village of 1949 had been orderly and constructive," he believed, "something more akin to the building of a new anti-bourgeois morality." In contrast, the "human denigration" and "aimless rutting" of the seventies was deeply troubling in its hedonism, its nihilism, its destructiveness. It was "not calculated or whimsical or aesthetic," Harrington lamented. His observations may have been fueled by more than a whiff of nostalgia on the occasion of his forty-ninth birthday, but he feared that what he saw around him was "a fate, not a choice, one more by-product of the urban (the societal?) disintegration in which I—and millions of New Yorkers—live."[3]

Officially, Harrington maintained his optimism about the long-run triumph of the working-class Left, but these musings of America's most prominent left-wing intellectual contained a corrosive fear about the incapacity of dissent. The radical Left, he believed, could only succeed as much as it could rely upon the strength of the liberal establishment (as opposed to rejecting it wholesale as had so many of his comrades in the sixties). The New Deal, he believed, had not just been an amalgam of programs but a way of making sense of the world—it gave order, vision, architecture, and direction to social life. In lieu of that collapsing sensibility, he feared that the nation could only look forward to "a period of continuous, nerve-wracking disequilibria, and so long as we do not know how to cope with that fact, the society will be pervaded by a certain kind of social meanness." The seventies were the "years in-between" in which "some of the most basic of the old truths—about religion and art and sex as well as politics and economics—decayed." The combined impact of Watergate, the fall of Saigon, the oil crisis, and the drift of the Democratic Party drew Harrington to two starkly different possibilities: "one must retreat back to Herbert Hoover; or, therefore one must proceed far beyond Franklin Roosevelt." He undoubtedly hoped for the latter but lived to watch the former unfold.[4]

Harrington began to fear his intellectual and political incapacity as early as the transitional year 1974, but he could only fall back on the old answers. "What is obviously required," Harrington noted in an essay in *Dissent* called "A Collective Sadness," "is an offensive by the labor movement aimed, not simply at bettering the position of this or that segment of the working people, but at changing the rules of the game so that there can be some kind of rational solution to the inflationary challenge." Yet 1974 marked not a rise in working-class militancy but its recession. For workers, the strike wave, stopped dead in its tracks by the economic crisis, faded into cultural conflicts with battles over abortion, pornography, busing, out of wedlock birth, affirmative action, rising crime, women's liberation, and gay rights moving into the spotlight. These quickly eclipsed an older order, one infused with a vision of collective economic rights that had itself been deeply compromised at its New Deal birth by its racial and gender limitations. In lieu of the labor "offensive" Harrington longed for, he admitted, "the dominant mood is one of scrambling to make the best of a bad lot. This corrodes what solidarity does exist; it privatizes social struggles and it makes people sad. It also creates the basis for a similar disintegration in our political life. Here, too, the centrifugal forces seem to predominate."[5]

Throughout the cultural and intellectual storms, Harrington maintained his hope that the "sense of foreboding and fear" seeping through western consciousness in the seventies might still lead to what he called the *Twilight of Capitalism* (1976). Some force had to seize control of the crisis, he believed, and it would either be the snowballing liberal state (leading eventually toward socialism) or the complete corporate takeover of all aspects of society. It had to cut one way or the other. "The next America is at hand," Harrington admitted, and it was both "inevitable and indeterminate." He may have remained unsure as to the direction, but he was sure that "the last America, a coherence inherited from the 1930s, is going, going, almost gone." In Harrington's continued hopes for socialism, the optimism of his will may have been betting heavily against the pessimism of his mind. By the end of the decade, it looked a lot more like the twilight of the working class than the twilight of capitalism. A political economy more redolent of pre–New Deal forms was poised to return, not just destroying Harrington's hopes of socialism, but enervating the very liberalism, and the type of working-class identity, on which his plans for more radical change rested.[6]

The intellectual ambivalence of the mid-1970s went far beyond Harrington's shrinking circle of left-wing politicos and encroached on much of mainstream civil society. Confusion, fragmentation, indulgence, and self-absorption were seeping into the cracks of the nation's fragile sense of collective destiny. Daniel Bell, in his *The Coming of Post-Industrial Society* (1973), pointed to the cultural rootlessness of a society whose social framework had shifted from goods producing to service work, from the labor of production to the control of technical knowledge. Bell noted that the nation, caught in a culture of interregnum, had allegedly become, variously, postmodern, post-historic, post-capitalist, post-collectivist, post-ideological, post-Puritan, post-Christian, post-traditional, or even post-civilized depending on whom one wished to believe. Yet the adoption of the prefix "post" had already conceded that nobody knew where the culture was going—it was, for better or worse, "pre" nothing. A few years later in Bell's *Cultural Contradictions of Capitalism* (1976), he argued that the pursuit of expressive individualism had undermined the common good, leading to a culture of hedonism and pleasure that had delivered the nation to the edge. There was an absence of a "transcendental ethic" of the sort that had animated Harrington in the forties, that could guide the morals, politics, and culture of dissent toward an emancipatory vision for mankind (other than what might, at best, lead to some kind of tepid multicultural capitalism or a more tolerant and expansive incarnation of competitive corporate individualism).[7]

The problem was not simply that other aspects of social identity—race, gender, sexuality, religious faith—were eclipsing class as points of reference in political life, but that working people, having transcended basic material deprivation of the sort they had struggled against in the 1930s, faced a form of class conflict that was more internal and psychological, pivoting on social power and self-worth rather than outward contests with powerful forces. Two sociologists of the seventies, Richard Sennett and Jonathan Cobb, called it *The Hidden Injuries of Class*. With class dissolving into ethnicity and resentment, inequality began to be perceived as a personal fate rather than collective responsibility. "This represents the 'internalizing' of class conflict," they explained, "the process by which struggle between men leads to struggle within each man." The politics of this were elusive. "The burden of class today is thus a strange phenomenon," continue Sennett and Cobb; "social inequality is maintained by creating a morality of anxiety," and "the logic of discontent leads people to turn on each other rather than on the 'system.'" The new "inner class warfare" helps to explain the turn of white, male workers toward the politics of resentment and promises of a Reaganesque golden age restoration in the late seventies and eighties. "The psychological motivation instilled by a class society is to heal a doubt about the self rather than create more power over things and other persons in the outer world." Figures like George Wallace, Richard Nixon, and Ronald Reagan offered psychic salve to the wounds of pride, while the new path of liberalism seemed to offer little more than to deepen the threats of that outer world.[8]

In other hands, the same problems that Harrington and Sennett and Cobb explored sympathetically could readily be twisted into condescension and outright dismissal. Among the dismissive was writer Tom Wolfe, who divined the zeitgeist of the era when he dubbed the seventies "The Me Decade" in his famous 1976 essay. Wolfe appropriately defamed the era as a time in which individual emancipation trumped the idea of the civic good, in which decadence looked liked politics, and glitter could be mistaken for substance. If the political revolution could not be realized in post-sixties America, Wolfe argued, the only thing left was the "alchemical dream" of revolutionizing the self. As if to confirm Wolfe's analysis, the seventies would often be symbolized by a spinning mirrored disco ball reflecting a mosaic of "hundreds of little me's"—swirling fragments of individualism that made a mockery of the antediluvian dream of solidarity.[9]

Wolfe's Me Decade epithet stuck as the unofficial moniker of the decade, but often overlooked in his famous essay is his sentencing of workers to the ashbin of history. With reasoning simultaneously flawed and indicative of a deeper ideological shift, he banked his entire conceptualization of the Me Decade not on the agency but on the profligacy of the American worker, a theme that many economists and policy makers echoed throughout the inflationary decade. "In America truck drivers, mechanics, factory workers, policemen, firemen, and garbagemen make so much money," Wolfe breathlessly proclaimed, "that the word 'proletarian' can no longer be used in this country with a straight face. . . . One can't even call workingmen 'blue collar' any longer. They all have on collars like Joe Namath's or Johnny Bench's or Walt Frazier's."[10]

Wolfe's analysis of the Me Decade thus leaned on one of the biggest myths in postwar America: the assumption that postwar affluence had solved the problems of class. The dazzling success of the postwar boom meant that working people could now spend their time, like royalty of yore, "dwelling on the self." Never mind the imprisoning assembly lines at Lordstown, the dreary row houses defended by the anti-busers, the wage earners condemned to the lowest end of the corporate machinery, inner cities bereft of manufacturing, women and minorities facing down unresponsive union leadership, or those on the frontlines of the nation's churning racial tensions. The postwar era undoubtedly delivered a new level of affluence for blue collar America, but it hardly meant that workers had few concerns beyond blithely lining up for consciousness raisings, est seminars, therapy sessions, and encounter groups as Wolfe charged. His argument was more than a misguided portrayal of working-class decadence—it was also a glib "I told you so" to generations of leftists who believed that in the breast of the worker burned the hope of emancipation from capitalism. "Once the dreary little bastards started getting money in the 1940s," Wolfe lectured, "they did an astonishing thing—they took their money and ran!" Wolfe banked his entire argument on conflating prosperity with the end of class and did so just when the boom was collapsing into what he admitted to be the "grim slide" of the seventies.[11]

More sophisticated commentators neither blamed working people for the dawning culture of rampant individualism nor held out grandiose hopes for a proletariat whose heart beat to the call of freedom. Christopher Lasch, who elaborated a more refined version of the "me" jeremiad in his *Culture of Narcissism: American Life in an Age of Diminishing Expectations* (1979), identified the same cultural pathogen as Wolfe but reversed the class diagnosis. He, too, feared that hedonism, consumption, cultural radicalism, and an obsession with the therapeutic had drained modern life of much of its meaning. For Lasch, it was a crisis of the elites, not working people, one professionals foisted onto the rest of the society in a sort of inter-class cultural imperialism. Lacking a sense of history and direction—neither past nor future—the knowledge class possessed little more than a capacity to dwell on the self. For Lasch, the one element of hope rested not with the politicians, the new radicals, the corporate elite, but in the hands of everyday people. He admitted, however, that when "the common man thinks about his prospects, we find plenty of evidence to confirm the impression that the modern world faced the future without hope." As he summarized the emerging paradigm, "Class consciousness declines; people perceive their social position as a reflection of their own abilities and blame themselves for the injustices inflicted upon them. Politics degenerates into a struggle not for social change but for self-realization."[12]

Even as recalcitrant a figure as George Meany could feel the post-1974 malaise as the hope of the early part of the decade dissolved into the despair of the latter half. After Watergate and the inglorious end to the war in Vietnam, Meany lamented that the nation "has sounded the trumpet of retreat and withdrawal—retreat from decency at home and withdrawal from principle everywhere else." President Gerald Ford, in his 1975 State of the Union address, concurred. "I must say to you that the state of the Union is not good: Millions of Americans are out of work. Recession and inflation are eroding the money of millions more. Prices are too high, and sales are too slow. This year's Federal deficit will be about $30 billion; next year's probably $45 billion. The national debt will rise to over $500 billion. Our plant capacity and productivity are not increasing fast enough. We depend on others for essential energy. Some people question their Government's ability to make hard decisions and stick with them; they expect Washington politics as usual." Plunging into the heart of his speech, Ford continued, "I've got bad news, and I don't expect much, if any, applause." Another chronicler put Ford's litany more succinctly. The mid-1970s were shaping up to be "the age of the rip-off."[13]

There may have been even bigger historical changes at work. The authors of *Habits of the Heart,* a study of the pain and promise of American individualism conceived in the latter half of the seventies, recognized "a widespread feeling that the promise of the modern era is slipping away from us." Questions about the direction of liberal democracy could only be compared to the crisis in European thinking in the disastrous interwar years. "Progress, modernity's master idea," the authors felt after extended interviews with ordinary American citizens, "seems less compelling when it appears that it may be progress into the abyss." The problem was not stifling conformity as it may have been in the fifties, but an overabundance of "expressive individualism" that eroded commitment to community and responsibility. Similarly, the noted historian Henry Steele Commager wondered if the nation perhaps stood at the "divide of disillusionment" in 1974, while Harvard University president Derek Bok lamented the "obvious dearth of people who seem able to supply convincing answers, or to point to directions toward solutions."[14]

Taken together, the economic, social, and cultural problems of the seventies were brewing into what Andrew Levison called the "sociological perfect storm" for working people. The insurgent energies of the first part of the decade lost traction in the labor movement; the white, male Nixonian working class was quickly veering right on cultural grounds; the attempts to marry the New Politics with old labor proved barren; and understandings of how race and gender worked tended to lack a touch point of class analysis. As one disturbing 1976 study of the dynamics of the working-class family summarized it, "The affluent and happy worker of whom we have heard so much in recent decades seems not to exist." More troubling, however, were the shrinking outlets, the diminished civic space, for the problems of that worker as the decade progressed. "Everything now is 'was,'" wrote novelist Philip Roth about the decade. "The old system that made order doesn't work anymore. All that was left was . . . fear and astonishment, but now concealed by nothing." The weakened culture of economic dissent and a Democratic Party "losing its class-based strength" proved weak opponents to a revitalized business lobby and economic thinkers brandishing new ideological weapons, determined to regain the upper hand in the hearts and minds of both Washington's policy circles and the nation's workplaces. The sense of foreboding blanketed much of the political spectrum, but it was the conservative movement that would eventually seize the upper hand in the mid-decade shift.[15]

Five months after Harrington took his troubling stroll, his worst fears about the state of civil society came true when, on a sweltering July night, New York City exploded into chaos. A lightning bolt struck, the city's infrastructure failed, the lights went out, and the city descended into another one of its blackouts. The day had been over one hundred degrees, and the night was moonless. The unemployment rate was high, and the city teetered on the brink of insolvency—it had been less than two years since the *Daily News'* famous headline, "Ford to City: Drop Dead" when a federal bailout was denied. The mood was already distinctly uncharitable, and then everything went bad in the darkness and the silence. After the night was over, the police had arrested several thousand looters, the firefighters responded to over one thousand fires, entire car lots were looted, stores ransacked, and the main boulevards of the boroughs were a parade of people struggling to run weighed down with as much merchandise as they could carry. Most everyone got away, as the police were outnumbered and fearful that a more aggressive response would end in an escalation of the violence. In the night of "shared sense of outrage and impotence," as the *Times* called it, only the newly emerging hip-hop industry seemed to profit. The genre got its first major material boost as young men swiped mountains of stereo equipment, giving birth to new DJs across the Bronx. "Everybody was out to get theirs," remarked one looter in an epigram for the new mood; "I wanted to get mine."[16]

Bestial metaphors swirled around the press and white popular discourse to describe the looters and arsonists on the "night of the animals." Historian Herbert Gutman, writing in the *New York Times*, tried to remind the city that Jewish women taking part in a 1902 kosher meat riot had also been described as "animals" and "beasts," "vultures" and a "jackal pack." He was not even trying to create a direct comparison between the events, merely arguing that animal metaphors served to separate "the behavior of the discontented poor (striking, rioting, looting, boycotting) from the conditions that shape their discontent." He noted how "history teaches us that a thin line connects the orderly and the disorderly, but the animal metaphor transmutes that thin line into a space—a crevice"—that separates "us" from "them." The piles of letters arriving at the *Times* proved the city's white ethnic population would have nothing of the comparison. Their ancestors worked hard and made something of themselves; their ancestors rose above; their ancestors' protests were moral acts. These people, came the white consensus, were different.[17]

I

Economists, the priestly figures of postwar policy, seized the moment to recast the mid-century working-class hero from the protagonist of postwar theology into the biblical scapegoat of the seventies. Many were determined to lay the economic sins of the era upon his head and banished him into the political wilderness. Using terms not dissimilar to those of Tom Wolfe, economists quickly found their way to accusing workers of becoming coddled and spoiled, apparently the source of not just wage-push inflation but a larger national rot. The 1970s ended up as the first decade in which, according to many elite opinion makers, working people simply made too much money, were too protected from the discipline of the market, and were so demanding as to destabilize the entire economy. As *Fortune* put it, "The gravest problem facing the Western world in the early 1970's is cost-push inflation powered by excessive wage increases." The source, the "overreaching" demands of organized labor, had to be disciplined. For the first time in world history, to take the claims seriously, the (comparatively weak) American welfare state and collective bargaining system had pampered its citizenry to the point of endangering the stability of the entire political economy. The workers, it seemed, had to take their medicine.[18]

So, the seventies became, in policy terms, almost the reverse of the thirties. Since under consumption and over production were the problems of the thirties, the political solutions ultimately settled on full employment and modest redistribution of wealth (through collective bargaining and the welfare state) in order to stimulate consumer demand. In the seventies, however, the dance was more economically complicated and politically vexing. When inflation, theoretically created by the rising prices of an overheated economy, went up, unemployment was supposed to go down as the demand for labor increased to meet the greater demand for goods. By mid decade, however, it was clear that a stagnant economy had joined forces with high inflation, leading to a new, and heretofore improbable, term: stagflation (stagnation plus inflation). As Arthur Burns, the Federal Reserve Chair under Nixon, explained, "the rules of economics are not working quite the way they used to." In 1975, the unemployment rate had shot up to 8.5 from only 3.5 percent in 1969, setting the record high for the postwar era to that date (it would be surpassed again in 1980). The inflation rate was 9.2 percent in 1975, which had fallen since 1974's record of 11 percent (a figure that would again be topped at the end of the decade). The combined inflation and unemployment figures—the "misery index" as it was coined—for 1975 was a shocking 17.7.[19]

The Great Inflation of the seventies absolutely dominated all political concerns, yet to this day there is debate between two general interpretations of its causation. One places the blame on the extreme supply shocks—most obviously caused by the 1973 Arab oil embargo. Another, which would dominate labor discussions, blamed excessive demand created by the commitment to full employment and high wages. Both of these built upon the over-spending during the 1960s on the Vietnam War. Liberal economist Robert Solow placed himself in the latter category, explaining that, "the single most important reason for inflation is that we are a society that has tried to prevent deep recessions, to provide income security for people and to help those who suffer. We no longer let big businesses go bankrupt or people go unemployed for a long time." Others, such as Ray Marshall, Carter's labor secretary, pinned the problem indisputably on the oil crisis. "You would have to really strain to argue that wages caused that inflation," Marshall explained. "That inflation was caused by external oil price shocks and therefore what they wanted to do was to let the workers pay for it with high unemployment. But it wouldn't be just the workers paying for it. The Democratic Party was going to pay for it." Perhaps the most honest answer was that what to do was any expert's guess. "In the 1970s, particularly that period at the end of the seventies," explained Alice Rivlin, director of the Congressional Budget Office during the Ford, Carter, and early Reagan years, "It was just almost impossible to say what good economic policy would have been. Nobody had thought through what you do when we have stagflation. . . . It was easy to criticize what they were doing, but it wasn't clear, even in hindsight, what should have been done."[20]

Despite the confused sense of causation about inflation, it provided a political opening for those interested in disciplining the labor market. Since solving the energy component of the inflationary spiral would require either a reconfiguration of the global order or a massive commitment to alternative energy, restraining demand became the experts' favorite tactic. It was the type of political opening that anyone interested in containing cost pressures in the labor market had been waiting for. Postwar governments' unwillingness to toss economies into cleansing recessions, a very successful strain of logic went, resulted in inflationary economies that created an ongoing conundrum: the Keynesian economics designed to make the labor market more just ended up introducing a pattern of escalating wages and prices that necessitated the undoing of those earlier remedies. The confusion opened up the space for a new argument: the New Deal would have to go.

Business Week captured perfectly the new mood. Inflation, reasoned the weekly's writers in 1974, was caused by "the world wide commitment to full employment and maximum production. Without exception, the governments of the world have consistently chosen to risk inflation rather than risk unemployment." Yet even those sympathetic to the workers' plight, like Nobel laureate Paul A. Samuelson, who remained puzzled by the seventies economy, put the problem this way: inflation "is a terrible blemish on the mixed economy and a sad reflection on my generation of economists that we're not the Merlins that can solve the problem. Inflation is deep in the nature of the welfare state. Even when there is slack in the system, unemployment doesn't exert downward pressure on prices the way it did under 'cruel capitalism.' But I don't think that anyone wants to turn the clock back."[21]

Many did prefer to turn back the clock, as history would unfold, finding that the old disease of low wages of the thirties was now the new cure for bloat in the seventies. They saw workers' growing sense of entitlement, especially union power, at the root of the nation's problems. "The insistence of strong, aggressive unions on keeping wages rising faster than prices is one of the underlying forces that give the U.S. an inflationary bias," explained *Business Week*. Unions, once the booster of Keynesian consumption and the tamers of the savageness of the industrial order, had now become the problem. "Organized labor has now become a destabilizing and dislocating force— made more unmanageable by large political influence," explained *Fortune*. "Some people will obviously have to do with less," editorialized *Business Week*; "Yet it will be a hard pill for many Americans to swallow—the idea of doing with less so that big business can have more."[22]

In essence, full employment, high wages, and high consumption, the pillars of the postwar success story, many experts argued, were in the process of killing prosperity. Doing the right thing had unintended consequences. Economists on the right could not agree fast enough. Former Federal Reserve official Milton Hudson pinned the problem on "the almost universal commitment to the objective of 'full employment' . . . and the welfare-state idea which holds that government ought to have a continuing active concern with the poor, the sick, the aged and the chronically unemployed." Inflationary factors such as the funding for the Vietnam War or the oil shocks faded into the need to discipline the labor market. The take-home message at mid decade was that weakening the policy network that offered security to the nation's citizens and redistribution of the nation's income was the only path out of the deepening economic morass. A return to cruel capitalism it would have to be.[23]

An unequal battle quickly ensued over which side of the economic equation deserved attention. Conservatives tended to look at inflation, and liberals toward unemployment. When the UAW's Irving Bluestone sat before a House subcommittee, for instance, and argued that the nation was close to returning to the dark days of the Depression, he was advocating for the resurrection of New Deal politics. "It is now widely recognized that our nation is going through the worst recession since the 1930s. Many people scoff at any comparison between the current slump and the Great Depression. While it is true that by absolute measures of human misery we have not sunk to the depths experienced then, it is no time to be smug—the parallels are getting closer." Any remedy that sought to address the jobs side of the problem, however, risked exacerbating the inflationary side. As President Ford explained in politically viable logic, "Unemployment is the biggest concern of the 8.2 percent of American workers temporarily out of work, but inflation is the universal enemy of 100 percent of our people." The early seventies therefore marks the time in which unemployment, long the bugaboo of capitalism, was being eclipsed in the minds of mainstream economists, policy makers, and politicians by fears of its near enemy—inflation.[24]

At the same time, the nation running out of energy was both a reality and a metaphor, and the problem of limits shaped the entire discussion. It haunted Richard Nixon, stymied Gerald Ford, all but destroyed the Carter presidency, and opened up the space for the Reagan restoration of the new Gilded Age, an era reminiscent of the nineteenth-century robber barons. Walter Lippman, the aged journalist-philosopher, noted that Nixon's role in history would be "to liquidate, defuse, deflate the exaggerations of the romantic period of American imperialism and American inflation. Inflation of promises, inflation of hopes, the Great Society, American supremacy—all that had to be deflated because it was all beyond our power and beyond the nature of things." Whether it was beyond any essential "nature" of the universe to have hope, it certainly seemed beyond the nature of the decade as Nixon's humiliation in Watergate and defeat in Vietnam seemed to go to great lengths to prove. By the time Ford filled in after Nixon's resignation, the litany of a restricted future had become less abstract and more particular until Carter was forced to concede that "dealing with limits" was the "subliminal theme" of his presidency. Yet it was often not that subliminal. As he explained in 1979, "We have a keener appreciation of limits now—the limits of government, limits on the use of military power abroad; the limits on manipulating, without harm to ourselves, a delicate and balanced natural environment. We are struggling with a profound transition from a time of abundance to a time of growing scarcity in energy."[25]

The pervasive sense of limits led readily to the need for austerity, fueled by skepticism of the efficacy of the post-Watergate state. The bookstores, for instance, were replete with titles from every scholarly and journalistic field proclaiming the age of limits: *Social Limits to Growth* (1976), *An Inquiry into the Human Prospect* (1974), *Limits to Satisfaction* (1976), *The Limits to Growth* (1972), *Ecology and Politics of Scarcity* (1977) *The Zero-Sum Society* (1980), *How to Prosper in the Coming Bad Years* (1979), and *The Broken Covenant* (1975). Most people had a hard time imagining the state that brought Vietnam, Watergate, and the inflated hopes of the Great Society would be of much help. "During most of the 1960s, the prevalent belief was that some kind of federal budgetary program could be designed to deal with almost any social problem," explained the Brookings' Charles Schultze, who would proceed to be Carter's chief economic advisor. "This conventional wisdom of a few years ago seems now to have been replaced by its polar opposite: most federal programs do not work well and consist principally in 'throwing money' at problems." In 1976, the Nobel Prize–winning economist Wassily Leonteif noted that the "real trouble at present is that the government not only does not know what road it wants to follow, but does not even have a road map." As the *New York Times* declared in 1977 under the headline "Paralyzed Economists, Stagnant Economy," the stagflation crisis proved the "bankruptcy of modern theory" that had governed economic thinking since World War II. "The resulting intellectual vacuum," the paper editorialized, "has pushed economic policy to the right, by default."[26]

Befitting the moment, libertarian economist and conservative intellectual Milton Friedman was awarded the Nobel Prize for economics in 1976 as his thinking flooded into the intellectual void. Echoing some of the stark policy logic that Harrington laid out from the left, Friedman argued in his Nobel address, "the present situation cannot last. It will either degenerate into hyperinflation and radical change; or institutions will adjust to a situation of chronic inflation; or governments will adopt policies that will produce a low rate of inflation and less government intervention into the fixing of prices." He believed that the crisis of stagflation opened the door to much more conservative policies than at any other time. "The watershed in the abandonment of Keynesian doctrine," he told historian Godfrey Hodgson, "was the conflict between Keynesian orthodoxy and the Phillips curve," which was the model that predicted the tidy trade-off between employment and inflation. Friedman claimed that by solving inflation, the nation would also take care of a preposterously large basket of mid-1970s rot, including the "generalized erosion in public and private manners, increasingly liberalized attitudes toward sexual activities, a declining vitality of the Puritan work ethic . . . explosion of the welfare rolls, widespread corruption," all of which derived from the "devil-take-tomorrow attitude fostered by rising prices." The shift in economic thinking away from postwar orthodoxy came slowly to the nation's attention, but, by the time of the collapse of liberal alternatives advocated by some during the Carter years, there was already a vibrant policy school in exile waiting to seize the ear of the nation's leaders and overturn liberal economic thinking.[27]

The remobilization of the business leadership was one of the most dramatic shifts in postwar policy history, recasting the legislative landscape for generations to come. If the New Deal was the revolution, this was the counter-revolution. Having contained labor policy for the entirety of the postwar era, corporations lost key legislative battles during the Johnson and Nixon years, fought to a stalemate during the transition period from 1975–77, and, by 1978, got reorganized and stood poised to win almost every battle on taxation, spending, regulation, and inflation for decades to come.[28]

II

Despite the draconian demands of policy makers, few working people were immediately abandoning the Keynesian ship—there was not a large-scale lurch to the right in *popular* economic thinking. The conservative movement made substantial inroads into white workers' cultural identity in the late sixties and early seventies, but it was still a long way from scoring points on economic grounds. This is where Nixon's groundwork on wooing working-class voters paid off, and where conservative strategists began to learn what country musicians already knew. Economics may have broken the policy levees and convinced policy elites, but it was the social issues that delivered working people to the new political waters. As the New Right's media guru Richard Viguerie noted, "We never really won until we began stressing issues like busing, abortion, school prayer and gun control. We talked about the sanctity of free enterprise, about the Communist onslaught until we were blue in face. But we didn't start winning majorities in elections until we got down to gut level issues." In a similar vein, Pat Buchanan continued his earlier work for Nixon, plowing terrain and sowing seed for a working-class right—often consciously setting the poorer and the more affluent elements of the New Deal coalition off from one another. The future of the Republican Party, he argued, would be as "the party of the working class, not the party of the welfare class." The federal government and know-it-all cultural elitists were well on their way to eclipsing the bosses as the workingman's enemy. As M. Stanton Evans, the president of the American Conservative Union, put it, the key was finding a common ground of anti-statism: "some of them reach their political position by reading Adam Smith while others do so by attending an anti-busing rally, but . . . all of them belong to a large and growing class of American citizens: those who perceive themselves as victims of the federal welfare state and its attendant costs."[29]

William Rusher, in his 1975 book *The Making of the New Majority Party*, argued, like Tom Wolfe, that the politics of old class divisions were over. An odd cross-class coalition of business, industrialists, blue-collar workers and farmers stood in opposition to a McGovernite "new class led by elements that were essentially non-productive" members of the chattering classes— like academics, intellectuals, government bureaucrats, and the media elite— who claimed to know what was good for the nation. The modern welfare state, Rusher argued, "exists simply as a permanent parasite on the body politics—a heavy charge on both its conscience and its purse, carefully tended and for-ever subtly expanded by the verbalizers as justification for their own exis-tence and growth." Although strategists like Rusher and Viguerie had hoped that they might be able to entice former actor and California governor Ron-ald Reagan as the standard bearer for a new Conservative Party (sharing a dream ticket with George Wallace, they hoped), Reagan finally rejected the tactic of a new party but fully embraced the white working-class Republican ideal. In 1976, Reagan failed to win the nomination of his party for the presidency, but he was en route to capturing its soul.[30]

As Reagan told the Conservative Political Action Conference in 1977, "And let me say so there can be no mistakes as to what I mean:

> The New Republican Party I envision will not be, and cannot be, one limited to the country club-big business image that, for reasons both fair and unfair, it is burdened with today. The New Republican Party I am speaking about is go-ing to have room for the man and the woman in the factories, for the farmer, for the cop on the beat and the millions of Americans who may never have thought of joining our party before, but whose interests coincide with those represented by principled Republicanism. . . . The Democratic Party turned its back on the majority of social conservatives during the 1960s. The New Repub-lican Party of the late '70s and '80s must welcome them, seek them out, enlist them, not only as rank-and-file members but as leaders and as candidates.

The New Right's coalition linked worker and businessman, shop floor and Wall Street, tavern and country club, cultural conservative and economic libertarian. Roosevelt's famous "Forgotten Man" was becoming a Republican, his enemy less the "economic royalists," the class *elites*, against which Roose-velt inveighed in his landslide 1936 victory, than the cultural *elitists* who would look down on the politics and culture of blue-collar America. Not all of even the white, male working class joined the New Right, of course, but certainly enough to make a viable coalition on the margins where elec-tions are won.[31]

Meantime, as one wag put it, like the old labor radical Joe Hill, business leaders did not mourn; they got organized. Following, sometimes quite consciously, the structure of power set up by organized labor's political action committees (PACs) in the forties and fifties, business awoke to its own political power and found renewed unity and class consciousness. Figures such as Nixon's secretary of the Treasury John Connally and Federal Reserve chairman Arthur Burns warned business leaders as much, explaining to them that they had "to shape up in sophistication and techniques in Washington or else go down the political tube." The degree of business unity, pushed by the economic crisis and the disillusionment with corporations, was at an extraordinary high level by any twentieth-century measure. One of the convenient tools came from the unintended consequences of the Campaign Finance Reform Act (1971)—as expanded by the Federal Election Commission in 1975—which, by increasing the number of business PACs dramatically, "effectively handed business a license to print political money." The number of PACs quadrupled in the four years following Watergate, from 248 to 1,100. Between 1968 and 1978, corporations with offices in Washington, DC, increased from one hundred to over five hundred, and those offices increased in staff from one or two people to six or seven. GM only had three staffers lobbying the capitol in 1968; a decade later they had twenty-eight. From a nadir of political power in the early seventies, business "achieved virtual domination of the legislative process in Congress" by the end of the decade.[32]

Building a vigorous political agenda for corporate America in the 1970s was neither a foregone conclusion nor an easy task. Not only did it take beating back the labor insurgencies of the first half of the decade and the policy attempts to come in the latter half (see Chapter 6), but it required rebuilding confidence in the corporation during a decade marked by faith lost in all institutions. The number of people expressing a great deal of confidence in corporate leadership in 1966 stood at 55 percent, falling to 21 percent in 1974, and a mere 15 percent by 1975. In fact, the decade that eventually marked such a sharp turn to the right began not with the success of conservative policies but with a flood of liberal regulations during the Nixon administration designed to tame corporate excess. Nixon may have been trying to romance the New Right worker of the day on cultural grounds, but he also had conceded a great deal of actual policy to the liberals. Between 1969 and 1974, the federal government passed the National Environmental Policy Act, the Clean Air Act Amendments, the Occupational

Safety and Health Act, the Consumer Product Safety Act, the Federal Water Pollution Control Act, the Noise Pollution and Control Act, the Equal Employment Opportunity Act, the Campaign Finance Amendments, and the Employment Retirement Income Security Act. Liberalism was still very much at full tide even if this was mostly focused on corporate regulation rather than redistributive policy. As a 1975 *Fortune* magazine article complained in somewhat hysterical terms, the wave of new laws was "putting the cuffs on capitalism." The magazine continued, "through streams of legislation, spreading and minutely detailed regulation, frequent application of moral suasion, and various other means, the government is now present—either in person, or somewhat like Banquo's ghost, in disturbing spirit—at every major business meeting."[33]

It was not until the second half of the decade that management's plans—meshing with labor's growing weaknesses and the deepening economic crisis—began to yield success, and the creation of the Business Roundtable embodied businesses' efforts to act concertedly and aggressively. The Roundtable consolidated three different, and sometimes competing, streams of activity. First and most important was the Construction Users Anti-Inflation Roundtable (CUAIR), which emerged in the late sixties from an effort to stop the wage-driven inflationary spiral in the construction industry. U.S. Steel's Roger Blough, who made it his personal mission to tame the construction unions through CUAIR, declared to Congress in 1971, "The No. 1 domestic problem of the country is the effect of the wage push on the total lives of everyone." CUAIR's enemies were the powerful building trades unions and their hiring halls, the "anachronistic, obsolete and inflationary" Davis-Bacon Act (born of the Depression and which guaranteed prevailing union wages in public works projects), and fear of a common-situs picketing bill that, if passed, would allow a single striking union to shut down all of the various trades at a single construction site. Nixon had suspended Davis-Bacon for almost a month in 1971 in an attempt to get the unions to moderate their wage demands (and attempted to open up the construction labor market with minority hiring); CUAIR and the executive branch had failed to make much of a dent in the structure of the industry. Both Davis-Bacon and the building trades formed a bit of a lock on the construction labor market, but they also served as bastions of white privilege and minority exclusion in those coveted high-paying jobs in big construction. The dire need to open up the building trades to minority workers meant that a natural alliance emerged between racially conscious liberals and the new free-market lobbyists, lined up against the old building trades unions who reacted paro-chially to defend privileged access to the construction labor market.[34]

"Restoration of the Management Role in the Construction Industry" may have been the official reason behind the attack on construction wages, but the broader concern was that those high wages formed a psychological virus that, if not checked, could spread through the entire labor market. Blough spoke of the "magnet-like pull" of construction wages on industrial pay that would help to galvanize other business leaders to join the fight. GM's vice president and director of labor relations argued, "We have building trade union mem-bers rubbing shoulders with our own auto worker union skilled mechanics who perform the same jobs. The building trades people were not above say-ing: 'Hey, buddy. If you were a member of the electrical workers union in-stead of the auto workers, you'd have this kind of check.' They jab them and they irritate them, so that our electrician goes down to his UAW local and says, 'Goddamn. How come that guy gets $8.50 an hour and I get $5.80?'"[35]

After the CUAIR, the second and third elements in the creation of the Business Roundtable were the Labor Law Study Committee, which was trying to match organized labor's political influence on policy issues, and the "March Group," founded by the chairmen of Alcoa and General Electric in order to find ways to improve the tarnished image of big business in both government and the media. Seeing their concerns allied, the three groups incarnated as the Business Roundtable in 1973, advancing the cause of the group above the trench warfare in the construction industry to the broader issues of corporate image and business climate—what they called telling "business's story." The Business Roundtable became a nationally recognized phenomenon when it blocked the AFL-CIO in its struggle to pass labor law reform in 1978. The defeat of that bill (detailed in Chapter 6) as Senator Orrin Hatch remarked, served as the foundation for "a starting point for a new era of assertiveness by big business in Washington." With over one hundred of the nation's biggest corporations—from U.S. Steel and GM to AT&T and Bank of America—united in an alliance to sway the federal government and public opinion, it was "like a populist's nightmare come true." The group linked up high-profile CEOs with a series of think tanks, academic studies, and outlets like *Reader's Digest*, all aimed at the Business Roundtable's principle political adversary, which had expanded well beyond the building trades to become the entirety of organized labor.[36]

Unlike older business lobbying groups like the National Association of Manufacturers or the Chamber of Commerce or the National Right to Work

Committee, the Business Roundtable was not known simply to oppose everything that came its way. More than a player, it sought to define the playing field. As David Vogel argues, it was more akin to a vanguard party than a simple trade union, advancing the larger issues of the business class rather than the narrow concerns of any particular interest or sector. It could modify its demands, help shape legislation to its advantage at the earliest stages, and, most importantly, deliver blue chip CEOs to Capitol Hill instead of paid lobbyists. The power of elite lobbying, as one legislative aide explained, is that "you can be sure that there would be very few members of congress who would not meet with the President of the Business Roundtable," even if there were no district connection. The CEO of the seventies, they envisioned, would have "one foot in the boardroom and the other in Washington."[37]

By the end of 1976, just before the inauguration of a new Democratic administration, *Business Week* declared the Business Roundtable to be "Business' Most Powerful Lobby in Washington." Liberals and labor would try to rebuild working-class power through economic planning, labor law reform, and plans for national health insurance and industrial policy, but the combination of the liberals' incapacity, the obstacle of inflation, and waning power of unions, allowed business to pull ahead in the beltway class struggle. Labor, unprepared for the onslaught of business lobbying, tended to see the Business Roundtable as a "terrible conspiracy" by the end of the decade. George Meany derided Roger Blough's mission to keep wages down as coming from a man who "drew $916,000 in wages his last three years at U.S. Steel." Yet, he noted, "If he were to succeed, America would become a low-wage country. The progress of America has been made on high wages. Now, as far as I'm concerned, I'd rather have inflation than deflation because I know the difference." His sardonic remarks turned out to be prophetic.[38]

Organizations like the Business Roundtable were joined by the growth of corporate PACs. After Watergate, reformers passed laws barring office seekers from accepting large contributions from individuals. Instead, they turned to PACs, which represented group interests—and the dominant group interest in 1974 was still the AFL-CIO. But after 1974, corporations formed their own PACs, which backed Republican candidates and left Democrats worse off than before they passed campaign finance reform. As *The Wall Street Journal* explained in September 1978, the new business lobby was not just a Republican operation but was making deep inroads into the Democrats as well. "Business PACs aren't experiencing any difficulty in finding outstretched hands, and they seem to be getting their money's worth from a growing contingent of Democrats. Many observers, looking at the pro-business tone of the current Congress, have concluded that PAC dollars have something to do with it. Says one Democratic member of the House Ways and Means Committee: 'These PACs are influencing a lot of Democrats. You're seeing people from mainstream Democratic districts, elected with labor support, who are now voting with business.'" The shifting balance of power in Washington was obvious in the number of PACs representing labor and business. In 1974, there were 201 pro-labor PACs, compared to only 81 corporate PACs. Four years later, there were 784 corporate PACs, plus about 500 trade association PACs, as compared to only 217 pushing labor's agenda.[39]

Comparing the political responses to the two major recessions of the seventies illustrates how the shifting logic in Washington was boosted by the growing success of the business lobby. In the 1974–75 recession of the Ford years, following the 1973 oil embargo, the federal government actually chose to increase spending to reduce unemployment and boost demand, despite fears of inflation from both President Ford and the business community. The second recession of the decade, following the Iranian revolution in 1979, led to the lifting of a host of controls and regulations and to launching tax cuts to spur investments. There was irony in a Republican administration increasing spending and a Democratic administration choosing deregulation and tax cuts. In between, however, was not just a growing exhaustion with inflation, but a watershed in postwar history.[40]

The management offensive of the second half of the seventies was hardly contained on Capitol Hill. The macro-level struggle for control of both Washington and the political imagination had its parallel fights on the ground, as firms engaged anti-union consultants in unprecedented numbers. Union busting became a sophisticated big business, with mass market seminars and crash courses, anti-union law firms that pushed workers into legal quagmires, industrial psychologists who tooled with the hearts and minds of the rank and file, consulting firms that walked employers through every step of an organizing drive in order to defeat it, and trade associations that customized each step for a particular industry. "At one time I think the unions had it all over business in terms of grass-roots activity," explained an official from the U.S. Chamber of Commerce. "That is now reversed." The AFL-CIO reported, "Almost gone are the days of the Pinkertons, the blacklist and the yellow-dog contracts. In their place stands a man in a three-piece suit, sporting a briefcase and perhaps a Ph.D. in industrial psychology or a law degree. He is the labor relations consultant."[41]

The corporations' accelerating use of anti-unionism, claimed the federation, was "double barreled." First was the twisting of the NLRA until it became reduced, in the later words of one historian, to "a management tool." The other was targeting the minds of the workers through direct anti-union appeals to the employees. "Neither leaves a mark on their target but each is effective in accomplishing the goal—kill the union." As a researcher for the Machinists noted after infiltrating a seminar on working union free, "Our enemies now wear button-down collars and Brooks Brothers' clothes. . . . Their goals are not different from those 19th century industrialists who espoused the Gospel of Wealth and gave American labor history such names as Haymarket, Homestead and Pullman. . . . This is not a game, it is a war and the side which attempts to play fair and follow the rules is going to end up the loser."[42]

Social scientists concluded that the figures on union decline had less to do with the changing labor market, and a lot more to do with management aggressiveness as hand-to-hand combat over unionism took place on the shop floors. "Unfair Labor Practices" (ULPs) acts, which the NLRB determined to impair workers' rights to make free decisions about unionization, accelerated dramatically in the 1970s. In the early fifties, there had been roughly three thousand charges of illegal dismissal over union activity; by 1980, it was up over eighteen thousand. For every twenty workers voting for a union in 1980, one lost his or her job. By the end of the decade, unions, accustomed to winning two-thirds of union votes, were losing a majority of the elections that they brought before the NLRB. Equally traumatic, workers were voting out unions in decertification elections. The 583 cases in which employees voted to throw their union out in 1978–79 was twenty times what it had been during the glory days of the early 1950s. From a high of over 35 percent in 1955, union density dipped below 25 percent in the mid-1970s, and even then public sector gains masked private sector losses. While that tumble was cause for alarm, few would have predicted a plummet to the single digits for private sector density in the decades to come.[43]

Expectations about rewards of the job were faltering, employer resistance was up, and faith in unions was down. As was the case for Dewey Burton, individual advancement was in tension with stable income. "Paradoxically then," reports sociologist Lillian Breslow Rubin, "the 'good money, good benefits, seniority' that come with long tenure on the job also serve to limit his choices—to bind him to it, trading the dream for this stagnant stability." Faith in the unions was not much better. In 1979, industrial relations scholar Thomas Kochan concluded that "unions are seen by a large number of workers as a strategy of last resort rather than as a natural or preferred means of improving job conditions."[44]

Meanwhile, business was rewarding "good" labor markets and punishing "bad" ones with their business decisions. They preferred the non-union, low tax, and least regulated areas they could find. In the sixties and seventies, the Northeast non-metropolitan areas gained 100,000 jobs, but the metropolitan areas *lost* 600,000 as many of the old industrial cities hemorrhaged employment. The major industrial cities that once responded to the clarion of the CIO—places like Camden, Pittsburgh, Toledo, Akron, Detroit, Flint—began to look like industrial mausoleums, and their housing stock was reduced to warehouses for unemployed African-Americans who had once taken the train from the deep South to the freedom of a northern industrial job during the Great Migrations of the two world wars. At the same time, the South gained about a million manufacturing jobs in both metropolitan and non-metropolitan areas. The "heartland" of the Midwest and Northeast gained 14 percent of the job growth, while the Sunbelt gained 86 percent of the new jobs drawn by the "right to work" laws, tax abatements, subsidies, union free promises, and low taxes. International and regional competition pushed employees hard to compete with each other, whipsawing community against community. When employers pushed to raise productivity or lower wages, workers often fought back, tightening management's push to search out cheaper locations. Firms in the most highly competitive sectors—especially garments, textiles, and electronics—simply jumped to "offshore" locations in Puerto Rico, Taiwan, and Mexico. Within the national context, it would not be long before the Americanization of Dixie looked a lot more like the Dixification of America.[45]

At the same time that the right was emboldened on economic policy and well organized on political grounds, there was little cohesive counterargument from the new breed of Democrats for the material interests of working people. The landslide Democratic congressional class of 1974, which picked up an additional forty-nine seats after Nixon's resignation, may have been strongly liberal, young, well-educated, and pro-civil rights, but few had much truck with pro-labor or pro-worker policies. The new Democrats came out of the anti-war protests and the McGovern campaign, the Peace Corps and the women's movement, the professions and the suburbs, but not the union halls and the wards. Union lobbyists knew they had a different animal on their hands—much less reliable politically and ideologically than the old postwar breed of New Deal liberals. As the AFL-CIO's lobbyist Kenneth Young explained in 1975, "The freshman Democrat today is likely to be an upper-income type, and that causes some problems with economic issues. It's not that they don't vote what they perceive to be working class concerns, but I think a lot of them are more concerned with inflation than with unemployment. They aren't emotionally involved with unemployment." These suburban, post-sixties, "new class" Democrats also had anti-institutional tendencies, pre-ferring to guard their independence against the political machinery of either the Democratic Party or organized labor. "There's no way you can get them to follow leadership," lamented Young; "You just run into one frustration after another." Gary Hart, who piloted the McGovern campaign to defeat in 1972, won one of five new Democratic Senate seats. His 1974 campaign speech was titled, "The End of the New Deal." Reflecting the New Politics, Hart de-clared, "labor can't deliver votes anymore; nobody can."[46]

III

Class, always a fragile concept in American civic life, died the death of a thousand cuts in the 1970s, but few problems sliced as deeply as how race and class were set against each other. Class and race are fundamentally in-tertwined social identities, mutually constructing each other, marbled to-gether into a sociological whole, but a whole that has proven to be one of the most elusive identities in American history. White working people have typically chosen their race over their class; black workers have generally ex-pressed themselves through a politics of racial oppression that has had more traction in American politics than class. Despite the Roosevelt coalition's linking of black and white working people politically, the tensions within the coalition ran very deep, and, in popular discourse, "working class" still meant white. In the 1970s, race and class were often at odds, trumping any possibility of drawing together the class-based politics of the thirties with the racial freedom of the sixties into that most elusive of things in American history—an interracial class identity. This is not to say that civil rights undermined the cohesion of class—far from it. It is to say that the nation proved incapable of speaking of both at the same time. Rather than synthe-sis, the seventies were a time of eclipse.

Although race and class are lived as a unified social reality, the separation between labor rights and civil rights is hard-wired into postwar policy. The two legislative landmarks that shape occupational justice are the NLRA (1935) and Title VII of the Civil Rights Act (1964). The former held out the right to form unions during the Great Depression and delivered immigrant Europeans to a sense of economic and political citizenship during the New Deal period. The latter created the Equal Employment Opportunity Commission during the black freedom struggle, which prohibited employment discrimination by race, sex, creed, or national origin. A coherent labor market policy would confront both collective economic rights and the right to non-discrimination, but the two pieces of legislation were products of separate struggles, separate policy traditions, and separate judicial spheres. And they were often in an unfortunate zero-sum tension. As Paul Frymer argues, the two acts are products of "two vectors of power," and the failure to build a strong and diverse labor movement was not a product of isolated individuals or events, but was "the outcome of a political system that, in its effort to appeal to civil rights opponents, developed a bifurcated system of power that assigned race and class problems to different spheres of government." The two acts, and the trajectory of the movements that gave birth to each, tended to institutionalize the divisions rather than build bridges between them. By the 1970s, the division was growing into an unbridgeable chasm.[47]

The roots of the problem stem back to the New Deal itself. The passage of each piece of New Deal labor legislation came with the political cost of keeping blacks, and, less consciously, women, from joining unions. Having left out agricultural and service workers, who were mostly black and women, as a necessary sop to the southern wing of the Democratic Party, the Wagner Act also shunned any connections to the question of employer discrimination. Both the National Association for the Advancement of Colored People (NAACP) and the Urban League fought to make racial discrimination in union membership an unfair labor practice under the Wagner Act— but to no avail. The NAACP, in fact, complained that unions were using the Wagner Act "to organize a union for all the white workers, and to either agree with the employers to push Negroes out of the industry or, having in effect an agreement with the employer, to proceed to make a union lily-white." The AFL also fought the non-discrimination provision in order to protect segregated locals, which helped seal the fate for much of the black working class. As the NLRB fulfilled its role in the postwar era, it continued to see discrimination within unions as outside of the board's purview. By the postwar period, it led to the absurdity, in the NLRB's *Bess F. Young* case of 1950, of an employer explicitly, and successfully, arguing that he fired his workers *because* they were black—not due to their union activities. Twenty-five years later, the opposite would be true—one could readily be fired for union activities, but discrimination remained a legal flashpoint.[48]

In the postwar era, a dual labor market maintained occupational segregation. Women and minorities—especially but certainly not solely those in the South—generally remained restricted to peripheral, non-unionized occupations, while white men enjoyed the fruits of the booming industrial work organized by the CIO. The end of World War II and the passage of the Taft-Hartley Act's "right to work" provision (and the CIO's failed organizing campaign, "Operation Dixie") further perpetuated the problem as the South remained largely outside of the New Deal framework. The solidly Democratic South voted en bloc with northern Republicans for fear that any advances in the New Deal would result in advances in civil rights and perhaps even the unionization of southern industry, thus blocking the political advance of New Deal or civil rights legislation. Across the nation, white working-class men enjoyed a sense of security and presence in civic life to the degree that it was wholly unremarkable—it was the very foundation of social life. "The white men who monopolized good employment were considered the core of the nation," argues historian Nancy MacLean. "Their needs and interests were taken into account because they belonged. They were the constituency assumed when politicians, business leaders, and intellectuals spoke of 'Americans'"—or, we can add, "workers." Employers listed their jobs by race and gender, unions were complicit in racial hiring practices, and wage structures followed suit. With all-white textile mills, strictly gendered office spaces, lily-white construction sites, and segregated hiring practices at steel mills, the occupational world was defined by gender and race. The postwar golden age, as the political scientist Ira Katznelson put it, was an age in which "affirmative action was white."[49]

The most uplifting chapters in the history of the 1970s chronicle how activists, the courts, working people, unions, and civil rights groups finally shattered the structures of the occupational world, not only gaining a seat at the lunch counter but gaining adequate employment to afford the hamburger as well. When the political logjam broke in 1964 and the Civil Rights Act was passed, it was at the height of liberalism and a point at which few would have imagined the wholesale decline of organized labor. Although there were brief syntheses of labor and civil rights struggles in the

1960s and 1970s—most notably the sanitation workers' strike in Memphis where Martin Luther King Jr. was killed, and the UFW's dual cries of "La Huelga" and "La Raza." Those syntheses were promising but rare. The struggle for occupational justice turned then almost solely on breaking down exclusion—gaining access to better and more skilled jobs for women and minorities—rather than linking the project of integration with that of structural change.

Thus, the seventies brought forth a dual movement: the revolution in minority and women's occupational rights took place at the same time as the counter-revolution in labor rights. And one cannot be understood without the other. By the 1980s, labor rights descended to "lawlessness," in the words of one sober historian, while a corporation that was caught in systematic discriminatory practices meant massive court settlements. In short, the new occupational opportunities for women and minorities arrived just as the call for broad economic justice was in decline. The result was heightened competition for dwindling opportunity. The political calculation shifted in the sixties and seventies from changing the division of the pie to making sure everyone had an equal chance to *compete* for a slice. The old system of collective economic rights was "fading away," as legal scholar Katherine Van Wezel Stone explains, replaced by "a plethora of new employment rights for individual workers" that promised protection from discrimination and sexual harassment. The new workplace justice movements found themselves in an uneasy relationship to the long-held, if elusive, dream of working-class collective uplift and, by necessity, strategically shifted the struggle to a more individualistic terrain of "occupational justice"—equal employment opportunity, diversity, affirmative action, and anti-harassment. All of these important and hard-won victories transformed the complexion and gender makeup of the wealth pyramid, but as the eighties would later prove, they were unable to have an impact on its all-important shape.[50]

Ironically, as the hope for a genuinely integrated manifestation of working-class identity rapidly faded, the actual sites of work were becoming more integrated than ever before. By the end of the seventies, the changes were profound: diversity and inclusion, to return to historian Nancy MacLean, "seeped deep into the culture. . . . From assembly lines and union halls to college lecture podiums and corporate boardrooms, African Americans and white women, especially, and Latinos, Asian Americans, and lesbians and gays to a lesser degree," had "a presence and a voice as never before." Unions, dwindling in strength and numbers to their pre–New Deal status, also grew to become some of the most diverse institutions in American life. As fundamental as inclusion, identity, and diversity were, an emphasis on gender and racial equity alone tended to allow jobs, pay, and labor rights to fall out of the equation, leaving workers with a set of individual rights to non-discrimination amidst a more brutal economy—a multi-cultural neo-liberalism.[51]

As a result, post-seventies struggle for diversity has been an inherent good but has simultaneously served as an unwitting "alibi" for the lost strain in American politics: the fight against economic inequality. Diversity and individual employment rights have carried a great deal of misplaced political freight that should be shared with questions of class and structural economic inequality. As Wendy Brown explains, when class falls out of the equation a certain displacement happens as "other markers of social difference may come to bear and an inordinate weight; indeed, they may bear all the weight of the sufferings produced by capitalism in addition to that attributable to the explicitly politicized marking." An unspoken risk inherent in the mono-politics of "diversity" was that white guys, too, would avail themselves of their own form of identity politics, taking shelter from the storm of cultural conflict in the politics of nostalgia, resentment, and authority. By defining themselves in opposition to women and minorities, the "working class" becomes, in essence, negatively defined: an "other" dwelling outside of the New Politics built by and upon minorities, women, youth, and sexuality.[52]

Many see the shift away from material politics toward identity, values, and social issues as part of a broad-based historic shift toward the culture of postmodernity. While such a historic transformation challenges stale narratives and breaks down falsely rigid identities, opening up a radically pluralist cultural space, the shift fails to challenge the core elements of working life and economics. Slavoj Žižek writes that "postmodern politics definitely has the great merit that it 'repoliticizes' a series of domains previously considered 'apolitical' or 'private,'" but "it does not in fact repoliticize capitalism, because the very notion and form of the 'political' within which it operates is grounded in the 'depoliticization' of the economy." Significantly, that popular depoliticization has allowed economic elites nearly uncontested control over civic life, making postmodern politics the cultural handmaiden of the neo-liberal order.[53]

Just as the demands for inclusion in the job market reached their apex, the economy also reached its nadir. By mid decade, the labor market could not adequately support those who enjoyed skin and gender privilege in the first place, let alone the new pressures to hire historically excluded workers. Piling more job seekers onto an economy that could not sustain the existing jobs proved a risky, zero-sum, political gamble. The so-called reverse discrimination protests of the seventies challenged the new rights discourse in discomforting ways. When white workers filed charges with the Equal Employment Opportunity Commission (EEOC) or in state and federal court, they made counterclaims about the meaning of equality and social justice, most typically on the question of union contractual arrangements.

In areas where the occupational world became more brutally competitive and restrictive in the seventies, like public sector Detroit, the idealism of affirmative action dwindled to a vicious logic. White Detroit police department officers sought to protect their jobs by maintaining seniority lists during layoffs rather than allowing African-Americans, who had just managed to get a toehold on hiring in the department, to keep their jobs. In such cases, affirmative action was a post-material solution in the midst of material crisis. "The opposition that makers of equal employment opportunity policy faced in the late 1960s over who should be hired," argues Dennis Deslippe, "gave way in the 1970s to a more intense opposition over who should be *fired*."[54]

IV

What became known as the "blue collar Bakke" case (named after the more famous case on public college admissions) suggests some of the complexities of integrating the workplace in the midst of declining economic opportunity. In 1974, Brian Weber, a young, white laboratory analyst working in a chemical plant in Gramercy, Louisiana, sued both his employer, the Kaiser Aluminum & Chemical Corporation, and his union, the United Steel Workers of America, for what was colloquially referred to as "reverse discrimination." The court had already banned the unfair application of tests and standards in *Griggs v. Duke Power Co.* (1971) and thus opened up the application of the Civil Rights Act to the private employment arena (and, implicitly, affirmative action since the burden of proof for non-discrimination fell to employers). Black workers at Weber's plant accounted for a mere 2 percent of skilled trades—such as repairman or electrician—even though African-American workers made up 39 percent of the labor force. To bring some equity to the gross history of discrimination, both the company and the union decided to admit white and black workers into the training program in a one-to-one ratio, thus taking affirmative action in admissions decisions to help correct the history of discrimination at the plant. Weber was denied a spot in the training program. He lacked the seniority necessary to obtain a slot reserved for white workers but had more seniority than most blacks accepted for a position. This, he argued, constituted a form of discrimination: he had been denied a position based on his color. Interestingly, Weber himself was no racist. He was active in his union local and had a good record on civil rights. The courts upheld his claim, arguing that Title VII of the Civil Rights Act of 1964 bans discrimination of any kind—even that designed to assist minorities to overcome the history of employment discrimination. The Supreme Court ultimately ruled on the case in 1979.

In contrast to the muddled real Bakke decision, the Supreme Court sent a clear message in the more far-reaching *United Steelworkers of America v. Weber* (1979). The court found that employers could give African-Americans special preference for jobs that had been historically dominated by whites. Even if there had not been a history of discrimination at the workplace, the employer could use race in its hiring and promotion decisions to right historic racial imbalances. The decision released employers from an impossible bind. If they engaged in affirmative action in hiring decisions, they risked being sued by white workers like Weber. If they did not use affirmative action, they faced being sued by minority workers or the EEOC.

Advocates of minority and women's employment rights cheered the decision. As James Nailor, a black electrician who was among the first hired under the Kaiser training program, said, "The decision means my children will have a chance to do better than I will. That's the American dream." Yet the new regulatory systems and the courts could only provide access to jobs; they could not create them. Diversity arrived to American industry just as industry was leaving America. One year after beginning the program of promoting inside candidates to the skilled trades, the company suspended the program that Weber had protested—the courts had been ruling on a program that no longer existed. The company found it significantly cheaper to hire skilled workers from outside. Corporations in general began to discover that it was cheaper and produced less legal exposure to contract outside the plant for work rather than taking responsibility for the workers within their plants. Most of all, affirmative action, the EEOC, and the Brian Webers of the world were no match for a steel industry that was about to enter a global crisis. As Judith Stein put it, "The Supreme Court sustained the USWA-Kaiser plan, but the recession of 1975–76 did not."[55]

A parallel problem of opening up access to shrinking opportunity came with the Consent Decree in steel. Union seniority had been the bedrock of contractual protection for industrial workers in the postwar era, but it was also a system that protected a host of ills, not the least of which was a rigid racial hierarchy on the job. In 1974, nine steel companies and the USW signed a Consent Decree with the federal government in the face of over four hundred discrimination cases pending before the EEOC. The Consent Decree allowed for simpler paths to advancement (seniority accruing plantwide rather than by department), more transparency in hiring and promotion, goals and timetables for the admission of women and minorities to the skilled positions, and over $30 million in back pay to the women and minorities covered by the agreement. The Consent Decree, of course, fueled plenty of Wallacite sentiments against the government, the company, and the union as white workers felt their job security and skin privilege under attack.[56]

The problems were much more profound than increasing the breadth of the seniority queue. Just a few years after the new system of racial hiring and promotion was set up, the steel mills began to shut down across Ohio and Pennsylvania creating Depression-like conditions in communities that once appeared to be incontrovertible proof of a stable and affluent working class. For African-Americans and women, the right to equal employment opportunity, as fundamental and important and hard won as those struggles were, suddenly became irrelevant in the old steel towns where there were few jobs. The steel industry had already been cutting back on employment throughout the seventies, then on "Black Monday," September 19, 1977, the first of the big steel mill shutdowns, that of the Campbell Works of Youngstown Sheet and Tube, was announced. The mills just kept folding "like broken promises" through the early eighties. As a journalist described it, "the dead steel mills stand as pathetic mausoleums to the decline of American industrial might that was once the envy of the world." While there may have been greater diversity in the steel industry after the Consent Decrees and the Weber decision, the number of African Americans with jobs in steel plummeted. In 1974, there were 38,096 African American steel workers; by 1988, that figure had fallen by more than three-quarters to 9,958 workers. One could tout the increase of blacks in the electrical trades from 5.3 to 8.4 percent of the workforce, but that only made sense if one examined the real numbers of black electricians, which had declined by 40 percent. Women workers also increased by percentage but showed slight declines in real numbers. The economics of the steel industry rarely entered into the questions of equal employment. Individual rights to non-discrimination smacked head-on into the need for industrial planning or structural adjustment in an era in which capital was being withdrawn from basic industry or relocated out of the rustbelt.[57]

Without a shared economic vision to go hand-in-glove with the urgent demands of equal access to jobs, both people of color and those often referred to as the "white ethnics" laid claim to race as a political resource in the wake of the civil rights movements. In a political world largely defined by the success of the civil rights movement, many working-class whites turned to the same tactics as minorities to maintain affirmation and political power. Whites mobilized along ethnic, racial, and historical lineages, in a sort of Ellis Island revivalism, as a pale entry in America's great oppression derby. As ethnic Americans clawed their way up from steerage, they not only had a proud history of oppression conquered, but, they often claimed, climbed the occupation ladder with liberty, hard work, and loyalty burning in their bellies. This simultaneously undercut black demands for equality and affirmative action with a combination of racial innocence and cultural superiority, while further reframing politics away from shared economic destiny and toward an inter-ethnic competition for jobs and resources.[58]

V

Boston became the national focal point for racial retrenchment in the face of the busing crisis, as working-class blacks and whites battled it out over access to education. J. Anthony Lukas, who wrote a Pulitzer Prize–winning book on the crisis, explained that the courts' decisions "assured that the burden of integration would fall disproportionately on the poor of both races. One need not proceed from a Marxist perspective—as I do not, to observe that class is America's dirty little secret, pervasive and persistent, yet rarely confronted in public policy." Like so many of the policies in the 1970s, the destructive logic of busing pitted interest against interest. There was no space to incubate the more tenuously generous racial impulses of a Dewey Burton or a white Boston woman who explained to Judge Garrity, who ruled on the plans for Boston's busing program, "I live and work with blacks. I have no objection to my child going to school with black children. I feel in this world, where we have to live with all kinds of people, that an integrated education is an advantage. I do not and shall not support forced busing to achieve racial balance in the schools. You cannot force people to get along." Many social scientists, politicians, white citizens, black citizens, and important civil rights leaders agreed that busing was simply not worth the extreme social costs of the ugly and often violent reactionary populism it unleashed on the land. The studies of the costs of segregation and the decisions by the courts continued forth, however, with a sense of urgency that the nation could not retreat to its sordid past of "separate but equal."[59]

So racialized had the debate become, that rarely discussed were ideas about improving poor education through *material betterment* rather than simply racial integration. An alternative was to move dollars rather than people. In the hotbed of racial politics of the 1970s, it was difficult to see beyond the problem of race alone and into the allied issue of class inequality. On busing, policy makers continued to believe that moving people was a better and easier solution than moving money and resources. If the problem was poverty—and, as black nationalists argue, one that would not be solved (possibly exacerbated) by simply rubbing shoulders with whites—then shifting resources to impoverished areas rather than shifting people might have been a reasonable strategy.

Solving educational inequality by focusing on the economics of it was the strategy of a group of Texas community activists who argued that unequal school funding violated their right to equal protection under the law. Gathering evidence of gross inequality between districts in classroom size, number of books per pupil, teacher-student ratios, counselor-student ratios, and overall expenditures per pupil, the parents took their case all the way to the Supreme Court in *San Antonio v. Rodriguez* (1973). Unlike most seventies cases, the focus of this one was not racial inequality per se but economic inequality. In yet another narrow 5–4 decision, the Court upheld the crazy quilt of inequitable local school funding by finding that education was not a right protected by the Constitution. There were no direct correlations between the wealth of families and expenditures on education, the court found, because even though there were generalities one could make about wealth between the districts, the logic did not hold up to specific individuals within the districts (i.e., there are poor people in rich districts and rich people in poor districts). The court held that the class of people at stake in the discussions was simply too large, diverse, and amorphous. Instead of the potential logic of economic equality held out by *Rodriguez*, the nation would continue on its racial struggle that pitted working-class whites and blacks against each other by trying to move people rather than resources. Even though race is the most socially constructed of all social categories (there is no biological dimension to race, it is a cultural phenomenon), the courts found racial identities absolute, while class boundaries were too diffuse to address.[60]

Pay equity by sex, especially in blue-collar and service work, fell into the same ideological trap. In the early seventies, women earned only sixty cents for every dollar earned by men. The raw pay gap shrank in the ensuing decades as women worked, protested, and lobbied their way up to something more like seventy-eight cents per dollar three decades later. Unfortunately, the long-standing demand for pay equity for women is most typically measured as a percentage of men's earnings (making male earnings the gold standard). Yet 1973 was the height of real male earnings—those earnings would tumble during the bad years or stagnate in the good ones for decades to come as unions declined, manufacturing closed, and the labor force shifted to less remunerative service work. So, working-class women in the private sector were comparing themselves to a declining or stagnant standard, basically gaining on a target that was either immobile or slipping backwards.[61]

Furthermore, the women's movement faced its own internal class divides. The "other women's movement," as Dorothy Sue Cobble labeled the brand of feminism that came out of the labor unions and looked to both class and gender as reference points of political mobilization, was a minor chord. The feminism that got the most attention, most notably during the decade-long debates over the Equal Rights Amendment (ERA), had a distinctly professional middle-class hue. The unintentional parody of upper-class feminism was the notorious Enjoli perfume commercial with a sexy woman variously clad in a robe, business attire, and an evening dress, singing:

I can bring home the bacon
(Enjoli!)
Fry it up in a pan
(Enjoi!)
And never, never, never, let you forget you're a man
Because I'm a woman

Such media images drove home the idea of professional "have it all" feminism that had little resonance with working people. As Debby D'Amico wrote in an essay, "To My White Working-Class Sisters," the problems were wholly different for working-class women. "We are the invisible women, the faceless women, the nameless women . . . the female half of the silent majority, the female half of the ugly Americans, the smallest part of the 'little people,'" explained D'Amico. Working-class women suffered a double dose of the hidden injuries. "As white people who haven't made it, we are living proof of the American lie and we hate ourselves for it."[62]

Labor feminists originally opposed the ERA on the grounds that it would eliminate special occupational protections for women. They eventually added their voices to the ERA effort, and unionists came around to support, often quite strongly, the ratification of the ERA in the second half of the decade. Women also finally grew to a third of all union members, but, again, it was a percentage of shrinking real numbers. Yet Second Wave feminism basically had the same problem the civil rights groups had in the seventies— identity with the class left out (or, in this case, assumed to be professional). As Alice Kessler-Harris explains, "In following the model of a civil rights movement that advocated individual rights [feminists] chose an effective politics that did not, perhaps could not, equalize social conditions among women. In so doing, the NOW [National Organization for Women] and the political wings of the newly formed women's movement may have helped to exacerbate divisions among [women] and to earn the new feminism . . . the . . . opprobrium of being white and middle class."[63]

VI

God, as Michael Harrington noted in his walk across Manhattan, had become a renewed source of moral anchorage in the midst of the confusion in a decade gone bad. In the 1960s, the political mobilization of churchgoers ran in multiple directions—pro-war and anti-war, pro-integration and pro-segregation. In the 1970s, with all of the decisions liberating "licentious" public behavior, it appeared to Evangelicals "that the Court was now waging a war on God." By the early 1980s, therefore, politics of churchgoers ran demonstrably conservative. Even though there were a great number of different denominational affiliations and theological perspectives, there was a remarkable coherence in their political activities (leading often to a sense of their being monolithic).[64]

Religion was far from new in American life, but the brand of revivalism of the late seventies was one of the most important and complex transformations in the nation's postwar culture. Even the most famous evangelical minister of the postwar era, Billy Graham, largely kept out of politics (though was a counselor to presidents), and, unlike future evangelicals, remained a registered Democrat (though he was very close to Richard Nixon). For the period of the New Deal order, then, the church largely rendered onto Caesar that which was Caesar's, as the evangelical movements focused on saving souls. As the secular cultural revolution of the seventies found support in the courts and the legislatures, however, Christians became politicized. As the *Christian Harvest Times* put it in 1980, "To understand humanism is to understand women's liberation, the ERA, gay rights, children's rights, abortion, sex education, the new morality, evolution, values clarification, situation ethics, the separation of church and state, the loss of patriotism, and many of the other problems that are tearing America apart today." So, they took up arms at the ballot box.[65]

The memberships of venerable liberal denominations like the Episcopalian, Methodist, and Presbyterian traditions declined by 20 to 30 percent from the late sixties to the early eighties. The growth faiths, in contrast, were organizations like the Southern Baptists and Assemblies of God, which jumped in membership from 50 to 100 percent. The roots of megachurches and new dominations can be found in the seventies, as well as the televangelical phenomenon featuring figures such as Jim Bakker, Rex Humbard, and Oral Roberts declaring the word of God while soliciting funds on the new cable outlets. Pat Robertson's immensely successful Christian Broadcasting Network even had its own satellite earth station built in 1977. Jerry Falwell, the most important minister of the lot, used his mailing list from his program "The Old Time Gospel Hour" to launch the Moral Majority in 1979, a group often credited with delivering the white evangelical vote from the born-again Jimmy Carter to Hollywood divorcé Ronald Reagan. Most of the growing fundamentalist sects looked to a literal interpretation of the Bible and orthodox theologies. Others turned to a wide variety of cults, eastern mystics, and non-western faiths of the type pilloried by Tom Wolfe in his famous "Me Decade" screed. It was just as Wolfe claimed, however, the "Third Great Awakening."[66]

Few issues mobilized Christian conservatives more than the abortion debate as it emerged after the Supreme Court found the practice legal in *Roe v. Wade* (1973). It was seen as an attack not just on some of the fundamental principles of family and motherhood but as a larger assault on human values that tapped into dormant wells of populism. As Garry Wills noted about the seventies, "The Rights Revolution had struck fear into Christian conservatives. They felt that their country was being taken from them, their children were being turned against them, the Bible was being mocked, the moral foundation of their world was being undermined." For pro-choice advocates, the right to choose offered liberation from patriarchal claims on women's reproductive choices. Many working-class families saw it in different terms, however: it was not only a question of the sacredness of human life, but also one of diminishing male responsibility in the blue-collar household and an attack on the meaning of motherhood. "Pro-life" women tended to value family and to be homemakers who were threatened by the sexual revolution and the transformation of motherhood into a discretionary choice rather than a sacred calling. "A social ethic that promotes more freely available sex undercuts pro-life women in two ways," explained one researcher; "it limits their abilities to get into a marriage in the first place, and it undermines the social value placed on their presence once within a marriage."[67]

Much of the cultural divide over abortion grafts readily, but not perfectly, onto tensions over class. Of a large survey of pro-life and pro-choice activists, 94 percent of pro-choice women worked outside of the home, and half of them enjoyed incomes that placed them in the top 10 percent of all working women in the nation. Many were in the most affluent percentiles in the country. In contrast, 63 percent of pro-life advocates did not work outside of the home (and those that did were unmarried). The personal income of pro-life women activists was very low, if there was any at all. The story was similar in terms of education and occupation. Where pro-choice women tended to be well-educated professionals, pro-life activists tended to be housewives or in traditional female occupations. For working-class families, "family values" was not a political slogan but a belief in sacrifice, fate, belonging, character, and the sanctity of parenthood. For pro-choice people, abortion rights freed women up to strive and become, to escape the restrictions of sexual tradition, and to fulfill their potential as human beings. As Kristin Luner explains, "Pro-life people really do want to see 'less' sexuality—or at least less open and socially unregulated sexuality—because they think it is morally wrong, they think it distorts the meaning of sex, and they feel that it *threatens the basis on which their own marital bargains are built.*"[68]

Further shaping the gender dimensions of class in the seventies were the new financial pressures, which meant more women had to move into the paid labor force—whether or not it was part of either partner's values. Most men did not question their role as bread winners, and many felt psychologically challenged by the new need to have two wage earners in the house during the seventies. "For the working-class man," writes Lillian Rubin in *Worlds of Pain*, "that often means yet another challenge to his already uncertain self-esteem—this time in the only place where he has been able to make his authority felt: the family. For his wife, it means yet another burden in the marriage—the need somehow to shore up her husband's bruised ego while maintaining some contact not only with her own desires but with family needs as well." Rough times bring sporadic unemployment, a reduction in overtime that allowed for the bills to be paid, debt, marital stress, divorce, drinking, and deferred dreams—and, not surprisingly, turns to faith.[69]

VII

The fog seeping into the national consciousness enveloped even the brightest beacons of union renewal—those that Harrington looked to for hope in 1974. As the *New York Times* reported, "Paradoxically, the recession has engendered new expressions of labor-management collaboration" rather than dissent. Similarly, public support withered. A San Francisco woman who had served as a volunteer to support the UFW boycotts in the chain stores put it this way: "I was really a believer. My kids had never even tasted grapes, and for three years I used spinach to make salads. I will wish Chavez well, but I'm out of it now." The cultural exhaustion crept in alongside the decline in union victories. "Maybe Vietnam, the civil-rights thing, Watergate and all the rest of it wore me out," she continued. "I worry more now about the price of a head of lettuce than the issue of who picked it." The decline was hard to take. By the late 1970s, the UFW, the beacon of so much hope earlier in the decade, had descended into strange cultish behavior. The old deliberative organizing model and its leaders were thrown out, and Chavez, following the brainwashing tactics of a religious group called Synanon, turned the union, in the words of the former organizing director, "into a community of unpaid cadre, loyal to a single leader, governed by groupthink rituals, and enjoying the apparent efficiency of unquestioning obedience." As the public employees' Jerry Wurf echoed Sadlowski's assessment of the new mood, "The recent traumas in our society have fomented resignation—not rebellion."[70]

Two of the most notable and hopeful insurgencies of the decade, those among the mine workers and the steelworkers, soldiered on into the second half of the decade in final swan songs of activity. Yet it was a very different political and social climate. Both ended in defeat: one was ignominious, the other simply disappointing. Steel Workers Fight Back tried to project Ed Sadlowski's regional victory to the international leadership of the union in 1977. Arnold Miller, who rode to victory on the Miners for Democracy Movement, marched the entire bituminous coal industry out in the biggest mining strike in U.S. history only to find that the feet of its insurgent leader were made of clay and the rank and file beyond his control.

In 1975, steel workers interested in building a permanent rank-and-file organization launched Steel Workers Fight Back and backed Ed Sadlowski, the fair-haired boy of labor revitalization in the seventies, for international president of the USW. Against tremendous odds—and with the help of a Department of Labor mandated re-running of the election—Sadlowski had beaten the steel workers' bureaucratic inertia and gained the head of District 31 in 1974 (see Chapter 1). Now, he was poised to bring his synthesis of old and New Lefts to the 1.4 million members of the USW and, undoubtedly, the Democratic Party. The man in power, I.W. Abel, ironically won election to international office in 1965 by attacking his predecessor's "tuxedo unionism." In comparison to the Sadlowski insurgency, however, Abel's was merely a palace coup. Since Abel faced mandatory retirement, "Oil Can Eddie" squared off against the official candidate and heir apparent, Lloyd McBride. Sadlowski accused the union of being not so much corrupt as "soft, pompous, dull, a bit lazy, and distant from the membership." Writer and radio commentator Studs Terkel called the election more significant than that between Ford and Carter.[71]

Labor's officialdom, inside and outside of the steel workers, went berserk over Sadlowski's maverick campaign. AFL-CIO secretary-treasurer Lane Kirkland warned against "a latter-day romance" with the radicalism and popular frontism of the 1930s that Sadlowski represented. Like so many of Sadlowski's opponents, Al Shanker, president of the United Federation of Teachers, inveighed against the "outsiders" involved in Steel Workers Fight Back. He portrayed it as a choice between a "president who has been chosen by the workers themselves or one who has really been put in office by the money and publicity of wealthy tax-exempt foundations, Harvard professors, radical chic movie stars, anti-union employers in other industries, leaders of the left wing of the Democratic Party, and newspapers and TV stations which had had strong anti-union histories." Even A. Philip Randolph, grandfather of the March on Washington Movement, urged "my fellow trade unionists to do everything in their power to repel this attack by destructive outside elements on basic trade union principles and policies in their efforts to capture control of the United Steelworkers." Randolph went so far as to claim, in a patent falsehood, that the "Steelworkers have a record second to none in advancing racial and economic quality."[72]

The accusation of "outsiders" seizing control of the USW—a term that applied variously to attorney Joseph Rauh, Victor Reuther, economist J.K. Galbraith, and the media who fawned over Sadlowski's working class heroics—spoke to the degree to which organized labor's official hierarchy had become insular and self-referential. Joe Rauh, Sadlowski's attorney, had to write to Randolph, his old mentor from the civil rights days, with "heavy heart," hoping that Randolph's name had been used to race bait Sadlowski without his permission. Reminding Randolph that the USW did not back the March on Washington, Rauh pointed out that it had been he (Rauh) and Victor Reuther (Walter's brother) who were the two key outsiders that were constantly being accused of meddling and that they had been the ones to support the March on Washington. George Meany, who refused to interfere in the internal politics of any unions whenever it suited his purpose, claimed it was "impossible to keep silent" about Sadlowski's "unethical" solicitation of outside money.[73]

As the official family attacked the "limousine liberals" and "cocktail party circuit" types who supported Sadlowski, they attempted to reverse the class discourse, presenting the pro-Sadlowski forces as a Park Avenue takeover of the traditionally working-class leadership of the USW. Sadlowski countered with his own class analysis. USW President I.W. Abel, he argued, "spends so much time drinking dry martinis with R. Heath Larry [vice chairman of United States Steel] that he's forgotten he's supposed to be fightin' the bosses. He lives like one himself, making $75,000 a year. And no S.O.B. district director is worth $35,000 either. There's no room in this union for bodyguards and limousines. And the staff guys, once they go from drinking beer and lugging lunch buckets to carrying briefcases, they forget where they came from. . . . We don't need any more actuarial experts and lawyers or any more strike agreements," he proclaimed, indicting the no-strike clause in Abel's Experimental Negotiating Agreement.[74]

Sadlowski generated wide support in basic steel but overreached, ideologically, when he told a *Penthouse* interviewer that he'd like to see fewer steel jobs. Not more—fewer. His vision for fewer guys sweating in the mills was based on the premise that the country could use more doctors and fewer furnace workers, more teachers and fewer miners, more scientists and fewer assembly line workers, more environmentalism and fewer poisons in the air. "With technology," he argued, "the ultimate goal of organized labor is for no man to have to go down into the bowels of the earth and dig coal. No man will have to be subjected to the blast furnace." Historically, the loss of jobs in American history meant unemployment, not new opportunity, and, even though Sadlowski had a more radical vision, it left him very vulnerable to attack. "It's one hell of a thing for me to say—we just don't need any more steel mills. We don't *need* that kind of industrial growth, at the expense of what the environment should be. We can't as a matter of fact, consume what the existing steel mills produce; so let's call a halt. Enough with the car!" He was thinking broadly, systematically, beyond collective bargaining and toward a reorganization of power, training, employment, stewardship, and the distribution of wealth. For Ed Sadlowski, demanding more perfunctory wage increases was a dead end.[75]

Taking those comments out of context, however, meant trouble for Oilcan Eddie. It could easily sound, for instance, like the insurgent candidate wanted fewer jobs and more "liberal" environmentalism. Yet he countered that labor had been "hoodwinked" into believing that environmentalism meant throwing a few people out onto the street, when what it meant was a massive reorganization of industrial society. Nobody likes working in a steel mill, he claimed. "I never met anyone in his right mind who loved working in the steel mill or who said he did. And I have a feeling that if such a guy exists, he's some liberal punk who will last two months—and feel like a he-man because he's sweated for once in his life." McBride merely avoided issues such as the Experimental Negotiating Agreement and took Sadlowski's words out of context in his speeches. And they were damning: "We have reduced labor forces from 520,000 fifteen years ago to 400,000 today. Let's reduce them to 100,000."[76]

The real obstacles were much larger. Former USW president David J. McDonald prophesized a rough road for the Fight Back insurgency. "Unless Sadlowski would have an overwhelming victory in the United States, he will not win the presidency. The Canadian return sheets will carry enough votes in favor of Lloyd McBride that he will be declared elected. I know how to run elections," McDonald explained. "I stole four elections for Joe Germano as director for District 31." Fight Back focused its campaign on the big locals, their natural constituency in basic steel with over a thousand members—which Sadlowski largely won. Large locals only accounted for a plurality of the union's members, however, as the union had a lot of locals outside of basic steel. And, as McDonald warned, the real variable was the Canadian locals.[77]

The Sadlowski forces begged the Department of Labor for supervision of the election, and, when that was not forthcoming, presented a lengthy indictment of the election process. It was to no avail. When the Canadian locals came in, it was all over. Although it is not clear at all that there was enough fraud to have stolen a victory from Sadlowski, the Department of Labor actively stonewalled Rauh's requests for a review of the election. Although the department finally did do an investigation, the Fight Back found it inadequate. Sadlowski nailed the bigger problem in an interview he did in 1977 just months before the election. "Do you think there's an increased consciousness among American workers as to the conditions under which they are working and how these might be ameliorated?" His answer was, "If you had asked that question five to seven years ago, I would have answered yes. Today, however, the economic situation dissipates a consciousness that needs to take better root. The 'consciousness' now is just wanting to have a job."[78]

VIII

The hope of renewal began with the mine workers, and it ended there, too. Arnold Miller, the man from Cabin Creek who rose upon the winds of Miners for Democracy to defeat the Boyle loyalists after the Yablonski murders in the early seventies, rapidly descended from working-class hero to symbol of despair and heartache in the second half of the decade. *Business Week* originally compared the UMWA under Miller's leadership to "Portugal after it was released from dictatorship" with all that one might expect after the end of authoritarian system of governance: a robust democracy of turmoil, power disputes, and uncertainty—all wrapped up in a lilting sense of hope and expectation.[79]

Toward the end of his first term, however, Miller grew listless and indifferent, then confused and overwhelmed. When he took the leadership in 1973, he ceremonially sold off all of the union's Cadillacs, but by 1976 his expenses became extravagant, returning the plague of decadence that he had purged from the national offices. He began to grow suspicious, some say paranoid, about the loyalties of his confidants and allies as early as 1976. Miners are a tumultuous, democratic, and strike-prone lot, and, fearing the instability and unrest he had helped to unleash, Miller also began to centralize functions at the UMWA headquarters in Washington. Trapped between the rank and file and the old opponents of the MFD, Arnold was in a tight political space. The organization spiraled out of control. As one staffer put it,

> For most people, it was the first time they had been involved in anything that they won. They didn't know what the hell to do with it. The potential, the commitment, all those things were there. People really gave a shit, but there was a lot of naivete, a total disregard for anything that had been there before, a total disregard of history.

In echoes of the Boyle administration he had risked his life to defeat, Miller started to hire personal security men to enforce his directives, serve as his bodyguards, and prowl and snoop around headquarters. As Miller prepared to run for his second five-year term in 1977 (after promising to serve only one term), things grew so bad that the union's actual work ground to a halt, and the young and gifted reformers from inside and outside the labor movement who had flocked to the MFD cause either quit or were fired. Arnold Miller was in over his head.[80]

Attorney Joe Rauh, who had fought so hard in the UMWA and USW democratization struggles, began to fear a "return to the old Boyle domination of the Union," as he described it in a letter to Miller. "You can still pull the reform group together," he pleaded; "they are waiting for a call from the Arnold Miller of 1969 and '70 and '71 and '72." Rauh enclosed in his letter to Miller a note from one Frank Ortiz, who was engaged in his own struggle to democratize the Operating Engineers and had heard reports of Miller's drift away from MFD principles. "The U.M.W. Reformers became our light and inspiration," Ortiz lamented to Rauh. "We had hoped that they would extend their Victorious Arms out to all the Brothers that fought for Democracy in Unions and in any possible [way] keep us striving for our goals." Rauh begged Miller not to "betray all the Frank Ortizes around the country who are fighting for union democracy."[81]

Rauh's pleas failed, as Miller drifted far not just from the rank and file, but the day-to-day running of the union office as well. When Miller ran for his second term in 1977, his campaign style had shifted from his visits to the bathhouses during shift changes to appearances before large audiences orchestrated by a big Washington public relations firm. He even failed to show up to any of the four debates scheduled with the two men opposing him. He ultimately won another term in 1977 in a tight three-way race, but he had largely ceased to function as union president before his first term was up. Miller's one-time staunch ally, Secretary-Treasurer Harry Patrick, who carried on the MFD tradition by running against him, explained of his former comrade, "I'm not a doctor so I can't say if he's sick or not. What I can say is unfortunately he reminds me of Hitler in his last days when he gathered all his lieutenants together in the bunker. I'm sorry to see what's happened to him. I think it's very obvious to members of this union, especially to those who've seen him in person lately, that something is very, very wrong." Former allies began to openly refer to Miller as "paranoid" (as did some of the staff of the UFW refer to Cesar Chavez about the same time). The union leader who overthrew the bureaucrats, installed a rank-and-file miner, cut their own salaries, fired the thugs, and auctioned off the union Cadillacs could not be found.[82]

Miller's story was, in many ways, a human tragedy: a veteran of Normandy who never finished high school rising humbly to the leadership of a union that had prevented anyone from gaining real experience in leadership who was not willing to bend to the autocracy. His early potential seemed limitless, but his limits were real, the obstacles large, and the complexities overwhelming. "It was all lying there waiting for him to pick up. He could have been not only a great labor leader, he could have been a tremendous force for good in this country, another Martin Luther King," one former aide exclaimed. "And here he let it all get away just because he didn't want to stand up and be counted."[83]

Simultaneous to the meltdown in national leadership, labor relations in coal—then in the midst of a recording-breaking wildcat epidemic—had tipped from hopeful ferment to foreboding chaos. The coal operators, like much of the rest of the business world, were ready to discipline the unions. Joseph Brennan, president of the Bituminous Coal Operators' Association, explained in 1977, "We must come to grips with the cancer of the wildcat or we will assuredly face the inevitability of continuing chaos and, more tragically, lost opportunity. . . . To do this, BCOA must stand as a monolith in the upcoming negotiations." Indeed, wildcat strikes were running rampant in the industry, as the miners struggled against the operators' abuse of the grievance and arbitrations procedures, changes in the law, and ineffective national leadership. In 1973, 419,200 man days were lost to wildcat actions; by 1976, that figure had jumped over four and half times to 1,940,300 man days. The operators made the containment of the workers' wildcat actions their number one concern in national contract negotiations; the miners, however, regarded their right to strike as sacrosanct, even during a contract, and the only weapon they wielded against management's push. By 1977, the coal operators and the union had played to a draw on the question of the right to strike.[84]

Not only were the coal companies out to restrict the miners' right to strike, so was the Supreme Court. For generations prior to the Great Depression, the core of American labor law consisted of the courts' willingness to issue injunctions—an order to refrain from organizing or picketing—as a way to stop union activity. If workers violated the court order to press their demands or defend their union, then they would be in violation of the courts. The troops could then be called in to suppress the union activity. The federal injunction, upheld by the Supreme Court after the Pullman Strike of 1894, basically created "government by injunction" until the passage of the Norris-LaGuardia Act in 1932, which finally did away with the much-hated practice—did away with it, that is, until the 1970s.[85]

In 1970, the Supreme Court ruled in *Boys Markets, Inc. v. Retail Clerks Union, Local 770* that a contract that included a grievance procedure with binding arbitration effectively barred strike activity for the duration of the contract. In essence, even if there was not a "no strike" clause in the contract, which there was not in UMWA agreements, workers were barred from striking for the duration of the agreement. Any strike during a contract period therefore became illegal and subject to injunction. Since the power of the strike played a key role in what standards and issues would be used in arbitrations, this not only weakened workers' ability to press demands during a contract, but it also weakened, *a priori*, the strength of labor's position in arbitration. *Boys Markets* basically made the wildcat strike subject to federal intervention, a blow to the main source of vitality for the UMWA. Suggestive of the reversal of labor's fortunes in the seventies, the Court argued simply that Norris-LaGuardia "was a response to a situation totally different from that which exists today" and so the courts could return to enjoining strikes. Tragically for the Miller administration, many in the democratically inclined rank and file came to believe that the right to strike had been bar-gained away by the new union administration, a belief that Miller went to great lengths to correct.[86]

Miners continued to walk out in an unprecedented number of wildcats de-spite the *Boys Markets* decision, resulting in injunctions, fines, and jail time. The union quickly elevated a contractual "right to strike" clause to the top of their demands in 1977. The number one issue for the operators was "labor stability"—or no wildcats—which they believed they could impose given the weak state of the national union leadership. The union proposed that a local could vote whether to arbitrate (a long and enervating process) or strike (within some specific parameters, including a cooling off period). The stalemate on the right to strike was further complicated by the operators' cutback on the health benefits just months before negotiations began, which the union needed to win back. With the right of miners to strike over grievances during a contract and the future of the health benefit system at stake, the two parties locked horns for the longest strike in the UMWA's history, 110 days, topping the previous record just after World War II. "I want to work, believe me," ex-plained Paul Fowler, a miner at the Old Ben No. 21 in Illinois. "I want to work so bad it hurts. But my dad was a coal miner since he was 15. He's picked at the coal and he's done it the hard way. If ever I voted for this contract, he'd come up out of his grave and beat hell out of me. I have to get back the things my father fought for or his life didn't mean anything."[87]

Chaos ruled on every level of the strike. Miller, whom a staffer called a "tower of indecision" during negotiations, proved openly uninterested and unprepared for negotiations. He was even known to disappear on car trips around Washington to avoid dealing with the tough issue before him. The bargaining committee rejected one contract agreement, and then the rank and file rejected the second by a 2:1 margin—with photos of workers burn-ing or tearing up their contracts on the cover of major papers across the country. This happened all while the nation was facing both an energy crisis and debating national labor law reform legislation. The strike began in December 1977, and by March, Jimmy Carter, envisioning coal as a central component of his energy plan, invoked the national emergency provision of the Taft-Hartley Act. A federal district court then ordered the miners back to work, but this, too, was roundly ignored by the rank and file. As one miner from West Virginia put it, "Taft can mine it, Hartley can haul it, and Carter can shove it." Washington insiders began to talk seriously about the federal seizure of the mines as Truman had done after World War II. The

Washington Post referred to the "almost comic opera disarray" of the top union leadership, which was incapable of controlling "160,000 independent, free-thinking angry people." It was, the paper explained, "democracy in full cry" with the "rank and file, running roughshod over its leaders" having "brought the industry to its knees, thumbed its nose at President Carter and the federal courts and caused some shivers and jitters in a dozen coal dependent eastern and Midwestern states."[88]

Few have a clear idea who won the strike. The final contract settlement was not an easy sell to the rank and file, but the miners were itching to work and desperate for income after months of idleness. During bargaining in January, Miller called for a National Day of Prayer in the coalfields. Then, aware that he would be hawking an unpopular product, Miller arranged for country star Johnny Paycheck, whose hit "Take This Job and Shove It" was very popular on coal country radio, to promote the contract. Without irony, the leadership claimed that they would be leaning on the "Silent Majority" of coal miners to vote in favor of the unpopular contract. With the 1978 settlement passed, wildcat strikes dropped quickly, but the UMWA was able to make little headway against its next nemesis: non-union western coal. Secretary of Labor Ray Marshall had warned that "the unionized sector of the coal industry must resolve some of their problems or the non-unionized sector is going to grow." It did. Productivity of non-UMWA miners was higher than that covered by the national agreement by 39 percent in underground mining and 55 percent in surface mining operations, factors that were crucial to the fact that the amount of coal mined under the national agreement fell to just 45 percent by 1981 from over 70 percent when Arnold Miller took office.[89]

Facing Miller's further health problems and erratic behavior, the UMWA secured his retirement in 1979. Sam Church, an old Boyle loyalist who switched over to the Miller camp when it became clear that Boyle had been part of the Yablonski murders, became president. The Cadillacs came back. As a UMWA member said after the 1978 strike, "There's a real motion to the right among a lot of these guys that are good fighters. That doesn't mean they have to stay that way; it just means that there's nothing else for them to grasp onto right now, and they're so anti-Miller that anything looks good compared to Miller." Although lasting institutional changes and democratic reforms stuck with the UMWA, the spirit and élan of the reform days was never successfully instituted in the labor movement broadly conceived. The *Washington Post* speculated as to the "'big message' for the era of union reform" that the UMWA was supposed to be ushering in, concluding that "the era never really developed."[90]

An attorney friend once asked labor lawyer Tom Geoghegan, "What do you think historians will say when they try to figure out why, in the seventies, these guys in the Mineworkers and the Steelworkers rose up the way they did?" Looking at him as if he were "nuts," Geoghegan replied, "What historians? It's as if the whole thing never happened now."[91]

6

The New Deal that Never Happened

"Is there any way the President can redeem himself in your eyes?" a journalist queried William "Wimpy" Winpisinger, the president of the International Association of Machinists, in the spring of 1979. Eyes were already turning toward what would become the watershed 1980 presidential race, with grave concerns among labor leaders about the unions' failed political agenda, Jimmy Carter's inability—perhaps unwillingness—to make his mark on labor-liberal grounds, the faltering economy, and the rising heat of conservatism boiling up throughout the nation. "Yes, there's one way he can do it," replied the maverick union leader.

"What's that?"
"Die."

"I don't wish that on him," Wimpy qualified his remarks, "but that's the only goddamn way I know that he can." He was a rare breed of union leader whose confrontational politics combined blunt rhetoric and sharp wit. He dismissed Carter as the "The best Republican President since Herbert Hoover." Wimpy later organized for Ted Kennedy's insurgency against Carter and, failing that, led a walkout of the 1980 Democratic Convention when Carter was re-nominated.[1]

Rumor had it that when Jimmy Carter appeared to have the 1976 nomination sewn up, he asked George Meany who he would like to have as vice president. Meany pulled his cigar out of his mouth and said, "You!" Three years later, Meany's ambivalence and Wimpy's naked hostility were shared, in varying degrees, by much of organized labor and a great number of work-ing people.[2]

In 1977, the first year of the Carter administration, *Time* had already noted labor's "rapid decline in political clout," and a few months into the Carter administration it was clear that working-class issues were not on the president's short list. Carter then faced "open rebellion" from the unions because of what they regarded as his miserly stimulus package, his parsimo-nious minimum wage, and his tepid endorsement of common situs picketing (which would have allowed one striking union to shut down the myriad of contractors and subcontractors at a single construction site—a bill that Ford had vetoed). As a result, union leaders lashed out. George Meany gave him a grade of "C-" for his first year's performance, explaining, "I think the President is a conservative." As the relationship between the White House and the AFL-CIO soured further, Carter's aides privately dismissed Meany as a "senile old man." For several months after 1978, Meany and Carter were said not even to be on speaking terms. When Carter was elected, *Business Week* expressed its concern—and labor leaders' hopes—about Carter push-ing for "the 1970s version of the New Deal." He ended up, however, as the first president to govern in a *post*–New Deal framework. Rather than the last attempt to revive the New Deal faithful, the Carter administration marked, as Melvyn Dubofsky put it, "the death of industrial pluralism and the New Deal system."[3]

The relationship between organized labor and the Carter administration did not begin with such acrimony, but rarely had it been smooth. What be-came labor's tortured relationship with the White House started out with a mix of caution and hope. With a Democrat in the executive branch and the substantial 1974 post-Watergate Democratic majorities still in both houses, hopeful whispers of a labor-liberal comeback solidified for 1976. Less than two years later, those hopes crashed hard. Labor law reform, which promised to breathe life back into the gasping efficacy of the Wagner Act, would be routed by a Senate filibuster; the Humphrey-Hawkins Full Employment Act, an homage to the economic security promised in FDR's Economic Bill of Rights, would be made into political hash by its supposed allies; and industrial policy and national health insurance never even got off the ground. By 1978, the attempts to revive postwar liberalism became the New Deal that never happened. It all ended far from a liberal revival and something closer to a requiem for a collective economic vision for the Amer-ican people.

Advocates of full employment and labor law reform, in ways both separate and overlapping, hoped that these policies would create a unified national labor market—overcoming competition by race, gender, and region that was threatening the economic foundation of postwar liberalism. The Humphrey-Hawkins Act would guarantee planning for full employment, which would mitigate the divisiveness of inter-racial competition for jobs in the midst of record unemployment. Full employment offered a firmer economic foundation for the otherwise divisive calls for racial equality and diversity. Labor law reform would not simply breathe new life into the deflated power of the Wagner Act but would help unions to organize new categories of workers in areas like the post-civil rights South—a region to which jobs were rapidly draining from the unionized Northeast—as well as in the service sectors replacing shuttered industry. In the best light, a growth in unionization, argued *The Nation*, "represents nothing less than the economic consolidation and extension of the limited legal and political gains won by the civil rights movement in the 1960s. By alleviating the poverty of both blacks and poor whites, unions can allay the economic enmity which lies at the roots of so much of the South's racial tension. The labor movement's self-interest lies in aggressively promoting integration in the region." As Monsignor George Higgins—Pittsburgh's famous "labor priest"—hoped, "The struggle to achieve a more humane economic order will not be fought along racial lines but will be defined by broader class interests."[4]

In contrast to the more technocratic mode of Jimmy Carter, the perfect—indeed, mythic—candidate to unite working-class America in the latter part of the seventies would probably have been an impossible amalgam of the "three Georges": George McGovern, moralist, social democrat, peacenik, and practitioner of the New Politics of gender and racial equality; George Meany, cold warrior, realist, and militantly parochial defender of the system of collective bargaining; and George Wallace, populist hero of the white man, capable of sticking it to elites of any stripe. The contradictions in such an amalgam are suggestive of the complexities and contradictions involved in uniting working-class America.[5]

Despite the political lift of Watergate that delivered strong majorities, the Democratic Party actually remained quite fragmented. The 1976 primary process had a smattering of individuals representing a smattering of interests—"a very pale imitation of Franklin Roosevelt's New Deal coalition" at every turn. Morris Udall, a congressman from Arizona, weighed in on behalf of college educated liberals and environmentalists; Scoop Jackson advocated on behalf of cold warriors and organized labor; Jerry Brown represented the multi-cultural fiscally conservative neo-liberals; and George Wallace pushed the cultural and racial resentments of working-class whites. Jimmy Carter, however, had "a foot in every camp and a face for every constituency," but his was less a coalition than a thin imitation of the old politics.[6]

Mistakenly, UAW president Leonard Woodcock, still traumatized by Wallace's 1972 victory in the Michigan primary, saw Carter as pretty close to that triptych of working-class Georges—at least in his endorsement rhetoric. "If a political genius had offered to produce a candidate who could carry the working class as well as the crucial black, moderate, and liberal votes in the North, and at the same time defeat the strident segregationists of the South, he would have been called a dreamer," Woodcock gushed. "And yet that is what Jimmy Carter had done." When Carter narrowly beat the wheel-chair-bound Wallace in the Florida primary and agreed to back the UAW's program for national health insurance, Woodcock had found his candidate.[7]

Since the McGovern debacle, the old Democratic establishment had recaptured the party machinery with a vengeance, returning the cold warriors and the anti-New Politics crowd back to positions of power in the Democratic National Committee. Labor's old guard hoped for Cold War liberal Henry "Scoop" Jackson but had little success. Carter received support from the McGovern coalition of unions, in particular Jerry Wurf's AFSCME—always on the margins of the AFL-CIO—and the UAW, which had abandoned the AFL-CIO back in 1968. Carter, it was hoped, could corral the Wallaceites; eventually be tolerated by the labor leadership; and, despite his personal attempt to sabotage the McGovern candidacy in 1972, run as a progressive Southerner who, like McGovern, was ready to embrace liberal social issues. As a dark horse candidate, Jimmy Carter had to sneak around the Democratic machinery; maximize the McGovern-Fraser reforms; and present himself as a fresh Washington outsider who, in the wake of Watergate, promised never to lie to the American people. Once he stopped being known as "Jimmy Who?" and captured the nomination, the AFL-CIO, unlike in 1972, fell into place behind him, determined to get him elected. Carter always knew, however, that he was not labor's first choice. Unions, not hostile as they had been to McGovern, remained suspicious of a Southerner and someone who had not risen to prominence without the support of organized labor.

Once Carter won the nomination, he eschewed the old campaign launch site of Detroit's Cadillac Square, and turned to Warm Springs, Georgia—

selected because it was both in Carter's home state and because it was one of Franklin Delano Roosevelt's favorite retreats. Cynics noted that the site had other meanings: it was in the heart of a region that had limited political support for labor liberalism and in the place that FDR had passed away. His eventual victory over unelected incumbent Gerald Ford was surprisingly fragile, given the aftermath of Watergate, the state of the economy, and Ford's widely unpopular pardon of Nixon. He narrowly won the national race (Ford received 48.0 percent of the popular vote against Carter's 50.1 percent) in a year that political logic suggested should have been owned by the Democratic Party. Like FDR, Carter won the South (trumping the Wallace problem and the rise of the Southern Republicans), the industrial cities, and organized labor (with 62 percent of union members). Ford, beating back a close insurgency from Ronald Reagan in a party deciding how far right it wanted to go, won core industrial and liberal states such as New Jersey, Michigan, California, and Illinois. Pat Caddell, who had polled for McGovern and moved on to Carter, recognized that this was not the revitalization of the Democratic coalition. "Carter's performance among traditional groups is impressive when compared to McGovern's showing in 1972," he explained; "but when placed in long-term historical perspective [of New Deal voting patterns it] simply cannot explain the victory." Rather, Carter gained moderate in-roads into a Republican electorate only temporarily demoralized by Watergate. He completely lost the West, except for Texas, and made up for his many losses in the Midwest and Northeast by his easier victories in the southern states—wins that only Southern Democrats would have a chance of replicating in the future.[8]

Much of the inflated liberal hopes about what was possible in the 1970s were informed by an unconscious and misguided New Deal triumphalism that allowed the surface glimmers of a Carter presidency to appear like something more substantial. As a new kind of Democrat, Carter ran and governed more in the mode of the Progressive Era good government steward—"attempting to make the government more competent and administratively more rational" rather than the anti-Washington populist crusader that he sometimes ran as or as the incipient New Dealer many hoped he might become. Unlike previous Democratic administrations, which tended to work with labor, Carter had very little experience with unions and felt hamstrung by his pro forma commitments to New Deal constituents. "Carter saw unions as just another interest group," remarked Chief Domestic Policy Advisor Stuart Eizenstat; "They did not have a special call on his heartstrings.

They were a group that had to be dealt with, but that was all." He had always understood race much better than class, did not understand unions at all, and felt caged rather than empowered by coalitional politics. His hope had been, in virtuous Wilsonian fashion, to rise above interest groups so as to become the moral steward of the nation in his battles with stagflation and the spiritual malaise he outlined in his famous 1979 "Crisis of Confidence" speech.[9]

By the end of the decade, the Carter administration teetered on the brink of failure, but the problems he faced were nearly intractable. Carter "needed to deal at the same time with a catalogue of competing and inherently contradictory claims on government and his administration," explains one biographer: "to promote employment while halting inflation; to reduce taxes while meeting pressing social needs; to maintain business confidence without alienating traditional Democrats; and to stabilize the dollar abroad without undercutting his economic program at home." As Stuart Eizenstat explained, the president's contradictory and confusing goals made it worse. "One always knew that [Carter] wanted to spend as little money as possible, and yet at the same time he wanted welfare reform, he wanted national health insurance, he wanted job training programs." Lacking both the willingness to chart a bold new course and the political winds to drive innovative policy (speechwriter James Fallows dubbed it the "passionless presidency"), Carter emerged as a new brand of conservative Democrat of the type that would go on to dominate the party, tempered by a personal disposition ill-suited to the structural crisis he faced. As a result, what some hoped would be a New Deal revival ended up as the "last hurrah" of the New Deal faithful.[10]

I

During World War II, I.F. Stone called full employment "that new, glamorous, and socially explosive slogan" for progressives. The political struggle to plan for a full employment economy represented liberals' hopes to advance economic security and solidify political power in the postwar era. The Full Employment Bill of 1945 blossomed out of President Roosevelt's famous Economic Bill of Rights in his 1944 State of the Union Address, in which he declared it the nation's duty to establish "the right to a useful and remunerative job in the industries or shops or farms or mines of the nation."

Under the bill, the president was to prepare a production and employment budget and calculate the number of jobs necessary in the upcoming year and the economic growth necessary to fulfill that estimate. If it looked as though the private sector would not be capable of fulfilling the nation's needs, the government would step in with an aggressive program of federal spending designed to deliver the economy to full employment. Opposition ran high, however, for a host of reasons: employers feared that it would drive up the price of labor, conservatives balked at the cost, economists questioned any-one's ability to create accurate forecasts, the long-feared postwar depression seemed not to be happening, and liberal Democrats lost power in Congress. The bill ended up as the gutted Employment Act of 1946. Absent from the act was the word "full" and, in the historian Alan Brinkley's terms, "In its place was a statement of purpose so filled with qualification and ambiguities that it was almost meaningless"—phrasing that foreshadowed the fate of the Humphrey-Hawkins Full Employment Act in the 1970s.[11]

The embers of the full employment idea remained buried but alive in the postwar era despite the fact that mainstream U.S. manpower policy empha-sized growth—and later fair employment practices—rather than planning. Whenever the slumps came or the need for Cold War spending justified, planning again flared up. The embers glowed brightly when the civil rights movement continued A. Phillip Randolph's World-War-II–era theme of "Jobs and Freedom" for the 1963 March on Washington. Bayard Rustin, in his 1965 defense of coalition politics, "From Protest to Politics," declared full employment to be a fundamental civil rights issue. "I fail to see how the movement can be victorious," he argued, "in the absence of radical programs for full employment, the abolition of slums, the reconstruction of our educa-tional system, new definitions of work and leisure." When those dreams ended in the flames of the long hot summer in the urban north, the Kerner Commission echoed calls for a massive investment in public employment and planning to boost private sector job growth.[12]

Old-school liberals began to try to imagine what Hubert Humphrey called "common denominators—mutual needs, mutual wants, common hopes, the same fears" to bring the Democrats back together after Vietnam, civil rights, busing, and a growing white blue-collar defection. As Humphrey believed in 1972, "The Democratic Party got in to trouble when its internal reforms came to be perceived as establishing specific quotas that favored young people, women, and blacks over the more traditional elements of the party, particu-larly ethnic American, blue collar workers, the elderly, and elected Democratic officials." He rejected the idea that 1960s-style politics ought to become the organizing principle of the Democratic Party. "There just aren't enough blacks, Chicanos, Indians and Puerto Ricans to form an electoral majority." For Humphrey, Nixon's landslide victory over George McGovern proved such a theory largely correct, and his project became one of finding new common ground. He feared that Nixon and Wallace seemed to have outmaneuvered the Democrats on the "common man" theme as they effectively tagged liberals with the label of elitism and softness on the "law and order" issue. As he appropriately framed it, "We must create a climate of shared interests between the needs, the hopes and the fears of the minorities, and the needs, the hopes and the fears of the majority."[13]

Many could see that placing affirmative action onto a world of declining opportunity was little more than a zero-sum game—and most likely a fast track to further racial resentment. The problem, as Bayard Rustin put it in 1974, was overcoming the divisiveness of "Affirmative Action in an Age of Scarcity." As Andrew Levison made the connection between the future of racial progress and the limits on economic opportunity in the *New Yorker* in 1974, "until progressives deal seriously with the idea of full employment and government guaranteed jobs, black representation in skilled jobs will remain a question of throwing a white carpenter out of work in order to employ a black, or making a Pole with seniority continue to tend the coke ovens while a black moves up to a better job." A few years later, when that same hypothetical coke oven shut down permanently in the plant closings of the late seventies and early eighties, the problem became even more profound.[14]

Cleveland Robinson, one of the founders of the Coalition of Black Trade Unionists, put it equally as forcefully. "The basic ingredient to successful affirmative action is full employment," he explained. Otherwise "you will have both blacks and whites fighting for the same jobs."

> Consequently, you will have a situation where the white worker who is hungry cannot see any reason why he shouldn't have the job, just because the black worker has traditionally been left out. It's actually asking too much to say to that white unemployed, "You should understand [how important it is for a black person to have this job]." So together with the struggle for affirmative action, we have to struggle for full employment.

The forward march of racial justice, many activists and politicians believed, could only proceed under conditions of both full employment and equality of opportunity—otherwise it risked the continuation of a politically fatal backlash as white blue-collar workers sought to protect what they had in trying economic times.[15]

The attempt at seventies alchemy—turning the leaden and divisive politics of race into the golden unity of class—began when Minnesota senator Hubert Humphrey and California congressman Augustus Hawkins introduced what would be known popularly, despite several iterations and various official titles in the 1970s, as the Humphrey-Hawkins Full Employment Bill (as well as the short-lived variation, the Humphrey-Javits bill). The proposed law featured a federal guarantee of a job and coordinated national planning to achieve a full employment economy—including, in the earliest versions, the right to sue the federal government for a job. Although the law did pass (in a very different form), its almost non-existent post-1978 legacy remains an artifact of a bygone political world buried deeply in the ideological layers of a neoliberal order.

Keenly aware of the defection of white blue-collar workers from the Democratic Party, advocates of full employment specifically tried to design and promote it as a bill that was actually *not* about race. Strategically, the legislation sought "targeting through universalism," in Theda Skocpol's terms, by constructing politically tenable mechanisms for creating minority employment through expanded rights for all workers. Humphrey-Hawkins also had the virtue of working within the same "rights consciousness" framework that some have seen as bringing an end to the politics of the common good. Rather than rights derived of gender or race, this bill sought to grant the universal right to a job—a melding of 1960s rights consciousness with the unfinished economic agenda of the late New Deal. Since organized labor was the number one financial backer of the push for Humphrey-Hawkins, and the civil rights groups had moral persuasion on their side, it also, in theory, set the unions in partnership with the civil rights community around an expansive political vision.[16]

Humphrey was trailing a path already blazed by Congressman Augustus Hawkins, a key voice in the new Congressional Black Caucus whose district included the blighted and riot-torn area of Watts in Los Angeles. Like Humphrey, Hawkins grew to be a consummate New Dealer, though he had launched his political career volunteering for Upton Sinclair's End Poverty in California campaign. He won a seat in the California assembly in 1934 and remained in elected office continuously until 1991, having switched to a seat in the House of Representatives in 1962. He attributed his own success to early support from A.P. Randolph and unionized African-American workers, and the folding of black voters into the Democratic Party under Franklin Roosevelt. Throughout his life, Hawkins never wavered from his deeply held belief in the New Deal coalition, its politics, and its principles. As a quiet but tireless legislator who worked largely outside the limelight, he slowly amassed a reputation as "the dean of the nation's elected black officials."[17]

Hawkins believed, above all, in the tradition of A. Phillip Randolph, that civil rights and economic rights were the twin requirements of social justice. He thought the 1963 March on Washington and the subsequent Civil Rights Act emphasized only the latter half of the "Jobs and Freedom" equation. As he recalled about his agitation to include fair employment rights in the bill, "We pushed to get employment into the Act because we thought it wouldn't make any sense to be able to eat in a public restaurant . . . if one didn't have the money. We felt that jobs were really the key to making the Civil Rights Act meaningful, so we pushed for that," he explained about the creation of the Equal Employment Opportunity Commission.[18]

The plan the two leaders came up with in 1974 combined two key elements: nationally coordinated economic planning to bring about full employment at "prevailing" (i.e., high) wages, and a federally mandated and legally enforceable right to a job for every American backed by the right to sue for employment in the appropriate U.S. district court by any person who felt deprived of work. "Full employment" in the bill was not some abstract goal, but rather was explicitly and ambitiously defined as 3 percent unemployment to be achieved in an incredibly ambitious eighteen months after the legislation went into effect. The umbrella of economic planning required that the president annually submit to Congress a nationwide full employment and production program to ensure an adequate demand for labor, as well as an expanded role for the congressional Joint Economic Committee in reviewing and challenging the full employment and production program that would be put forth by the president. Under the bill, planning councils on the local level would initiate public and private projects to meet community needs, an idea that, in later incarnations of the bill, evolved into a long list of national priorities that full employment would help meet, including child care, transportation, conservation, housing, education, and recreation. Although based largely on the private sector, the bill also expanded the federal role in providing jobs through the creation of local reservoirs of public service and private employment projects developed by local planning councils, the creation of Job Guarantee Offices able to fund these projects, and a Standby Job Corps for temporary placement of workers.[19]

The attempt to unite employed with unemployed and black with white required tremendous political imagination—nothing short of a social democratic America. Proponents had to create new economic logic that defied the limits of market discipline and, most importantly, overcome fears of the expansive role of government, increased taxes, and, especially, the acceleration of inflation. They also had to overcome the weakness of the very idea of planning within the intellectual and institutional history of postwar liberalism, which itself had a shaky foundation on the rest of American history. Believers in the power of full employment also faced serious obstacles in the entrenched interests that opposed planning—interests that were aggressively re-organized in the 1970s.

"Above all," wrote Senator Humphrey in staking out the broad philosophical terrain he hoped the bill would inhabit, full employment "means a spelling out of all the many kinds of goods and services—in housing, mass transportation, daycare facilities, health education, research and the arts—which are not now available but could be made available to the American population in a genuine full employment economy." This, he concluded, will allow the "economics of abundance" to replace the "economics of scarcity." It was a bold, even grandiose plan for a social democratic America in an age that was defining itself by its limitations and in which people were questioning the ability of the state to deliver on its promises.[20]

II

All of the pieces for the ready, if contentious, passage of Humphrey-Hawkins appeared to fall into place in the spring of 1976. It was a symbolically auspicious year to push it through Congress: it was not only the year of the nation's bicentennial but also the thirtieth anniversary of the eviscerated 1946 Employment Act. It was also an election year, and the Democrats hoped to pass it and force President Gerald Ford into a veto on the eve of a national presidential election against a Democratic candidate who would be, presumably, adamantly in favor of national planning. Polls also showed that in 1976, for the first time in forty years, the electorate was more concerned with matters domestic than foreign. The *New York Times* had given the bill a reasonably warm endorsement, and even the House Republican Research

Committee feared the proposal's "appealing rhetoric" and went so far as to argue that full employment proposals "underline a valid concern in an economy plagued by high rates of unemployment and concomitant social costs." On top of these favorable trends, a *New York Times* poll in early 1976 showed that 70 percent of voters believed in the much vaguer concept that the government should provide jobs for all who wanted them. There were some important storm clouds on the horizon, however, as polling also showed that inflation *and* unemployment were the nation's top two concerns, but the two remained in an irreconcilable trade-off in most policy makers' minds. Furthermore, polls suggested that the third most important issue in post-Vietnam, post-Watergate America was dissatisfaction with government—a fact that would make it hard for government intervention to solve the first two.[21]

Humphrey-Hawkins would proceed nowhere in 1976 or beyond without the backing of the AFL-CIO, so in weeks of quiet negotiations among the bill's sponsors, the AFL-CIO, and the Congressional Black Caucus, Humphrey-Hawkins was retooled and toned down for the labor federation. The definition of "unemployed" was narrowed to include only adults, and the targeted period for achieving full employment was moved from eighteen months to four years after it became law. The right to sue the government for employment was removed, but the legal guarantee of a job—certainly the heart and the most politically and philosophically charged element in the bill—remained. Unlike the gutted 1946 bill, the 1976 incarnation set up specific and mandatory processes for achieving full employment and contained concrete numbers and definitions to back it up. It also included a series of job programs, counter-cyclical state aid mechanisms, and calls for increased coordination with the Federal Reserve in planning matters.[22]

The most important, and probably fatal, concession the sponsors of the bill made in preparing for the 1976 legislative session was to organized labor when they gave up federal controls on wages and prices. The bill's sponsors were stuck in a Catch-22: Humphrey-Hawkins could not proceed legislatively without the support of organized labor, but mandatory controls on prices and wages would instantly kill labor's support since it would restrict the unions' ability to bargain for wage increases (and since prices were more difficult to control than wages, leave the membership vulnerable to actual wage losses). Without controls, however, the bill would be vulnerable to attack by economists and fiscally conservative members of Congress who feared that without controls the bill was a recipe for runaway inflation. As

Humphrey groused in a private letter about the 1976 rewriting of the bill, "The AFL and CIO were adamant as you can well imagine, and the Black Caucus wanted everything they could possibly think of plus another ten to fifteen percent." So the sponsors eliminated any talk of controls and received labor's support but left themselves vulnerable on the fatal problem of inflation. They did get George Meany on board, without whom the bill did not stand a chance. The aging labor leader declared, with questionable conviction, that Humphrey-Hawkins would be the unions' number one legislative priority and that labor would be mobilizing for "the biggest fight for the future of America."[23]

The new version of the bill attracted a broad coalition of supporters that read like a mailing list for the Democratic faithful. Key liberal senators promoted the bill to a central position in the Democrats' 1976 platform and the Platform Committee concurred, adopting the idea of full employment—complete with the 3 percent unemployment figure—"without a murmur of protest from the floor." House Majority Leader Tip O'Neill proclaimed that Humphrey-Hawkins was "the centerpiece of our party's 1976 platform." The Democratic consensus on full employment legislation illustrated the political intent of the bill—to paper over more controversial and divisive issues like the draft amnesty, abortion, and busing—as much as it did actual support. The *Wall Street Journal* explained the bill offered a life raft for liberals sinking in the troubled water of race in the 1970s. "As they go over the side on busing, the liberals can yell: 'But I'm for Humphrey-Hawkins.'"[24]

At the same time that the Democratic elite were getting ready to push the bill, the Full Employment Action Council (FEAC) tried to become a national vehicle to mobilize grassroots support for Humphrey-Hawkins. As a national coordinating body, FEAC brought together grassroots organizations and local and national rallies, gatherings, conferences of all sorts, editorials and articles in the national press, and a barrage of pamphlets, posters, and literature in support of the bill, all of which added up to substantially less than the sum of its parts. The co-chairs of the committee, much like the co-sponsors of the bill, symbolized the attempt to fill the breach in progressive politics by bringing the labor and civil rights groups together. Coretta Scott King, widow of the slain civil rights leader and head of the Martin Luther King Center for Social Change, embodied the civil rights side of the struggle, while Murray H. Finley, president of the Amalgamated Clothing Workers of America, symbolized the progressive labor side of the push. While much of the political muscle for FEAC's efforts on Humphrey-Hawkins came from the Congressional Black Caucus, most of the money came from organized labor.[25]

The Congressional Joint Economic Committee, chaired by none other than Hubert Humphrey, also took to the road in early 1976 and held regional field hearings on the problem of unemployment to build pressure and evidence for the bill. Not surprisingly, the committee unearthed evidence that demonstrated the immediate need for full employment policies. In Fall River, Massachusetts, the mayor declared, "We are running out of thumbs and the sieve-like dikes are cascading us with the drowning waters of poor economic policies and leadership that are not our own doing." In Chicago, listening to testimony about inner-city unemployment, Humphrey declared, "it is obvious to me that the old economic rules no longer apply." In Los Angeles, a union plumber declared his industry to be in "a state of no growth or no work at all. . . . We are really down at rock bottom." Later that year, research for the Joint Economic Committee found that unemployment sponsored a wide array of social ills. The 1.4 percent increase in unemployment in 1970 was supposedly directly responsible for: 51,570 premature deaths in a five-year period, including 1,740 homicides, 1,540 suicides, 5,520 mental hospitalizations. The same rise in unemployment cost the nation $7 billion in lost income and added prison and hospital outlays, to which had to be added another $2.8 billion in jobless and welfare payments.[26]

"The heavy rhetorical guns are being wheeled into place on Capitol Hill," reported the *Congressional Quarterly* in May 1976; "statistical arms are being stockpiled and lobbying troops deployed" for the battle over full employment. The bill moved through the House committees with Democratic support, and with Republican lawmakers making no attempt to amend it on the grounds that it was simply "irredeemable." The chief opponents of the bill were largely economists of all stripes. Alan Greenspan, Ford's Council of Economic Advisors (CEA) chair (the CEA had been created under the 1946 Employment Act), for instance, opposed it in his congressional testimony on the grounds that the logic of the bill falsely assumed that employment was always productive, a flaw that could lead to serious inflation problems. The numerical goals in the bill were either useless or harmful and based on a notion of detailed, scientific forecasting that did not exist. For most people, unemployment was a short-term phenomenon, so critics believed it was "foolish" to take workers out of the labor market semi-permanently with public jobs. Other attacks from the Right followed similar logic, though typically with an even sharper political edge. Ford's secretary of the Treasury William E. Simon criticized congressional Democrats for offering what he called "an instant panacea to all our economic woes" that played upon "the economic illiteracy of the American people." Milton Friedman characterized it as "close to a fraud." The sponsors' harping on the tragedy of the unemployed meant that the "whole subject of the bill has become so smothered in sentimentality that anyone who speaks out against it runs the risk of being considered brutal," proclaimed Richard Nixon's former CEA head, Herbert Stein. President Ford, recognizing that he was being set up for a veto on a sensitive issue, declared it a "vast election year boondoggle." Liberal economist Arthur Okun claimed that the bill was little more than "beautiful poetry."[27]

While conservative assaults on full employment were predictable and even useful to the bill's proponents, what undid the hopes of Humphrey-Hawkins for 1976 was the testimony of what *Business Week* declared "a *"Who's Who* of liberal economics." Particularly damning was the testimony of Charles Schultze, who had been Lyndon Johnson's budget director and a trusted liberal insider. Schultze was particularly concerned about the "prevailing wage" clause, which threatened to draw people out of low-paying private sector employment and into higher-wage public sector jobs, fomenting further inflation. As he emphasized in his statement to a Senate subcommittee, Humphrey-Hawkins supporters had given up wage and price controls in order to win support for the bill, which meant, "*The stumbling block to low unemployment is inflation; the supporter of a full employment policy must of necessity become a searcher for ways to reduce the inflation that accompanies full employment.*"[28]

Schultze's testimony proved devastating to hopes for the 1976 bill, as liberal congressional representatives chose to deny it a vote until it could be retooled to gain the support of the former Great Society economist and those like him. Humphrey saw it differently, claiming privately that full employment supporters had been "stabbed in the back" by their erstwhile Keynesian allies in the economics profession. Yet even J.K. Galbraith pleaded with his fellow liberals not to invest too much faith in Humphrey-Hawkins' ability to transcend the iron laws of economic reasoning. "Let all who advocate this legislation be mature," he pleaded. "Let us not imagine that God is a liberal gentleman who will work miracles for liberals merely because He loves His own."[29]

The logic of the economists' opposition to the idea of legislating full employment rested on the most influential explanation of the relationship between employment and inflation, the Phillips Curve, named after A.W. Phillips and a paper he wrote in 1959. In short, the curve demonstrated a trade-off between the inflation rate and the unemployment rate: a lower inflation rate could be manufactured by slowing down the economy and increasing unemployment, which placed a downward pressure on both wages and prices. According to the Phillips-Curve faithful, the opposite was also true: a low unemployment rate tightened the labor market, drove up the price of labor, and ignited inflation. Since the curve posited a nonlinear relationship, the closer the unemployment rate approached the "frictional" rate of unemployment, the faster the inflation rate would rise. In the push-button logic of postwar economic thinking, the Phillips Curve offered a spectrum of policy options depending upon political priorities and alliances. Groups could advocate targeting different places on the curve depending on whether full employment or disciplining inflation was more important to a given set of political interests.[30]

In a time of inflation like the 1970s, putting more people to work—especially at federal expense—was not what the fiscally prudent doctor ordered. According to critics of Humphrey-Hawkins, to absorb the unemployed into federal jobs at prevailing wages would tighten the labor market, drive up wages, and exacerbate an already inflationary economy. Moreover, the "prevailing wages" language often meant higher wages than many existing private-sector jobs. Such a stipulation would therefore attract workers out of the private sector and, in the process, actually violate the coveted "natural rate" of unemployment. According to mainstream economists, Humphrey-Hawkins would not only push the economy too far down the employment side of the equation but would actually drive inflation to unprecedented heights by drawing workers out of the private sector. This scenario was exacerbated by the fact that economists generally believed that the natural rate of unemployment had gone up in the 1970s as women and youth entered the labor market. To try to drive unemployment legislatively to "artificial lows" defied the conventional wisdom.

Advocates of full employment legislation marshaled a host of arguments against the prevailing wisdom of the Phillips Curve, most of which began with the fact that the curve was incapable of explaining the economy of the 1970s. Both inflation and unemployment were rising during the decade—a situation that already defied the logic of the tradeoff. The economy was so out of sync with what was supposed to be happening that the popular term "stagflation" unified two trends—stagnation and inflation—that theoretically should have been in opposition. The inflation of the 1970s was not caused by a tight job market, argued Humphrey-Hawkins' proponents, but by issues such as the oil shocks and crop shortages. One logic stream argued that the supply-and-demand price mechanism simply no longer worked. In times of low demand, producers did not lower prices as theory predicted; rather, oligopolistic industries actually increased prices to make up for lost revenue. Unemployment therefore actually fed inflation. Putting people to work, these advocates argued, actually increased the supply of goods and thus would drive down their price, essentially using policy to subvert the impulses of executives of large corporations. Ray Marshall, for instance, who would become secretary of labor under Jimmy Carter, explained that the causes of inflation were not employment related, but a product of too much money chasing too few goods: "If you have people not working, then they're sure not producing any goods but they are living so they are getting money. And that's inflationary." This approach contained an argument against non-productive welfare payments since they did not add to the aggregate supply of goods and tended to be more inflationary than the type of productive employment promised under Humphrey-Hawkins.[31]

The most persuasive approach to beating the Phillips Curve could be found on the populist moral high ground. Should throwing people out of work (most typically under the euphemism "cooling the economy") be the way to keep things on the right track? Proponents of Humphrey-Hawkins argued that sacrificing jobs on the altar of economic orthodoxy was politically and ethically irresponsible. Leon Keyserling, the major torch bearer for the cause of full employment who went all the way back to the Truman years, called the whole idea of the curve playing "games with the human misery of unemployment." Former member of the CEA and Harvard economist, Otto Eckstein, explained that Humphrey-Hawkins was a realistic alternative "to telling the public we've got to live with high unemployment for years" and that we "are so intellectually bankrupt we won't even try to do something." Even Charles Schultze, who personally did more to undermine the bill than anyone in 1976, still wanted to be known as a "friendly critic" and believed that despite the bill's flaws, "we must keep rubbing the government's nose in the problem of chronic unemployment." Humphrey continued his struggle to push the debate beyond the "sterile and misleading exercise" involved in economic statistics. "If price stability is to be gained at the price of 7 million, 8 million, 10 million people being left unemployed, then that policy is politically and morally indefensible."[32]

Even if full employment advocates could beat the "upside-down theory of the 'immoral trade-off'" found in orthodox economic thinking, they had to convince politicians, voters, and especially the business community that the risk of gambling on such macroeconomic planning was worth it given that the unemployed—however large their number and terrible their condition— remained a relatively small part of the population, especially as compared to those contending with inflation. Yet it raised questions about what the role of the market was—does it serve the people or do people serve the market? "If the greatest free nation in the history of mankind has to get down on its knees in fear of something as abstract and as arbitrary as these so called 'free market forces,' well, then we're through," Humphrey explained to Congress. "We might just as well haul down the flag, lock up the Capitol, go home and admit that we don't have the courage or the imagination to govern ourselves."[33]

Polling data showed a consistently high concern for employment issues throughout the decade, topped only by concerns about its obverse, inflation. In 1975, the two issues were almost in a dead heat when pollsters asked which one the government ought to be paying greater attention. Inflation was selected by 46 percent of those surveyed and unemployment selected by 44 percent. Among Democrats, however, unemployment was of greater concern (48 percent) than was inflation (44 percent). Yet it was not typically that close. In a 1977 poll, just as the unemployment rate was falling and inflation was heating up again, 58 percent selected inflation as the more important issue, while 39 percent chose unemployment. By the time Humphrey-Hawkins came up for a vote in the House, the split had widened to 54–18. The bill's sponsors faced the same problem the bill was trying to avoid: creating liberal legislation that serviced a minority of people—even if it was trying to create a right for all. This made the bill vulnerable to populist attack. Ronald Reagan ripped into Humphrey-Hawkins on his radio show with the type of rhetoric that would help get him elected in 1980. Claiming that the bill was "as persuasive and grandiloquent in it's [sic] promises as the label on a bottle of patent medicine," he concluded, slyly invoking Friedrich Hayek's Road to Serfdom, "Maybe it is a full employment program—but so was slavery."[34]

III

Despite such rhetorical heat from the right, for a brief period in 1976, Humphrey-Hawkins looked like a sure thing—at least until congressional Democrats scotched it in the face of growing opposition within their own party. In retrospect, it turned out to be more of an election year weapon than a political vision for a generation. As Margaret Weir argues, "it quickly became evident that the ideas it embodied had no political or institutional ground in which to germinate." Arguably, effective leaders have been able to plow new terrain to allow for that germination, but if ever there was a head of state destined to do so in the name of government planning, it certainly was not Jimmy Carter. The hostility from Gerald Ford, the Republicans, and the mainstream economists was much easier for liberals to overcome than was the tepid cooptation that Humphrey-Hawkins received from the thirty-ninth president, who, in the end, reduced the bill from substance to symbol.[35]

During the Democratic primaries, Carter cautiously declared the goals of Humphrey-Hawkins "laudable" and claimed he supported the "aims" of the bill and congratulated the sponsors "for their concern about what I have long stated was the key issue confronting this country." His television spots for the primary race included vague but passionate references to jobs as the key to the future. It was hardly a rousing endorsement, but candidate Carter had little interest in backing the full employment act. Not long after his tepid endorsement of the general idea of full employment, Carter found himself in the midst of an odd controversy that forced him left and into the Humphrey-Hawkins fold. Caught by a political stumble in which he said he supported the "racial purity" of neighborhoods, he strategically had to tack left to shore up his African-American support, which he did by backing Humphrey-Hawkins. Mostly, the candidate maintained vague support coupled with a face-saving official agnosticism on the bill since the final version always remained under negotiation.[36]

As the fall campaign season heated up, Carter still proclaimed ambivalence and only qualified support for the bill. "I am for the concept of Humphrey-Hawkins as it shows the consequence of unemployment on the present scale," he explained. "It is too expensive and I do not favor the kind of overall planning by the federal government that it would mean." Cornered by union officials at the end of September 1976, Carter gave his "complete endorsement" to the revised bill, since new changes had made it more palatable than it had been earlier in the year. As the Democratic challenger turned to a sort of bread-and-butter populism late in the campaign, he began to attack the Republicans on their employment record. In echoes of New Dealism, explaining that "Mr. Nixon and Mr. Ford have made these people poor in the same way Mr. Hoover made them poor in the 1930s—by denying them the chance to work."[37]

Whatever his campaign posturing, the inflation debate placed the president in an impossible political position. His core constituents on the left wing of the Democratic Party, including organized labor, the civil rights community, and a host of religious and community-based organizations, were in favor of it. The bulk of his middle-class supporters were most likely sympathetic skeptics but who were much more concerned about inflation. Carter himself, by upbringing, training, temperament, and philosophy, was certainly opposed. For a leader, in James Fallow's terms, who "thinks in lists, not arguments" and whose views of problems were "technical, not historical," the idea of watershed legislation and the leadership necessary to implement it simply did not exist. Although backers of full employment legislation thought they had Carter on their side after the election, the president moved away from the campaign populist and more toward the technocratic governor once in office. "For more than three and a half years," Carter recalled after the fact, "my major economic battle would be against inflation, and I would stay on the side of fiscal prudence, restricted budgets, and lower deficits." He confessed his alienation from the Democratic base at the beginning of the second year of his administration in his diary: "In many cases I feel more at home with the conservative Democratic and Republican members of Congress than I do with the others," he wrote, "although the others, the liberals, vote with me much more often."[38]

Vice President Walter Mondale and Secretary of Labor Ray Marshall strongly favored a meaningful employment bill, but virtually every other key player in the administration came together to form a formidable wall of opposition to the idea, including Treasury Secretary Blumenthal, Budget Director Bert Lance, and, above all, Humphrey-Hawkins' nemesis from 1976, Charles Schultze, who became Carter's CEA chair. Carter's staff and cabinet saw it as inflationary, hostile to business, and expensive; Schultze went so far as to declare it "economically illiterate." Yet the Democratic base wanted it. As Schultze recalled, the administration was, at best, hamstrung by the demands of the party's base, and, at worst, in open battle with its major constituencies. "Exactly where one came down between the necessi-

ties of the times and the political necessities of holding the coalition together and having had no experience in national politics on this would make
it even tougher," recalled the CEA head. It was a problem Reagan would not
have to face, Schultze recalled, since he could politically afford to put the
economy "through the ringer" rather than trying to achieve the "modest
austerity balancing act" Carter attempted. Basically, concluded Schultze,
"the Democratic party has never quite sorted out what its image is in those
kind of [inflationary] times."[39]

In March 1977, just a few months after taking office, the Carter administration privately reached the conclusion "that the Humphrey-Hawkins bill
is both unnecessary and undesirable." The internal White House consensus
was that it "would have undesirable side effects on the rate of inflation, on
private labor markets, on the quality of policymaking, and on the size of
government." But the administration remained uncertain what to do about it
given that it could not afford to alienate its key constituents. Carter officials
contemplated opposing the bill, offering an alternative bill, and negotiating
a compromise bill. Administration officials at least wanted to remove nu-
meric employment goals, focus the bill on inflation, drop the idea of the
federal government as employer of last resort, and emphasize flexibility over
requirements and timetables. In sum, the administration wanted Humphrey-
Hawkins in name only.[40]

In June 1977, Humphrey, Hawkins, and FEAC sought to call Carter's
campaign commitments and push him to act on the legislation. "Despite
long and persistent efforts on our part," declared the bill's sponsors in a
forceful letter to the president, "we have not obtained a reaffirmation of your
position on the Bill this year, nor any specific suggestions for further im-
provements in it from your representatives." Humphrey and Hawkins
warned that if full agreement was not forthcoming, some of their other concessions might have to be withdrawn, leading to a public confrontation
between the Administration and the Black Caucus. The bill's sponsors
requested a meeting and attached a resolution signed by almost the entirety
of the progressive wing of the Democratic Party—including the Urban
League, the AFL-CIO, the NAACP, key figures in the Congressional
Black Caucus, several Hispanic and Mexican-American organizations, a
host of religious groups including the National Council of Churches, several
women's groups, and the National Education Association, among dozens of
others. Much of that support was wider than it was deep. Coretta Scott
King threatened "serious trouble" if the administration did not make good

on promises for full employment legislation. With vintage George Meany sarcasm, the AFL-CIO president publicly derided Carter's backing away from full employment with a mock endorsement of the president's obsession with balancing the budget in 1977. "We have to balance the budget by 1981," quipped the labor leader, "and if we do all our problems will be over. . . . There will be dancing in the streets of the ghettos, and I think Moscow might even put up a white flag and surrender."[41]

Although Charles Schultze remained adamantly opposed to the legislation, he understood the political importance of problem. "This is a very sensitive issue, much broader than the legislation," a policy staff memo to Schultze explained. "It involves the leadership of major organizations throughout the country who suddenly feel cut off from this administration, an administration which they feels [sic] shows little concern about domestic issues. We are treading on very unstable grounds politically and socially. I'm getting nervous because we're going to be blasted soon, due to our inactivity in this area." There was a clear sense that the administration was torn between what it felt it ought to do economically and what it needed to do politically—especially as the bill's backers threatened a public confrontation with the administration. "We have been stretching out this matter for some time now, but I think the string may have run out," concluded the economist.[42]

Aware of the price to be paid by not controlling the agenda on Humphrey-Hawkins, Schultze masterminded a plan to drain the lifeblood from the bill. By transforming the bill into something symbolically important but economically meaningless, the administration could prove its commitment to full employment, service the Democratic constituents that threatened Carter's presidency, and still keep inflation the number one priority. Schultze's strategy was to replace concrete plans with long-term "targets" and "goals" under the rubric of "full employment" that would serve as little more than suggestions—far from the goal of national planning put forth in earlier iterations of the bill but hopefully enough to appease the Democratic base. Throughout the summer and into the early fall of 1977 the question of just how far they could go with this strategy hung over negotiators from both the administration and the bill's sponsors. Originally Humphrey and Hawkins appeared unwilling to budge, but as negotiations continued for months, they began to concede ground to Carter. The two parties' major sticking points were the legal right to employment, the inflationary pressures that they believed were inherent in the ambitious employment agenda, and the lack of flexibility in the timetables and goals. To save the legislation they had labored for years to support, Humphrey and Hawkins ended up caving in on all of the administration's major issues, even reducing the already watery "right to full opportunity for employment," which had already been stripped of its legal guarantees, into nothing more than an abstract "national goal." When the president's official statement endorsing the new 1977 bill finally came in November, it was clear to all observers how far the legislation had traveled. Humphrey-Hawkins had evolved into a mere economic suggestion put into legislative form—barely recognizable as the ambitious social vision that had inspired its original proponents.[43]

Since the Carter administration won the closed-door battle of the negotiators, full employment advocates were left to choose whether to continue to mobilize on behalf of an anemic bill, a political symbol, or simply to give up. Having poured years of mobilization efforts into the bill and hoping that even the eviscerated Humphrey-Hawkins would be a useful weapon for progressive policy makers—or at least a platform from which to continue the struggle—advocates chose to continue their national push as if nothing had changed. The new bill was a "fact," FEAC leaders explained in an internal memo; it could not be compared with any theoretically perfect bill desired by full employment activists. This approach left advocates pleading with their allies not to jump ship by arguing shrilly, in the phrase that dominated later campaign materials, that Humphrey-Hawkins was "Not a Paper Tiger." FEAC continued to organize aggressively for the bill, launching a national mobilization called Full Employment Week for the week of Labor Day 1977. Coordinating a national network of rallies, breakfasts, picnics, leafleting brigades, church services, radio and television addresses, and even a series of "work-ins" to show that there was meaningful public work to be done by the unemployed, they attempted to put grassroots pressure on the administration.[44]

Despite the public spin advocates put on the bill, the 1977 incarnation revealed how hollow the politics of economic planning had become. The negotiations with the administration had turned the tables against full employment advocates, leaving them to fight a rear-guard action, and giving Carter adequate room to appease concerns on the right. The president announced that "the achievement of full employment and price stability must be sought through the use of monetary and fiscal policies, together with structural measures designed to improve the function of the Nation's labor and capital markets—not through government planning or control of private production, wages, and prices." Even the inflation-jobs debate had been tilted toward those who favored price stability as the 1977 version of the bill declared that inflation was "a major national problem requiring improved government policies." In the 1977 draft, there was not even a mechanism to require a given administration to adopt a policy that favored full employment. Echoing the events of 1946, an unnamed administration official publicly confessed, "This bill requires Carter to do nothing that it wasn't already planning to do to increase employment."[45]

The press rightly named the political hash they saw before them. The *New York Times* called the bill "a hollow promise"; *Business Week* explained that it had been "sanitized of all references to economic planning"; the *Washington Post* said it was "full of nice thoughts" though the real impact on joblessness would be "zero"; *Time* magazine called it a "declawed bill"; and *Newsweek* argued that it was "so watered down as to be almost meaningless." Rather than making the government the employer of last resort, quipped Edward Cowan of the *New York Times*, Humphrey-Hawkins ended up as the "political symbol of last resort for President Carter, Congressional liberals and the Congressional Black Caucus." Many pulled their support. Jesse Jackson of Operation PUSH rejected Carter's endorsement, claiming that the president, in failing to put real money and real plans into achieving full employment, was trying "to get the greatest political mileage at least economic cost." The *New York Times* turned against the bill, editorializing that it "would play a cruel hoax on the hard-core unemployed, holding before them the hope—but not the reality—of a job. For that reason alone, Humphrey-Hawkins should be rejected." As the historian Gary Fink has aptly summarized, "Ultimately, Carter sought to have it both ways—to endorse the principle of Humphrey Hawkins while retaining the flexibility to establish economic priorities at odds with the concept of full employment."[46]

Remarkably, and despite continued support from congressional liberals, the already battered bill still faced even more torturous treatment. In March 1978, Humphrey-Hawkins finally passed the House on a vote of 257–152, but not before it was laden with so many amendments that one representative claimed it had grown into an "unmanageable Christmas tree," an "unworkable monster" that ought to be destroyed. Despite further evisceration, Carter still remained hesitant about many provisions in the bill, forcing labor and civil rights groups to demand his support of what remained. Clearly, had the administration had the courage of its political convictions, it would have ended the debate over full employment much earlier. Stuart Eizenstat and Charles Schultze explained to Carter, however, that he had to stand behind the remaining bill for his own political survival: "If the Administration does not fight hard to secure passage of a bill that is acceptable to them, backers of the bill will view this as a betrayal and publicly say so." Eizenstat emphasized the trap the Democratic coalition had placed them in. "This is one of the few bills in which we are clearly aligned with our major constituencies—labor and the minority community," he argued. "To disappoint them . . . on a bill on which we have already taken whatever heat we will take would be a dramatic mistake." So the political farce marched on.[47]

The Congressional Black Caucus brought to life many of Charles Schultze's worst fears about unruly Democratic constituents as the Senate geared up for the vote in the fall of 1978. The caucus had very high expectations about what it would get from the president—the first Democrat to hold the office in the caucus's history—but the entire relationship between the president and the caucus, as one biographer put it, was "especially nasty." Jody Powell, Carter's press secretary, condescendingly described the administration's "outstretched hand and open door policy" toward the Congressional Black Caucus as "more often than not, to spit in the hand as they tracked mud through the door." On the other hand, Hawkins recalled that they had to "almost hit him over the head with a baseball bat" to get Carter to sign the bill. In a stormy meeting, the caucus demanded that Carter back Humphrey-Hawkins with the same energy that he had given other issues. Representative John Conyers Jr., an African-American Democrat from Michigan, urged Carter to convene a Humphrey-Hawkins summit conference similar to the Middle East summit at Camp David and, when he felt that Carter was not adequately forthcoming, he walked out of the meeting. The gathering ended with Carter being forced to commit to Humphrey-Hawkins, but, as negotiations turned out, only as a political symbol that would be stripped even further of economic substance.[48]

When Hubert Humphrey passed away early in 1978, the bill became a bit of a monument to the liberal senator, though not until it faced its own ignoble death by even further amendment. By the final vote in the fall of 1978, Senate wags were referring to it as the Humphrey-Hawkins-Hatch bill since Orrin Hatch, the conservative Republican senator from Utah, was able to shape the terms on which the bill would be considered. By the final Senate vote on the last day of the 1978 session, time was working against the bill's proponents. The final bill was so full of commitments to balanced budgets, competitiveness, business incentives, and fighting inflation, that even the AFL-CIO confessed that it was "more symbol than substance." While FEAC and the bill's sponsors continued to promote it as a landmark victory, everyone else knew that what some hoped would be a second New Deal had ended as little more than a legislative farce. The words of Ohio Republican senator Robert Taft spoken during the final debate over the Employment Act of 1946 echoed into 1978. "I do not think any Republican need fear voting for the bill because of any apprehension that there is a victory [for proponents] in the passage of the full employment bill, because there is no full-employment bill any more."[49]

IV

What began as the nation's second attempt at full employment planning ended in an empty bill that silenced talk of a collective economic vision for working people. Since joblessness tended to be regarded as either an individual or a racial problem rather than a structural one, a macro-planning approach was simply too radical a prospect in the 1970s and one that squandered great doses of political energy. There was simply no political tradition on which to lean for such a marked departure—especially in an era of inflation. For liberals, a more politically viable answer to the economic and political puzzles of the 1970s may not have been schemes like Humphrey-Hawkins, but in sectoral planning, industrial policy, and aggressive support for the expansion of jobs programs like the Comprehensive Employment and Training Act of 1973 (CETA) (which Carter backed). Another angle, disciplined tripartite leadership that brought labor, management, and government together to mitigate the crisis of plant closures in the late seventies might have proved effective as well. Humphrey-Hawkins, in contrast, smacked too much of supervision, too much of control, and too much of the rational in a decade marked by their opposites. As one critic put it, full employment appeared to be such an unwieldy vision as to resemble "a Donizetti opera: There are hundreds of people on stage, each convinced that a magic elixir will solve all his problems. The magic elixir of Humphrey-Hawkins was central planning. Simply by setting national goals, unemployment would be magically reduced, recessions would disappear, exports would expand, the energy crisis would go away and the trade balance would improve. These factors, in turn, would lead to increased real income, 'balanced growth,' a balanced federal budget and zero inflation."[50]

Symbolic of the sea change in the politics of economic planning, the Humphrey-Hawkins story ended in bitter irony for liberals who had poured their hopes into the bill. Thrown into the final mix was the requirement that the Federal Reserve would be required to appear twice each year before the House and Senate banking committees to explain deviations from the Federal Reserve's annual target ranges for growth in the money supply—one aspect of the bill that Carter seriously wanted. Although intended to keep tabs on the Federal Reserve's control of the money supply, the famous "Humphrey-Hawkins reports" evolved into a source for key data for supply-side economic policy makers. As William Greider notes, "conservative insiders were amused: their ascendant doctrine of monetarism was riding to victory on the legislative carcass of the fading orthodoxy of Keynes."[51]

Yet of all the sins of Humphrey-Hawkins, the most egregious was emblematic of postwar liberalism: its lack of democratic participation and grassroots support. Michael Harrington, one of the bill's supporters on the Left, noted the problem during an early organizing meeting for the bill. Looking around, he noted "only paid staffers from the unions came." It was haunting.

> We had encountered one of the strangest, almost eerie, aspects of the recession-inflation of the Seventies. Those most intimately, even tragically, involved in the collapse had not been galvanized into action. Logically, the highest unemployment rates in a generation—an average of 8.5 percent out of work in 1975—should have sent both the jobless and the threatened workers out into the streets demanding full employment planning. Yet when people get fired, they often lose contact with the union, becoming dropouts rather than militants. And in the first stages of a downturn, those with the jobs are primarily looking for ways to hold on to what they have. It is a time when solidarity forever has less appeal than a bird in the hand.[52]

Despite the bill's failures, Gus Hawkins and the FEAC leadership continued to declare victory in an effort to grant some discursive meaning where legally there was absolutely nothing. While distressed about what was left out of the bill, they took considerable comfort in the fact that the inflation targets remained separate from the employment goals, thus rejecting the trade-off between the two factors that plagued full employment advocates throughout the seventies. "Even its most ardent critics," Hawkins naively wrote to FEAC co-chairs Murray Finley and Coretta Scott King, "are already admitting that this Act is now the center piece of Federal economic policy law and a standard for measuring official conduct." Coretta Scott King went so far as to proclaim that the signing of Humphrey-Hawkins was "perhaps as significant as the signing of the Civil Rights Act of 1964 and the Voting Rights Act of 1965" and that "perhaps in the future, history will record that it may be even more significant." As Hawkins and FEAC continued a quixotic fight in the years to come, they declared the succeeding austerity budgets to be violations of the intent of the law. But nobody listened.[53]

The full employment advocates' optimism, even if genuine, could not possibly have been more misplaced, as the context of the Carter administration's other actions in the fall of 1978 quickly revealed. Almost simultaneous to the passing of the full employment bill, Carter announced a three-part anti-inflation strategy that included restrictive fiscal and monetary policy, voluntary wage-price guidelines, and regulatory reform—almost all of which cut against the spirit of the original Humphrey-Hawkins Full Employment Act. Congress, for the first time since it went Democratic in 1932, passed a tax cut not to redistribute wealth but to give relief to the upper middle class, suggesting a very new mood among Democrats more broadly. With inflation climbing into the double digits in 1979 (topping out at 13.5 percent in his last year in office), Carter had, according to Herbert Stein, "assumed the look of a conservative in economics." Yet he found himself in an untenable bind: having lost the Left, he still did not have adequate support on the Right since his policies were "not acceptable or credible, especially to people who considered themselves conservatives." His middle-of-the-road anti-statism quickly fell into the breach of the widening chasm of late seventies American politics.[54]

V

Labor law reform, the other liberal pillar of the 1977–78 legislative sessions, did not fare any better than full employment. With union density falling, organizing efforts also had generally failed to break out of the stagnating Northeast industrial sector (except for the very notable exception of the public sector). Capital investment was flowing to the non-union South. Corporations had selected to engage in often quite militant anti-union practices (and hiring consulting firms to do the job), quietly folding the fines and penalties from an enervated legal system into the cost of business rather than face the unionization of their workforces. The rate of successful organizing efforts had fallen from about 80 percent in the first ten years of the Wagner Act (1935) to 61 percent in the 1950s to only 46 percent by 1977.[55]

Labor leaders preferred to see their decline as a product of the corruption of labor law, which was certainly one important part of the equation. As the AFL-CIO executive council accurately declared, "Worker protections geared to the conditions of the 1930s are inadequate in the face of employer tactics of the 1970s." More significantly, the Wagner Act had lost its teeth, transformed from a mechanism for "encouraging" unionization and collective bargaining to a legal cul-de-sac from which workers never emerged, falling victim to delay tactics, intimidation, and aggressive employers. "Employers violate the rights of workers with virtual impunity," continued the AFL-CIO. "They disregard those rights secure in the knowledge that procedural delays will prevent the NLRB from enforcing the law for several years. Employers know that if that day of reckoning eventually arrives, the price of settling up will be cheap. They count on the fact that by that time the workers will have come to believe that the Act's promises of protection are just words on a piece of paper."[56]

The 1977–78 political struggle to reform the sclerotic legal system rekindled tremendous hope on a variety of fronts—not the least of which was shoring up the New Deal's southern flank. Making unionization easier, they believed, would bring the high wage, high union-density model of the postwar era to the South where jobs and investment had been flowing to since unions began to form in the industrial Northeast. In the seventies, many were referring to the heightened battle over jobs as the "second war between the states" as the low wage, low regulation, non-union, low taxation Sunbelt was attracting jobs from the areas of high union density, regulation, and taxation. The project to integrate the South into the New Deal paradigm would also serve to advance the civil rights struggles of the sixties by bringing collective bargaining to southern workers in the seventies. As civil rights activists Bayard Rustin and Norman Hill put it, "the opponents of labor law reform—especially those in the South—hope to preserve a system of occupational segmentation by keeping unions out of low-wage manufacturing and service enterprises." These opponents were not necessarily "racists," they argued, but that "defeat of the reform package will have an especially adverse economic impact on black workers."[57]

The focal point for labor law reform efforts therefore focused, not surprisingly, on a southern case—the J.P. Stevens campaign, which became the poster child for advocates of labor law reform. Among the remarkable labor insurgencies of the early seventies was the successful organizing drive at the J.P. Stevens textile plant in Roanoke Rapids, North Carolina. The struggle, part of which was fictionalized in the film *Norma Rae* (1979), stands, in the words of one historian, as "a defining confrontation between labor and capital in the United States." The South, where organizing had been hobbled by the problems of race and employer militancy, had been the labor movement's weak link for generations. In a dramatic inter-racial struggle in 1974—the first meetings were held in a black church—the workers broke through the textile industry's vicious anti-unionism and won the election at the plant in Roanoke Rapids. It looked as though the South would finally be organized. "It was a new day in Dixie—first J.P. Stevens, then the textile industry, then the South," proclaimed a Carolina unionist.[58]

Rather than a new day, however, the victory in Roanoke Rapids came to symbolize the futility of working within the tangled web of a legalistic industrial relations system. J.P. Stevens simply refused to bargain and instead embarked on a notorious war of attrition in the courts. The U.S. court of appeals concluded that the company's "campaign has involved numerous unfair labor practices, including coercive interrogation, surveillance, threat of plant closing and economic reprisals for union activity. Moreover, the threats have been made good by extensive discriminatory discharges." It won the company the aphorism, "the nation's number one labor law violator." Despite winning case after case in the courts and the NLRB, the union ended up drained of it resources, having established the moral high ground but gaining little in the way of new union members.[59]

With faint echoes of the famous LaFollette Commission hearings that exposed the horrors of management's abuse of workers rights in the 1930s, Congress was awash in such testimony in 1977. Representative Frank Thompson, a liberal New Jersey Democrat and long-time labor ally, brought the House Subcommittee on Labor-Management Relations to Roanoke Rapids, home of J.P. Stevens, for nine days. The congressmen, the press, lobbyists, and staff piled into buses and motored down to North Carolina, site of the lowest wages and the lowest union density in the nation. There, a parade of workers and civic leaders told stories of "sinister, subversive, and un-American" collusion between business and state government to prevent unionization, in the words of local clergy. Back in Washington, Reverend Bouie, a black Episcopal priest from McComb, Mississippi, told of employees at the Croft Metals Company who voted for a union and then struggled for six years, struck the firm for another six months, and still did not have a contract. The company, he explained, "has ignored the law with total impunity." A woman formerly employed at Craftool in Fort Worth, Texas, described how "We've been cheated, and the NLRB has yet to get one of its many orders enforced. We are out on a limb, and the employer is sawing it off." The many workers, organizers, and union officials concurred with Robert Muehlencamp, the organizing director of hospital workers Local 1199, that "the promise and dream for these workers has turned into a complete nightmare."[60]

The crisis of underconsumption shaped the politics of the 1935 Wagner Act—it had been, at its core, less of a labor rights initiative than it had been a prod to redistribute wealth to foster increased demand during the Great Depression. By 1977–78, however, wage demands were taking the heat for rising inflation. The seventies again appeared to be the thirties inverted. Even with inflation and unemployment at postwar highs, Carter's pollster, Pat Caddell, explained to the president that there were more "haves" than "have-nots" in the seventies and that for American voters the central issues were socio-cultural in nature, not economic. Nonetheless, one of the great things about labor law reform for the fiscally prudent Carter was that it cost the government little. It could redistribute wealth, bring representation to the nation's neediest workers, support working people of color, and all the while not cost the government a dime in direct outlays. It was in line with his good government and regulatory reform themes, even if outside of his political vision.[61]

The labor law reform bill of the AFL-CIO's dreams included repeal of section 14(b) of the Taft-Hartley Act (the "right to work" provision that helped to keep the South non-union), along with "card check" union certification (a process by which workers could select a union by signing membership cards rather than going through the drawn-out and legalistic system of the NLRB). Much of this was a return to the pre–Taft-Hartley days, as the original Wagner Act did not include the right-to-work provision nor require secret ballots, but they had become required by both law and tradition since. A final component of the hoped-for reform package, which would require new owners of a firm to honor the old union contract, provided for some stability during the growing number of mergers, acquisitions, and bankruptcies. Finally a package of smaller reforms designed to increase the efficiency, though not the overall mechanisms, of Wagner included increasing the number of members of the NLRB, placing calendar limits on elections, and increased penalties for noncompliance with the board's rulings.[62]

In the summer of 1977, Jimmy Carter endorsed the principles of labor law reform, but in its most tepid form, backing only the smaller provisions rather than any of the core principles labor hoped for. The AFL-CIO agreed, having learned its lessons from a long string of previous failures at labor law reform from the forties through the sixties mostly from the threat or practice of the filibuster. The unions learned that they would prefer anything to nothing, so three core provisions were dropped—14(b), card check, and the honoring of a previous union contract among recently acquired firms. Including the elimination of 14(b) alone would have immediately torpedoed the effort by guaranteeing forty instant votes against it from the senators from the twenty right-to-work states. What remained was a bill with six basic provisions, all of which added up to a fairly minor reform bill designed to increase efficiency and bring stiffer penalties to labor law violators. Unlike the 1965 attempt to repeal 14(b), this bill would largely shore up the slippage in the efficacy of the act since the 1960s but not offer any true restoration, let alone expansion, of the original Wagner Act.[63]

The compromise bill was lean, moderate, and basically unchallenging to the corporate order, which is why the opposition it raised was so historically significant. Seven former secretaries of labor gave their endorsement of the bill. "While the business community will certainly oppose the bill," Eizenstat noted to the president, "they view it as much more acceptable than earlier versions and will therefore be less vociferous in condemning the administration for its position." By trimming their expectations, the unions and the administration believed they had a bill that had a very good chance of passing. They misunderstood the historical moment.[64]

After facing a few more modifications, the bill sailed through the House in October 1977 on a final vote of 257–163 with good support from liberal Republicans. As attention turned to the Senate, things began to fall apart. The national miners' strike erupted in December, redoubling concerns about the availability of fuel, leaving a question mark over whether giving more power to the unions was a good idea. Then President Carter had to choose whether to bring up the Panama Canal Treaty or labor law reform for a vote first. Whichever came first would have the better chance, as well as giving opponents more time to organize against whichever would be delayed. The Canal Treaty generated very strong feelings on the right as many felt that returning the Canal Zone to the nation of Panama was the equivalent of some sort of American surrender of power. Carter chose to bring Panama up first, meaning that those on the fence would be unlikely to vote for two controversial measures in succession.[65]

Business lobbies, reeling at the early success of reform in the House, seized upon the Canal Treaty delay and began plotting to defeat labor law reform in the Senate. The Business Roundtable, the National Association of Manufacturers, the Chamber of Commerce, and a host of conservative anti-union groups like the National Right to Work Committee, marshaled their forces. Largely avoiding the substance of the bill, as Ray Marshall predicted, the opponents concentrated their campaign on "'union bosses,' 'labor racketeering,' 'inflation,' 'destroying small business,' and other matters which cut to the heart of our national policy of fostering industrial democracy." The Chamber of Commerce's labor attorney explained that "delay has dissipated the momentum caused by the easy victory of similar House legislation in October" and "given the Chamber additional time to mobilize grass-roots opposition." Then four militantly conservative senators, Orrin Hatch, Richard Lugar, John Tower, and Jesse Helms decided "to talk the bill to death." It would face the same fate as most labor and civil rights legislation: a filibuster. If that failed, opponents said they had five hundred amendments ready in order to sink the bill. The anti-reform campaign was immense, well orchestrated, and well funded. In an open letter/advertisement in the *Wall Street Journal*, George Meany asked American business leaders, "Why should law-abiding companies seek to continue a system that allows some employers to break the law with impunity? . . . Do you secretly seek a death sentence for the collective bargaining system you so often hail in public forums?"[66]

With forces dissipating and a Senate filibuster imminent, all international union presidents were summoned to Washington for a war council. The idea that by weakening the bill dramatically it would become acceptable to business turned out to be unsound. Instead the business lobbies smelled blood in the political waters. Meany told everyone that he wanted this understood for what it was, "an all out attack on the American labor movement. This is no longer a fight on the bill but an attack by every anti-union group in America to kill the labor movement."[67]

A filibuster then became inevitable, and labor law reform advocates needed to drum up a supermajority of sixty votes necessary to invoke cloture. After several votes, reform advocates got their tally up to fifty-eight. Another senator, perhaps Lawton Chiles (Florida), agreed to change his vote if one vote more could be found. Four people were targeted: three Southern Democrats—John Sparkman (Alabama), Dale Bumpers (Arkansas), and Russ Long (Louisiana)—and one conservative Nebraskan, Edward Zorinksy, who had just switched from Republican to Democrat in 1976. Days before the last cloture vote, Carter's advisors pleaded with the president to do what he could to round up the last votes for the bill. "We are within one vote of defeating the most expensive and powerful lobby ever mounted against a bill in the nation's history," they told him. The day of the final vote, the staff had to admit that "we are in trouble."[68]

As with full employment legislation, the Carter administration appears to have been motivated more by the desire to do what was necessary to appear on labor's side rather be truly committed to the cause. "The present circumstances do present us with an unusual opportunity to show the depth of our commitment to labor," the staff explained to the president. "To the labor unions, this bill is the most important one Congress has considered in a great many years." The staff urged President Carter to "become more involved in the effort to get cloture," but throughout the discussion they showed far more concern about appearing supportive of labor than they did about being invested in the bill. "To the extent that we may not be able to fully satisfy labor on issues like National Health Insurance, we will have built a recent reservoir of good will with the labor movement."[69]

The final vote was never found. Carter made calls and hosted a labor law reform breakfast but never quite pulled out the stops for the bill. Labor law reform went down as one of the great near misses in a decade of near misses. *Congressional Quarterly* called it "the most stinging humiliation for the unions in a Congress that was marked by a string of defeats for labor" and spoke casually of labor's "loser image." Meanwhile, Senator Hatch believed it was "a starting point for a new era of assertiveness by big business in Washington." The inability to check the erosion of labor liberalism meant the hardening of management-labor relations for the indefinite future.[70]

The causes of the defeat of labor law reform are multiple, not the least of which was the filibuster itself, which had been dragged out regularly to block labor and civil rights laws in the twentieth century. "The biggest thing working against us," declared a UAW lobbyist, "was an undemocratic system." The filibuster or the threat of it had thwarted both labor law and civil rights legislation in the twentieth century, and the 1978 effort added one more to the list of the minority's ability to block legislation. Because of the filibuster, the southern senators enjoyed disproportionate representation and their voting was completely predictable given historical patterns. As Taylor Dark argues, "The solid southern opposition, grounded in generations of regional antipathy to unionism was therefore a major cause of the bill's defeat."[71]

Opinions in both the administration and in the union leadership differed as to whether Carter could have done more to help push the bill or whether such a push would have even worked. As was the case with Humphrey-Hawkins, internal White House memos show a clear pattern of backing the bill to appear to be helping the Democrats' key constituents rather than acting out of political conviction or even genuine coalition-building. As was the case with Humphrey-Hawkins, the administration wanted to keep the coalition together with minimum political outlay. He offered only limited promises or deals to make it happen and clearly placed much more emphasis and did much more arm-twisting on the Panama Canal Treaty. Timing also mattered. Many congressmen felt that they had risked significant political capital for the Canal Treaty and were hesitant to do it again for labor. Carter also risked little personally for the bill, leaving the lobbying effort to Secretary of Labor Ray Marshall and Vice President Walter Mondale, already two of labor's obvious allies. A similar timing problem hit with the prolonged coal strike during the winter of 1978, which made many people who were already fearful of an energy shortage wary of giving labor any more power.

Most labor leaders simply blamed the business lobbies' new found power in Washington. The opposition delivered a fearless lobbying campaign to defeat the bill, successfully portraying the tepid reform package as a "naked power grab" by "union bosses;" senators received as many as four million pieces of mail from the National Right to Work Committee alone. Senator Lawton Chiles, a key Florida Democrat, felt the heat from the newly aggressive business lobbies. "I can't remember when we last experienced a lobbying effort like this. It is so well-structured, so well-organized, and I don't think they missed a single possible opponent of that bill in our state." The opposition was particularly stunning since business groups such as the Business Roundtable and the National Chamber of Commerce had been brought to the table on the original draft of the bill, so most supporters and the administration figured that the bill would face a minimum of opposition from the business lobby. Stuart Eizenstat, Carter's domestic policy chief, "clearly misjudged the venomous character of these groups, which, after securing concessions from the administration, used all the resources at their command to kill the legislation."[72]

The year 1978, as a business historian succinctly noted, was "'Waterloo' for unions, regulators, Keynesian tax reformers." On the one hand, the failure of labor law reform is consistent with all of postwar legislative history; southern conservatives, business lobbies, ambivalent presidents, and competing legislation are all constants—especially with regard to labor law. On the other hand, 1978 was the last major attempt to leap the hurdles that had prevented the labor-liberal coalition from expanding beyond its postwar limits. The defeat of the bill's calculated moderation was stunning. The legislation merely tinkered around the edges of a deeply flawed and legalistic labor relations regime and was offered to a Congress with strong majorities in both houses. Labor law seemed more than just another legislative failure; in it one could hear the death rattle of American working-class political power. Until then, there had always been at least the hope of revitalization. Instead, the failure opened up the floodgates of the 1980s. The turbulent waters that made life for unions difficult in the 1970s roared with vengeance by the 1980s.[73]

VI

"I believe leaders of the business community, with few exceptions, have chosen to wage a one-sided class war today in this country—a war against working people, the unemployed, the poor, the minorities, the very young and the very old, and even many in the middle class of our society," declared UAW president Douglas Fraser just after the failure of labor law reform in July 1978. "The leaders of industry, commerce and finance in the United States have broken and discarded the fragile, unwritten compact previously existing during a past period of growth and progress." As Fraser explained, the reform bill had been "an extremely moderate, fair piece of legislation that only corporate outlaws would have had need to fear." Fraser's flurry of angry rhetoric was part of his public resignation from John Dunlop's Labor-Management Group. The group had been set up under the Nixon administration to seek out cooperative solutions to labor-management problems and to pass advice along to the White House. Although the group was supposed to reflect the postwar consensus in labor-management relations, Fraser's public resignation and the press conference that accompanied it shredded the fiction of that consensus with brilliant rhetorical barbs that sent shudders of concern all the way to the Carter White House.[74]

Promising to forge a new social movement to combat the corporate offensive of the seventies, Fraser explained, "I would rather sit with the rural poor, the desperate children of urban blight, the victims of racism, and working people seeking a better life than with those whose religion is the status quo, whose goal is profit and whose hearts are cold. We in the UAW intend to reforge the links with those who believe in struggle: the kind of people who sat-down in the factories in the 1930's and who marched in Selma in the 1960's."[75]

Fraser's letter is often used to demarcate the end of the postwar golden age, the sunset of the "fragile, unwritten compact" as Fraser called it, which shaped over three successful decades of industrial relations. The phrase "one-sided class war" has often been cited as evidence of business abrogating its end of the deal as they went on the offensive in both workplaces and the nation's legislatures. And, in many ways, this end of the golden age scenario is true. The events of 1978–79 do serve as a historical bookend to the heady days of 1935–36. In the latter, the Wagner Act came to life, Franklin Roosevelt became the workers' president, and the autoworkers began their occupation of GM. Fast forward a couple of generations, and inflation not employment was the touchstone of American politics, significant attempts to rekindle the old politics failed, the industrial heartland faced an enormous wave of plant shutdowns, and progressive pushes for national health insurance and industrial policy never made it out of committee. On one side a social compact was being born; on the other it was falling apart. In between, as organized labor ascended to its apex of power, dreams of fundamental changes in the structure of American capitalism withered on the vine of industrial pluralism.[76]

From the vantage point of a new century, a different interpretation of the Fraser letter suggests itself. Rather than the beginning of a revival or the collapse of a compromise, the document reflects, in ways that may not have been intended by the author, the historic limits of U.S. organized labor. Weighing just how different the postwar era was from earlier and later eras of labor history, David Brody stresses an odd continuity in the guiding philosophy of the labor movement across eras. "It is the underlying perspective that carried on, the assumption that labor's place was inherently limited, that its sphere was necessarily circumscribed in the nation's industrial life. And, if one listened closely, Gompers' words could be heard echoing long decades after his death. . . . If the Walter Reuthers voiced a headier social rhetoric, if they grew restless under the burden of Meany's philosophy, in practice they adhered to the same trade-union precepts confining the power of the labor movement." Seen in this light, Fraser's letter represents neither the moment of turn-around that he hoped it would initiate nor the end of the postwar compact of which it has become emblematic. Rather, it is actually a rather stunning admission of how limited organized labor was during even the loftiest heights of its powers in the postwar period. The historian Robert Zieger once referred to the labor movement that burst upon the national stage during the 1930s and 1940s as a "fragile juggernaut." Perhaps no better metaphor could describe the broader political culture that came of age under Franklin Roosevelt. The New Deal alliances seemed like an all-powerful force capable of implementing its progressive liberal policy regardless of conservative opposition. Yet simultaneously, when challenged, this same juggernaut shattered, its central contradictions revealed in its own compromises with the very real complexities of American history and politics.[77]

Fraser's letter almost unconsciously reversed the sense of historical agency from the unions' power and shrewdness to business' temporary tactical tolerance. The *New York Times*' A.H. Raskin picked up labor leaders' realization that much of their power rested on an ephemeral deal, not a permanent realignment of class power:

> What galled labor beyond measure, oddly enough, was not the treason of politicians who had taken labor's shilling at election time. It was the defection to the anti-union camp of a raft of chief executives from the Fortune 500—men whom the unions had come to think of almost as allies. As many labor leaders see it, that crucial battle marked the end of a thirty-year entente cordiale. During this era of good feelings, many big companies had come to depend on the unions as a primary force for stabilization, both in equalized basic labor costs within each major industry and in maintaining uninterrupted production for the life of the contract. In return, management became the principal recruiting agenda for a labor movement that had run out of steam. The operation of union shop contracts automatically delivered over tens of thousands of new employees, the ultimate in push-button unionism.[78]

The next year Fraser did, as promised, reach out to new groups and form new alliances in the creation of the Progressive Alliance. Representatives from over one hundred organizations from unionists to environmentalists and from feminists to civil rights advocates came together in Detroit in the fall of 1978. The alliance was part think tank, part political caucus, and part coordination center for mobilization aimed at ending the "despair at the failure of the political process to respond to the needs of the American people." Fraser called for a "broad yet targeted anti-corporate offensive" based on inter-coordination of social groups and movements in order to overcome the fragmentation of progressive forces; a host of positions on issues of importance to the broad membership, including budgets, housing, welfare, national health insurance, plant closure, tax reform, and the Equal Rights Amendment; and an agenda to keep the Democrats accountable to the official party platform, from which they had been wandering for the better part of the decade. The *Economist* declared it "a conclave of American liberalism such as it has been impossible to assemble since before the Vietnam war."[79]

Just over two years after it began, the Progressive Alliance folded shop. The crisis in the auto industry, the old left-right split in the labor unions (the AFL-CIO did not get on board the alliance), and the victory of Reagan all undermined the effort. Some important work came out of the alliance, including the lobbying efforts on plant closings and the very important study by Barry Bluestone and Bennett Harrison, *The Deindustrialization of America: Plant Closings, Community Abandonment, and the Dismantling of Basic Industry* (1982). Fraser's eloquent but stumbling search for a place to lay the blame for the debacle of 1978 and his stillborn efforts to find a way out of his entanglements with the Democratic Party suggest how difficult it was to find ways to regain the initiative while still trapped in the confines of the system he stridently criticized. The efforts were in the right direction, but they were at least a decade too late.[80]

The national mood certainly did not augur well for Fraser's plans as anti-tax rebellions roiled through the land. Tax reform efforts, which often started as progressive movements to shift the burden onto the wealthy, began to move to the right in the late sixties and early seventies. The new calls were for tax cuts and smaller government rather than progressive tax equity. Then inflation rapidly pushed property values up and incomes crept up the tax brackets, both of which drove individual's tax burdens up while their standards of living did not change. Tax rates for homeowners in California doubled and even tripled. Howard Jarvis, the eccentric conservative, led the charge for California's Proposition 13 in 1978, which won by a massive two-to-one margin. The proposition rolled back property taxes to 1 percent of market value, and limited assessments to only 2 percent per year (unless sold). California lost $7 billion in property taxes overnight. Nationwide, any politician thinking about raising taxes had to look over his shoulder. The ill-defined populist rage of the first half of the decade had found its target. "Democratic liberalism ran into a brick wall" with the tax revolts, explain Edsall and Edsall, which placed taxpayers at odds with tax recipients and public sector workers against everybody else. Pat Caddell, Carter's pollster, put it succinctly: "This isn't just a tax revolt, it's a revolution against government." Although polling suggested that Proposition 13 was not a cry for less government but for better government, as justifiable as the anger at runaway property taxes may have been, it was the beginning, as Robert Kuttner labeled it, of "the Revolt of the Haves."[81]

After the tax revolts, the failure of labor law, the gutting of Humphrey-Hawkins, and the quarreling over national health insurance, the administration did get labor's allegiance on its central priority: fighting inflation. Toward the end of the administration, high-level meetings between organized labor and the Carter administration resulted in a document that most, at the time, would have pointed to as the pinnacle of the labor-Carter relationship but which is now largely forgotten: the National Accord designed to foster a spirit of cooperation and consultation in fighting inflation.

Signed in September 1979 after months of negotiations, the accord was modeled after the "social contracts" of Britain and Western Europe. For labor, the core of the accord was the recognition that unemployment would not be used to fight inflation and assurances that "the austerity arising from battling inflation is fairly shared, while protecting those members of society who are least able to bear the burden." The administration, meantime, hoped to get more wage restraint out of the unions than they had under voluntary wage-price controls (which, Carter's advisors were quick to mention, were already reasonably high). It also formalized labor's special role in a Democratic administration and quelled the bickering and suspicions that had emerged between the AFL-CIO and Carter. Yet the accord smacked of a formalized, perhaps forced, version of the informal social contract that cemented the labor-liberal coalition in the postwar era—faint echoes of what Fraser called the "fragile, unwritten pact." Having to codify what was once a working relationship suggested something of its late seventies weakness.

Like so much of the seventies, it stood as an inverted homage to the triumphs of the thirties and forties. Rather than FDR's compact for working-class plenty, the accord looked to shared austerity to overcome political hostility. Added into the smoothing of relations late in the Carter administration was the final retirement of the cantankerous George Meany in the fall of 1979. His successor, cold warrior Lane Kirkland, proved more diplomatic than the old Bronx plumber, but the AFL-CIO inherited a leader who had never been an elected officer of a union that he actually held a membership card in and who had barely ever earned wages for a living—the bureaucrat's bureaucrat. Carter gained the unions' allegiance just when the most progressive of them went to work for Ted Kennedy.[82]

"I am thinking of 1979," recalled Thomas Geoghegan, "that damned, horrible year, the last year organized labor could have saved itself, although not many in labor may realize it now. This was the year, 1979, when Iran imposed the oil embargo; when OPEC then tripled the price of oil to $30 a barrel; when the U.S. economy then crashed in flames, with double-digit inflation *and* unemployment; when mobs started forming to throw Jimmy Carter out of the White House; and when Paul Volcker became chairman of the Federal Reserve Board and could more or less run the country under martial law. After 1979, everything was lost." Indeed, snubbing commitments to full employment, Jimmy Carter adopted an austerity budget and appointed Paul Volcker to the Federal Reserve, who saw his job as wringing inflation out of the economy. Unemployment again hit double digits. J.K. Galbraith once remarked, "what is called sound finance is very often what mirrors the needs of the respectably affluent." Volcker was even more explicit, declaring, "The standard of living of the average American has to decline" as fighting inflation trumped all other social and economic concerns. Carter's inflation czar, Alfred Kahn, declared labor one of the administration's "natural enemies."[83]

VII

In July 1979, as the nation buckled under the strain of the second great energy crisis of the decade, President Jimmy Carter cancelled a scheduled public address on energy policy. He then disappeared somewhat mysteriously for ten days. The press and the public were bewildered, and rumors swarmed about his physical and mental state. Carter already had a reputation for not being in control of events, and suddenly, as gas prices shot through the roof, he was absent from his post. Facing a nearly impossible set of political and economic problems, unable to govern either through the old Democratic coalition or outside of it, he watched the nation's approval of his job erode to that of Nixon in the throes of Watergate. In most voters' minds, gone was the honest and plainspoken Southerner who promised never to lie to the people; in his place was an overwhelmed, if moral and sincere, technocrat who appeared to be in over his head. Nobody, it appeared, was in charge.

The president could be found at Camp David, engaged in one of the more interesting experiments in presidential history. Rather than simply announcing policies to confront the energy crisis, he had gone hunting for answers to what he believed to be a more profound issue: the nation's spiritual crisis.

He had already hosted a White House reading group and dinner to discuss the spiritual state of the nation with leading intellectuals concerned with the problem, three of whom formed the touchstones of his thinking: Daniel Bell, whose *The Cultural Contradictions of Capitalism* (1976) had warned of the corrosive effects of the pursuit of affluence and self-gratification; Christopher Lasch, whose best seller *The Culture of Narcissism: American Life in An Age of Diminishing Expectations* (1979) diagnosed the nation with a case of enervating self absorption; and Robert Bellah, whose *The Broken Covenant* (1975) explained the loss of civic virtue and the need for the connections of community and religious faith. Together, the three thinkers shared a concern with consumption and hedonism; each, in different ways, searched for paths toward preserving waning traditional values—work, community, family, faith—but felt the most likely way to do so was through radical economic measures. The nation was poised to achieve the opposite: return to very conservative economics that would unleash an orgy of consumerism that made concerns about materialism in the seventies seem quaint.[84]

President Carter's readings, combined with his own view from the White House, convinced him, in one historian's words, "that something was truly amiss in the nation's psyche." He invited over 130 leaders from religious, community, business, labor, and academic communities to talk to him at Camp David about the American malaise. He also made secret visits by helicopter to two "average" families to find out what they thought. The "Crisis of Confidence" speech was, by far, the most important speech of his presidency. It was also one of the riskiest.[85]

A vigorous debate erupted within the administration about what was going on with the nation, and what the president was doing and why. Was the "crisis" of the seventies a meltdown in the economic and political structure or some sort of profound spiritual malaise? Perhaps both? Even if some malady could be found in the national conscience, was it actually a matter of national political concern? Pollster Pat Caddell led one camp with a seventy-five page, intellectually serious, memo to Carter titled "Of Crisis and Opportunity," which argued that the president needed to shake the nation out of its national torpor, its obsession with materialism, its diminished faith in the future, and its disconnection with the past. Taking his clues from Bell, Bellah, and Lasch, Caddell argued that the problems were more psychological than material. Another camp, led by Vice President Walter Mondale, an old-school Minnesota liberal in the New Deal tradition, and Senior Domestic Policy Advisor Stuart Eizenstat, argued that scolding the American people for their moral failings was neither on target nor politically wise. Interest group politics may have gummed up the postwar political machinery, they believed, but that did not mean that Democrats should blame the people for Washington's failures or offer philosophy in lieu of governance. Besides, they argued, why talk about confidence when the nation was in a severe material crisis—an identifiable and disastrous shortage of real energy? Mondale had already come close to resigning from the Carter administration earlier that spring because of his opposition to what he believed was Carter's abandonment of the Democratic Party's commitment to the material needs of working and poor people. As Mondale wrote to the president about the "Crisis of Confidence," "the draft speech in its present form sounds too much like an old scold and a grouch." Staffers referred to it variously as "Apocalypse Now" or the "America is going to hell speech."[86]

It was almost preposterous to discuss a cultural crisis when the material world of the late seventies was spiraling apart. When the president disappeared to Camp David to plan for his talk, wholesale prices were pushing toward a 13.7 percent increase; inflation was raging at over 12 percent annually; and unemployment was at about 6 percent (though down considerably from the mid decade high of 9 percent, a figure it would soon return to). OPEC appeared to have a stranglehold on the nation's fate, while manufacturing suffered from excess capacity, sharp foreign competition, and high interest rates. Plants were shutting down, and Chrysler, the nation's number three automaker, teetered on bankruptcy. People were buying goods and ignoring savings as much for immediate gratification of their spiritual emptiness, as Carter would charge, as they were buying immediately as a hedge against rising prices. Better to abandon savings and buy now. Even debt made sense since one could pay back loans in inflated dollars. The lines at the pump returned with a vengeance, this time coupled with shorter tempers, violence, a rash of gasoline theft, and unpredictable closings of gas stations. There was a national independent trucking strike to protest the rising cost of diesel, which exploded in the blue-collar suburb of Levittown, Pennsylvania, as thousands of motorists clashed with police and cars burned in the street.[87]

Yet, even given the obvious meltdown in material life, there was nonetheless something in the idea of a moral and spiritual breakdown that resonated with the American people in 1979. In the final address, which Carter gave eleven days after his retreat to Camp David, the president confessed to listening closely to people's criticisms of his presidency, including a southern governor who said, "Mr. President, you are not leading this Nation—you're just managing the Government." Carter went on to argue that the cultural crisis was "deeper than gasoline lines or energy shortages, deeper even than inflation or recession." Sounding in cadence, tone, and rhetoric like an old-fashioned preacher delivering a jeremiad, he intoned, "Owning *things* and consuming *things*, does not satisfy our longing for meaning." With a particularly disdainful intonation on the repeated use of the word "things," he claimed that desire for escalating consumption was the nation's undoing. With passion and eloquence, he argued that pursuit of material possessions could not "fill the emptiness of lives which have no confidence or purpose." The nation faced a crisis of faith in democracy, progress, and purpose; it was unmoored from its past, uncertain of its future. "Our people are losing that faith, not only in government itself but in the ability as citizens to serve as the ultimate rulers and shapers of our democracy." He spoke of energy policy as well, proclaiming a successful implementation of his energy policy to be the first test of American renewal. He appeared a bit preachy but also decisive, strong, and impassioned in ways that too often he had not.[88]

Although most of the intellectuals Carter consulted in the making of his address put working people at or near the center of their analysis, Carter did not. Lasch, for instance, found the whole class diagnosis at the heart of the speech misguided. Carter, he believed, should have addressed "more directly the groups that have a real stake in change—poor people, working-class people, and any others whose minds have not been wholly paralyzed by the culture of 'self-expression' and self gratification." The target is more appropriately "the ascendancy of corporate interests as a whole, and more broadly of the managerial and professional elite. . . . What I have called the culture of narcissism is above all the culture of this class." Rather than pinning a lust-for-self on everyone, Lasch argued that the professional middle class had begun to colonize the rest of the nation with its anxious self-absorption, betrayal of the common good, and crippled sense of sacrifice. "These people have sold the rest of us on their way of life, but it is their way of life first and foremost, and it reflects their values, their rootless existence, their craving for novelty and contempt for the past, their confusion of reality with electronically mediated images of reality, their essentially gossipy approach to politics, their 'other-directed' round of life and bureaucratic setting (corporate or governmental) in which it unfolds." He concluded that Carter's message of "hard work, discipline, and sacrifice," offered as a way out of what he called the nation's "crisis of spirit," was likely "to fall on deaf ears when addressed, not to those who most need to hear them, but to people who already work hard and undergo sacrifices every day through no choice of their own."[89]

For Lasch, the roots the problem went all the way back to the Fordist bargain. In the 1920s, Taylorism and Fordism removed the skill and the independence from the workplace. Workers' mental and physical labors were separated through advanced management techniques, leaving a decline from the all-around craftsman capable of designing and building a product to workers as modern day appendages to machinery. It was the very problem that caused the Lordstown workers to rebel and that Harry Braverman had brilliantly outlined as the "degradation of work in the twentieth century" in his 1975 study *Labor and Monopoly Capital* (which influenced Lasch). In exchange for leaving their souls at the plant gate, workers were promised a cornucopia of consumption, Lasch explained in a letter to the White House. What Caddell had noted as the "ennui of affluence" (quoting an editor at *U.S. News and World Report*) was actually a crisis of the collapse of the bargain based on consumption in exchange for soul-killing work—that is, the crumbling of an entire paradigm upon its own vacuity. The system urged gratification but could not deliver. To correct the course of the nation, Lasch urged "a decisive turn to the left." Carter instead turned rapidly to the right.[90]

If Carter could not find a way to advance to a future framed by limits, Reagan was at work trying to restore a limitless past. Rather than chastising the citizenry for their desires, the New Right promised a restoration to the way things used to be—a return to an optimistic and limitless future, led with a combination of paternalism and authority. Richard Wirthlin, Reagan's campaign pollster, argued in June 1980, "Traditional Americans are finding themselves beset by a vocal minority who find it chic to denigrate family solidarity, parental respect and familial intradependence." In lieu of the bedrock of community and family, people were lost in a fog of disillusionment and fragmentation. The forces for victory could be found in the votes of "Southern white protestants, blue collar workers in the industrial states, urban ethnics, and rural voters"—that is, the old working-class constituents of the Democratic Party. The American people, he argued, wanted to "follow some authority figure," someone who could "take charge with authority; return a sense of discipline to our government; manifest the willpower needed to get this country back on track." Working Americans, he argued in echoes of Nixon, are "no longer solely motivated by economic concerns but by larger social issues as well." Like Nixon's strategists, the Reaganites would have to "differentiate between the official position of the unions and the rank and file members of the unions." The hope, as it was in Nixon's time, was to create a post–New Deal coalition that included working people willing to follow an authority figure who could turn back the clock on all that had gone wrong. The Reagan administration even debated deploying Nixon-style overtures to labor and working people, including another prominent White House celebration of Labor Day for the unions. Instead, they would choose a frontal assault in the summer of 1981 when they attacked the Professional Air Traffic Controllers Organization (PATCO).[91]

For Carter, criticizing the American people for their socio-spiritual failings and their hedonism, oddly enough, worked—at least temporarily. He received a nice boost in the polls after his speech (up eleven points but still only to a mere 37 percent approval), and the public response in phone calls and telegrams was exceedingly supportive. He had undoubtedly touched a deep nerve of concern. Two days after the speech, however, he squandered his advance. As part of his bold new leadership initiative, he sought to shake up his cabinet. He asked for "pro forma" resignations of every member, from which he would decide those to accept. In the end, he accepted five resignations of people who appeared less than committed to the president or suffered loose tongues. Yet the request for mass resignations appeared more like things were still falling apart than it did a decisive move. Carter, who had been criticized for micro-managing the White House, also appointed Hamilton Jordan to be his chief of staff. Jordan then circulated a silly questionnaire about the job performance of each staff member's supervisor, which felt like a loyalty test and the making of yet another purge to come. By the time the palace intrigue was over, Carter's approval ratings were lower than before the "malaise" speech. Events then cascaded into frustration over getting the energy program through Congress. By October of 1979, a key poll had Carter receiving the lowest rating of any of a series of potential candidates for the highest office in 1980, including Republicans John Connally, Ronald Regan, George Bush, Howard Baker, and what appeared to be the biggest threat, Democratic senator Ted Kennedy, who received the highest rankings.[92]

Then it all got worse for the remainder of 1979. UN Ambassador Andrew Young had to resign due to an unauthorized meeting with the Palestine Liberation Organization (PLO), Hamilton Jordan was charged with using cocaine at a trendy New York disco, and Ted Kennedy announced his candidacy to unseat Carter from the Left. In November, militant Iranian students seized the embassy in Tehran and took fifty hostages. At first, Carter's cool and purposeful response to the hostage crisis bolstered his position in the polls. As the crisis dragged on into the campaign season the following fall, it became his final undoing. Then the Soviets invaded Afghanistan. The next year, 1980, would be even worse than the fall of 1979 as the hostage crisis dragged on, a rescue attempt went terribly bad, unemployment crept up to 8 percent, and Miami exploded in a massive three-day race riot after an all-white jury acquitted a white police officer in the killing of a black man. Carter's brother, Billy Carter, who played the hard-drinking good ol' boy to the hilt, then seemed to be receiving money from the Libyan government in what Republicans dubbed "Billygate." The administration appeared in disarray, the party deeply divided. By the end of his presidency, people began to refer to him as "Jimmy Hoover," not simply because he was overseeing a new form of economic crisis without solution, but also because he served as the "hardworking but uninspiring technocrat and numbers cruncher" who was "fixated on detail" and moral principles much like his Depression-era counterpart. Like Hoover, Carter would be swept away with the old politics to make room for a new patronly figure who, like Roosevelt, would claim to heal the nation's wounds.[93]

Prior to the 1980 contest against Republican Ronald Reagan and third-party candidate John Anderson, Carter had to beat back Ted Kennedy's attempt to dethrone him for the Democratic nomination. Kennedy, concerned that Democratic fundamentals of jobs and health care had been left by the wayside, sought to revive the New Deal faithful. For the duration of Carter's term, Kennedy and the administration had been warring over the quality of a proposal for national health insurance that never came to a vote. In the process, Kennedy gained the support of the old Reuther wing of the labor movement that had supported McGovern, and he won key primaries such as Michigan and Pennsylvania. Yet his mistakes on the campaign trail, and the lingering fears of his moral failures at Chappaquiddick, made unseating Carter impossible. As the political director of SEIU said, "Kennedy says all the things that the labor movement needs to have said. He's taken over Hubert Humphrey's role. He's right on all the issues." Even though he lost the primary challenge, he still got the biggest applause for the most famous lines of his political career at the 1980 Democratic Convention. "Our cause has been, since the days of Thomas Jefferson, the cause of the common man and the common woman," Kennedy declared. "We cannot let the great purposes of the Democratic Party become the bygone passages of history."[94]

Despite the disastrous year, Carter remained confident in his ability to defeat someone he believed to be politically reckless and intellectually incapable—Ronald Reagan, former governor of California. On this, too, he was wrong. As Pat Caddell warned the president on the eve of the election, "We're losing the undecided voters overwhelmingly, and a lot of working Democrats are going to wake up tomorrow and for the first time in their lives vote Republican." The *New York Times* reported that Ford Motor Company worker "Dewey Burton has become a happy man" who "will gladly vote for Ronald Reagan for President" even though he is "a strong union man, a Democrat by upbringing and conviction." As if to bookend the New Deal order, Carter was the first president since Herbert Hoover to stand for re-election and not win. He lost by a much larger margin than anyone had dared to predict.[95]

The political warriors for labor liberalism rode Carter's coattails out of office. Five of the senators who supported cloture in the labor law reform fight had already lost their seats in the 1978 midterm elections, including some of labor's strongest allies. Then, in 1980, sixteen more voters for cloture lost their seats, among them politicians with very high COPE rankings. Not only did Reagan carry forty-four states, but Republicans gained twelve Senate spots and defeated a host of liberal Democrats, including George McGovern, the party's left-wing standard bearer in 1972. The Republican Party enjoyed a fifty-three to forty-seven seat majority in the Senate (as well as the

Democrats losing the all-important committee chairs), a margin not seen since 1928, and they narrowed the Democratic lead in the House by thirty-three seats. Even moderate Republicans took a beating. Then the 1980 census reflected the rising demographic power of the Sunbelt and the loss of population and political representation in the Northeast. Most symbolically, Orrin Hatch, the leader of the filibuster effort and labor's biggest political enemy, became chair of the Senate Labor Committee.[96]

In 1980, the Democrats failed to place any real ideas in competition with the swelling support of the New Right. By shifting to the right, they gave ideological ground to the opposition, especially by conceding that high wages, full employment, and deficit spending caused inflation. If their major policy weapons were the cause of inflation, then the Democrats were effectively disarmed. As James D. Savage argues, by 1980, "in the name of short term political gain the Democrats discredited the very foundation of their macroeconomic policy, leaving nothing substantial in their place." They discredited their own policy history and therefore their future. "For any new Democratic budget proposal that added a single dollar to the deficit instantly lost legitimacy on the grounds . . . that it helped cripple the economy." Having lost the battle over full employment and labor rights, the Democrats had sacrificed their highest political ground for the indefinite future. Then, with the rise of the Democratic Leadership Council, the party shifted to a socially liberal but economically conservative position in the 1990s. As a result, they spent the decades that followed fighting on the other party's turf.[97]

Americans, it turned out, preferred to have their spiritual crisis cured by someone who thought it only existed in the political imagination of a Democratic White House. On the night before the 1980 election, Ronald Reagan declared, "Americans are asking: does history still have a place for America, for her people, for her great ideals? There are some who answer 'no'; that our energy is spent, our days of greatness at an end, that a great national malaise is upon us. . . . I find no national malaise, I find nothing wrong with the American people. Oh, they are frustrated, even angry at what has been done to this blessed land. But more than anything they are sturdy and robust as they have always been." America, for Ronald Reagan, was still a "shining city on a hill," a beacon of hope for the world in covenant with God, as Puritan John Winthrop declared in the sermon "A Model of Christian Charity" on board the *Arabella* in 1630. Reagan claimed that he would unleash the genius of the American individual by freeing him from the shackles of the state. That individual initiative, in turn, would put the factories back in operation, restore full employment, tame inflation, and rebuild the nation's image abroad.[98]

VIII

After the convulsions of the seventies—"Ten Years that Shook America," *Newsweek* headlined its retrospective cover story—it perhaps should not be surprising that the nation chose authority, calm, and order. As Andreas Killen portrays it, the "institutional failures of American society routinely evoked expressions of systemic, perhaps irreparable crisis. And yet the re-markable thing was how quickly the nation reconstituted itself, and, more-over, did so along lines that reflected continuity with the deepest myths of the American past." It was the selection of mythology over the real chal-lenges that irked those devoted to reimagining what might have come of the hope and possibility of the decade. Michael Harrington, for one, countered that the Reagan restoration was more Disney than Puritan. The future would not be "Reagan's utterly sincere, utterly irrelevant vision of a new city on the hill," he argued, "but Disney World . . . a reactionary and very modern future in the fantastic costume of a dead past."[99]

After Reagan's inaugural address, Washington descended into an unpre-cedented orgy of conspicuous consumption as the richest of the rich re-turned to power, showing up for inaugural balls that one critic prophetically described as the "Bacchanalia of the haves." It had once been the "the 'revolt of the masses' that was held to threaten social order and the civilizing tradi-tions of Western culture," explained Christopher Lasch in *The Revolt of the Elites* (1995). "In our time, however, the chief threat seems to come from those at the top of the social hierarchy, not the masses." Lasch believed that professional and managerial elites subverted the nation's democratic poten-tial with their rapacious greed, their asocial cultural values, and their vacu-ous civic responsibility. Many economic elites had opted out of the public in the way they educated their kids, traveled the city, gated their communities, and imagined their citizenship, he argued. Indeed, it was difficult to imag-ine a time when the concerns of elites were less connected to everyday people since the ostentatious displays of wealth at the end of the nineteenth century—privilege without responsibility; wealth without obligation; no-blesse without oblige. As Michael Douglas' iconic character Gordon Gekko said in *Wall Street* (1987), "The point is, ladies and gentlemen, that greed, for lack of a better word, is good. Greed is right. Greed works. Greed clarifies, cuts through, and captures the essence of evolutionary spirit." Yet it was hardly fiction—Gekko's speech had been retooled from one originally given by convicted inside trader Ivan Boesky.[100]

As alt-country singer Steve Earle complained in the eighties, "nowadays it just don't pay to be a good ol' boy." Between 1949 and 1979, the inflation-adjusted average hourly wage for production workers rose *75 percent*. Between 1979 and 2005, in contrast, the average production-worker's wage rose a mere *2 percent*. During the same time, executive compensation and productivity, which are supposed to be linked to wages, went up dramatically. Personal savings topped out at 11.2 percent of household income in 1982, before plummeting into negative numbers. Measures of inequality dropped to their nadir in the early seventies, only to skyrocket to new highs. Unions lost not just the percentage of workers they covered but lost real numbers in the seventies. Unions also began to lose the majority of elections held by the NLRB in the 1970s, and wage settlements in the eighties went back to what they had been in the 1960s. With stagnating income, decreased saving rates, and the end of usury laws (1978), it should not be surprising to see negative savings rates, the rise of payday lending agencies, and a flood of capital into finance rather than production. Dewey Burton, reflecting on Reagan's action against PATCO, remarked, "in hindsight, that's only one of the things, like what he done with the income tax system in this country has basically devastated the workingman." Tom Geoghegan quipped that workers lost their union cards in the seventies just in time to pick up their credit cards for the eighties.[101]

One of the many ironies of the period was that one of the people who recoiled most dramatically at the massive rise of economic inequality since the 1970s was Kevin Phillips, one of the key strategists behind the white identity politics of Nixon's "New Majority" strategy. "The 1980s were the triumph of upper America," decried Phillips, "an ostentatious celebration of wealth, the political ascendancy of the richest third of the population and a glorification of capitalism, free markets and finance." The new "plutocracy" of the eighties, he believed, had initiated a "new Gilded Age." Phillips, who lit populist fires and jabbed pitchforks at the "liberal elite" in the 1970s, had shifted to attacking the capitalist elite after their merciless triumph in the 1980s. Yet there was a fundamental difference between the old Gilded Age and the new. The old one hosted some of the most dramatic labor disputes in American history at places like Haymarket and Homestead, Pullman and Coeur d'Alene. It gave birth to the Knights of Labor, the American Federation of Labor, the Populist Party, the Socialist Party, and the Industrial Workers of the World. The new "Gilded Age," in contrast, has had a deafening silence about what elites once whispered to each other with concern: "the labor question." Even post-1970s expressions of that deepest of veins in American politics—populism—was filled with the cultural rage of the people but stripped of questions of class inequality.[102]

7

The Important Sound of Things
Falling Apart

In 1975, rock journalist Nik Cohn embarked on an underground tour of the working-class disco scene in Brooklyn with a black dancer named Tu Sweet. "Some of those guys," explained Tu Sweet, "they have no lives. Dancing is all they got." That idea sunk into Cohn, whose British roots gave a class edge to his understanding of pop music. "I'd always thought of teen style in terms of class," Cohn reported; "Rock, at least the kind that mattered to me, attains its greatest power when have-nots went on the rampage, taking no prisoners. *'Dancing's all they got.'* It sounded to me like a rallying cry." His adventures at a club named 2001 Odyssey ended with a stellar piece of reportage for *New York* magazine about living to dance and dancing to escape called "The Tribal Rights of the New Saturday Night." The theme of the piece was that only a select few were capable of rising above the "vast faceless blob" of humanity that does most of the nation's working and dying. Only a select few "faces" knew "how to dress and how to move, how to float, how to fly. Sharpness, grace, a certain distinction in every gesture." As Vincent, king of the 2001 Odyssey explained, "The way I feel, it's like we've been chosen." The *New York* article became the foundation for the most popular movie of the decade, *Saturday Night Fever* (1977).[1]

There was only one problem: Cohn fabricated the entire story—from the characters to their performances, from their looks to their dreams. His editors did not know of his deceit. Concerned that the public might not buy the veracity of Cohn's tales of the disco underground, the editors went so far as to include an inset, claiming "everything described in this article is factual and was either witnessed by me or told to me directly." But Cohn's journalism was just one more part of the seventies hustle. He did show up at the club to do his research with Tu Sweet after wandering lost in the "dead land" of Brooklyn, but when he stepped out of his gypsy cab, there was a brawl taking place in the parking lot, and then someone spun around and threw up on his pants. Figuring nothing could be worth such a price, he immediately headed back to Manhattan. After other failed attempts to penetrate the scene, he gave up and decided to make up his tale from thin air and a few fragments that were burned into his mind from his unsuccessful excursion over the class divide.

One particular image provided the inspiration for the fiction of "Tribal Rights." Before retreating to his cab, Cohn recalled "a figure in flared crimson pants and a black body shirt standing in the back doorway, directly under the neon light, and calmly watching the action. There was a certain style about him—an inner force, a hunger and a sense of his own specialness. He looked, in short, like a star." This random encounter with seventies street-cool would be transformed into the quintessential icon of the decade, *Saturday Night Fever*'s Tony Manero (Vincent in the article). Although Cohn later failed in his efforts to transfer his myth making into a screenplay (Norman Wexler, who had done two other seventies blue-collar scripts, *Joe* and *Serpico*, had to be brought in to do the job), his brief moment in a Brooklyn parking lot was the spark that made pop culture history.

Tony Manero, as played by John Travolta in the screen adaptation of Cohn's story, became not simply the definitive seventies icon but also one of the most revealing and popular working-class heroes of the decade. Two critics described the white-suited disco king as a "high-powered fusion of sexuality, street jive, and the frustrated hope of a boy-man who can't articulate his sense of oppression." The film, they suggest, gives "the impression that it knows more about the working class psyche and ethos than it is willing to risk showing us." The classic cinematic theme of imprisonment or escape is pitch perfect, and the disco setting makes it emblematic of the seventies. The urgency and desperation of its themes make the movie more than a dance flick: *Saturday Night Fever* is both symptom and exploration of the most important breaking points in the nation's white, male, working-class identity.[2]

The film begins with one of the great opening scenes in American cinema, featuring Travolta strutting confidently through Bay Ridge to the beat of the Bee Gees' "Stayin' Alive." He then works the customers at a hardware store with the same grace and ego that he later reveals on the dance floor of the renamed Club 2001. All of his spark and charm contrast markedly with the world of fixed values and social limits that constantly contain his expressive individuality. His slick salesmanship and confidence are interrupted only by the horrific realization that he could be stuck peddling paint for the rest of his life like his broken down co-workers. Begging his boss for an advance so he can buy a new shirt for his true passion, the weekend festivities in the disco, Tony gets a lecture from his boss about not frittering away his money. "Fuck the future!" Tony angrily retorts. The boss fires back that no, "The future fucks you." It was a refrain heard often in the shrinking seventies, not the least significant of which was the chorus of the Sex Pistols' riot anthem of the same year, "God Save the Queen:" "No future, no future, no future for you."

The workplace is only a minor set in *Fever*'s blue-collar teen drama, as the plot centers on Tony's attempt to conquer the discotheque, win over an upwardly mobile dancer, Stephanie (Karen Lynn Gorney), deal with his gang of futureless buddies, and, most importantly, find some sense of himself. Stephanie, the object of his affections, continually rebuffs him, explaining, "You're a cliché. You're nowhere on your way to no place." Tony's attempt at impromptu self-improvement quickens as he tries to fake his way through a conversation with someone who is, herself, trying to fake her way rather sadly across the river to upwardly mobile Manhattan. Before heading to the disco, Tony carefully prepares his look surrounded by posters of Bruce Lee, Farrah Fawcett-Majors, and Sylvester Stallone, inserting himself into the galaxy of stars by imagining himself as the Pacino of Bay Ridge. As Cohn originally wrote, "Whenever he gazed into the mirror, it was always Pacino who gazed back. A killer, and a star." The twinkling allure of fame is his hope. He and his friends, explained one critic, stuck with unemployed fathers, an economy in the dump, and a vacuum in national leadership, "are part of the post-Watergate working-class generation with no heroes except in TV-show-biz land; they have a historical span of twenty-three weeks, with repeats at Christmas."[3]

Once Tony is finished preening (looking "as sharp as I can look without turning into a nigger"), the true action of the film happens on the dance floor. He bursts with the creativity and sense of self that he cannot find anywhere else in his life. Bathed in the immediacy of the backlit floor, Tony gets the attention and adulation missing in both his job and his home life as the crowd parts in celebration of his prowess. "The bodies, the drugs, the heat, the sweat, the sunrises, and the throb of the music all conspired to create a heated sense of nowness," explained one writer on the disco experience, "a sense that nothing existed outside of that room. No past, no future, no promises, no regrets, just right now and those strings from 'Love's Theme' cascading all over you and prickling your skin." Tony is no longer pretending to be Pacino; the working-class hero has become king.[4]

The film turns as Tony's claustrophobia begins to build as the walls of ethnic and sexual violence close in on him. Enraged when the first-place trophy in the dance contest is given to him (like the judges, a fellow Italian) rather than the obviously better Puerto Rican couple, he turns over the trophy to the reviled ethnic newcomers and storms out of the club. With this act of betrayal—choosing merit over ethnic loyalty—he has begun a path toward individualism, mobility, and independence, an escape from his shrinking and intolerant working-class world toward an expansive, even open-minded, new life. As he storms out of the dance contest, Tony harangues his partner Stephanie with a furious, primitive, Marxist sociology that explains gender, race, and class in a few easy pieces: "My Pa goes to work, he gets dumped on. So he come home and dumps on my mother, right? Of course, right. And the spics gotta dump on us, so we gotta dump on the spics, right? Even the humpin' is dumpin' most of the time." Tony proceeds to prove his point about oppression rolling downhill, when, in a rage of frustration, he attempts to rape Stephanie. By the time an insane night of gang-banging and suicidal behavior is over, the drama concludes with a tightly wrapped, if largely improbable, plot resolution. Unable to contend with either dwindling economic opportunity or the dead-end racial, ethnic, and gender hatreds around him, Tony chooses to sever all ties to his working-class community and create himself anew. "They're all assholes," he declares as he escapes the limits of Brooklyn after riding the subway all night, emerging in Manhattan in the early morning light.

When Tony resurfaces from his subterranean ride, bruised and battered from his inter-ethnic street warfare, he is all but reborn with a new day dawning in the upper-class world of Manhattan. Stephanie's apartment (borrowed from an older boss whom she seems to be sleeping with in the exchange) is a place where a Matisse print hangs on the wall, and jazz is in the air. The nation as a whole was asked to make a similar journey by the dawn of the 1980s, and like Tony and his new friend Stephanie, they had to fake it. The characters are sitting in a borrowed apartment—literally inhabiting somebody else's world. In this new place, their identity as members of a class—such a salient aspect of their lives just an endless train ride ago—is on its way to being denied or covered up. Their old blue-collar community is relegated to some forgotten past to which neither they nor the viewer will return. Tony and Stephanie are in the midst of a fantasy that they can remake themselves by changing their surroundings and abandoning their past. Even the violence of their sexual encounter melts into a new platonic relationship. Class is neither community nor culture nor occupation nor power but a mere affect that the select few, the chosen ones, can drop. A Matisse print, a borrowed apartment, and the ability to do the hustle are all that is needed.

The theme of relegating class to some distant geographic or temporal past is driven home by the Bee Gees' disco anthem "Stayin' Alive" from the film's immensely successful soundtrack. The song thumps through the opening scene of Tony strutting down the street, seemingly in control of his tiny world. "Music loud and women warm / I've been kicked around / Since I was born," they declare in their famous helium falsetto. "Life goin' nowhere. Somebody help me," they plea in the lower ranges with just a splash of social-realist pain. But then comes the twist; rather than a call to act, the Bee Gees, like the film itself, offer permission to forget: "And now it's all right. It's OK. And you may look the other way" as Tony, Stephanie, and the audience turn their back on the unseemly race-class stew of Brooklyn, pointing their faces toward a future purged of the working class. Not to worry, this is a pain I can carry myself, the narrator of "Stayin' Alive" mutters beneath the pulse and the chorus. The megahit of 1977 allowed the nation to begin to move toward the eighties celebration of working-class heroes who managed to get out, while casting those who could not into cinematic (and political) darkness.[5]

Just as the song offered permission to cover up, to deny, and to forget—and then rolled it all up in polyester and cast it under swirling lights—so the discotheques themselves inhabited the former physical settings of the old industrial working class by inhabiting the buildings of a once mighty occupational past. "Despite its veneer of elegance and sophistication, disco was born, maggot-like, from the rotten remains of the Big Apple," explains the genre's otherwise sympathetic historian Peter Shapiro. As New York's manufacturing base evaporated into empty factories and bolted warehouses of New York City, discotheques moved into those abandoned locations, "recolonizing the dead industrial space, replacing the production of goods with the production of illusions. The economy was in tatters and people wanted to do what they did during the Great Depression—dance."[6]

The Depression analogy, alive through much of seventies pop, obfuscates important differences in the meaning of dance, cinema, and politics in the thirties and the stagflation era. Like so many of the constant echoes and re-verberations of the thirties and forties in seventies popular culture, Tony's love affair with the Verrazano Narrows bridge, the frequency of trains in the film, the grit and violence, and the urban skyline that precedes Tony's famous Bay Ridge strut are suggestive of the social-realist motifs and iconography of a previous generation. In many ways, however, *Fever*'s runaway individualism is the opposite of the notorious dance marathon contests of the thirties, as depicted most famously in Horace McCoy's novel *They Shoot Horses Don't They?* (1935). McCoy explored the collective dehumanization and degradation of the unemployed who dance for days and weeks for the entertainment of others—a far cry from dancing as a showcase for individual stardom. Like the ever down-and-out but suave Fred Astaire, perhaps Tony's best Depression-era analogue, the thirties dancer, served a different function. Astaire possessed a tuxedoed panache with a huckster's edge—always demonstrating control of his social environment like Tony. Unlike Tony Manero, Astaire's characters were not "clichés going nowhere" but guides for common people to the world of the affluent. "One function of the song-and-dance man in the 1930s films," explains Joel Dinerstein, "was to resolve and mediate class differences in his role as well-dressed entertainer." As much as Astaire's performances served to keep society together, Manero functions as the opposite. He is neither a go-between nor a class interpreter; he is an escape artist.[7]

As much as curmudgeonly Archie Bunker was the definitive character of the first half of the seventies, doomed to be on the losing side of history, Tony Manero served that role for the second half by battling his way toward the winning side of history. He showed that, for the able, "working-class" may be something that could simply be rejected like any other style choice in the world of self-constructed identities, and that the cost was merely severing all connections to the past. And not only *could* it be rejected but, if possible, it *should*. "These are not nice people for the most part," admitted a perceptive film critic about the characters of Bay Ridge, "but they are alive and striving—it is a mistake to ignore them or, maybe worse, pretend that their lives have no meaning." As Tom Wolfe proclaimed, the decade belonged to those who did pretend, those willing to ignore, and those who found meaning in "remaking, remodeling, elevating and polishing one's very self." For those with the resources or the talents, the malleability of the seventies self might have been liberating. For others, however, the Maneroesque fantasy was simply mean. And, we might recall, a deception from the very start.[8]

I

Disco, of course, was much larger than one immensely successful film and its runaway sound track, and the supersonic flight of the craze across the cultural skies of the 1970s revealed much about class and the cultural shifts of the second half of the decade. The same disturbing scenes of decline and despair that chilled Michael Harrington as he strolled across the Greenwich Village in 1977 were embraced by the disco movement in celebratory ways: a sense of cultural dissent without direction, and an anti-bourgeois sentiment without a need to build an alternative to the status quo. Such points of despair for Harrington provided a sense of freedom for others. "The 60s were clutter. The seventies are very empty," explained noted artist and denizen of disco palace Studio 54, Andy Warhol. Disco attempted to fill the emerging cultural void of the 1970s with the glitter of a multicultural individualism, the shimmer of aristocracy, the promise of physical ecstasy, and the possibility of forgetting. And its promise of personal liberation proved more lasting than the "come together" spirit of the sixties.[9]

Discotheques negated the gloom and the emptiness by manufacturing a spectacle of meaning out of the very same void that others feared. Yet it was "false promise," explains Anne-Lise Francois, whose "total fulfillment in the fictive realm of the strobe-globe precludes and always exceeds its realization elsewhere." The experience of the discotheques dissolved the pain of the past into the celebration of the present, allowed indulgence to be the salve for the wounds of hope, and embraced the cult of celebrity in lieu of a generation's search for authenticity—all mixed with a splash of Weimaresque fatalism. "The postindustrial, inflationary '70s spawned their own fantasy factories," explains Peter Shapiro, "combining nostalgia and extravagance with devil-may-care attitude that not only perfectly summed up the times, but also foreshadowed the bleakness of what was on the horizon." Christopher Lasch noted how hedonism and spectacle, fantasy and celebrity, came "to dominate the modern psyche" in the seventies in such a way that living "for the moment" had become "the prevailing passion." Disco certainly made a good case. The beautiful people, the glamour, the drugs, and the big party all trumped the waning struggle over meaning—just as the empire tipped toward disaster.[10]

Disco was a contradiction. It too easily gets conflated with the affluent hedonism of the beautiful people, but it was also one of the few integrated working-class cultural movements of the second half of the decade—particularly its earliest forms. The alter ego to its aristocratic exclusiveness was actually the promise of a new inclusiveness that could bring together the races, the sexualities, the classes, and the ideologies into one big—if fleeting—social triumph over the fragmentation of social life. Since the eclipse of the integrated rock scene of the early seventies, most popular music had fractured into insular societies—"white rock was sounding whiter and black music was sounding blacker," as Craig Werner explains. The exception was disco, which formed a temporary bridge between what George Clinton famously called the chocolate cities and the vanilla suburbs, encouraging women, gays, blacks, Latinos, and ethnic whites to enjoy a polyrhythmic point of integration—even if it was based on erasing, as the Bee Gees sang, that "the price of meat is higher than the dope on the street."[11]

Although disco may have begun with an inclusive impulse, it drifted toward the exclusive and the aristocratic, and was plagued with a nagging sense of whether poppers, beats, sex, and coke could amount to a social vision. Dancing was, as one aficionado explained, "a way of communicating with people you might not have anything to say to if you sat down to talk." If the basis of that communication merely amounted to ecstasy and desire, however, it may have offered less of a vision than a punctuation point to the end of a larger narrative. Disco, continues Shapiro, "attempted to suggest answers to questions posed by a society in the process of abandoning a universalist communitarian model for a vision based on cutthroat individualism; disco's glitter queens and escapist working-class teens were kicking against the pricks the only way they knew how." The redemption it could offer was not spiritual, political, or material, but corporeal. In its hedonistic and solipsistic response to an economy gone bad, a state revealed as corrupt, and a nation bereft of its mission, disco was like "being trapped in the headlights of the oncoming cultural paradigm shift—not quite dancing through the apocalypse, but something similar." Like liberals' failed efforts to stitch their vision back together with full employment and labor law reform, disco "was liberalism's last hurrah, the final party before the neocon apocalypse."[12]

And the more popular the genre became, the less content it had. Between the pretensions of royalty and the promise of a people's dance movement erupted a routinized corporate drumbeat in place of the genre's dwindling polyrhythmic complexity. Quickly, as disco went from underground movement to craze, the studios took the roots of the music and drained funk of its funk, soul of its soul, and the blues of its rhythm. The music devolved into the most manufactured art form, representing the triumph of the producer over the artist, and the victory of those who were willing to pander to the market to the point of destroying what they purported to love. Disguised as liberation, it was the ultimate triumph of capitalism over art. "It is a riot of consumerism," acknowledged Richard Dyer in a critical defense of the genre, "dazzling in its technology (echo chambers, double and more tracking, electric instruments), overwhelming in its scale (banks of violins, massed choirs, the limitless range of percussion instruments), lavishly gaudy in the mirrors and tat of discotheques, the glitter of denim flash of its costumes. . . . Gone are the restraint of popular song, the sparseness of rock and reggae, the simplicity of folk." But, as Dyer explained, it felt good when little else did.[13]

If disco contained more than hints of the Weimar Republic, the heartland's "Disco Sucks!" movement was its Beer Hall Putsch. By the late seventies, disco had moved from an innovative art form to a fad and finally to a cultural volcano with heat, swell, and territorial ambition—taking over radio stations, rock bands, clothing styles, and mating patterns. Perhaps not the least significant absorption was the seizure of the affectations of working-class masculinity by the campy ensemble the Village People. Many traditionalists fought back without much generosity of spirit, and one of the first and most notable was a small-time country-rock outfit called Chuck Wagon and the Wheels. While playing at the Stumble Inn in Tucson, Arizona, a polyester-studded heckler demanded that the band "Play some disco!" Chuck and the boys volleyed back with a disco beat and a spontaneous chant of "Disco Sucks!" The combination struck a nerve as the several hundred people in the club roared with approval. Realizing their potential new market, the band then tossed off another in a long line of painfully bad novelty songs littering the decade called, of course, "Disco Sucks." "I like songs about drivin' trucks," Chuck Wagon sings of the feelings of the heartland working class, "And I don't make a whole lotta bucks / But I know enough to know that disco sucks." The song got immediate airplay on album-oriented FM rock stations in 1978, and the "Disco Sucks" uprising was born.[14]

The most public face of the anti-disco movement was a disc jockey at Chicago's WLUP named Steve Dahl, who quickly adopted Chuck Wagon and the Wheels' song as the anthem for a new movement. Dahl had been fired from an album-oriented station just before Christmas Eve when the station suddenly turned to a disco format, and he exacted his revenge publicly with regular anti-disco rants and the playing of "Disco Sucks" during his new show on WLUP. Dahl organized his shock troops, which he called the Insane Coho Lips Army, named after the salmon responsible for ridding Lake Michigan of the parasitic and destructive lamprey eel. The height of the rebellion came during the 1979 baseball season at a double header with the Detroit Tigers. The fortunes of the White Sox were sagging, so, as part of a promotional deal, fans were let in for 98 cents if they brought a disco album for Dahl to destroy between games in what he called a Disco Demolition Derby. The usually empty seats of the ballpark were crammed with fans (and tens of thousands more denied access were milling around outside the park and even more stuck on the surrounding expressways trying to get there). Ten thousand disco records piled up on the field for mass destruction—fans brought so many that they were allowed to keep their discs, which readily turned into Frisbees when things got wild. Dahl took to the diamond in full military regalia, including fatigues, helmet, and a jeep. As he blew up the records, a riot ensued as thousands of rock/baseball fans poured out onto the field, lighting bonfires, ripping down the backstop, stealing bases, tearing up the grass, and even, it was alleged, engaging in oral sex on home plate. The mayhem was such that the White Sox made baseball history by forfeiting the second game to the Detroit Tigers because the field was rendered unplayable.[15]

Dahl's disco riot was another pillar in the bridge between Nixon and Reagan, offering an addition to the identity of the white everyman on the road to the counter-revolution. Not far below the shrill aesthetic critique of the musical genre could be found deep wells of homophobia, racism, and long-standing anti-Eastern establishment sentiments dating back to the dawn of the republic. In Detroit, a group had originally wanted to go so far as to call itself the Disco Sucks Klan but agreed to change its name to the less racially charged DREAD (Detroit Rockers Engaged in the Abolition of Disco). They still held mock on-air electrocutions of disco fans by name (and even traveled with an electric chair as a promotional prop)—only a few degrees of separation from the Klan analogy. Along with the constant references among disco-phobes to the music "lacking balls," it was difficult to find any distinct line between where the aesthetic critique stopped and the larger cultural backlash began. As Craig Werner writes, "Driving disco from the charts, the alliance [of disco haters] also succeeded in destroying the last remaining musical scene that was in any meaningful sense racially mixed. After nearly a quarter century of doubt, white America had recovered its sense of self."[16]

The "Disco Sucks" rallies and the various burnings, steamrollings, and smashing of disco records (by the "Saturday Night Cleaver" no less) seemed like the last stand of white blue-collar Midwestern males against all that was cosmopolitan, urbane, racially integrated, and, most of all, gay. Disco's challenge to both segregation and straight identity created an open forum for the celebration of the different, the outcast, and the wild, while simultaneously creating a focal point for young, white, male, blue-collar kids who fetishized the phallic guitar solos of rock, despised the producer-driven mechanized format of disco, and felt secure in the increasingly white envelope of seventies rock. The guys in the "Shoot the Bee Gees," "Disco Sucks," and "Kiss Army" t-shirts were ingredients in a larger rage of Midwestern males against the system, but like Dewey Burton's commitments to the anti-busing cause, it was more complicated than just race or just sexuality—it tipped into economic power, class, and cultural authority. It was also a raised middle finger to the decadence of those who would party through double digit unemployment and the deindustrialization of America.

The anti-disco movement was less about the materiality of working-class identity than what white, male, blue-collar identity had morphed into: a populist grab bag of resentments based on region, race, economics, and sexuality. White guys, already insecure about their employment future, now faced threats to everything else they thought they could rely upon: racial identity, masculinity, and, what by then had become a safely white genre, rock 'n' roll. The protest was not simply about racism or deviance; it was about something far more threatening, explains Shapiro: "impotence."

Detroit had once been the shining industrial beacon of the American economic miracle. Its massive car factories provided high-paid blue-collar jobs to just about everyone, and the images of third-generation Germans, Jews, recent Polish immigrants, and newly arrived African Americans from the Deep South working side by side on the shop floor were enduring symbols of both the might and beneficence of American capitalism. . . . The high falsettos of disco stars like the Bee Gees and Sylvester sounded the death knell for the virility of the American male. Disco came from New York, "Sodom on the Hudson," the home of both namby-pamby knee-jerk liberals and Spiro

Agnew's "Northeast liberal media elite." Viewed in this context, Dahl's military pomp makes a bit of sense: He was waging a war on the enemy within that was draining America of its life force.[17]

Vying against both the disco craze and the homogenized landscape of corporate rock was the underground scene of the New York City club, CBGB's. There the Ramones, a bunch of long-haired, leather-clad, white boys from Archie Bunker's Queens, stripped rock of fifteen years of accumulated commercial bloat and artistic pretense and boiled it down to two-minute songs made of three chords and a hurricane of energy. *Creem*, the famous Detroit rock 'n' roll magazine, summed up the Ramones' aesthetic as set against "ponderous middle-aged labor unions like Zep, Bad Co. and Foghat."[18]

The Ramones returned rock 'n' roll to its proper garage setting, promising a do-it-yourself kit for those interested in emancipation from the chains of mainstream seventies music that Greil Marcus could dismiss as little more than "a habit, a structure, an invisible oppression." They were the United States' most important contribution to, and much of the catalyst for, the Anglo-American punk movement, but what was curious about the band, especially as opposed to their British cousins, was their distinct lack of class politics—and, when they had them, their often conservative bend. Rather than being class conscious or even political, they tended to embrace simply being "dumbbell pillhead teenagers" stripped of any sentimentality and who could whipsaw angst into contempt and farce. It is not that the Ramones were not often witty or even brilliant, but simply, in contrast to much of the punk movement across the Atlantic, they were part of the breakdown of class as a category of analysis rather than a re-imagining of it.[19]

In many ways, one could take away the drugs, the leather, and the long hair, and imagine Johnny Ramone, at least, relating pretty well to his old neighbor back in Queens, Archie Bunker. Despite their distinct edge and their time with the avant-garde CBGB's crowd, the Ramones wallowed in their American provincialism. On a European tour with the cerebral art school band the Talking Heads, they demonstrated their parochial view of the world. "The Ramones hated Europe," reported the Talking Heads manager. "They didn't like the idea that people didn't speak English. The Talking Heads adored it. It was really yuppie chic at work. The Ramones were like Archie Bunker at the Vatican. They were not amused. They hated the food and just looked for hamburgers everywhere." When they got to Stonehenge, the Ramones did not even bother to leave the bus. Joey Ramone would go on to criticize the Reagan administration in the eighties, but Johnny, who left his job as a construction worker in 1974 to don his trademark bad haircut and leather jacket, became a vocal right-wing Republican.[20]

The limits of the American punk scene only make sense when compared with their UK equivalent, where the Clash and the Sex Pistols proved to be the driving forces of innovation. While the Ramones were always detached from issues of class, preferring a fury of irony and a mess of fun, British punk was all about an expansive—and explosive—vision of it. British punk voiced working-class anger—of the sort that would have its direct analogue in the 1978–79 British strike wave known as the Winter of Discontent—and it was a direct assault on the pomp of the upper classes. In the case of the Clash, the music was also global, strongly influenced by reggae, ideologically aligned with the class struggle, and proclaiming revolutionary solidarity through albums such as the sprawling *Sandinista!* The band's first single, the 1977 "White Riot" urged white working-class youth to quit taking it out on black people and find their own cause: "Are you taking over / Or are you taking orders? / Are you going backwards / Or are you going forwards?" Even the nihilism of the Sex Pistols derived its edge from class. The Ramones, in contrast, gave us intentionally dumbed-down, anti-social irony, such as the 1977 cut "Commando," which offered up four basic tenets of social behavior: "First rule is: The laws of Germany. Second rule is: Be nice to mommy. Third rule is: Don't talk to commies. Fourth rule is: Eat kosher salamis." West Coast hardcore bands like the Dead Kennedys did offer an unyieldingly savage critique of the United States (including a cover of a modified version of Johnny Paycheck's "Take This Job and Shove It"), but American punk never became a national outlet for class antagonism even when it shared some of the aesthetics and anger of the British insurgency.

The most important thing that a band like the Clash had that almost all American music of the late seventies lacked was a conscious infusion of black musical traditions. As rock critic Lester Bangs put it, "Somewhere in their assimilation of reggae is the closest thing yet to the lost chord, the missing link between black and white noise, rock capable of making a bow to black forms without smearing on the blackface." Unlike the musically integrated London scene, there was zero funk in American punk and barely any in new wave either. The integrated band sound of the seventies, like the hope of a multi-cultural class identity more generally, was lost. In the United States of America, there was little hope of a progressive working-class identity without confronting its full racial complexity, and on those grounds the nation's music failed to offer assistance. Punk and "classic" rock, on the one hand, and disco and hip-hop, on the other, were re-segregating audiences. The occasional, antediluvian, but "heroic," acts of some bands, like the Talking Heads, of covering songs like Al Green's "Take Me to the River," was the moral equivalent of attempting to re-unite the shifting tectonic plates of American culture. Its brilliance was also an isolated one, accepted mostly on college campuses and the club scene, far from the antidisco shock troops commandeering Comiskey Park.[21]

II

Given the black-blue tensions in the air at mid decade, it ought not to be surprising that the pop culture fantasy for the bicentennial year 1976 rested upon the ability of a down and out, golden hearted, dim-witted white guy to go the distance with a gorgeous and talented black man. The measure of success for the great white hope of seventies America, according to the smash hit boxing movie *Rocky* (1976), had been reduced from victory merely to be still standing at the end of the day. *On the Waterfront*'s (1954) Terry Malloy, to whom Rocky was inevitably compared in reviews, "coulda been a contender" if he had not been sold out by the mob and his brother. Rocky, however, really does get his chance—plucked out of the white ghettos of Philadelphia with the fortune of a lottery winner—to take on the fast-talking and commercially savvy black superstar Apollo Creed in a testament to "the dream of uplift to the common man through individual initiative." He proves himself a contender in this cinematic version of the *Bakke* case—though not quite a full winner until the growing absurdity of later sequels.[22]

What is amazing about *Rocky* is its triple layer of Cinderella-like fantasy—from the fight that inspired it, to the writer who maintained his claim to it, to the film itself. The film was based on reality, created out of necessity, and spoke directly of the issues of the day. Like films from *Dog Day Afternoon* to *Blue Collar* to *Saturday Night Fever*, Rocky's working-class plot came straight out of the headlines. In 1975, the African American boxing promoter Don King (who had orchestrated the famous Rumble in the Jungle in Zaire between Muhammad Ali and George Foreman) decided, as he saw it, to give a white guy a break. Declaring that world heavyweight champion Ali was "an equal opportunity employer" he looked for a white boxer to give him an opportunity to slug his way to the title. "I am," explained King with a wink, "for the heavy-laden and downtrodden." The sacrificial white man selected for the job was Chuck Wepner, a club fighter and liquor salesman who, far from an athletic star, got up in the morning and went to work like everyone else selling his goods in the bars of New Jersey. He was also a highly ranked journeyman fighter with forty-one fights to his name and over three hundred stitches holding his face together. They called Wepner the "Bayonne Bleeder" after his New Jersey hometown and his propensity to get his face ripped open. Thickly built, scarred, ungraceful, and thinning in hair, he was a marked contrast to the smooth-skinned beauty and dancing grace of Muhammad Ali. Just as in *Rocky*, the champ would make $1.5 million for the stunt and the challenger would earn $100,000 for taking the beating.[23]

"Here I am going in with a damn legend," explained the thirty-five-year-old Wepner. "You know, most people live dull lives, never get a break, but with one punch I could be a millionaire, and my wife wouldn't have to work on the post office night shift anymore, and my name would mean something for a long, long time." The advertising posters called it "The Chance of a Lifetime." On fight day, Wepner defied all odds and almost went the distance; he was only the sixth person in boxing history to answer the bell for the fifteenth round with Ali. Wepner was also one of the very few to have ever knocked the champion down (although many others say Ali simply tripped over Wepner's feet). But it was a grueling marathon—"more a transfusion than a boxing match." Ali mugged, teased, taunted, and ridiculed Wepner throughout the fight, while the challenger clumsily lunged his powerful fists at the champ. His sweaty strings of thinning hair bouncing from his bleeding head with each punch, Wepner took Ali's merciless punishment into the fifteenth round. In the final nineteen seconds of the final round, Ali finally managed a knockout, bringing the horrific contest to a close. When they dragged the Bayonne Bleeder semi-conscious to his corner, Ali came over to congratulate him for almost going the distance. "None of my fights was tougher than this one," Ali later said. Making it to the fifteenth round was a moral victory, commentators seemed to agree, for what everyone called "the ordinary guy."[24]

The cinemagraphic quality of the fight was obvious to many watching it—especially a young and hungry actor named Sylvester Stallone. He watched the fight intently in a theater with closed circuit television, amazed at the support the embattled Wepner received from the screaming crowd. Stallone rushed home afterward and, in a four-day writing frenzy fueled by caffeine pills, created one of the most popular and metaphorical films of the decade. Stallone took Wepner's second tier, outsider status and amplified it to create the doe-eyed Rocky Balboa as a loser with a heart, out to prove, if he could, that he was not "just another bum from the neighborhood." In the inverted cultural world of the seventies, boxing was not a vehicle to explore corruption and oppression—its typical role in American social problem film—but a setting for hope and possibility. Like Wepner, Stallone's title character did not have to win but merely prove that a white working-class hero could go the distance with a black superstar.

The studios were anxious to buy Stallone's script, but the author punched back with his own underdog's gamble: he refused to sell it unless he got to play the lead. Completely broke and with very few acting credits to his name, Stallone's prospects to play the lead were as much of a long shot as Wepner's with Ali. With a mere $106 in the bank, Stallone refused everescalating offers from the studio that reached $150,000. As Stallone recalled telling his wife, "If you don't mind going out in the backyard and eating grass, I'd rather burn this script than sell it to another actor." The studio eventually caved and let Stallone have the part, but, in the process, sliced the budget for the film down to bare bones.[25]

In *Rocky*, the heavyweight champion of the world, Apollo Creed (Carl Weathers), loses his planned-for opponent due to an injury and decides to turn the stroke of bad luck into a spectacle of good fortune. By plucking the second-rate "Italian Stallion" out of a book of club fighters, Creed hopes to revive (manipulate) the American dream for the bicentennial year. "I'm sentimental," explains Apollo Creed, a thinly veiled Muhammad Ali figure. "A lot of other people in this country are sentimental and would like nothing more than to see Apollo Creed give a boy from Philadelphia a chance at the biggest title in the world on this country's biggest birthday." Apollo likes Rocky's Italian ancestry, since Columbus discovered America. "What would be better than getting it on with on with one of his descendents?" As a tale about a dead-end Italian street fighter who manages to go fifteen rounds with an arrogant, commercially manipulative, and beautiful black super hero, the film easily lent itself to white ethnics who wanted a crack at redemption after feeling themselves to have been sacrificed to the cause of racial justice.

Rocky was a racially charged film, but it appeared to be less about racial redemption than hope, while really being about the intersection of the two. A brilliantly assembled hodgepodge of cinematic clichés, *Rocky* is often compared with Frank Capra's movies about the triumphs of the little man (and Capra liked *Rocky*), yet Capra's characters battled greedy businessmen and corrupt politicians, not black men. Like the politics of the late seventies, the film combines white blue-collar renewal with what borders on revenge against the success and power of black people. Rocky's patriotic mission becomes all the more clear at the beginning of the fight when Apollo shows up dressed as George Washington and Yankee Doodle Dandy, while the Italian hero can merely mutter and watch. African-Americans, it would seem, own Americana. Rocky is an inversion of the black ghetto superstars like *Shaft* (1971) and *Superfly* (1972), whose fantastic powers of masculinity allowed them to take on all challengers. With Rocky's quiet blue-collar attitude, however, he is determined to get the job done without fanfare and despite all odds.[26]

The film's director was John Avildsen, who also directed the clunky backlash film *Joe*. The warm-hearted Rocky lacks the meanness of Joe; that role is left for the often overlooked supporting role of the grim and violent Paulie, the brother of Rocky's love interest, the painfully timid Adrian. Again, like *Saturday Night Fever*, the audience is presented with a choice between the future heroics of a star or the psychological burdens of the past. As Stallone explained, he wrote Paulie to serve as "a symbol of the blue collar disenfranchised, left-out mentality, a man who feels life has given him an unfair amount of cheap shots." Both Tony Manero and Rocky Balboa have the opportunity to escape, and Paulie is, in many ways, like the same characters Tony left behind. As Stallone said, "when they're cheering for Rocky, they're cheering for themselves." Rocky, as another critic put it, is "for but not really of the working class. . . . He gives substance to our escapism."[27]

Stallone continued his working-class studies with a biopic about the Teamsters' leader Jimmy Hoffa called *F.I.S.T.* (Federation of Inter-State Truckers). The film begins with the noble origins of the truckers' union on the docks where it has to battle the arrogance of management—"That damned Roosevelt; what this country needs is Douglas MacArthur," says the boss as his workers assert their power to strike. Although the subject choice—one of the most notoriously corrupt labor leaders of the century— might imply a certain anti-labor bias, the film is actually a sympathetic treatment of the origins of organized labor in the 1930s and a compassionate and even endearing portrait of working-class life. Stallone, as the fictional-ized Hoffa character Johnny Kovak, is a rare figure in American cinema: a valiant, militant, sharp, and much needed voice for working people. Even the Faustian pact he stumbles into with the mob seems a reasonable turn given the power of management. The *mise-en-scène* appears to have been taken straight out of a piece of thirties agitprop, with an overdose of smokestacks, folk songs, picket lines, rich social life, and girls serving up soup, coffee, and sandwiches to the deserving strikers.

The overarching theme of the film, however, is that worker militancy is a thing of the past, and organized labor—however necessary it may have been at one time—achieved its success illegitimately. In *F.I.S.T.*, explains histo-rian John Bodnar, "The entire union movement is held up to ridicule for betraying the noble goals of the Depression decade." In the second half of the film, Kovak moves to the plush union headquarters in Washington, DC, and he and his union sink deeper into the mob and pursuit of power for its own sake. Material concerns trump all others. At national negotiations, Ko-vak wants an 8 percent wage increase when the cost of living is only 5 percent. He gets his 8 percent but only with a no-strike pledge and the agreement to end all wildcats—the rank and file's main source of power—in forty-eight hours. Throughout the film, another character, Abe, serves as Johnny's con-science. He stays connected to the rank and file and remains very suspicious of Johnny's new world. Toward the end, in a nod to the seventies insurgen-cies, Abe calls his West Coast local out on a wildcat in violation of Kovak's national contract. The union sends in the thugs to rough them up. By the end, the union has Abe, the last democratic voice, killed. Whatever death labor experiences after this film—by subpoena, legislative act, or business offensive—seems reasonable and justified. Militancy may have once been a beautiful thing but not any more.[28]

III

After Arthur Bremer shot George Wallace in a shopping mall parking lot, investigators found his journal, published the next year as *An Assassin's Diary* (1973). Bremer, the son of a truck driver who had most recently worked as a janitor and busboy, filled his journal with the rage of the lonely. "ALL MY EFFORTS & NOTHING CHANGED. Just another god Damn failure," he wrote in his diary. He longed "to do SOMETHING BOLD AND

DRAMATIC, FORCEFULL & DYNAMIC, A STATEMENT of my manhood for the world to see." That something was to shoot either Nixon or Wallace for the fame it would deliver. He speculated that his excuses when caught would be "'I don't know,' or 'Nothing else to do,' or 'Why not?' or 'I have to kill somebody.'" Bremer's story became the inspiration for the bicentennial year's neo-noir anti-hero character, Travis Bickle (Robert De-Niro), in one of the decade's most iconic films, *Taxi Driver* (1976).[29]

The film centers almost exclusively on Travis's occupational life as a cabbie who plies his trade through the New York City at its socio-economic nadir, the metropolis teetering on bankruptcy and engulfed in crime. Travis, a feverish combination of cowboy, terrorist, soldier, and street warrior, is the common man traveling through a world of filth and injustice. He wanders through a tortured existential crisis before performing his own gory spectacle of violence. "Loneliness has followed me my whole life, everywhere. In bars, in cars, sidewalks, stores, everywhere. There's no escape. I'm God's lonely man." He despises the world he inhabits—the "whores, skunk pussies, buggers, queens, fairies, dopers, junkies, sick, venal. Someday a real rain will come and wash all this scum off the streets," he grunts. Bickle looks for a way to assert his masculinity over the degradation, and—armed with rage and guns and loneliness—he sets out to purge New York of its filth. "Listen you fuckers, you screwheads. Here is a man who would not take it anymore," he exclaims. "A man who stood up against the scum, the cunts, the dogs, the filth, the shit, Here is someone who stood up." In this film, the only thing more frightening than the social degradation Bickle rails against is Travis Bickle himself.

At first Bickle seems to be trying on everyone else's identity, searching for belonging, then finally succumbing to his fantasy of power and bloodthirsty redemption. His is a world of overblown realism without the social. We live the film and travel the streets through Travis' eyes; it is wholly his world detached from all other points of social reference, and we have no idea what made him the creature that he is beyond vague suggestions of his experience in Vietnam. He is the opposite of those other famous cabbies from American letters in Clifford Odets' *Waiting for Lefty*. Odet's taxi drivers, "the storm birds of the working class" as one character puts it, were struggling toward a collective identity that would deliver them to a strike—if not socialism. Travis, in contrast, is suspicious of all institutions and stifled by his alienation; he is driven by an impossible longing, as he tells us, to "become a person like other people." As Barbara Mortimer suggests, "what *Taxi Driver* documents is not only the desire of people today to create 'authentic selves,' but the impossibility of doing so."[30]

The lonely, alienated tones of seventies films like *Taxi Driver* might be related to the production process brought about by the much-honored individualism of the auteur cinema movement. Rejecting the studio production process as too stiff and stultifying to the creative process, the great young directors of the seventies, like Martin Scorsese, Robert Altman, Francis Ford Coppola, and Stanley Kubrick, were given free hand to make their own adventurous cinematic statements unfettered by the constraints of the old Hollywood. "Although the collapse of the studios has allowed filmmakers to confront cultural and aesthetic problems in ways that would not have been possible under the determining control of the old Hollywood," writes Robert Phillip Kolker, "they have had to undertake their confrontations alone—not only without secure financial support, but without creative support, without a community among which ideas and concerns might be shared. In the true spirit of American individualism they work in a creative vacuum." Without all of the old craftsmen, who shared the experience of making many films together and played central roles in the creative process, the occupational culture of the filmmakers affected the end product. The new artistic freedom was the freedom to be alone. "The power is with the people now," George Lucas argued with unintended irony and ideological confusion. "The workers have the means of production."[31]

In addition to *Assassin's Diary*, Scorsese's inspiration for *Taxi Driver* was John Ford's classic Western *The Searchers* (1956) in which the cowboy-soldier-hero cannot enter the community, condemned to wander unconnected; and part of screenwriter Paul Schrader's inspiration was Sartre's *Nausea*, which he called the "model" for the film. Like Bremer, Schrader, too, was lost in social isolation, and the diary must have spoken to him (and the film would go on to inspire yet another psychotic shooting, that of John Hinckley's attempt on Ronald Reagan). Schrader, once the darling of New Left film circles, had drifted into the worst aspects of failed idealism that the decade had to offer—all of which he freely projected directly onto his proletarian anti-hero: "I was very enamored of guns," he recalled, "I was very suicidal, I was drinking heavily, I was obsessed with pornography in the way a lonely person is, and all those elements are upfront in the script." Schrader was also obsessed with film noir—having written one of the most highly regarded essays on the subject—and Bickle was meant to be "the last noir man in the ultimate noir world: closed and dark, a paranoid universe of perversion, obsession, and violence."[32]

As much as America celebrated *Rocky*, *Taxi Driver* is about the Paulies of the world. Politically, the film captures the inversion of the blue-collar themes of an earlier era, as Schrader explains, since Travis "takes out his anger on the guy below him rather than the guy above." The film's rejection of class as either a political or an economic category makes Travis a strange new antihero in a strange new cultural class war.[33]

The alternative, political outlets for Travis' concerns were empty at best and cynical at worst. He pursues a beautiful campaign worker (Cybill Sheperd) who works for a presidential candidate named Palantine, a McGovern-like figure but of the worst, most plastic, sort. His campaign slogan, "We are the people" appears frequently throughout the film, but it is the opposite of what his campaign really is. As Palantine condescendingly proclaims in one speech, "The people are rising to the demands I am making on them!" "We the people suffer," he declares, "from Vietnam, inflation, crime, corruption." In reality, "the people," if they exist at all, suffer from Palantine. The chasm between occupational life and politics cannot be crossed. When Palantine gets into Bickle's cab, they talk right past each other. Even his fellow cabbie, The Wizard (Peter Boyle again), unlike Odets' cabbies, only talks in circular nonsense.

Given this lineage of alienation, it is not surprising that Travis Bickle is simultaneously sympathetic and pathological, endearing and murderous. By the time viewers warm to Travis, it is too late—he has hatched his angel-of-death plans. Unlike his inverse, the true proletarian hero, he is not of the people but against them; his line of vision is always filled with unredeemable prostitutes, junkies, and criminals. Unable to win the woman he knows he cannot have, he turns to saving the girl he does not want. By the end of the film, he is the twisted working-class vet turned vigilante, attempting to purge society of its filth as a way to redeem his own failure to be a part of society. Rather than the classic Capraesque Hollywood theme of a pure commoner in battle with a corrupt world, here is the working-class hero out to make the world that much more sordid. The "final phase" of noir, writes Schrader, "was the period of psychotic addiction and suicidal impulse" caused by "the loss of public honor, heroic conventions, personal integrity, and finally, psychic stability." As much as film noir is about, as George Lipsitz writes, the "presumption that society will blame and punish the hero for acts he never committed," *Taxi Driver* turns the genre on its head. In the end, Travis is made into a hero for the bloody acts of misguided vigilantism that he did do. Ironically, as Bremer explained to the judge after sentencing for his attempt on Wallace, the assassin actually longed for the social cohesions and constraints of civil society. "Looking back on my life," he told the judge, "I would have liked it if society had protected me from myself."[34]

IV

"Then one day I came across the Lordstown, Ohio, strike, the Chevy Vega plant," screenwriter Paul Schrader reported after the success of *Taxi Driver*. "All the autoworkers were under twenty-five, they were not interested in what the union had done for dad and grandpa. What it had done for them was nothing," he recalled in a somewhat vengeful reading of the strike. "Yes, we hate management, but you know who we hate worse? Our union. It betrays us," Schrader concluded with a projection of his own post-sixties anti-institutional sentiments. Schrader's success as a screenwriter for *Taxi Driver* gave him the Hollywood credibility to make his first movie, and Lordstown gave him his topic. The result was the controversial *Blue Collar* (1978), featuring three autoworkers, Jerry (Harvey Keitel), Smokey (Yaphet Kotto), and Zeke (Richard Pryor in a rare dramatic role), who try to buck the system.[35]

The original Lordstown dispute contained all the variables of the new labor politics: youth, inter-racial solidarity, and protest against the quality of production rather than the quantity of compensation. In the hands of filmmaker Paul Schrader, the event was reinterpreted from one of hope and agency to one of the bleakest meditations on blue-collar America ever made. Schrader's contemptuous manipulation of working-class reality is typical of many of Hollywood's professional middle-class productions, but the film's twisting cinematic daggers also spoke to some larger truths. Despite Schrader's re-interpretation of seventies labor history, the film is beautifully crafted in a classic social-realist style. Like many seventies artists, Schrader looked to the old imagery and narratives of workers from the thirties and forties to provide the tools, tropes, style, and comparative backdrops for the new seventies worker albeit for different purposes.

Like most seventies films dealing with working-class themes, the sense of psychological violence and claustrophobia are quickly established with char-

acters literally squeezed into the scenes. There are also occasional borrow-
ings of some of the anger and language from the 1960s. Particularly obvious
is the influence of the League of Revolutionary Black Workers' documentary film *Finally Got the News* (1970)—including Richard Pryor calling the
plant, the "plantation." Part of the source of the claustrophobia of the film
came from Schrader's autobiography. "Even though I was a middle-class
kid," Schrader explained, "the fact that we lived in a poor part of town gave
me the sense that rich people aren't going to give you anything, you're gonna
have to take it. That Animals song, 'We've Gotta Get Out of This Place,'
was a real strong song for me, and a real strong feeling for me."[36]

The imagery may be social-realist and the energy of the sixties, but the
plot shows the influence of a post–New Left intellectual that has given up on
the working class. The movie revolves around the disintegration of a once
very solid inter-racial camaraderie among three autoworkers—two black and
one white—as a sort of New Deal coalition on the shop floor. *Blue Collar*
begins commandingly with an overhead shot of the auto plant that directly
quotes the opening scene of Sergei Eisenstein's immortal film *Strike* (1925)
and features a Muddy Waters/Bo Diddley blues song blaring over the din of
the assembly work (juiced up in volume, lyrics, and profanity by Captain
Beefheart sounding like a psychedelic Howlin' Wolf). The story turns on
the three workers who are alienated from their work beyond measure, pun-
ished by inflation, and floundering for solutions. As *Cineaste* explained, "The
three heroes of the movie are the kind of workers who abound in cities like
Detroit. They have an ingenuous American moral sincerity, a camaraderie
that transcends personal racism, drive that defies resignation, and refusal to
be suckered. They have only the common illusions about their place in capitalist society: that one person or a bunch of buddies can beat the system.
They are the kind of people who need and are ready for political consciousness, who sustain our belief in an impending class struggle."[37]

At first they do seem like perfect seventies workers. They defend their
union, they despise their foreman, and they support each other; but Schrader
quickly shifts the plot to cynicism and betrayal as the workers turn to rob-
bing their union to solve their problems. Schrader envisioned the film as one
about workers "who commit metaphorical suicide by stealing from the union,
the organization which is supposed to protect him." The three men rob the
union, finding only $600 in the safe, but then realize they have something
even more valuable: the ledger of the union's loan sharking activities. The
workers try to blackmail the union, the union tries to rip off the insurance

company, and the company gets off with nary a scratch. Schrader believed that the film was an exploration of the "self-destructiveness" of workers who "attack the organization that was supposed to defend them. And how that kind of dead-end mentality is fostered and engendered by the ruling class in order to keep the working class at odds with itself."[38]

While that plot line is considerably far from any form of 1970s reality other than, maybe, the democratization movements in unions like the United Mine Workers or the Teamsters, the political sensibility of the film does capture the decade well. "Its politics are the politics of resentment and claustrophobia, the feeling of being manipulated and not in control of your life," Schrader explained. The otherwise depressing sets are laden with symbols of past struggles that haunt the present moment (resulting in the same nostalgic affect as *F.I.S.T.*)—as photos of Martin Luther King, John F. Kennedy, the sit down strikes, and UAW president Walter Reuther drift throughout the picture. Those are images of a once mighty past; in the film, the 1970s class war is against the union, not the company or even, potentially, both the company and the union. Even the scene in which Zeke is seduced by the union into selling out takes place on an overpass, reminiscent of the infamous 1937 "Battle of the Overpass" when Walter Reuther and three UAW organizers were assaulted by Ford Motor Company goons while the press looked on. Rather than the place union organizers fought off company goons this overpass is where Zeke sold his soul to union corruption.

Blue Collar delivers a working-class stripped of agency other than the ability to destroy itself. There are no avenues to liberation possible here, merely a crushing sense of hopelessness. By the end, all hope for inter-racial solidarity that opened the film is destroyed. The union has the street-wise militant Smokey murdered in a gruesome scene of suffocation in the paint room, killed by a collusion of the union and workplace technology. Zeke ends up selling out to the union bosses who have sold out long ago when he accepts their offer to become shop steward. And Jerry, now "thinking white," as Zeke tries to explain to him, ends up turning to the FBI out of fear for his life. With black militancy dead, reformism co-opted, and the white working-class siding with state authority, the cohesion that once animated these workers has turned into racial hatred. In a review of the film called "On the Auto Front," the *New York Times* critic—like so many others—compared the film to Elia Kazan's classic *On the Waterfront*. "The emphasis on inevitability, which is one step away from complete passivity, may be the essential difference between a certain kind of pop culture today and that of the mid-

50's when Elia Kazan made his furious, idealized film about crooked locals on NY piers."[39]

In the final scene of *Blue Collar*, former friends Jerry and Zeke, having called each other every racial slur in their imaginations, pick up tools and go after each other in open conflict. Solidarity is destroyed, and the one-time glue of class has become the solvent of race. The movie ends in a freeze frame of white worker against black worker. Smokey's prophetic lesson for his co-workers, imparted to his comrades earlier in the film, returns in an overdub from the grave: "They pit the lifer against the new boy, the young against the old, the black against the white. Everything they do is to keep us in our place," he explained in what Schrader called the *Waiting for Lefty* moment. In a complete inversion of 1930s proletarian drama, however, the working class is in the midst of meltdown, not unification. Without a hint of irony, Schrader called the violent freeze frame of workers assaulting workers a "classic social-realist poster" that "should be in a post office somewhere."[40]

The ending of the film could not be further from the dignity of a Works Progress Administration (WPA) mural. Schrader may have derived his working class from real life and captured its tone with perfect pitch, but his use of social realism was so refracted through New-Left cultural resentments as to be unrecognizable. The specifics of the film do not connect with reality, and the anger of the film as well as its anti-unionism are palpable. Yet if we accept *Blue Collar* as more allegorical than literal, the confusion of identity, the questions of agency, and the dissolution of the limited racial solidarity make it one of the more successful explorations of working-class identity of the decade.

V

Like Paul Schrader, one of Bruce Springsteen's anthems was The Animals' hit "We Gotta Get Out of This Place." After the success of *Born to Run* (1975), a rock 'n' roll fantasy of escape, Springsteen turned to those trapped in the reality of home. In crafting his next album, he turned to observations of friends and family "living the lives of my parents in a certain way," in the types of "everyday kind of heroism" necessary "to lead decent, productive lives." If *Saturday Night Fever* was about "the chosen ones" who could escape, Springsteen's late seventies characters are the opposite. Here was a study of those left in what he dismissed as a "town full of losers" in *Born to Run*'s

"Thunder Road." Trapped somewhere between the political potential of *Grapes of Wrath* and the underground estrangement of film noir, they live in a world in which expressions of inequality have not disappeared—merely been pushed inward, smoldering in characters who lack any means of expression for their position. The cars are still there and so are the girls of the emancipatory *Born to Run*, but his end-of-the-decade recordings are drained of optimism and hope, driving through the *Darkness on the Edge of Town* (1978).[41]

Springsteen explicitly placed his claustrophobic blue-collar world in a creative tension with the sources of his own performative optimism: sixties pop—especially soul. Although this last of the great working-class heroes is typically seen as a descendent of blue-collar troubadours like Walt Whitman, Woody Guthrie, and Bob Dylan, the more appropriate—or at least coequal—lineage would be Sam Cooke, Smokey Robinson, and James Brown, artists who adapted gospel traditions—sometimes scandalously—for secular pop. "It seemed like in those songs by The Drifters and Smokey Robinson, there was a promise, and it was just the promise of a right to a decent life," he recalled about his youth spent glued to top-forty radio. "That you didn't have to live and die like my old man did, working in a factory until he couldn't hear what you were saying anymore." Musicians like Springsteen who are connected to the gospel impulse bear witness to the shared struggles and despairs and burdens of secular life but call audiences upward toward a better day. The feelings of redemption, communal belonging, and suffering open up what Joel Dinerstein calls the sacred/secular crossroads, holding out the promise of a new day. His epic performances sought to conquer the alienation evident in his own lyrics, with shows that were what he called "part political rally, part dance party, and part religious revival."[42]

In the confined, airless lyrical domain of *Darkness on the Edge of Town*, however, the stories are not of emancipation or redemption as much as they are digging in to survive the long haul of working-class adulthood. Springsteen himself had escaped his working-class roots via the power of rock 'n' roll and his performances urged others to do the same, but, shaken by fame and the corruption of the record machine, he returned to the setting of those he grew up with who were now charged less with rebellion than with resignation. An album "suffused with class consciousness," according to his biographer, the characters of *Darkness* face making their peace with their entrapment in a place, according to the title track, "Where no one asks any questions / Or looks too long in your face." He was one of the few artists to explore the "trouble in the heartland" of those people who did not get out, who were not Manero (or Springsteen). As Dave Marsh explains, "for all the cars, the violence and the search, the dominant image of *Darkness on the Edge of Town* is labor."[43]

In writing *Darkness*, the Jersey rocker used the social-realist themes of an earlier generation and the expressive modes of the hopeful spirit of the sixties in order to study the shrinking sense of opportunity that defined working-class life in the seventies. Musing about influences on the album, Springsteen pointed to "early pop class consciousness" of some of the British invasion bands, as well as the car songs of both Chuck Berry and the Beach Boys. "I wanted my street racers to carry the years between the car songs of the 60s and 1978 America." While pop car songs were fun, they did not explain the world he grew up in: "the stress and tension of my father's and mother's life that came with the difficulties of trying to make ends meet." To explain those lives, he turned to earlier constructions of working-class characters. While making *Darkness*, he explained, "I discovered Hank Williams. I'd seen John Ford's the *Grapes of Wrath* for the first time. Film Noir." "I was searching for a tone somewhere between *Born to Run*'s spiritual hopefulness and 70s cynicism," Springsteen explained. "I wanted my new characters to feel weathered, older, but not beaten. The sense of daily struggle in each song greatly increased. The possibility of transcendence or any sort of personal redemption felt a lot harder to come by. I intentionally steered away from any hint of escapism and set my characters down in the middle of a community under siege."[44]

The songs on *Darkness* are about surviving, of not surrendering; it is all a struggle with neither defeat nor victory. "You can just tell some of these guys are looking for trouble. But they're not looking to punch anybody out. They want to *be* punched." The album is infused with themes of work and futility. Six of the ten cuts mention labor, and almost all the rest deal with wealth inequality in some capacity. These are working people without control, hungry for something that they cannot stop chasing but with little hope of deliverance beyond survival. "Something in the Night" breathes the stale, claustrophobic air of working-class seventies in deeply, exhaling little more than futility. "You're born with nothing," the character wails, "and better off that way / Soon as you've got something they send someone to try and take it away."[45]

"Racing in the Street," one of the artist's favorites and a cult hit among fans, begins with a particular image: a '69 Chevy parked outside of a 7–11 store. One could envision Dewey Burton at the wheel. The automobile is stationary, but we feel its rumbling power ready to screech out of the most generic of postwar consumer landscapes. Simply reading the lyrics of "Racing" would lead one to presume that the song is another anthem, but it is, in fact, a melancholy lament that, like another cut, "Factory," approaches a funeral dirge in cadence and tone. It consciously upends the bragging of the Beach Boys' "Little Deuce Coupe" or the pursuit of the girl in Chuck Berry's "Maybelline." It is, in essence, a meditation on survival:

> *Some guys they just give up living*
> *And start dying little by little, piece by piece*
> *Some guys come home from work and wash up*
> *And go racin' in the street*

Here the open road appears to be the salvation but only in the most limited terms: it offers not freedom but a momentary piece of ownership of one's own life. Street racing is merely an escape from the dreary existential suicide of the work-a-day world.[46]

The meaning of the plodding lyricism of "Racing in the Street" can only be gleaned from juxtaposing it to its creative opposition: Martha and the Vandellas' Motown party anthem "Dancing in the Street." While the sound of the two songs could not be more different—one a public celebration and the other a private struggle to stay alive—Springsteen's paraphrasing of the Motown hit is overt: "Summer's here and the time is right, for racing in the street," and "Calling out around the world, we're going racin' in the street" are obvious quotes. Springsteen was well aware of not just the power of the Motown dance song but also how "Dancing in the Street" took on political significance as a declaration of public presence for African Americans as the civil rights movement moved into the urban North. No longer hidden from the public view, black America sent out "An invitation across the nation / A chance for folks to meet / There'll be laughing, singing, music swinging / Dancing in the street." "Racing in the Street" inverts the Motown message for white working-class men; while "Dancing" is public, social, joyful, and adopted for the political, that of "Racing" is desolate, alone, and somewhere below politics. Like film noir characters, the people of "Racing" are in the grips of a private pain, a closeted agony buffeted only by the love and compassion they are able to muster for each other.[47]

The automobile functions as a metaphor for limits in "Racing" at a point in time in which hopes were deflated and the price of energy was inflated. Tinkering with cars was one of the great postwar refuges for the victims of Fordism and Taylorism—the last place for armchair craftsmen to use their hands against the swelling tide of the "degradation of work." As Dewey Burton readily grasped, car building and modifying was a hobby, a preoccupation to prevent the dire truths of the assembly line from creeping in, a tool to prevent the all-powerful "they" of the shop floor from taking over. No matter how many hot rods were built or modified, however, it could not prevent the inevitable: "But now there's wrinkles around my baby's eyes / And she cries herself to sleep at night" laments Springsteen. "She sits on the porch of her daddy's house / But all her pretty dreams are torn / She stares off alone into the night / With the eyes of one who hates for just being born." The song ends with the narrator driving off toward the sea with his aging "girl" to "wash these sins off our hands." The sense of pain and isolation remains inescapable. As Jim Curtis argues, the holy trinity of Girl, Car, and Night are broken. If "Dancing in the Street" made African-Americans visible, "Racing in the Street" portrayed the white working class in a desperate and dark silence—perhaps even a new invisible man.[48]

Yet Springsteen is about nothing if not faith. In the title track to *Darkness on the Edge of Town*, his main character is alone on the hill, struggling against all odds. As opposed to the plodding pace of "Racing," "Darkness" is delivered with all of the faith and power that is rock 'n' roll. In performance, the individual pain becomes collective triumph as the fans respond to the promise of a soul-based deliverance from the darkness. His character is alone, on a hill, determined to struggle forward. Forward toward what—other than simple survival—is unknown:

Tonight I'll be on that hill 'cause I can't stop
I'll be on that hill with everything I got
Lives on the line where dreams are found and lost
I'll be there on time and I'll pay the cost
For wanting things that can only be found
In the darkness on the edge of town

He is invisible in the night, searching for what comes with great sacrifice but appears to promise little in the way of payoff. This working-class hero is a perpetual motion machine of struggle, pushing toward what may be a fruitless hope.

The core theme that spans much of Springsteen's working-class studies is the disconnection—real and feared—of working people from the things that ground them: job, family, home, and community. "I live now only with strangers," he sings in "Streets of Fire," "I talk to only strangers / I walk with angels that have no place." As Springsteen explained, "I think what happened during the seventies was that, first of all, the hustle became legitimized"— and he did not mean the disco dance. By the time of his follow up *The River* (1980), when his character receives his "union card and a wedding coat" for his nineteenth birthday, that union card was a symbol of a failure to get out, a source of entrapment. What was a source of material liberation in the 1930s, membership in a trade union, had become a symbol of those *not* chosen, those left behind.[49]

VI

Just before the complete economic collapse of Akron's faltering rubber tire industry, the improbably vibrant music scene of eastern Ohio coughed up a phenomenon that was part rock band, part postindustrial ideology, part sci-fi kitsch, and part media art known as Devo. Springsteen may be the most iconic—and arguably, romantic—artist to examine working-class communities under siege in the 1970s, but he was known to show up in the late seventies to witness Devo's stone-cold vivisection of American culture. The band neither criticized nor shied away from the socio-economic failures they saw around them; instead, explicitly rejecting the neo-realism of a Springsteen, Devo embraced the decline, marching fearlessly into the oblivion of repetition, commodification, and vacant fun. The band was named after the process of "de-evolution" in which humankind, descended from brain-eating apes, was claimed to be regressing toward some backward state. Devo neither praised the glory days nor held out hope for what was about to unfold; for the band, there was little salvageable from the past, little romance in the present, and even less in the offerings of the future. "Of all the bands who came from the underground and made it in the mainstream," declared Kurt Cobain later, "Devo were the most challenging and subversive of all." That subversion had little to do with working-class solidarity or an assault on capitalism.[50]

Devo emerged at the time when rock 'n' roll was something akin to the aural wallpaper of American life, and they challenged stadium "cock rock" by performing as tweaky, demasculinized oddballs. Acting like spasmodic—if synchronized—short-circuited mutants in industrial jumpsuits and 3-D industrial safety goggles, the members of Devo presented "a deliberately opaque vision of mass braindeath" with an infectious pop drive. As pioneers in the music video genre, they made their music into a visual artistic experience, and their performances exhibited unnervingly high levels of control and discipline. Their Dadaesque anti-agitprop, as front man Mark Mothersbaugh put it, was a sort of "guerrilla behavioralist experiment," and the band's music, as they repeatedly said, was "the important sound of things falling apart."[51]

The pop eggheads' first video performance, *In the Beginning Was the End: The Truth About De-evolution*, which won a prize at the 1976 Ann Arbor film festival, contained two separate songs: their cover of "Secret Agent Man" and their breakthrough, "Jocko Homo." The video begins with band members as bored and indifferent factory workers doing their repetitive labors while waiting for quitting time. Realizing the hour has finally arrived, they hop into their beat-up car, leaving the rusting hulk of a factory behind them. Still wearing their blue workmen's suits and eerie clear face masks (except for Mothersbaugh, who appears in the creepy man-child Booji Boy mask that will become a Devo staple), they head to a broken down club to play "Secret Agent Man." The song is an oddly brilliant choice, retooling the sixties pop narrative as radical critique: "They've given me a number / But they've taken away my name / I've got one hell of a job to perform for the U.S. of A." The original song of adventure and dedication to the security state becomes, in their hands, a trenchant critique of American identity and fantasy. "Every night and day / I salute the flag and say / Thank you Jesus / Cause I'm a secret agent man." The performance of the song is interspersed with a panoply of wild visuals—two men in monkey masks spanking a waitress with Nixon and Mao ping pong paddles, a clichéd rock star playing a double-neck guitar, Booji Boy disco dancing with a waitress, an ape eating a popsicle.

The "Jocko Homo" half of the film starts as Booji Boy urgently runs through an Akron parking lot and up the fire escape in front of a massive mural proclaiming "Shine on America." Once in the office, he meets General Boy and gives him the news. "In the past this information has been suppressed," explains the General, "but now it can be told. Every man, woman, and mutant on this planet shall know the truth about de-evolution." Named after an obscure anti-evolutionary pamphlet from the twenties, *Jocko-Homo Heavenbound* (1924) by B.H. Shadduck, the song turns to a mad scientist—Mothersbaugh again—lecturing at Kent State with the medical classroom bordering on a riot. The professor asks "Are we not men?" with exclamations of "We are Devo!" ricocheting in a call and response ritual as far removed from its origins in the black church as one might get.

"Are we not men?" a question focused more on evolution than masculinity, informs all of Devo's creative works. The question came from the 1933 sci-fi horror film *Island of the Lost Souls* (adapted from H.G. Wells' *The Island of Dr. Moreau*) where scientific experiments to turn animals into humans on a remote island go terribly awry. There the doctor creates horrific man-beasts, and one of them, played by Bela Lugosi, asks, "Are we not men?" The mutant creatures eventually storm the doctor's compound and perform a savage bloodbath of revenge.

For Devo, the working class people of Akron were much like the evolutionary disasters of the *Island of the Lost Souls*. "Those mutants were fucked with," the band explained. "They looked like people from Akron." The industrial landscape for the twin videos of *In the Beginning was the End* "worked as an art-directed backdrop for this kind of music we were making," band member Jerry Casale said about the dying rubber town where the glory days of economic success meant sweeping up the black tire soot from workers' front porches. It "had this hellish, depressing patina. . . . and the people in Akron seemed—their spirits were depressed; they were desperate; their kids were kind of like the characters in the *Island of Lost Souls* that rebelled in the pit. In other words, they were just ready to go over the edge at any moment. They were so beaten down that they were gonna freak out. And it fit in with the early-20th century art movements—Expressionism, Dada and others that were influenced by those kinds of environments in Germany and England. We had our very own backyard version of it. A rubber version."[52]

Not so ironically, the terrain that fostered Devo's surrender of agency was the same place that the American working-class hero had originally come of age. Akron was the genesis point for the dramatic sit downs, the mass pickets in sub-zero temperatures, and the guerrilla warfare against the rubber tire magnates in the 1930s that made the tire builders "the first to fight their way to freedom," in the words of one chronicler. Their struggle blazed the path for the rest of industrial America to join the great leap forward in working-class organizing in the thirties—the coming of the CIO. As one of the key flashpoints in labor history, the workers opened up a new world of opportunity, and the city in turn pried opened the hope of unionization for the rest of the nation's industrial workers. Using words like pride, class, skill, and freedom, which Devo would later only be able to use with irony, Ruth McKenney romantically extolled the meaning of the rubber workers' victory in Akron in the 1930s:

> The CIO was first a bulwark for the working people of Akron and, after them, for the small businessman who was dependent upon their wages; but beyond that, union organization taught the rubberworker pride of class. . . . Mass industry has not crushed the spirit of the free-born. Rubberworkers, no matter how skillfully they work on the conveyor belt, are not robots. A membership card in the [union] is the rubberworker's declaration of freedom. The union is the answer of American workingmen to the impersonal dictatorship of a faraway Board of Directors. . . . the rubberworker has learned how to defend liberty. In his hands, and in the hands of his friends and allies everywhere, lies the future of our country.[53]

Fast forward four decades, and Devo, staring out at the same location before them, stripped their subjects not just of romance but even their humanity, declaring the citizens of Akron (and themselves) to be mere "Spuds." The days of such working-class heroics, and the artistic and political popular front that supported them, had gone the way of the smoldering stench of the prosperous rubber tire industry—and the wages and the jobs that accompanied them—receding into rusting industrial hulks and boarded up downtown windows. A city in which nearly two out of three workers once carried union cards, in an exceptional distribution of class power, had since lost the entire automobile tire industry by the late seventies and was en route to losing the rest of tire production by the early eighties.

The culture that Devo identified was as vacuous as the empty hulking tire factories around them. This one-time postwar success story was based on the two things that Devo went on to mock with absolute irreverence: industrial and consumer cultures. These were the twin pillars of the high modern postwar success story in America, the high tide of American white guy, lunch-bucket labor liberalism that Devo watched in the throes of death. Not to say the promise of industrialism and consumerism did not have their massive hollow spots, but simply that they appeared all the more absurd after the hope had been drained from them. As fellow Akron rocker Chrissie Hynde of the Pretenders put it, when she went back to Akron, "My city was gone / There was no train station / There was no downtown . . . A O, way to go, Ohio."

According to Devo, there was no nobility in the suffering of the people, no working-class agency—just regression to corporate stasis, blue collar fading to colorless grey. As one critic put it, Devo "astutely observed that American consumer society had become enslaved to some falsely idealized sense of the 'good life' that supposedly could be attained through a stringent, mechanized work ethic and the conspicuous consumption of material products and goods." And that was when things were going well. Devo's brilliantly robotic, dehumanized, musical and video landscape is a product of life saturated in a corporate culture. Their hometown was so dominated by the rubber tire industry that a worker could "wake up at a house in Goodyear Heights, settle into a car with Goodyear tires, drive down Goodyear Boulevard to the Goodyear factory, grab a quick haircut at the Goodyear barbershop before clocking in at the Goodyear plant, then drive home later with the Goodyear blimp watching above." "Look we are spuds," explained one of the band members. "We're very average looking, normal gene pool. In Akron, it's the Goodyear Museum and the Soapbox Derby and McDonald's and women in hair rollers beating their kids in supermarkets. We were products of it and used it."[54]

Akron's disillusioned pallor was only part of the equation of origins—the rest belonged to the vibrant arts scene at Kent State University and the tragic shooting of four student protestors there by the Ohio National Guard. "I would not have started the idea of Devo unless [the shootings] had happened," explained Jerry Casale. The shooting "was just the defining moment. Until then I might've left my hair long and been a hippie. When you start to see the real way everything works, and the insidious nature of power, corruption, injustice, brute force, you realize it's just all primate behavior." The local events and national response, explained the band, "showed human beings at their worst. It was real Devo."[55]

The sixty-seven shots unleashed in the infamous thirteen seconds at Kent State University were the bloodiest battle of the early seventies internecine class war: angry and desperate blue-collar students at the modern multiversity, outraged by the escalation of the war into Cambodia, confronted by a terrified National Guard filled with blue-collar kids avoiding the draft, all of which earned the enmity of the "Silent Majority" in Kent and the nation. Polling suggested that a large majority of the nation blamed the protestors for their own deaths; "the only mistake they made was not to shoot all the students and then start in on the faculty" was a popular sentiment. Students compared it to *Easy Rider*—the apocalyptic revenge of the rednecks upon the counterculture. It then spilled into the streets of the financial district of New York in the notorious Hard Hat Riot as the construction workers pursued war protestors upset about the Kent State killings through lower Manhattan. This was followed by a month of pro-Nixon rallies. When Nixon named the head of the New York building trades, who promoted the demonstrations, to the position of secretary of labor, the deal was done. "I'm scared," explained one student. "If this is what the class struggle is all about . . . there's something wrong somewhere." No wonder Devo embraced the politics of the absurd.[56]

Yet Devo played their status politics from both ends. The references to "spuds"—as an epithet for themselves and others—placed them in a category with basic earth-dwelling humanity, but the band, like much of new wave, was fundamentally elitist in many ways. The "simple act of pointing out dullards put them in a position of superiority," explains the band's historian. In Devo's lexicon, "there were Readers, and there were Breeders, and it's safe to assume Devo didn't consider themselves Breeders." The band's performances toyed with "a certain populism," even as they disdaned the populace. The concept of "Real humans" was a moniker of a bygone era and "rebellion" an "outmoded and obsolete" artifact. While simultaneously rejecting rebellion and detesting the way ordinary people lived ("getting fat, getting mellow, getting drugged out, getting married. Getting real Devo") they left themselves a space to be part and parcel of the system they were as much entwined in as critical of. Rather than advancing into the promise of modernity, according to Devo, the nation and its workers were turning into a bunch of idiotic, infantile, backward sliding stooges, and all the band could do was buckle in for the ride.[57]

For Devo, like the social critic Jean Baudrillard, the autonomous position of critique was gone; there was nothing outside of the system—no leverage, no purchase, no vantage point. "We learned something from the hippies that, unfortunately, the punks at the same time didn't learn," explained Mothersbaugh, "and that is that rebellion is obsolete. In a healthy capitalistic world, rebellion is just something else to market." When the band covered the Rolling Stones' "Satisfaction" in a brilliant testament to how white the nation's rock could be, they also delivered one of the finest comments on the moment: a "shriveling, ice-cold absurdity [that] might not define the Seventies as much as jump the gun on the Eighties."[58]

VII

Just above Lordstown on the list of the seventies' most famous labor disputes is the organizing drive at J.P. Stevens. The film that captured the initial hope of these events was the remarkable, Academy Award–winning *Norma Rae* (1979). Sally Field earned an Oscar for her portrayal of the title character, which, for a Hollywood production, was modeled very closely on one of the real protagonists from the 1974 organizing drive: labor activist Crystal Lee Sutton. Like other films of the blue-collar seventies, the realism in *Norma Rae* is particularly real: she did stand on that table and hold a UNION sign over her head, the police did take her to jail, the campaign did overcome the divisiveness of race while still beginning in an all-black church, and she did have the famous heart-to-heart with her children in which she confessed all of her past indiscretions so that they would not be hurt by the town gossiping about her. Most of all, the film does accurately trace Crystal Lee's rising consciousness as both a woman and a labor organizer and does an extraordinary job of showing the difficulties in union organizing. Director Martin Ritt also did a masterful job in capturing the confinement, the noise, and the struggles of southern mill town life.

Norma Rae was thus a distinct oddity in seventies popular culture: an optimistic message about the capacity of working people and one of the very few unabashedly pro-labor movies of the decade. As film critic Stanley Kauffmann put it, "Norma Rae shows that, at least within the frame of limited objectives, heroism is still possible, which means that hope is still possible."[59]

Several issues make *Norma Rae* unique, and the first was director Martin Ritt. While most of the pieces discussed in this book were by filmmakers coming out of the New Left and auteur cultures, Ritt was one of the very few remaining filmmakers coming out of the *Old* Left. His credentials were complete: he was a veteran of both WPA theater and Group Theater, an assistant stage manager on Clifford Odets' *Golden Boy*, and, if not a member of the Communist Party, certainly a fellow traveler and a victim of the Hollywood blacklist. This places him in a completely different political tradition than the other artists and helps to account for his other sympathetic portraits of the working class in the 1970s in *The Molly Maguires* (1970) and *Sounder* (1972). By the 1970s, Martin Ritt was, in essence, an anachronism making wonderfully anachronistic projects. For Ritt, the power of Crystal Lee's story, which first surfaced the *New York Times*, was literally the melding of thirties realism with the new social movements of the seventies—a conscious intervention into the missing dialectical synthesis of the seventies. "When I first heard about the situation in this industry," Ritt wrote, "I could not believe that I was not reading a period piece, and was further excited to find how many women were in the forefront of the struggle for civil and economic rights." No matter how compelling the mill drama was, however, the issues never would have made it to the screen had Fox studios not been flush with cash after the runaway success of *Star Wars*.[60]

In addition to Ritt's exceptionalism, one of the most important aspects of the film is the subtle way that both individualism and feminism subtly trump workerism in the film. Rather than creating a solid foundation for the merging of gender and class, as Ritt had hoped for, this film was backed and marketed as a women's picture. Like all Hollywood productions, the film focused on the rising consciousness of the lead heroine at the expense of the rest of the workers' efforts. Crystal Lee found this so problematic that she came close to suing Martin Ritt and launching a competing narrative of the events in collaboration with the Academy Award–winning documentary filmmaker Barbara Kopple. The narration of individual uplift also became the center of the marketing strategy. There were, for instance, two promotional posters for the film. One was a classic social-realist image with Sally Field's shadowy face behind a large mill, and the other was Sally Field as a liberated woman with up-stretched arms feeling happy and free (a scene that never even happened in the film). The former was almost never used, while the latter was *the* promotional image for the movie. The overdub for the film's trailer sounded like it was straight out of *Saturday Night Fever*: "Norma Rae is a survivor and for the first time in her life she has the chance to become something more—a winner!" In fact, the up-stretched arms image of Sally Field was even used as an advertisement for a new brand of (non-union!) women's clothing: Norma Rae jeans: "The Work n Class jeans and slacks at the Work n Class price." As the historian Robert Brent Toplin sums up, *Norma Rae* was promoted as "a story about a female 'Rocky' and as a film that exuded feminist spirit while not overtly preaching feminism."[61]

Suggestions as to the gender-class problem can also be found in the male lead. In the film, Norma Rae's fictionalized union mentor, Reuben Warsovsky, is a New York intellectual who reads poetry, enjoys opera, and eats Chinese food. Ruben has all of the cultural trappings of the smart-talking but ultimately new sensitive male of the seventies—a sort of upper-West Side Jewish Alan Alda. He is not only prepared to accept a liberated woman, but he is a man who can help in the process of consciousness raising. As one film critic ranted, "Despite its claim to being a serious examination of the working man's situation, Norma Rae is really a post-women's lib love story. A man representing a superior culture (political awareness, good literature) enlightens a downtrodden woman and then graciously refuses to take advantage of her: Cinderella, with a truly liberating ending, he frees her from her chains and from himself as well."[62]

Crystal Lee continues to have deep respect for the real Reuben, a man named Eli Ziskevich, whom she has called "the most intelligent person I've ever met." The real union organizer, however, was a former coal miner who could not have been more different than the hip New Yorker. Criticizing the groovy, sixties-influenced re-invention of his image on film, he recalled, "Sneakers, I didn't wear. I don't happen to own a pair of jeans. I'm pretty conservative in my dress and I've never worn what they call a shoulder bag in my life, and I stay away from people who wear shoulder bags. He [his fictional representation] would have never worked for me because, frankly, I would have fired him." By the 1970s, was it impossible for a man of old-school union sympathies—rather than a man of post-sixties therapeutic self-awareness and literacy—to be able to play a role in Crystal Lee's transformation?[63]

As one of the best and most sympathetic portraits of work and unions in mainstream American cinema made since *Grapes of Wrath*, *Norma Rae* stands as an exception to the rule of the 1970s. As Crystal Lee argued, she may not have seen a nickel from its production, it may not have dealt with the other workers adequately (choosing instead to focus on her as the hero), and it failed to deal with Brown Lung disease, one of the core issues in the mills during the seventies. But, as she explained despite her ambivalence, "It made me laugh and it made me cry. . . . It's the best pro-union movie ever made and for that I'm grateful."[64]

Gender overwhelms class more definitively in the popular pink-collar farce *9 to 5* (1980), which was also based on the real experiences—and revenge fantasies—of women office workers. In this film, three office workers, played by an amazing ensemble cast (Lily Tomlin, Jane Fonda, and Dolly Parton), fantasize about exacting revenge on their chauvinist boss in an often hilarious romp through the demeaning world of patriarchal corporate culture. The boss (Dabney Coleman), as the workers call him, is a "sexist, egotistical, lying, hypocritical bigot." As the three co-workers get very stoned (on a single joint), they fantasize about what style of torturous treatment they would like to inflict upon him as the film fades to some wonderful dream/fantasy sequences. Dolly Parton's character, the victim of endless sexual advances, wants to hog tie him like a Wild West heroine; Jane Fonda dreams of hunting him down like a safari animal; and, in the best of the lot, Lily Tomlin's character poisons him in Snow-White-style animation while little furry woodland creatures look on. Slowly, their fantasies come true throughout the movie, and they have to deal with the consequences. As Violet (Lily Tomlin) says, "I killed the boss. Do you think they're not going to fire me for that?" The end result is a screwball comedy in which the office workers manage to take hold of the corporate reins and remake the office altogether by introducing flex time, day care, and a host of reforms while stashing the idiot boss away in a crazy S&M rig made out of an electric garage door opener.

The idea for the farcical *9 to 5* also came from the struggles of real women office workers. The movie was based on interviews of a group of Cleveland office workers called Working Women. "Jane [Fonda] wanted to know more about what office workers thought about their jobs," recalled organizer Karen Nussbaum, "and so early on, we invited her to come to Cleveland." There, about forty office workers, Fonda, Nussbaum, and a script writer spent a long night discussing women's problems with the boss on the job. "And then," explained Nussbaum, "ultimately, every detail in the movie, with the exception of hanging the boss up by a garage opener system, actually came from these women." The film helped bust open an issue—sexual discrimination and harassment on the job—that was just beginning to get recognition. "You had to fight hard on this issue about whether there was discrimination or not," continued Nussbaum, "and then Jane Fonda makes a movie that mocks discrimination in the workplace and the argument is over, because women have been poised on the edge of their chairs, ready to understand it this way and then this capped it and made it, the behavior of the bosses and the discrimination, the object of ridicule." It switched the debate from whether the problem existed to what to do about it. Nussbaum and Fonda did national tours to support the film and the cause, hitting the local morning talk shows. "It was the best example I've ever seen of popular culture helping to lift organization and movement," concluded Nussbaum.[65]

What is fascinating about *9 to 5* is the degree to which it succeeds wonderfully as a feminist comedy but fails as a film about class—better and female management is all that is needed. In fact, compared with movies like the similar comedic workplace fantasy *The Devil and Miss Jones* (1941) (and its connections to the real-life Woolworth sit-down strikes of 1937) *9 to 5* could have been produced in a modern Human Resources Department. As Michael Rogin explains, *The Devil and Miss Jones* "affirms two new working-class institutions, union organization at work and urban public pleasure. The result is not a traditional carnivalesque but one that generates a new deal." In the hands of Jane Fonda, who piloted *9 to 5* from idea to screen, the film advocates new solutions outside of the New Deal by making the movie about women's rights stripped of any connection to the political economy. "Forget the energy crisis, inflation, recession, job shortages, the disappointing sales of the Chrysler 'K,' urban blight and the price of gold," exclaimed the *New York Times* reviewer; "There's no problem with capitalism that these three liberated Nancy Drews can't solve if they don't have to keep running out to get coffee for their superiors." Indeed, the bad guy here is not capitalism at all, but sexism stripped of its economic setting. Once the sexist pig of a boss is removed from power, and a fine thing that, feminism is allowed to work its magic in the transformation of the workplace. Indeed, enlightened feminism is compatible with the modern workplace where unionism is not. As the *Times* reviewer continues, the film actually inverted the social-realist message for the seventies: *9 to 5* "begins as satire, slips uncertainly into farce . . . and concludes by waving the flag of feminism as earnestly as Russian farmers used to wave the hammer-and-sickle at the end of movies about collective farming."[66]

VIII

"The world promised in the 1950s, a world apparently on the verge of real-ization in 1965, seemed like a cruel joke by 1975," explained rock critic Greil Marcus in his eclectic world history of the underground score of dissent, *Lipstick Traces*. "Panic set in . . . so did the urge to seek revenge." While the punks Marcus celebrated went on rampages of brilliant anger, the broader polity sought their comfort in the overstuffed armchairs of nostalgia.

For years Ford autoworker Dewey and his wife Ilona held annual parties in honor of one of the first popcorn blockbusters of the 1970s, George Lucas's rock 'n' roll nostalgia tour, *American Graffiti* (1973). Although made in the seventies, the film was the inauguration of that decade's love affair with the "Happy Days" of the fifties (though set in 1962, arguably the last year of the "fifties"). As the United States teetered on what Francis Wheen calls the "pungent mélange of apocalyptic dread and conspiratorial fear" of the seventies, Lucas created a mythic, comic book community of youth untainted by parents, war, civil rights, or protest. Cruising on the strip in a hot rod, searching for the blond in the white T-Bird, listening to the Wolfman spin disks, and drag racing was all there was to be concerned about. On the last night of cruising before heading off to college—and on to Vietnam, urban riots, Watergate, and energy crises—the assemblage of characters provide the audience with what they want most: permission to forget.[67]

Lucas's successful exploitation of his audience's longing for safety and predictability made *American Graffiti*'s "effacement of history," as Fredric Jameson argues, the "inaugural film of postmodern nostalgia." The music (fifties rock 'n' roll) and the setting (Modesto, California) serve to convey a mood but not a history, a style disembodied from conflict, a recent past unconnected to the present. Yet not completely so. The James Dean like character, John Milner (Paul Le Mat), visits a foreboding car graveyard strewn with totaled dragsters. "The whole strip is shrinking," he laments. It was an appropriate epitaph for the exact moment that the oil embargo was brewing, bringing an end to a wave of car culture. The symbol of America's strength was becoming the symbol of its decadence.[68]

For Dewey Burton, *American Graffiti* captured "the last time the world was ran right." The combination of design, manufacture, power, influence, speed, pay, glory, purpose, reward, and power all made sense. In the disorganized culture of post-1970s capitalism, fifties auto culture was Dewey Burton's Archimedean point, the position from which all the world might be made sensible. His own custom hot rods function as the material embodiment of that alternative world.

There was one person who, as if captured in a cultural bell jar and protected from the upheavals of history, unified the late postwar blue-collar narrative: one time rock 'n' roll rebel, Elvis Presley. To many he was a gaudy joke by mid decade, but if the majority of white working people got their vote, the real working-class hero of the postwar era would not have been Bruce Springsteen or John Lennon (both of whom were too serious to carry the title) but Elvis. Yet it was not the man who once kicked down the nation's doors of sexual mores and square taste in 1956, who freed the teenage body, and performed the synthesis of the nation's racial dialectics but who, by the time of the 1970s, had become a beacon of safety, whiteness, and postwar affluence. No matter how many top hits he had or B movies Colonel Parker stuck him in, Elvis remained loved as the "sharecropper's son in the big house," that truck driver who made it big. When he arrived to stardom he brought his friends, and he did not donate his wealth away to elusive foundations but showered it freely upon friends and strangers alike, bestowing Cadillacs and expensive jewelry on those who happened to be within eyesight, while building a gaudy personal empire and playground that flew in the face of every kind of taste—except that of the people.[69]

When Elvis died in 1977, he was grossly overweight and with the better part of a pharmacy running through his veins—"bloated by the American ambrosia—peanut butter, Pepsi, pills and success," as *Newsweek* put it. A thousand and one newspapers wondered what happened to the glory days of the "King" who once oozed "sexuality and redneck chic," as the *Philadelphia Inquirer* recalled; "The Elvis Presley of 1956 was a lean, mean, whip-like young man, whose greasy hair, sideburns, white pants, purple shirts and all around low-rent, drugstore-hood appearance set teenage America on fire." Transformed into the "hillbilly Faust" when he sold his soul to the Colonel, he lost his revolutionary powers of cultural transformation just when the nation was beginning to think about the barricades. When he returned to touring in the seventies, he often simply performed Elvis Presley performing Elvis in rudimentary ways, but other times he belted out some of the most transcendent shows of his career. As his gluttony even pushed him from his standing as a Las Vegas spectacle, he began touring the little cities across the nation by mid decade, hitting the types of places that never would have had a visit from the King otherwise, declaring his love for both the people and the establishment all along the way.[70]

Seventies Elvis became a sacrament for those, like the King himself, whose gratitude for postwar success had mutated into a defensive conservatism. The performer who had dissolved the adhesives of American culture, who sexualized performance, mixed the races, and even gave straight male fans what Lester Bangs called an "erection of the heart" had by the seventies become the traditionalist, the patriot, the totem of once great dreams. His many concerts—from the massive 1973 television extravaganza "Aloha from Hawaii" to his last swing through life in places like Lincoln, Rapid City, Montgomery, and Johnson City—served, as Greil Marcus explained, as "a kind of unifying ritual, as if Elvis, through his charisma and commitment, could bind the nation's wounds and heal the divisions that had racked America since the mid-1960s." By the 1970s, Elvis had become a living repository of fifties virtue, a time capsule of values, a specimen preserved throughout the cultural turmoil of the sixties who reemerged, however bloated, gilded, caped, and bell-bottomed, singing the good old stuff to women in beehive hairdos, men who still buzz cut their hair, and rock fans who needed a glimpse of where it all began. His outlandish costumes and garish sets expressed Elvis' unique combination of the southern, the working class, and the evangelical along with a "penchant for excess derived from the 'populuxe' aesthetic of postwar consumer culture."[71]

As one of Elvis' biographers wrote, many working class fans "had lived through dramatic changes during the postwar economic boom, when widespread affluence had lifted countless poor and working-class people into the ranks of the comfortable middle class. In a sense, Elvis's success epitomized their own. . . . The distance many had traveled from their often humble origins left them nostalgic and sentimental, emotions expressly evoked by Elvis's show[s]." When he died in Graceland in August 1977, so did a point of cultural unity, a symbol of the postwar dream. In the midst of a key moment of cultural breakup, he was, arguably, the last unifying vision of what the nation was for white working-class America. As cultural tastes scattered into its many cul-de-sacs in the seventies, he was the only figure capable of carrying the crown. In the King's passing, the irrepressible rock critic Lester Bangs found the unhinging of the nation's culture and arguably the final word on a postwar dream gone bad:

We will continue to fragment in this manner, because solipsism holds all the cards at present; it is a king whose domain engulfs even Elvis's. But I can guarantee you one thing: we will never again agree on anything as we agreed on Elvis. So I won't bother saying good-bye to his corpse. I will say goodbye to you.[72]

8

Dead Man's Town

In the summer of 1984, Ronald Reagan campaigned toward his landslide victory over liberal Democratic challenger Walter Mondale. That same summer, America's foremost working-class hero appeared on stages across the nation, dwarfed, Patton-like, by an enormous American flag, pounding his fist in the air like it mattered. Tens of thousands of voices united to chant the most popular song of the summer, the year, and the decade: "Born in the U.S.A." This audience sometimes drowned out the marshal tones of the E Street Band itself, heightening the pitch of an event that was already equal parts rock concert, spiritual revival, and nationalist rally. Replacing the skinny greaser-poet of his earlier tours, Bruce Springsteen had become a superhero version of himself, his new pumped-up body accentuated by exaggerated layers of denim and leather, his swollen biceps working his guitar like a jackhammer. Fists and flags surged into the air at the first hint of the sing-song melody, as thousands of bodies shadow-boxed the empty space above the crowd to the rhythm of the song, the deafening refrain filling stadiums around the world. Whether one chose to compare the spectacle to the horror of a Nuremburg Rally or the ecstasy of an Elvis Presley show, rock 'n' roll felt almost powerful again—more like a cause than an escape.[1]

On the surface, the performance seemed obvious evidence that working-class identity had been swept out into the seas of Reaganite nationalism. The toughness, the whiteness, the chant, the fists, the flags, the costume, all pointed to the degree to which this figure, once hailed as "the new Dylan," had, like so much else in the 1980s, been stripped of even the pretense of authenticity. Instead, Springsteen, dubbed "rock and roll's future" only a decade earlier, had been painted red, white, and blue, and packaged as an affirmation of American power and innocence to an eagerly waiting market-place. "Like Reagan and Rambo," writes Bryan Garman, "the apparently working-class Springsteen was for many Americans a white hard-body hero whose masculinity confirmed the values of patriarchy and patriotism, the work ethic and rugged individualism, and who clearly demarcated the boundaries between men and women, black and white, heterosexual and homosexual." The many and complex labor questions of the 1970s seemed to have found easy answers in the 1980s with the narrowing and hardening of white working-class identity into a blind national pride that sounded like belligerence.[2]

Yet these surface elements of "Born in the U.S.A." and its performance belie a profound complexity—much like political discourse and popular cul-ture in the 1980s masked the intricacies of post-New Deal working-class identity more generally. The song's story line, buried beneath the pounding music and the patriotic hollers of the chorus, explores the muffled tale of a socially isolated working-class man, burning within the despair of deindus-trialized, post-Vietnam America: a social history of white working-class identity unmoored from the elements that once defined it. Though Spring-steen projects the chorus with all his might, the tale told by the verses barely manages to peek over the wall of sound, like a man caught in a musical cage, overpowered by the anthem of his own country. Like the neo-patriotism of the Reagan era itself, the power of the national chorus, "I was Born in the U.S.A.," dwarfs the pain of the "dead man's town" below it. "You end up like a dog that's been beat too much / Til you spend half your life just coverin' it up."

The juxtaposition of this unemployed worker's dire, muted narrative, and a thundering patriotic chorus sparked battles among rock critics, pundits, and fans. Was the song part of a patriotic revival or a tale of working-class betrayal? A symptom of Reagan's America, or the antidote to it? Protest song or nationalist anthem? Both sides assumed that the words and the mu-sic could not go together, and in picking one over the other denied the song's unity—and its subject's—in favor of its far less compelling individual parts.

Conservative columnist George Will famously fired the first shots in the Springsteen wars with a September 1984 opinion column that claimed the singer as a repository of Republican values. Will's assertion of the song's conservatism was a product of his one-night stand with the E Street Band, a concert he admittedly heard through ears packed with cotton. "I have not got a clue about Springsteen's politics, if any, but flags get waved at his concerts when he sings songs about hard times," Will explained. "He is no whiner, and the recitation of closed factories and other problems always seems punctuated by a grand, cheerful, affirmation: 'Born in the U.S.A.!'" Casting this "working class hero" as a paragon of what workers should be—a little more patriotic, a lot more hardworking, and much more grown-up—he saw Springsteen as "vivid proof that the work ethic is alive and well" in the "hard times" of 1984. A few days later, when Will's informal advisee Ronald Reagan requested the song for his presidential campaign (and was turned down) the president invoked Springsteen anyway during a campaign stop in the singer's home state of New Jersey.[3]

Liberals, leftists, and rock critics responded in kind and, ridiculing conservatives, claimed the song and the singer for their own by shoehorning the rock anthem into the withering protest song tradition. Springsteen's most devoted chroniclers admitted that the song functioned more for the Right in the Reagan years, but with apologies: "Released as it was in a time of chauvinism masquerading as patriotism, it was inevitable that 'Born in the U.S.A.' would be misinterpreted, that the album would be heard as a celebration of 'basic values,'" explained one critic, "no matter how hard Springsteen pushed his side of the tale." Even Walter Mondale presumed (incorrectly) to have Springsteen's endorsement for the presidency.[4]

Lost to listeners on the Right and the Left was the fact that "Born in the U.S.A." was consciously crafted as a conflicted, but ultimately indivisible, whole. Its internal conflicts gave musical form to contradictions that grew from fissures to deep chasms in the heart of working-class life during the '70s and their aftermath. The song was first written and recorded with a single acoustic guitar during the recordings for *Nebraska* (1982)—a critically acclaimed collection of some of Springsteen's starkest and most haunting explorations of blue-collar despair, faith, and betrayal during the economic trauma of the early Reagan era. "That whole *Nebraska* album was just that isolation thing and what it does to you," Springsteen explained. "The record was basically about people being isolated from their jobs, from their friends, from their families, their fathers, their mothers—just not feeling connected to anything that's going on—your government. And when that happens, there's just a whole breakdown. When you lose that sense of community, there's some spiritual breakdown that occurs. And when that occurs, you just get shot off somewhere where nothing seems to matter."[5]

Most of the lyrics of the original *Nebraska*-period "Born" remain the same in the popular electric version released two years later, but the first recording lacks the pounding accompaniments, and, with them, any reason for pumping fists. "To me," Springsteen explained of the earlier version, "it was a dead song. . . . Clearly the words and the music didn't go together." So the first draft was shelved, only to emerge again, in a much stormier, amplified form, as the title track of its own album, *Born in the U.S.A.*, in 1984.[6]

In the intervening time, the song had found its soul. As producer Jon Landau explained, Springsteen had "discovered the key, which is that the words were right but they had to be in the right setting. It needed the turbulence and that scale—*there's* the song!" The electrification, projection, and anthem-ification of the first draft placed the chorus-lyrics tension at the center of the song. For Springsteen's project of giving voice to working-class experience, then, the words of working-class desperation "went together" with the music of nationalism—the "protest" only worked within the framework of the "anthem." For the song to convey its message, the worker had to be lost in the turbulence of the nation's identity. As Springsteen once explained, the narrator of "Born in the U.S.A." longs "to strip away that mythic America which was Reagan's image of America. He wants to find something real, and connecting. He's looking for a home in his country." Putting the pieces together, as Greil Marcus recognized, the song was about "the refusal of the country to treat Vietnam veterans as something more than nonunion workers in an enterprise conducted off the books." As loud as the final product was, then, "Born in the U.S.A." was actually more about silence—both existential and political.[7]

"Had a brother at Khe Sanh," Springsteen sings, "Fighting off the Vietcong / They're still there / He's all gone." When Springsteen singles out one of the bloodiest and most closely watched battles of the Vietnam War, he has also selected one of the most pointless. The siege of Khe Sanh forced American combat soldiers to live in their own labyrinth of holes and trenches while waiting in fear of the moment when an estimated twenty thousand enemy soldiers amassed outside of the perimeter would storm their position in the winter of 1968. Two and a half months of constant attack ended with American carpet-bombing around Khe Sanh, turning the area around the fort into a sea of rat-chewed bodies, shrapnel, and twisted ordnance. Despite the heroism of the soldiers' stand, a mere two months after the battle, General Westmoreland ordered the fort destroyed and abandoned. The gruesome defense was for naught. "A great many people," explains Michael Herr, "wanted to know how the Khe Sanh Combat Base could have been the Western Anchor of our Defense one month and a worthless piece of ground the next, and they were simply told that the situation had changed."[8]

Springsteen's song was never a ballad of the foreign and faraway, however, but an anthem of the U.S.A.—the reality of a war, yes, but also a metaphor for domestic working-class life under assault. Khe Sanh and deindustrialized places like Youngstown or Flint (or Cleveland, Toledo, St. Louis, Buffalo, South Chicago, or any one the other battle zones across the Rustbelt) were not that different. The site of the song is not "Khe Sanh," but a war-torn land in which, economist Barry Bluestone explains, "entire communities" were forced "to compete for survival" as shuttered factories, abandoned downtowns, and whitewashed windows were physical evidence of continued double-digit unemployment. By 1984, a city like Detroit, once of such strategic national importance to be known as the "Arsenal of Democracy," had, like Khe Sanh, become an abandoned pile of twisted refuse.[9]

"Came back home to the refinery," he laments, but the "Hirin' man said, 'Son, if it was up to me.'" It is not surprising, for a nation out of gas, that Springsteen chose a refinery as his character's workplace. Yet things were little better in other industries: across the industrial sector, global competition steadily increased as advanced industrial countries recovered from the industrial devastation of World War II, and third world nations turned toward manufacturing as a development strategy. Corporations decentralized, moved to the South, relocated abroad, replaced workers with technology or diversified into non-manufacturing sectors where the return on investment was higher. Communities began a downward spiral in the competition to create a better "business climate" than the next community down the interstate. Meanwhile, U.S. research and development sagged, complacency trumped innovation, growth rates shriveled, profits sagged, foreign competition took market share, plant technology proved grossly antiquated, and federal policy remained incoherent—even at odds with itself. Unionized manufacturing, stumbling since the mid-fifties, dropped off at a vertiginous pace. But many of the biggest firms that shut down were nowhere near bankruptcy, merely demonstrating a return on investment that was inadequate for the capitalist reformation already under way.

When, for instance, Ford announced the final closure Dewey Burton's Wixom assembly operation in 2006, the factory had already lost two shifts and several models from its assembly lines—this despite having been named the most efficient of all of Ford's plants and the third best auto plant in both North and South America by J.D. Power and Associates (a title that included beating all of the Toyota transplants). Odes to efficiency and hard work rang hollow when even the jewel of the system did not survive. Not surprisingly, given the culture such logic engenders, Richard Sennett's follow up to the 1970s analysis *The Hidden Injuries of Class* (1972) was called the *The Corrosion of Character* (1998). By the time the next generation of Detroit residents looked for work, there was little hope of finding the kind of security and remuneration that Dewey Burton finally settled into at Ford after the restlessness of a restless decade. When the shutdown finally came, one of Dewey's fellow skilled tradesmen sent him a DVD disc memorializing the plant and the modest protests to keep it open. It was labeled "Glory Days," and Springsteen's pop hit was its bootlegged soundtrack.[10]

For all of the melodrama of deindustrialization, however, the decline of major industrial manufacturing should not be conflated with the decline of the working class. Making industrial workers synonymous with the working class not only smacks of nostalgia ("Glory Days") but eclipses the possibility of a more expansive notion of working class identity. Those steel mills and their surrounding communities may be gone, but the workers are still out there—part of the new Wal-Mart working class. Women, immigrants, minorities, and, yes, white guys, all make up the "new working class" that succeeded that of basic industry, but there is no discursive, political place for them comparable to the classic concept of the industrial working class. Absent a meaningful framework in civic life, fear and anger can quickly take the place of the pride and honor of work. The issues defining working class life, argues Lillian Rubin, are "unnamed, therefore invisible" even to working people themselves. "It is after all, hard to believe in the particularity of the class experience if there's no social category into which it fits."[11]

The decline of industry went fist-in-glove with the siege of working-class institutions, an assault that took its most literal form when eleven thousand members of PATCO went on strike in the summer of 1981. In one of the boldest acts of his administration, President Ronald Reagan responded in no uncertain terms by firing the strikers wholesale and banning them from future federal employment. Their union leaders were taken away in chains and jailed. Well before the release of "Born in the U.S.A.," the workers turned to military assault metaphors. "I'm really surprised at how bloodthirsty they've been," exclaimed Frank Massa, a controller from Long Island. "It's such overkill—they brought in the howitzers to kill an ant," explained controller Jon Maziel. "It's like, 'Don't sit down and talk to people like human beings, just bring in the howitzers and wipe them out.' There's no reason for this situation to be like this, and I feel scared of a system of government that turns me off as a human being and says, 'O.K., if you don't play the game our way, you're a nonentity.'"[12]

The PATCO disaster revealed the confusion of enemy and ally at the heart of Springsteen's guerrilla combat metonym. During his 1980 campaign, candidate Reagan declared his sympathy with the "deplorable state of our nation's air traffic control system." He claimed that if elected, he would act in a "spirit of cooperation" and "take whatever steps are necessary to provide our air traffic controllers with the most modern equipment available and to adjust staff levels and work days so that they are commensurate with achieving a maximum degree of public safety." Given Carter's failures on the labor and economic fronts, PATCO even endorsed Ronald Reagan in 1980. When the controllers finally walked off the job in the summer of 1981, Reagan, like his hero Calvin Coolidge in the 1919 Boston police strike, attacked them for engaging in an illegal strike "against the public good." Yet it was the size and drama of Reagan's response that shocked even the most jaded labor commentator: the administration's firing the striking workers, smashing the entire organization designed to represent both employees' interest and public safety, and, ultimately, giving the nod to business to declare open season on organized labor. The otherwise bureaucratically calm new AFL-CIO president, Lane Kirkland, recognized war when he saw it, describing the federal response as having the "massive, vindictive, brutal quality of the carpet bombing."[13]

After the PATCO defeat, the national strike rate plummeted, and Eddie Sadlowski's nightmare of an economically disarmed working class became a reality. At the beginning of the seventies, about 2.5 million workers across the country were engaged in large strikes—strikes of over one thousand workers. By the 1980s, that same statistic was a tiny fraction of the earlier rate, hovering between one and three hundred thousand workers total out in major strikes. The number of large walkouts fell from around four hundred at the early years of the story to only about fifty by the mid-1980s.[14]

The most famous private sector strikes and lockouts that did take place in the 1980s truly smacked of isolated guerrilla battles in hostile economic terrain. These disputes were mostly an attempt to preserve some semblance of the status quo among the copper miners in Clifton-Morenci, Arizona; the meat packers in Austin, Minnesota; and the cannery workers in Watsonville, California. Their heroic stories unfolded along remarkably similar lines. First, various industries, emboldened by Reagan's move against PATCO, demanded concessions from their employees. One of the communities in the pattern bargaining settlement inevitably fought back—standing up for standards that rose above the pattern settlement. Those communities then found themselves fighting against the company but also against the very uncertain ally of the international union, which was still trying to keep wages and working conditions even across the nation. By the end of their heart-breaking community-based struggles, all three movements ended in more or less the same place: a broken strike, with striking workers facing "permanent replacement" by non-union workers, a demoralized community, and an inferior (or nonexistent) contract that drained all the gold out of the golden age of collective bargaining. One of the theme songs of the Austin meatpackers' struggle was Springsteen's "No Retreat, No Surrender," though the workers ended up doing both. As Jonathan Rosenblum concludes his detailed analysis of the 1983 Clifton-Morenci dispute in Arizona, the copper miners' defeat marked "the decline of two vital achievements of the American labor movement: solidarity and right to strike."[15]

What other recourse did working-class Americans have in the face of lost wars, rusting factories, wilting union strength, and embattled hometowns? One answer was to accept the New Right's retooled discourse of what it meant to be born in the U.S.A.: populist nationalism, protection of family, and traditional morality. This retooling often utilized terms first drafted by segregationist George Wallace, then refined by Richard Nixon, and ultimately perfected by Ronald Reagan, a framework designed to provide symbolic sanctuary for a white working class that felt itself embattled. This discourse tapped into the material as well as the social and moral concerns of its targets but actively and strategically reformulated the terms of resentment away from the economics of class and almost soley onto social issues. While "politics and identity" were being pulled "free from the gravity of class," the screaming chant of "Born in the U.S.A." allowed national mythology to drown out the realities of lived working-class experience. As George Lipsitz argues, the "'new patriotism' often seems strangely defensive, embattled and insecure" based as it was on "powerlessness, humiliation, and social disintegration." At a time when the traditional working class political ally, the Democratic Party, proved capable of precious little material comfort, the New Right offered soothing tonic for the injured pride and diminished material hopes of America's workingmen. Yet it was just that: tonic that promised to sooth cultural queasiness, rather than cure collective economic illnesses.[16]

"Born in the U.S.A." ends with a hidden eulogy to an inter-racial republic, the promise of which drew to a close at the end of the decade along with the potential for an honest, multi-racial rendition of working-class identity. As the song draws to a close, the narrator finds himself "ten years burning down the road / Nowhere to run ain't got nowhere to go." The reference to Martha and the Vandellas' Motown hit, "Nowhere to Run" makes explicit the theme of being adrift. He then quickly turns to the other tributary of American pop, by invoking the great country and western chronicler of loneliness and alienation, Hank Williams. As "Born in the U.S.A." trails off, its narrator cites the title of a Williams tune when he declares, "I'm a long gone Daddy." In setting up Motown and Nashville as the poles of working-class identity, Springsteen unites black and white experiences—not in triumph or social unity, but in their shared but separate experiences of rootlessness within American culture. Springsteen, who never indulged in the white racial victimization common in the seventies, suggests that politics—just like rock 'n' roll—work best when integrated. However, the next line uneasily transforms his lament for the dream of unity. He sings, "I'm a cool rocking daddy in the U.S.A." "Long gone" in social, economic, political, and even human senses, the narrator here clings to the "cool"—a bit of defensive and elusive cultural flotsam left over from the glory days of postwar triumph. The collapse of meaningful, shared, and vernacular social patriotism is driven home as the narrator wails, seems to take punches, and becomes lost as the relentless rhythm of the song finally breaks down—only to be reconstituted, oblivious to the narrator's story.

Despite a complex revival of labor issues that resonated from Detroit to Hollywood to Washington, by the end of the decade, workers—*qua* workers—had eerily been shaken out of the national scene. The aging labor intellectual J.B.S. Hardman, reflecting on his involvement in organized labor since the beginning of the century, predicted such a fate when he declared that labor stood "at the Rubicon" at the start of the decade. The crossing, he cautioned, would be fraught with treacherous obstacles, but he believed that, win or lose, the decade would represent a watershed in the fortunes of workers. It did. The seventies whimpered to a close as the labor movement had failed in its major initiatives; deindustrialization decimated the power of the old industrial heartland; market orthodoxy eclipsed all alternatives; and promising organizing drives proved limited. The redefinition of "the working class" beyond its high modern, New Deal, form failed, leaving out the "new" working class of women and minorities—as well as almost all of the service sector. Workers occasionally reappeared in public discourse as "Reagan Democrats"—later as "NASCAR Dads" or the victims of another plant shutdown or as irrational protectionists and protestors of free trade, but rarely did they appear as workers. "The era of the forgotten worker," in the words of one journalist, had begun.[17]

Andrew Levison, who had contributed to the revival of working-class studies in the seventies with *The Working Class Majority* (1974) and *The Full Employment Alternative* (1980), asked in 2001, "Who Lost the Working Class?" It was too big and complex a question for a single answer. He cited simply the sociological "perfect storm" of post-sixties working-class politics. Indeed, there are points in history in which the confluence of events suggests a transformation that is beyond a single causal explanation, but that requires a multilayered narrative to capture the complexity. The American working class, a fragmentary but untamed force before the Great Depression, empowered and contained by the New Deal collective bargaining system, ideologically assimilated to the middle class in the fifties, and objectified as an enemy of social change in the 1960s, had always been a vulnerable and malleable thing in American history. Perhaps one of the primary interpretive problems of working-class history was that the baseline of comparison had too often been the extraordinary postwar period. As Eric Hobsbawm wrote of the decline of the golden age:

> it was not until the great boom was over, in the disturbed seventies, waiting for the traumatic eighties, that observers—mainly to begin with, economists— began to realize that the world, particularly the world of developed capitalism, had passed through an altogether exceptional phase of its history; perhaps a unique one. . . . The gold glowed more brightly against the dull or dark background of the subsequent decades of crisis.[18]

With the failure of union insurgencies and the intransigence of labor leaders of the seventies, the sirens of the Nixon administration, the political divisions and blinders that created the McGovern fiasco, and the dissolution of work in popular culture, the post-New Deal working class never regained its footing. After the seventies, labor's officialdom promised transformations— through the promises of Solidarity Day, John Sweeney's New Voice slate, and the breakaway coalition known as Change to Win—but these were largely intra-palace machinations. The promise had already passed by the time labor got serious. Talk of labor law reforms under Clinton and Obama raised further, unfulfilled, hopes. Roseanne Barr, Michael Moore, and Homer Simpson all tried to remind us of the void in popular culture, but the jokes really played off of what we as a society had already agreed to forget. "First we stopped noticing members of the working class," wrote one critic, "and now we're convinced they don't exist."[19]

* * *

By the time the Great Recession began in 2008, with the return to double-digit unemployment, staggering public spending poured in to prop up Wall Street with nary a word of the needs of working people. The political response was nothing like that of either the Great Depression of the 1930s, which placed workers at the center of the nation's consciousness, or even the debates of the Great Stagflation crisis of the 1970s, where working-class concerns were raised but ultimately defeated. Rather, the election, despite the endless alleged parallels with the New Deal made by commentators, was really evidence of the "curious forgetting" about working people.[20]

Stock working-class characters continued to be dragged out when political campaigns required them but rarely within any real content. One was "Joe the Plumber," one of the stars of 2008, who happened to be playing football with his son outside of his modest house near Toledo when candidate Barack Obama came to the neighborhood. Making about $40,000 per year, Joe had dreams of buying his employer's firm for $250,000 (even though, as it later came out, he owed back income taxes). He criticized Obama for undermining the American dream with his burdensome tax policies and thus blocking entrepreneurial ambitions of people like himself. Even though Obama explained to Joe that 95 percent of businesses made below the $250,000 mark, he became a national symbol for workers whose future rested on fuzzy dreams of affluence. Although Joe succeeded briefly as a media star, he had yet to even make it as a plumber, having never held a plumber's license (a requirement in Toledo and several surrounding municipalities), never completed an apprenticeship, and was not a member of the plumbers' union (which had endorsed Obama). Yet, Joe the Plumber, barely keeping it together economically, became a semi-official member of the Republican campaign, the party's emblem of everyman's discontent who, like the disgruntled lottery players at the convenience store, was a man on the margins of success who feared that when he did strike it big and managed to transcend the rigidities of the American class structure, the nation's tax policies would one day punish him.

The Democrats' working-class hero was similarly one-dimensional. When Barack Obama spoke at a West Coast campaign fundraiser, he described the people he met with a certain detachment that could readily be twisted as contempt. "You go into some of these small towns in Pennsylvania, and like a lot of small towns in the Midwest, the jobs have been gone now for 25 years and nothing's replaced them," the candidate honestly explained. "And they fell through the Clinton Administration, and the Bush Administration, and each successive administration has said that somehow these communities are gonna regenerate and they have not." All true. Then, however, Obama explained, "And it's not surprising then they get bitter, they cling to guns or religion or antipathy to people who aren't like them or anti-immigrant sentiment or anti-trade sentiment as a way to explain their frustrations." While the displacement of material concerns onto cultural questions was not an unreasonable interpretation of the politics of the heartland, there was an inescapable condescension when it came to speaking *about* other people rather than *to* them, which perpetuated the problem of the "liberal elite" who discussed and dissected working people but actually knew precious few—and dared to act on behalf of even fewer. The needs of both McCain's Joe the Plumber and Obama's disgruntled worker largely vanished once the vote harvesting was over.

Today, workers, people with "no right to be," as one novelist put it, chart their course on what Mike Davis calls a "survivalist" social axis, reduced to calling it freedom. Liberty has largely been reduced to an ideology that promises economic and cultural refuge from the long arm of the state, while seemingly lost to history is the logic that culminated under the New Deal: that genuine freedom could only happen within a context of economic security. "It is absurd to conceive liberty as that of the business entrepreneur, and ignore the immense regimentation to which workers are subjected," argued John Dewey in 1935. "Full freedom of the human spirit and of individuality can be achieved only as there is effective opportunity to share in the cultural resources of civilization." For Dewey, one of America's greatest philosophers, any political system that failed to make "full cultural freedom" available through "genuine industrial freedom as a way of life" was little more than "degenerate and delusive."[21]

How a republic of anxiety overtook a republic of security may be the seventies' greatest, and most tragic, legacy. The social and political spaces for the collective concerns of working people—the majority of the citizenry—dissolved from American civic life when the nation moved from manufacturing to finance, from troubled hope to jaded ennui, from the compromises and constraints of industrial pluralism to the jungle of the marketplace. The seventies marked the end of a political order, the end of a movement, and the end of an era. Most of all, it was the end of a historically elusive ideal: the conscious, diverse, and unified working class acting as a powerful agent in political, social, and economic life. This dream, ever deferred but always an animating feature of modern politics, was that collective working-class agency could guarantee basic economic security for all as the foundation of a greater freedom.

Moving away from merely staying alive and toward John Dewey's vision of cultural and economic sharing is hardly simple. Autoworker Dewey Burton was right when he said that the working class he knew was "gone and it's not gonna happen again." Whatever working-class identity might emerge from the postmodern, global age will have to be less rigid and less limiting than that of the postwar order, and far less wedded to the bargaining table as the sole expression of workplace power. It will have to be less about consumption and more about democracy, and as much about being blue collar as being green collar. It will have to be more inclusive in conception, more experimental in form, more nimble in organization, and more kaleidoscopic in nature than previous incarnations. The chapter of the modern working class has closed; the page of imagination is open; and the future is unwritten.

Acknowledgments

Since this project has made me acutely aware of the costs of inflation, I will try to keep my acknowledgments brief. To the countless people who provided comments on many papers, leads on sources, rare documents, places to crash, quick reads, and more felicitous phrasing—all of whom made this a better book—I offer my gratitude to the collective spirit of scholarship and writing. Many of the ideas here had their first outings with several semesters of students in "Recent History of American Workers," and then got subsequent workouts in a number of conference talks and invited paper presentations. Miscellaneous fragments of several of these chapters appeared previously in *American Quarterly*, *New Labor Forum*, *Labor History*, *Labor: Studies in the Working Class History of the Americas*, and *America in the Seventies*, edited by Beth Bailey and David Farber.

For material support, I am indebted to fellowships from the Society for the Humanities at Cornell University and the American Council of Learned Societies-Andrew W. Mellon Foundation. The ILR School at Cornell University provided an ideal place to work and teach, as well a special research grant award, and the assistance of a sizable number of bright and talented student assistants, including: Keith Becker, Joshua Glick, David Klesh, Matthew Loeb, Amanda Magee, Stephen Mak, Michael O'Donnell, Richard Scherer, and Jarrett Taubman. Lauren Boehm, disappearing girl and itinerant brainiac, tops the list and has continued to engage these ideas well after her official duties were complete. Thanks, too, Lauren, for letting me borrow a little of the stuff we worked on together. Anyone engaged in historical research must quickly come to terms with debts owed the professional staffs of the archives (which are listed before the endnotes on pages 375–76).

A very special thanks goes to Dewey and Ilona Burton who first sprang from the pages of the *New York Times*, then opened their home to me with trust and good will. I hope that in this book you can see a few fragments of lives well lived. Marc Favreau, most patient of editors, sent painful messages about long-overdue chapters like, "Do you really need the last 20 pages?" and, after a few deep breaths, I found my writing more focused and the book leaner because of him. Anyone who has read to this point should toast Marc for not having to read more. Ethan Stephenson has kept the wheels on the Keeton House bus and, moreover, proved to be an inspiring intellectual partner on the trip.

Cornell may be "far above Cayuga's waters" as the Alma Mater goes, but half way up the hill is a worn out old pub with dozens of taps, free popcorn, and a group of historians I could trust regularly to shred weak ideas, puncture turgid prose, and share the conquests and setbacks of personal and professional life. To the gang of "beer and history," you are that rarest of all things, a true intellectual and creative community. Heartfelt thanks to Derek Chang, Aaron Sachs, Michael Smith, Michael Trotti, and Rob Vanderlan, as well as group alumni Joel Dinerstein, Finis Dunaway, Adriane Lentz-Smith, and Jason Sokol. They're probably almost as happy to see this out the door as I am. Michael Trotti and Rob Vanderlan, in particular, were there when I needed them. They not only deepened and enlivened a manuscript but also a friendship. Comrades of the Chapter House, the next round's on me.

My profound thanks goes out to a small number of a people who sustained me, challenged my ideas, and, occasionally, gave me a good kick in the pants. Jack Metzgar—friend, mentor, working-class hero—felt that this book was too important to allow me to screw it up (though his verb choice was earthier). As a result, Jack did everything in his power to prevent that tragedy by reading the manuscript in various pieces and arguing, largely unsuccessfully, with me about all aspects of it. Joel Dinerstein, comrade, soul brother, confidant, tramp, believer, and gatekeeper to the alternative justice league, not only helped me think through many aspects of this book, he helped me think through core aspects of my life. Similarly, the buoyant good faith of Nick Salvatore sustains me daily. His laugh echoes through the halls of Cornell, as do his ideas through the universe.

More than anyone, Madeleine Casad proved strong enough to get me through the scary parts with a whole new twist on social realism—the type of humane love, earthy faith, and sensual being that one finds only rarely in life. Fortunately, she doesn't walk like Bo Diddley, but she sure has been my soulful mama, "bringing me everything and more." Mik, I'll never confuse shelter from the storm with the view from a Buick 6.

Finally, Aidan and Aliya probably cannot remember a time when I was not working on this book. There is nothing to add to the dedication, except to say that writing this book was an attempt to excavate hope, but I need not have looked any further than you two.

Notes

Abbreviations of Some Primary Materials Used in Notes

Abbreviations used in notes	Collection Name	Location of Collection
AHP	Augustus Hawkins Papers	Special Collections, University Research Library, University of California Los Angeles
AUAIC	Arthur Unger Audio Interview Collection	Arthur Unger Audio Interview Collection, Special Collections Research Center, Syracuse University Library
BRP	Bayard Rustin Papers	Library of Congress
CRP	Cleveland Robinson Papers	Tamiment Library & Robert F. Wagner Labor Archives, New York University
DPCC	Diamond Political Commercials Collection	Special Collections, Syracuse University
FCWEC	Frank Cormier and William Eaton Collection	Walter P. Reuther Library of Labor and Urban Affairs, Wayne State University
FEAC	Full Employment Action Council	Kheel Center for Labor-Management Documentation, Cornell University
GMMA	George Meany Memorial Archives	George Meany Memorial Archives, National Labor College, Silver Spring, Maryland

Abbreviations used in notes	Collection Name	Location of Collection
GSMP	George S. McGovern Papers	Seeley G. Mudd Manuscript Library, Princeton University
HHHP	Hubert H. Humphrey Papers	Minnesota Historical Society
JCP	Jimmy Carter Papers	Jimmy Carter Library, Atlanta, Georgia
JHLL	*John Herling's Labor Letter*	Catherwood Library, Cornell University
JHP	John Herling Papers	Walter P. Reuther Library of Labor and Urban Affairs, Wayne State University
JLRP	Joseph L. Rauh, Jr. Papers	Library of Congress
JPSP	J.P. Stevens Papers	Kheel Center for Labor-Management Documentation, School of Industrial and Labor Relations, Cornell University
JWP	Jerry Wurf Papers	Walter P. Reuther Library of Labor and Urban Affairs, Wayne State University
KCLMD	Kheel Center for Labor-Management Documetation	School of Industrial and Labor Relations, Cornell University
KLRM	Kroch Library Rare Manuscripts Collection	Kroch Library, Cornell University
Local 1112	United Auto Workers Local 1112 Papers	Walter P. Reuther Library of Labor and Urban Affairs, Wayne State University
MCI	Miller Center Interviews	Miller Center of Public Affairs, University of Virginia
MFP	Murray Finley Papers	Kheel Center for Labor-Management Documentation, Cornell University
RFKP	Robert F. Kennedy Papers	John F. Kennedy Presidential Library, Boston, Massachusetts
RGP	Robert Guthridge Papers	Walter P. Reuther Library of Labor and Urban Affairs, Wayne State University
RNP	Richard Nixon Presidential Materials	Richard Nixon Presidential Materials, National Archives II, Suitland, Maryland (since moved to the Nixon Library in Yorba Linda, California)

Introduction: Something's Happening to People Like Me

1. *New York Times* 1 June 1970, *New York Times* 2 April 1972, *New York Times* 14 May 1972; Pete Hamill, "The Revolt of the White Lower-Middle Class," in Louise Kapp Howe, ed., *The White Majority: Between Poverty and Affluence* (New York: Random House, 1970), 22.

2. The first article was Agis Salpukas, "Workers Increasingly Rebel Against Boredom on Assembly Line," *New York Times* 2 April 1972. Burton's profiles were as follows: Nan Robertson, "A Wallace Backer Stirred by Busing," *New York Times* 14 May 1972; "2 Wallace Backers Unsure on Their Votes," *New York Times* 7 November 1972; "Auto Worker and Wife Decide on McGovern," *New York Times* 8 November 1972; "A Michigan 'Primary Jumper' Explains Why He Is Planning to Vote for Reagan," *New York Times* 18 May 1976; "One Man's Road to a Vote for Reagan," *New York Times* 15 October 1980. One article not written by Robertson was James T. Wooten, "Pre-Election Mood: There's No Time for Dreams," *New York Times* 17 October 1974. Burton also appeared on the David Susskind talk show in New York City for a discussion of industrial discontent; see Susskind Show, 27 May 1973, DSP. The author also interviewed him by phone in Florida on 27 July 2006 and conducted a recorded oral history in person: Dewey Burton and Ilona Burton, interview by the author, 30 September 2006, Fort White, Florida, tape recording, author's possession (hereafter Burton Oral History).

3. "Labor 1970: Angry, Aggressive, and Acquisitive," *Fortune*, October 1969, 95; Andrew Levison, "The Rebellion of Blue Collar Youth," *Progressive* 36 (October 1972): 38–42; Jim Jacobs and Larry Laskowski, "The New Rebels in Industrial America," *Leviathan*, March 1969, 5–7, 51–54; statistics from Bureau of Labor Statistics, *Handbook of Labor Statistics* (Washington, DC: GPO, 1983), 380, and table "Work stoppages involving 1,000 workers or more, 1947–2002" Bureau of Labor Statistics, Table 1: Work Stoppages Involving 1,000 or more Workers, 1947–2008, 11 February 2009, http://www.bls.gov/news.release/wkstp.t01.htm; "Blue-Collar Blues on the Assembly Line," *Fortune Magazine*, July 1970, 69–71, 112–17; "The Blue Collar Worker's Lowdown Blues," *Time*, 9 November 1970, 68; *New York Times* 19 May 1970; *Newsweek* special edition on the "The Troubled American," 6 October 1969, 60.

4. Dennis H. Wrong, "How Important Is Social Class?" in *The World of the Blue-Collar Worker*, ed. Irving Howe (New York: Quadrangle, 1972), 300; Gil Scott-Heron lyrics from "B Movie," on the album *Reflections* (Arista Records, 1981); Gus Tyler, "White Workers/Blue Mood," in *The World of the Blue-Collar Worker*, ed. Irving Howe (New York: Quadrangle, 1972), 207.

There have been a great number of studies trying to establish an objective definition of "the working class." Erik Olin Wright's massive body of research is among the most prominent (for a useful primer, see Wright and others, *The Debate over Classes* [New York: Verso, 1989]. Taking a cue from gender and race studies, in contrast, this study uses "the working class," as a socially, politically, culturally, and economically constructed category with multiple possible meanings, expressions, and outlets. The elastic nature of class in politics and social life—especially in the elusive American context—is, arguably, more important than defining the term with statistical accuracy. As David R. Roediger has argued, however, both workers and organized labor "in iconography, public discourse, and historical writing ha[ve] often been assumed to be white and male"; see Roediger, "What if Labor Were Not White and Male?" in Roediger, *Colored White: Transcending the Racial Past* (Berkeley: University of California Press, 2002), 181. See also Richard F. Hamilton, *Class and Politics in the United States* (New York: John Wiley and Sons, 1972); Michael Zweig, *The Working Class Majority: America's Best Kept Secret* (Ithaca, NY: ILR Press, 2000) Jack Metzgar, "Politics and the American Class Vernacular," *Working USA* 7 (August 2004): 49–80; Reeve Vanneman and Lynn Weber Cannon, *The American Perception of Class* (Philadelphia: Temple University Press, 1987); most useful has been John R. Hall, ed., *Reworking Class* (Ithaca, NY: Cornell University Press, 1997).

5. Brendon and Patricia Cayo Sexton, "Labor's Decade—Maybe," in *The Seventies: Problems and Proposals* [*Dissent* compilation], ed. Irving Howe and Michael Harrington (New York: Harper and Row, 1972), 269; *New York Times* 14 May 1972.

6. *New York Times* 14 May 1972. On the Charlotte case, see Mathew D. Lassiter, *The Silent Majority: Suburban Politics in the Sunbelt South* (Princeton, NJ: Princeton University Press, 2005).

7. Daniel Carter, *The Politics of Rage: George Wallace, the Origins of the New Conservatism, and the Transformation of American Politics* (New York: Simon and Schuster, 1995); *New York Times* 14 May 1972; Kevin Phillips, *The Emerging Republican Majority* (New Rochelle, NY: Arlington House, 1969).

8. On Wallace, see Michael Kazin, *The Populist Persuasion: An American History* (New York: Basic Books, 1995), 221–42; Carter, *The Politics of Rage*; Wallace quote from Richard M. Scammon and Ben J. Wattenberg, *The Real Majority* (New York: Coward-McCann, 1970), 62; on conservatives and Wallace, see Christopher Lasch, *The True and Only Heaven: Progress and Its Critics* (New York: Norton, 1991), 505; trucker, quoted in Kim Phillips-Fein, *Invisible Hands: The Making of the Conservative Movement from the New Deal to Reagan* (New York: Norton, 2008), 155.

9. *New York Times* 14 May 1972; *New York Times* 7 November 1972; Burton Oral History.

10. Breslin, quoted in Ronald P. Formisano, *Boston Against Busing: Race, Class, and Ethnicity in the 1960s and 1970s* (Chapel Hill: University of North Carolina Press, 2004 [1991]), 177; on white ethnic revival, see Matthew Frye Jacobsen, *Roots Too: White Ethnic Revival in Post-Civil Rights America* (Cambridge, MA: Harvard University Press, 2006), Michael Novak, *The Rise of the Unmeltable Ethnics* (New York: Macmillan, 1971); on the transformation in gender and race in the workplace, see Nancy MacLean, *Freedom Is Not Enough: The Opening of the American Workplace* (Cambridge, MA: Harvard University Press, 2006), 2; Katherine Van Wezel Stone,

"The Legacy of Industrial Pluralism: the Tension between Individual Employment Rights and the New Deal Collective Bargaining System," *University of Chicago Law Review* 59 (Spring 1992): 576; Judith Stein, *Running Steel, Running America: Race, Economic Policy and the Decline of Liberalism* (Chapel Hill: University of North Carolina Press, 1998), 195. Thanks to Rick Perlstein for the "postscarcity" framing here.

11. *New York Times* 7 November 1972.

12. Ibid.; *New York Times* 8 November 1972; see Patrick Buchanan, *The New Majority: President Nixon at Mid Passage* (Philadelphia: Girard Bank, 1973), 55–68.

13. *New York Times* 2 April 1972, *New York Times* 14 May 1972.

14. On Lordstown, see David Moberg, "Rattling the Golden Chains: Conflict and Consciousness of Auto Workers," (PhD diss., University of Chicago, 1978); the unrest is surveyed in Aaron Brenner, "Rank and File Rebellion, 1966–1975" (PhD diss., Columbia University, 1996); Heather Ann Thompson, "Auto Workers, Dissent, and the UAW: Detroit and Lordstown," in *Autowork*, ed. Robert Asher and Ronald Edsforth (Albany: SUNY Press, 1995), 181–208; Judith Coburn, "Ed Sadlowski Strides Toward Bethlehem," *Village Voice* (7 February 1977): 27; Joe Klein, "Old Fashioned Hero of the New Working Class," *Rolling Stone* (18 December 1975), 51.

15. Abel, quoted in *New York Times* 1 June 1970; David Brody, *Workers in Industrial America: Essays on the Twentieth Century Struggle*, 2nd ed. (New York: Oxford University Press, 1993), 185; machine quote in Thomas Geoghegan, *Which Side Are You On?: Trying to Be for Labor When It's Flat on Its Back* (New York: Farrar Straus Giroux, 1991), 67; Alice and Staughton Lynd, *Rank and File: Personal Histories by Working-Class Organizers* (Boston: Beacon Press, 1973).

16. Godfrey Hodgson, *America in Our Time* (Garden City, NY: Doubleday, 1976), 83; Steve Fraser, "The Labor Question," in *The Rise and Fall of the New Deal Order*, ed. Fraser and Gary Gerstle (Princeton, NJ: Princeton University Press, 1989), 55–84; for the most subtle analysis of how class was not simply contained but defined the social architecture of the postwar era, see Jack Metzgar, *Striking Steel: Solidarity Remembered* (Philadelphia: Temple University Press, 2000).

17. *New York Times* 14 May 1972; Burton Oral History.

18. *New York Times* 17 October 1974; Peter Marin, "The New Narcissism," *Harper's* (October 1975): 46; the idea is developed most thoroughly in Christopher Lasch, *The Culture of Narcissism: American Life in an Age of Diminishing Expectations* (New York: Norton, 1978).

19. On the limits of the New Deal and the postwar era, see Richard Oestreicher, "The Rules of the Game: Class Politics in Twentieth-Century America," in *Organized Labor and American Politics, 1894–1994: The Labor-Liberal Alliance*, ed. Kevin Boyle (Albany: SUNY Press, 1998), 29. For the quotes on the spectrum of thought on the seventies, David Frum, *How We Got Here: The 70s: The Decade That Brought You Modern Life (For Better or Worse)* (New York: Basic Books, 2000); Bruce J. Schulman, *The Seventies: The Great Shift in American Culture, Society, and Politics* (New

York: Free Press, 2001); Stephen Paul Miller, *The Seventies Now: Culture as Surveillance* (Durham: Duke University Press, 1999), 45.

20. Andreas Killen, *1973 Nervous Breakdown: Watergate, Warhol, and the Birth of Post-Sixties America* (New York: Bloomsbury, 2006), 4–5; *New York Times* 17 October 1974; Michael Harrington, "A Collective Sadness," *Dissent* 21 (Fall 1974): 486–91.

21. Robert Collins, *More: The Politics of Economic Growth* (New York: Oxford University Press, 2000), 132–65; Daniel H. Weinberg, "A Brief Look at Postwar U.S. Income Inequality," *Current Population Reports* June 1996, Bureau of the Census (P60–191); Daniel H. Weinberg, Charles T. Nelson, and Edward J. Welniak Jr., "Economic Well-Being in the United States: How Much Improvement—Fifty Years of U.S. Income Data from the Current Population Survey: Alternatives, Trends, and Quality," *American Economic Review* (May 1999): 18–22; for a brief overview of postwar Gini coefficients, see Thomas Frank, *One Market Under God* (New York: Doubleday, 2000), 6; Frum, *How We Got Here*, 331–32; U.S. Census Bureau, *Income, Poverty, and Health Insurance Coverage in the United States: 2005* (Washington, DC: GPO, 2005), 38; Francine D. Blau and Lawrence M. Kahn, "Gender Differences in Pay," *Journal of Economic Perspectives* 14 (Fall 2000): 84–85.

22. *New York Times* 17 October 1974.

23. Ibid., Robert Nisbet, *Twilight of Authority* (New York: Oxford, 1975), 1, 9, 23, 230.

24. *New York Times* 18 May 1976.

25. Ibid., *New York Times* 15 October 1980.

26. UAW President Leonard Woodcock, quoted in Martin Halpern, *Unions, Radicals, and Democratic Presidents: Seeking Social Change in the Twentieth Century* (Westport, CT: Praeger, 2003), 120. The tensions between labor and Carter are laid out in Taylor Dark, "Organized Labor and the Carter Administration: The Origins of Conflict," in *The Presidency and Domestic Policies of Jimmy Carter*, ed. Herbert D. Rosenbaum and Alexej Ugrinsky (Westport, CT: Greenwood Press, 1994), 775; Interview with Charles Schultze, Miller Center Interviews, Carter Presidency Project, vol. XI, January 8–9, 1982, 2, 38–39, 80, Jimmy Carter Library, Atlanta, Georgia; W. Carl Biven, *Jimmy Carter's Economy: Policy in an Age of Limits* (Chapel Hill: University of North Carolina Press, 2002).

27. George Meany interviewed on *Face the Nation*, CBS Television, 6 September 1970, Collection 5498m, KCLMD.

28. *New York Times* 15 October 1980.

29. Burton Oral History; see also Gil Troy, *Morning in America: How Ronald Reagan Invented the 1980s* (Princeton, NJ: Princeton University Press, 2005), 50–83.

30. See Richard Sennet and Jonathan Cobb, *The Hidden Injuries of Class* (New York: Vintage, 1972), 98, 105.

31. Nelson George, *Hip Hop America* (New York: Viking, 1998), 3; *Time* 14 December 1981, 64–65; the claustrophobic mood contrasts with popular culture in the

postwar era, see Lary May, *The Big Tomorrow: Hollywood and the Politics of the American Way* (Chicago: University of Chicago, 2000).

32. André Gorz, *Farewell to the Working Class: An Essay on Post-Industrial Socialism* (London: Pluto, 1982); Eric Hobsbawm, ed., *The Forward March of Labour Halted?* (London: Verso, 1981).

33. Burton quote from phone interview with the author, July 28, 2006, follow-up discussion in Burton Oral History.

Chapter 1: Old Fashioned Heroes of the New Working Class

1. The Yablonski murder story appears in many sources, including Joseph E. Finley, *The Corrupt Kingdom: The Rise and Fall of the United Mine Workers* (New York: Simon and Schuster, 1972), 272–79; Brit Hume, *Death and the Mines: Rebellions and Murder in the United Mine Workers* (New York: Grossman, 1971), 240–41; Trevor Armbrister, *Act of Vengeance: The True Story Behind the Yablonski Murders* (New York: Saturday Review Press, 1975); *Time* 15 May 1972; *Time* 17 September 1973; *New York Times* 6 January 1970, *New York Times* 8 January 1972; *New York Times* 5 March 1972, including a Home Box Office (HBO) movie starring Charles Bronson, *Act of Vengeance* (1986).

2. *New York Times* 29 May 1972, *New York Times* 8 January 1970.

3. *JHLL* 10 January 1970; Paul F. Clark, *The Miners' Fight for Democracy: Arnold Miller and the Reform of the United Mine Workers* (Ithaca, NY: ILR Press, 1981), 25; Hume, *Death and the Mines*, 173.

4. *New York Times* 17 July 1974; Leon Fink and Brian Greenberg, *Upheaval in the Quiet Zone: A History of Hospital Workers' Union, Local 1199* (Urbana: University of Illinois Press, 1989).

5. *Washington Post* 30 May 1969; Paul John Nyden, "Miners for Democracy: Struggle in the Coal Fields" (PhD diss., Columbia University, 1976), 496–98; *New York Times* 30 May 1969.

6. When Boyle later came under investigation, it also came out he had made illegal contributions to Humphrey's campaign. *Washington Post* 29 February 1972; *Washington Post* 25 July 1972; *JHLL* 14 June 1969; Hume, *Death and the Mines*, 169–71, 174; Nyden, "Miners for Democracy," 499; Hunter S. Thompson, *Fear and Loathing: On the Campaign Trail '72* (San Francisco: Straight Arrow Books, 1973), 207.

7. Rauh's work for Negotiate Now! is in Kevin Boyle, *The UAW and the Heyday of American Liberalism, 1945–1968* (Ithaca, NY: Cornell University Press), 231–33; on Rauh and MFD, see John Dittmer, *Local People: The Struggle for Civil Rights in Mississippi* (Urbana: University of Illinois Press, 1994), 272–302.

8. *Washington Post* 10 January 1970.

9. *Washington Post* 6 January 1970; *Washington Post* 7 January 1970; *Washington Post* 10 January 1970; the only UMWA official present was Marion Pelligrini, a sub-district board member in Yablonski's home District 5; Clarice R. Feldman,

"Miners for Democracy," *Autocracy and Insurgency in Organized Labor* (New Brunswick, NJ: Transaction Books, 1972), 11–12; Thomas Geoghegan, *Which Side Are You On?: Trying to Be for Labor When It's Flat on Its Back* (New York: Farrar Straus Giroux, 1991), 115.

10. *New York Times* 26 November 1972. On the break with the AFL and the early rise of the CIO, see Robert H. Zieger, *The CIO, 1935–1955* (Chapel Hill: University of North Carolina Press, 1995), 22–41.

11. Saul Alinsky, *John L. Lewis, An Unauthorized Biography* (New York: Putnam, 1949), 74, 76–80, quotes Lewis as saying that the infamous punch was premeditated. David Brody, *Workers in Industrial America: Essays on the Twentieth Century Struggle* (New York: Oxford University Press, 1980), 90.

12. Nelson Lichtenstein, *State of the Union: A Century of American Labor* (Princeton, NJ: Princeton University Press, 2002), 52–53.

13. Jack Metzgar, *Striking Steel: Solidarity Remembered* (Philadelphia: Temple University Press, 2000), 4, 39.

14. Table A-2, "Real Median Earnings of Full-Time, Year-Round Workers by Sex and Female-to-Male Earnings Ratio: 1960–2005," in *Income, Poverty, and Health Insurance Coverage in the United States* (Washington, DC: U.S. Census Bureau, GPO, 2005), 38; Economic Policy Institute, "Hourly and weekly earnings of production and nonsupervisory workers, 1947–2005," http://www.epi.org/page/-/old/datazone/06/earnings.pdf; Emmanuel Saez and Thomas Piketty, "Income Inequality in the United States, 1913–1998," *Quarterly Journal of Economics* 118 (2003):1–39; Emmanuel Saez, Wojciech Kopczuk, and Jae Song, "Earnings Inequality and Mobility in the United States: Evidence from Social Security Data Since 1937," *Quarterly Journal of Economics* 125 (2010): 91–128; Alan Brinkley, *End of Reform: New Deal Liberalism in Recession and War* (New York: Knopf, 1995), 4–7; Metzgar, *Striking Steel*, 62, 146–47; the result, in Lizabeth Cohen's terms, was *A Consumer's Republic: The Politics of Mass Consumption in Postwar America* (New York: Knopf, 2003).

15. For "pork chop solidarity," see A.H. Raskin in *New York Times* 20 February 1972; Joseph A. Beirne, *Challenge to Labor: The New Roles for American Trade Unions* (Englewood Cliffs, NJ: Prentice-Hall, 1969), 135, 137–38; on pluralism, see Melvyn Dubofsky, *The State and Labor in Modern America* (Chapel Hill: University of North Carolina Press, 1994), 212–17, 226–31; Clark Kerr, "Industrial Relations and the Liberal Pluralist," in Clark Kerr, *Labor and Management in Industrial Society* (New York: Anchor Books Doubleday, 1964); Milton Derber, "Collective Bargaining: The American Approach to Industrial Democracy," *Annals of the American Academy of Political and Social Science* 431 (May 1977): 83–94.

16. *New York Times* 26 November 1962; Clark, *Miners' Fight*, 19; Finley, *Corrupt Kingdom*, 538; *JHHL* 8 May 1971.

17. This was not the first time that Boyle had made foolish remarks. One of his first public appearances as UMWA president was at an explosion that killed thirty-

seven men at U.S. Steel's Robena mining complex. There, Boyle asked "Did a trapper boy leave the door open?" Trapper boys, who manually managed mining ventilation, had not been used for decades. Word quickly spread that Boyle was out of touch with the everyday operation of a mine. See Richard Jay Jensen, "Rebellion in the United Mine Workers: The Miners for Democracy, 1970–1972," (PhD diss., Indiana University, 1974), 18; Hume, *Death and the Mines*, 16; Clark, *Miners Fight for Democracy*, 23–24; Nyden, "Miners for Democracy," 476–77.

18. Yablonski, quoted in Armbrister, *Act of Vengeance,* 13; historian is Alan Derickson, *Black Lung: Anatomy of a Public Health Disaster* (Ithaca, NY: Cornell University Press, 1998), 150.

19. Hume, *Death and the Mines*, 66–69, 162.

20. Miners for Democracy, 6058 Oral History (1972), Box 12, FF: MFD #1144, 12, KCLMD; Derickson, *Black Lung*, 144; Barbara Ellen Smith, *Digging Our Own Graves: Coal Miners and the Struggle over Black Lung Disease* (Philadelphia: Temple University Press), 77–114.

21. Derickson, *Black Lung*, 160–61; Smith, *Digging Our Own Graves*, 114–44.

22. Derickson, *Black Lung*, 181; Paul J. Nyden, "Rank-and-File Rebellions in the Coalfields, 1964–1980," *Monthly Review* 58 (2007): 38–53.

23. Oral History 6058 (1972), Box 12, FF: MFD #1144, 18, KCLMD; Dixiana quote *Washington Post* 12 December 1972; block quote from George Williams Hopkins, "The Miners for Democracy: Insurgency in the United Mine Workers," (PhD diss., University of North Carolina, 1976), 426.

24. "Comment," Rauh to Davis, 16 February 1971, Box 86, FF: Miners for Democracy, JLRP; Rauh to Hodgson, 7 May 1971, Box 116, FF: United Miner Workers Correspondence, JLRP; an invaluable trove of material on the UMWA conflict is *United Mine Workers' Election, Hearings Before the Subcommittee on Labor and Public Welfare*, United States Senate, 91st Cong., 2nd Sess., February 5–September 1970 (Part 1) and 92nd Cong. 1st Sess., July 12–13, 1971 (Part 2) (Washington, DC: GPO, 1971, 1972); *Washington Post* 7 January 1970; *Washington Post* 7 March 1970.

25. *New York Times* 26 November 1972; *New York Times* 17 December 1972; *Washington Post* 24 December 1972.

26. *New York Times* 26 November 1972.

27. Jensen, "Rebellion in the United Mine Workers," 120; Hopkins, "Miners for Democracy," 520, 567–68.

28. *New York Times* 15 August 1972; *New York Times* 26 November 1972.

29. Brit Hume, "Uncommon Sense," *Ramparts* 11 (February 1973): 10; *Washington Post* 17 December 1972.

30. Rauh to Dubinsky, 27 October 1972, Box 17, FF: 39, JHP; *The National Observer* 30 December 1972; Fred Barnes, "The UMWA Dictatorship on the Defensive," in *Autocracy and Insurgency in Organized Labor*, ed. Burton Hall (New Brunswick, NJ: Transaction Books, 1972), 21–29; *Washington Post* 29 February 1972.

31. *New York Times* 9 December 1973; *Proceedings of the Forty-Sixth Consecutive Constitutional Convention of the United Mine Workers of America*, 3–4 December 1973, 318. Meanwhile, Tony Boyle was wheel-chair bound after a suicide attempt in the fall of 1973. Already facing three years in prison for corruption, he was then finally convicted of three counts of murder with a mandatory sentence of life imprisonment in April of 1974. *Washington Post* 20 December 1973; *Washington Post* 12 April 1974.

32. Geoghegan, *Which Side Are You On?* 15, emphasis original; Benson, quoted in Hopkins, "Miners for Democracy," 480.

33. Joe Klein, "Old Fashioned Hero of the New Working Class," *Rolling Stone* 18 December 1975, 51; Philip W. Nyden, *Steelworkers Rank-and-File: The Political Economy of a Union Reform Movement* (South Hadley, MA: Praeger, 1984), 65. David Ignatius, in "The Press in Love," *Columbia Journalism Review* 16 (1977): 26, argues that Sadlowski's working class "puffery" made him a "momentary liberal culture figure" among a press hungry for such presentations of blue collar authenticity.

34. "Penthouse Interview: Ed Sadlowski," *Penthouse*, January 1977, 191–92; Edgar James, "Sadlowski and the Steelworkers: Notes for the Next Time," *Working Papers for a New Society*, Spring 1977, 31; *New York Times* 19 December 1976; Judith Coburn, "Ed Sadlowski Strides Toward Bethlehem," *Village Voice*, 7 February 1977, 27; Sidney Lens, "The Coming Revolt in Labor," *Progressive*, April 1977, 26–29; *Newsweek*, 10 May 1976; Philip Nyden, "Rank-and-File Organizations and the United Steelworkers of America," *Insurgent Sociologist* 8 (Fall 1978): 15–24; *New York Times* 1 September 1975.

35. Nyden, *Steelworkers Rank-and-File*, 72–73.

36. *UMWA Proceedings 1973*, 176; Nyden, "Miners for Democracy," 857–59; Nyden, *Steelworkers Rank-and-File*, 62; I.W. Abel, *Collective Bargaining: Labor Relations in Steel, Then and Now* (New York: Columbia University Press, 1976), 58; I.W. Abel, *ENA: The Experimental Negotiating Agreement* (Pittsburgh, PA: United Steel Workers of America, 1973), Archives Union File (AUF) Pamphlet Collection, KCLMD.

37. Coburn, "Ed Sadlowski Strides Toward Bethlehem," 27; David Bensman and Roberta Lynch, *Rusted Dreams: Hard Times in a Steel Community* (Berkeley: University of California Press, 1988), 132–34.

38. Klein, "Old Fashioned Hero," 50.

39. Coburn, "Ed Sadlowski Strides Toward Bethlehem," 27.

40. "Protest of Edward Sadlowski, Candidate for District Director of District 31, member of Local 65, concerning the conduct of the Election and the Counting of the Votes" 23 February 1973, Box 12, FF: 16, JHP; *Washington Post* 23 November 1974.

41. Stephen Singular, "Man of Steel," *New Times*, 4 February 1977, 41; "Penthouse Interview: Ed Sadlowski," 191–92.

42. Russell W. Gibbons, "Showdown at Lordstown," *Commonweal*, 3 March 1972, 523–24; Peter B. Levy, *The New Left and Labor in the 1960s* (Urbana: University of Illinois Press, 1994), 157.

43. Nelson Lichtenstein, *The Most Dangerous in Detroit: Walter Reuther and the Fate of American Labor* (New York: Basic Books, 1995), 396–419; Kevin Boyle, *The UAW and the Heyday of American Liberalism, 1945–1968* (Ithaca, NY: Cornell University Press, 1995), 234–56.

44. John Herling, "George Meany and the AFL-CIO," *New Republic* 4 October 1975; *JHLL* May 18, 1968; *JHLL* 12 April 1969; Haynes Johnson and Nick Kotz, *The Unions* (New York: Pocket Books, 1972), 50; Gil Green, *What's Happening to Labor* (New York: International Publishers, 1976), 122; George Morris, *Rebellion in the Unions: A Handbooks for Rank and File Action* (New York: New Outlook Publishers, 1971), 102–103; Reuther said of Meany, "He belongs in another period in human history. And that doesn't make him a bad person. It makes him an inadequate labor leader." William Eaton interview with Walter Reuther, February 1968–August 1969, 16, Box 2, FF: 35, FCWEC. Reuther's burst of energy in the late sixties contrasted markedly with the stolid plans for the future exhibited by his nemesis. In 1972, *U.S. News and World Report* asked AFL-CIO president George Meany why the total membership of the labor movement had not grown at the same rate as the nation's labor force, allowing for a downward creep in union density since its apex in the mid-1950s. Usually Meany combined political craftiness with his curmudgeonly tones, but in this interview his callousness was revealed. "I don't know and I don't care." As Meany continued, "Frankly, I used to worry about the size of the membership. But quite a few years ago I just stopped worrying about it, because to me it doesn't make any difference." The nation's number one labor leader showed shades of indifference reminiscent of his ally Tony Boyle. As the journalist John Herling noted, Meany was "light years away from labor's historic struggle." *JHLL* 26 February 1972.

45. Boyle, *The UAW and the Heyday of American Liberalism*, 247; for an analysis of ALA's organizing, see Victor G. Devinatz, "To Find Answers to the Urgent Problems of Our Society: The Alliance for Labor Action's Atlanta Union Organizing Offensive, 1969–1971," *Labor Studies Journal* 31 (2006): 69–91. The ALA's plans may have been doomed, but the rhetoric was pitch-perfect. The new organization spoke of organizing the South, pushing into low-paid white-collar work, bringing collective bargaining to agricultural workers, and it pledged to combine the new social movements with labor by mending "the alienation of the liberal-intellectual and academic community and the youth of our nation in order to build and strengthen a new alliance of progressive forces." *New York Times* 24 July 1968; *New York Times* 25 May 1969; *New York Times* 21 June 1970.

46. William Serrin, *The Company and the Union: The Civilized Relationship of the General Motors Corporation and the United Automobile Workers* (New York: Alfred A. Knopf, 1973), 24, 260.

47. Ibid., 19, 188–89, 306, emphasis in original; Brody, *Workers in Industrial America: Essays on the Twentieth Century Struggle* (New York: Oxford University Press, 1993), 185. On strike classes, see *New York Times* 18 October 1970; *New York Times* 8 November 1970.

48. *Washington Post* 2 August 1970.

49. "Press Release by Paul Cubellis—Shop Chairman of Bargaining Committee," n.d., Local 1112 Box 8, FF: 2, Local 1112. For the most detailed overview of Lordstown, see David F. Moberg, "Rattling the Golden Chains: Conflict and Consciousness of Auto Workers," (PhD diss., University of Chicago, 1978), 321; Mike Davis, *Prisoners of the American Dream: Politics and Economy in the History of the U.S. Working Class* (New York: Verso, 1999), 55.

50. Geoffrey Norman, "Blue-Collar Saboteurs," *Playboy*, September 1972, 98.

51. *Time*, 7 February 1972; *New York Times* 6 February 1972; *Wall Street Journal* 31 January 1972; "Boredom Spells Trouble," *Life*, 1 September 1972; *Newsweek*, 7 February 1972; *Newsweek*, 23 October 1972; "Sabotage at Lordstown," *Time*, 7 February 1972; *Business Week*, 4 March 1972; *New York Times* 7 March 1972; Moberg, "Rattling the Golden Chains," 321, and passim; Clark, *Miners for Democracy*, 19, 15, 89; Special Task Force to the Secretary of Health, Education, and Welfare, *Work in America* (Cambridge, MA: MIT Press, 1973); Norman, "Blue-Collar Saboteurs," 251; for a sampling of the newspaper press, see the sizable clipping collection in Box 1, FF1, RGP.

52. Judson Gooding, "Blue-Collar Blues in the Assembly Line," *Fortune*, July 1970, 112–13; *JHLL* 3 January 1970; *Worker Alienation, Hearings Before the Subcommittee of Employment, Manpower, and the Poverty of the Committee on Labor and Public Welfare*, U.S. Senate, 192nd Cong. (Washington, DC: GPO, 1972), 15–18; Neal Q. Herrick and Michael Maccoby, "Humanizing Work: A Priority Goal of the 1970s," in Louis E. Davis, Albert B. Cherns and Associates, *The Quality of Working Life: Problems, Prospects and the State of the Art* (New York: Free Press, 1975), 63–90.

53. Studs Terkel, *Working* (New York: Pantheon, 1972), 193; Barbara Garson, "Luddites in Lordstown," *Harper's Magazine*, June 1972, 68–73; B.J. Widick, "The Men Won't Toe the Vega Line," *The Nation* 27 March 1972; *Wall Street Journal* 31 January 1972; Stanley Aronowitz, *False Promises: The Shaping of the American Working Class Consciousness* (New York: McGraw-Hill, 1973), 21–50.

54. "Press Release by Paul Cubellis—Shop Chairman of Bargaining Committee," UAW Local 1112, Box 8, FF: 2, Local 1112.

55. Aronowitz, *False Promises*, 43–44; *New York Times* 9 September 1973; Moberg, "Rattling the Golden Chains," 322–31. The issues and settlement are well discussed in Heather Ann Thompson, "Auto Workers, Dissent, and the UAW: Detroit and Lordstown," in *Autowork*, ed. Robert Asher and Ronald Edsforth (Albany, NY: SUNY Press, 1995), 205. The real defeat at Lordstown, however, may have been one of political imagination. As Victor Reuther explained to Stan Weir, at the same time as the Ohio auto dispute, the West Coast longshoremen were in the midst of the longest strike in their history, a 130-day long conflict led by Harry Bridges. The autoworkers sent a delegation out to the coast to support the strike and to keep Japanese cars out of the United States until they had won their strike

at GM. UAW President Leonard Woodcock would have none of it. The Lordstown workers then decided to mobilize a group to go to Japan to discuss the setting of international work rules for automobiles—thus ending the whipsawing of the workers of one country against another. Woodcock rejected that idea too, noting that he was going to go to Japan himself. There, percolating up from the rank and file, was an imaginative solution to what would, a generation later, be called globalization. As Weir notes, "The Lordstown men and women have never been given proper credit for the genius of their commonsense approach, anticipating the need for an alternative unionism that draws its strength from solidarity agreements rather than cooperation with employers." See Stan Weir, *Singlejack Solidarity* (Minneapolis: University of Minnesota Press, 2004), 70–71.

56. *UMWA Proceedings 1973*, 59.

57. Susan Ferriss and Ricardo Sandoval, *The Fight in the Fields: Cesar Chavez and the Farmworkers Movement* (New York: Harcourt Brace, 1997), 149; Levy, *The New Left and Labor*, 128–34; Sam Kushner, *Long Road to Delano* (New York: International Press, 1975).

58. Jacques E. Levy, *Cesar Chavez: Autobiography of La Causa* (New York: Norton, 1975), 325; Ferriss and Sandoval, *Fight in the Fields*, 178.

59. Levy, *Chavez*, 487, 441; Jerry J. Berman and Jim Hightower, "Chavez and the Teamsters," *The Nation* 2 November 1970.

60. Marshall Ganz, *Why David Sometimes Wins: Leadership, Organization, and Strategy in the California Farm Worker Movement* (New York: Oxford University Press, 2009), 231–33.

61. *New York Times* 17 April 1974; *New York Times* 22 February 1972; *New York Times* 10 May 1973; Ganz, *Why David Sometimes Wins*, 231–33.

62. *New York Times* 15 September 1974; Ferriss and Sandoval, *Fight in the Fields*, 188; *New York Times* 8 February 1975; *Time*, 3 September 1973; "wearing thin" is from Cletus Daniel, "Cesar Chavez and the Unionization of California Farm Workers," in *Labor Leaders in America*, ed. Melvyn Dubofsky and Warren Van Tine (Urbana: University of Illinois Press, 1987), 376.

63. *New York Times* 15 May 1975; *New York Times* 8 May 1975; *New York Times* 30 May 1975; Ganz, *Why David Sometimes Wins*, 235–37.

64. Ferriss and Sandoval, *Fight in the Fields*, 209.

65. Ganz, *Why David Sometimes Wins*, 243–48.

66. *UMWA Proceedings 1973*, 288; "Farah: The Strike that Has Everything," *Texas Observer*, 29 December 1972 (the article was made into a widely circulated pamphlet by the ACW, see Box 1, FF: Union Documents, MFP.

67. On the development of "twin plants" on the border, see Leslie Sklair, *Assembling for Development: The Maquila Industry in Mexico and the United States* (Boston: Unwin Hyman, 1989); Jefferson Cowie, *Capital Moves: RCA's Seventy Year Quest for Cheap Labor* (New York: The New Press, 2001), 108–113.

68. Bill Finger, "Victoria Sobre Farah," *Southern Exposure* 4 (1976): 45–49; Rex Hardesty, "Farah: The Union Struggle in the 70's," *American Federationist* 80 (June 1973): 1–13; *New York Times* 15 February 1973; "The Strike that Has Everything," *UMWA Proceedings 1973*, 290.

69. Laurie Coyle, Gail Hershatter, and Emily Honig, "Women at Farah: An Unfinished Story," in *Mexican Women in the United States*, ed. Magdalena Mora and Adelaida R. Del Castillo (Los Angeles: UCLA Chicano Studies Research Center Occasional Paper No. 2, 1980), 137.

70. Coyle, Hershatter, and Honig, "Women at Farah," 136.

71. Jennifer Rebecca Mata, "Creating a Critical Chicana Narrative: Writing the Chicanas at Farah into Labor History," (PhD diss., Washington State University, 2004), 128.

72. Coyle, Hershatter, and Honig, "Women at Farah," 137.

73. See the interview with Bustamante, a critic of the union, in George I. Serebrenik, "The Unionization of Farah in the Early Seventies," Professional Report, University of Texas, Austin, Graduate School of Business, 54–85, 137; Coyle, Hershatter, and Honig, "Women at Farah," 137; Emily Honig, "Women at Farah Revisited: Political Mobilization and Its Aftermath Among Chicana Workers in El Paso, Texas, 1972–1992," *Feminist Studies* 22 (1996): 448.

74. *UMWA Proceedings 1973*, 239–40.

75. See, for instance, August Meier and Elliott Rudwick, *Black Detroit and the Rise of the UAW* (New York: Oxford University Press, 1979); Thomas J. Sugrue, *Origins of the Urban Crisis: Race and Inequality in Postwar Detroit* (Princeton, NJ: Princeton University Press, 1996); Bruce Nelson, *Divided We Stand: American Workers and the Struggle for Black Equality* (Princeton, NJ: Princeton University Press, 2001); Michael K. Honey, *Black Workers Remember: An Oral History of Segregation, Unionism, and the Freedom Struggle* (Berkeley: University of California Press, 1999); Zaragosa Vargas, *Labor Rights are Civil Rights: Mexican American Workers in the Twentieth Century* (Princeton, NJ: Princeton University Press, 2005); Ruth Needleman, *Black Freedom Fighters: The Struggle for Democratic Unionism* (Ithaca, NY: ILR Press, 2003). Other founders of CBTU were William Lucy of AFSCME, Jack Edwards of the UAW and William Simons of the Washington Teachers Union.

76. Robinson quotes from undated *Ledger-Star* clipping, FF: Clippings, misc., 1955–1986, Box 9, CRP; *UMWA Proceedings 1973*, 238–41; on formation of CBTU, see *New York Times* 12 September 1972.

77. A. Philip Randolph, Bayard Rustin, and Norman Hill, "A Call to Action" Working Paper for Conference of Black Trade Unionists 1–2 May 1972, Box 48, FF: Black Trade Unionists, BRP; *JHLL* 19 December 1970; remarks on differences with CBTU are from Rustin to Lucy, 7 April 1976 and Lucy to Rustin, 29 April 1976, Box 48, FF: Black Trade Unionists, BRP; William Lucy, "The Black Partners," *The Nation* 7 September 1974; John D'Emilio, *Lost Prophet: The Life and Times of Bayard Rustin* (New York: Free Press, 2003), 414–39; Rustin's thinking is out-

lined effectively in Bayard Rustin, "The Blacks and the Unions," *Harpers Magazine* (May 1971): 73–81; for a critique of Rustin from the left, see Julius Jacobson, "From Protest to Politicking," *New Politics* 5 (Fall 1966): 47–65.

78. Kate Karl, "The Unquenchable Spark: The UAW, Revolutionary Union Movements, and the Rank and File in Detroit, 1968–1973 (honors thesis, Cornell University, 1999), 27–28, 38, 43.

79. Thompson, "Auto Workers, Dissent, and the UAW: Detroit and Lordstown," 190; Boyle, *UAW and the Heyday of American Liberalism*, 254.

80. "An Appeal to the Community from Black Trade Unionists" (full page ad) *New York Times* 19 September 1968.

81. Irwin Ross, "Those Newly Militant Government Workers," *Fortune*, August 1968, 131, 134.

82. Wurf in *Fortune*, August 1968, 104.

83. Quoted in Richard N. Billings and John Greenya, *Power to the Public Worker* (Washington, DC: Robert B. Luce, Inc., 1974), 13; Richard B. Freeman, "Unionism Comes to the Public Sector," *Journal of Economic Literature* 24 (March 1986): 43; Joseph C. Goulden, *Jerry Wurf: Labor's Last Angry Man* (New York: Atheneum, 1982).

84. Joseph A. McCartin, "A Wagner Act for Public Employees: Labor's Deferred Dream and the Rise of Conservatism, 1970–1977," *Journal of American History* 95 (June 2008): 123–48.

85. Wurf, quoted in John Herling, "Change and Conflict in the AFL-CIO," *Dissent* (Fall 1974): 482; Joseph A. McCartin, "Bringing the State's Workers Back In: Time to Rectify an Imbalanced US Labor Historiography," *Labor History* 47 (February 2006): 73–94; Lichtenstein, *State of the Union*, 182.

86. Karen Nussbaum interview by Kathleen Banks Nutter, December 2003, transcript, Voices of Feminism Oral History Project, Sophia Smith Collection, Smith College, 18–19, 33.

87. Ibid.

88. Dorothy Sue Cobble, *The Other Women's Movement: Workplace Justice and Social Rights in Modern America* (Princeton, NJ: Princeton University Press, 2004), 222; Dorothy Sue Cobble and Alice Kessler-Harris, "Karen Nussbaum," in *Talking Leadership: Conversations with Powerful Women*, ed. Mary S. Hartman (New Brunswick, NJ: Rutgers University Press), 135–55; see also Mary Margaret Fonow, *Union Women: Forging Feminism in the United Steelworkers of America* (Minneapolis: University of Minnesota Press, 2003), 95–111.

89. *Wall Street Journal* 15 March 1971; *Detroit Free Press* 16 March 1971; *Detroit Free Press* 17 March 1971; *Detroit Free Press* 18 March 1971; *Detroit Free Press* 22 March 1971; Serrin, *Company and the Union*, 153; *Cleveland Plain Dealer* 30 July 1972. As a 1978 study showed, women accounted for half of the increase in union membership between 1956 and 1976 but barely made inroads into leadership. See Linda H. LeGrande, "Women in Labor Organizations: Their Ranks are Increasing," *Monthly Labor Review* 101 (August 1978): 8–14.

90. Cobble, *Other Women's Movement*, 201; Ruth Milkman, "Women Workers, Feminism and the Labor Movement Since the 1960s" in *Women, Work & Protest*, ed. Ruth Milkman (Boston: Routledge & Kegan Paul, 1985), 314; Patricia Cayo Sexton, "Workers (Female) Arise!" *Dissent* (Summer 1975): 380–95.

91. Alice Kessler-Harris, *In Pursuit of Equity: Women, Men, and the Quest for Economic Citizenship in the 20th Century America* (New York: Oxford University Press, 2001), 294; Cobble, *Other Women's Movement*, 205.

92. Susan Reverby, "An Epilogue . . . or Prologue to CLUW?" *Radical America*, November–December 1975, 112–14; Cobble, *Other Women's Movement*, 205; Diane Balser, *Sisterhood & Solidarity: Feminism and Labor in Modern Times* (Boston: South End Press, 1987), 186, 193, 195. Similarly, flight attendants struggled both within the unions and against the notorious sexism of the airlines, which often used them as sex objects to sell seats on airplanes with ploys such as National Airlines' ad campaign featuring stewardesses saying slogans such as, "Hi, I'm Linda, and I'm going to FLY you like you've never been flown before" or Continental's, which claimed, "We really move our tail for you." As a result, airline workers launched Stewardesses for Women's Rights and, in conjunction with the Equal Employment Opportunity Commission, were able to redefine their work from the realm of the sexualized "sky muffin" to that of flight attendant. See Dorothy Sue Cobble, "A Spontaneous Loss of Enthusiasm: Workplace Feminism and the Transformation of Women's Service Jobs in the 1970s," *International Labor and Working-Class History* 56 (Fall 1999): 23–44; Lindsy Van Gelder, "Coffee, Tea, or Fly Me," *Ms.*, January 1973, 86–91; *Newsweek*, 18 March 1974; Louise Kapp Howe, "No More Stewardesses—We're Flight Attendants," *Redbook*, January 1979, 65, 70–74.

93. Mazzacchi, quoted in Les Leopold, *The Man Who Hated Work and Loved Labor* (White River Junction, VT: Chelsea Green, 2007), 333.

94. U.S. Census Bureau, *Income, Poverty, and Health Insurance Coverage in the United States: 2005*, 38; Francine D. Blau and Lawrence M. Kahn, "Gender Differences in Pay," *Journal of Economic Perspectives* 14 (Fall 2000): 84–85.

95. Staughton Lynd, "Blue-Collar Organizing," *Working Papers for a New Society* 1 (Spring 1973): 28.

96. James R. Green, *Taking History to Heart: The Power of the Past in Building Social Movements* (Amherst: University of Massachusetts, 2000), 44, 48; Steve Early, "Thoughts on the 'Worker-Student Alliance'—Then and Now," *Labor History* 44 (2003): 9.

97. Hopkins, "Miners for Democracy," 46; Early, "Thoughts on the 'Worker-Student Alliance,'" 9.

98. Green, *Taking History to Heart*, 44.

99. Davis, *Prisoners of the American Dream*, 127; Michael Goldfield, *The Decline of Organized Labor in the United States* (Chicago: University of Chicago Press, 1987), 238.

100. Paul Krugman, "For Richer," *New York Times Magazine*, 20 October 2002. For an elaboration of this argument, see Jefferson Cowie and Nick Salvatore, "The Long Exception: Rethinking the New Deal in American History," *International Labor and Working-Class History* 74 (2008): 3–32, with five commentaries and response, "History, Complexity, and Politics: Further Thoughts."

101. Singular, "Man of Steel," 41.

102. Moberg, "Rattling the Golden Chains," 363, 604: a large group interview done eighteen months after the strike confirmed that the problems had largely never been solved; see *New York Times* 9 September 1973; Joshua Freeman, *Working-Class New York* (New York: The New Press, 2000), 281.

Chapter 2: What Kind of Delegation Is This?

1. Jack Newfield, *RFK: A Memoir* (New York: Thunder's Mouth Press/Nation Books, 2003 [1969]), 8.

2. David Frost, *Presidential Debate 1968* (New York: Stein and Day, 1968), 114; Newfield, *RFK*, 9.

3. The Torres anecdote introduces Lester David and Irene David, *Bobby Kennedy: The Making of a Folk Hero* (New York: Dodd, Mead & Company, 1986), 3; Ronald Steel, *In Love with Night: The American Romance with Robert Kennedy* (New York: Simon and Schuster, 2000), 16–128.

4. Cowan and Coles, quoted in Arthur M. Schlesinger, Jr., *Robert F. Kennedy* (New York: Houghton Mifflin, 1978), 891; similar sentiments in Mathew Maxwell Taylor Kennedy, "Introduction," in *Make Gentle the Life of this World: The Vision of Robert F. Kennedy* (New York: Harcourt Brace & Company, 1998), vx; William Vanden Heuvel and Milton Gwirtzman, *On His Own: Robert F. Kennedy 1964–1968* (Garden City, NY: Doubleday, 1970), 203. For criticism of the "black and blue-collar" alliance, see Dominic Sandbrook, *Eugene McCarthy: The Rise and Fall of Postwar American Liberalism* (New York: Knopf, 2004), 199–202; Steel, *In Love with Night*, 173–76; Vanden Heuvel and Gwirtzman, *On His Own*, 379, 348–49; Samuel Flaks, "Searching for Bobby Hoosier: Robert Kennedy's 1968 Indiana Primary Campaign" (honor's thesis, Cornell University, 2006); David R. Roediger, *Colored White: Transcending the Racial Past* (Berkeley: University of California Press, 2002), 181, 62.

5. Doris Kearns, *Lyndon Johnson and the American Dream* (New York: Signet, 1976), 359, for LBJ's "Bobby problem," see 208–10.

6. Joseph A. Palermo, *In His Own Right: The Political Odyssey of Senator Robert F. Kennedy* (New York: Columbia University Press, 2001), 174–77; Taylor Branch, *At Canaan's Edge* (New York: Simon and Schuster, 2006), 689; William H. Chafe, *The Unfinished Journey*, 4th ed. (New York: Oxford University Press, 1999), 365.

7. Bayard Rustin, "From Protest to Politics: The Future of the Civil Rights Movement," *Commentary*, February 1965, in Rustin, *Down the Line: The Collected*

Writings of Bayard Rustin (Chicago: Quadrangle Books, 1971), 111–22; Chavez and Kennedy from Susan Ferriss and Ricardo Sandoval, *The Fight in the Fields: Cesar Chavez and the Farmworkers Movement* (New York: Harcourt Brace, 1997), 145.

8. Newfield, *RFK*, 80; on the "liberal consensus," see Godfrey Hodgson, *America in Our Time* (Garden City, NY: Doubleday, 1976), 67–98.

9. Pete Hamill, "Wallace," *Ramparts,* 26 October 1968, 48; Michael Kazin, *The Populist Persuasion: An American History* (New York: Basic Books, 1995), 238, 240–41. Some of the early concern over Wallace can be seen in Michael Rogin, "Wallace and the Middle Class; the White Backlash in Wisconsin" *Public Opinion Quarterly* 30 (Spring 1966): 98–108; Rogin, "Politics, Emotion, and the Wallace Vote," *British Journal of Sociology* 20 (March 1969): 27–49; Margaret Conway, "The White Backlash Re-examined: Wallace and the 1964 Primaries," *Social Science Quarterly* 49 (December 1968): 710–19.

10. Kazin, *Populist*, 238, 240–41; on Wallace in general, see Dan T. Carter, *The Politics of Rage: George Wallace, The Origins of the New Conservatism, and the Transformation of American Politics* (Baton Rouge: Louisiana State University Press); for Wallace and labor, see "The Wallace Labor Record," Box 7, FF: 20, JHP; Welder, quoted in Kazin, *Populist Persuasion*, 221; Harris, quoted in Jonathan Rieder, "Politics and Authenticity," *Dissent* (Summer 1975): 292; Doug Fraser, UAW president, remarked that the backlash was real but not hard to overcome. The workers "accepted the inevitability" of integration. "Now that it's integrated and they meet the blacks and socialize with the blacks and they say, 'What the hell was the fuss about? They're human beings just like me, or much like me." Doug Fraser Oral History by John Barnard, Archives of Labor and Urban Affairs, Walter P. Reuther Library, Wayne State University, 86, Detroit, Michigan.

11. "Bobby-LBJ" and Smith to Barkan, 4 May 1968, FF 13, Box 39, RG 1–038, President Files, GMMA; many polls showed substantial rank-and-file support for Kennedy, see "Why Unions Are Running Scared in 1968," *Nation's Business* 56 (June 1968): 36–39.

12. Newfield, *RFK*, 302; *JHLL* 11 May 1968.

13. Greenberg, Orren, Mollenkopf, and Solomon, "Voting Prediction Model: Kennedy and McCarthy in Indiana" 14 May 1968, RFK Presidential Campaign National Headquarter Files, Media Division, Box 2, Primary Surveys, RFKP; John F. Kraft, Inc., "Presidential Primary Preferences of Indiana Voters," late March 1968, RFK Black Boxes, RFKP; 1968 Presidential Campaign, Indiana other, Box 1, Presidential Primary Preference, RFKP; Palermo, *In His Own Right*, 205.

14. The Romero story is revisited in *Time*, 8 June 1998.

15. 12 October 1968 *JHHL;* Barkan to Meany, 5 August 1968, FF: 15, Box 39, RG 038, GMMA; 2 November 1968 *JHLL*.

16. As Theodore White put it with regards to labor's mobilization in 1968: "The dimension of the AFL-CIO effort, unprecedented in American history, can be

caught only by its final summary figures: the ultimate registration, by labor's efforts, of 4.6 million voters; the printing and distribution of 55 million pamphlets and leaflets out of Washington and 60 million more from local unions; telephone banks in 638 localities, using 8,055 telephones, manned by 24,611 union men and women and their families; some 72,225 house-to-house canvassers; and on elections day, 94,457 volunteers serving as car-poolers, materials-distributors, baby-sitters, poll-watchers, telephoners." See Theodore H. White, *The Making of the President, 1972* (New York: Atheneum Publishers, 1973), 453; Mike Davis, *Prisoners of the American Dream* (New York: Verso, 1986), 265; Haynes Johnson, *The Unions*, 80, 87; 9 November 1968 *JHLL*, 23 November 1968 *JHLL*.

17. Edmund F. Wehrle, *Between a River and a Mountain: The AFL-CIO and the Vietnam War* (Ann Arbor: University of Michigan Press, 2005).

18. Robert Sam Anson, *McGovern: A Biography* (New York: Holt, Rinehart and Winston, 1972), 2–11; George McGovern, *Grassroots: The Autobiography of George McGovern* (New York: Random House, 1977), 109–12; William Chafe, *Never Stop Running: Allard Lowenstein and the Struggle to Save American Liberalism* (New York: Basic Books, 1993), 271.

19. White, *Making of the President*, 40; Anson, *McGovern*, 2, 10; McGovern, *Grassroots*, 109–10, 117.

20. McGovern, *Grassroots*, 3–32; McGovern's remarkable time as a bomber pilot is covered in Stephen E. Ambrose, *The Wild Blue: The Men and Boys Who Flew B-24s over Germany* (New York: Simon and Schuster, 2001), 187–89, 234.

21. Anson, *McGovern*, 57.

22. McGovern, *Grassroots*, 29; on the South Dakota Democratic Party, see Valerie R. O'Regan and Stephen J. Stambough, "From the Grassroots: Building the South Dakota Democratic Party," in *George McGovern: A Political Life, A Political Legacy*, ed. Robert P. Watson (Pierre: South Dakota State Historical Society Press, 2004), 38–49.

23. Gordon Lee Weil, *The Long Shot: George McGovern Runs for President* (New York: Norton, 1973), 13–16.

24. McGovern, *Grassroots*, 133–54; William J. Crotty, *Decision for the Democrats: Reforming the Party Structure* (Baltimore: Johns Hopkins University Press, 1978), 33–58.

25. *New York Times* 17 July 1972; the neo-conservatives' views are outlined in Nelson W. Polsby, *Consequences of Party Reform* (New York: Oxford University Press, 1983); Norman Podhoretz, *Breaking Ranks: A Political Memoir* (New York: Harper and Row, 1979); Byron E. Shafer, *Quiet Revolution: The Struggle for the Democratic Party and the Shaping of Post-Reform Politics* (New York: Russell Sage, 1983), Ronald Radosh, *Divided They Fall: The Demise of the Democratic Party, 1964–1996* (New York: Free Press, 1996*)*; for the Wurf quote, see Joseph C. Goulden, *Jerry Wurf: Labor's Last Angry Man* (New York: Atheneum, 1982), 216.

26. Crotty, *Decision for the Democrats*, 52–53.

27. Barkan and COPE official quote in Haynes Johnson and Nick Kotz, *The Unions* (New York: Pocket Books, 1972), 83, 77. For further discussion of this, see Taylor Dark, "Organized Labor and Party Reform: A Reassessment," *Polity* 28 (Summer 1996): 512. Despite the war and the reform commission, there was still some room for reconciliation a year before McGovern won the primary. During McGovern's meeting with the AFL-CIO in 1971, the senator bowed and scraped as Democratic leaders were supposed to do before labor's monarch, referring to Meany as "a tower of strength for the working men and women of this country." George Meany was visibly pleased with McGovern's denunciations of Nixon's New Economic Policy, and the senator was still on Meany's short list of "acceptable" candidates. The immense improbability of McGovern winning the nomination and the hope that the war would be over by 1972 probably prevented the AFL-CIO apparatchik from seriously vetting him at a point so far from election year.

28. For a strategic outline of how McGovern's coalition might look like RFK's as the Democratic center was collapsing, see Herbert Hill to Joe Floyd, 30 June 1972, FF: Issues-Various, Box 898, GSMP; Joseph L. Rauh, "Liberals and 1972," FF: Campaign Suggestions 1971, Box 1115, GSMP.

29. White, *Making of the President 1972*, 312, 317–18.

30. Anson, *McGovern*, 266 (fn).

31. Frederick G. Dutton, *Changing Sources of Power: American Politics in the 1970's* (New York: McGraw-Hill, 1971), xv.

32. Dutton, *Sources of Power*, 142, 222, 225.

33. Charles A. Reich, *The Greening of America* (New York: Random House, 1970), 334, 378.

34. Richard M. Scammon and Ben J. Wattenberg, *The Real Majority* (New York: Coward-McCann, Inc., 1970), 21, 40–43, 44, 76, 81.

35. Kazin, *Populist Persuasion*, 1; Jack Newfield and Jeff Greenfield, *A Populist Manifesto: The Making of a New Majority* (New York: Praeger, 1972), 204.

36. Newfield and Greenfield, *Populist*, 9, 10, 11.

37. Fred R. Harris, *Now Is the Time: A New Populist Call to Action* (New York: McGraw-Hill, 1971), 147–148.

38. Kristi Witker, *How to Lose Everything in Politics Except Massachusetts* (New York: Mason & Lipscomb, 1974), 202; Mankiewicz quoted in White, *Making of the President*, 44.

39. Gary Hart, *Right from the Start: A Chronicle of the McGovern Campaign* (New York: Quadrangle, 1973), 4, 45; Hunter S. Thompson, *Fear and Loathing: On the Campaign Trail '72* (San Francisco: Straight Arrow Books, 1973), 127.

40. *Business Week* 27 May 1972; White, *Making of the President*, 118–20; Milton Friedman, *Capitalism and Freedom* (Chicago: University of Chicago Press, 1962), 192–95; Nee to Mankiewicz, "How the $1,000 Income Plan will win McGovern the Election," Box 329, NF, GSMP.

41. Weil, *Long Shot*, 97–101.

42. White, *Making of the President*, 95.

43. *New York Times* 11 August 1972; *New York Times* 2 February 1972; *New York Times* 3 March 1972; the *Manchester Union-Leader* attributed his success in New Hampshire to support for parochial schools, see 19 February 1972; *Washington Post* 8 March 1972; Hart, *Right from the Start*, 127.

44. *Washington Post* 15 February 1972, *Washington Post* 20 February 1972, *Washington Post* 12 May 1972, *New York Times* 19 May 1972; the *Post* reported that of 42 percent of all American school children bused to school, 39 percent were bused voluntarily, and only 3 percent were bused for the purposes of desegregation. *Washington Post* 29 March 1972; *New York Times Magazine* 14 May 1972; *New York Post* 27 April 1972; Ronald P. Formisano, *Boston Against Busing: Race, Class, and Ethnicity in the 1960s and 1970s* (Chapel Hill: University of North Carolina Press, 1991), 225.

45. George McGovern, "The Message They Sent," 23 March 1972, Milwaukee, in George McGovern, *An American Journey, The Presidential Campaign Speeches of George McGovern* (New York: Random House, 1974), 178–90; Thomas Byrne Edsall and Mary D. Edsall, *Chain Reaction: The Impact of Race, Rights, and Taxes on American Politics* (New York: Norton, 1991), 89.

46. Reuther quote from letter to Willy Brandt, quoted in Stephen Amberg, "The Labor-Liberal Alliance at Work," in *Organized Labor and American Politics, 1894–1994*, ed. Kevin Boyle (Albany, NY: SUNY Press, 1998), 181–83; on the transformation of the urban north, see Thomas J. Sugrue, *The Origins of the Urban Crisis: Race and Inequality in Postwar Detroit* (Princeton, NJ: Princeton University Press, 1996).

47. McGovern, "The Message They Sent," 178–90.

48. Hart, *Right from the Start*, 141, 144; *New York Times* 29 March 1972.

49. *Face the Nation*, CBS News transcript, 2 April 1972, Milwaukee, FF: Labor 1972, Box 790, GSMP; George McGovern, "A Personal Reflection," 11–12, unpublished ms, FF: December 1972, Box 774, GSMP; Hart, *Right from the Start*, 144.

50. *Newsweek* 29 May 1972; Carter, *Politics of Rage*, 437.

51. Jody Carlson, *George C. Wallace and the Politics of Powerlessness: The Wallace Campaigns for the Presidency, 1964–1976* (New Brunswick, NJ: Transaction Books, 1981), 148–49; Stephan Lesher, *George Wallace: American Populist* (New York: William Patrick, 1994), 485; Richard M. Scammon, *America Votes 10: A Handbook of Contemporary American Election Statistics (1972)* (Washington, DC: Congressional Quarterly, 1973), 19. The subsequent vote-getting attempts of the Wallace campaign produced a further 401,064 votes for a grand total of 3,755,424 votes for Wallace in the 1972 primaries. Wallace ran third in the post assassination California primary, though he received 216,000 write-in votes in California.

52. *New York Times* 19 April 1972, *New York Times* 6 May 1972; Weil, *Long Shot*, 240.

53. *Washington Post* 28 April 1972; *New York Times* 30 April 1972.

54. White, *Making of the President*, 123; *JHLL* 6 May 1972; *JHLL* 17 June 1972; labor's relationship to the war is covered in Edmund F. Wehrle, *Between a River and a Mountain: The AFL-CIO and the Vietnam War* (Ann Arbor: University of Michigan Press, 2005).

55. David J. McDonald, *Union Man* (New York: E.P. Dutton, 1969), 287.

56. White, *Making of the President*, 178; *New York Times* 17 July 1972.

57. Delegate percentages from McGovern, *Grassroots*, 149 and Crotty, *Decision for the Democrats*, 143; Clark to Harris, "Black Delegate Representation," 5 July 1972, FF: 11, Box 55, JWP; union delegate numbers from The Ripon Society and Clifford W. Brown, Jr., *Jaws of Victory: The Game-Plan Politics of 1972, the Crisis of the Republican Party, and the Future of the Constitution* (Boston: Little, Brown and Company, 1973), 173; *Washington Post* 2 September 1972; Stephen C. Schlesinger, *The New Reformers: Forces for Change in American Politics* (Boston: Houghton Mifflin, 1975), 90; descriptions of labor's privileges at the convention are in the handwritten notes in Box 55, FF: 11, JWP.

58. "McGovern: A Good Labor Record," Box 789, FF: Labor 1972 #1, GSMP; George S. McGovern and Leonard F. Guttridge, *The Great Coalfield War* (Boston: Houghton Mifflin, 1972); on the platform, see Denis G. Sullivan, Jeffrey L. Pressman, Benjamin I. Page, and John J. Lyons, *The Politics of Representation: The Democratic Convention of 1972* (New York: St. Martin's, 1974), 95–96.

59. "McGovern: A Good Labor Record," Box 789, FF: Labor 1972 #1, GSMP; Sullivan, Pressman, Page, and Lyons, *The Politics of Representation: The Democratic Convention of 1972*, 95–96; "Senator McGovern on Article 14b of Taft-Hartley Act," Box 790, FF: Labor 1972, GSMP; Taylor E. Dark, *The Unions and the Democrats: An Enduring Alliance* (Ithaca, NY: Cornell/ILR, 1999), 56–63.

60. *Washington Post* 10 July 1972; Lester Spielman to Senator, 10 July 1972, Box 790, FF: Labor 1972, GSMP.

61. *JHLL* 15 July 1972; Dark, *The Unions and the Democrats*, 87–92.

62. White, *Making of the President*, 165; Thomas Byrne Edsall and Mary D. Edsall, for instance, use the Royko quote as anecdotal evidence of a party gone awry, see *Chain Reaction*, 94.

63. Thompson, *Fear and Loathing*, 280–81, 284.

64. Hart, *Right from the Start*, 233; McGovern, quoted in Thompson, *Fear and Loathing*, 470–71.

65. *New York Times* 12 July 1972; McGovern, *Grassroots*, 194.

66. McGovern, *An American Journey*, 24; White, *Making of the President*, 187.

67. Nixon, *RN, the Memoirs of Richard Nixon* (New York: Gosset and Dunlap, 1978), 657.

68. *New York Times* 17 July 1972; *JHLL* 22 July 1972; *Wall Street Journal* 27 February 1969.

69. Jerry Wurf, "What Labor Has Against McGovern," *New Republic*, 5–12 August 1972; Wurf statement in McGovern for President release, 4 July 1972, FF:

Labor 1972, FF 789, GSMP; see also Harry McPherson, "The Democrats' Dilemma: Watergate Has Undone the Republicans, Right?" *New York Times Magazine*, 9 September 1973; *JHLL* 22 July 1972; Schlesinger, *New Reformers*, 95; Barkan to Keefe, 14 August 1972, RG21–001, FF: 6, Box 14, GMMA. The ideas are echoed by political scientist Taylor Dark who argues, "the behavior of the AFL-CIO leaders largely, if not exclusively, grew out of their desire to maintain the power-broker role to which they had grown accustomed, and which buttressed their organizational status." See Dark, "Organized Labor and Party Reform," 512.

70. *New York Times* 27 July 1972; White, *Making of the President*, 200–208.

71. *Haldeman Diaries*, 28 July 1972, 29 July 1972; Nixon, *RN*, 658; Carter, *Politics of Rage*, 450.

72. Press Release, "National Labor Committee for the Election of McGovern-Shriver," 16 August 1972, Box 725, FF: Major Labor Unions, GSMP; "Remarks by Senator George McGovern to Labor for McGovern Meeting," 25 August 1972, Box 790, FF: Labor 1972, GSMP; "Official Union Endorsements," Box 727, FF: Official Union Endorsements, GSMP; *JHLL* 30 September 1972; Communication Workers of America, "A Response to McGovern's Critics," (Washington, DC: CWA, 1972), FF: Labor 1972, Box 790, GSMP; on McGovern's attempt to woo Meany, see "Before Wed AFL-CIO Executive Council," FF: Labor 1972, Box 790, GSMP.

It was headed by Joseph D. Keenan, Secretary of the International Brotherhood of Electrical Workers, a figure from the typically conservative building trades who could hopefully work on the rightward drifting working-class vote. Joseph Beirne, President of the Communication Workers of America, was elected secretary-treasurer, and Howard D. Samuel of the ACWA was appointed executive director.

The list of members of the National Labor Committee for the Election of McGovern-Shriver includes AFSCME; Communication Workers of America; Machinists; Oil, Chemical and Atomic Workers; International Union of Electrical Workers; Retail Clerks; and the Auto Workers. This core expanded to include Amalgamated Meat Cutters, Amalgamated Clothing Workers, International Ladies Garment Workers, United Rubber Workers, and the Service Employees to name a few of the thirty-nine internationals that had joined by the height of the national campaign.

73. *New York Times* 23 October 1972; Schlesinger, *New Reformers*, 95.

74. *JHLL* 19 and 26 August 1972.

75. "McGovern Positions on Labor Issues," FF: Labor 1972 #1, Box 789, GSMP; "A Campaign White Paper," FF: Labor 1972 #1, Box 789, GSMP; "McGovern: A Good Labor Record," F: Labor 1972 #1, Box 789, GSMP; "How in the Hell Can You Vote for Nixon?" FF: Campaign Literature Directed at Special Groups, Box 87, GSMP. First poll cited in Robert Mason, *Richard Nixon and the Quest for a New Majority* (Chapel Hill: University of North Carolina Press, 2004), 187; second poll in Jean Westwood to Senator George McGovern, "Recapturing the Democratic Vote and Victory," 30 August 1972, Box 898, FF: Issues: Various, GSMP; see also "National Opinion Survey," n.d., Box 898, FF: Economy '72, GSMP.

76. Ken and Gerry to Senator McGovern, "Bringing the Ethnic Vote Home to the Democratic Party," 28 August 1972, Box 785, FF: Ethnic Issues 1972, GSMP.

77. Jean Westwood to Senator George McGovern, "Recapturing the Democratic Vote and Victory," 30 August 1972, Box 898, FF: Issues: Various, GSMP; see also "National Opinion Survey," n.d., Box 898, FF: Economy '72, GSMP; John Douglas to Senator McGovern, "August Schedule" 20 July 1972, Box 329, no folder, GSMP; Ted Van Dyk to Senator McGovern, "Your Principal Campaign Theme," 23 August 1972, Box 898, FF: Issues: Various, GSMP; Milt Gwirtzman to Senator McGovern, "Talk to Labor Leaders," 24 August 1972, Box 790, FF: Labor 1972, GSMP.

78. White, *Making of the President*, 317–18.

79. "Remarks of Senator George McGovern, Youngstown, Ohio, August 15, 1972," Reel no. 185, Box 752, FF: Tape Transcript, GSMP; *Washington Post* 16 August 1972; *New York Times* 16 August 1972.

80. "A Campaign White Paper," FF: Labor 1972 #1, Box 789, GSMP; "McGovern: A Good Labor Record," FF: Labor 1972 #1, Box 789, GSMP; Many of the advertisements for the 1972 campaign are archived at The Living Room Candidate, http://livingroomcandidate.movingimage.us/; Guggenheim quote from Kathleen Hall Jamieson, *Packaging the Presidency: A History and Criticism of Presidential Campaign Advertising*, 3rd ed. (New York: Oxford, 1996), 324.

81. Jamieson, *Packaging the Presidency*, 303–304.

82. Timothy Crouse, *The Boys on the Bus* (New York: Random House, 1973), 268–89.

83. Stephen E. Ambrose, *The Wild Blue: The Men and Boys Who Flew the B-24s over Germany* (New York: Simon and Schuster, 2001), 192–93; Labor Day Speech, Barberton and Chippewa Lake, Ohio and Alameda County, California, 4 September 1972, in McGovern, *An American Journey*, 31–42.

84. Richard Dougherty, *Goodbye, Mr. Christian* (Garden City, NY: Doubleday, 1973), 213; Gordon to Senator, 30 July, re: Status of Campaign, Box 898, FF: Issues-Various, GSMP.

85. *Newsweek* 6 November 1972, 43–44.

86. George McGovern, "They, Too, Are Created in the Image of God," 26 September 1972, Los Angeles, in *An American Journey*, 119–27; Jamieson, *Packaging*, 326–27.

87. George McGovern, "Sources of Our Strength," 11 October 1972, Wheaton College, in *An American Journey*, 205–13. While Ronald Reagan would invoke the same quote in 1974 and again at the Republican National Convention in 1984, it came tinged with American chauvinism, smacked of material greatness, and certainly dripped with visions of American exceptionalism. Even Mario Cuomo responded to Reagan at the 1984 Democratic Convention with the idea that the United States was not a "City on Hill" but really "a tale of two cities," one rich and one poor. Yet Cuomo's conceptualization was a material idea vanishing from American politics.

88. *New York Times* 6 August 1972, *New York Times* 5 November 1972.

89. Denis G. Sullivan and others, *The Politics of Representation*, 95–96; Jeffrey L. Pressman and Denis G. Sullivan, "Convention Reform and Conventional Wisdom: An Empirical Assessment of Democratic Party Reforms," *Political Science Quarterly* 89:3 (Fall 1974): 559; on the divisions among the unions, see Andrew Battista, "Political Divisions in Organized Labor, 1968–1988," *Polity* 24 (Winter 1991): 173–97.

90. Gallup Poll, "Vote by Groups, 1968–1972," http://www.gallup.com/poll/trends/ptgrp6872.asp. The southern vote for Nixon had the most dramatic increase of any category for Nixon—thirty-five points—but this can be attributed largely to the absence of George Wallace, who garnered 33 percent in 1968. The only other category approaching this type of increase was the high-school-educated vote, with a 23 percent increase, but this category is not an unreasonable proxy for "manual worker." The only other substantial jump that matches these categories is in the age category thirty-to-forty-nine-year-old, which saw a disproportionate twenty-six-point increase.

91. *JHLL* 18 November 1972; Schlesinger, *New Reformers*, 98; *Washington Post* 4 November 1974.

92. "A Personal Reflection," Box 774, FF: December 1972, 25–26, GSMP; Dougherty, *Mr. Christian*, 247; *Newsweek,* 16 October 1972, 29–30; *Time,* 2 October 1972, 13–14; "Who Speaks for the Union Voter? *Newsweek,* 18 September 1972, 21; polling discussed in Jon D. Schaff, "A Clear Choice: George McGovern and the 1972 Presidential Race," in *George McGovern,* ed. Robert P. Watson (Pierre: South Dakota State Historical Society Press, 2004), 131–32. Thompson, *Fear and Loathing,* 469; quote on 1968 from Thompson, *Fear and Loathing,* 478.

93. Raymond Price, *With Nixon* (New York: Viking Press, 1977), 122.

Chapter 3: Nixon's Class Struggle

1. There are extensive notes on the conversation in *The Haldeman Diaries: Inside the Nixon White House* CD-ROM (Santa Monica: Sony Electronic Publishing, 1995), 8 January 1970, 21 July 1971; Charles Colson, "Memorandum for the President's File," FF: Nixon and Labor/Political, Contested Documents, Colson Files Box 96, RNP. "There would be no more rhetoric from the Administration but contained any kind of anti-union implications," Nixon confirmed shortly afterward. See FF: Meeting, Peter Brennan w/ President, 26 July 1971, Contested Documents, Colson Files Box 23, RNP; William Safire, *Before the Fall: An Inside View of the Pre-Watergate White House* (Garden City, NY: Doubleday, 1975), 266.

2. *Haldeman Diaries,* 8 January 1970, 21 July 1971; Colson, "Memorandum for the President's File"; Safire, *Before the Fall,* 266.

3. Raymond Price, *With Nixon* (New York: Viking Press, 1977), 121.

4. On Wilson, see Steve Fraser, "The Labor Question," in *The Rise and Fall of the New Deal Order*, ed. Steve Fraser and Gary Gerstle (Princeton, NJ: Princeton University Press), 55; for Nixon's use of Wilson as a model, see Garry Wills, *Nixon Agonistes: The Crisis of the Self-Made Man* (Boston: Houghton Mifflin, 1970), 419–95. Nixon made clear in his first inaugural address that while the nation faced "only" material problems under FDR, Nixon would have deal with moral and social problems. See Richard Nixon, "Inaugural Address" January 20, 1969, *Public Papers of the Presidents of the United States: Richard Nixon, 1969* (Washington, DC: GPO, 1971), 2; on Nixon declaring a ban on anti-labor rhetoric, see FF: Meeting, Peter Brennan w/ President, 26 July 1971, Contested Documents, Colson Files Box 23, RNP. Scholars can roughly be divided into three camps on Nixon. One group emphasizes the semi-authoritarian figure with regard to foreign policy and the illegal means he used to achieve his political ends that resulted in Watergate. In contrast, considering "Nixon without Watergate," as historian Joan Hoff has conceptualized the problem in *Nixon Reconsidered* (New York: Basic Books, 1994), creates a compelling portrait of a president pushing for a revised New Deal liberalism that in reality increased social spending, reconceptualizing (rather than defund) welfare through the Family Assistance Plan, and signing such benchmark legislation as OSHA and the EPA. His labor strategy links the two and shows Nixon's strategic mind at work. His liberal domestic policies were indeed remarkably liberal by the standards of the early twenty-first century. His goals, however, were framed less out of any political conviction than out of an attempt to take flight on the political winds of his time in order to build his political majority. As Allen Matusow argues, "The whole point of Nixon's domestic presidency was to create a New Majority by taking the center and recruiting Democrats to his cause." Allen J. Matusow, *Nixon's Economy: Booms, Bust, Dollars, and Votes* (Lawrence: University Press of Kansas, 1998), 203; Robert Mason, *Richard Nixon and the Quest for a New Majority* (Chapel Hill: University of North Carolina Press, 2004); Rick Perlstein sees him as building that majority by profiting and fomenting from the culture wars. See *Nixonland: The Rise of a President and the Fracturing of America* (New York: Scribner, 2008).

5. Safire, *Before the Fall*, 579; Richard Reeves, *President Nixon: Alone in the White House* (New York: Simon and Schuster, 2001), 12–14; on the reformulation of populism in this period, see Michael Kazin, *The Populist Persuasion*, rev. ed. (Ithaca, NY: Cornell University Press, 1995), 248–55.

6. On Nixon's ethnic appeals, see "Republican Ethnic Buttons, 1972" in Collection 3334, Box 2, Political Campaigns, U.S. presidential, miscellany, 1972, KLRM.

7. Reeves, *Alone in the White House*, 138–39; Dent to Nixon, 16 October 1969, President's Office Files, Box 79.

8. Todd Giltin, *The Whole World Is Watching: Mass Media in the Making and Unmaking of the New Left* (Berkeley: University of California Press, 2003), 205, 229, 279; Mason, *New Majority*, 48.

9. Reeves, *Alone in the White House*, 149; *Time*, 21 November 1969; Richard Nixon, *RN: The Memoirs of Richard Nixon* (New York: Simon and Schuster, 1978), 402–13; Mason, *New Majority*, 65–66; on Agnew, see Jules Witcover, *White Knight: The Rise of Spiro Agnew* (New York: Random House, 1972), 362.

10. Stephen Lesher, *George Wallace: American Populist* (Reading, MA: Addison-Wesley 1994), 395; Dan T. Carter, *The Politics of Race: George Wallace, the Origins of the New Conservatism and the Transformation of American Politics* (New York: Simon and Schuster, 1995), 378.

11. Kevin P. Phillips, *The Emerging Republican Majority* (New Rochelle, NY: Arlington House, 1969), 463; Wills, *Nixon Agonistes*, 265.

12. On how the Wallace issue plagued Nixon and his attempt to outflank the Alabama governor, see Carter, *The Politics of Race*, 371–414; *JHLL* 9 March 1969. As the blue-collar strategy took shape, Kevin Phillips recognized it as the "Post-Southern Strategy," *Washington Post* 25 September 1970; Phillips still believed in the liberal economic measures even as he sought to guide the nation toward social conservatism. He pushed for national health insurance, welfare reform, aid to ailing industrial and agricultural areas. Roland Evans Jr. and Robert Novak, *Nixon in the White House: The Frustration of Power* (New York: Random House, 1971), 322–23; Kevin P. Phillips, "Middle America and the Emerging Republican Majority," Box 46, Dent Files, RNP; Mason, *New Majority*, 48, 117; Philip Jenkins, *Decade of Nightmares: The End of the Sixties and the Making of Eighties America* (New York: Oxford University Press, 2006), 94.

13. Richard M. Scammon and Ben J. Wattenberg, *The Real Majority* (New York: Coward-McCann, 1970), 195–97; Pete Hamill, "Wallace," 7 *Ramparts* (7 October 1968): 44–48.

14. Pete Hamill, "The Revolt of the White Lower Middle Class," *New York Magazine*, 14 April 1969, 28–29, reprinted in *The White Majority, Between Poverty and Affluence*, ed. Louise Kappe Howe (New York: Random House, 1970), 10–22.

15. Huston, quoted in Mason, *Nixon*, 74, 47; "The Problem of the Blue Collar Worker," 16 April 1970, FF: Blue Collar, Colson Files Box 39, RNP. See Rosow's speech on the matter as well: "Rosow Calls on American Business to Help Solve the Problem of Blue-Collar Workers," U.S. Department of Labor Office of Information, press release, 29 October 1970, FF: Blue Collar, Colson Files Box 39, RNP; Scammon and Wattenberg, *The Real Majority*; as Nixon noted in his diary, "We should set out to capture the vote of the forty-seven-year-old Dayton housewife." Nixon, *Memoirs*, 491. Nixon learned about the New Majority from Pat Buchanan in August 1970, long after he had already acted on Pete Hamill's ideas. For a typical disproportionate emphasis on the New Majority and the date Nixon read it, see Bruce J. Schulman, *The Seventies: The Great Shift in American Culture, Society, and Politics* (New York: Free Press, 2001), 37–38; similarly, see Reeves, *Alone in the White House*, 261–62.

16. *Wall Street Journal* 30 June 1970 and 17 July 1970. The much more modest coverage of the administration's official endorsement of the Rosow Report is covered on 14 August 1970. The story behind the report is covered in Charles Culhane, "White House Report/Nixon eyes Blue-Collar Workers as Potential Source of Votes in '72," *National Journal*, 30 January 1971, 236.

17. Burns to President, 26 May 1969, FF: [Welfare Book], Ehrlichman Files Box 39, RNP; "Memorandum for the Director," n.d., FF: Blue Collar, Colson Files Box 39, RNP. For another powerful iteration of the administration's thinking on the labor issue, see "The Nixon Administration and the Working Man," 11 June 1971, FF: Blue Collar, Colson Files Box 39, RNP.

18. *New York Times* 9 May 1970; *New York Times* 10 May 1970; *New York Times* 11 May 1970; *New York Times* 12 May 1970; *New York Times* 13 May 1970; *New York Times* 21 May 1970; *Business Week,* 16 May 1970; for an insightful discussion of the issue of masculinity in the hard hat image, see Joshua B. Freeman, "Hardhats: Construction Workers, Manliness, and the 1970 Pro-War Demonstrations," *Journal of Social History* 26 (Summer 1993): 726–44; see also Joshua B. Freeman, *Working-Class New York* (New York: New Press, 2000), 237–46. It is interesting to note that Hamill condemned the riots as the "work of cowards," see Vincent J. Cannato, *The Ungovernable City: John Lindsay and His Struggle to Save New York* (New York: Basic Books, 2001), 448–53.

19. *New York Times* 21 May 1970; Christian G. Appy, *Working-Class War: American Combat Soldiers and Vietnam* (Chapel Hill: University of North Carolina Press, 1993), 299; tradesman quoted in Freeman, *Working-Class New York*, 242.

20. Bull to Colson, 22 May 1970, FF: Hard Hats-Building and Construction Trades, Colson Files Box 69, RNP.

21. Richard Sennett and Jonathan Cobb, *The Hidden Injuries of Class* (New York: Knopf, 1972), 146.

22. *Haldeman Diaries*, 10 May 1970; Safire, *Before the Fall*, 38; Charles W. Colson, *Born Again* (Old Tappan, NJ: Chosen Books, 1976), 39–40.

23. Colson to President, 26 October 1970, FF: Broder Articles, Colson Files Box 40, RNP.

24. Haldeman to Chapin, 31 July 1971, FF: 14, Chronological Files, Contested Documents, Haldeman Files Box 197, RNP; Memo from Colson to O'Hara, 21 September 1970 in Bruce Oudes, ed., *From the President: Richard Nixon's Secret Files* (New York: Harper and Row, 1989), 161; Haldeman Notes, 24 July 1970, FF: H Notes July–December '70, Haldeman Files Box 42, RNP; Colson claims that no Teamsters were hired. *New York Times* 24 September 1981; Summers, *Arrogance*, 356–57. There seemingly could be many more such ploys that may never come to light, with unresolved hints sprinkled throughout the Nixon papers such as Charles Colson's cryptic correspondence about a meeting with New York building trades leader Peter Brennan in the fall of 1970 regarding "some political chicanery that we should get going on as fast as possible."

The only "smoking gun" that ties the administration to the revolts uncovered in this research is a small piece of correspondence between the staff member Steve Bull and one of Nixon's most trusted advisors, Charles Colson. "Obviously," Bull wrote to Colson, "more of these [hard hat protests] will be occurring throughout the Nation, perhaps partially as a result of your clandestine activity." Biographer Anthony Summers, for instance, implies that Nixon did orchestrate the protests, and even Ehrlichman "assumed" that the some of the hard-hat attacks were "laid on" by the White House. No concrete evidence has proven the case that the original protests were directed by the White House, but it is not unlikely that the administration helped, in whatever ways necessary, to insure their continuation. Whether or not the administration actually assisted in the development of the protests, it was easy to see how, in the combination of working-class backlash, police sympathy, apparent employer support (the workers were off the job and still getting paid), and some mysterious gray-suited individuals, they added up to what *The Nation* called a pattern evincing "the classic elements of Hitlerian street tactics." See Anthony Summers, *The Arrogance of Power: The Secret World of Richard Nixon* (New York: Viking, 2000), 358, 590; Fred J. Cook, "Rampaging Patriots," *The Nation*, 15 June 1970, 712; Bull to Colson, 22 May 1970, FF: Hard Hats-Building and Construction Trades, Colson Files Box 69, RNP.

25. *New York Times* 27 May 1970; Freeman, *Working-Class New York*, 239.

26. Robert Collins, *More: The Politics of Economic Growth in Postwar America* (New York: Oxford, 2000), 103; *New York Times* 17 August 1969; Mason, *New Majority*, 57.

27. Nixon quote on OSHA in Mason, *New Majority*, 118; Charles Noble, *Liberalism at Work: The Rise and Fall of OSHA* (Philadelphia: Temple University Press, 1986), 68–98.

28. *Haldeman Diaries*; Mason, *New Majority*, 57; Hoff, *Nixon Reconsidered*, 129–44; Vincent J. Burke, *Nixon's Good Deed: Welfare Reform* (New York: Columbia University Press, 1974).

29. On the postal workers' strike, see, Aaron Brenner, "Rank-and-File Rebellion, 1966–1975" (PhD diss., Columbia University, 1996), 112–46; National Association of Letter Carriers, *Carriers in a Common Cause: A History of the Letter Carriers and the NALC* (Washington, DC: National Association of Letter Carriers, 1989), 72–77; *Time* 30 March 1970.

30. Ibid.; *New York Times* 24 March 1970; *Newsweek*, 30 March 1970; In the end, although the workers did not gain all they were promised when they returned to work three weeks later, they did receive a hefty raise that hedged their inflation problems, a decrease in the number of years necessary to reach top rates of pay, and, most importantly, collective bargaining rights (although without the right to strike or the union shop). "You can't jail thousands of workers," declared a postal workers' spokesman about the implicit power of their numbers. It turned out, however, that one could. When a similar massive strike against the federal government

happened ten years later, Ronald Reagan jailed thousands of federal strikers of PATCO. Compared with what would happen under Reagan just a decade later, the postal workers enjoyed a remarkable victory, and Nixon, whittling out a space between his blue collar strategy and his policy desires, came across as a passable liberal.

31. Safire, *Before the Fall*, 584; *Washington Post* 31 August 1970. Not to be suckered, Haldeman scrawled across the Meany interview, "Don't be totally taken in by this—What he's trying to do is force the Dems back to the right—not to help us." Brown to Colson, 23 September 1970, FF: Labor Campaign (2 of 2), Colson Files Box 77, RNP.

32. Office of the White House Press Secretary, "Exchange of Toasts Between the President and George Meany," 7 September 1970, FF: Blue Collar, Colson Files Box 39, RNP.

33. *Haldeman Diaries*, 7 September 1970; Haldeman to Colson, 8 September 1970, FF: Labor Campaign (2 of 2), Colson Files Box 77, RNP.

34. Colson also revealed intelligence at this time that Meany was already positioning "himself to be at least neutral in the 1972 election" (well before McGovern had been selected as the presidential candidate), news seemingly confirmed by a confidential FBI memo a few weeks later. For descriptions of Colson, see *Wall Street Journal* 15 October 1971; Colson, *Born Again*, 31–32, 57; Colson, "Thank God for Watergate," Part II, cassette tape, Life Story Foundation, Sumas, Washington, http://www.lifestory.org/cols2.html. Nixon, *Memoirs*, 496; *New York Times* 24 September 1981. For administration's discussions, see Colson to Haldeman, 14 September 1970, FF: Hodgson/Elsrey/Colson meeting with President, Folder 2 of 6, Contested Documents, Colson Files Box 22, RNP; Brown to Colson, 23 September 1970, FF: Labor Campaign (1 of 2), Colson Files Box 77, RNP.

35. Colson to Haldeman, 14 September 1970, FF: Hodgson/Elsrey/Colson meeting with President, Folder 2 of 6, Contested Documents, Colson Files Box 22, RNP.

36. Ibid.

37. *Haldeman Diaries*, 13 May 1971; John Ehrlichman, *Witness to Power: The Nixon Years* (New York: Simon and Schuster, 1982), 239; Colson to Haldeman, 14 September 1970, FF: Hodgson/Elsrey/Colson meeting with President, Folder 2 of 6, Contested Documents, Colson Files Box 22, RNP. There was a host of smaller plans. Personal letters were sent out to all of the guests explaining Nixon's unemployment plan; the leaders of all sizable unions were to be put on the list to be invited to major White House social functions (with published guest lists); lesser leaders would be invited to Sunday worship, photo opportunities, and brief words with the president; and influential figures would get thirty-minute discussions with him. "Recognition and reward be made to those who publicly support us; this by means of legislative favors and additional invitations, appointments to boards, commissions, task forces, and honorary delegations," Colson explained. They kept

careful track of what local, state, and national leaders needed help or were proving their loyalty to the president or other Republican candidates. They also kept track of where COPE funds were going and how well Meany was able to control them from being used to support liberal candidates. Often through tips from Jay Lovestone, the Nixon image makers were well aware that "Meany was under intense pressure for his behind-the-scenes relationship with the Nixon Administration while ignoring struggling liberal Democrats," but they remained confident that, despite his policy "blasts" against the administration, he would continue to refuse to help Democrats. See Colson to Haldeman, 14 September 1970, FF: Hodgson/ Elsrey/Colson meeting with President, Folder 2 of 6, Contested Documents, Colson Files Box 22, RNP; see the memos of implementation of Colson's strategies in Brown to Colson, Brown to Ehrlichman, Brown to Flemming, Brown to Magruder, Brown to Shultz, Brown to Chapin, Brown to Klein, Brown to Dent and Chotiner, Brown to Flanigan and Flemming, Brown to Flemming, all 26 September 1970, FF: Labor Campaign (2 of 2), Colson Files Box 77, RNP; Colson to Haldeman, 9 October 1970, FF: Labor Campaign (2 of 2), Colson Files Box 77, RNP; Colson to Haldeman, 3 November 1970, FF: Nixon and Labor/Political, Colson Files Box 96, RNP.

38. Safire, *Before the Fall*, 584, 587; Kissinger to Ehrlichman, 15 January 1970, "Confidential Intelligence Analysis," 9 July 1970, FF: SACB (Subversive Activities Control Board), (Folder 4 of 4), Dean Files Box 70, RNP; see all attached memos, especially, Hoover to Huston, 30 September 1970, FBI Surveillance Letter, 1 September 1970, FBI Surveillance Letter 9 September 1970, Brown to Dean, 26 September 1970, FF: Subversive Activities Board (4 of 4), Contested Documents, Dean Files Boxes 46–71, RNP; see also Hutson to Dean, 28 September 1970, Dean to the Attorney General 2 October 1970, Dean to Hoover, 2 October 1970, Dean to Attorney General, 2 October 1970, Dean to Staff Secretary, 2 October 1970, all in FF SACB, Dean Files Box 70, RNP. For a discussion of the enemies list, see Stanley I. Kutler, *The Wars of Watergate* (New York: Knopf, 1990), 104; for Nixon on Jews at the Bureau of Labor Statistics, see Matusow, *Nixon's Economy*, 96–98.

39. For a discussion of the 1970 elections, see Mason, *New Majority*, 77, 109–12; *Haldeman Diaries*, 10 and 11 July 1970.

40. Colson to Bell, 26 July 1971, FF: State Labor Leaders (5 of 6), Contested Documents, Colson Files Box 114, RNP; Walker to President, 30 November 1970, FF: President's Handwriting (16–30 December 1970), President's Office Files, Contested Documents, Boxes 1–13, folder 1 of 4, RNP; Keogh to Haldeman, 25 November 1970, FF: Labor Campaign (1 of 2), Colson Files Box 77, RNP; Shultz to Brown, 30 December 1970, FF: President's Handwriting (16–30 December 1970), President's Office Files, Contested Documents, Boxes 1–13, RNP.

41. Keogh to Haldeman, 25 November 1970, FF: Labor Campaign (1 of 2), Colson Files Box 77, RNP; Shultz to Brown, 30 December 1970, FF: President's Handwriting

(16–30 December 1970), President's Office Files, Contested Documents, Boxes 1–13, RNP; for a succinct breakdown of all of the key players' positions on the labor question, see Kehrli to Haldeman, 31 December 1970, FF: HRH-Higby/Kehrli memos, Haldeman Files Box 69, RNP.

42. Keogh to Shultz, 4 December 1970, FF: Labor Campaign (1 of 2), Colson Files Box 77, RNP.

43. Colson to President, 7 December 1970, FF: President's Handwriting December 1970, President's Office Files, Contested Documents, Boxes 1–13, RNP.

44. Safire, *Before the Fall*, 586. On voting analysis, see Colson to Haldeman, 22 December 1970, FF: "Nixon and Labor/Political," Colson Files Box 96, RNP; Colson to Haldeman, 16 February 1971, FF: Labor Campaign (1 of 2), Colson Files Box 7, RNP; Colson, *Born Again*, 63; Colson to Haldeman, 22 December 1970, FF: Nixon and Labor/Political, Colson Files Box 96, RNP.

45. Colson to Howard and "Public Thinking on Unions and Labor Legislation," 26 July 1971, FF: Unions and Labor Legislation, Barker Files Box 3, RNP; Colson to Bell, 26 July 1971, FF: Unions and Labor Legislation, Contested Documents, Barker Files Box 3, RNP.

46. The suspension was hotly debated by his advisors as Arthur Burns recommended Nixon "wave a big stick at the building trades unions," while Shultz, then at the Bureau of the Budget, "argued that antagonizing the hard-hat unions would be bad politics." See Evans and Novak, *Nixon in the White House*, 370–71; "Statement by the President" (suspension of Davis-Bacon Act), 23 February 1971, FF: Building and Construction Trades, Colson Files Box 39, RNP; Colson to President, 23 February 1971, FF: Building and Construction Trades, Colson Files Box 40, RNP; Colson to Chapin, 25 February 1971, FF: Hard-Hats-Building and Construction Trades, Colson Files Box 69, RNP; *New York Times* 24 February 1971 and 25 February 1971; *Wall Street Journal* 30 March 1970.

47. *New York Times* 30 March 1971; Matusow, *Nixon's Economy*, 95–96, Safire, *Before the Fall*, 587–88; for a complete discussion of the wage controversy in the construction industry, see Marc Linder, *Wars of Attrition: Vietnam, the Business Roundtable, and the Decline of the Construction Unions* (Iowa City: Fanpihua Press, 1999), 304–27.

48. Safire, *Before the Fall*, 266; and Dean J. Kotloswki, "Richard Nixon and the Origins of Affirmative Action," *Historian* 60 (Spring 1998): 523–41; Mason, *New Majority*, 53–54; Hugh Davis Graham, "Richard Nixon and Civil Rights: Explaining an Enigma," *Presidential Studies Quarterly* 26 (1996): 103; on the grassroots origin of the Philadelphia Plan, see Thomas J. Sugrue, "Affirmative Action from Below: Civil Rights, the Building Trades, and the Politics of Racial Equality in the Urban North, 1945–1969," *Journal of American History* 91 (June 2004): 145–74.

49. *New York Times* 19 August 1971; Matusow, *Nixon's Economy*, 158; Meany clarifies his stance on controls on "NBC's Meet the Press," 11 July 1971, transcript, RG 1, Box 83, FF 10, GMMA.

50. Quotes from Matusow, *Nixon's Economy*, 158–59; see also *Washington Post* 27 August 1971.

51. *Haldeman Diaries*, 12 October 1971; Matusow, *Nixon's Economy*, 157, 160; Chotiner to Mitchell, 2 September 1971, FF: Press Reports, Haldeman Files Box 303, RNP; Colson to President, 4 November 1971, FF: Charles Colson, November 1971, Haldeman Files Box 86, RNP; Melvin Small, *The Presidency of Richard Nixon* (Lawrence: University Press of Kansas, 1999), 211. Frank Fitzsimmons of the Teamsters stayed on the board.

52. *Haldeman Diaries*, 17 November 1971, 19 November 1971.

53. *New York Times* 20 November 1971; *JHLL* 20 November 1971, 27 November 1971. When the press later fired back at Meany that he had been at best discourteous to Nixon, the Bronx plumber claimed to the convention, "I have the impression the President did not come here to make a speech. He came here to contrive a situation under which he could claim that he had been unfairly treated," he explained. See the discussion of a leaked memo to Meany, which suggested that Nixon was trying to set Meany up in Archie Robinson, *George Meany and His Times* (New York: Simon and Schuster, 1981), 318–19. In Meany's backpedaling, he claimed that they did not have the sheet music for "Hail to the Chief," but the Teamsters later gave Colson a photograph of the sheet music sitting on the piano at the convention.

54. *Haldeman Diaries*, 20 November 1971, 22 November 1971, and 30 November 1971; *New York Times* 20 November 1971; the *Miami Herald*'s headline proclaimed "Big Labor Blows the Game with an Intentional Foul." Meany wanted to patch things up afterward; see analyses on 11 January 1972 and 28 January 1972 in FF: Political Miscellaneous 1971, Haldeman Files Box 303, RNP; *Los Angeles Times*, 25 November 1971.

55. *Haldeman Diaries*, 20 November 1971. When Nixon met with Fitzsimmons after the Teamsters' endorsement of the president in 1972, Colson told Nixon to take Fitzsimmons aside and "tell him that we are with him all the way and that there will be no concessions with Hoffa. Obviously no one else should hear this." See Colson to President, 17 July 1972, FF: Meeting with Pres of Teamsters, San Clemente, Colson Files Box 24, RNP. See Arthur A. Sloane, *Hoffa* (Cambridge, MA: MIT Press, 1991), 362. Fitzsimmons was responsible for a period of drift and dramatic reduction in the Teamsters' organizational power.

56. "Letter from Cesar Chavez," *New York Review of Books*, 31 October 1974; *New York Times* 22 February 1972; *New York Times* 15 December 1972; *New York Times* 16 April 1973; Marshall Ganz, *Why David Sometimes Wins: Leadership, Organization, and the Strategy in the California Farm Worker Movement* (New York: Oxford University Press, 2009), 232.

57. Chotiner to Mitchell, 29 November 1971, FF: Press Reports, Haldeman Files Box 303, RNP; *Haldeman Diaries*, 22 March 1972; Strachan to Bell (and attachments), 14 March 1972, FF: George Bell March 72, Haldeman Files Box 93, RNP.

58. Safire, *Before the Fall*, 591–92.

59. *Washington Post* 10 October 1972; David Broder, "The Story that Still Nags at Me—Edward S. Muskie," *Washington Monthly*, February 1987; Jules Witcover, "William Loeb and the New Hampshire Primary: A Question of Ethics," *Columbia Journalism Review* (May/June) 1972, 14–27; *Manchester Union Leader* 24 February 1972.

60. The details of this potential conspiracy are laid out in Dan Carter, *From George Wallace to Newt Gingrich*, 49–51; *Haldeman Diaries*, 20 July 1972.

61. "Why Unions Are Running Scared in 1968," *Nation's Business* 56 (June 1968): 36–39; Mason, *New Majority*, 164; Taylor Dark, *The Unions and the Democrats: An Enduring Alliance* (Ithaca, NY: Cornell University Press, 1999), 87–92; J. David Greenstone, *Labor in American Politics*, 2nd ed. (Chicago: University of Chicago Press, 1977), xxv; see also, Jerry Wurf, "What Labor Has Against McGovern," *New Republic*, 5 and 12 August 1972.

62. *JHLL* 23 September 1972; *New York Times* 29 July 1972; Robinson, *Meany*, 322–23.

63. Notes on the memo in Safire, *Before the Fall*, 592–93.

64. Buchanan/Kachigian "Assault Strategy," 8 June 1972, in Oudes, *From the President*, 466. On tensions between Meany and McGovern on 14(b) and communism, see *Washington Post* 28 April 1972.

65. Theodore H. White, *The Making of the President, 1972* (New York: Atheneum Publishers, 1973), 239–40; *New York Times* 15 October 1972.

66. Broder quote, ibid., 268.

67. Poll cited in Mason, *New Majority*, 187; Address by Secretary of Labor James D. Hodgson, 3 October 1972, FF: Labor (1 of 2) Barker Files Box 2, RNP.

68. *Haldeman Diaries*, 10 October 1972; Rodgers to Colson, 5 September 1972, FF: Nixon and Labor/Political, Colson Files Box 96, RNP.

69. Colson, *Born Again*, 15. Calculations made from Gallup Poll, "Vote by Groups, 1968–1972," http://www.gallup.com/poll/trends/ptgrp6872.asp. The southern vote for Nixon had the most dramatic increase of any category for Nixon—thirty-five points—but this can be attributed largely to the absence of George Wallace, who garnered 33 percent in 1968. The only other categories approaching this type of increase were the high-school-educated vote, with a 23 percent increase, but this category is not an unreasonable proxy for "manual worker." The only other substantial jump that matches these categories is in the age category thirty-to-forty-nine-year-olds, which saw a disproportionate twenty-six point increase.

70. Patrick J. Buchanan, *The New Majority: President Nixon at Mid-passage* (Philadelphia: Girard Bank, 1973), 63–64.

71. Colson article, 19 January 1973, Colson Files Box 17, RNP, cited in Mason, *New Majority*, 195; Peter Carroll, *It Seemed Like Nothing Happened* (New Brunswick, NJ: Rutgers University Press, 1990 [1982]), 56–70; Chilton Williams, Jr., "To the Nashville Station," *National Review* 30 (9 June 1978): 713.

72. *JHLL* 2 December 1972; Mason, *New Majority,* 194; Kutler, *The Wars of Watergate,* 245; *Haldeman Diaries,* 20 November 1972, 13 February 1973; Robinson, *Meany,* 329–30. William Gould, "Moving the Hard-Hats In," *Nation,* 8 January 1973.

73. For the infamous "cancer" on the presidency discussion, see "Transcript of a Recording of a Meeting Among the President, John Dean, and H.R. Haldeman in the Oval Office, on March 21, 1973," 5, RNP; for Meany speech, see Safire, *Before the Fall,* 596.

74. "New Majority Squandered," *National Review* 26 (15 March 1974): 298–302; Safire, *Before the Fall,* 596.

75. David Farber, "The Silent Majority and Talk about Revolution," in *The Sixties from Memory to History,* ed. David Farber (Chapel Hill: University of North Carolina Press, 1994), 295; Farber applies Jean Baudrillard's post-Marxist conceptualization that controlling the means of production is less important than the means of "controlling the code"; David Halle, *America's Working Man* (Chicago: University of Chicago Press, 1984), 301, 292. See a very useful similar theoretical formulation that helps situate the politics of class with the new social movements, J. Craig Jenkins and Kevin Leicht, "Class Analysis and Social Movements: A Critique and Reformulation" in *Reworking Class,* ed. John R. Hall (Ithaca, NY: Cornell University Press), 369–92, esp. 382–84.

76. Judith Stein, *Running Steel, Running America* (Chapel Hill: University of North Carolina Press, 1998), 6.

77. "Nixon Wooing of Labor Vote Dates to 1970," 12 October 1972, FF 14, Box 031, Cope Research Files, GMMA; Rieder, "Silent Majority," 265; Schulman, *The Seventies,* 24–32; Colson, *Born,* 31–32. There was talk of using Nixon's biography as a "common man" to bolster the blue-collar strategy.

78. The tape is Conversation Number 153–20, 14 November 1972, Camp David Study Table, Nixon Presidential Library & Museum, Sample Conversations, Fifth Chronological Release, Part II, http://www.nixonlibrary.gov/virtuallibrary/tape excerpts/fifthchron_part_ii.php.

Chapter 4: I'm Dying Here

1. For the accounts of the White House appearance, see Merle Haggard, *Sing Me Back Home* (New York: Times Books, 1981), 238–41; Merle Haggard, *Merle Haggard's My House of Memories: For the Record* (New York: Cliff Street Books, 1999), 193.

2. *Haldeman Diaries: Inside the Nixon White House* CD-ROM (Santa Monica: Sony Electronic Publishing, 1995), 17 March 1973; Steve Turner, *The Man Called Cash* (Nashville: W Publishing Group, 2004), 153–54; on the dismissive tendency of most critics, see Florence King, "Red Necks, White Socks, and Blue Ribbon Fear," *Harper's,* July 1974, 30–34.

3. Bryan Di Salvatore, "Ornery" *New Yorker,* 12 February 1990, 54.

4. Aaron A. Fox, *Real Country: Music and Language in Working-Class Culture* (Durham, NC: Duke University Press, 2004), 25–32; Patrick J. Huber, "'Redneck': A Short Note from American Labor History," *American Speech* 69 (1994): 106–12; Bill C. Malone, *Don't Get Above Your Raisin': Country Music and the Southern Working Class* (Urbana: University of Illinois Press, 2002), 48–49, 210–11, 242. While the term "redneck" is generally associated with a rural laborer's sun-burned neck, it was also used to describe the red bandana clad miners at the Battle of Blair Mountain, West Virginia, in 1921, the largest armed uprising of the American working class. So, although there is a left-wing dimension to the term—as there was a left-wing dimension to its revival in the seventies—it mostly connoted a "white supremacist, antimodern, and antiurban politics and culture of the Confederacy," as ethnographer Aaron A. Fox put it.

5. Malone, *Above Your Raisin'*, 238–39; Paul DiMaggio, Richard A. Peterson, and Jack Esco, Jr., "Country Music, Ballad of the Silent Majority," in *The Sounds of Social Change: Studies in Popular Culture*, ed. R. Serge Denisoff and Richard Peterson (Chicago: Rand McNally, 1972), 38–55.

6. Paul Hemphill, *The Good Old Boys* (New York: Simon and Schuster, 1974), passim; Bruce Schulman, *The Seventies: The Great Shift in American Culture, Society, and Politics* (New York: Free Press, 2001), 102–17.

7. On Hag's body (and one of the best portraits of him), see Hemphill, *The Good Old Boys*, 134.

8. Haggard, *My House of Memories*, 192.

9. Ben Marsh, "A Rose Colored Map," *Harper's*, July 1977, 80–82; Paul Hemphill, "Merle Haggard," *Atlantic*, September 1971, 98–103; Don Cusic, ed., *Merle Haggard: Poet of the Common Man* (Milwaukee, WI: Hal Leonard Corporation, 2002), xxxix.

10. Gerald W. Haslam, *Workin' Man Blues: Country Music in California* (Berkeley: University of California Press, 1999), 249–50; and Malone, *Above Your Raisin'*, 242.

11. James N. Gregory, *American Exodus: The Dust Bowl Migration and Okie Culture in California* (New York: Oxford University Press, 1989), 247–48.

12. The "reddening" phrase appears in Roger Shattuck, "The Reddening of America," *New York Review of Books*, 30 March 1989, 3–6 (a review of V.S. Naipual, *Turn in the South*) and invoked as a direct play on Charles A. Reich's counterculture manifesto (discussed in Chapter 2), *The Greening of America* (New York: Random House, 1970); John Egerton, *The Americanization of Dixie: The Southernization of America* (New York: Harper's Magazine Press, 1974), xx.

13. Schulman, *The Seventies*, 117.

14. Marsh, "A Rose Colored Map," 80–82; Robert Christgau, "A Boogie Band that Loves the Governor (Boo Boo Boo)," in *Grown Up All Wrong: 75 Great Rock and Pop Artists from Vaudeville to Techno*, ed. Robert Christgau (Cambridge, MA: Harvard University Press, 1998), 145–46.

15. Nat Hentoff, *Village Voice*, quoted in "The Battle over 'Okie from Musk-ogee,'" *Weekly Standard*, 19 August 1996. Emphasis added. Walter Carter, "The Story Behind the Song: 'Okie from Muskogee,'" *Country Music*, February/March 2003, J10.

16. William Safire, *Before the Fall: An Inside View of the Pre-Watergate White House* (Garden City, NY: Doubleday, 1975), 582; DiMaggio, Peterson, and Esco, Jr., "Country Music: Ballad of the Silent Majority," 50.

17. Christopher Lasch, *The Culture of Narcissism: American Life in an Age of Diminishing Expectations* (New York: Norton, 1978), 4.

18. *Washington Post* 17 March 1974, *Washington Post* 18 March 1974; King, "Red Necks, White Sox, Blue Ribbon Fear," 30–34.

19. Raymond Price, *With Nixon* (New York: Viking Press, 1977), 121.

20. Peter Doggett, *Are You Ready for the Country: Elvis, Dylan, Parsons and the Roots of Country Rock* (New York: Penguin, 2000), 87–88; King, "Red Necks, White Sox, Blue Ribbon Fear," 30–34.

21. Bob Allen, quoted in Cusic, *Poet of the Common Man*, xl–xlii; Gerald W. Haslam, *Workin' Man Blues*, 205.

22. Mark Marqusee, *Chimes of Freedom: The Politics of Bob Dylan's Art* (New York: The New Press, 2003), 202, 215–16.

23. Jessica Hundley with Polly Parsons, *Grievous Angel* (New York: Thunder's Mouth Press, 2005), 210; Ben Fong-Torres, *Hickory Wind: The Life and Times of Gram Parsons* (New York: Pocket Books, 1991), 109; as Emmy Lou Harris said about Parsons, "You have to draw on the past and you have to come up with something new. Gram's music was very contemporary and modern, but it was music that tipped its hat to the heart and soul of traditional country." See Nicholas Dawidoff, *In the Country of Country* (New York: Vintage, 1997), 279.

24. Doggett, *Are You Ready for the Country?* 150.

25. Rich Wiseman, *Jackson Browne: The Story of a Hold Out* (Garden City, NY: Dolphin Books, 1982), 79.

26. Janet Maslin, "For Everyman," *Rolling Stone*, 22 November 1973.

27. The refrain of the song, "waiting here for everyman," echoes in important ways with both the Chilean poet Pablo Neruda's "For Everyone" and Clifford Odets' 1935 agitprop play *Waiting for Lefty* (also discussed in Chapter 7). Neruda, who devoted his poetry to the Chilean people, believed in their emancipation and lived to see socialist Salvador Allende elected to the presidency (and died the year of the 1973 U.S.-backed coup against him). Browne was known to be reading Neruda while writing "For Everyman," and the inspiration of the poet's similarly titled, though more gender neutral, "For Everyone" is palpable. The poet explains the need to wander and to travel but promises that when the moment comes and his countrymen need him, he will be there and die among them if necessary. Yet Browne's problem with America was darker and more tangled than Neruda's with his beloved Chile. The Chilean people were struggling alongside their

"Compañero Presidente" to build a new society, while Browne had to search out "some hearts" where "love and truth remain" while sticking it out with the silent majority.

The classic Odets' play *Waiting for Lefty*, in contrast, was about taxi drivers on the verge of an important strike vote in 1934. The workers each recall what led them to the union and their rising class consciousness as they wait for Lefty Costello, the leader of the union's strike faction. The inverted narrative of *Waiting for Lefty* and "Waiting for Everyman" explains much of the distance between the thirties and the seventies. In the former, the workers are in search of their leader (which turns out to be themselves); in the latter, the sensitive troubadour cannot find workers ready to struggle for a better world and is resolved to remain in silent vigilance for the people.

28. Greil Marcus, *Mystery Train: Images of America in Rock 'n' Roll Music* (New York: E.P. Dutton, 1975 [first edition]), 50.

29. Ibid., 62; See interviews, sleeve notes, and miscellania in Peter Viney, "King Harvest (Has Surly Come)" (1997), http://theband.hiof.no/articles/king_harvest_viney.html.

30. John Street, *Rebel Rock: The Politics of Popular Music* (New York: Basil Blackwell, 1986), 212–13.

31. Robert Christgau, *Rock Albums of the Seventies: A Critical Guide* (New York: Da Capo Press, 1981), 120.

32. Quoted in Doggett, *Are You Ready for the Country?* 103–104, 157; Eric Lott, *Love and Theft: Blackface Minstrelsy and the American Working Class* (New York: Oxford University Press, 1993).

33. Richard Bach, *Jonathan Livingston Seagull* (New York: Avon Books, 1970), 14, 30–31, 39, 81; Doggett, *Are You Ready for the Country?* 161.

34. Southern, quoted in Peter Biskind, *Easy Riders, Raging Bulls: How the Sex-Drugs-and-Rock-'n'-Roll Generation Saved Hollywood* (New York: Simon and Shuster, 1998), 68.

35. Barbara Ehrenreich, *Fear of Falling: The Inner Life of the Middle Class* (New York: Pantheon, 1989), 121, 142–43.

36. *New York Times* 2 August 1970; David Denby, "New York Blues," *Atlantic Monthly*, November 1970, 126; Peter Lev, *American Films of the 70s: Conflicting Visions* (Austin: University of Texas Press, 2000), 22–27; J. Hoberman, *The Dream Life: Movies, Media and the Mythology of the Sixties* (New York: The New Press, 2003), 281–86; *New York Times* 30 July 2000.

37. "Meet the Bunkers," also discussed in Josh Ozersky, *Archie Bunker's America; TV in an Era of Change, 1968–1978* (Carbondale: Southern Illinois University Press, 2003), 67–68.

38. The firestorm around *All in the Family* is covered in Richard P. Adler, ed., *All in the Family: A Critical Appraisal* (New York: Praeger, 1979); Stuart H. Surlin and

Eugene D. Tate, "'All in the Family': Is Archie Funny?" *Journal of Communication* 26 (Autumn 1976): 61–68; Roger Rosenblatt, "All in the Family," *New Republic*, 24 May 1975, 30–31; Michael J. Arlen, "The Media Dramas of Norman Lear," *New Yorker*, 12 March 1975, 89–94; Arnold Hano, "Can Archie Bunker Give Bigotry a Bad Name?" *New York Times Magazine*, 12 March 1972; Charles L. Sanders, "Is Archie Bunker the Real White America?" *Ebony*, June 1972, 186–92; Howard F. Stein, "'All in the Family' as a Mirror of Contemporary Culture," *Family Process* 13 (September 1974): 279–315.

39. Sanders, "Is Archie Bunker the Real White America?" 192; on the psychology of the Bunkers, see Stein, "'All in the Family' as a Mirror of Contemporary American Culture," 298.

40. E.E. LeMasters, *Blue Collar Aristocrats: Life-Styles at a Working-Class Tavern* (Madison: University of Wisconsin Press, 1975), 90.

41. Unger, Interview with Carroll O'Connor #4968 and #4743, Unger, Interview with Jean Stapleton #4968, in Arthur Unger Audio Interview Collection, Television History Collection, Syracuse University; *Christian Science Monitor* 3 September 1974, 9 September 1974; *Variety* 28 August 1974, 18 September 1974; the CBS dispute is covered in *Variety* 7 August 1974, 28 August 1974, 11 September 1974.

42. Unger, Interview with O'Connor #4968.

43. Unger, Interviews with O'Connor #4968 and #4743; *Christian Science Monitor* 3 September 1974, 9 September 1974. O'Connor continued his labor sympathies late in life. He wrote a play in the late nineties called *A Certain Labor Day* about a New York labor union official, which was panned by the critics and quickly closed. Carroll O'Connor, *I Think I'm Outta Here: A Memoir of All My Families* (New York: Pocket Books, 1998), 1–2. He made two television commercials for Mayor John Lindsay's candidacy during the Florida primaries to help defeat the runaway success of the Wallace campaign; in it, he moved between himself and his famous character, complete with cigar in mouth. *New York Times* 8 March 1972, *New York Times* 13 March 1972.

44. Unger, Interview with O'Connor, #4698, AUAIC.

45. The episodes are "The Bunkers and Inflation," "Archie Underfoot," "Edith the Job Hunter," "Archie's Raise," archived at Moving Image Collection, Motion Picture and Television Reading Room, Library of Congress, Washington, DC.

46. For the conversation on homosexuality, see 13 May 1971 Oval Office tape transcript, published as "All the Philosophers' Men," *Harper's Magazine*, February 2000, 22–24.

47. Review quotes in Jack Shadoian, "Dirty Harry: A Defense," *Western Humanities Review* 28 (1974): 166, 172; Hoberman, *Dream Life*, 324–25.

48. Hoberman, *Dream Life*, 325, 376 fn; Judith Crist, "Git 'Em Up, Move 'Em Over," *New York*, 30 April 1973.

49. *New York Times* 23 August 1972; *New York Times* 24 August 1972; *New York Times* 25 August 1972.

50. *New York Times* 25 August 1975; P.F. Kluge and Thomas Moore, "The Boys in the Bank: A Fouled-up Holdup Moves Step by Step from Threats to Farce to Violence," *Life Magazine*, September 22, 1972, 66–70; Frank R. Cunningham, *Sidney Lumet: Film and Literary Vision*, 2nd ed. (Lexington: University Press of Kentucky, 2001), 24.

51. Jay Boyer, *Sidney Lumet* (New York: Twayne Publishers, 1993), 56.

52. Charles Champlin, *Hollywood's Revolutionary Decade* (Santa Barbara, CA: John Daniel, 1998), 118–21.

53. Kluge and Moore, "The Boys in the Bank," 66.

54. Peter Roffman and Jim Purdy, *The Hollywood Social Problem Film: Madness, Despair, and Politics from the Depression to the Fifties* (Bloomington: Indiana University Press, 1981), 17; George Lipsitz, *Rainbow at Midnight: Labor and Culture in the 1940s* (Urbana: University of Illinois Press, 1994), 279–85.

55. Fredric Jameson, "Class and Allegory in Contemporary Mass Culture: *Dog Day Afternoon* as a Political Film" *College English* 38 (April 1977): 854.

56. Lev, *American Films of the 70s*, 45–47.

57. Champlin, *Hollywood's Revolutionary Decade*, 112–14.

58. *Time*, 27 October 1975, *Newsweek*, 27 October 1975; *New York Times* 15 August 1975; *New York Times* 29 August 1975; *New York Times* 5 October 1975.

59. Dave Marsh, *Bruce Springsteen: Two Hearts: The Definitive Biography* (New York: Routledge, 2004), 139.

60. Springsteen quoted in Louis P. Masur, *Runaway Dream: Born to Run and Bruce Springsteen's American Vision* (New York: Bloomsbury Press, 2009), 112–13.

Chapter 5: A Collective Sadness

1. Michael Harrington, *The Next America: The Decline and Rise of the United States* (New York: Holt, Rinehart, and Winston, 1981), 1, 129; one of the defining dimensions of Old Left/New Left tensions was the idea of working-class agency. C. Wright Mills threw down the gauntlet in his "Letter to a New Left" by urging the Left to get rid of its "labor metaphysic"—rejecting the idea that the power and will for society's emancipation burned in the breast of the proletariat. C. Wright Mills, "Letter to the New Left," *New Left Review*, 5 (September–October 1960): 18–23.

2. Harrington, *Next America*, 2.

3. Ibid., 1; Michael Harrington, *Fragments of the Century* (New York: Saturday Review Press, 1973), 228–29.

4. Michael Harrington, *Decade of Decision: The Crisis of the American System* (New York: Simon and Schuster, 1980), 37; Harrington, *Next America*, 6; Michael Harrington, "Why the Welfare State Breaks Down," *Dissent* 27 (Winter 1980): 47.

5. Michael Harrington, "A Collective Sadness," *Dissent* (Fall 1974): 490.

6. Michael Harrington, *Twilight of Capitalism* (New York: Simon and Schuster, 1976), 11; Harrington, *Next America*, Harrington, "Collective Sadness," 486–91.

7. Daniel Bell, *The Coming of Post-Industrial Society: A Venture in Social Forecasting* (New York: Basic Books, 1973), 53–54; Daniel Bell, *The Cultural Contradictions of Capitalism* (New York: Basic Books, 1976); Andreas Killen, *1973 Nervous Breakdown: Watergate, Warhol and the Birth of Post-Sixties America* (New York: Bloomsbury, 2006), 216.

8. Richard Sennett and Jonathan Cobb, *The Hidden Injuries of Class* (New York: Vintage Books, 1972), 98, 105, 171–73; Otto Feinstein and Rolland H. Wright, "The Ethnic Revival: Work and Community Satisfaction and the Work Ethic," in *Immigrants and Migrants: The Detroit Ethnic Experience*, ed. David W. Hartman (Detroit: New University Thought Pub, 1974), 245; Colin Greer, "Remembering Class: An Interpretation," in *Divided Society: The Ethnic Experience in America*, ed. Colin Greer (New York: Basic Books, 1974), 6, 34; Richard Sennett and Jonathan Cobb, "The Hidden Injuries of Class," in Greer, ed., *Divided Society*, 268.

9. Tom Wolfe, "The Me Decade and the Third Great Awakening," in *Tom Wolfe: The Purple Decades* (New York: Farrar Strauss Giroux, 1982), 277; Andy Warhol, *The Philosophy of Andy Warhol: From A to B and Back Again* (New York: Harcourt Brace Jovanovich, 1975), 26; for the context of Warholism in the 1970s, see Killen, *1973 Nervous Breakdown*, 137–62; for the mirrored ball, see Craig Werner, *A Change Is Gonna Come* (New York: Plume, 1998), 177–78.

10. Wolfe, "Me Decade," 271–73.

11. Ibid., 292–93.

12. Lasch, *The Culture of Narcissism: American Life in an Age of Diminishing Expectations* (New York: Norton, 1978), xiii–xiv, 28; see what Richard Wightman Fox called the "hedonism of the knowledge class" as discussed in Richard Wightman Fox, "Breathless: The Cultural Consternation of Daniel Bell," *American Quarterly* 34 (Spring 1982): 70–77.

13. Harrington, "A Collective Sadness," 486–91; Paul Buhle, *Taking Care of Business: Samuel Gompers, George Meany, Lane Kirkland, and the Tragedy of American Labor* (New York: Monthly Review Press, 1999), 187; *Proceedings of the Tenth Constitutional Convention of the AFL-CIO* (Washington, DC: AFL-CIO, 1973), 15, 39; the release of the "Church Committee Report" on the abuse of the intelligence agencies did not help the national spirit; see the *Final Report of the Select Committee to Study Governmental Operations with Respect to Intelligence Activities*. United States Senate, 94th Congress, 2nd Session, April 26 (legislative day, April 14), 1976. [AKA "Church Committee Report"], http://www.icdc.com/~paulwolf/cointelpro/churchfinalreport IIa.htm, transcription and HTML by Paul Wolf (accessed 7 July 2007); Gerald R. Ford's Address Before a Joint Session of the Congress Reporting on the State of the Union, 15 January 1975, http://www.fordlibrarymuseum.gov/ford_full_search.html; Tad Szulc, *Innocents at Home: America in the 1970s* (New York: Viking Press, 1974), 43.

14. Robert N. Bellah and others, *Habits of the Heart: Individualism and Commitment in American Life* (Berkeley: University of California Press, 1985), 22–23, 49, 277; *Time* 15 July 1974.

15. Andrew Levison, "Who Lost the Working Class?" *The Nation* 26 April 2001; Thomas Byrne Edsall and Mary D. Edsall, *Chain Reaction: The Impact of Race, Rights and Taxes on American Politics* (New York: Norton, 1991), 104; Phillip Roth, *American Pastoral* (New York: Vintage, 1997), 422; Lillian Breslow Rubin, *Worlds of Pain: Life in the Working-Class Family* (New York: Basic Books, 1976), 204.

16. James Goodman, *Blackout* (New York: North Point Press, 2003), 92; Jonathan Mahler, *Ladies and Gentlemen, The Bronx Is Burning: 1977, Baseball, Politics, and the Battle for the Soul of a City* (New York: Farrar, Straus and Giroux, 2005), 256, passim.

17. *New York Times* 21 July 1977; *New York Times* 3 August 1977; Goodman, *Blackout*, 157–60; Mahler, *Bronx*, 229–30; Joshua B. Freeman, *Working Class New York: Life and Labor Since World War II* (New York: The New Press, 2000), 276, 281–82.

18. *Fortune*, quoted in Kim Phillips-Fein, *Invisible Hands: The Making of the Conservative Movement from the New Deal to Reagan* (New York: W.W. Norton, 2009), 156.

19. Burns quote in Kim McQuaid, *Uneasy Partners: Big Business in American Politics, 1945–1990* (Baltimore: Johns Hopkins University Press, 1994), 140; Charles L. Schultze, "Federal Spending, Past, Present, and Future," in *Setting National Priorities*, ed. Henry Own and Charles L. Schultze (Washington, DC: Brookings Institution, 1976), 324.

20. Solow in *Wall Street Journal* 19 June 1979; Carl W. Biven, *Jimmy Carter's Economy: Policy in an Age of Limits* (Chapel Hill: University of North Carolina Press, 2002), 197, 22; Alan S. Blinder, *Economic Policy and the Great Stagflation* (New York: Academic Press, 1979); Interview with Ray Marshall, Miller Center Interviews, Carter Presidency Project, vol. XXV, 4 May 1988, 42, Jimmy Carter Library, Atlanta, Georgia; Martin Neil Baily and Arthur M. Okun, eds., *The Battle Against Unemployment and Inflation*, 3rd ed. (New York: W.W. Norton, 1982).

21. *Business Week* 12 October 1974; *Business Week* 14 September, 1974; *Business Week* 29 June 1974; *Wall Street Journal* 19 June 1979; Robert M. Solow, "The Citizen's Guide: The Trade-Off View," in Baily and Okun, eds., *The Battle Against Unemployment and Inflation*, 40–44.

22. John Carson-Parker, "The Options Ahead for the Debt Economy," *Business Week* 12 October 1974, 120–21; "The 1970s: A Second Look," *Business Week*, 14 September, 1974, 51–53; Phillips-Fein, *Invisible Hands*, 156.

23. *Wall Street Journal* 19 June 1979; Harrington, *Twilight of Capitalism*, 331; Harrington, *Decade of Decision*, 11; Patrick J. Akard, "Corporate Mobilization of Political Power: The Transformation of U.S. Economic Policy in the 1970s," *American Sociological Review* 57 (October 1992): 597–615.

24. Irving Bluestone Testimony to House Subcommittee on Equal Opportunities on the Equal Opportunity and Full Employment Act (H. 50) 24 March 1975, Box 55, FF 2, Irving Bluestone Papers, Reuther Archives, Wayne State University; Ford, quoted in Collins, *More*, 155.

25. Collins, *More*, 101, 158.

26. Fred Hirsch, *Social Limits to Growth* (Cambridge, MA: Harvard University Press, 1976); Robert L. Heilbroner, *An Inquiry into the Human Prospect* (New York: Norton, 1974); William Leiss, *The Limits to Satisfaction: An Essay on the Problems of Needs and Commodities* (Toronto: University of Toronto Press, 1976); Donatella H. Meadows, *The Limits to Growth: A Report for the Club of Rome's Project on the Predicament of Mankind* (New York: Universe Books, 1972); William Ophuls, *Ecology and the Politics of Scarcity: Prologue to a Political Theory of the Steady State* (San Francisco: W.H. Freeman, 1977); Lester C. Thurow, *The Zero-Sum Society: Distribution and the Possibilities for Economic Change* (New York: Basic Books, 1980); Howard J. Ruff, *How to Prosper During the Coming Bad Years: A Crash Course in Personal and Financial Survival* (New York: Times Books, 1979); Robert Bellah, *The Broken Covenant: American Civil Religion in a Time of Trial* (New York: Seabury Press, 1975); Interview with Charles Schultze, MCI, Carter Presidency Project, 8 January 1982–89 January 1982, Jimmy Carter Library, Atlanta, Georgia; Wassily Leontief, "National Economic Planning: Methods and Problems," *Challenge* (July/August 1976): 10; *New York Times* 24 September 1977.

27. Milton Friedman, "Inflation and Unemployment," Nobel Memorial Lecture, 13 December 1976, accessed at http://nobelprize.org/nobel_prizes/economics/laureates/1976/friedman-lecture.html; Godfrey Hodgson, *The World Turned Right Side Up: A History of the Conservative Ascendancy in America* (New York: Mariner Books, 1996), 201–203; William Greider, *Secrets of the Temple: How the Federal Reserve Runs the Country* (New York: Simon and Schuster, 1987), 87–88, 91–92.

28. Edsall and Edsall, *Chain Reaction*, 167; McQuaid, *Uneasy Partners*, 150.

29. Richard Viguerie, quoted in *Guardian*, 1 April 1981, 5; Patrick Buchanan, quoted in Michael Kazin, *The Populist Persuasion: An American History* (New York: Basic Books, 1995), 245; Phillips-Fein, *Invisible Hands*, 216–27.

30. William A. Rusher, *The Making of the New Majority Party* (New York: Sheed and Ward, 1975); Phillips-Fein, *Invisible Hands*, 218–19; Philip Jenkins, *Decade of Nightmares: The End of the Sixties and the Making of Eighties America* (New York: Oxford, 2006), 94, 97.

31. Governor Ronald Reagan, Conservative Political Action Conference, Washington, DC, 6 February 1977; see Samuel G. Freedman, *The Inheritance: How Three Families and America Moved from Roosevelt to Reagan and Beyond* (New York: Simon and Schuster, 1996).

32. Robert Weissman, "Don't Mourn, Organize: Big Business Follows Joe Hill's Entreaty to U.S. Political Dominance," *Multinational Monitor* 26 (January/February

2005) accessed at: http://www.multinationalmonitor.org/mm2005/012005/weiss man.html; Kim McQuaid, "Big Business and Public Policy in Contemporary United States," *Quarterly Review of Economics and Business* 20 (Summer 1980): 59–60; Mark Blyth, *Great Transformations: Economic Ideas and Institutional Change in the Twentieth Century* (New York: Cambridge, 2002), 155; David Vogel, "The Power of Business in America: A Re-Appraisal," *British Journal of Political Science* 13 (January 1983): 21; As Ian Maitland argues, however, this did not always mean business was unified—especially in the 1980s; see Ian Maitland, "Self-Defeating Lobbying: How More Is Buying Less in Washington," *Journal of Business Strategy* 7 (Fall 1986): 67–68; Thomas Byrne Edsall, *The New Politics of Inequality* (New York: W.W. Norton, 1984), 108; Phyllis S. McGrath, *Redefining Corporate-Federal Relations* (New York: Conference Board, 1979).

33. Vogel, "The Power of Business in America," 24; Theodore Lowi, "American Business, Public Policy, Case-Studies, and Political Theory," *World Politics* 16 (1964): 677–715.

34. Phillis Payne, "The Plot to Subvert Labor Standards," *AFL-CIO American Federationist* (July 1979): 20; Marc Linder, *Wars of Attrition: Vietnam, the Business Roundtable, and the Decline of Construction Unions* (Iowa City, IA: Fanpihua Press, 1999), iv, 199; McQuaid, "Big Business and Public Policy in Contemporary United States," 59–60.

35. George B. Morris, quoted in Haynes Johnson and Nick Kotz, *The Unions* (New York: Pocket Books, 1972), 137; borne out by Linder, *Wars of Attrition*, 187, 197–200; *New York Times* 12 July 1970.

36. Linder, *Wars of Attrition*, 209; James Gross, *Broken Promise: The Subversion of U.S. Labor Relations Policy, 1947–1994* (Philadelphia: Temple University Press, 1995), 217–41; McQuaid, "Big Business and Public Policy in Contemporary United States," 59–60, 64; Walter Guzzardi, Jr., "A New Public Face for Business," *Fortune*, 30 June 1980, 48–52; Peter Slavin, "The Business Roundtable: New Lobbying Arm of Big Business," *Business and Society Review* (Winter 1975/1976): 28; "Business' Most Powerful Lobby in Washington," *Business Week*, 20 December 1976: 60–63; Kim McQuaid, "The Roundtable: Getting Results in Washington," *Harvard Business Review* (May–June 1981): 114–23.

37. Kim McQuaid, "Back-Door Policymaking," *Working Papers for a New Society* 7 (July/August 1979): 53; David Vogel, "The Power of Business in America: A Re-Appraisal," *British Journal of Political Science* 13 (January 1983): 32, 35; David Vogel, *Fluctuating Fortunes: The Political Power of Business in America* (New York: Basic Books, 1989), 198–99.

38. *Business Week* 20 December 1976; Johnson and Kotz, *The Unions*, 139.

39. James T. Patterson, *Restless Giant: The United States from Watergate to Bush v. Gore* (New York: Oxford, 2005), 85–86; *Wall Street Journal* 11 September 1978; Akard, "Corporate Mobilization of Political Power," 602.

40. Vogel, "Power of Business," 42.

41. Kim Moody, *An Injury to All: The Decline of American Unionism* (New York: Verso, 1988), 130; George Meany, "Common Sense in Labor Law," *Labor Law Journal* 27 (1976): 603–608; Richard Prosten, Research Director, Industrial Union Department, AFL-CIO, "The Longest Season: Union Organizing in the Last Decade a/k/a How Come One Team has to Play with its Shoelaces Tied Together," 30 August 1978, Box 12, FF: 23, JHP; AFL-CIO, "Special Report: The Right Wing," (1977) RG 98–002, Box 2, FF 19, GMMA; Charles McDonald and Dick Wison, "Peddling the 'Union-Free' Guarantee," *AFL-CIO Federationist*, April 1979, 12–19.

42. John Logan, "Consultants, Lawyers, and the 'Union Free' Movement in the USA Since the 1970s," *Industrial Relations Journal* 197 (August 2002): 197–214; and Phillis Payne, "The Consultants Who Coach the Violators," *AFL-CIO Federationist*, September 1977, 22–30; Center to Protect Workers' Rights, *From Brass Knuckles to Briefcases: The Changing Art of Union-Busting in America* (Washington, DC: Center to Protect Workers' Rights, 1979).

43. Michael Goldfield, "Labor in American Politics—Its Current Weakness," *Journal of Politics*, 48 (February 1986): 2–29; Henry S. Farber, "The Recent Decline of Unionization in the United States," *Science* 238 (November 1987): 915–20; Mike Davis, *Prisoners of the American Dream* (New York: Verso, 1986), 131–32.

44. Farber, "The Recent Decline of Unionization in the United States," 915–20; Rubin, *Worlds of Pain*, 163; Thomas Kochan, "How American Workers View Labor Unions," *Monthly Labor Review* 102 (April 1979): 30.

45. Davis, *Prisoners of the American Dream*, 130; Timothy Minchin, *Fighting Against the Odds: A History of Southern Labor Since World War II* (Gainesville: University Press of Florida, 2005), 117–46; Kirkpatrick Sale, *Power Shift: The Rise of the Southern Rim and Its Challenge to the Eastern Establishment* (New York: Random House, 1975); John Egerton, *Americanization of Dixie: The Southernization of America* (New York: Harper's Magazine Press, 1974), xx; Jefferson Cowie, *Capital Moves: RCA's Seventy Year Quest for Cheap Labor* (New York: The New Press, 2001), 73–99, 127–51; Earl Black and Merle Black, *The Rise of the Southern Republicans* (Cambridge, MA: Harvard University Press, 2002).

46. Harrison H. Donnelly, "Organized Labor Found 1978 a Frustrating Year, Had Few Victories in Congress," *Congressional Quarterly*, 30 December 1978, 3539; *Wall Street Journal* 18 October 1978; *Washington Post* 3 November 1974; Hart would have a hard time with organized labor right through his 1984 race for the Democratic nomination.

47. Paul Frymer, *Black and Blue: African Americans, the Labor Movement, and the Decline of the Democratic Party* (Princeton, NJ: Princeton University Press, 2008), 2–3, 9.

48. Ibid., 29.

49. Ira Katznelson, *When Affirmative Action Was White: An Untold History of Racial Inequality in Twentieth-Century America* (New York: W.W. Norton, 2005); Nancy

MacLean, *Freedom Is Not Enough: The Opening of the American Workplace* (New York: Russell Sage Foundation and Harvard University Press, 2006), 7.

50. David Brody, *Labor Embattled* (Urbana: University of Illinois Press, 2005), 107; Katherine Van Wezel Stone, "The Legacy of Industrial Pluralism: the Tension between Individual Employment Rights and the New Deal Collective Bargaining System," *University of Chicago Law Review* 59 (Spring 1992): 576; Timothy J. Minchin, *Hiring the Black Worker: The Racial Integration of the Southern Textile Industry, 1960–1980* (Chapel Hill: University of North Carolina Press, 1999), 56; Thomas J. Sugrue, "Affirmative Action from Below: Civil Rights, the Building Trades, and the Politics of Racial Equality in the Urban North, 1945–1969," *Journal of American History* 91 (2004): 145–83; *New York Times* 28 August 1969; Reuel E. Schiller, "The Emporium Capwell Case: Race, Labor Law, and the Crisis of Post-War Liberalism," *Berkeley Journal of Employment and Labor Law* 25, no. 1 (2004): 129–65.

51. MacLean, *Freedom Is Not Enough*, 346; as the social theorist Nancy Fraser argues, recognition (that is, remedies for cultural forms of oppression) must go together with issues of redistribution (remedies for socio-economic injustice). Nancy Fraser, "From Redistribution to Recognition?" in *Justice Interruptus: Critical Reflections on the Post-Socialist Condition* (New York: Routledge, 1997), 11–40.

52. Ruy A. Teixiera and Joel Rodgers, *America's Forgotten Majority: Why the White Working Class Still Matters* (New York: Basic Books, 2000); Walter Benn Michaels, *The Trouble with Diversity: How We Learned to Love Identity and Ignore Inequality* (New York: Holt, 2006), 6–7. Jefferson Cowie, "From Hard Hats to NASCAR Dads," *New Labor Forum* (Fall 2004): 9–17; Richard Harvey Brown, *Culture, Capitalism, and Democracy in the New America* (New Haven, CT: Yale University Press, 2005), 62; Wendy Brown, *States of Injury* (Princeton, NJ: Princeton University Press, 1995), 14, 60.

53. Slavoj Žižek, "Class Struggle or Postmodernism? Yes, Please!" in *Contingency, Hegemony, Universality*, ed. Judith Butler, Ernest Laclau, and Slavoj Žižek (New York: Verso, 2000), 98; Ronald Inglehart, *Modernization and Postmodernization: Cultural, Economic, and Political Change in 43 Societies* (Princeton, NJ: Princeton University Press, 1997), 35; Geoff Eley, *The Future of Class in History: What's Left of the Social* (Ann Arbor: University of Michigan Press, 2007), 59; Craig Calhoun offers a useful correction, arguing that class became an overcentralized discourse, overshadowing the complexity of other social movements even in the nineteenth century. See Craig Calhoun, "Postmodernism as Pseudohistory," *Theory Culture Society* 10 (1993): 75–96; as Foucault argues, "There is no single locus of great Refusal, no soul of revolt, source of all rebellions, or pure law of the revolutionary." Michel Foucault, *The History of Sexuality* (New York: Vintage, 1980), 95–96.

54. Emphasis added. Dennis A. Deslippe, "'Do Whites Have Rights?': White Detroit Policemen and 'Reverse Discrimination' Protests in the 1970s," *Journal of American History* 91 (2004): 932–960; Matthew Frye Jacobson, *Roots Too: White Ethnic Revival in Post-Civil Rights America* (Cambridge, MA: Harvard University Press, 2006); Jonathan Rieder, *Canarsie: The Jews and Italians of Brooklyn Against Liberalism* (Cambridge, MA: Harvard University Press, 1985).

55. "What the Weber Ruling Does," *Time,* 9 July 1979; Judith Stein, *Running Steel, Running America: Race, Economic Policy, and the Decline of Liberalism* (Chapel Hill: University of North Carolina Press, 1998), 191.

56. The complexities of steel, race, and public policy are best understood in Stein, *Running Steel, Running America,* 169–95; see also Bruce Nelson, *Divided We Stand* (Princeton, NJ: Princeton University Press, 2001), 280–86.

57. Dale Maharidge and Michael Williamson, *Journey to Nowhere: The Saga of the New Underclass* (New York: Hyperion, 1996); 17, 20; Stein, *Running Steel,* 195.

58. Jacobsen, *Roots Too: White Ethnic Revival in Post-Civil Rights America* (Cambridge, MA: Harvard University Press, 2006), 1–10; Katherine Van Wezel Stone, "The Legacy of Pluralism: The Tension Between Individual Employment Rights and the New Deal Collective Bargaining System," *University of Chicago Law Review* 59 (1992): 575–644; Edsall and Edsall, *Chain Reaction,* 95; Michael J. Piore and Sean Safford, "Changing Regimes of Workplace Governances, Shifting Axes of Social Mobilization, and the Challenge to Industrial Relations Theory," *Industrial Relations* 45 (2006): 299–325.

59. Ronald P. Formisano, *Boston Against Busing: Race, Class, and Ethnicity in the 1960s and 1970s* (Chapel Hill: University of North Carolina Press, 1991), 12; J. Anthony Lukas, "A Touch of Class," *Boston Observer,* June 1985, 8; J. Anthony Lukas, "Boston in Turmoil: A Matter of Class," *Yale Review* 76 (Autumn 1986): 56–61; J. Anthony Lukas, *Common Ground: A Turbulent Decade in the Lives of Three American Families* (New York: Knopf, 1985); Edsall and Edsall, *Chain Reaction,* 89; Matthew Lassister, *The Silent Majority: Suburban Politics in the Sunbelt South* (Princeton, NJ: Princeton University Press, 2006), 315.

60. Paul A. Sracic, *San Antonio v. Rodriguez and the Pursuit of Equal Education: The Debate over Discrimination and School Funding* (Lawrence: University Press of Kansas, 2006).

61. Francine D. Blau and Lawrence M. Kahn, "The Gender Pay Gap: Going, Going . . . but Not Gone," in *The Declining Significance of Gender?* ed. Francine D. Blau, Mary C. Brinton, and David B. Grusky (New York: Russell Sage Foundation, 2006), 52; Nicole M. Fortin and Thomas Lemieux, "Are Women's Wage Gains Men's Losses? A Distributional Test," *American Economic Review* 90 (2000): 456–60.

62. Debby D'Amico, "To My White Working-Class Sisters," in *"Takin' it to the Streets:" A Sixties Reader,* ed. Alexander Bloom and Wini Breines (New York: Oxford University Press, 1995), 520–25.

63. Dorothy Sue Cobble, *The Other Women's Movement: Workplace Justice and Social Rights in Modern America* (Princeton, NJ: Princeton University Press), 194–95, 221; Alice Kessler-Harris, *In Pursuit of Equity: Women, Men, and the Quest for Economic Citizenship in 20th-Century America* (New York: Oxford University Press, 2001), 268–69; Beth Bailey, "She 'Can Bring Home the Bacon,'" in *America in the Seventies*, ed. Beth Bailey and David Farber (Lawrence: University Press of Kansas), 107–28; by the early eighties, however, it seemed that labor needed the women's movement rather than the other way around; see Edsall, *The New Politics of Inequality*, 161.

64. Robert Wuthnow, *The Restructuring of American Religion: Society and Faith Since World War II* (Princeton, NJ: Princeton University Press, 1988), 237–39.

65. Garry Wills, *Head and Heart: American Christianities* (New York: Penguin Press, 2007), 485.

66. Jenkins, *Decade of Nightmares*, 83–84; Wolfe, "Me Decade"; Wills, *Head and Heart*, 483.

67. Kristin Luker, *Abortion and the Politics of Motherhood* (Berkeley: University of California Press, 1984), 209.

68. Ibid., 194–210; Jack Metzgar, "Politics and the American Class Vernacular," in *New Working Class Studies*, ed. John Russo (Ithaca, NY: ILR Press, 2005), 201.

69. Rubin, *Worlds of Pain*, 183–84; Arlie Russell Hochschild, *The Second Shift* (New York: Viking, 1989).

70. *New York Times* 15 September 1974; *Time*, 21 March 1977; Marshall Ganz, *Why David Sometimes Wins: Leadership, Organization, and Strategy in the California Farm Worker Movement* (New York: Oxford University Press, 2009), 243–44. Jerry Wurf, "Labor and 1980: We Must Not Be Spectators," remarks for the National Press Club, 12 July 1979, Box 7, FF: 19, JHP.

71. Stephen Singular, "Man of Steel," *New Times*, 4 February 1977; John Herling, *Right to Challenge: People and Power in the Steelworkers Union* (New York: Harper and Row, 1972).

72. Rauh to Randolph, 28 January 1977, Box 131, FF: USWA v. Sadlowski, misc., 1976–1977, JLRP; *New York Times* 26 December 1976; News from the McBride Team, press release, 29 December 1976, Box 131, FF: USWA v. Sadlowski: post-election prospects, JLRP; Msgr. George G. Higgins, "A Look at the Outside Interference in Recent United Steelworkers of America Union Elections," 14 February 1977, Box 12, FF: 15, JHP; *New York Times* 1 September 1975; Edgar James, "Sadlowski and the Steelworkers: Notes for the Next Time," *Working Papers for a New Society*, Spring 1977, 31.

73. See the packet of correspondence and press releases pertaining to the presence of "outsiders" in FF: USWA v. Sadlowski, misc. 1976–1977, Box 131, JLRP; *Wall Street Journal* 13 January 1977; NBC, *Meet the Press* with Lloyd McBride and Ed Sadlowski, transcript of TV show printed as pamphlet (January 1977).

74. Judith Coburn, "Ed Sadlowski Strides Toward Bethlehem," *Village Voice*, 7 February 1977, 27; Sideny Lens, "The Coming Revolt in Labor," *Progressive*, April 1977, 26–29; Philip Nyden, "Rank-and-File Organizations and the United Steelworkers of America," *Insurgent Sociologist* 8 (Fall 1978): 15–24.

75. "Penthouse Interview: Ed Sadlowski," *Penthouse*, January 1977, 182; "Oilcan Eddie Is Running for President and the Union Bosses in Tuxedos are Running Scared," *Seven Days*, 28 February 1977, 5–12.

76. "Penthouse Interview: Ed Sadlowski," 162, 183; James, "Sadlowski and the Steelworkers," 37; Thomas Geoghegan, *Which Side Are You On?: Trying to Be for Labor When It's Flat on Its Back* (New York: Farrar Straus Giroux, 1991), 79–80. Sadlowski's musings on the reduction of steel employment, which raised the hackles of the rank and file, were prophetic. When he spoke them, steel consumption was very high, but imports were cutting substantially into U.S. market share, as a surge of European and Japanese steel flooded the U.S. market in 1977. More than fourteen major mills shut down in late summer and fall as the North American steel market remained unprotected and became a dumping ground for foreign steel. Names and places that had served as metaphors for American working class success—like Bethlehem Steel and Johnstown, Pennsylvania; the Campbell Works of Youngstown Sheet and Tube, the Alan Wood Steel Company (the oldest producer in the nation), went bankrupt; Kaiser closed three mills. Jones and Laughlin shutdown a mill in Michigan. U.S. Steel ceased three operations at three mills in the East and threatened to close its South Works plant in Sadlowski's backyard, which would soon come to pass. In the fall of 1979, U.S. Steel announced that it was closing fifteen mills in eight states.

77. *New York Times* 9 September 1976; Philip W. Nyden, *Steelworkers Rank-and-File: The Political Economy of a Union Reform Movement* (New York: Praeger, 1984), 88–89; Coburn, "Ed Sadlowski Strides Toward Bethlehem," 27–30.

78. Steelworkers Fight Back, Press Release, 21 November 1976, Box 131, FF: USWA v. Sadlowski, misc., 1976–1977, JLRP; Rau to Miller, 29 December 1976, FF: USWA v. Sadlowski: post-election prospects, Box 131, JLRP; the insurgents' complaints are detailed in Steelworkers Fight Back to Ray Marshall, 17 June 1977, Box 12, FF: 14, JHP.

79. Paul F. Clark, *The Miners' Fight for Democracy: Arnold Miller and the Reform of the United Mine Workers* (Ithaca, NY: ILR Press, 1981), 85; Nyden, "Rank-and-File Organization," 30–36.

80. Miller to Meany 12 December 1975, FF: United Mine Workers Correspondence, Box 116, JRP; UMWA Press Release 8 September 1975, Miller to members 4 September 1975, Federal Court Injunctions under the National Bituminous Coal Wage Agreement (memorandum), all in FF: 5, Box 12, JHP; Barbara Ellen Smith, *Digging Our Own Graves: Coal Miners and the Struggle over Black Lung Disease* (Philadelphia: Temple University Press, 1987), 189; Clark, *Miners' Fight for Democracy*, 123–24; *Wall Street Journal* 3 January 1978; *New York Times* 17 February 1978.

81. Rauh to Miller 28 December 1976, Ortiz to Rauh 13 December 1976 in Box 116, FF: United Mine Workers Correspondence, JRP.

82. *Washington Post* 16 January 1977; Clark, *Miners' Fight for Democracy*, 93; Kim Moody and Jim Woodward, *Battle Line: The Coal Strike of '78* (Detroit, MI: Sun Press, 1978), 27, 37–40, 69.

83. *Washington Post* 16 January 1977.

84. Bituminous Coal Operators' Association, "Open Letter to the American People, The Congress, the President," n.d., FF: 5, Box: 12, JHP; Moody and Woodward, *Battle Line*, 12.

85. William Forbath, *Law and the Shaping of the American Labor Movement* (Cambridge, MA: Harvard University Press, 1991), 59–97; Christopher L. Tomlins, *The State and the Unions: Labor Relations, Law, and the Organized Labor Movement in America, 1880–1960* (New York: Cambridge University Press, 1985), 32–59.

86. See the correspondence, 8 September 1975 press release, and memorandum "Federal Court Injunctions Under the National Bituminous Coal Wage Agreement," in FF: 5, Box 12, JHP; William B. Gould, *A Primer on American Labor Law* (Cambridge, MA: MIT Press, 2004), 157.

87. *Washington Post* 14 March 1978.

88. Moody, *Battle Line*, 66; *Washington Post* 14 March 1978; *Washington Post* 21 March 1978.

89. *Washington Post* 18 January 1978; *Washington Post* 28 February 1978; Moody, *Battle Line*, 38, 48, 81, 42; Charles R. Perry, *Collective Bargaining and the Decline of the United Mine Workers* (Philadelphia: Wharton School, 1984), 231; John A. Ackermann, "The Impact of the Coal Strike of 1977–1978," *Industrial and Labor Relations Review* 32 (January 1979): 175–18.

90. Moody, *Battle Line*, 94; *Washington Post* 16 January 1977.

91. Geoghegan, *Which Side Are You On?* 82.

Chapter 6: The New Deal that Never Happened

1. Winpisinger, quoted in Alexander Cockburn and James Ridgeway, "Is There Hope for the Eighties?" *Village Voice,* 26 March 1979; Carter as Republican remark in *New York Times* 13 December 1977; James W. Singer, "The Latest Humphrey-Hawkins Bill—What Hasn't Changed Is the Name," *National Journal*, 10 December 1977, 1929–1931.

2. Interview with Ray Marshall, MCI, Carter Presidency Project, vol. XXV, 4 May 1988, 26, Jimmy Carter Library, Atlanta, Georgia.

3. *Washington Post* 9 April 1977; "Labor's Rising Anti-Carter Mood," *Business Week* 21 April 1978; Butler to the President, "Mr. Meany's Comments," 28 February 1978, FF: AFL-CIO 1/12/78–5/30/78, Box 86, Chief of Staff Butler, JCP; Melvyn Dubofsky, *The State and Labor in Modern America* (Chapel Hill: University of North Carolina Press, 1994), 226; Taylor Dark, *The Unions and the Democrats: An Enduring*

Alliance (Ithaca: ILR Press, 1999), 116; *Time*, 11 April 1977; "Unions' Sweet Hopes Turn Sour," *U.S. News and World Report*, 11 April 1977; "Behind Big Labor's New Attack on Carter," *U.S. News and World Report*, 27 February 1978; "Labor 'Disappointed' in Carter's Performance," *Congressional Quarterly*, 9 April 1977, 640; when Meany attacked Carter's treatment of the coal strike, Carter scrawled, "I'm getting tired of this. What is behind it?" Chief of Staff Landon Butler argued that labor leaders' "cheap shot[s]" were not about "substantive" disagreement on policy—an inaccurate read. See Butler to President, "Meany's Comments," 28 February 1978, Coll Chief of Staff Butler, FF: AFL-CIO, 1/12/78–5/30/78, Box 86, JCP.

4. Quote from Ed McConville originally in *The Nation*, excerpted in Msgr. George G. Higgins, "Struggle for Economic Justice Rests on Broad Class Interests," *AFL-CIO News*, 6 November 1976.

5. The "three Georges" reference belongs to Michael Harrington. See Maurice Isserman, *The Other American: The Life of Michael Harrington* (New York: Public Affairs, 2000), 345.

6. Burton Kaufman, *The Presidency of James Earl Carter* (Lawrence: University of Kansas Press, 1993), 34–36.

7. Woodcock, quoted in Martin Halpern, *Unions, Radicals, and Democratic Presidents* (Westport, CT: Praeger, 2003), 120; Kaufman, *Presidency of James Earl Carter*, 12–14 (on campaign); the complex landscape of 1976 is captured in Richard Reeves, *Old Faces of 1976* (New York: Harper and Row, 1976).

8. Paul R. Abramson, "Class Voting in the 1976 Presidential Election," *Journal of Politics* 40 (1978): 1066–72; Cadell quote in Robert Mason, *Richard Nixon and the Quest for a New Majority* (Chapel Hill: University of North Carolina Press, 2004), 233; William C. Berman, *America's Right Turn: From Nixon to Clinton*, 2nd ed. (Baltimore: Johns Hopkins University Press, 1998), 34–36.

9. Kaufman identifies Carter as in the Progressive mold in *Presidency of James Earl Carter*, 19, 28; Eizenstat, quoted in Taylor Dark, "Organized Labor and the Carter Administration: The Origins of Conflict," in *The Presidency and Domestic Policies of Jimmy Carter*, ed. Herbert D. Rosenbaum and Alexej Ugrinsky (Westport, CT: Greenwood Press, 1994), 775.

10. Eizenstat, quoted in Bruce Schulman, *The Seventies: The Great Shift in American Culture, Society, and Politics* (New York: Free Press, 2001), 129; on the contradictions, see Kaufman, *Presidency of James Earl Carter*, 77; W. Carl Biven, *Jimmy Carter's Economy: Policy in an Age of Limits* (Chapel Hill: University of North Carolina Press, 2002), 33; James Fallows, "The Passionless Presidency: The Trouble with Jimmy Carter's Administration," *Atlantic*, May 1979, 33–48.

11. Alan Brinkley, *The End of Reform: New Deal Liberalism in Recession and War* (New York, 1995), 228–29, 261–63.

12. Timothy N. Thurber, *The Politics of Equality: Humbert H. Humphrey and the African American Freedom Struggle* (New York, 1999), 235; on the postwar history of full employment and its champion Leon Keyserling, see Edmund F. Wherle,

"Guns, Butter, Leon Keyserling, the AFL-CIO, and the Fate of Full-Employment Economics," *Historian* 66 (Winter 2004): 730–48.

13. On the March on Washington Movement, see Beth Tompkins Bates, *Pullman Porters and the Rise of Protest Politics in Black America, 1925–1945* (Chapel Hill: University of North Carolina Press, 2001), 148–74; Bayard Rustin, "From Protest to Politics: the Future of the Civil Rights Movement," in *Down the Line: the Collected Writings of Bayard Rustin* (Chicago: Quadrangle Books, 1971), 118; *Report of the National Advisory Commission on Civil Disorders* (New York: Bantam, 1968), 24; Remarks of Hubert H. Humphrey, American Bar Association, 11 August 1970, Box 1, 1970 Campaign Files, HHHP; "Political Power and the Middle Class in the '70s: As former Vice President Humphrey Sees It," *U.S. News and World Report*, 24 November 1969, 57–58; Remarks by Senator Hubert H. Humphrey, Civil Rights Symposium, LBJ Library, 11 December 1972, Box 3, Subject Files 1971–1977 HHHP; "Remarks by Senator Humphrey," Congressional Breakfast for Full Employment, 15 January 1975, Washington, DC., Box 40, Speech Files, HHHP; U.S. Congress, Joint Economic Committee, *National Economic Planning, Balanced Growth, and Full Employment*, 94th Cong, 1st Sess. (Washington, DC: GPO, 1976), 194; Humphrey to Wilkins, 27 June 1975, Box 2 1975, Legislative Files, HHHP; Thurber, *Politics of Equality*, 223–31.

14. Andrew Levison, "The Working-Class Majority," *New Yorker*, 2 September 1974, 48; Bayard Rustin and Norman Hill, "Affirmative Action in an Economy of Scarcity," testimony to the House of Representatives Special Subcommittee on Education, 17 September 1974, House Committee on Education and Labor, Special Subcommittee on Education-Affirmative Action Programs; see similar sentiments in Augustus F. Hawkins, "Full Employment Is the Answer," *Adherent*, 2 August 1975, 18; for fuller development, see Andrew Levison, *The Full Employment Alternative* (New York: Coward, McCann and Geoghegan, 1980). On deindustrialization, see Barry Bluestone and Bennett Harrison, *The Deindustrialization of America* (New York: Basic Books, 1982); Jefferson Cowie and Joseph Heathcott, eds., *Beyond the Ruins: The Meanings of Deindustrialization* (Ithaca, NY: Cornell University Press, 2003).

15. Cleveland Robinson, Interview by Janet Green and Joe Wilson, "New Yorkers at Work" Oral History Project, Robert F. Wagner Labor Archives, New York University, 28 October 1980, 53.

16. Theda Skocpol, "Targeting Within Universalism: Politically Viable Policies to Combat Poverty in the United States," in Christopher Jencks and Paul E. Peterson, eds., *The Urban Underclass* (Washington, DC: Brookings Institute, 1991), 411–36. For an elaboration and critique of "rights consciousness," see Nelson Lichtenstein, *State of the Union: A Century of American Labor* (Princeton, NJ: Princeton University Press, 2002), 178–211. Margaret Weir persuasively argues that the postwar framework "provided little groundwork upon which to build such new policies: the institutional framework and the organization of interests would have had to be

substantially reoriented to support policies that expanded the government role." See Margaret Weir, *Politics and Jobs: The Boundaries of Employment Policy in the United States* (Princeton, NJ: Princeton University Press, 1992), 131.

17. Quote from *Los Angeles Times*, 13 June 1976; biographical material from Oral History interview with August F. Hawkins by Clyde Woods, transcript, 1992, special collections, University Research Library, UCLA, Los Angeles, California; Oral history interview with Augustus F. Hawkins by Carlos Vásquez, transcript, University Research Library, UCLA.

18. Vásquez interview with Hawkins, 63.

19. It was officially called the "Equal Opportunity and Full Employment Act." See some of the sponsors' early testimonies in *Congressional Record*, Senate, 93rd Cong. 2nd Sess., 9 October 1974, 34588–91; *Congressional Record*, House, 93rd Cong., 2nd Sess., 26 June 1974, 21278–83; Hawkins speech to NAACP, 2 July 1975, Washington, DC, FF: Speeches, Box 35, AHP.

20. These three factors are the core of Gary Mucciaroni, *The Political Failure of Employment Policy, 1945–1982* (Pittsburgh: University of Pittsburgh Press, 1990). Hubert H. Humphrey, "Guaranteed Jobs for Human Rights," *Annals of the American Academy of Political and Social Science*, 418 (March 1978): 24.

21. *Washington Post* 27 April 1975; "Jobs Now! Rally," FF: Jobs Now Rally, Box 21, MFP; *New York Times* 16 February 1976; *New York Times* 23 April 1975; House Republican Research Committee, 25 November 1975, clipping in FF: Opposition, Box 82, AHP; *The Gallup Poll: Public Opinion 1972–1977* (Wilmington, DE, 1976), 760–61, for year 1976.

22. Hawkins had tried to bring Meany on board (the AFL-CIO had editorialized in favor of full employment in *AFL-CIO News*, 17 May 1975), but Meany "snubbed" Hawkins's requests. Hawkins speculated that Meany wanted to be the architect of the bill. See FF: George Meany, Box 35, AHP; Hawkins, "Full Employment Is the Answer," 16. On the 1976 bill, see *New York Times* 14 March 1976; 24 March 1976; U.S. Congress, Joint Economic Committee, *National Economic Planning, Balanced Growth, and Full Employment*, 94th Cong., 1st Sess. (Washington, DC: GPO, 1976); *U.S. News and World Report*, 16 February 1976, 21; David Ignatius, "National Economic Planning: Must It Be Orwellian?" *Washington Monthly,* January 1976, 55–61; *Business Week*, 31 May 1976, 14 June 1976; "Changes Adopted in the Full Employment and Balanced Growth Act," 16 September 1976, FEAC, fiche 9 of set 14, MFP.

23. *New York Times* 24 March 1976; Humphrey to Walter W. Heller, 6 August 1976, FF: 4, Box 2, HHHP; Melville J. Ulmer, "Taking a Dim View of Humphrey-Hawkins," *New Republic*, 12 June 1976, 17–19; *Congressional Record*, 94th Cong., 2nd Sess., 24 May 1976, 15188; *Business Week*, 31 May 1976; *New York Times* 14 March 1976: *New York Times* 16 February 1976; *New York Times* 24 March 1976.

24. *New York Times* 19 May 1976; *Newsweek*, 31 May 1976. The text of the platform did not use Humphrey-Hawkins by name. "The Democratic Party," it read, "is committed to the right of all adult Americans willing, able and seeking work to

have opportunities for useful jobs at living wages. To make that commitment mean-ingful, we pledge ourselves to the support of legislation that will make every re-sponsible effort to reduce adult unemployment to 3 per cent within 4 years."

25. The FEAC materials are enormous, stored on microfiche as part of the Murray Finley Papers. They cover strategy, mobilization, outreach, clippings, copies of the Full Employment Advocate, financial information, targeting of congressman, ral-lies, campaigns, and relations to other groups in the full employment coalition. For an overview of activities for 1976, see "Report of Activities of the Full Employment Action Council—1976," FEAC, fiche 1 of set 2, MFP.

26. See U.S. Congress, Joint Economic Committee, *Jobs and Prices in Atlanta*, *Jobs and Prices in Chicago*, and *Jobs and Prices in the West Coast Region*, (Washing-ton, DC: GPO, 1976); U.S. Congress, Joint Economic Committee, *Estimating the Social Costs of National Economic Policy: Implications for Mental and Physical Health, and Criminal Aggression* 94th Cong., 2nd Sess. (Washington, DC: GPO, 1976), vi, ix.

27. "Full Employment Bill Stirs Partisan Battle," *Congressional Quarterly*, 12 May 1976, 1171–75; *Congressional Digest*, June 1976, 179–91; *New York Times* 5 March 1976; *New York Times* 27 April 1976; *New York Times* 21 June 1976; *New York Times* 13 August 1976; *New York Times* 26 August 1976; *Business Week*, 31 May 1976.

28. Charles Schultze, statement before the Senate Committee on Public Welfare, Subcommittee on Unemployment Poverty, and Migratory Labor, 14 May 1976, 94th Cong., 2nd. Sess., 154 (Washington, DC: GPO, 1976); *Congressional Quar-terly*, 15 May 1976, 1174; *Congressional Digest*, June 1976, 179–83; Mucciaroni, *Po-litical Failure of Employment Policy*, 97; Thurber, *Politics of Equality*, 239–40.

29. *Washington Star*, 7 July 1976.

30. The original paper is A.W. Phillips, "The Relation Between Unemployment and Rates of Change in Money Wages in the United Kingdom, 1862–1957," *Eco-nomica* 25 (November 1958): 283–99; for discussion, see Bruce E. Kaufman, *The Economics of Labor Markets and Labor Relations* (Chicago: Dryden, 1988), 597–99; Albert Rees, "The Phillips Curve as a Menu for Policy Choice," *Economica* 37 (Au-gust 1970): 227–38; John Burton and John T. Addison, "The Institutionalist Analy-sis of Wage Inflation: A Critical Appraisal," in *Research in Labor Economics*, ed. Ronald G. Ehrenberg 1 (1977): 333–76; for a more institutional approach, see Mi-chael J. Piore, ed., *Unemployment and Inflation: Institutionalist and Structuralist Views* (White Plains, NY: M.E. Sharpe, 1979).

31. Mrs. Coretta Scott King, Testimony, Senate Labor Committee 19 May 1976, fiche 3 of set 5, FEAC; examples of arguments marshaled against the Phillips Curve include Gus Tyler, "The Phillips Curve Falls Flat" pamphlet, n.d., Special Full Employment Files, fiche 5 of set 19, MFP; *Congressional Record*, 94th Cong., 1st Sess., July 22, 1975, 24152; *Full Employment* (newsletter), April 1976, 4, MFP; "Arguments For and Against H.R. 50" Democratic Study Group 3 March 1978,

MFP, Special Full Employment, fiche 17 of set 19; "Facts and Myths on Full Employment" United States Secretary of Labor Ray Marshall Speaks Out, Full Employment Week 1977 pamphlet, fiche 7 of set 14, FEAC; Tom Wicker, "How Jobs Could Fight Inflation" FEAC handout (text from *New York Times* editorial), FF: Martin Luther King, Box 20, MFP; 16 November 1975 *New York Times*; Position Paper No. 1 issued by Senator Hubert H. Humphrey and Congressman Augustus F. Hawkins on the "Full Employment And Balanced Growth Act of 1976," fiche 1 of set 2, FEAC.

32. Leon Keyserling, *Toward Full Employment Within Three Years: Restrain Inflation, Reform Federal Reserve Board Policies, Improve Federal Budget Policies* (pamphlet) (Washington, DC: Conference on Economic Progress, 1976) in fiche 1 of set 11, FEAC; *Business Week*, 31 May 1976; Mucciaroni, *Employment Policy*, 96–97; Joint Economic Committee, *Twentieth Anniversary of the Full Employment Act of 1946—A National Conference on Full Employment* (Washington, DC: GPO, 1976), 156; *Minneapolis Tribune* 19 May 1976. The Congressional Budget Office, after studying the potential economic impacts of the bill, concluded that it could lower unemployment at the risk of substantially higher inflation, particularly given the goals of the bill. Congressional Budget Office simulations showed that reaching a 3.5 percent overall unemployment rate instead of 5.0 percent by 1980 might add roughly two percentage points to the inflation rate by 1982. It also said that, "In the long run, on the other hand, it is possible that careful development of employment programs targeted at pockets of high structural unemployment could reduce these inflationary risks. Training programs, if successful, could shift workers from situations of labor surplus to those of labor shortage. Further, vigorous pursuits of anti-inflation measures might increase the feasibility of achieving a 3 percent unemployment goal in a non-inflationary environment." See *Congressional Record*, 94th Cong., 2nd Sess., 3 June 1976, 16348.

33. Keyserling, *Toward Full Employment Within Three Years*, 22; *Congressional Record*, 94th Cong., 2nd Sess., 11 June 1976, 1709.

34. *Gallup Poll: Public Opinion 1972–1977*, 1040 (1977); Ronald Reagan, "Humphrey Hawkins Bill," in *Reagan's Path to Victory: The Shaping of Ronald Reagan's Vision: Selected Writings* (New York: Free Press, 2004), 71–72.

35. Margaret Weir, *Politics and Jobs*, 136.

36. For the analysis of the Warm Springs launch, see William Leuchtenberg, *In the Shadow of FDR*, 2nd ed. (Ithaca, NY: Cornell University Press, 1993), 177–79. "Statement by Jimmy Carter at Full Employment Press Conference," fiche 1 of set 6: FEAC; Jimmy Carter, *The Presidential Campaign 1976, Vol. I* (Washington, GPO, 1978), 156–57, 299–300, 368; Carter Campaign Spots, videotape D1153, DPCC; *Congressional Quarterly Weekly Report*, 21 May 1977, 967; *New York Times* April 1976.

37. *Washington Post* 7 September 1976; *Wall Street Journal* 28 September 1976.

38. Fallows, "The Passionless Presidency," 42, 44; Jimmy Carter, *Keeping Faith: Memoirs of a President* (New York: Bantam Books, 1982), 78, 102.

39. John Dumbrell, *The Carter Presidency: A Re-Evaluation* (New York: Manchester University Press, 1993), 100; Interview with Charles Schultze, MCI, Carter Presidency Project, vol. XI, 8–9 January 1982, 2, 38–39, 80, Jimmy Carter Library. Schultze's reasoning contrasts with that of Secretary of Labor Ray Marshall's. Marshall believed that the administration should have built a consensus, especially with labor, early on in order to have the political goodwill to do what was necessary. See Interview with Ray Marshall, MCI, Carter Presidency Project, vol. XXV, 4 May 1988, 20–21, Jimmy Carter Library.

40. Eizenstat and Schultze to Carter, 10 October 1977, Box LA-2, White House Central Files, Subject File—Executive, JCP.

41. *Baltimore Sun* 23 November 1977; *New York Times* 31 August 1977.

42. Charles Schultze, "Memorandum for the Economic Policy Group," 14 March 1977, FF: Humphrey Hawkins, Martha Mitchell Box 11 JCP; Schultze to President, 23 May 1977, Box 221 Domestic Policy Staff (DPS), Staff Office Files-Eizenstat; Hawkins to Schultze, 11 May 1977, Box 221, DPS-Eizenstat; Hawkins and Humphrey to Carter (and attachments), 9 June 1977, Box 221 DPS-Eizenstat; Schultze to Pinson, 30 June 1977, Box 221 DPS-Eizenstat; Blumenthal to President, DPS, Box 221, JCP.

43. Eizenstat to Carter 9 June 1977, DPS-Eizenstat, Box 221, JCP; Lance to President, 31 May 1977, DPS-Eizenstat, Box 221, JCP; Pinson to Schultze, 30 June 1977, DPS-Eizenstat, Box 221, JCP; on the legality of the phrase "right to full opportunity for employment," see Larry A. Hammond, "Memorandum to Margaret A. McKenna," 26 October 1977, Staff Office Files-Counsel's Office, Box 132, JCP.

44. Confidential Memo, 7 November 1977, Box 124, FF: Humphrey-Hawkins Bill, MFP; Eizenstat to President 6 October 1977, JCP; Lance to President, 31 May 1977, DPS-Eizenstat, Box 221, JCP; Pinson to Schultze, 30 June 1977, DPS-Eizenstat, Box 221, JCP; Confidential Memo, 7 November 1977, Box 124, FF: Humphrey-Hawkins Bill, JCP; Eizenstat to President 6 October 1977, DPS-Eizenstat, Box 221, JCP; on the debate over the legality of the phrase "right to full opportunity for employment," see Larry A. Hammond, "Memorandum to Margaret A. McKenna," 26 October 1977, Staff Office Files-Counsel's Office, Box 132, JCP; *Full Employment Advocate* 11, no. 3 (October 1977), fiche 5 of set 14, FEAC.

45. Singer, "The Latest Humphrey-Hawkins Bill," 1929–31.

46. *New York Times* 19 November 1977; *New York Times* 21 February 1978; Singer, "The Latest Humphrey-Hawkins Bill," 1929–31; *Chicago Defender* 17 November 1977; *New York Amsterdam News,* 26 November 1977; Gary Fink, "Fragile Alliance: Jimmy Carter and the American Labor Movement," in Rosenbaum and Uginsky, *The Presidency and Domestic Policies of Jimmy Carter,* 793.

47. *New York Times* 17 March 1978; *Congressional Quarterly Almanac*, 95th Cong., 2nd Sess. (Washington, DC: GPO, 1978), 275.

48. Kaufman, *Presidency of James Earl Carter*, 110; Robert Singh, *The Congressional Black Caucus* (Thousand Oaks, CA, 1998), 86–90; Woods interview with Hawkins, 291; Bob Schieffer, "White House Tiff," *New Leader*, 9 October 1978, 3.

49. Mark Blyth, *Great Transformations: Economic Ideas and Institutional Change in the Twentieth Century* (New York: Cambridge University Press, 2002), 181; *AFL-CIO News* 21 October 1978; Helen Ginsburg, "Congressional Will-O'-the-Wisp, *The Nation*, 5 February 1977, 139.

50. The Donzetti comparison in *Wall Street Journal* 22 February 1995; Gary Gerstle, "The Protean Character of American Liberalism," *Journal of American History* 99 (October 1994): 1073; Bruce Bartlett, "America's New Ideology: 'Industrial Policy'" *American Journal of Economics and Sociology* 44 (January 1985): 1–7.

51. Humphrey quoted in *Congressional Record*, 94th Cong., 2nd Sess., 11 June 1976, 1709; Gary Gerstle argues that the United States vacillated between two visions: civic and racial nationalism. "By 1970," he writes, "neither civic nor racial traditions of American nationalism retained enough integrity to serve as rallying points for those who wished to put the nation back together." Gary Gerstle, *The American Crucible: Race and Nation in the Twentieth Century* (Princeton, NJ: Princeton University Press), 10, 345. The notion of limits comes from many of Carter's policy staff and was used effectively as the theme for Biven, *Jimmy Carter's Economy*, 259–63; the founding document of the idea of governing in an age of limits, which had a profound impact on Carter, is Donella H. Meadows and others, *The Limits to Growth: A Report for the Club of Rome's Project on the Predicament of Mankind*, 3 vols. (New York: Universe Books, 1972); William Greider, *Secrets of the Temple: How the Federal Reserve Runs the Country* (New York: Simon and Schuster, 1987), 96–97.

52. Robert M. Collins, *More: The Politics of Growth in the Postwar America* (New York, 2000), 166–213; for a full treatment of the economic policies of the Carter administration, see Biven, *Jimmy Carter's Economy*.

53. Hawkins to King and Finley, 23 October 1978, FF: Humphrey-Hawkins Bill, Box 124, MFP; Carr to FEAC Executive Committee, 26 October 1978, FF: Humphrey-Hawkins Bill, 124, MFP; "Remarks of the President at a Signing Ceremony for H.R. 50" 27 October 1978, FF: Signing Ceremony for Humphrey-Hawkins, Box: 36, Speechwriter Chronological Files, JCP.

54. Thomas Edsall, *New Politics of Inequality* (New York: W.W. Norton, 1984), 65; Herbert Stein, *Presidential Economics: The Making of Economic Policy from Roosevelt to Clinton*, 3rd ed. (Washington, DC: American Enterprise Institute, 1994), 232.

55. *Wall Street Journal* April 19, 1978; Lichtenstein, *State of the Union*, 178–211.

56. "Labor Law Reform," Statement by the AFL-CIO Executive Council, 22 February 1977, Bal Harbour, Fla., FF: 7, Box 167, JWP.

57. On capital flows, see Jefferson Cowie, *Capital Moves: RCA's Seventy Year Quest for Cheap Labor* (New York: The New Press, 2001); Tami J. Friedman, "Exploiting the North-South Differential: Corporate Power, Southern Politics, and the Decline of Organized Labor after World War II," *Journal of American History* 95 (September 2008): 323–48; Beth Anne English, *A Common Thread: Labor, Politics, and Capital Mobility in the Textile Industry* (Athens: University of Georgia Press, 2006); *Miami Times* 9 March 1978; Bayard Rustin and Norman Hill, "A Black Perspective on Labor Law Reform," FF: Labor Law Reform, Box 25, BRP.

58. James A. Hodges, "J.P. Stevens and the Union: Struggle for the South," in *Race, Class and Community in Southern Labor History*, ed. Gary M. Fink and Merl E. Reed (Tuscaloosa: University of Alabama Press, 1994), 59; Clete Daniel, *Culture of Misfortune: An Interpretive History of Textile Unionism in the United States* (Ithaca, NY: Cornell University Press, 2001), 264.

59. Timothy J. Minchin, *Don't Sleep with Stevens!: The J.P. Stevens Campaign and the Struggle to Organize the South, 1963–1980* (Gainesville: University Press of Florida, 2005); Peter E. Kenseth, "The Politics of Injustice: The J.P. Stevens Campaign and Its Impact on Labor Law Reform in the United States, 1976–1987" (honors thesis, Dartmouth College, 2007).

60. *New York Times* 12 August 1977; *AFL-CIO News*, 30 July 1977; *Oversight Hearings on the National Labor Relations Act*, Subcommittee on Labor-Management Relations of the Committee on Education and Labor, House of Representatives, 94th Cong., 2nd Sess., 17 February–5 May 1976 (Washington, DC: GPO, 1976); *Labor Reform Act of 1977*, Hearings before the Subcommittee on Labor-Management Relations of the Committee on Education and Labor, House of Representatives, 95th Cong., 1st Sess. (Washington, DC: GPO, 1977); Archie Robinson, *George Meany and His Times* (New York: Simon and Schuster, 1981), 372; "Statement of the ACTWU, AFL-CIO Before the Senate Subcommittee on Human Resources on the Need for Labor Law Reform," Washington, DC, 21 September 1977, KCLMD; Schlossberg to Butler, 15 March 1977, Coll: Chief of Staff Butler, Box 138, FF: UAW, JCP.

61. Steven M. Gillon, *The Democrats' Dilemma: Walter F. Mondale and the Liberal Legacy* (New York: Columbia University Press, 1992), 178–79.

62. Eizenstat to President, "Labor Law Reform," 30 June 1977, Staff Secretary, Box 35, FF: 7/1/77; Jordan to President, 29 June 1977, Domestic Policy Staff—Eizenstat Box 232, FF: Labor Law Reform, JCP; see also Eizenstat and Johnston to President, "Labor Law Reform," 6 April 1977, Domestic Policy Staff—Eizenstat Box 231, FF: Labor Law Reform; the principles are laid out publicly in Carter White House to Congress, 18 July 1977, Staff Offices Administration—Hugh Carter, Box 38, FF: Labor Law Reform Act, JCP; *Wall Street Journal* 17 August 1977. On the history of card check, see David Brody, *Labor Embattled: History, Power, Rights* (Urbana: University of Illinois Press), 99–109.

63. The bill finally introduced to Congress in the summer of 1977 included

- expansion of NLRB from five to seven members,
- elections within thirty days after a union presented membership cards signed by a majority of employees,
- back pay of up to 150 percent to workers fired for union activity,
- provisions for union organizers to gain equal time to address workers who were required to attend anti-union meetings,
- award of back pay to workers if the NLRB found that the employer did not negotiate in "good faith" with a new union for a first contract,
- withholding of federal contracts from labor law violators.

64. For the negotiations on the bill, see "Analysis of Proposals to Amend Labor Laws" and "Comparison of Labor Law Reform Bills," FF: Labor Law Reform, Box 231, DPS Eizenstat Labor Dept., JCP; Jordan to President, 29 June 1977, FF: Labor Law Reform, Box 232, Domestic Policy Staff-Eizenstat, JCP; Eizenstat and Johnston to the President, 6 April 1977, FF: Labor Law Reform, Box 231, Domestic Policy Staff-Eizenstat, JCP; Eizenstat and Johnston to President, 11 July 1977, FF: Labor Law Reform, Box 232, DPS-Eizenstat; Office of the White House Press Secretary to Congress, FF: Labor Law Reform Act, Box 38, Staff Offices Administration—Hugh Carter, JCP; Dark, *Unions and the Democrats*, 109; Gary Fink, "Labor Law Revision and the End of the Postwar Labor Accord," in *Organized Labor and American Politics, 1894–1994: The Labor-Liberal Alliance*, ed. Kevin Boyle (Albany, NY: SUNY Press, 1998), 247.

65. Steven Lee Lapidus, "Politics, Lobbying and the Labor Reform Act of 1977–1978" (honors thesis, Cornell University, 1981), 84–86; Fink, "Labor Law Revision and the End of the Postwar Accord," 248–49.

66. *Wall Street Journal* 4 May 1978.

67. Fink, "Labor Law Revision and the End of the Postwar Accord," 250; Stetin to Sheinkman, 10 May 1978, "Re: Labor Law Reform," FF: Labor Law Reform—1978, Box 563, Coll: 5619c, KCLMD.

68. Eizenstat and Johnston to President, 19 June 1978, "Labor Law Reform Bill," FF: 6/19/78, Box 91, Coll: Staff Secretary Box, JCP; Moore and Thomson to President, "Labor Reform—Status," 19 June 1978, FF: Labor Law, Box 232, Coll: DPS E12; Ref. Jordan, Moore and Vice President to President, 22 June 1978, FF: 6/22/78, Box 92, JCP.

69. Eizenstat to President, 30 June 1977, FF: 7/1/77, Box 35, Staff Secretary, JCP; Jordan to President, 29 June 1977, FF: Labor Law Reform, Box 232, Domestic Policy Staff, JCP; Eizenstat and Johnston to President, 19 June 1978, FF: Labor Law Reform, Box 232, Domestic Policy Staff, JCP.

70. "Filibuster Kills Labor Law 'Reform' Bill," *CQ Almanac* 34 (1978): 284. Kim McQuaid, "Big Business and Public Policy in Contemporary United States," in *Regulatory Issues Since 1964: The Rise of the Deregulation Movement*, ed. Robert F. Himmelberg (New York: Garland, 1994), 184; Harrison H. Donnelly, "Organized

Labor Found 1978 a Frustrating Year, Had Few Victories in Congress," *Congressional Quarterly*, 30 December 1978, 3542.

71. Ibid., 3540; Dark, *Unions and Democrats*, 111.

72. Edsall, *New Politics of Inequality*, 125; *U.S. News & World Report*, 10 April 1978; Fink, "Labor Law Revision and the End of the Postwar Accord," 247; Lapidus, "Politics, Lobbying and the Labor Reform Act of 1977–1978," 117–19; Jeffrey H. Burton, *Labor Law Reform in the 95th Congress* (Washington, DC: Congressional Research Service, 1979), 75.

73. Kim McQuaid, *Uneasy Partners: Big Business in American Politics, 1945–1990* (Baltimore: Johns Hopkins University Press, 1994), 156.

74. For a fuller analysis and the text of the Fraser letter, see Jefferson Cowie, "'A One-Sided Class War': Rethinking Doug Fraser's 1978 Resignation from the Labor-Management Group," *Labor History* 44, 3 (2003): 307–14; see also Victor G. Devinatz, "Doug Fraser's 1978 Resignation Letter from the Labor-Management Group and the Limits of Trade Union Liberalism," *Labor History* 45, 3 (2004): 323–31.

75. Fraser letter reprinted in Cowie, "A One-Sided Class War," 311–13.

76. Jack Metzgar, *Striking Steel: Solidarity Remembered* (Philadelphia: Temple University Press, 2000), 39.

77. David Brody, *Workers in Industrial America: Essays on the Twentieth Century Struggle*, 2nd ed. (New York: Oxford University Press, 1993), 220–21; Robert Zieger, *The CIO: 1935–1955* (Chapel Hill: University of North Carolina Press, 1995), 1; Nelson Lichtenstein, "Class Politics and the State during World War Two," *International Labor and Working Class History* 58 (Fall 2000): 270; for an argument about the fragility of the postwar settlement, see Jefferson Cowie and Nick Salvatore, "The Long Exception: Rethinking the New Deal in American History," *International Labor and Working-Class History* 74 (2008): 3–32.

78. A.H. Raskin, "Big Labor Strives to Break Out of Its Rut," *Fortune*, 27 August 1979, 33; see the discussion in Dark, *The Unions and the Democrats*, 113. Dark's argument is similar to the one put forth here, except that he sees continued power with the Democratic alliance, whereas Fraser saw the continuation of a pattern of weakness.

79. The Progressive Alliance and all labor liberal caucuses are ably covered in Andrew Battista, *The Revival of Labor Liberalism* (Urbana: University of Illinois Press, 2008), 83–102.

80. On the formation of the Progressive Alliance, see the coverage in *UAW Solidarity*, July 1978, 15–30 October 1978, and February 1979; Progressive Alliance, "A Call to Action," (1979) in FF: 40, Box 17, JHP.

81. *New York Times* 26 November 1978; Peter Carroll, *It Seemed Like Nothing Happened: America in the 1970s* (New Brunswick, NJ: Rutgers University Press, 1982), 324–25; Robert Kuttner, *Revolt of the Haves: Tax Rebellions and Hard Times* (New York: Simon and Schuster, 1980); Thomas Byrne Edsall with Mary Edsall, *Chain*

Reaction: The Impact of Race, Rights, and Taxes on American Politics (New York: Norton, 1992), 116–36.

82. "A National Accord" FF: Labor Consultation/National Accord, Box 108, Coll: Chief of Staff Butler, JCP; "President's Statement on Inflation and National Accord, 28 April 1979, FF: National Accord 9/28/79–11/79, Box 30, Special Advisor Inflation, JCP; the accord was quickly "strained to the limits"; see Butler to the President, "Status of the National Accord," 10 April 1980, FF: Labor Consultations/National Accord, Box 108, COS Butler, JCP; Gary Fink, "Fragile Alliance: Jimmy Carter and the American Labor Movement," in Rosenbaum and Ugrinsky, eds., *The Presidency and Domestic Policies of Jimmy Carter*, 798; John Herling, "Change and Conflict in the AFL-CIO," *Dissent* (Fall 1974): 482.

83. John Kenneth Galbraith, *Money: Whence It Came and Where It Went* (New York: Houghton Mifflin and Company, 1975), quoted in Greider, *Secrets of the Temple*, 56; Volcker, quoted in *New York Times* 18 October 1979; Alfred Kahn, MCI, Carter, Jimmy Carter Library, 10–11 December 1981, 69; Geoghegan, *Which Side Are You On?* 223. Around 1980, a visitor to Volcker's office noticed a small mountain of bricks in his outer office, yet he could not see any remodeling going on. Volcker explained that they had been sent over by the bricklayer's union with a note saying the bricks were no longer needed. The Reagan era had already begun—under Carter. See Brian Trumbore, "Volcker Part II," http://www.buyandhold.com/bh/en/education/history/2000/paul_volker2.html.

84. Daniel Horowitz, *The Anxieties of Affluence: Critiques of American Consumer Culture, 1939–1979* (Amherst: University of Massachusetts Press, 2004), 223–24.

85. J. William Holland, "The Great Gamble: Jimmy Carter and the 1979 Energy Crisis," *Prologue* 22 (Spring 1990): 63–79.

86. Horowitz, *Anxieties of Affluence*, 93, 95; Jack W. Germond and Jules Witcover, *Blue Smoke and Mirrors: How Reagan Won and Why Carter Lost the Election of 1980* (New York: Viking, 1981), 23–46.

87. David M. Anderson, "Levittown Is Burning!: The 1979 Levittown, Pennsylvania, Gas Line Riot and the Decline of the Blue-Collar American Dream," *Labor: Studies in Working-Class History of the Americas* 2, no. 3 (2005): 47–65; *Time*, 9 July 1979.

88. Daniel Horowitz, ed., *Jimmy Carter and the Energy Crisis of the 1970s: The "Crisis of Confidence" Speech of July 15, 1979* (Boston: Bedford/St. Martin's, 2005), 109–19.

89. Lasch to Cadell, 18 July 1979; Bellah, "A Night at Camp David," 27 July 1979, in Horowitz, ed., *Jimmy Carter and the Energy Crisis of the 1970s*, 152–61.

90. Christopher Lasch, *Minimal Self: Psychic Survival in Troubled Times* (New York: Norton, 1984), 27; Horowitz, *Anxieties of Affluence*, 236–37, 239–44; Lasch to Caddell, 18 July 1979, in Horowitz, ed., *Jimmy Carter and the Energy Crisis*, 158–61; Robert Bellah concurred with Lasch, declaring that he was "terribly disappointed" with the speech. Like conservatives, Bellah believed a return to religion, family, and community was the only path out of the mess of the decade,

but he was disappointed that Carter had "no social vision" to go with his piety. Bellah recalled that the guests at Camp David said, "Look, don't just invoke spiritual values and sacrifice if you're not going to say anything about the structural conditions that force people to be more selfish than they might want to be, like building the whole economy on the profit motive." Bell suspected that Carter's studies may have allowed him to conclude that there was something wrong with the people—not his leadership. According to Daniel Horowitz, "Carter's reading provided him a kind of intellectual cover and justification for his own political instincts, personal convictions, and ideological commitments, offering ways of articulating his moralism without compromising his perspective as an engineer." Ironically, both Bellah and Lasch believed that Ted Kennedy would serve their ends more effectively.

91. Kim Phillips-Fein, *Invisible Hands: The Making of the Conservative Movement from the New Deal to Reagan* (New York: W.W. Norton, 2009), 252–53; on the administration's early debates about tactics with labor, see "Nofziger/Murphy suggestions re emphasis on jobs/labor," 13 July 1981, Dole Labor File 1, and Bonitati to Dole, 11 June 1981, Dole Labor File 2, Ronald Reagan Library, Simi Valley, California. Thanks to Joe McCartin for providing these documents to me. Even after PATCO, Reagan told the United Brotherhood of Carpenters, "I want to express again my belief in our American system of collective bargaining and pledge that there will always be an open door to you in this Administration." See Reagan's address to the United Brotherhood of Carpenters and Joiners of America, 34th General Convention, 31 August–4 September 1981, Chicago, Illinois, 447.

92. Kaufman, *Presidency of James Earl Carter*, 145–50.

93. James T. Patterson, *Restless Giant: The United States from Watergate to Bush v. Gore* (New York: Oxford University Press, 2005), 111.

94. Address of Senator Edward M. Kennedy, Democratic National Convention, New York City, 12 August, 1980; A.H. Raskin, "After Meany," *New Yorker,* 18 August 1980, 36–76; Elizabeth Drew, "1980: The Final Round," *New Yorker*, 23 June 1980, 50–77; Carter had promised a "universal and mandatory" national health insurance plan during the campaign but quickly backed away, which alienated Kennedy. Carter faced the same problem of lower expectations of labor and liberals; see Bourne to President, "Meeting with Senator Kennedy," Box 92, FF: 6/26/78, Staff Secretary, JCP; the national health insurance debate is covered in David Carroll Jacobs, "The United Auto Workers and the Campaign for National Health Insurance: A Case Study of Labor in Politics" (PhD diss., Cornell University, 1983); Statement of Doug Fraser, Chair of the Committee for National Health Insurance, 28 July 1978, Box 7, FF: 19, JHP; James W. Singer, "Carter in 1980—Not Ideal, But Maybe Labor's Best Hope," *National Journal*, 28 July 1979, 1252–55.

95. Caddell, quoted in Kaufman, *Presidency of James Earl Carter*, 207; *New York Times* 15 October 1980.

96. AFL-CIO Committee on Political Education, "A Report on Congress-1980," *AFL-CIO News*, 30 August 1980; *New York Times* 9 November 1980.

97. James Savage, *Balanced Budgets and American Politics* (Ithaca, NY: Cornell University Press, 1988), 195. As Michael Piore put it, Carter's "neo-classical economic philosophy made it impossible to see social programs and institutions (at least those who like unions abridged market mechanisms) as anything more than pay-offs to the special interest constituencies which had been responsible for the President's election." Michael J. Piore, "Can the American Labor Movement Survive Re-Gomperization?" in Industrial Relations Research Association, *Proceedings of the Thirty-Fifth Annual Meeting*, 28–30 December 1982, New York City (Madison, WI: IRRA, 1983), 38–39.

98. Ronald Reagan, "A Vision for America" (Election Eve Address, 3 November 1980), http://www.reagan.utexas.edu/archives/reference/11.3.80.html.

99. Andreas Killen, *1973 Nervous Breakdown: Watergate, Warhol, and the Birth of Post-Sixties America* (New York: Bloomsbury, 2006), 261; *Newsweek*, 19 November 1979; Michael Harrington, *The Next America: The Decline and Rise of the United States* (New York: Holt, Rinehart, and Winston, 1981), 151.

100. Haynes Johnson, *Sleepwalking Through History: America in the Reagan Years* (New York: Anchor Book, 1992), 20; Christopher Lasch, *The Revolt of the Elites and the Betrayal of Democracy* (New York: Norton, 1995), 25; Lasch extracted the title from Jose Ortega y Gasset's *The Revolt of the Masses* [trans.] (New York: Norton, 1932).

101. Economic Policy Institute, *State of Working America 2006–2007* (Ithaca, NY: ILR Press, 2006), table 3.3; Dewey Burton and Ilona Burton, interview by the author, 30 September 2006, Fort White, Florida, tape recording, in author's possession; Thomas Geoghegan, "Infinite Debt: How Unlimited Interest Rates Destroyed the Economy," *Harper's*, April 2009, 31–39.

102. Kevin Phillips, *The Politics of Rich and Poor: Wealth and the American Electorate in the Reagan Aftermath* (New York: Random House, 1990): xvii–xviii; Ruy Teixeira and Joel Rogers, *America's Forgotten Majority: Why the White Working Class Still Matters* (New York: Basic Books, 2000), 62–63.

Chapter 7: The Important Sound of Things Falling Apart

1. Nik Cohn, "Feverish," in *Rolling Stone: The Seventies*, eds. Ashley Kahn, Holly George-Warren, and Shawn Dahl (Boston: Little, Brown & Co., 1998), 202; Nik Cohn, "Tribal Rites of the New Saturday Night, *New York*, 7 June 1976, 31–43.

2. Al Auster and Leonard Quarter, "Saturday Night Fever," *Cineaste* 8 (Summer 1978): 36–37.

3. Cohn, "Tribal," 32; Pauline Kael, "Nirvana," *New Yorker*, 26 December 1977, 60.

4. Peter Shapiro, *Turn the Beat Around: The Secret History of Disco* (New York: Faber and Faber, 2005), 68.

5. Even the entrepreneurs behind the disco's most famous monument to decadence, Studio 54, lived out Tony Manero's dreams of escape. Steve Rubell and Ian Schrager, small-time restaurant owners from the depths of Brooklyn, were "quintessential bridge and tunnelers out for revenge on the world that excluded them—except the only revenge they ever exacted was on the world that they came from." Shapiro, *Turn the Beat Around*, 207.

6. Ibid., 4, 195.

7. Tom Wolfe, "The Me Decade and the Third Great Awakening" in *The Purple Decades: A Reader* (New York: Farrar Straus Giroux, 1982), 277. See Joel Dinerstein, *Swinging the Machine: Modernity, Technology, and African American Culture Between the World Wars* (Amherst: University of Massachusetts Press, 2003), 221–26, 237–38.

8. Martin A. Jackson, "Saturday Night Fever," *Intellect* (June 1978): 509.

9. Warhol, quoted in Andreas Killen, *1973 Nervous Breakdown: Watergate, Warhol, and the Birth of Post-Sixties America* (New York: Bloomsbury, 2006), 146–47.

10. Anne-Lise Francois, "Fakin' It/Makin' It: Falsetto's Bid for Transcendence in the 1970s Disco Highs," *Perspectives of New Music* 33 (Winter-Summer 1995): 443; Shapiro, *Turn the Beat Around*, 196; Christopher Lasch, *The Culture of Narcissism: American Life in an Age of Diminishing Expectations* (New York: W.W. Norton, 1978), 5, 231–32.

11. Nelson George, *Death of Rhythm and Blues* (New York: Pantheon, 1988), 150–55, 157–59; Craig Werner, *A Change Is Gonna Come* (New York: Plume, 1999), 219; Alice Echols, *Shaky Ground: The 60s and Its Aftershocks* (New York: Columbia University Press, 2002), 181.

12. Ed McCormack, "No Sober Person Dances," in *Dancing Madness*, Abe Peck, ed. (New York: Anchor Press, 1976), 13; Shapiro, *Turn the Beat Around*, 252, 247.

13. Richard Dyer, "In Defense of Disco," *Gay Left* (Summer 1979), reprinted in *The Faber Book of Pop*, ed. Hanif Kureishi and Jon Savage (Boston: Faber and Faber, 1995), 526.

14. Chuck "Wagon" Maultsby published "The Story of 'Disco Sucks'" (August 2006) on his Web site, http://www.chuckmaultsby.net/ (accessed 15 January 2010).

15. *Chicago Sun-Times* 13 July 1979; *Chicago Sun-Times* 14 July 1979; *New York Times* 13 July 1979; Don McLeese, "Anatomy of an Anti-Disco Riot," *In These Times,* 29 August–4 September 1979, 23; "Disco-Haters to the Barricades," *Newsweek,* 23 July 1979; Frank Rose, "Discophobia: Rock & Roll Fights Back," *Village Voice,* 12 November 1979, 33.

16. Gillian Frank, "Discophobia: Antigay Prejudice and the 1979 Backlash against Disco," *Journal of the History of Sexuality* 16 (2007): 276–306; Shapiro, *Turn the Beat Around*, 236; Werner, *Change Is Gonna Come*, 211; Echols, *Shaky Ground*, 163.

17. Shapiro, *Turn the Beat Around*, 236–37; for white working-class backlash tastes, see Seth Sanders and Michael O'Flaherty, "44,000,000 Ronald Reagan Fans Can't Be Wrong! Rock and the Backlash" *The Baffler* 15 (2002): 81.

18. Brian J. Bowe, *Creem: America's Only Rock 'n' Roll Magazine* (New York: Harper Collins, 2007), 124.

19. Greil Marcus, *Lipstick Traces: A Secret History of the Twentieth Century* (Cambridge, MA: Harvard University Press, 1990), 47–48; Tom Smucker, "Pop Music,' *The Nation*, 31 May 1980.

20. David P. Szatmary, *Rockin' Time: A Social History of Rock-and-Roll*, 4th ed. (Upper Saddle River, NJ: Prentice Hall, 2000), 224.

21. Ken Tucker called the Talking Heads' cover of Greene "heroic" in *Rolling Stone* 11 December 1980; Werner, *Change Is Gonna Come*, 225.

22. Peter Biskind and Barbara Ehrenreich, "Machismo and Hollywood's Working Class," in *American Media and Mass Culture: Left Perspectives*, ed. Donald Lazere (Berkeley: University of California Press, 1987), 201–15; John Bodnar, *Blue-Collar Hollywood: Liberalism, Democracy, and Working People in American Film* (Baltimore: Johns Hopkins University Press, 2003), 195; the Bakke analogy is from Matthew Frye Jacobson, *Roots Too: White Ethnic Revival in Post-Civil Rights America* (Cambridge, MA: Harvard University Press, 2006), 101.

23. *New York Times* 23 March 1975, *New York Times* 25 March 1975, *New York Times* 26 March 1975; Mark Kram, "They Have Kept Him in Stitches," *Sports Illustrated*, 24 March 1975, 22–24.

24. Ibid., *Time* 11 April 1977.

25. Daniel J. Leab, "The Blue Collar Ethnic in Bicentennial America: Rocky (1976)," in *American History/American Film: Interpreting the Hollywood Image*, ed. John E. O'Connor and Martin A. Jackson (New York: Unger, 1979), 261.

26. Leab, "Blue Collar Ethnic," 267; Rocky, argues Ed Guerrero, is about "white yearnings for a 'great white hope' and a nostalgic return to a bygone racial order." See Ed Guerrero, *Framing Blackness: The African American Image in Film* (Philadelphia: Temple University Press), 104–105, 116.

27. Peter Aufderheid, "Rocky," *Cineaste* 8 (Summer 1977): 40–41; Leab, "Blue Collar Ethnic," 265, 269; *Time*, 11 April 1977; *Christian Science Monitor*, 22 November 1976, 31 March 1977.

28. Bodnar, *Blue Collar Hollywood*, 198; Al Auster and Leonard Quart, "The Working Class Goes to Hollywood: 'F.I.S.T.' and 'Blue Collar,'" *Cineaste* 9 (Fall 1978): 4–7.

29. Arthur H. Bremer, *An Assassin's Diary* (New York: Harper's Magazine Press, 1973), 94–96, 119; the manhood quote is in the unpublished manuscript of the diary, quoted in Dan T. Carter, *The Politics of Rage: George Wallace, the Origins of the New Conservatism, and the Transformation of American Politics* (New York: Simon and Schuster, 1995), 422.

30. Barbara Mortimer, "Portraits of the Postmodern Person in Taxi Driver, Raging Bull and The King of Comedy," *Journal of Film & Video* 49 (1997): 29.

31. Robert Phillip Kolker, *A Cinema of Loneliness: Penn, Kubrick, Coppola, Scorsese, Altman* (New York: Oxford University Press, 1980), 7, 224; see Lary May, *The Big Tomorrow: Hollywood and the Politics of the American Dream* (Chicago: University of Chicago Press, 2000), 4; Derek Nystrom argues that the auteur directors of the seventies reasserted their class power over both production and content of films, weakening unions' power on the set and undermining working-class representation on the screen while reasserting professional middle-class power in both arenas. See Derek Nystrom, "Hard Hats and Movie Brats: Auteurism and the Class Politics of the New Hollywood," *Cinema Journal* 43 (Spring 2004), 18–41. Lucas quoted in Killen, *1973 Nervous Breakdown*, 170–71.

32. Kevin Jackson, ed., *Schrader on Schrader* (London: Faber and Faber, 1990), 117; Scorcese notes from *Taxi Driver* script, vertical files, Television and Motion Picture Reading Room, Library of Congress, Washington, DC; Kolker, *Cinema of Loneliness*, 255; the famous "Are you talkin' to me?" sequence that DeNiro improvised in front of the mirror derived from DeNiro watching a recent Bruce Springsteen concert in which the rock star asked the same question of his audience. See Rob Kirkpatrick, *Magic in the Night: The Words and Music of Bruce Springsteen* (New York: St. Martin's Griffin, 2007), 59.

33. Jackson, *Schrader on Schrader*, 117; in the original screenplay, in fact, all the characters Travis was supposed to kill were black, but, given the racial tensions in the seventies, Scorsese was afraid that the film would incite a riot.

34. George Lipsitz, *Rainbow at Midnight: Labor and Culture in the 1940s* (Urbana: University of Illinois Press, 1994), 283; Peter Lev, *American Films of the 70s: Conflicting Visions* (Austin: University of Texas Press, 2000), 22–39. Kolker, *Cinema of Loneliness*, 225; Bremer, *An Assassin's Diary*, 142.

35. Studs Terkel, *Working* (New York: Pantheon, 1972), 193; Barbara Garson, "Luddites in Lordstown," *Harper's Magazine*, June 1972, 68–73; for the broadest overview of Lordstown, see David F. Moberg, "Rattling the Golden Chains: Conflict and Consciousness of Auto Workers," (PhD diss., University of Chicago, 1978), 321; rummaging around for a theme for a script, Schrader took (some say stole) an idea from another young screenwriter about the suicide of an autoworker and combined it with the themes of the famous 1972 Lordstown struggle.

36. Schrader discusses the influences on the film, including "Finally Got the News," in "Blue Collar: An Interview with Paul Schrader," *Cineaste* 8 (Winter 1977–1978): 34–37; Jackson, *Schrader on Schrader*, 148; Dan Georgakas, "Finally Got the News: The Making of a Radical Film," *Cineaste* 5 (Spring 1972): 2–6.

37. "Blue Collar: An Interview with Paul Schrader" *Cineaste* 8 (Winter 1977–1978): 34–37; "Blue Collar: Detroit Moviegoers Have Their Say," *Cineaste* 8 (Summer 1978): 28–31.

38. "Blue Collar: An Interview with Paul Schrader," 34–37; Jackson, *Schrader on Schrader*, 142.

39. *New York Times* 10 February 1978.

40. Jackson, *Schrader on Schrader*, 148; Paul Schrader, director's comments on "Blue Collar," DVD release, Anchor Bay Entertainment/Universal City Studios, [1978] 2000; *New York Times* 10 February 1978.

41. Bryan K. Garman, *A Race of Singers: Whitman's Working-Class Hero from Guthrie to Springsteen* (Chapel Hill: University of North Carolina Press, 2000), 199–200.

42. Joel Dinerstein, "The Soul Roots of Bruce Springsteen's American Dream," *American Music* 25 (Winter 2007): 441–76.

43. Dave Marsh, *Two Hearts: Bruce Springsteen, the Definitive Biography, 1972–2003* (New York: Routledge, 2004), 368, 195.

44. Bruce Springsteen, *Songs* (New York: Avon Books, 1998), 65–69; Marsh, *Two Hearts*, 193–98, 228.

45. Springsteen's quote and insights on the amount of work in "Darkness" from Marsh, *Two Hearts*, 194–95.

46. *Darkness* illustrates many of the themes of Richard Sennett and Jonathan Cobb, *The Hidden Injuries of Class* (New York: Vintage, 1973) and Johnny Paycheck's novelty song, "Take This Job and Shove It," which saturated the radio stations, workplaces, and bars of the nation. The songs are less about open rebellion than about a "hidden transcript" of resistance that takes place internally, far from the outward contest of power relations that defined the first half of the seventies. Paycheck's narrator is unable to act; the rebellion is only a fantasy: "I'd give the shirt right off of my back / If I had the nerve to say / Take this job and shove it!"

47. For a discussion of the politics of Motown—with particular emphasis on Martha and Vandellas, see Suzanne E. Smith, *Dancing in the Street: Motown and the Cultural Politics of Detroit* (Cambridge, MA: Harvard University Press, 1999).

48. Jim Curtis, *Rock Eras: Interpretations of Music and Society, 1954–1984* (Bowling Green, OH: Bowling Green State University Popular Press, 1987), 273.

49. Chet Flippo, "Bruce Springsteen," *Musician*, November 1984, 53–58.

50. Pat Long, "We are Legend," *Guardian* (UK), 2 May 2009.

51. Theo Cateforis, "Performing the Avant-Garde Groove: Devo and the Whiteness of the New Wave," *American Music* 22 (Winter 2004): 581; *Newsweek*, 30 October 1978; *Rolling Stone*, 25 January 1979; Diane Moroff, "Devo Biography," *Musician Guide*, http://www.musicianguide.com/biographies/1608000419/Devo.html.

52. *Rolling Stone*, 25 January 1979; Jade Dellinger and David Giffels, *Are We Not Men? We Are Devo!* (London: SAF Publishing Limited, 2003), 20.

53. Ruth McKennedy, *Industrial Valley* (New York: Harcourt, Brace and Company, 1939), 373, 376, 379.

54. Cateforis, "Performing the Avant-Garde Groove," 565; *Rolling Stone*, 25 January 1979; Dellinger and Giffels, *Are We Not Men?* 20.

55. Ibid., 34; *Newsweek*, 30 October 1978.

56. Rick Perlstein, *Nixonland: The Rise of a President and the Fracturing of America* (New York: Scribner, 2008), 487–89; Marc Linder, *Wars of Attrition: Vietnam, the Business Roundtable, and the Decline of Construction Unions* (Iowa City, IA: Fanpihua Press, 1999), 283.

57. Dellinger and Giffels, *Are We Not Men?* 81; *Rolling Stone*, 25 January 1979.

58. James Wessinger, "New Traditionalists: Baudrillard, Devo, and the De-Evolution of the Simulation," *Haverford Journal* 3 (April 2007): 64; Cateforis, "Performing the Avant-Garde Groove," 583; Dellinger and Giffels, *Are We Not Men?* 176.

59. Stanley Kauffmann, "Well-Organized Labor," *New Republic*, 17 March 1979, 24.

60. Robert Brent Toplin, "Norma Rae: Unionism in an Age of Feminism," *Labor History* 36 (Spring 1995): 287; Gabriel Miller, *The Films of Martin Ritt: Fanfare for the Common Man* (Jackson: University Press of Mississippi), 170–71.

61. As the promotional materials claimed, "*Norma Rae* is not a film merely about unions or the South, anymore than it is a film merely about love and bravery. It is, instead, a multidimensional study of one woman's attempts to rise above oppression without losing sight of who she is or what she stands for. . . . She grows into herself." In the end, however, Crystal Lee went on tour as "The Real Norma Rae," barnstorming the country trying to drum up support for the J.P. Stevens boycott in radio and television interviews. Her television interviews are archived in video format at the KCLMD, including *Good Morning America*, 2 April 1980; *The Bob McLean Show*, 10 December 1979; *Speaking Frankly*, 13 December 1980; *The Gallery Show*, 13 March 1980.

62. Robert Asahina, "Cinematic Delusions," *New Leader*, 9 April 1979, 20.

63. Manuscript of *60 Minutes* interview, attached to: Burt Beck to The Offices, 14 August 1979, Box 367, unnamed file, JPSP, KCLMD; Miller, *Films of Ritt*, 189.

64. Videotape interview, KCLMD, AM Chicago, WLS-TV 7, 12 May 1980, "Amalgamated Textiles" (Norma Rae).

65. Karen Nussbaum, interviewed by Kathleen Banks Nutter, Voices of Feminism Oral History Project, 18–19 December 2003, transcript, 29–31, Sophia Smith Collection, Smith College, Northampton, Massachusetts.

66. *New York Times* 19 December 1980; Michael Rogin, "How the Working Class Saved Capitalism: The New Labor History and The Devil and Miss Jones," *Journal of American History* 89 (June 2002): 113; Dana Frank, "Girl Strikers Occupy Chain Store, Win Big: The Detroit Woolworth's Strike of 1937," in *Three Strikes: Miners, Musicians, Salesgirls, and the Fighting Spirit of Labor's Last Century*, ed. Howard Zinn, Dana Frank, and Robin D.G. Kelley (Boston: Beacon Press Books 2001), 57–118.

67. Francis Wheen, *Strange Days Indeed: The Golden Age of Paranoia* (London: Fourth Estate, 2009), 9.

68. Fredric Jameson, *Postmodernism, or, The Cultural Logic of Late Capitalism* (Durham, NC: Duke University Press, 1991), 181, see also xvii, 18–19; David R. Shumway, "Rock 'n' Roll Sound Tracks and the Production of Nostalgia," *Cinema Journal* 38 (Winter 1999): 42.

69. Greil Marcus, *Lipstick Traces: A Secret History of the Twentieth Century* (Cambridge, MA: Harvard University Press, 1989), 45; Linda Ray Pratt, "Elvis, or the Ironies of a Southern Identity," in *The Elvis Reader: Texts and Sources on the King of Rock 'n' Roll*, ed. Kevin Quain (New York: St. Martin's Press, 1992), 97.

70. Neal and Janice Gregory, *When Elvis Died: Media Overload and the Origins of the Elvis Cult* (New York: Pharos Books, 1980), 136, 213.

71. Charles L. Ponce de Leon, *Fortunate Son: The Life of Elvis Presley* (New York: Hill and Wang, 2006), 172–73.

72. Ibid., 173–75; Lester Bangs, "Where Were You When Elvis Died?" in Kevin Quain, ed., *The Elvis Reader*, 89.

Chapter 8: Dead Man's Town

1. For a full elaboration of "Born in the U.S.A." and working-class identity, see Jefferson Cowie and Lauren Boehm, "Dead Man's Town: 'Born in the U.S.A.,' Social History, and Working-Class Identity," *American Quarterly* 28 (June 2006): 353–78.

2. Bryan Garman, *Race of Singers: Whitman's Working-Class Hero from Guthrie to Springsteen* (Chapel Hill: University of North Carolina Press, 2000), 225.

3. *Washington Post* 13 September 1984.

4. Jefferson Morely, "The Phenomenon," *Rolling Stone*, October 10, 1985, 74–75; Dave Marsh, *Bruce Springsteen: Two Hearts: The Definitive Biography, 1972–2003* (New York: Routledge, 2004), 430–33; Jim Cullen, *Born in the USA: Bruce Springsteen and the American Tradition* (New York: Harper Collins, 1997), 5.

5. Marsh, *Two Hearts*, 378–82.

6. Ironically, given the song's departure from Springsteen's often-used cinematic structure, the song was originally supposed to be for a Paul Schrader film called *Born in the U.S.A.*, a title that Springsteen took from Schrader. See Springsteen, *Songs*, 163; Dave Marsh, *Glory Days: Bruce Springsteen in the 1980s* (New York: Pantheon, 1987), 93, 431.

7. Marsh, *Glory Days*, 102; Springsteen, *Songs*; Eric Alterman, *It Ain't No Sin to Be Glad You're Alive* (New York: Little, Brown, 1999), 157; Amiri Baraka, "The Meaning of Bruce," *Spin Magazine*, November 1985, 51, 80; Chet Flippo, "Bruce Springsteen: A Rock 'n' Roll Evangelist for Our Times," *Musician* 73 (November 1984): 54–55.

As Erich Fromm argues, by surrendering one's freedom and identity to an outside force such as national identity, one can participate in the "strength and glory" of a power that is "unshakably strong, eternal, and glamorous." The costs, however, are

444 NOTES FOR PAGES 360–363

great. "One surrenders one's own self and renounces all strength and pride connected with it, one loses one's integrity as an individual and surrenders freedom." The losses are offset, Fromm continues, by "a new security and a new pride in the participation in the power in which one submerges. One gains also security against the torture of doubt." Erich Fromm, *Fear of Freedom* (London: Routledge & Kegan Paul, 1942), 134.

8. Michael Herr, *Dispatches* (London: Pan Books, 1978), 103, 163.

9. Thomas Sugrue, *Origins of the Urban Crisis: Race and Inequality in Post-War Detroit* (Princeton, NJ: Princeton University Press, 1996), 17, passim; Barry Bluestone, "Deindustrialization and Unemployment," in *Deindustrialization and Plant Closure*, ed. Paul D Staudohar and Holly E. Brown (Lexington, MA: D.C. Heath, 1987), 13; for a broader historical perspective, see the essays in Jefferson Cowie and Joseph Heathcott, eds., *Beyond the Ruins: The Meanings of Deindustrialization* (Ithaca, NY: Cornell University Press, 2003). In Dale Maharidge and Michael Williamson, *Journey to Nowhere: The Saga of the New Underclass* (Garden City, NJ: Dial Press, 1985), a study of photos and reportage about unemployed workers' exodus from the Rustbelt, two laid-off Youngstown steelworkers, Joe Marshall Sr. and Jr., World War II and Vietnam vets, respectively, who were poking through the rubble of the Campbell Works. The factory's six ten-story blast furnaces had been blown up by order of the corporate executives, and it was Joe Sr., the WWII vet, who applied a clear military metaphor to the action: "What Hitler couldn't do, they did it for him."

10. Harold Meyerson, "Doing Good Jobs, But Losing Them," *American Prospect* online, 16 February 2006, http://www.prospect.org/cs/articles?article=doing _good _jobs_but_losing_them; *Washington Post* 15 February 2006. A verse in the original version of "Glory Days" (that did not make it into the recorded version), spoke directly to the Wixom experience:

My old man worked 20 years on the line and they let him go
Now everywhere he goes out looking for work they just tell him that he's too old
I was 9 years old when he was working at the Metuchen Ford plant assembly line
Now he just sits on a stool down at the Legion Hall, but I can tell what's on his mind

11. Jack Metzgar, "Blue-Collar Blues: The Deunionization of Manufacturing," *New Labor Forum* (Spring 2002): 20–23; Lillian B. Rubin, *Families on the Fault Line: America's Working Class Speaks About the Family, the Economy, Race, and Ethnicity* (New York: Harper Perennial, 1995), 42.

12. *New York Times* 6 August 1981, *New York Times* 13 August 1981, *New York Times* 16 August 1981.

13. *New York Times* 6 August 1981, *New York Times* 13 August 1981, *New York Times* 16 August 1981; Ronald Reagan to Robert E. Poli, President, PATCO, 20 October 1980, reprinted by UAW-CAP, in author's possession.

14. In 2003, Federal Reserve Chairman Alan Greenspan, speaking on the legacy of Ronald Reagan, placed PATCO as the most important initiative of Reagan's first term: "But perhaps the most important, and then highly controversial, domestic initiative was the firing of the air traffic controllers in August 1981. . . . President Reagan prevailed, as you know, but far more importantly his action gave weight to the legal right of private employers, previously not fully exercised, to use their own discretion to both hire and discharge workers. There was great consternation among those who feared that an increased ability to lay off workers would raise the level of unemployment and amplify the sense of job insecurity." Remarks by Chairman Alan Greenspan at the Ronald Reagan Library, Simi Valley, California, 9 April 2003, http://www.federalreserve.gov/boarddocs/speeches/2003/200304092/default.htm.

15. Jonathan Rosenblum, *The Copper Crucible: How the Arizona Miners' Strike of 1983 Recast Labor-Management Relations in America* (Ithaca, NY: ILR Press, 1995), 217; Kim Moody, *An Injury to All: The Decline of American Unionism* (New York: Verso, 1988), 303–330; Jeremy Brecher, *Strike!* (Boston: South End Press, 1997), 305–35.

16. George Lipsitz, "Dilemmas of Beset Nationhood," in *Bonds of Affection: Americans Define Their Patriotism*, ed. John Bodnar (Princeton, NJ: Princeton University Press, 1996), 255, 260; Seth Sanders and Mike O'Flaherty, "44,000,000 Ronald Reagan Fans Can't Be Wrong! Rock and the Backlash," *Baffler* 15 (2002): 81.

17. Maharidge and Williamson, *Journey to Nowhere*, 7; Jefferson Cowie, "The Enigma of Working-Class Conservatism: From the Hard Hats to the NASCAR Dads," *New Labor Forum* 13 (Fall 2004): 9–17.

18. Eric Hobsbawm, *The Age of Extremes: A History of the World, 1914–1991* (New York: Vintage, 1996), 257–59.

19. William Deresiewicz, "The Dispossessed," *The American Scholar* 75 (Winter 2006): 17–24.

20. Michael Denning, *The Cultural Front* (London: Verso, 1997), 467.

21. Dean Bakopoulos, *Please Don't Come Back from the Moon* (New York: Harcourt, 2005), 184–85; Davis, *Prisoners of the American Dream*, 178; John Dewey, "The Future of Liberalism," *Journal of Philosophy* 32, no. 9 (April 1935): 230; see also the discussion in Michael J. Thompson, *The Politics of Inequality: A Political History of the Idea of Economic Inequality in America* (New York: Columbia University Press, 2007), 188 and passim.

Index